Immigration and Exile Foreign-Language Press in the UK and in the US

Immigration and Exile Foreign-Language Press in the UK and in the US

Connected Histories of the 19th and 20th Centuries

Edited by
Stéphanie Prévost and Bénédicte Deschamps

BLOOMSBURY ACADEMIC
LONDON • NEW YORK • OXFORD • NEW DELHI • SYDNEY

BLOOMSBURY ACADEMIC
Bloomsbury Publishing Plc, 50 Bedford Square, London, WC1B 3DP, UK
Bloomsbury Publishing Inc, 1385 Broadway, New York, NY 10018, USA
Bloomsbury Publishing Ireland, 29 Earlsfort Terrace, Dublin 2, D02 AY28, Ireland

BLOOMSBURY, BLOOMSBURY ACADEMIC and the Diana logo are trademarks
of Bloomsbury Publishing Plc

First published in Great Britain 2024
This paperback edition published in 2025

Copyright © Stéphanie Prévost and Bénédicte Deschamps, 2024

Stéphanie Prévost and Bénédicte Deschamps have asserted their right under the
Copyright, Designs and Patents Act, 1988, to be identified as Editors of this work.

Cover images: Glasshouse Images/Alamy Stock Photo and David Pollack/Getty.

All rights reserved. No part of this publication may be: i) reproduced or transmitted in
any form, electronic or mechanical, including photocopying, recording or by means of any
information storage or retrieval system without prior permission in writing from the publishers;
or ii) used or reproduced in any way for the training, development or operation of artificial
intelligence (AI) technologies, including generative AI technologies. The rights holders expressly
reserve this publication from the text and data mining exception as per Article 4(3) of the
Digital Single Market Directive (EU) 2019/790.

Bloomsbury Publishing Plc does not have any control over, or responsibility
for, any third-party websites referred to or in this book. All internet addresses
given in this book were correct at the time of going to press. The author and
publisher regret any inconvenience caused if addresses have changed or sites
have ceased to exist, but can accept no responsibility for any such changes.

A catalogue record for this book is available from the British Library.

A catalog record for this book is available from the Library of Congress.

ISBN: HB: 978-1-3501-0704-5
PB: 978-1-3503-2525-8
ePDF: 978-1-3501-0705-2
eBook: 978-1-3501-0706-9

Typeset by RefineCatch Limited, Bungay, Suffolk

For product safety related questions contact productsafety@bloomsbury.com.

To find out more about our authors and books visit www.bloomsbury.com
and sign up for our newsletters.

Contents

List of Illustrations   vii
List of Charts and Tables   ix
List of Contributors   x

General Introduction – Print Media in a Foreign Language across the Atlantic: Common Grounds, Diverging Approaches
Bénédicte Deschamps and Stéphanie Prévost   1

Section One – Journalism Without Borders: Wandering Titles and Transnational Journalistic Networks

1. The Hebrew 'Wandering Press' in Europe: *Ha-Levanon* from Jerusalem to Paris, Mainz and London (1863–86)   *Gideon Kouts*   27
2. A Transnational Radical Print Culture: French-Language Anarchist Periodicals between London, Paris and the United States before 1914   *Constance Bantman*   45
3. Collaborating across the Atlantic: Gigi Damiani and the Italian Anarchist Press in the United States (1909–45)   *Isabelle Felici*   63

Section Two – Community Building and Transculturation: Allocating Foreign-Language Communities' Needs

4. French-Language Almanacs in the United States, from the Eighteenth Century to the Beginning of the Twentieth Century: Genres, Social Dimensions and Transcultural Adaptations *Hans-Jürgen Lüsebrink*   81
5. 'A modest sentinel for German interests in England': The Anglo-German Press in the Long Nineteenth Century *Susan Reed*   93
6. The Soul of the Colony: Origins and Cultural Imaginary of the Portuguese-Language Press in the United States (1877–2019) *Alberto Pena-Rodríguez*   109
7. 'Spotlight on Jim Crow': Radical Slovak and Polish Immigrant Newspapers in Solidarity with Black Civil Rights   *Robert M. Zecker*   125

8   Manufacturing Identities of Poles in the UK in Polish-Language
    Online Media Following the Brexit Campaign *Katarzyna
    Molek-Kozakowska*   143

Section Three – Betwixt Local Politics and the Home Country's Politics:
Extraterritorial Media Staging of Political Conflicts

9   Betwixt Spain and England: The Spanish Liberals'
    Spanish-Language Media Strategies in London (1810–50)
    María José Ruiz Acosta   163
10 The *Megali Idea* in New York's Greek-Language Press (1915–22):
    Doing Greek Politics from a Distance? *Nicolas Pitsos*   177
11 Barzini Overseas: The *Corriere d'America*, from Promoting
    Italianità to Fascist Propaganda *Lorenzo Benadusi*   193

Section Four – Monolingualism, Plurilingualism and Rivalling
Languages: Language Choice and Identity Framing

12 Why French? The Multiple Uses of French-Language Periodicals
    in London (UK) and Sydney (Australia) during the Nineteenth
    Century and Beyond *Valentina Gosetti*   207
13 Revolutionizing Women's Roles in the Late Nineteenth-Century
    US-Based Spanish-Language Press *Kelley Kreitz*   223
14 Divergency in Russian Emigré Publishing in Late Victorian
    Britain: The Case of the *Narodovolets* and *The Anglo-Russian*
    Robert Henderson   237
15 *Le Haïasdan*, *L'Arménie*, *Armenia* and *Hnch'ak*: Language
    Choice and the Construction of a Cosmopolitan Armenian
    Diasporic Identity in London and Paris (1888–1905)
    Stéphanie Prévost   259
16 The Power of the Transnational Native Tongue in Exile: Belgian
    Refugees during the First World War, Their Exile Press and Their
    Fragmented Identity *Christophe Declercq*   279

Selected Bibliography   297
Index   323

Illustrations

0.1 Photograph by Ian J. Dennis of 'International free newspaper stands on the Strand, 6 October 2011', Flickr, © Ian James Dennis 2013.   2
0.2 *Freiheit*, New York and London, 10 March 1888, 1 [Serials IISG ZF 1078], Courtesy of the International Institute of Social History (Amsterdam).   14
0.3 'Languages in the Directory of US Newspapers of American Libraries', National Digital Newspaper Program, Library of Congress website, December 2022.   18
1.1 *Halbanon*, 5 March 1863, Jerusalem, issue 1. By courtesy of the Historical Jewish Press website (www.Jpress.org.il) founded by the National Library and Tel Aviv University.   28
1.2 *Libanon*, Masthead, 6 January 1865, Paris. By courtesy of the Historical Jewish Press website (www.Jpress.org.il) founded by the National Library and Tel Aviv University.   30
1.3 *Ha-Levanon, Hebreische Ausgabe des ‚Israelit'* (The Hebrew edition of *Der Israelit*), Masthead, Mainz, 16 August 1871. *Libanon*, Masthead, 6 January 1865, Paris. By courtesy of the Historical Jewish Press website (www.Jpress.org.il) founded by the National Library and Tel Aviv University.   37
1.4 *The Lebanon*, Masthead, 1 September 1886, London, last issue (771). By courtesy of the Historical Jewish Press website (www.Jpress.org.il) founded by the National Library and Tel Aviv University.   39
3.1 Masthead of *Cronaca sovversiva*, 19 August 1916. Author's personal collection.   64
3.2 Masthead of *Il Martello*, 16 August 1924 (New York). Courtesy of Il Ministero della cultura – Pinacoteca di Brera –Biblioteca Braidense, Milano.   66
3.3 Masthead of *L'Adunata dei refrattari* (New York), 26 June 1926. LC_FPR_0394_1926 « Collection La Contemporaine » (Nanterre, France).   67
3.4 Masthead of *L'Adunata dei refrattari* (New York), 31 January 1931. Source: gallica.bnf.fr/BnF.   67
3.5 Masthead of *Germinal* (Chicago), 15 May 1928. LC_GFP_5101_1936 « Collection La Contemporaine » (Nanterre, France).   67
14.1 V. L. Burtsev. *The Anglo-Russian*, vol. 8, no. 11 (November 1904), 859. Courtesy of the British Library Board. Shelfmark General Reference Collection 1904 LOU.LON 744 [1898].   238
14.2 J. M. Prelooker. Frontispiece from *Russian Flashlights*. London: Chapman and Hall, 1911.   239
14.3 *Anglo-Russian*, vol. 7, no. 1, 1898, 1. Courtesy of the British Library Board. Shelfmark General Reference Collection 1898 LOU.LON 744 [1898].   241

14.4 *Narodovolets*, no. 1, April 1897, 1. Courtesy of the British Library Board. Shelfmark General Reference Collection P.P.3554.ec. 243

15.1a and 15.1b *Le Haiasdan*, issue 1, 1 November 1888, 1 (Armenian and French versions). Courtesy of the AGBU Nubar Library, Paris. 262

Charts and Tables

2.1 Key French-language anarchist communist papers published in Britain and the United States, 1880–1914. ... 46
3.1 Number of articles published each year (1923–39) by Damiani in *L'Adunata dei refrattari, Il Martello* and *Germinal*. ... 68
8.1 Table of main sources of *MojaWyspa* articles. ... 148
8.2 Table of main thematic categories in *MojaWyspa* articles. ... 149
10.1 Greek-language newspapers published in the United States of America from the late nineteenth century to the first half of the twentieth century (non-exhaustive list). ... 177
16.1 Year by year periods for the publication of the Belgian exile press in Britain, ordered alphabetically. ... 286
16.2 List of Belgian exile press in France and the Netherlands (not exhaustive). ... 288
16.3 Selected overview of transnational networks of Belgian exile press in France, Britain and The Netherlands and their nationalist affiliation. ... 290

Contributors

María José Ruiz Acosta is Professor of Spanish Journalism at the University of Seville, Spain. Her works and publications address the relationship established between communication, political discourse and culture in nineteenth-century Spain. She is currently doing research in three areas: exile and journalism (particularly in the 1823–33 Spanish Liberal exile in England); the representation (and construction) of national identity in the nineteenth-century Spanish press; and aspects of the representation of society in radio and television during the Spanish transition to democracy. She is the author of *Sevilla e Hispanoamérica. Prensa y opinión pública tras el Desastre de 1898* (CSIC, 1996) and *La prensa hispánica en el exilio de Londres* (Comunicación Social Ediciones, 2016).

Constance Bantman is Associate Professor in French at the University of Surrey, UK. Her research focuses on the social and political history of French anarchism as a networked and transnational movement. Her most recent monograph is *Jean Grave and the Networks of French Anarchism, 1854–1939* (Palgrave, 2021), a biography of the influential French editor Jean Grave exploring the transnational print culture of the anarchist movement. She is also the author of *The French Anarchists in London 1880–1914. Exile and Transnationalism in the First Globalisation* (LUP, 2013) and the co-editor of *The Foreign Political Press in Nineteenth-Century London, Politics from a Distance* (Bloomsbury, 2017).

Lorenzo Benadusi is Professor of Contemporary History and European Cultural History at Roma Tre University. His research has focused on gender and sexuality studies, intellectual history and history of journalism, with particular interest in Liberal and Fascist Italy. He is author of several books and essays, and his publications include *Respectability and Violence: Military Values, Masculine Honor, and Italy's Road to Mass Death* (University of Wisconsin Press, 2021), *The Enemy of the New Man. Homosexuality in Fascist Italy* (University of Wisconsin Press, 2012), *Il Corriere della Sera di Luigi Albertini. Nascita e sviluppo della prima industria culturale di massa* (Aracne, 2012) and, with Paolo Bernardini, Elisa Bianco and Paola Guazzo, *Homosexuality in Italian Literature, Society, and Culture, 1789–1919* (Cambridge Scholars Publishing, 2017).

Christophe Declercq is Assistant Professor at the University of Utrecht and Senior Honorary Research Fellow at University College London. After his PhD (Imperial College London) on the linguistic and socio-cultural identity of a temporary displacement during the First World War, Christophe moved into the domain of cross-cultural communication at times of conflict, either in a historic setting (including three books on *Languages and the First World War*, co-edited with Julian Walker, Palgrave-MacMillan, 2016, Bloomsbury, 2021) or in a contemporary setting (including *Intercultural Crisis Communication: Translating, Interpreting and Languages in Local Crises*, co-edited with Federico Federici, Bloomsbury, 2019). During the Centenary of the First World War, several outreach projects on Belgian refugees at the time were valorized by the media (BBC and VRT). With Koen Kerremans, he is preparing the *Routledge Handbook of Translation, Interpreting and Crisis* (2023).

Bénédicte Deschamps is Associate Professor at the Université Paris Cité (France) where she teaches US history, US immigration history and Italian-American studies. She is a member of the Centre National pour la Recherche Scientifique (LARCA UMR 8225) and of the Institut Convergences Migrations. Her research focuses on the history of Italian immigration in the United States from the Risorgimento to the Second World War, the US ethnic press, and the diplomatic relationships between Italy and the US. Her two latest books deal with the history of the Italian immigration press in the United States and Italian immigrant journalism in the world: *Histoire de la presse italo-américaine du Risorgimento à la Grande Guerre* (Paris, L'Harmattan, 2020) and *Voci d'Italia fuori dall'Italia. Giornalismo e stampa dell'emigrazione*, co-edited with Pantaleone Sergi (Cosenza, Pellegrini, 2021). For more details on her publications, see https://u-paris.academia.edu/B%C3%A9n%C3%A9dicteDeschamps.

Isabelle Felici is Professor of Italian Studies at the Paul-Valéry University in Montpellier, France. Her works and publications address cultural representations of Italian migratory movements from nineteenth- to twenty-first-century-century migration and Italian Anarchism in exile. She is currently doing research on the Italian Anarchist Press in France and in other French-speaking countries (1872–1950 Switzerland, Tunisia and Belgium). Her publications, mainly in French, Italian and Portuguese, include two chapters in English: 'Strangers at Home. A Reading of Marco Turco's Film, *La Straniera*, Italy 2009' (in Seyed Javad Miri (ed.), *Orientalism, A Eurocentric Vision of the 'Other'*, International Peace Studies Centre Press, 2013, 61–78) and 'Anarchists as Emigrants' (in Bert Altena and Constance Bantman (eds), *Reassessing the Transnational Turn. Scales of Analysis in Anarchist and Syndicalist Studies*, Routledge, 2014, 83–99 and AK Press, Chico, California, 2016, 83–99).

Valentina Gosetti works on the unceded country of the Dharug people. She is Associate Professor in French at the University of New England in Australia, where she is the recipient of a Discovery Early Career Researcher Award from the Australian Research Council (DE200101206: 'Provincial Poets and the Making of a Nation'), funded by the Australian government. Her research so far has been aimed at revaluing the contribution of lesser-known provincial poets and the importance of the provincial and transnational press in and beyond nineteenth-century France. She authored *Aloysius Bertrand's 'Gaspard de la Nuit': Beyond the Prose Poem* (2016), co-edited *Still Loitering: Australian Essays in Honour of Ross Chambers* (2020) and co-edited/co-translated the bilingual anthology *Donne: Poeti di Francia e oltre. Dal Romanticismo* *a Oggi* (2017). With Patrick McGuinness, she co-edits the Oxford Peter Lang book series 'Romanticism and After in France'.

Robert Henderson gained an MA in Russian and a Diploma in Slavonic Languages at the University of Glasgow before taking up the post of Russian Curator at the British Library. Some twenty years later he returned to academic studies in the School of History, Queen Mary University of London and in 2009 completed his doctoral research into the Russian political emigration in late nineteenth-century London. He has published extensively in that field, the latest being the monographs *Vladimir Burtsev and the Struggle for a Free Russia: A Revolutionary in the Time of Tsarism and Bolshevism* (Bloomsbury Academic, 2017) and *The Spark that Lit the Revolution: Young Lenin in London and the Politics that Changed the World* (I.B. Tauris/Bloomsbury Academic, 2020).

Gideon Kouts is Emeritus Professor of Modern Jewish History, Culture and Communication at Paris 8 University and lectured at the Jerusalem Hebrew University (1992–4). He is Head of the European Institute of Hebrew Studies and a research fellow at Tel Aviv University Center for International and Regional Studies. He is the editor of *REEH* (the European Journal of Hebrew Studies) and *Kesher* (the International Journal of Jewish Press and Communications History Research). He serves as senior international correspondent for the Israel Public Broadcasting Corporation and *Maariv* daily, and is Honorary President of the French Foreign Press Association. His research focuses on the Jewish press and Communications History. Aside from numerous articles and chapters in Hebrew, French, English, Polish, Russian, German and Spanish, his books include *News and History: Studies in History of Hebrew and Jewish Press and Communications* (Bialik Institute, 2013, in Hebrew), *The Hebrew and Jewish Press in Europe-Select Problems in Its History* (Suger University Press, 2006), *Editors and Journals: Studies in History of the Hebrew and Jewish Press* (World Hebrew Union, 1999, in Hebrew), *La presse hébraïque en Europe: ses origines et son évolution de 1856 à 1897* (Septentrion, 1997) and *Les grands périodiques hébraïques en Europe* (Maisonneuve et Larose, 1993).

Kelley Kreitz is Associate Professor of English and an affiliate faculty member in Latinx Studies at Pace University in New York City, where she also directs the university's digital humanities centre, Babble Lab. Her research on print and digital cultures of the Americas has appeared in *American Literary History*, *American Periodicals*, *English Language Notes* and *Revista de Estudios Hispánicos*. She steers a digital mapping project on New York City's nineteenth-century Spanish-language press, C19LatinoNYC.org. She serves on the board of the Recovering the US Hispanic Literary Heritage Project at the University of Houston and on the steering committee of New York City Digital Humanities (NYCDH). She is completing a book on the leading role played by US-based writers of Latin American descent in the media innovation of the late nineteenth century.

Hans-Jürgen Lusebrink studied Romance languages and literature and history at the universities of Mainz, Paris and Tours, doctorate (1981) and habilitation in Romance languages and literatures at the University of Bayreuth (1987) and in history at the EHESS in Paris (1984). He held the Chair of Romance Cultural Studies and Intercultural Communication at the University of Saarbrücken (1993–2018), where he has been senior professor since 2018. He is also a member of the Scientific Committee of Transfopress. His main research interests include theories of intercultural communication, Franco-German cultural relations, cultural transfers between Europe and the non-European world, Enlightenment cultures and media (especially almanacs, encyclopaedias and popular media), francophone literatures and media outside Europe (especially in Africa and Québec). His recent book publications include *Le livre aimé du peuple. Les almanachs québécois de 1777 à nos jours* (Québec, 2014), *Jesuit Accounts of the Colonial Americas. Intercultural Transfers, Intellectual Disputes, and Textualities*, edited with Marc-André Bernier and Clorinda Donato (Toronto, 2014), *Intercultural Communication* (Stuttgart, 2005, 4th ed. 2017), *Écrire l'encyclopédisme, du XVIIIe siècle à nos jours*, edited with Susanne Greilich (Paris, 2020) and *Translation and Transfer of Knowledge in Encyclopedic Compilations, 1680–1830*, edited with Clorinda Donato (Toronto, 2021).

Katarzyna Molek-Kozakowska is Associate Professor and Head of the Department of English, Institute of Linguistics, University of Opole, Poland and Senior Research Fellow at the Department of Creative Communication, Vilnius Gediminas Technical University, Lithuania. With a background in English studies, she specializes in discourse analysis, political communication and media studies, with a special interest in Polish media in the UK. She co-edits the international open access Scopus/WoS-indexed journal *Res Rhetorica*. With Jan Chovanec, she co-edited a monograph on *Representing the Other in European Media Discourses* (Benjamins, 2019). She is a communication manager for the multinational consortium FORTHEM Alliance coordinating a Horizon 2020 project FIT FORTHEM (2020–3).

Alberto Pena Rodriguez is Professor of Media Studies at the University of Vigo, Spain. His research is particularly focused on the History of Social Communication in the Lusophone world. Among other publications, he is the author of *Comunicar en la diáspora. Inmigración, periodismo, exilio y propaganda entre los inmigrantes portugueses en Estados Unidos (1877–1950)* (Comares, 2021) and *News on the American dream. A history of the Portuguese press in the United States* (University of Massachusetts Press, 2020). He is also the co-editor of *Para uma história do jornalismo português no mundo* with António Hohlfeldt (Livros Icnova, 2021).

Nicolas Pitsos is Associate Researcher at the Center for Studies on Europe and Eurasia (CREE/Inalco) and at the Center for Cultural History of Contemporary Societies (CHCSC/Université Paris-Saclay) in Paris. He is currently teaching on the history of the Eastern question at the ICES (Institut Catholique d'Études Supérieures) and he is a member of the Transfopress, a transnational network for the study of foreign-language press. His latest publications include *Le Magasin pittoresque: kaléidoscope d'études grecques* (L'Harmattan, 2022). He was also co-editor of a special of *Cahiers Balkaniques* entitled *La presse allophone dans les Balkans* (Inalco Presses, 2020). At the same time, he is pursuing his research on Greek-speaking newspapers around the world, as well as British, French and Greek perceptions of the Eastern question during the nineteenth and twentieth centuries.

Stéphanie Prévost is Senior Lecturer in long nineteenth-century British history and culture at Université Paris Cité in France. Alongside her membership of LARCA (a CNRS research group on histories, literatures, arts and cultures of English-speaking countries), she sits on the scientific committee of the Transfopress network, which studies the allophone press as a historical and global phenomenon (https://www.chcsc.uvsq.fr/transfopress). She has published extensively on British-Ottoman relations (long nineteenth century) and has developed an interest in the English-language press of the Ottoman Empire in that context. In 2017–18, she co-curated a public exhibition (with Dr Bénédicte Deschamps) entitled 'Language Matters' at the Grands Moulins Library in Paris, which associated more than seventy institutional partners throughout the world. The exhibit was in two parts, with part 1 proposing the first-ever retrospective of the English-language press (broadly considered) since its inception in 1760 and part 2 offering an inkling into the ethnic press in the UK and the US since the seventeenth century. A follow-up virtual exhibition will be released in 2023 (http://www.language-matters.fr). Her research is now also geared towards nineteenth-early twentieth-century histories of humanitarianism and liberal internationalisms as part of the junior fellowship of the Institut universitaire de France that she was recently awarded.

Susan Reed is Lead Curator of Germanic Collections at the British Library. Her research interests include broadsides and ephemera from the revolutions of 1848 in Germany, and German-language printing and publishing in nineteenth-century London. On the latter topic she has published 'Printers, Publishers and Proletarians: Some Aspects of German trades in Nineteenth-Century London' in Barry Taylor (ed.), *Foreign Language Printing in London 1500–1900* (Boston Spa and London, 2002) and 'German Printers, Publishers and Booksellers in 19th Century Britain' in Stefan Manz et al. (eds), *Migration and Transfer from Germany to Britain 1660–1914* (Munich, 2007).

Robert M. Zecker is Professor of History at Saint Francis Xavier University, Nova Scotia, Canada, where he teaches courses on race, immigration, social movements, and US history. His research includes immigration, radicalism and the popular culture of immigrants on the left. He is the author of four books, including *America's Immigrant Press: How the Slovaks Were Taught to Think Like White People* (Continuum, 2011) and most recently *'A Road to Peace and Freedom': The International Workers Order and the Struggle for Economic Justice and Civil Rights, 1930–1954* (Temple University Press, 2018) He is the author of many book chapters, as well as many articles in journals such as the *Journal of American Ethnic History*, *American Communist History*, *The Journal of the Canadian Historical Association* and *The Journal of Social History*. Zecker is currently working on a book on the history of the Workers' Schools of the Communist Party USA. Before entering academia, he was a journalist in his native New Jersey.

General Introduction – Print Media in a Foreign Language across the Atlantic: Common Grounds, Diverging Approaches

Bénédicte Deschamps
Université Paris Cité-LARCA, CNRS, Institut Convergences Migrations

Stéphanie Prévost
Université Paris Cité-LARCA, CNRS/Institut Universitaire de France

What do the London tube stations Charing Cross, Victoria, Queensway and Temple have in common? They all used to offer distribution points for *El Ibérico Gratuito* (The Free Iberian), a Spanish-language free periodical published in London meant for Spanish-speakers residing or visiting the British capital.[1] Launched in 2010, *El Ibérico Gratuito* was quickly financially successful and has been promoting Spanish and Latin American culture ever since, while providing British and international news to its readers, and is now only digital.[2] *El Ibérico Gratuito* is by no means an isolated case. Outside of Charing Cross train station, it used to sit side by side with free London-based Lithuanian-language *Tiesa* (Truth, 2010?–), and Russian-language titles like weekly Áнглия (Angliya/England, 2011–), weekly Пульс UK (Pulse UK, 2005–) and Elvira Polyanskaya's bilingual Russian-English *The Business Courier* (2012–). Change stations, and other free press titles were available from street dispensers. On the Strand, the free weekly Romanian-language *Ziarul romanesc* (The Financial Newspaper) could usually be found, or Polish language free titles like *The Polish Express* (weekly) or *The Polish Observer* (2007–). If you're looking for the *UK Chinese Times*, dash to Gerrard Street in Chinatown!

The list could go on, as it offers just a snapshot of the numerous non-English-language periodicals that still exist in Britain today (in Arabic, Urdu, Gujarati, Bengali, Punjabi, Turkish, Bulgarian, Greek, Italian, French, German, Hebrew, Yiddish, Bulgarian, Armenian, Portuguese, etc. to name but a few of languages not discussed before). In a way, the alignment of these street dispensers in the public space gave to see and spatialize a contemporary multilingual press in Britain as a phenomenon that otherwise remains largely off-centre, even in media studies. Yet these free non-English-language press titles available in the public space (now mostly digital) represent but the tip of the iceberg, which has a long, but so far largely unrecognized history.

Figure 0.1 International free newspaper stands on the Strand, 6 October 2011, Flickr, © Ian James Dennis 2013.³

On the other side of the Atlantic, this iceberg is the size of a continent. Indeed, it is on a wider scale that the phenomenon can be observed in the United States, where there is a long-standing tradition of distributing free community press and where printing papers in a language other than English dates back to the times of the American British colonies with Benjamin Franklin's German-language *Die Philadelphische Zeitung*, published in Pennsylvania as early as 1732. It is common knowledge that US history has been shaped by millions of immigrants, but rarely is it recorded that the latter have all sought a voice in the choir of American journalism by creating organs in their own languages. The panel of their papers is as rich as their origins are variegated. Drawing a list of all the US-based non-English-language titles would thus require more than one volume. For the sole Italian-language press, the only existing catalogue compiled in 1983 by historian Pietro Russo is already 180 pages long and yet incomplete, if anything because new periodicals were issued after the 1980s.⁴ Two and a half centuries have not quenched the various ethnic/nationality/language groups' thirst for launching their own media, be they in paper or online. In the late nineteenth century, the *Rowell* and the *Ayer and Son* periodical directories already inserted a section listing the 'foreign-tongue' newspapers, which could be of use to the potential advertisers. In the early 2000s, the periodicals published by and for Hispanics represented such an important issue that the major newspaper companies invested in expanded Spanish editions to 'crack the burgeoning market' by 'dismantling the language barrier', as journalist Tim Porter puts it.⁵ In 2014, the New York *Intelligencer* celebrated the vitality of New York City's ninety-five 'ethnic' papers which reached a combined circulation of no fewer than 2.9 million copies.⁶ Today in New York City, like in London, newsstands still display papers whose titles in Portuguese (*24 Horas*), Italian (*America Oggi*), Arabic (*Cedar News*), Urdu (*The Pakistani Newspaper*), Spanish (*El Diario/La Prensa*), Russian (русские новости), Nepali (*US Nepali News*) or Greek (*ΚΑΛΑΜΙ*) testify to the local diversity.

Language does matter

The United Kingdom and the United States are not the only countries that can boast having a rich multilingual press, though not always in the same proportions. In Brazil, Argentina, Australia, Germany, France, Italy, Canada and even Peru, migration and exile have also planted the seeds of thousands of journalistic ventures that gave birth to newspapers published in hundreds of different languages. Such a profusion has made the question of terminology when referring to this press even more complex. In fact, giving a name is a process that is never neutral and that often reveals more about the name givers than it succeeds in describing the object that is being defined. Both in Europe and in the Americas, the emergence of a press issued in a language other than what was – or was perceived – as the official language of the country it was printed in led to the use of different terms. Each of them evinces a specific approach to the phenomenon, be it historical, sociological, or political. Each of them reveals how multicultural societies envision themselves and relate to their immigrants.

The most commonly used terms to qualify this press are 'immigrant', 'ethnic', 'minority' and 'foreign-language', yet none of them is fully satisfactory. The first appeared in the early studies of US immigration, in particular in sociologist Robert Park's seminal *The Immigrant Press and Its Control* (1922). While it adequately depicts the papers issued by the first generations of migrants, it makes no distinction between the English-language and the foreign-language periodicals published by the various communities, and it fails to address appropriately the journalism of second and third generations who have become full citizens or subjects or the countries where their parents settled. Today, historians, sociologists and politicians in the United States tend to privilege the word 'ethnic', which matches the American concept of 'ethnic group', a concept that is widely referred to in US government reports but is sometimes seen as controversial in other countries with a colonial history like France.[7] The North American papers themselves seem to have appropriated it, using the term 'ethnic' in the names of their associations.[8] Although quite handy, this adjective is too wide here as it encompasses in the same category African-Americans and Native Americans, while those groups' experiences differ from those of immigrants.

The compound 'foreign-language' puts the emphasis on the linguistic choice made by the editors and therefore could seem more accurate, especially for the earlier period, to refer to press titles set up by foreign exiles and immigrants who had just settled in Britain or the US. Nonetheless, it is equally questionable as its use implicitly dismisses the fact that the nationals of the same country may speak various languages (not to mention the regional tongues) and supports the idea that there is such a simple thing as an 'official' language. In the case of the United States, the constitution says otherwise and while Congress regularly discusses 'English-only' bills, education, media and government information agencies are bound to acknowledge the multilingual background of American society.[9] Another limit to the locution 'foreign-language' is that it merges in the same category the papers produced in the host countries and those imported from abroad. Both *El País* and *El Diario* can be bought at a New York newsstand, and both belong to the Spanish-language press. Yet the first is a Madrid-based national Spanish daily, while the second is a leading US Hispanic newspaper. They share only a few characteristics with one another, aside from language. In reality, even the idea that they are printed in the same language is debatable as *El Diario* contains articles written in Latin American varieties of Spanish. As surprising as it might seem, *El Diario* might have more in common with its American counterpart *The Pakistani News* or even the London-based Spanish-language *Express News* as they have similar ambitions, needs and problems that are specific to the lives of their readers.

Quite revealingly, in times of political turmoil and international crises, the leaders of anti-immigration and nativistic movements further blur the distinction between local immigrant periodicals and organs produced abroad, referring to the former no more as 'foreign- language' but as 'foreign' or 'alien' papers, to justify the request that they be suppressed.

In Europe, the terminology 'minority press' or 'minority language newspapers' focuses on the immigrant groups' place in host societies. Those groups are thus presented as smaller distinct cultural entities to be dealt with in relation to the larger context of European states' dominant cultures. However, the notion of 'minority language' remains rather unclear. The 1992 European Charter for Regional and Minority Languages (effective since 1998) aims at protecting 'Europe's rich linguistic diversity, including its traditional regional and minority languages (RML)'[10] and defines the latter as languages 'traditionally used within a given territory of a State by nationals of that State who form a group numerically smaller than the rest of the State's population and different from the official language(s) of that State'. Interestingly, that category does not include 'either dialects of the official language(s) of the State or the languages of migrants'.[11] In line with this restrictive definition, the European Association of Daily Newspapers in Minority and Regional Languages (MIDAS) was formed in 2001 to promote and protect the rights of minority language communities' papers.[12] MIDAS welcomes among its members the editors of Italian-language *La Voce del Popolo* published in Croatia and Polish-language *Kurier Wilenski* printed in Lithuania, because Italian- and Polish-speaking communities have long been established in Fiume and Vilnius, respectively. Although both based in London, neither *La Voce degli Italiani* nor *The Polish Express* could join this association, not just because they are not dailies but above all because they are published by immigrants, therefore not in what the European Union calls RMLs. This is just one example of how delicate it is to define the newspapers studied in this book.

The EU definition is as clear as it can be in a legal context, but, as Malika Pedley and Alain Viaut underline, the terms 'minority' and 'minority language' are in reality used more loosely and often extend to immigrants, their languages and their media.[13] In *The Other Languages of Europe,* Guus Extra and Durk Gorter thus refer to 'immigrant minority languages', and stress the more inclusive approach embraced by the 1996 Barcelona Universal Declaration on Linguistic Rights.[14] This text was signed by non-governmental organizations, and challenges the 1992 EU charter by defining a 'language group' as 'any group of persons sharing the same language which is established in the territorial space of another language community but which does not possess historical antecedents equivalent to those of that community', i.e. 'immigrants, refugees, deported persons and members of diaspora'.[15] The same declaration reiterates the need to guarantee the right of each language group to enjoy – and therefore produce – media of their own. Indeed, such a right has repeatedly been challenged in the course of history and it happens to be still debated today on the ground of national security by states fearing the subversive potential of news published in a language that mainstream media do not understand. Yet Sally Holt and John Packer recall that, as part of the human rights protected by the European Union, 'freedom of expression guarantees not only the right to impart and receive information, but the right to do so in the chosen medium, including language and form'.[16] That freedom applies to all media, whatever the definition of 'minority language' be, including immigrant papers. The EU debates over the naming of the groups producing information in an alternative language, as much as the efforts made by various institutions to define the place of those languages in a State's life are far from being anecdotal, because those very definitions may also induce the granting or deprivation of rights and support.

In the UK, where linguistic and cultural diversity is a well-known feature, but where a comprehensive history of immigrant media is yet to be written, definitions are also an issue. While the Multilingual Manchester project led by Yaron Matras (2010–21) promotes language awareness in a city whose inhabitants speak no fewer than 150 idioms, finding the right terminology is still a challenge, as language for multilinguals is also very much context-dependent.[17] In the early 1980s, Ming Tsow, an official of the Commission for Racial Equality, addressed the urge for British governments to acknowledge British 'ethnic minority community languages'.[18] More recently, Viv Edwards's discussion of the terminology problem serves as a reference in the field. In her analysis of Britain's ever-growing linguistic vitality, she highlights the inadequacy of the often-used terms 'immigrant language' for the reasons mentioned earlier in this introduction, and dismisses the terms 'community language', because the groups speaking another language than English may not necessarily picture themselves, nor act, as 'communities'. She further underlines the limits of expressions like 'minority languages', which include 'older tongues' such as Welsh, Gaelic or Irish, and therefore chooses to define the languages of groups that have recently settled in the United Kingdom as 'new minority languages'.[19] Whatever the field of research or the country of reference, so unsatisfactory are the terms referring to the non-mainstream language press that compounds have become a rule: Catherine Dewhirst and Richard Scully speak of 'minority community printed press' for the Australian context, while Alicia Ferrández Ferrer and Jessica Retis prefer discussing the case of 'ethnic minority media' in North America.[20] Insisting on its position as an alternative to the dominant information business, other authors identify this press as an 'outsider', an 'other voice' in national journalism, and categorize this press as 'dissident', 'specialized', 'diverse' or 'distinctive'.[21] In this book, the terminology also varies according to authors, research fields, time periods, countries and topics. We are aware of the terminology debate, but must admit there is as yet no definition that is entirely connotation-free and that might cover fully the width of what this press is. The phrase 'non-English-language press' is perhaps an acceptable alternative (especially for the contemporary period), but stills relies on the assumption that in Britain and the United States, the *de facto* official language is English.

Writing the history of the foreign-language press across the Atlantic: compared perspectives

Writing the history of this press is no easier than defining it. Even in the US where the literature in the field is richer than anywhere else, there were few attempts to analyse the path of ethnic newspapers from a scholarly perspective until the late 1980s. In fact, more than two centuries elapsed between the birth of Benjamin Franklin's German-language paper and Robert Park's report on the 'immigrant press'. A number of testimonies published by newspapermen themselves partly make up for this original void. Indeed, journalists were the first to reconstruct the histories of the periodicals they created or with which they collaborated. Quite self-celebrative, their recollections were essentially relating the epic of a difficult enterprise. They focused on the challenges editors heroically faced: the lack of funding, the inexperience of their first steps, and the struggle for shaping their fellow compatriots into a cohesive political force. Last but not least, they insisted on the glorious deeds they had achieved in the name of what they then labelled their 'colony'. The articles and books that resulted from those narratives are valuable documents, but their hagiographic tone as much as the numerous factual errors they contain dismiss them as reliable histories of the newspapers they explore.

Equally biased are Robert Park's study and Edward Hunter's *In Many Voices: Our Fabulous Foreign-Language Press*, two of the only three volumes taking up the gauntlet of discussing the immigrant/ethnic press globally. The former was innovative for the 1920s not only because it dealt with a material that had always been deemed marginal, but also because it attempted to analyse it comprehensively, not limiting itself to one specific group. Yet it was part of a research programme led by the Chicago School of Sociology which was funded by the Carnegie Foundation, i.e. by the US captains of industry. It aimed at assessing immigrants' assimilation in society, and presented the foreign-language press as an instrument to be controlled by business and government agencies when necessary. Park believed immigrant editors should be educated – not to say manipulated – so that they would serve the needs of the big industries and help mould their readers into good and productive American citizens. Written with the help of various immigrant journalists, Park's volume can be credited for shedding precious light on periodicals that had been discarded until then by the academia, but it remains nonetheless patronizing and has served as the foundation stone for the literature justifying the existence of immigrant papers only on the basis of their willingness to qualify as assimilating tools. As to Hunter's poorly documented essay, it was published in the aftermath of the Second World War, when McCarthyism was raging and when the loyalty of the foreign-language press was subjected to close scrutiny. Its main purpose was to check the political orthodoxy of non-English newspapers which Hunter suspected of potentially supporting 'foreign' ideologies like communism. The book compared the 'reader of a foreign language newspaper' to 'a small boy in a five-and-ten-cent store, clasping a dime in his hand', whose excitement at seeing the profusion of 'toys and candies' at the counter confused him to the point that he could 'end up picking what isn't good for him'.[22] In other words, foreign-language papers were appraised as potential weapons in the hands of an immature readership that was unable to select decent food for thought. Rather emblematic of the Cold War literature and preoccupations, Hunter displayed blatant contempt for immigrants and reinforced the idea that the latter's press should play a specific role by guiding its readers into making the 'right' political choice. Breaking from this connoted approach, the last of the three books dealing globally with the US ethnic press studies how newspapers 'recorded the movement from immigrant populations moving from acculturation to assimilation to cultural pluralism by shaping the American dream'.[23] Yet in this very short volume published in 2010, media specialist Leara D. Rhodes does not try to offer an in-depth history of the ethnic press but limits herself to analysing its functions by drawing from the existing literature on single groups.

It is indeed a challenge to try to give a wide panorama of thousands of periodicals printed in hundreds of languages, even in one country only. The required multilingual skills therefore justify collective initiatives such as historian Sally Miller's *The Ethnic Press in the United States: a Historical Analysis and Handbook*.[24] While it dates back to the 1980s and does not cover all language groups, this collection of essays brings together noteworthy contributions to the history of the press by twenty-six of them from Chinese to Ukrainian immigrants and is still the most comprehensive book in the field. In the same decade, as scholars continued the reflection that the civil rights movement had ignited in humanities, Christiane Harzig and Dirk Hoerder documented the immigrant workers' input to US radical print culture in a transatlantic perspective.[25] Their ground-breaking work has shown how rich and interactive labour migrants' journalism was in Europe and North America between the 1840s and the 1980s, and it has paved the way for numerous other studies focusing on non-English titles produced by foreign-born anarchists, communists, unionists and socialists established in the Americas. Those investigations made clear that the immigrant/ethnic press was multifaceted as much linguistically as in its format and motivations. What transformed sweat into ink was also the need to protest. Not all of the periodicals were meant to act as integration facilitators, as Jerzy Zubrzycki suggested, or to disappear with the taken-for-granted assimilation of migrants, as Robert Park or Oscar Ban maintained.[26]

The rise of ethnic studies and the preservation programmes led by institutions such as the Immigration History Research Center in Minneapolis, the Balch Institute in Philadelphia or the Center for Migration Studies on Staten Island (to mention just a few of them) fostered further research which led, in the long run, to the publication of a number of studies, each centred on one language group.[27] Aside from the linguistic choice, all those books opt for a different angle. For instance, Peter Connolly-Smith focuses on the role played by German editors in interpreting the American way of life to immigrants, Nicolàs Kanellos makes a significant contribution to the mapping of Hispanic periodicals, Elena Chadova probes the Russian-American media's coverage of political tensions between the US and Russia, and Robert Zecker examines how Slovak-language newspapers were used to teach 'White values' to their readers.[28]

In comparison to the rich literature on the non-English-language press in the United States, the historiography about Britain's non-English language press is very patchy and still in its infancy. At present, a global take is lacking, as is a full recognition of the long history of that phenomenon, which dates back to the midst of the seventeenth century. And yet, since the publication of the first foreign-language serial in Britain in June 1644 – a French-language political news bulletin entitled *Le Mercure anglois* and edited by the Huguenot community until 1648[29] – Britain has never really ceased to be home to non-English-language periodicals. An extreme and complex case is that of *Stobsiade*, a German-language newspaper produced in Stobs Internment Camp (in the Scottish Borders area) during the First World War by German internees and prisoners of war, declared 'enemy aliens' under the Defence of the Realm Act 1914. *Stobsiade* reads like a narrative of camp life – one that was subject to censorship at a time when publications in what was considered 'enemy languages' were theoretically outlawed, and one that was both meant for circulation within the camp and for distribution in Germany.[30] The high specialization and limited circulation of these two serials could easily lead to the dismissal of the phenomenon as an extremely marginal one by 'outsiders'. What, then, should we make of the longevity of the Polish-language *Tydzień Polski* ('The Polish Week'), published weekly since 1959 and frequently distributed at newsagents throughout the UK and with an estimated circulation of approximately 10,000?[31]

Since the 1970s, public bodies have paid attention to the non-English-language print heritage in the UK as part of a wider debate on multiculturalism, multilingualism and political identity, driven partly by the 1977 European Council Directive on the education of the children of migrant workers and the 1976 UK Race Relations Act, which barred discrimination in various contexts, including schools. In that context, the British Library issued a guide on material for 'ethnic minorities in Great Britain' in its collections, which included entries on non-English language serials available in Britain, including thirty-five published in Britain.[32] Interestingly, they primarily correspond to titles curated by the Asian and African Studies Department, which illustrates how intermingled the 1970s UK debate on multilingualism was with decolonization, immigration from former British territories, and an understanding of 'ethnic' as being more or less synonymous with 'race'/'colour' (ethnic as meaning 'non-White').[33] The British Library also started a soon-discontinued collecting campaign, for it realized that some of the current serial publications escaped national deposit. Yet the scope of its collection is in no way comparable to that of the US Library of Congress, and the British Library collections remain very uneven, although publication language is increasingly taken into account.[34]

While the 1988 Education Reform Act reinforced 'the dominance of English as the medium of education for all pupils' in England and Wales,[35] the debate on multiculturalism/multilingualism not only at school but also in the media has been kept alive ever since. Over the years, the acronym BAME (Black, Asian, Minority Ethnic) has been increasingly used in relation to discussions of building a 'plural Britain', as an interchangeable term for 'ethnic'.

Recent studies on 'ethnic media' in the UK have highlighted their transnational dynamics and central role towards integration. However, they rarely question how a non-English-language serial published in Britain may operate and relate differently to its targeted readers than a foreign-language newspaper published outside of Britain, but meant for a British market of multilinguals (like the London-based European edition of the Hong Kong *Sing Tao Daily*, for instance). Among exceptions is the work carried out by media specialist Myria Georgiou, who has been researching ethnic/diasporic media since the 1990s – a space that she finds central for self-representation and 'diasporic [taken broadly] consciousness', especially as mainstream media may be exclusive and/or discriminatory.[36] More than mainstream media, she argues that 'flexibility in the output of minority media, in the relation of their output to place, and in the use of new technologies, is directly related to the survival of minority media as corporations', and suggests that despite the overall lack of state funding and increased competition, the 'minority press, for example is not bounded by the strict regulations that bind broadcasting'.[37] In her attempt to give visibility to these 'diasporic mediascapes', Georgiou produced a list of media by type that included 105 ethnic newspapers and periodicals in 2002, thirty-eight of which were printed in another language than English (or were bilingual). She insisted on the difficulty of presenting a comprehensive list, 'as many media projects never manage to reach the attention of government and other bodies outside the community. Furthermore, this list cannot fully reflect the rapid changes among minority media, with some of them interrupting their publication and other new ones appearing all the time'.[38] Just like Katarzyna Molek-Kozakowska's analysis of the Polish-language glocal media portal for British Poles *MojaWyspa.com* ('My Island', 2003–) in this volume, Georgiou stresses the blurring between paper and digital, which is otherwise observed in the mainstream press. Not unlike the studies aiming at mapping the US immigrant newspapers during the New Deal, UK reports on minority media are rather geared towards contemporary study objects and policy change (here in favour of a more tolerant plural Britain). However, ethnic/diasporic serials tend to be analysed as a purely contemporary phenomenon that has little to no historicity.[39]

And yet, from the 1960s, historians of nineteenth-century immigration/exile to Britain started integrating mentions of the non-English-language press, both for the mine of information that such titles represented to document immigration, and as an object of study in itself.[40] One such pioneer was Lloyd Gartner, who regarded the Yiddish press as a 'practically uncharted field' in his *The Jewish Immigrant in England, 1870–1914* (1960).[41] A few years later, Leonard Prager, a Professor of English at the University of Haifa, researched the Yiddish press in Britain and found that more than 200 had appeared in Britain since 1867, while many of these titles were only known through mentions and had not survived in libraries, be it at the British Library or anywhere in the world. General indexes, such as *The Waterloo Directory of English Newspapers and Periodicals: 1800–1900*, can be of help, although they contain but a very small fraction of non-English-language titles. The non-preservation and dispersion of a large portion of this heritage accounted for long-lasting myopia, despite the fact that, as Prager argued, Britain had been the 'birthplace of the Yiddish radical press', whose readership was truly global.[42] Prager's work not only inspired further research in the Anglo-Jewish press, especially Josef Fraenkel's *Exhibition of the Jewish Press in Great Britain* (1963), but also placed the non-English-language print (perhaps more than the press specifically) in Britain in the limelight, at a time when multiculturalism was a hot topic on British governments' agenda.

It was not until the 1990s, however, that sustained interest in the non-English-language émigré press picked up among historians of print/political culture, centring on the French-language exile press at the turn of the eighteenth century, the Russian-language late nineteenth-century revolutionary press or the long nineteenth-century German-language immigrant press and, more recently, on the Spanish Liberals' press.[43] The purview was mostly the radical foreign-language press, which had strangely been left aside, whereas historians considered revolutions (especially the French Revolution), the printed word (especially journalistic texts) and the development of a public sphere indissociable.[44] In *French Exile Journalism and European Politics* (2001), a pioneering study of the French-language exile press in London, 1789–1814 (through thirteen titles out of nineteen existing then), historian Simon Burrows makes the émigré press the site of interconnected political spheres (French, French émigré, British and international).[45] From then on, foreign-language serials published in Britain would be appraised in their transnational dimensions, often sideways, through: biographies of editors;[46] discussion of interculturality, cultural transfers and mediators (travellers, diplomats, merchants, humanitarians);[47] and discussions of diasporic networks and their organs (especially the Jewish diaspora, the anarchist diaspora, or refugees) included by editors of that press.[48] Concomitantly, studies on the mainstream long nineteenth-century British press have shown growing awareness of trans-colonial and cross-border dynamics, with the *Dictionary of Nineteenth-Century Journalism* (2009) edited by Laurel Brake and Marysa Demoor making space to discuss the significant contribution of prominent European radicals in exile in Britain (Karl Marx, Giuseppe Mazzini, Louis Kossuth and Peter Kropotkin) to the British political press.[49] Most studies nonetheless still generally bypass the non-English language press in Britain.[50]

In 2017, two endeavours sought to investigate the phenomenon trans-language, thereby offering a new approach. First, Constance Bantman and Ana Cláudia Suriani da Silva's edited collection *The Foreign Political Press in Nineteenth-Century London: Politics from a Distance* included a series of essays on the anarchist press in French, in Italian and in German, and brought to the fore little-known exiles' periodical print, especially in Portuguese and Spanish. It allows us to see a very polyphonic London in periodical print, although authors (and contributors to this present volume) recognize that non-English-language serials are found across Britain. The approach takes space seriously and proposes the tag 'foreign political press' to suggest further how remote those titles were for the British society of the time. Operating from this idea of marginality and bordering, the collection includes an essay on the English-language Indian nationalist press. The main takeaway point is about how despite exile being 'marked by political stagnation and acrimony bred by defeat and expulsion from the patrie', remoteness creates 'opportunity for political reinvention' – including through cross-fertilization and hybridization between other émigré press in Britain and elsewhere, and the 'home' print culture.[51] Consideration of language choice, however, remains off-centre. This stands in contrast to 'Language Matters', a 2017 exhibition curated in Paris by the two authors of this introduction, as a side event to the annual meeting of the international Transfopress network, which researches the allophone press as a global phenomenon since 2012.[52] In a section devoted to the non-English-language press in the United States and in Britain since its early days, the exhibition was making a statement about the uninterrupted, diverse story, whereby newcomers could decide to start a serial publication as they settled in Britain for all sorts of reasons and purposes. Put differently, the political press is but one category. For instance, *La Staffetta Italiana: or, The Italian Post* (1728–9), a (bi-)weekly published in Italian and English by Italians working in the British opera trade, was a way to promote their art with a London cosmopolitan audience. More generally, the exhibition suggested that despite advances in the knowledge of certain allophone press titles in Britain, there was a desperate need for further research, better classification in library catalogues and reflection on that body of non-mainstream-language print as a specific category, not only in Britain and the United States but also in France and other countries of immigration.

Why this volume? The connected approach

This volume reflects on the specificities of foreign-language periodicals published by immigrants, refugees and exiles in the United States and in Britain in an era of mass mediatization (long nineteenth–early twentieth centuries), when the printed press was the main mediatic form and when language and nationalism were closely interconnected.[53] As the volume demonstrates, far from being a marginal phenomenon, even prior to the contemporary period, foreign-language journalism represents thousands of titles and tackles central political, linguistic and cultural issues. Building up on the vast yet uncomplete literature on the foreign-language press in the US and seeking to make up for the absence of a global study on the foreign-language press phenomenon in Britain, this volume offers a fresh perspective into this still-marginalized phenomenon in media history by its joint focus on the two countries.

Theoretically, the volume situates itself beyond the purely comparative approach and draws from the input of *histoire croisée*. The latter considers interconnections empirically and heuristically and, to use Michael Werner and Bénédicte Zimmermann's words, it

> breaks with a one-dimensional perspective that simplifies and homogenizes, in favour of a multidimensional approach that acknowledges plurality and the complex configurations that result from it. Accordingly, entities and objects of research are not merely considered in relation to one another but also through one another, in terms of relationships, interactions, and circulation. The active and dynamic principle of the intersection is fundamental in contrast to the static framework of a comparative approach that tends to immobilize objects.[54]

While each essay deals with a specific case study, the volume functions as a kaleidoscopic whole that interrogates the foreign-language press in Britain and the US as a distinct press category, one that is inherently dynamic and at many intercrossings (especially of different States, of different press cultures, of networks). Put differently, by assuming that, whether published in the US or Britain, whether printed then or now, such endeavours do share similarities, this volume retraces the multifaceted roles that the foreign-language press played in the print and political culture of these groups across boundaries, while still paying attention to specific political, economic or social contexts that may have influenced their existence.

The first reason for this heuristic rapprochement is twofold. The non-English-language press in North America pre-dates US history by more than half a century. But more importantly, both the US and Britain have a long history of being harbours to foreign political exiles and immigrants, who often set up newspapers and periodicals that engaged with aspects of community-building in their new environment and actively contributed to the political debates not only of their host countries, but also of their homelands. While both countries' central administration kept an eye on the non-English-language press over the period discussed (and even more so in times of war), they still seemed to offer their foreign-born editors and journalists more leeway than, say, the rest of Europe, Russia and the Ottoman Empire. Indeed, there, press censorship prior to publication was either still active, or the administration of press restrictions was still enduring for most of the nineteenth century. The case was obviously different in the United States, where the first amendment to the constitution protected the freedom of the press. As to Britain, despite the special press taxes (the stamp duty, the advertising duty and the paper excise) having long stifled the popular press until their definitive suppression in the 1861,[55] the foreign-language press seems to have been little affected. This can be accounted for, in some early cases, as it favoured the periodical publication frequency, which was less liable to censorship as registration applied primarily to newspapers and as it was thought to approach political affairs in the form of essays rather than as 'hard political news'.[56] But more centrally, Britain's self-celebration as 'the land of the free' and 'the asylum of nations' – a self-celebration they shared with the United States – ensured foreign-language press editors/journalists in exile a freer press than in their countries, where special taxes on the press could still be operative (until 1874 in Germany, 1881 in France and 1899 in Austria).[57] Valentina Gossetti in this volume situates the long nineteenth-century French-language press in a Greater British context (metropolitan Britain and Australia), herewith reminding us that the British Empire is polycentric (notably when it comes to its press) and inviting us to think about how foreign-language journalism may be affected by trans-colonial print dynamics.

Second, this volume considers foreign-language press titles (whatever their publication frequency) for their in-betweenness as prime sites of connections that place the US and Britain at the core of globalized media dynamics.[58] Building on actor-network theory and on recent developments in periodical press studies, the volume investigates the agency of these titles, which it considers as mediators that facilitate connections (typically between editors and their readerships, etc.), but which are themselves transformative.[59]

Perhaps even more than any serial of the period, foreign-language press titles travelled and established connections beyond editors' expectations at times, especially through cross-referencing. Many periodicals discussed in this volume operated a system of subscription that was worldwide. For instance, this would allow the small Armenian community in late nineteenth-century British India, the United States, France, the Ottoman Empire, Russia, etc. to know of the Armenian/Armenian-language press in Britain at the time, and cross-referencing on both sides of the ocean was frequent. The same was true of the German-language press, as Susan Reed suggests in this volume.

Beyond cross-referencing within a globalized same-language press community, several essays in this volume show that the mainstream press in English on both sides of the ocean made regular references to the non-English language press in their own country of publishing, as well as to the non-English-language press publishing elsewhere, especially in times of crises (typically war, episodes of violence or periods of anti-alienism): the non-English-language press then becomes a source of information for the mainstream English-language press, much as any foreign newspaper does thanks to news agencies services. As such, the foreign-language press in both countries may operate from the margins, but is never completely isolated from the mainstream press in both countries. With their respective essays on the turn-of-the-twentieth-century French-language anarchist press in Britain and on Damiani's global networks of news and contacts as facilitators of his Italian-language journalism in the USA, Constance Bantman and Isabelle Felici further insist on how Britain and the United States operated as hotspots of non-English language press publishing in the late nineteenth/early twentieth century, whereby titles activated myriads of interconnections, within the country (for instance, with the anarchist press in English, as well as with anarchist presses in other languages), as well as with anarchist presses elsewhere in the world (often of the same language of publishing). Similarly, Susan Reed analyses the German-language title *Der Kosmos* in a spatialized perspective, as a title that embodies the in-between position of Germans in London. Indeed, *Der Kosmos* considers them 'as standing between continental Europe and America, and thus being best placed to maintain communication between exiles across the Atlantic and radicals still in Europe'.[60]

Finally, the volume asks about the place of the foreign-language press in discussions of transatlantic journalism. One title discussed in this volume, German-language *Freiheit* ('Freedom'), brings this to the fore. Its editor, Johann Most, a leading figure of anarchism had to close his London-based paper after it rejoiced in the assassination of the Chief Secretary of State for Ireland in 1881. He decided to resettle it in New York. From then on, the masthead bore the mention of both London and New York and its subtitle changed to 'the international organ of the anarchists of German language'. The minute it moved to New York, it attracted the attention of New York correspondents, like Norris A. Clowes, the *New York Star*'s correspondent in Ireland, who approached Friedrich Engels about whether Most would give an interview to *The New York Star* regarding the *Freiheit* trial and his vision.[61]

But the phrase 'transatlantic journalism' means much more than staff collaboration across the Atlantic. It is multifaceted, covering its copy-and-paste dimension (as the bilateral copyright for news was long lacking), the extent to which the nineteenth-century British press became Americanized (through the intromission of a popular style of journalism, 'new journalism' that historian Joel H. Wiener sees as primarily

Figure 0.2 *Freiheit*, New York and London, 10 March 1888, 1 [Serials IISG ZF 1078], Courtesy of the International Institute of Social History (Amsterdam).

American, and with the impact of new technologies), or the multi-directional transatlantic exchanges which lead to a 'shared journalistic culture that retains important pockets of difference' (according to Mark Hampton).[62] Did the non-English language press remain impervious to these major changes? Though not a *fil rouge* per se, several chapters (Constance Bantman, Isabelle Felici, Lorenzo Benadusi on Luigi Barzini's promotion of 'Italianità' in *The Corriere d'America*, 1921–31) point to the impact of Americanization on the format and journalistic style of non-English-language titles they discuss. Many others suggest that hybridization was the norm, with adaptability and pragmatism being the rule to survive: just as today, publishing in a 'minority' language in the long nineteenth/early twentieth century implied a higher level of constraints (tolerance of the State towards the foreign-language press, niche market, multifarious competition as targeted readers may decide to subscribe to a newspaper published in their country of origin rather than a local paper, even if it be in their own language).

The foreign-language press: by whom, for whom and why?

This volume offers a global perspective on the experience of foreign-language journalism in Britain and the USA by bringing together historians, literature, media and translation specialists with skills in different languages. It demonstrates that the non-English-language journalism in both countries is more varied and complex than is sometimes assumed and that too little attention has been paid to the language(s) in which it is produced. It certainly provides a number of new bibliographical references, but its rationale is elsewhere. It argues that the foreign-language press in Britain and the United States serves similar purposes throughout time and mediatic forms, even though it also adapts to its environment.

Section 1 deals with 'journalism without borders'. The phrase is now commonly used to refer to journalistic endeavours in favour of global peace and human rights,[63] but it is used in a different way here to refer to wandering titles and editors, who were often forced to resettle due to their religious identity (Judaism) or political ideology (Communism, anarchism, etc.), especially in times of conflict. The section raises the question of whether the immigrant and exile foreign-language press may not be intrinsically wandering and transnational, since many titles were first published in the editors' home countries, before being revived in a more welcoming foreign land. Some periodicals keep being on the move, due to threats met by the editor(s), or to cosmopolitan journeying journalists – the two not being exclusive, as Gideon Kouts's analysis of Hebrew-language *Ha-Levanon* demonstrates: the newspaper was successively removed from Jerusalem to Paris, Mainz and London in between 1863 and 1886, and is very much a case of one-man journalism (a relatively common feature of the exile press). The trajectories of titles discussed in this section highlight cosmopolitan cities that were places of choice for late nineteenth-century exiles and mid-twentieth-century exiles, in particular Paris, London and New York. Constance Bantman's discussion of the French-language anarchist press in turn-of-the-twentieth-century London places the British capital in a series of dense, overlapping networks of editors, book-sellers and texts that have much to do with careers in exile and wandering journalism. These dynamics of print shape the global anarchist-communist diasporas. Finally, Isabelle Felici reflects on a different face of 'journalism without borders' through distant collaboration. She discusses Italian-born anarchist Gigi Damiani's contribution to the Italian-language anarchist press in the United States over the period 1909–45, when he moved from Italy to Brazil and back, finally ending his life in exile in Tunisia. In so doing, she questions the role of 'foreign correspondents' in the foreign-language press as another contribution to the globalized anarchist diaspora.

Section 2 leaves the political per se to reflect on foreign-language papers' role towards community building and allocating immigrant/ethnic groups' needs abroad. It suggests that foreign-language periodicals launched by immigrants first and foremost aim at binding an 'imagined community' together and do so in various ways: by giving news from home, but also by providing useful information for newcomers in their chosen countries. Bringing the community together is also about format. Indeed, as Hans-Jürgen Lüsebrink's essay demonstrates, French immigrants in the United States long continued the tradition of almanac printing (from the late eighteenth century to the twentieth century), which was an identity marker in French press printing. He insists on adaptations so that French-language almanacs in the United States – and Canada with which he offers a comparison – are not exactly similar to French-language almanacs published in France, while still remaining distinctively French. The four contributions in this section, whether on the long nineteenth-century German-language press in Britain (Susan Reed), the French tradition of French-language almanac printing (Hans-Jürgen Lüsebrink) and the Portuguese-language press in the long nineteenth century in the United States (Alberto Pena-Rodríguez) or Polish-language British online media today (Katarzyna Molek-Kozakowska), all reveal how this press most often helps bridge identities, rather than aiming at sedition, as was often assumed by early works on the ethnic press. They also allow us to see how titles may evolve over the long term, once a first generation of immigrants has settled and may have renewed expectations from its first-language press. From this perspective, Robert M. Zecker's essay on the radical Slovak- and Polish-Language immigrant newspapers in the United States (1910s–1960s) revises the borders of 'community' and challenges general assumptions regarding interracial conflicts, by showing that the struggle over Black-White equality could transcend ethnic boundaries. As Zecker makes clear, collaboration goes well beyond first-generation immigrants and may also be a way for foreign-language press editorial teams and readers to join forces and weigh in on American politics. Finally, with the recent advent of the digital press, the foreign-language press still allocates foreign-language communities' needs and is thus an essential aspect of immigrant culture, as revealed by Katarzyna Molek-Kozakowska's analysis of the British-based Polish-language portal *MojaWyspa.com*. All in all, the section pleads for us to reconsider the foreign-language press in Britain and in the United States as fully fledged part and parcel elements of the national presses of these two countries.

Section 3 reflects on what sociologist Stéphane Dufoix calls 'exopolities', i.e. the field of political action in emigration, and how the foreign-language press may be an instrument of such political campaigning. Originally the term referred to Hungarian,

Czechoslovak and Polish émigré political action in exile in the context of the Cold War,[64] but it has been lifted out of its historical context to apply more broadly to any 'politics from a distance' (to take up the subtitle of Bantman and da Silva's *The Foreign Political Press in Nineteenth-Century London*). Dufoix and others reconceptualize distance by analysing the transnational mechanisms of such political action and insist on its being 'an arena of political activity that is still fully embedded in state politics and politics between states, both sending and receiving, "home" and "host"', rather than its transcending nation-States (as the term 'transnational' originally meant).[65] Contributions in this section not only reflect on how immigrant and exile newspapers can try to influence the home politics, but expose how the British and the American governments can use such titles to forward their own takes on foreign policy issues. Nicolas Pitsos's chapter on the Greek-language press in the US just after the First World War and Lorenzo Benadusi's analysis of *Il Corriere d'America* reveal how tensions in the home politics of Greece after the First World War and fascist Italy are exported in Britain and the US. They analyse foreign-language titles as places of virulent advocacy and plurivocality, thereby dispelling the idea that immigrant/ethnic so-called communities in Britain and the US speak with a single voice regarding the politics of their 'home' country. British and American governments can thus decide to prop up the periodicals that would serve their own foreign policy interests. Relating to this, Maria José Ruiz Acosta's chapter on Spanish Liberal exiles in London tackles issues of financing, emphasizing how materially challenging publishing a foreign-language press title may be. Many of these periodicals only ran for a few issues, which account for such heritage having long remained off the radar of media history scholars. In such dire straits, financial backing from the 'host' country may be welcome, though thorny.

Finally, Section 4 interrogates language choice and identity framing, as ethnic newspapers also exist in English and in bi/trilingual versions. It reflects on reasons why serials were published in a foreign language at all, while such enterprise proved both difficult and potentially seditious. Whatever choice is made, publishing in a foreign language or in English, publishing a monolingual or plurilingual title, questions of linguistic strategies are often debated in the foreign-language press as they relate to the imagined identities of communities where it appears, but also sometimes that of the country of origin. Contributions in this section ponder on cases of foreign-language periodical publishing: at times of crises in their homelands – Russian revolutionists in late nineteenth-century Britain (Robert Henderson), Armenians in Britain trying to contribute to the national awakening of Ottoman Armenians in the 1880s (Stéphanie Prévost), Belgian refugees in Britain during the First World War, anti-Tsarist émigrés to London (Christophe Declercq); in liminal spaces – see Kelly Kreitz's discussion of Spanish-language periodicals in Florida and New Mexico upholding 'Latinidas' in the context of the Spanish-American war over Cuba in 1898; or in the context of imperial patterns of immigration (through a comparative study of French-language titles in nineteenth-century Britain and Australia by Valentina Gossetti). The point is to give examples of the vivacity of the debates (including about the risk of 'Englishing') and of solutions found. This section also highlights the status of certain languages as *lingua franca* and bears witness to how French was eventually superseded by English from this perspective at the turn of the twentieth century (Valentina Gossetti and Stéphanie Prévost).

Languages in Directory of US Newspapers in American Libraries

Refined by: Part of: Directory of US Newspapers in Amer...

Show: ☐ Alphabetically ☐ By Number of Matches

Languages: 1 - 66

English [149,410]	Croatian [60]	Ladino [10]
German [2,549]	Lithuanian [56]	Dakota [9]
Spanish [2,495]	Slovak [55]	Turkish [9]
French [809]	Dutch [42]	Germanic Languages [8]
Italian [384]	Flemish [42]	Syriac [8]
Swedish [300]	Hebrew [40]	Malayalam [7]
Polish [254]	Slovenian [38]	Samoan [7]
Yiddish [204]	Armenian [33]	Thai [7]
Chinese [182]	Iloko [33]	Austronesian Languages [5]
Russian [168]	Vietnamese [31]	Belarusian [4]
Norwegian [163]	Persian [30]	Engrpa [4]
Czech [155]	Romanian [26]	Undetermined [4]
Japanese [136]	Bulgarian [24]	Creek [3]
Hawaiian [90]	Serbian [24]	Creoles and Pidgins [3]
Hungarian [90]	Tagalog [17]	Creoles and Pidgins, French-Based [3]
Danish [84]	Cherokee [16]	Estonian [3]
Arabic [81]	Choctaw [16]	Gereng [3]
Korean [80]	Welsh [15]	Icelandic [3]
Finnish [78]	Latvian [14]	Indonesian [3]
Greek [73]	Bengali [11]	Multiple Languages [3]
Ukrainico [68]	Urdu [11]	Amseng [2]
Portuguese [62]	Albanian [10]	Basque [2]

Figure 0.3 'Languages in the Directory of US Newspapers of American Libraries', National Digital Newspaper Program, Library of Congress website, December 2022.[66]

The overall volume endeavours to make space to non-Latin-script periodical prints, which tend to be underrepresented in the historiography, although they account for a significant number of titles. As has already been made clear, it is near impossible to have clear and definitive statistics, all the more so for Britain where awareness has been growing slowly. Nonetheless, the table of languages represented in the periodical print found in the *Directory of US Newspapers in American Libraries* gives some insight into the variety of languages found, with Yiddish and Chinese featuring quite high in the list. Some caveats need to be added here. In this book, selections had to be made in terms of print and languages represented to keep the enterprise manageable, but also unfortunately depending on specialists' availability. It also leaves out discussion of print by 'subjects of British rule' in 'native' languages (for instance, in South-African language Xhosa), whose history jointly involved empire migration, missionary influence and nationalist struggle, but is somehow distinct and parallel to periodical print edited by foreigners settling on British soil.[67] While gender issues are addressed in Kelly Kreitz's innovative chapter on Latina press (where she reflects on women editors' choice of words in Spanish to express their feminism), they are not given here the space they deserve for lack of space, as the growing place of women in immigrant/ethnic media would require more investigations, and hopefully a dedicated volume.

The advent of the digital era has sparked renewed interest in the foreign-language press in the past few years.[68] The creation of hundreds of new titles and the increasing emergence on the web of long-existing newspapers has made it impossible for specialists of media studies to neglect immigrant/ethnic journalism any more. In that regard, Sherry Yu and Matthew Matsaganis's book entitled *Ethnic Media in the Digital Age* is an enlightening contribution to the field.[69] So is the handbook the same Matsaganis co-edited to help students understand these specific media.[70] The digital era also had a clear impact on historians as well, though in a slower way for the historic allophone press. With the development of digitizing programmes, the Library of Congress and other private and public institutions realized the abundance of US foreign-language titles and dedicated to them entire collections made available to researchers on the web.[71] The use of optical character recognition (mostly for Latin script at this stage[72]) also allows the tracing of mobile texts and ideologies, and helps reconstruct how journalists and contents crossed borders, switching from one periodical to another, one country to another and one language to another. There is no doubt that future scholarship will, as this book is intending to do, weave the threads of wandering journalism into new patterns and raise awareness to that still non-uniformly visible heritage worldwide.

Notes

1. 'Conoces El Ibérico Gratuito?', *Expat.com*, 1 October 2010 [Post]. https://www.expat.com/forum/viewtopic.php?id=48487 (accessed 1 August 2022).
2. Juan Calleja, 'No me veo con la misma ilusión por quedarme en Reino Unido que hace cinco años', CEXT, 22 July 2016, https://www.cext.es/posts/experiencias/no-me-veo-con-la-misma-ilusion-de-quedarme-en-londres-que-hace-cinco-anos (accessed 1 August 2022); Email, Paco De La Coba to Stéphanie Prévost, 'Information about *El Iberico* at Tube Stations', 8 August 2022.
3. Ian Dennoir, 'International free newspaper stands. The Strand, London 6th October 2011 12:56.59pm', photo on Flickr, https://www.flickr.com/photos/51282757@N05/6218461187 (accessed 10 December 2022).
4. Pietro Russo, *Catalogo collettivo della stampa periodica italo-americana (1836–1980)* (Rome: Centro Studi Emigrazione, 1983).
5. Tim Porter, 'Dismantling the Language Barrier: in an Effort to Crack the Burgeoning Hispanic Market, Major Newspaper Companies are Investing in New and Expanded Spanish-Language Editions', *American Journalism Review* 25 (2003), https://ajrarchive.org/Article.asp?id=%203415 (accessed 2 March 2022).
6. Alex Yablon, 'The Rise of New York's Foreign-Language Newspapers', *New York Intelligencer*, 9 October 2014, https://nymag.com/intelligencer/2014/10/rise-of-new-yorks-foreign-language-newspapers.html (accessed 2 March 2022).
7. For an early discussion of the terms 'ethnic media', see Lubomyr Wynar, 'The Study of the Ethnic Press', *Unesco Journal of Information Science* I, n°1 (1979). For a more recent approach, see Chapter 2 of John Budarick, *Ethnic Media and Democracy, From Liberalism to Agonism* (New York: Palgrave MacMillan, 2019), 27–42.
8. See for example the Canadian Ethnic Media Association, https://canadianethnicmedia.com.
9. See for instance, H.R.997 – English Language Unity Act of 2017 (https://www.congress.gov/bill/115th-congress/house-bill/997/text). For more details on the status of English in the United States, see Eduardo D. Faingold, *Language Rights and the Law in the United States and Its Territories* (New York: Lexington Books, 2018); Bryan Meadows, 'Neo-Nationalism and Language Policy in the United States: A Critical Discourse Analysis of Public Discourse Advocating Monolingual English Use', in Kyle McIntosh (ed.), *Applied Linguistics and Language Teaching in the Neo-Nationalist Era* (Palgrave Macmillan Cham, 2020), 17–49.

10 Magdalena Pasikowska-Schnass, *Regional and Minority Languages in the European Union*, European Parliamentary Research Service Briefing, September 2016, 3.
11 Council of Europe, *European Charter for Regional or Minority Languages*, ETS 148 – Regional or Minority Languages, 5.XI.1992, 2.
12 https://www.midas-press.org.
13 Malika Pedley and Alain Viaut, 'What Do Minority Languages Mean? European Perspectives', *Multilingua* 38, no 2 (2019), 133–9.
14 Guus Extra and Durk Gorter (eds.), *The Other Languages of Europe: Demographic, Sociolinguistic and Educational Perspectives* (Clevedon, Multilingual Matters, 2001), 23.
15 Universal Declaration of Linguistic Rights Follow-Up Committee, *Universal Declaration of Linguistic Rights*, Barcelona, 1998, 23–4.
16 Sally Holt and John Packer, 'OSCE Developments and Linguistic Minorities', *International Journal on Multicultural Societies* 3, no. 2 (2001), 122.
17 Matylda Wierietelny, *Being Part of the City: Multilingual Manchester*, Film, 2019, https://youtu.be/awUoeKJzxj4; 'Ethnicity', *Manchester Voices* Exhibition, Manchester Central Library, 2022.
18 Ming Tsow, 'Ethnic Minority Community Languages: A Statement', *Journal of Multilingual and Multicultural Development* 4, no 5 (1983), 361–84.
19 Viv Edwards, 'New Minority Languages in the United Kingdom', in Guus Extra and Durk Porter (eds.), *Multilingual Europe: Facts and Policies* (Berlin and New York: Mouton de Gruyter, 2008), 253–4.
20 Catherine Dewhirst and Richard Scully, 'Australia's Minority Community Printed Press History in Global Context: An Introduction', in Catherine Dewhirst and Richard Scully (eds.), *The Transnational Voices of Australia's Migrant and Minority Press*, Palgrave Macmillan, 2020, 1–17; Alicia Ferrández Ferrer and Jessica Retis, 'Ethnic Minority Media: Between Hegemony and Resistance', *Journal of Alternative and Community Media* 4, no 3 (2019), 1–13.
21 Frankie Hutton and Barbara S. Reed (eds.), *Outsiders in 19th-Century Press History: Multicultural Perspectives* (Bowling Green: Bowling Green State University Popular Press, 1995); http://nationalethnicpress.com/ethnic-press; James P. Danky and Wayne A. Wiegand (eds.), *Print Culture in a Diverse America* (Chicago: University of Illinois Press, 1998); Lauren Kessler, *The Dissident Press, Alternative Journalism in American History* (Newbury Park: Sage, 1990); Sally Miller, 'Distinctive Media: The European Ethnic Press in the United States', in Carl F. Kaestle and Janice A. Radway (eds.), *A History of the Book in America, Volume 4: Print in Motion: The Expansion of Publishing and Reading in the United States, 1880–1940* (Chapel Hill: University of North Carolina Press, 2009), 299–311.
22 Edward Hunter, *In Many Voices: Our Fabulous Foreign-Language Press* (Norman Park: Norman College, 1960), 30.
23 Leara D. Rhodes, *The Ethnic Press: Shaping the American Dream* (New York: Peter Lang, 2010).
24 Sally Miller (ed.), *The Ethnic Press in the United States: a Historical Analysis and Handbook* (New York: Greenwood Press, 1987).
25 Christiane Harzig and Dirk Hoerder (eds.), *The Press of Labor Migrants in Europe and North America 1880s–1980* (Lexington: Lexington Books, 1985); Dirk Hoerder (ed.), *The Immigrant Labor Press in North America 1840s–1970s* (New York, Greenwood Press, 1987).
26 Jerzy Zubrzycki, 'The Role of the Foreign-Language Press in Migrant Integration', *Population Studies* 22 (1958), 73–82; Oscar Ban, 'Death Comes to the Foreign Press', *New Outlook*, July 1933, 44–8.

27 For an overview on collecting, see Dominique Daniel, 'Elusive Stories: Collecting and Preserving the Foreign-Language Ethnic Press in the United States', *Serials Review* 45, no. 1–2 (2019), 7–25.
28 Robert A. Karlowich, *We Fall and Rise: Russian-Language Newspapers in New York City, 1889–1914* (Metuchen, NJ and London: Scarecrow Press, 1991); Nicolás Kanellos and Helvetia Martell, *Hispanic Periodicals in the United States, Origins to 1960: A Brief History and Comprehensive Bibliography* (Arte Público Press, 1999); Peter Conolly-Smith, *Translating America: an Ethnic Press and Popular Culture, 1890–1920* (Washington, DC: Smithsonian Books, 2004); Odd Sverre Lovoll, *Norwegian Newspapers in America: Connecting Norway and the New Land* (Saint Paul: Minnesota Historical Society, 2010); Elena Chadova, *Between the Eagle and the Bear: Coverage of U.S.-Russian Foreign Policy Disputes in Russian Ethnic Media in the United States* (Sarrebruck: VDM Verlag, 2010); Robert Zecker, *Race and America's Immigrant Press: How the Slovaks Were taught to Think like White People* (New York: Continuum, 2011); Peter Vellon, *A Great Conspiracy against our Race: Italian Immigrant Newspapers and the Construction of Whiteness in the Early 20th Century* (New York: New York University Press, 2014); Anna D. Jaroszyńska-Kirchmann, *The Polish Hearst: Ameryka-Echo and the Public Role of the Immigrant Press* (Urbana-Champaign: University of Illinois Press, 2015); Bénédicte Deschamps, *Histoire de la presse italo-américaine, du Risorgimento à la Grande Guerre* (Paris: L'Harmattan, 2020); Alberto Pena-Rodríguez, *News on the American Dream: A History of the Portuguese Press in the United States* (Tagus Press, 2020). For the sake of space, we have limited this list to books only.
29 Claire Boulard Jouslin, 'Du *Mercure Anglois* au *Paris Monthly Review*: Quelques réflexions sur les phénomènes de transfert et d'influence dans les presses anglaise et française du long XVIIIe siècle', *Études Épistémè* 26 (2014).
30 'Historical Background', *Stobsiade*, http://www.stobsiade.org/introduction/historicalBackground.html (last consulted 21 July 2022).
31 *Tydzień Polski* was originally a weekend edition supplement to the daily *Dziennik Polski* ('The Polish Daily', 1959–2015), which itself is heir to *Dziennik Polski i Dziennik Żołnierza* ('The Polish Daily and Soldier's Daily'), published in the United Kingdom from July 1940 shortly after the Polish government-in-exile arrived in London. The organ was the legal Polish authorities' official voice, recognized as such by the British Government and her Allies. Cf. 'Londyński "Dziennik Polski" staje się tygodnikiem', 17 July 2015, *Dzieje.pl*, https://dzieje.pl/aktualnosci/londynski-dziennik-polski-staje-sie-tygodnikiem (last consulted 21 July 2022).
32 Eric A. Clough and Jacqueline Quarmby, *A Public Library Service for Ethnic Minorities in Great Britain*, London: Library Association, 1978, 340–8.
33 Myria Georgiou, 'Mapping Minorities and Their Media: The National Context – The UK', 2002 [European Media, Technology and Everyday Life Network].
34 Luke Mckernan, 'Newspaper data and news identity', *The British Library Newsroom blog*, 18 October 2017. *Aptak* (The Slap) has been partly digitized by the British Library, in partnership with the National Library of Armenia, as part of the Endangered Archives Programme https://eap.bl.uk/collection/EAP180-3-3/search.
35 Jill Bourne, 'Languages in the School Systems of England and Wales', *Linguistics and Education* 3, n°1 (1991), 81.
36 Georgiou, 'Mapping Minorities and Their Media', 17. Also see Ola Ogunyemi (ed.), *Journalism, Audiences and Diaspora* (Basingstoke: Palgrave Macmillan, 2015), Ola Ogunyemi's 'Conceptualizing the Diaspora Media' (1–14) and Sanem Şahin's 'Journalism of Turkish-Language Newspapers in the UK', 68–83.

37 Georgiou, 'Mapping Minorities and Their Media', 19.
38 Ibid., 30-42. The quote is found in footnote 16, p. 30.
39 See, for instance, the Works Progress Administration's investigations in the San Francisco ethnic journalism: *The History of Journalism in San Francisco*, volume 1: *Foreign Journalism in San Francisco*, San Francisco, 1939. One exception is Serhiy Blavatskyy's article 'Constructing Victimization Grand-Narrative in the Ukrainian Foreign-Language Press (1901-1926)' (in French and English), published online in *Media History* (2022).
40 For a discussion of German-language periodical print, see Panikos Panayi's *German Immigrants in Britain during the Nineteenth Century 1815-1914* (Oxford 1995), 179-83.
41 Cited in Leonard Prager, 'A Bibliography of Yiddish Periodicals in Great Britain (1867-1967)', *Studies in Bibliography and Booklore* 9, no. 1 (1969), 3.
42 Ibid., 5.
43 Simon Burrows's *French Exile Journalism and European Politics, 1792-1814* (Suffolk: Royal Historical Society, 2001) and 'Les journaux des émigrés et la communauté francaisé des exilés, 1792-1814', in Nicolas Beaupré and Karine Rance (eds.), *Arrachés et Déplacés: Réfugiés Politiques, Prisonniers de Guerre, Déportés, 1789-1918* (Clermont-Ferrand: PUBP, 2016), 241-57; Martin A. Miller, 'The Transformation of the Russian Revolutionary Emigre Press at the End of The Nineteenth Century', *Russian History* 16, no. 2/4 (1989), 197-207; John Slatter, 'The Russian Émigré Press in Britain, 1853-1917', *The Slavonic and East European Review* 73, no. 4 (1995), 716-47; Dorothea Miehe and Christopher Skelton-Foord, 'A Press for Natives and Immigrants. German Newspapers in the British Library', *British Library Newspaper Library News* 27 (1999), 8-10; María José Ruiz Acosta (ed.), *La prensa hispánica en el exilio de Londres, 1810-1850* (Salamanca: Comunicación Social Ediciones y Publicaciones, 2016).
44 Burrows, *French Exile Journalism*, 1.
45 Burrows, *French Exile Journalism*, 1.
46 Fernando Durán López. 'Blanco White aconseja a los americanos. Variedades o el Mensajero de Londres', in Antonio Cascales Ramos (ed.), *Blanco White, El rebelde ilustrado* (Sevilla: Universidad de Sevilla, 2009), 53-62. See also the biographical entries in Constance Bantman and Ana Cláudia Suriani da Silva (eds.), *The Foreign Political Press in Nineteenth-Century London: Politics from a Distance* (London: Bloomsbury, 2017), 193-206.
47 Sylvie Aprile, '"Translations" politiques et culturelles: les proscrits français et l'Angleterre', *Genèses. Sciences sociales et histoire* 38 (2000), 33-55; see the mention of the Japanese-language *Taisei Shinbun* (1873) in Andrew Cobbing's *The Japanese Discovery of Victorian Britain: Early Travel Encounters in the Far West* (Richmond, UK: Japan Press, 1998), 133 ff.; Tsypylma Darieva, *Russkij Berlin. Migranten und Medien in Berlin und London* (Münster: Lit, 2004), 199-299.
48 Sajid Mansoor Qaisrani, *Urdu Press in Britain* (Islamabad: Mashal Publications, 1990); Gideon Kouts, 'La Presse hébraïque en Europe: ses origines et son évolution de 1856 à 1897', PhD dissertation, Université Paris 8, 1997; Constance Bantman, *The French Anarchists in London: Exile and Transnationalism in the First Globalisation* (Liverpool: Liverpool University Press, 2013); Christophe Declercq, *Belgian Refugees in Britain 1914-1919: A Cross-Cultural Study of Belgian Identity in Exile*, PhD dissertation, Imperial College London, 2015 and 'Belgian Exile Press in Britain' in Felicity Rash and Christophe Declercq (eds.), *The Great War in Belgium and the Netherlands Beyond Flanders Fields* (Basingstoke: Palgrave Macmillan, 2018), 121-41; William Pimott's

project 'The Yiddish Press 1890–1920: A Global History', https://bisa.bbk.ac.uk/research/item/the-yiddish-press-1890-1920-a-global-history.

49 In Andrew King, Alexis Easley and John Morton's edited *The Routledge Handbook of Nineteenth-Century British Periodicals and Newspapers* (Abingdon: Routledge, 2016), see their introduction (4), Michelle Tusan's 'Empire and the Periodical Press' (153–62), Bob Nicholson's 'Transatlantic Connections' (163–74) and Jane Chapman, 'Transnational Connections' (175–84). Also specific entries in Laurel Brake and Marysa Demoor (eds.), *DNCJ. Dictionary of Nineteenth-Century Journalism* (Ghent: Academia Press, 2009); Federico Ferretti, 'Publishing Anarchism: Pyotr Kropotkin and British Print Cultures, 1876–1917', *Journal of Historical Geography* 57 (2017), 17–27.

50 Just one example: David Finkelstein's edited volume *The Edinburgh History of the British and Irish Press, Volume 2. Expansion and Evolution, 1800–1900* (Edinburgh: EUP, 2020) misses references to the non-English press published in Britain, although Diana Cooper-Richet's chapter deals with the English-language press published in foreign countries (especially France).

51 Thomas C. Jones and Constance Bantman, 'From Republicanism to Anarchism: 50 Years of French Exilic Newspaper Publishing', in Constance Bantman and Ana Cláudia Suriani da Silva (eds.), *The Foreign Political Press in Nineteenth-Century London: Politics from a Distance* (London: Bloomsbury, 2017), 92.

52 Bénédicte Deschamps and Stéphanie Prévost, 'Language Matters: Presse anglophone en France/Presses d'exil et d'immigration aux Etats-Unis', Exhibition, Paris, 2017–18. A virtual updated exhibit, created by Karl Gosselet is forthcoming in 2023 at www.language-matters.fr.

53 Stephen Barbour, 'Nationalism, Language and Europe', in Stephen Barbour and Cathie Carmichael (eds.), *Language and Nationalism in Europe* (Oxford: OUP, 2000), 1–17.

54 Michael Werner and Bénédicte Zimmermann, 'Beyond Comparison: Histoire Croisée and the Challenge of Reflexivity', *History and Theory* 45 (February 2006), 38.

55 Martin Hewitt, *The Dawn of the Cheap Press in Victorian Britain: The End of the 'Taxes on Knowledge', 1849–1869* (London: Bloomsbury, 2015).

56 Laurel Brake, 'Writing the Contemporary in the Periodical Press: Art and News 1893–1906', *Journal of European Periodical Studies* 4, n°2 (2019), 34–5; Martin Hewitt, 'The Press and the Law', in Joanne Shattock (ed.), *Journalism and the Periodical Press in Nineteenth Century Britain* (Cambridge: Cambridge University Press, 2017), 154–5.

57 Robert J. Goldstein, *Political Repression in 19th Century Europe* (Abingdon: Routledge, 2010; first edition 1983), 35.

58 See part III of Joanne Shattock (ed.), *Journalism and the Periodical Press*.

59 Roland Wenzlhuemer, 'The Ship, the Media, and the World: Conceptualizing Connections in Global History', *Journal of Global History* 11 (2016), 165; Evanghelia Stead, 'Periodicals In-Between', *The Journal of European Periodical Studies* 4, no 2 (2019), 5–9.

60 Susan Reed in this volume.

61 Engels to Most, 22 July 1881, in Karl Marx and Friedrich Engels, *Collected Works, Volume 24: Marx and Engels 1874–83* (Lawrence & Wishart: Electric Book, 2001), 410.

62 Mark Hampton, 'Transatlantic Exchanges', in Martin Conboy and Adrian Bingham (eds.), *The Edinburgh History of the British and Irish Press, Volume 3: Competition and Disruption, 1900–2017* (Edinburgh: EUP, 2020), 151–70.

63 Ibrahim S. Shaw, '"Human Rights Journalism": A Critical Conceptual Framework', in Ibrahim S. Shaw, Jake Lynch and Robert A. Hackett (eds.), *Expanding Peace Journalism: Comparative and Critical Approaches* (Sydney: Sydney University Press, 2011), 107–8.

64 Stéphane Dufoix, *Politiques d'exil. Hongrois, Polonais et Tchécoslovaques en France après 1945* (Paris: PUF, 2002), 29.
65 Andy Byford and Olga Bronnikova, 'Introduction. Transnational Exopolities. Politics in Post-Soviet Migration', *Revue d'études comparatives Est-Ouest* 4, no. 4 (2018), 17–18; Nancy L. Green, *The Limits of Transnationalism* (Chicago: Chicago University Press, 2019), Chapters 1–2.
66 https://www.loc.gov/collections/directory-of-us-newspapers-in-american-libraries/?searchType=advanced.
67 For instance, see A. O. Adedeji, 'Analysis of Use of English and Indigenous Languages by the Press in Selected African Countries', *Arabian Journal of Business and Management Review* 4, no. 8 (2015), 35–45.
68 While US institutions had long developed ways of flagging allophone journalism in their catalogues, others have since followed suit, including the Bibliothèque nationale de France in Paris (https://presselocaleancienne.bnf.fr/html/anglais), the Libraries of Estonia through their shared catalogue ESTER (https://www.ester.ee/search/X) or again the Europeana portal (https://www.europeana.eu/en/collections/topic/18-newspapers). Early catalogues may have allophone press sections. One such example is *Bibliotheca Danica. Systematisk Fortegnelse over den danske Literatur fra 1482 til 1830*, which has been regularly updated since the nineteenth century (thanks to Jürgen Beyer for this information).
69 Sherry S. Yu and Matthew D. Matsaganis, *Ethnic Media in the Digital Age* (New York: Routledge, 2019).
70 Matthew D. Matsaganis, Sandra Ball-Rokeach and Vikki S. Katz, *Understanding Ethnic Media: Producers, Consumers, and Societies* (Thousand Oaks: Sage Publications, 2011).
71 Library of Congress, 'Chronicling America Ethnic Press Coverage', February 2022, https://public.tableau.com/app/profile/chronicling.america/viz/ChroniclingAmericaEthnicPressCoverageGraph/ethnicity_bar; Proquest, 'Ethnic Newswatch', http://www.proquest.com/products-services/ethnic_newswatch.html; Readex, 'American Ethnic Newspapers', http://www.readex.com/content/american-ethnic-newspapers.
72 Calfa was launched in 2014 by Chahane Vidal-Gorène as a DH tool specifically for Oriental languages. https://calfa.fr.

Section One

Journalism Without Borders: Wandering Titles and Transnational Journalistic Networks

1

The Hebrew 'Wandering Press' in Europe: *Ha-Levanon* from Jerusalem to Paris, Mainz and London (1863–86)

Gideon Kouts
Université Paris 8

Ha-Levanon ('The Lebanon') was the earliest Hebrew monthly published in Palestine (1863) and it was soon carried by its editor and one of the founders, Yehiel Bril, from the Holy Land to Paris, where it appeared between 1865 and 1870 as a strictly Orthodox Jewish weekly. Between 1871 and 1882, the paper was published in Mainz, Germany. It reached the end of its career in 1886 in London, where Bril passed away. In his wanderings, Bril, a British citizen, had to adjust to different countries and political regimes, a living example of the 'wandering Jew' embodied in the press. The first Jewish newspapers were one-man enterprises, where a single person filled all journalistic and managerial functions, and the paper's fortunes followed those of its creator. *Ha-Levanon* was no otherwise. Its trajectory embraces both transnational characteristics of the Jewish diaspora and the Jewish press: first, it advocated Jewish solidarity across borders; second, it emphasized diasporic alienation and instability within a given country. *Ha-Levanon* also expressed the centrality of *Eretz Israel* –Palestine and Jerusalem as a unifying symbol of the Jewish national identity revival. This chapter looks at how the wanderings of *Ha-Levanon* shaped the expression of its Jewishness.

Jerusalem: *Halbanon* facing community divisions and Ottoman press regulations

The 'Palestinian' orientation of *Halbanon/Ha-Levanon* was evident from the start, when it first appeared in Jerusalem. This is not surprising, since Bril's first journalistic occupation was as the first Hebrew foreign correspondent in Palestine of *Ha-Maggid* ('The Storyteller'), the first Hebrew weekly published in Prussia since 1856. The orientation towards Palestine-Israel even pre-dated the publication of *Ha-Levanon*'s first issue: editors (Bril, I. M. Salomon. Michal Hacohen) apparently published an advertisement beforehand,[1] which targeted a European readership and was inspired by their desire to satisfy the curiosity of their distant brethren.

Figure 1.1 *Halbanon*, 5 March 1863, Jerusalem, issue 1. By courtesy of the Historical Jewish Press website (www.Jpress.org.il) founded by the National Library and Tel Aviv University.

Following the traditions of the early Hebrew press, the subtitle of *Ha-Levanon* gave indication as to its contents and read: 'Messenger of Peace from Jerusalem, brings news from the entire Holy Land, reveals secrets from Syria, Yemen and India (later were added the words: and *Torah* [Jewish law] innovations from those who sit before the Lord in holy majesty). Everything that an Israelite would want to know.' Sections appeared in the order listed in the subtitle. Following a tradition, *Ha-Levanon* was written in the form of a pamphlet and was meant to be read as a book – in order, from the first page to the last. The paper's sections thus appeared in order of their importance, which explains why its morphological analysis may serve as an important tool to ascertain the paper's tendencies and orientations.

The first section was labelled 'Shlom Yerushalaim' ('The State of Jerusalem'), an editorial section that expressed the views of the leaders of the Ashkenazi-Pharisaic community regarding the question of Palestine and its settlement. After that, came news from Palestine and the Near East, with the assistance of Bril's 'traveling' father-in-law, serving as special envoy, Yaakov Sapir. Of note, news from Palestine included reports about nature and the weather.[2] In the European Hebrew press of the time, descriptions of nature usually surfaced within two contexts: (a) scientific articles on 'knowledge of Nature'; and (b) romanticized, highly lyrical descriptions, corresponding more to the editor's glamorous imaginings at times. By contrast, weather and season descriptions in *Ha-Levanon* dealt with natural disasters, such as drought that destroyed crops and brought about hunger and thirst. In so doing, Bril apparently took up the wish of the 'Old Establishment' (*HaYishouv Ha-Yashan*) to excite compassion among their brethren in Europe in order to spur donations towards the *Halukah*, a distribution-of-alms system aimed to support settlement in the Land of Israel. These specific reasons left aside, such journalism produced a realistic rendering of nature.

To return to the *Ha-Levanon*'s political agenda, its stance caused internal dissent within the Jewish community, as it was hard for Bril and his peers to remain neutral. Bril's commitment remained unfailing as he settled in Paris, after *Ha-Levanon* had lasted less than a year in Jerusalem. Falling prey to the strife among the Jewish factions in Jerusalem, it apparently succumbed to a denunciation from competitor title *Havatzelet* (The Crocus), run by Israel Bek. *Ha-Levanon* editors had not received a written licence from the Turkish authorities to publish a newspaper – which was required prior to publication – and had relied on a verbal authorization from a local official, who was almost certainly bribed. Consequently, Bril attempted to get a formal licence from Constantinople, the Ottoman capital, but when this effort failed, he decided to try his luck in Paris.

To Paris: from *Ha-Levanon* to *Le Libanon*, juggling with the French press regime

The established and legally protected status of the Jewish community in France since the time of Napoleon I was a seemingly favourable environment for a Hebrew newspaper seeking a haven in the tempestuous sea of migration. It was central to Bril, even though he did not wish to stress the differences between Jews and their surrounding society.

At the beginning of November 1864, Bril issued a prospectus in Paris on a sheet of paper printed on both sides, now held at the Bibliothèque nationale de France in Paris.[3] In this prospectus entitled *Qol mevasser. Perah Levanon* ('Voice announcing the flower of Lebanon'), Bril condemned the 'hidden informers' who had injured him. He described his personal tragedy with the following words: 'for this reason I was forced to wander abroad and to abandon my home, forsake my children, be separated from my loving and kind brothers'. Conversely, he thanked all those 'dignitaries of my people, scientists, notables and God-fearing men' who encouraged him to publish his newspaper in Paris. The back page of the prospectus (entitled 'For Knowledge and Testimony') included approvals and recommendations from well-known Rabbis, which appeared in both Hebrew and French. As for the future, 'The first fruits will be from the Holy Land, to inform faithfully, telling it truthfully and correctly... the news and also the old from the Holy Land, to inform about the situation of our brothers settled in the Lord's land'. Bril promised that from here on, '*Ha-Levanon* would bring news concerning the situation of our brothers in Europe, in addition to those living in Yemen, Ethiopia and India'.

However, between November 1864 and January 1865, it became clear that founding the newspaper was nowhere straightforward, which the close consultation of the *Ha Levanon/Libanon* file in the French Home Office archives (Press Department) confirm. For sure, Bril arrived in Paris at a strongly 'cosmopolitan' time, which proved auspicious for a flourishing press in foreign languages. Besides, Napoleon III's government was not opposed then, in principle, to the appearance of a Hebrew newspaper on the French soil. The status of the Jewish community was relatively secure, and the Emperor seemed quite amenable on that front. However, the situation was not so simple.

Licences to publish a newspaper in France were given only to publishers with a French nationality. Bril was a British subject. On 24 December 1864, a petition was submitted to the French Ministry of the Interior, as required by law, to publish a new bi-weekly with the name *Libanon* ('Le Liban'/'Lebanon'). For abovementioned reasons, Bril could not be the petitioner. A solution had to be found, so the petition was presented by a person named Michel Edinger, a Parisian Jewish merchant, who declared that he was the single editor of the paper. The petition was transferred, as usual, to the Attorney General. After that, following procedure, the Minister of the Interior requested the Chief of Police to conduct a background/character check into the petitioner's personal history.

The request for publication was eventually for a non-political newspaper, after a previous request from *Ha-Levanon* for a political serial had failed. To put it differently, Edinger covered (for) Bril, which was apparently fairly usual during the Second Empire. So does the Paris Chief of Police's reply of 19 January 1865 suggest. The police had discovered that the petitioner could not be the editor of *Ha-Levanon*. The Chief of Police was being ironic about this and wrote: 'The Petitioner is married and is father to five children. He is totally illiterate'.[4] The meaning here was that the person did not know how to write French. As in any good detective story, the Chief of Police's letter had a surprise ending. It revealed that, according to his own investigation, the real publisher of *Ha-Levanon* was no other than 'a German teacher – Mr. Weisselkopf… who arrived from Koln six months ago… he runs a school he has set up… his political ideas are unknown'.[5] Thus, Bril gained double cover. Interestingly, his name in French as editor of *Ha-Levanon* did not appear until March 1870, a short time before the paper closed and moved to its next publication site, Mainz in Germany.

Despite relocation, Bril wanted to stress continuation. To do so, when the first issue appeared in Paris on 6 January 1865, Bril took up the numbering of the Jerusalem *Lebanon* and the paper appeared in Paris as if in its second year. As already stated, *Ha-Levanon* was published in Paris during six years, from its second until its seventh year.

Figure 1.2 *Libanon*, Masthead, 6 January 1865, Paris. By courtesy of the Historical Jewish Press website (www.Jpress.org.il) founded by the National Library and Tel Aviv University.

During its first three years the paper appeared as a bi-weekly, and after that it became a weekly. From the beginning, Bril stressed its 'Jerusalem' character, and the paper carried a heading 'Brings light from the Holy Land Jerusalem', and the motto: 'Bless Jerusalem will say your lovers.' The subtitle brought some further clarification as to the newspaper's purpose: 'To announce and inform about everything a Jewish person should know as a Jew.'

Registration as a non-political journal impacted format and contents, as can be seen with the sections of the paper. The first part of the *Ha-Levanon* was called 'Divrey Ha-yamim' ('History'): it brought news from the Jewish communities, of which Palestine was always given precedence. The first section ('The Tower of Lebanon looks over Jerusalem') makes clear that Bril addressed Jewish readers through references to the Holy Land, which was cast as the main shared element/identifier. No matter the non-political label imposed by the newspaper's registration, Bril felt that he could not remain an outside observer of events taking place in (Ottoman) Palestine. In 'The Tower of Lebanon', thus appeared news about what was happening in Jerusalem, officially brought to readers 'by the Editorial staff'.

Coming out in the open, Bril made his own observations on and gave explanations to what seemed to be editorial news. In so doing, using arguments, he sought to even the score with various persons in the community, especially with regard to the Jewish settlement in Palestine. Bril himself pointed out the purpose of the section: 'We shall build in *Ha-Levanon* a tower overlooking Jerusalem, and even if somebody will hide his actions in darkness, the spectator will see them from there. I have a place in *Ha-Levanon*, from which I shall be able to display the entire Zion Mountain.'[6] This reflects Bril's mindset as a political exile, for whom Palestine was the natural tangible centre. This was in stark contrast with the mind frame of most European Jews at the time. *Ha-Levanon* was thus more Palestinian than European, to the point that, as historian and writer Samuel Leib Zitron (1860–1930) remarked that 'according to all that was printed on *The Lebanon* during its entire second year, it was impossible to know that in the world existed a country called Russia, where millions of Jews were living.'[7] This was a rather unique positioning at a time when all Hebrew newspapers that attempted to be transnational saw Russian Jewry as their main potential target audience – it was the rationale behind the establishment of *Ha-Maggid* in Lyck (Eastern Prussia) in 1856.

The second issue raised in the *Lebanon* file (at the Paris *Archives nationales*) is the paper's political column. At the beginning of the paper's Paris career, Bril had been forced to abandon the idea of it being registered as a political journal. Thus, he gave up on inserting a political section *per say*. He still followed closely the development of events in Palestine and was actively fighting against the Haskalah (Jewish Enlightenment) movement in Eastern Europe whose activities for integration in the general society were opposed by the orthodox Jews. Why then not try his luck again and have the newspaper registered as political? Apart from the already evoked difficulties (editor's nationality in particular), Bril's renunciation had at least two motivations. First, a *journal politique* had to pay the sum of fifty thousand French francs as irrevocable guarantee, in addition to a special 'stamp duty' payable on every copy. Secondly, a political journal would naturally attract closer attention from the authorities, and as we have seen, Bril's legal position was not at all clear. Nevertheless, as time went by, the absence of a political column became a true obsession for Bril, as he believed that this was the main reason for the paper's small circulation, compared to the success of *Ha-Maggid*, which in his eyes was his principal competitor.

On 12 June 1867, after many promises to his readers, editor Michel Edinger submitted a petition to the French *ministre de l'Intérieur* (Home Secretary), requesting authorization for *Ha-Levanon* to publish news and articles translated from the official government periodical, *Le Moniteur Universel* ('The Universal Monitor'), and to exempt him from duty. It appears that such an arrangement was already in force for some other foreign-language publications intended for circulation beyond the French borders. The petition was also supported by the Chief Rabbi of France, who stressed Bril's loyalty to the French State and insisted that the paper was mainly intended for circulation among the Jews of Poland and the Near East. Whoever is acquainted with the history of French journalism cannot avoid linking this petition with the renewed flourishing of the political press in France between 1867 and 1870, and the preparations for the Press Laws of 1868. In this context, the French Home Secretary weighed the petition of the Hebrew paper, but still with the characteristic hypocrisy of the Napoleonic government concerning the press. The Ministry of the Interior preferred to give *Ha-Levanon* a 'verbal authorization' that could be revoked at will 'even without any apparent reason'. On 16 August 1867, Bril informed his readers that 'yesterday the great French government, may its glory be uplifted, authorized me to publish in *Ha-Levanon* also political matters'.

The first political affairs section of the Parisian *Ha-Levanon* (the *Libanon*) concerned itself with international politics and not only with 'Jewish' news appeared in its third year in the French capital, on 30 August 1867. It was labelled 'Al hamedinot po ye-amer', which roughly translates as 'Get your international news here' and formed an obvious imitation of 'Al hamedinot bo ye-amer', an expression from the Jewish sources (from a Yom Kippur prayer) that carried the same meaning and was used by its rival, *Ha-Maggid*. As it appears from the documents in the *Ha-Levanon* file at the French Interior Ministry Archives, the (oral) go-ahead to publish the section was given with strings attached.[8] Its contents had to be copied over from the French press and, effectively, from one newspaper only, the official organ of the Second French Empire, *Le Moniteur Universel* – of which one of the senior writers, producing anonymously, was Emperor Napoleon III himself... In an editorial preceding the first political section, headlined 'A Word with the Reader', Bril explained why he would publish 'only what was known to one of the French journalists'. In so doing, he wanted to showsubstantive differences between the general press and the Hebrew press then – its limited influence, small readership, and scanty resources.[9] Proudly, however, he changed the subtitle of his newspaper to 'Everything a Jew and a Member of Human Society Needs to Know' and set out, from the very first edition, to tackle matters 'at the pinnacle of the ways of the world'. The section was written in the form of a narrative synthesis and shifted from topic to topic with the help of rhetorical connectives. The aggregated news was followed by a commentary written in an official and statist spirit. In the news items themselves, Bril allowed himself a little more licence and attempted to demonstrate a 'Jewish ethics' of his own in presenting matters that at times, seem to have been gleaned from various newspapers, other than *Le Moniteur Universel*.

An example is provided by the first article on international politics, when the *Libanon* section 'Al hamedinot po ye-amer' was introduced on 30 August 1867. It dealt with a summit meeting between the emperors of France and Austria in Salzburg and an open letter from the French Foreign Minister, officially denying allegations in the press that a military alliance between the countries and war preparations had been discussed *en tête-à-tête*. Bril stressed that it was 'a consolation visit', quoting the official iteration of the French Foreign Minister without questioning it in any way, of course.[10] He pursued that the talks had nothing to do with a military alliance, but were peace arrangements – which seemed to be a new fashion among the rulers of Europe to the disheartenment of the enemies of peace. The agreement that allowed France to annex Luxemburg was handed to Napoleon III with the consent of the Germans, in return for Napoleon III's neutrality in the German conflict with Austria.

Further on, Bril quotes remarks by the Prussian Foreign Minister about a series of meetings in the opposing camp – a journey by the King of Prussia to the principalities of eastern Germany 'to bring the kings of the east German lands into his alliance'.[11] Bril thus endorsed the idea of the King of Prussia's trip to the southern principalities as being just another 'pure family visit', which had nothing to do with preparations for a military and political alliance ahead of imminent war for the establishment of a German empire – this was the dream of Chancellor Bismarck, who had already managed to unify Northern principalities. For his part, Bismarck did not stand behind the balance of forces and diplomatic equilibrium in Europe and remained true to his famous motto: 'The great problems of our time will not be solved by speeches and majority votes but by iron and blood'. The southern principalities would join the northern union in a future war against France in 1870–1. Bril was duty-bound to accept this discourse verbatim, and the interpretation he gave remained true to the official line, as noted below:

> The words of the two ministers, France and Prussia's ones, penetrate the hearts of their listeners, who will not continue to smell war from afar. Truly, the entire content of the spirit of the mighty, wise, and great Emperor Napoleon III, May God protect him, knows that it pleases him even in wartime to choose peace.[12]

The two ministers should be trusted, Bril states, basing himself on the official press organs' reports. However, he reserved most of his praise for Emperor Napoleon III – following the manner of Diaspora Jewish communities, but also to keep his Hebrew newspaper safe and sound. Bril's account took up the traditional manner in which dispersed Jews described rulers of the countries they lived in: lines about Napoleon III thus recall Biblical descriptions of the Master of the Universe. The characteristics then attributed to Napoleon III were not those of a war hero, but the opposite: those of a peace-making heroic statesman. From here, Bril segues into an idyllic generalization about the 'new' Europe, where peace and prosperity have supplanted wars and conquests. He reserved his descriptions of an impending war for rival Britain, which was then waging a colonial war against the emperor of the 'land of the *Cushites*', i.e. Abyssinia/Ethiopia. The international politics section on 30 August 1867 contained the following:

> The English Empire, mistress of the sea, is preparing for a ground war against the emperor of the land of the *Cushites*, Theodoros, *Empereur de l'Abyssinie*, because travelers, a missionary, and also a British consul have been languishing in prison there for three years now and to this day are being tortured in jail. The emperor of the *Cushites* is a self-styled savant who says: I know the ways of the kings of Europe. When they set their eyes on a country, they first send envoys there, portraying them as visiting only for religious matters and the like, and then they send a consul who is related to their envoys, and afterwards they send their armies and occupy the country. Therefore, he said, I will not yield to the kings of Europe to the last moment, and I would do well not to let their envoys and travelers set foot on the ground. And he kept his word: for three years now, he has been holding English envoys and emissaries in prison and has not allowed them to return to their country, to the fury of the English Empire.[13]

In this passage, Bril aimed at a didactic and (quite) objective account, using irony and shared symbols that help readers understand current realities and the author's intentions. He then presents a sober analysis of Emperor Theodoros's motives for detaining the British subjects, which brought on Britain's fury. As a reminder, the Abyssinian Campaign was a rescue mission and punitive expedition carried out in 1868 decided on by Britain against the Ethiopian Empire (aka Abyssinia then), after Emperor Theodore II had imprisoned British subjects in an attempt to force the British government to comply with his requests for military assistance, and had refused to release them. The punitive expedition extraordinary logistics, including the transportation of a sizable military force hundreds of miles across mountainous terrain lacking any road system. Obstacles were overcome by the commander of the expedition, General Sir Robert Napier, who defeated Theodore's troops, captured the Ethiopian capital, and rescued all the hostages.[14] Here is Bril's rendering of the situation:

> Now that her requests to the Emperor of the *Cushites* to release her prisoners have been unrequited, she is preparing to declare war on him until he is defeated.... To wage war against this empire, the English Empire will have to prepare on a large scale. Nevertheless, it is confident that it will defeat the enemy, that the Kingdom of Egypt will not only allow it to cross through its upper portion on the way to *Cush*, that [Egypt] will also give 10,000 camels, ships of the desert, to help carry the needs of the war on their backs. What is more, 10,000 men from the British forces in India were chosen to be sent to *Cush*, and they will not be afraid of being sunburned because they, like the *Cushites*, were born in a very hot region. Apart from them, the British Empire will send a mighty fleet down the Red Sea to the coast of Massawa on the eighteenth of this month and will fight with the *Cushites* at sea and on land. If even now, after hearing that war is closing in on him, the emperor of the *Cushites* hardens his heart and fails to release the British prisoners, he will quickly smell the odor of the gunpowder made in England.[15]

The passage stands as a caricatured sketch of the colonization process (missionaries first, then a consul to protect their interests, followed finally by the army), reminiscent of the 3 Cs (Christianity, Commerce, Civilization). It provides a detailed account of the balance of forces, including economic, geopolitical and strategic aspects. The intermingling of political actors is rendered in picturesque explanations, couched in the typical racist language/tone of the time – see for instance, the remark about sending Indian soldiers against the Ethiopians because they, like the Ethiopians, come from a subtropical area ('a very hot region') and need not fear 'getting sunburned' (due to their skin colour).

By contrast, the account also demonstrates an understanding of the motives of Emperor Theodoros, who, despite his being described as a latter-day Pharaoh, feared an imperialist colonialist takeover. This description fits the underlying humanistic and sympathetic attitude of Hebrew journalists then towards dominated peoples and an understanding of their needs.[16] Switching to the commentary column however, Bril reverted to the colonialist-racist outlook of the time, the Orientalist and Eurocentric attitude that he encountered in the newspapers that served as his official and mandatory sources. Here he sanctioned imperialist and colonialist wars as vehicles for the dissemination of what he saw as the noble Western culture among the sub-cultured locals.

> May God inspire those kings who wish to live by their sword and display their valour on the battlefield to declare war on those lands that have not yet accepted the yoke of civilization, so that even those people far from urban man will know that man is differentiated from beast.[17]

Despite general desires for peace among European rulers, Bril's words operated as a *tour de force*, insisting that those 'who wish to live by their sword' should be allowed to fulfil their wishes through wars on faraway continents – all of which for the sake of peace in Europe. Reconciling European peace and European imperialism as compatible objectives, Bril endorsed European discourse on the imperial civilizing mission.

The political column did not produce the sweeping change in circulation Bril expected. To the problematic legal situation was now added the economic predicament, which was always an issue despite Bril's connections with personalities like the founder of the Jewish library Baron Yudil Ginsburg, French philosopher and historian Ernest Renan and leaders of the Alliance Israélite Universelle. Among the Rabbis of Paris, there were only seven subscribers to *Ha-Levanon* against ten non-Jews. Bril changed addresses in Paris four times, and he himself set the paper's type and proofread it. In 1868, he established his own printing press, registered in the name of Michel Edinger. The paper was very much a one-man journalistic enterprise.

At the beginning of its Parisian period (the first three years), *Ha-Levanon*'s 'History' section had preceded the 'Lebanon Honor'. From the fourth year of its Parisian period (1869), this changed, with 'Lebanon Honor' (*Kevod Ha-Levanon*) coming first before the secular section. Bril's foregrounding of religion was made explicit by the section's motto: 'This is the Lord's section – the righteous will come here.' Religion had always been at the heart of *Ha-Levanon*. From the beginning, in 'The Tower of Lebanon' section, Bril gave representation to the rulers of the *Halukah* (the distribution of alms to the poor Jews in Palestine), but also related scandals. In its fourth and fifth years, The

Lebanon made wide space to radical Rabbis' hostility against the *Haskalah* (as covered in the St Petersburg Jewish press title *Ha-Melitz*).

In its sixth year, Bril leaned more and more towards yellow journalism, but was careful not to turn the *Libanon* into a censorship office. To do so and thus save his journalistic venture, Bril reordered columns. For instance, the 'Lebanon Honor' was removed from the paper and started then being printed as four separate pages. The paper's motto was also softened to 'I chose the way of faith', which to him symbolized an equipoise between faith and reason, 'because pure Faith will not be hostile to its sister Reason'. Bril explained in a penetrating article, that he wanted to avoid turning his paper into a 'house of learning'.[18] Rather than a blind acceptance of the *Haskalah*, Bril was displaying journalistic and political flexibility when it came to salvaging his paper.

Only a year before, Bril had shed the mention of the paper's name in Osmanli (Turkish in Arabic characters), which had been used from its Jerusalem days. Bril constantly tried to adapt to the paper's context of publication and new readership. And yet, he still gave space to personalities such as Polish Orthodox Rabbi Zvi Hirsch Kalisher, one of the precursors of the 'Lovers of Zion' (*Hovevey-Zion*) ideology and movement that pre-dated the Zionist movement and advocated the settlement of Palestine, alongside his own articles, which then called for caution in that matter. Trying to strike a more balanced position, Bril also hoped that he would be considered an authority for his views printed in *Le Libanon* and would be consulted on such political questions. Just before the paper stopped its publication in Paris, Bril somehow recanted and pursued an acrimonious 'religious war' against the *Haskalah* leaders (mainly Moses Leib Lilienblum and Judah Leib Gordon) in the paper, this time making his position extremely clear. Such a war came to dominate the paper... only another war, the Franco-Prussian War – temporarily – altered Bril's perspectives and prospects.

Mainz, 1871: doing French politics from over the border?

The war whose menace he had striven to deny caught up with him. Reality knocked on his door: despite the diplomatic denials, the unification of the German principalities became a fact and the resulting union inflicted defeat on France and weakened her Austro-Hungarian ally even more. The Prussian-French War broke out in July 1870 and it lasted until the armistice – in fact, France's surrender – on 29 January 1871. In its course, Napoleon III was unseated after his defeat in the battle of Sedan and the French Third Republic was declared. (In March–May 1871, the Republic would entangle itself in a bloody civil war upon the rising of the Paris Commune.) On 18 January 1871 at the Versailles palace, victors announced the establishment of the German empire.

Due to the war, *Ha-Levanon* ceased to appear in Paris and Bril had to move to Mainz, in Bismarck's Unified Germany, bringing the newspaper with him – but not before the siege of Paris, which Bril experienced with his family at the end of his stay in the French capital. Bril could not rest satisfied with being a mere observer. By then, he had spent seven years in France. Notwithstanding his 'underground' status as the

Figure 1.3 *Ha-Levanon, Hebreische Ausgabe des ‚Israelit'* (The Hebrew edition of *Der Israelit*), Masthead, Mainz, 16 August 1871. *Libanon*, Masthead, 6 January 1865, Paris. By courtesy of the Historical Jewish Press website (www.Jpress.org.il) founded by the National Library and Tel Aviv University.

unofficial editor of a Hebrew newspaper in France, he had attempted to integrate into his country of adoption, without giving up his allegiance to *Eretz Israel* (Palestine). He was also unabashedly grateful to France for her historical role in empowering the Jewish people. Thus, he wished to link his fate to that of the French, including as a fighter, no matter how unsuitable this was for a litterateur of the Jewish persuasion.[19] He explained:

> I was already like a Frenchman in the sense of preferring death to a life of disgrace. I said that I too would set out amid the civilian force and be like one of the French. It is also my duty to do this – to help the French because they were the first to recognize our fellow Jews as equal citizens of the country. Does not Prussia also have a government minister who goes by a Jewish name? [an allusion to Adolphe Crémieux by his Hebrew name] Even in this country, where our brethren are not the last to excel in the proficiency of their wisdom in every matter and their mighty spirit in war – would a Jewish man be named a battalion commander as is the case in France?[20]

Notwithstanding his criticism, Bril did not hesitate to move his personal residence and that of *Ha-Levanon* to the other side of the border. His fighting spirit had to yield before his wife's opposition:

> For all these reasons, I resolved to join the fighters myself. My wife, however, did not let me act on my wish and my duty. She cried to me day in and day out until I promised her that I would respect her and stay home. Nevertheless, I could not hang around with the kids. To satisfy those around me, who gave a jaundiced look to any man who had not strapped his sword to his loins, I enlisted in the battalions

of the civilian force aged fifty and over... When the fighting in town wound down, before all the warriors had stopped and the town was opened up, our swords remained as rusty as the day we received them.[21]

This ironic and grotesque conclusion is an example of Bril's proficiency in critical writing, including self-criticism. However, he does not paper over the facts: the editor of the Jerusalem *Ha-Levanon* puts on a French sword, of all things – probably for the first time in his life – as a member of the Civil Guard in besieged Paris. In the pairing of book and sword, his book serves his people in Jerusalem while his sword does so for 'Gentiles' (non-Jews). He did promise to record all his observations in a book entitled *130 Days in the Siege of Paris*, but all he managed to produce were nine instalments about the siege in the first editions of the Mainz *Ha-Levanon*, which started appearing on 16 August 1871.[22]

In these episodes, he finally gave his pen full rein and unleashed a sober and sometimes powerful critical overview, skilfully written by a participant-eyewitness. The instalments combined mingling irony, sometimes-outright satire, with excitement. Bril provided full coverage of the crisis and the state of war. This time, he relies more liberally on the press that opposed the fallen emperor. He alternated field reportage with digests of information and analyses harvested from newspapers, which he also treats critically. He addressed the socio-psychological aspect of the state of war at length and even criticized propaganda.

In the very first instalment of the series, Bril attempted to tackle the question of his personal objectivity and the claims that things looked different in Germany, his current location, than they did in France, his erstwhile home: 'Do not say, enlightened reader, that from the day I tasted grain bread and barley beer I changed my stripes because now my eyes opened to see those things that had misled them.... Do not, my dear brother reader, take me for a traitor to the truth.' The mere fact of his having relocated from France to Prussia, he claims, did not prompt him to change his mind about the French people and his quondam benefactor, Emperor Napoleon III. Was he, however, able to convince the 'enlightened Hebrew reader', accustomed to self-censorship in his newspapers, that these publications could also cover the war even-handedly?[23]

Nonetheless, despite Bril's claims, *Ha-Levanon* lost its independence for the first time, now that it was published in Mainz. It indeed became the Hebrew supplement of Dr Meir Lehman's *Der Israelit* ('The Israelite'), the weekly organ of radical Orthodoxy, and continued appearing in Mainz until late 1882, when it was in its nineteenth year. In its last two years, Bril managed to restore *Ha-Levanon*'s independence and it again appeared as a newspaper in its own name (not as the supplement of another).

During this period, *Ha-Levanon* mostly targeted readers in Russia and Poland, where Orthodox Jews often read Hebrew. Bril seconded Lehman in his 'sacred mission' of 'curing the great ills of the Jewish world' – understand here Russian and Polish Judaisms – according to the German model. But Bril and Lehman's attempt at translating the struggle against Reform Judaism from Germany to Russia got a belittled echo, as they did not take into account Russian Orthodox Jews' specific concerns. To boost sales and spur newspaper readership, Bril bet on the arsenal of scandal sheets and starting printing scandalous news about his competitors that they betrayed Judaism and Jewry. At the same time, while still cajoling Orthodox positions, Bril moved closer to the 'Lovers of Zion' ideology. A fall-out with the radical Orthodox party followed and put an end to the collaboration with Lehman.

The Lebanon in London: short rebirth and final leg

Meanwhile, Bril had not abandoned the Holy Land. In 1883, he even headed the project of taking eleven farmers from Russia to Palestine, where they founded the colony of Ekron,[24] as he had reached an understanding with such hated competitors as *Ha-Maggid* on the subject of encouraging Jewish emigration from Russia to Palestine. Back in Europe after a three-year break, Bril now moved to London, where he started publishing issue number 1 of 'the 20TH year of *Ha-Levanon*' (with the title appearing also in English as *The Lebanon*) on 2 June 1886. The publishing office address was '82 Brick Lane, Spitalfields [sic]', in East London.

This final leg in the history of *Ha-Levanon* was perceived by Bril as a near spiritual rebirth. In his editorial ('Call to readers and contributors'), he considered his newspaper as a 'new born baby' and mainly focused on the burning subject of the year in the world of the Hebrew press: the switch from weeklies to dailies. The first Hebrew daily *Ha-Yom* (Today) appeared in 1886 in St Petersburg, quickly followed by *Ha-Melitz* (The Mediator) in St Petersburg and then *Ha-Zefira* (The Dawn) in Warsaw – the latter two being weeklies that were turned into dailies. Bril called to reflect on what he regarded as 'a big step' (*pessia gassa*) on the part of the *Ha-Melitz* and *Ha-Zefira* editors. The consequences of that change would be known in the future, but as far as *Ha-Levanon* was concerned, Bril preferred a weekly publication (to a daily) – even if he encountered

Figure 1.4 *The Lebanon*, Masthead, 1 September 1886, London, last issue (771). By courtesy of the Historical Jewish Press website (www.Jpress.org.il) – founded by the National Library and Tel Aviv University.

irregular publishing and faced difficulties in publishing in Hebrew. To a hypothetical question of its readers: 'So, if you can't bring us daily news, why publishing a weekly if you won't have readers', Bril answered that his intention was not to make money, but to awake love for *Eretz Israel* – the Jewish homeland – and the Hebrew language.

Bril's move to London was the occasion to reflect on the place of Jews in British society, as is particularly conspicuous in the first three issues. Bril's relocation to London took place at the time of mass emigration of Eastern European Jews fleeing persecution, with London operating as one sites of Jewish refuge, especially over the period 1880–1905. While overall, Jewish émigrés to Britain over the larger period of the 'Grand Jewish Migration' (1880–1914) only amounted to 120,000, restrictionist circles agitated much larger figures to create a panic and media attention on Jews in Britain soared. Bril's revival of *Ha-Levanon* in London took stock of that context. It so follows that in that very first London issue, Bril set out to criticize an article just published in the London *Globe* about 'Hebrew Journalism in London' (May 1886).[25] Despite its title, the *Globe* article, written by a non-Jew, actually derided the Yiddish rather than the Hebrew press – which was considered as being more cultivated, therefore as not being rivalling to the acquisition of the English language by Jews. An editor of both *Ha-Levanon* in Hebrew and formerly of the *Shulamith* in Yiddish, Bril outspokenly defended those who had not yet learnt English and spoke what was considered by detractors as 'jargon' (Hebrew).

In keeping with its transnational positioning, *The Lebanon* made space to correspondents, news about the Jewish world and international news. For instance, the 'Correspondents' section of the first London issue staged two correspondents from London and another one from Berlin. Letters from correspondents could highlight facts, events or documents of particular relevance to Bril's readers, such as the letter (in London issue n°2) by an important Paris contributor and sponsor, Schneur Sachs (1815–92), who was Head of the manuscripts section of the Jewish library founded by the Baron Yudil Guinsburg. The 'News from the Jewish world' section started with news from different Jewish meetings and institutions in London, like the crisis in Spital Square Synagogue, because of permission given to representatives of Reformed Judaism to pray there. Then followed long quotes from *Ha-Tzvi* ('The Deer') in Jerusalem about the settlements in *Eretz Israel*. This pattern, first giving news from the Jewish community in London and more widely Britain, and then from the world, was repeated over the following issues, which also included coverage of crises – as with the mention of the Anglo-Jewish association in London issue n°2, or criticisms of publications about *Halukah* scandals (issue n°4). The first issue also demonstrated Bril's desire to resurrect a political newspaper. It launched a series about Jews in China – which was continued – and included a political section, with news came from Great Britain about the Irish question, then came news from France, Germany, Spain and Greece. Over the London issues, political news from these countries was well represented.

Issued two weeks after the first one – publication in London was irregular – Bril launched 'a second call for readers and contributors'. He mentioned some reactions he had received, after having exposed his material difficulties in the first issue, and still complained that 'during all the years I have lived from my work, since the age of fourteen, I have never worked so hard – and under conditions of slavery – as since I have chosen the London darkness'.[26] Still, he announced that he would fight for the Hebrew language, even if that displeased some readers. Strategy-wise, he confirmed that he had chosen direct sales of his paper, he presented his only agent in St Petersburg who was still needed in Russia because of the censorship laws there, but asked those in London and Europe, who had received the first issue, to send it back, if they do not want to become its readers. Otherwise, they would be considered as subscribers... The following issues reproduced this warning, indicating how financially frail Bril's position was. To try to maintain his paper afloat and integrate readers more, Bril eventually proposed them a new financial model (11 August issue) in which readers would pay the writers directly, as he would only take a fee to ensure publishing. The swift interruption of *The Lebanon* shortly before Bril's death in November 1886 meant that he lacked time to test the viability of the new model.

No matter its transnational connections with the Jewish diaspora and its foregrounding international politics, *The Lebanon* was very much a British paper in its very structure and contents, which increasingly gave priority to British Jewish affairs. In issue n°2, Brill pursued his critique of the article 'The Hebrew press in London', insisting that knowledge of English did not mean elimination of Yiddish. He also denounced the condemnation of *Heder* (Jewish schools) that made them incompatible with successful assimilation. The third issue, published on 23 June (but six days after issue n°2) started with an editorial on Jews' massive migrations throughout the world and rekindled with the Palestinian theme. Indeed, Bril suggested not hurrying up and preparing the departure for *Eretz Israel*. In the 11 August issue, Bril argued with a published report of Claude Montefiore about the treatment of foreigners in the Jewish society, and discussed sir Lawrence Oliphant's Palestine settlement plans. As always, Bril connected the local, with more global and diasporic scales. The July and August 1886 issues sought to further reflect on The Lebanon's uniqueness as a newspaper, as a transnational, wandering paper which remained tinted by Bril's Jerusalem background and itineraries. For instance, the 'Correspondents' section of the July 1886 issues featured a presentation of the two London Jewish newspapers appearing in English, *The Jewish Chronicle* – presented as openly reformist – and *Jewish World* – which was criticized because of its false self-presentation. The 11 August issue opened with a reflective editorial about 'Jews in the British Politics', in which he presented them as different from 'the Typical Jew' drawing conclusions from a comparison with Jews' involvement in the politics of the main European countries. According to Bril, for British Jews, 'Money means (solves) everything' and so, British Jewish financiers (like Baron Rothschild) did not hesitate to enter in politics. Bril pursued that for British Jews, the biggest honour was to be a Member of Parliament: 'British Jews would like to count 10 MP's in their ranks, unlike the French who would prefer 10 academicians.'[27]

Overall, the section layout in *The Levanon* was fairly flexible, probably as Bril tried to find a voice in the London competitive and transnational markets. For instance, the general political news section, which was last and least in order, disappeared in early

August, but reappeared on 25 August. How much representation of international news depended on ongoing events, as well as to their impact for Jews. In the 1 September issue, Bril brought together the coverage of British General elections and parliamentary affairs and the situation in the Balkans – mainly Bulgaria. With ongoing persecution, a larger place was also given to Russian Jewry, but never to the detriment of settlements in Palestine – as is shown by Bril's decision to discuss a *Jewish Chronicle* issue honouring British Jewish leader and philanthropist Sir Moses Montefiore (who had died in 1885) and herewith contest the supposedly negative image of Palestinian Jews.

London was *Ha-Levanon*'s last stop. Bril suddenly passed away on 12 November 1886 aged 50, so that the London *Ha-Levanon* ended after only twelve issues, at a time when Bril was still trying to adjust the editorial line to its new publication location. In a way, *Ha-Levanon* was one extreme example of a wandering 'one-man newspaper', in which the Hebrew newspaper's destiny was linked with that of its founder. *Ha-Levanon* typifies the 'wandering Jew' as embodied in the press. One needs to remember that the Jewish press grew and developed in Europe in the nineteenth century within a hostile and uncertain environment, that it was a minority press subject to the benevolence of 'foreign' owners, in accordance with the legal situation of the local Jewish community.[28] As such, *Ha-Levanon* is a perfect example of how the nineteenth-century foreign-language/diasporic press – be they weeklies (as here) or dailies – could set up a transnational communication network between Jewish communities dispersed throughout the world thanks to a common language, here Hebrew, that *Ha-Levanon* was one of the early Jewish newspapers to resurrect for that purpose.

But Bril's trajectory is atypical, reverse somehow. Facing the religious, quasi-mystical diasporic quest of the return to Sion becoming increasingly political on the one hand, and the development of an assimilationist movement that pleaded for the integration of Jews in the countries they found themselves in, Bril's trajectory was other: he came from the 'imagined' and sought-after destination, so that Jerusalem and Palestine constituted a practical experience for Bril – one he could passionately write about in his paper. Contrary to other editors who lacked this background, Bril could give some realistic shape to the nostalgic myth of the ancient homeland. Out of comparison with other competitors throughout Europe, Bril's particular positioning conferred on *Ha-Levanon* its modernity and allowed his paper to remain an organ in the service of strict Orthodoxy, while advocating Jews' involvement in world affairs, their knowledge of national and international politics. As an editor of his time and of the world, Bril embraced new forms of journalism, especially the yellow journalism of the French popular press, as a way of promoting his ideas and reaching his objectives. As with other wandering foreign-language, diasporic newspapers, the general, and especially legal, documentation is often hard to find, often scarce and dispersed. This is particularly true of the Jewish press. As such, the voluminous archival file held at the French National archives about *Ha-Levanon* in Paris, has a unique value, thereby reminding anybody researching this type of press of the need to go to multifarious archival sources to give full life to serials whose histories would otherwise remain obscure(d).

Notes

1 Included in the Collection of articles on the history of the Press in Palestine, 2, 16–19.
2 Galia Yardeni dealt with this subject in her book *The Hebrew Press in Palestine (1860–1904)*, Hakibutz Hameuhad Publishers, Tel Aviv University, 1969.
3 I accidentally discovered the prospectus, held under the following reference: Archives nationales, Intérieur; Direction de la Presse. Presse parisienne et agences de presse: dossiers, des journaux (1820–1894) F/18/377, Dossier 58, LIBANON (LE) 1864–7.
4 Ibid. Items 310–16. The original is in French and the translation is the author's.
5 Ibid. Item 316.
6 *Ha-Levanon*, 6 January 1865.
7 In 'Notes on the history of Hebrew Press', *Haolam*, issue 30, 1912, 13.
8 Gideon Kouts, *News and History: Studies in the History of Hebrew and Jewish Press and Communication* (in Hebrew), Jerusalem: The Zionist Library and Tel Aviv University, 2013, 47–50, 55–68.
9 Ibid., 51–3.
10 'Words to the Reader', *Ha-Levanon*, 30 August 1867. (Pages not numbered.)
11 Ibid. The original is on Hebrew and the translation is the author's (as with other quotes from *Ha-Levanon*).
12 Ibid.
13 Ibid.
14 Christopher Brice, 'The Expedition to Abyssinia, 1867–1868', in *Queen Victoria's Wars: British Military Campaigns, 1857–1902*, edited by Stephen M. Miller, 62–82 (Cambridge: Cambridge University Press, 2021).
15 'Words to the Reader', *Ha-Levanon*, 30 August 1867. (Pages not numbered.)
16 For example, *Ha-Maggid* urged Jews to support British imperialism and repression of the Indian uprising in 1857, but harshly criticized its brutal nature and narrow horizons of the British administration in that country, which lacked the wisdom to bring 'progress' to its inhabitants. See analysis in Yaakov Shavit, 'A Window onto the World', *Kesher* 36 (2007), 18–23 (in Hebrew).
17 'Words to the Reader', ibid.
18 'To the Readers', *Ha-Levanon*, 1 January 1869, Paris. (Pages not numbered.)
19 Yehiel Bril, 'The Publisher Discourses with his Readers', in Todros Halevi Abulafia, *Ketab al-Rasil* (tr. From Hebrew: *Sefer Iggrot*), Paris, 1871, 3.
20 Ibid.
21 Ibid.
22 'Siege of Paris' in *Ha-Levanon* (Mainz edition): 16 August 1871 (volume 8, Issue 1, afterwards 8:1); 4 September 1871 (8:2); 11 September 1871 (8:3); 22 September 1871 (8:4); 28 September 1871 (8:5); 16 October 1871 (8:6); 2 November 1871 (8:8); 15 November 1871 (8:10); 29 November 1871 (8:12).
23 See also Getzel Kressel, 'Hebrew reverberations of the French-Prussian War and the Paris Commune', *Katif* 9–10 (1973), 180–95 (in Hebrew).
24 The story is told in his fascinating book: Yehiel Bril, *Yessod Hama'ala*, Mainz, 5643 (1883) – a new edition including an introduction, notes and index by G. Kressel, was published by the Itzhak Ben-Zvi Memorial, Jerusalem, 5738 (1978).
25 'Hajournalistic haivrit beLondon', *Ha-Levanon*, London, 2 June 1886, 1; 'Hebrew Journalism in London', *The Globe*, 18 May 1886, 6.
26 'To readers and contributors', *Ha-Levanon,* London, 16 June 1886, 2.

27 'Jews in British Politics', *Ha-Levanon*, London, 11 August 1886, 7. Bril forgets that until 1860, British Universities did not accept Jews, and that Lionel Nathan de Rothschild could take his seat in Parliament (House of Commons) only in 1858 after the passage of the Jews Relief Act, eleven years after he was first elected. Baron Nathan Mayer Rothschild became the first Jewish member of the House of Lords in 1885, after having served as a Liberal MP from 1865.
28 See Gideon Kouts, *The Hebrew and Jewish Press in Europe* (Paris: Suger Press, 2006), 43–4.

2

A Transnational Radical Print Culture: French-Language Anarchist Periodicals between London, Paris and the United States before 1914

Constance Bantman
University of Surrey

Between its emergence in the 1870s and the start of the First World War, the anarchist movement existed through and was informed by dense multidirectional transnational exchanges, as a result of ideological internationalism as well as labour mobility and political exile within its ranks.[1] Alongside direct contact largely concentrated in cosmopolitan cities and rare international congresses and conferences, periodicals were the prime medium for theoretical and strategic discussions, as well as the organization of the movement and construction of anarchist identities on a variety of scales. The multifaceted role of the press for anarchists, in return, fostered an elaborate, inventive and effective radical print culture, often operating on a shoestring and in adverse circumstances.

The anarchist press is often described by historians as fulfilling the role of the 'party' in anarchism, and its central, many-sided role in creating and sustaining a collective identity for its readers on a variety of scales, ranging from local group formation to anarchism as a cross-border, network-based internationalist movement, must be emphasized.[2] As summarized by Kenyon Zimmer, 'it would be difficult to overstate the functional importance of newspapers in the anarchist movement. The printed word created a transnational community of anarchists and transmitted the movement's ideology across space while sustaining collective identities across time.'[3] While a few wandering titles naturally appeared as a result of the intense mobility of personnel which was integral to late nineteenth-century anarchism, even more striking and widespread was the circulation of contents across different titles, languages and geographical areas. In order to shed light on the material and ideological contexts in which such circulations took place, this study explores the personal and print networks which created, sustained, disseminated and consumed these publications. Pre-1914 anarchist periodicals provide a striking illustration of a sophisticated transnational print culture in the face of disruptive mobility, intense surveillance, financial precariousness as well as linguistic and ideological hurdles. This, in return, allows us to interrogate anarchist periodicals as a sub-genre of radical journalism, and its variations.

Assessments of these periodicals in comparison to the 'national' anarchist press are also undertaken, in order to identify areas of innovation arising from displacement, and to highlight the specificity of this press-in-mobility.

Defining the transnational anarchist press: approaches and quandaries

The functioning of anarchist print culture is fruitfully examined through the example of late nineteenth-century transnational periodicals, with a focus on Anglo-French connections in Paris, London and Eastern US states, where nodes of such transnational publishing activities were located. This analysis follows a group of publications entangled through their editors, contributors and contents, which were part of wider exchanges within the global anarchist-communist diasporas.

A preliminary caveat is that this is a necessarily truncated view of the broader networks within which these papers were produced, disseminated and consumed, which routinely extended far beyond the sites examined here, typically into Argentina, Brazil, Spain, Italy, Switzerland, Belgium, often along linguistic diasporas. Conversely, while far-reaching transnational networks cannot be fully mapped out and analysed, the local and national editorial contexts of these publications is also partly lost through the angle adopted here. Nor is it straightforward to isolate a clearly discrete corpus based on ideological criteria, given the ideological fluidity of anarchism, especially in

Table 2.1 Key French-language anarchist communist papers published in Britain and the United States, 1880–1914.

Place of publication	Title of publication	Dates	Lead editors
London (previously in Paris)	Le Père Peinard (The Easy Father)	September 1894–January 1895; eight issues	Emile Pouget (1860–1931)
London	Le Tocsin (The Alarm)	December 1892–September 1894; nine issues, published irregularly	Charles Malato (1857–1938); Nicolas Nikitine (1852–?)
London	Le Rothschild (The Rothschild)	15 June 1891–31 July 1891; three issues	Lucien Weil (1865–?)
London	La Grève Générale/Lo Sciopero Generale (The General Strike)	18 March 1902–2 June 1902; three issues	Henry Cuisinier (?); Louis Depoilly (?)
Boston	The Rebel	20 September 1895–March/April 1896; six issues	Charles Mowbray (1857–1910); Harry Kelly (1871–1953)
Charleroi, Pennsylvania	La Tribune Libre (The Open Forum)	25 June 1896–14 August 1900; weekly publication.	Louis Goaziou (1864–1937); Louis Lambert (?)
Paterson, New Jersey	Germinal	1 October 1899–May 1902	Louis Goaziou (1864–1937)

the early 1890s when the individualist and communist strands of the movement still overlapped ideologically and organizationally, and therefore in print too. Thus, the decision was made to leave out the French-language, London-based *La Tribune Libre* (The Open Forum; London, 1890–1), a publication operating within the same networks as *Père Peinard* and *La Révolte* (Rebellion; 1887–94; Paris-based and produced by the French editor Jean Grave, with extensive national and international influence); *La Tribune Libre* advertised these publications in its first issue.[4] It also deployed many of the same editorial networking strategies as the other papers examined here. However, the paper defined itself as 'revolutionary anarchist' and printed bomb-making instructions, meaning that ideological differences over the use of violence in hastening the revolution soon evolved into open discord and the initial networking was short-lived. Lastly, examining periodicals offers a partial view of a wider print culture, as this type of publications was extended and enriched by other types of printed material, such as the books and pamphlets advertised in or resold through the paper – here too with multiple geographic links – and the pamphlets which they discussed. Intertextuality and transmediality were essential features of the journalistic and reading experience of anarchists and sympathizers.[5] Nonetheless, despite these unavoidable selections and omissions, a conclusive overview of processes of circulations and exchange and the networks underpinning them can be reached by focusing on a relatively small number of publications.

Despite shared networks, formal characteristics and strong ideological similarities, the papers examined here varied in size, production and elocutory contexts, as well as overall strategy. They were published in diverse transnational settings, falling into the broad categories of the exile press or immigrant publications, in terms of editorial staff, readership and formal characteristics. With specific reference to the corpus examined here, exile papers were characteristically found in Britain, a traditional harbour for French refugees from across the political spectrum throughout the nineteenth century, while US-based French-language anarchist papers mainly emerged from the French coal mining communities of Pennsylvania in the 1880s, and shared many features with the ethnic press. Louis Goaziou, who edited the US-based periodicals *La Tribune Libre* and *Germinal*, was an economic migrant who had left France for Pennsylvania as an adolescent in 1880, working as an anthracite miner; it is highly likely that he became politicized only after this relocation, by taking part in strikes, only gradually moving towards anarchism from the mid 1880s onwards.[6] *La Tribune Libre*, which Goaziou published in Charleroi, Pennsylvania, carried the subtitle '*organe hebdomadaire des travailleurs de langue française*' ('the weekly organ of French-language workers') and its inaugural editorial flagged its claim to be the only French-language paper in the entire country 'in the interest of the working-class' – a reference to occupational solidarity and anchorage in the country of migration which pointed to the long-term perspective of migration.[7] The distinction between exile and immigrant papers has significant limitations, if only because political exiles were also economic migrants equally pressed by material circumstances – as clearly indicated, for instance, in the exile paper *Le Tocsin* by the inclusion of ads for the various businesses set up by members of the French groups in London, as well as Paris and nearby Levallois-Perret.[8] Moreover, the distinction was complicated by publications that emphasized the status of anarchists as workers, even though they were in other respects known as exiles; this blend was increasingly frequent from the mid-1890s onwards, as syndicalist ideas such as the general strike pervaded anarchist communist circles. This was the case of the 1902 *La Grève Générale*, published in London by Henry Cuisinier and Louis Depoilly, who were deserters from France – that is to say exiles rather than economic migrants[9] – whose primary aim was the promotion of the general strike as a revolutionary labour strategy. The publication originated in the activities of the International Workingmen's Group, attended by about a hundred members, from Spain, Germany, Italy, Switzerland and Belgium, many of whom were de facto workers. The distinction between exiles and migrants did not have much bearing on the papers' editorial teams: all of these papers were associated with a lead editor, sometimes in partnership with a small group (a model which was typical of the anarchist press): Emile Pouget for *Père Peinard*, Charles Malato and Nicolas Nikitine for *Le Tocsin*, Charles Mowbray and American anarchist Harry Kelly for *The Rebel*, Louis Goaziou for his string of French-language publications in Pennsylvania.

Nonetheless, the distinction between immigrant and exile papers had implications for the format and contents of the publications. These publications were all in tension between the local and the international level, but these tensions played out very differently, depending on the groups which produced them, and the 'push' factor for their displacement. Thus, the short-term outlook and predominantly national focus of the exile press has often been stressed despite some recent qualifications,[10] in contrast to the long-term, integration-focused perspective which is more characteristic of papers created by and for immigrants. This is exemplified most convincingly by *Père Peinard*, which displayed a very national outlook. The London iteration of *Le Père Peinard* combined publication outside France with a very French-oriented outlook – a classic exilic stance, as the imperative of discretion and even reserve towards British politics as well as a focus on home politics combined into a seemingly blinkered national perspective, suggesting that 'refugees gave absolute priority to political action in the motherland'.[11] Thus, in early issues, the section 'Coups de tranchet' ('skiving-knife strikes') which dealt with current events, discussed primarily French matters and figures, such as the Baron de Rothschild, French politician Daniel Wilson (1840–1919), a recent mining law passed in France, and the case of a butcher from Abbeville (Northern France) selling contaminated meat. Even the internationally themed section 'La Sociale partout' (i.e. Labour and revolutionary news from everywhere) focused on the landmark August 1894 Paris-based Trial of the Thirty, which marked the peak of the repression of the anarchist movement in France, anti-anarchist legislations in France and deportations from Dijon and Le Havre; repression in Italy ('worse than in France!') and Spain ('a hint of détente', after some of the 250 anarchists arrested in Barcelona the previous year were released) and Switzerland ('the mini-republic is still *dégueulasse*!' [filthy]).[12] 'Coups de tranchet' developed a more international orientation in subsequent issues; demonstrations in London are mentioned in later issues, for instance, alongside those in Budapest, Lisbon, Terre-Neuve and Montreal. Overall, no clear sense of place and anchorage transpires from the paper, as a combined result of self-imposed discretion as a deliberately internationalist perspective. London-based *Le Tocsin* devoted substantial column space to the life of the French anarchist groups in

London, alongside a similarly international focus. In contrast, Goaziou's publications evidence his deep rootedness in American society. *La Tribune Libre* had a clear American anchorage, with a close grasp of US social and political events (for instance a long article on the South and racial issues from Houston[13]), and even technical articles (e.g. on the technicalities of patenting[14]). Its target readership and editorship were reflected in numerous articles on miners, their work conditions and trade news. Even the 'Echo d'Europe' ('Echoes from Europe') section focused on *labour* news from France and Britain, as well as, for instance, Prague;[15] in this thematic inclusion of organized labour in the context of an anarchist periodical pointed to the influence of the American context and the community associated with the paper. Similarly, *Germinal* asked European anarchists to communicate and send their news but the anchorage is clearly local, including in its readership.

Lastly, a brief terminological caveat is needed concerning the use of the terms 'periodicals' and 'newspapers': anarchist sheets and publications were not news-based and did not appear at fixed intervals (despite plans to do so), making the use of both terms problematic. The term 'serialized media' is more technically accurate, although 'paper' has often been preferred for expediency.

Personal and periodical mobility

The history of pre-1914 anarchist publishing includes numerous examples of 'wandering' periodicals which mirrored the often-forced mobility of their editors. Emile Pouget's Paris-based *Père Peinard* (1889–94) was relocated to London in 1894, when Pouget fled France after being sentenced *in absentia* in the August 1894 Trial of the Thirty. The paper was relaunched in London in September 1894 as a small brochure, still written in Pouget's distinctive French slang, and illustrated by the artist Lucien Pissarro (1863–1944). It did not carry the name 'Le Père Peinard' on its cover, most likely for reasons of discretion (although the signature 'Le Père Peinard' appeared at the very end of the brochure). A total of six brochures appeared over several months, with different titles; the first one carried the defiant title 'Il n'est pas mort' ('It is not dead'). Despite these formal variations, the continuity in content and writing style was obvious and references to London and exile life were nearly absent from the publication.

A more frequent scenario was for new periodicals to appear, but with clear evidence of them being integrated in pre-existing personal and publishing networks – a slightly different form of editorial mobility. Thus, Louis Goaziou launched *Germinal* (1899–1903) in Paterson, New Jersey, reactivating earlier networks, as *Germinal* followed from *Le Réveil des Mineurs* (The Miners' Awakening; Hastings, Pennsylvania, 1890–3), and *La Tribune Libre* (Charleroi, Pennsylvania, 1896–1900). These publications shared some personnel and large networks of local and international correspondents.[16] A clear instance of network activation can be observed in *The Rebel*, whose first issue appeared on 20 September 1895, not long after its editor, British anarchist Charles Mowbray (1857–1910), had relocated to the United States. The publication of this first issue had been postponed, but even with this delay, the paper manifested well-established national and international links: it contained inserts about England (by the anarchist and trade unionist John Turner) and France (translated from the anarchist sociologist Augustin Hamon's (1862–1945) paper *L'Humanité Nouvelle* [A New Humanity]), as well as news from Austria. By the second issue, its bibliographic section listed no fewer than twenty papers, based in Britain (four including one in Sheffield), France (two), Argentina (two), Germany, Austria, etc. This reflected the editors' pre-existing networks, and especially Mowbray's, which appeared subsequently through the links with British anarchist Agnes Henry (1850–1915), the citation of the Liege-based paper *Le Plébéien*[17] (The Plebeian) and countless others. Within four months of initial publication, in January 1896, the paper appeared to be operating within extensive multiscalar networks, extending to Latin America, featuring updates from France, Venezuela, but also Philadelphia and the Southern states, advertising papers from Liege, Buenos Aires (*Le Cyclone* [The Cyclone]), Amsterdam (*De Anarchist* [The Anarchist]) and publishing theoretical pieces by Peter Kropotkin (1842–1921) and Augustin Hamon. A similar, albeit less striking example is provided by London's *Le Tocsin* and *Le Rothschild*. Its editors, Charles Malato and Lucien Weil respectively, had both also edited papers in France prior to this exile. Weil had been the administrator and manager of *Le Père Peinard* in Paris, from 1889 to 1894.[18] When Malato, with Nicolas Nikitine, launched *Le Tocsin* in London, eight ads featured in the first issue, distributed into London (front) and Greater Paris sections (back); the paper's first appearance had even been moved forward ('current events, which cannot wait, precipitated our appearance').[19] The second issue included an expanded list of ads for both locations. Clearly, in all these instances, despite the upheavals of personal relocation, the publications evidence a level of connections which testified to their editors' prior networks.

Intertextual networks

A dense web of similarities and echoes – personal, ideological, lexical, bibliographical, textual – linked these publications, which were the product of highly collaborative modes of funding, production, diffusion and consumption. These features converged to establish anarchist periodicals as a recognizable genre.

Indeed, anarchist publications often followed a fairly set format (also characteristic of other sections of the left radical press), especially in their paratextual elements, which included correspondences notes, notices about gatherings taking place across various locations (including internationally), information about subscriptions, bibliographical recommendations. Some of the variations between the publications examined here were also characteristic of the 'national' anarchist press; for instance, the inclusion of illustrations (in *Le Père Peinard*), and that of commercial advertisements inclusion: such ads were found in *La Tribune Libre*, *The Rebel* and *Le Tocsin*. The latter featured ads from London-based anarchists of various nationalities, such as the Italian Giovanni Deffendi (1849–?), who advertised his French and Italian delicatessen in Islington, while Louis Bertgues (1866–?) worked as an electrician, Charles Capt (1855–97) as a plumber and others as a baker, a tailor and a framer. It is not possible to ascertain whether these ads were paid for; in any case, they point to the fact that the papers were also here to serve their local communities, especially in situations of economic duress. Equally telling, nonetheless, was the inclusion of ads for businesses run by individuals who were still in Paris, such as Achille Leroy's well-known Latin Quarter 'librairie internationale'. The editor clearly had in mind readers based in different areas: the paper was produced transnationally, with input from individuals who were based in France, with a French readership in mind. It is clear that, despite the stifling censorship imposed on anarchist literature circulating in and into France, these publications were smuggled across the Channel, as reflected in these contents.

These publications were connected, sometimes closely, by flows of information and intertextuality; these were so numerous that only a broad survey of their functions can be mapped out here. Their very titles testified to more or less overt onomastic circulation, which was characteristic of anarchist periodical culture: *Germinal*, *Tribune Libre*, *Le Tocsin* were all stock anarchist names at the time of publication, irrespective of the language of publication. Such onomastic nods were openly acknowledged: the first editorial explained the choice of the name 'Germinal', in reference to Italian anarchist Michele Angiolillo (1871–97), who had killed Spanish Prime Minister Antonio Cánovas in reprisals for the anti-anarchist persecutions which he oversaw in Spain. *Germinal*, which had been Angiolillo's dying word, encapsulated notions of resistance and revolutionary hope.[20] Even the sections of the papers were pervaded with transnational references: thus, *Germinal*'s column by Louis Goaziou, 'Au Palais d'Injustice' ('The Court of Injustice') was a reference to a similarly titled section in the original, Paris-based *Père Peinard*. Intertextuality extended far beyond the title, operating at all levels of the papers: for instance, the March-April issue of *The Rebel* was devoted to the Commune celebration, with a lead article by Louise Michel, which pointed to many levels of connections, through the shared celebration of key figures and symbolic dates, as well as the shared reporting on commemorative events. The commemoration and discussion of the 11 November Chicago executions (known as the Haymarket Massacre) across the international anarchist press fulfilled a similar community-building role.[21]

Direct citation and cut-and-pasting of articles were a common practice, for instance with *La Tribune Libre* citing from *Le Père Peinard* in an article on cooperatives written from Chicago and discussing the French Verrerie d'Albi (Albi Glass Factory), a widely held model for such initiatives.[22] *Germinal* reprinted material published by Harry Kelly in London's *Freedom*, having translated it into French.[23] It also contained material from Paris's *Les Temps Nouveaux*, for instance, a scathing insert reporting the rape of a child in a congregational school in Lille, France.[24] Such replications of contents and formal characteristics point to a strong degree of virality in the papers, which was integral to shared discourse and a generic characteristic.

Unsurprisingly, the papers carried traces of the personal links and mediators connecting them, and were clearly in correspondence. These mediators, in addition to the papers' staff, included Augustin Hamon,[25] 'l'ami Turner' (our friend John Turner, a correspondent of *The Rebel*, mentioned in *Tribune Libre*,[26] as well as a London exile alongside Pouget and Malato) during his tour in the US; it also published pieces by Louise Michel (1830–1905), who was a central figure in both London's anarchist circles and the international movement and, as such, an essential intermediary. Emile Pouget was in direct contact with Louis Goaziou, and their editorial exchanges, as documented in *Tribune Libre* testified to a regular partnership, and extended readership networks which they both facilitated. 'Terrenoire from Bishop does not receive [Paris-based] *Le Libertaire*. Did you pass on the message? He did not receive the almanac [a yearly almanac for *Le Père Peinard*] either.'[27] Networks of paper exchange also connected the papers: *Tribune Libre* was clearly in dialogue with Paris's *Temps Nouveaux*,[28] *Le Père Peinard*, *L'Humanité Nouvelle*, *Le Libertaire*, all of which were fixtures of the international press. Vendors who sold the international anarchist press were also part of these networks: for instance, *La Tribune Libre* was sold at Pelletier's Librairie internationale on Goodge street, in London, alongside all the London-based and more international papers. These connections also included readership networks. Shared networks, creating further networks of entanglement. For instance, *Le Père Peinard* was distributed internationally, and clearly read in some of the places where Goaziou's paper were read, and more generally in places of French migration, with contacts in Liege, Hastings, Ougree, Brighton, Brooklyn, Jeannette and Paterson, and subscriptions from Pittsburgh, Seraing.[29]

Organizing and sustaining the movement

The papers performed an essential organizing role for the anarchist movement on various scales, fulfilling several of the functions of a political party. This was inscribed in many aspects of the papers, such as daily organization and coordination, tactical debates, the management of financial support through fundraising, the resale of printed material. A hallmark of transnational publications was precisely this emphasis on various scales and many facets of activism, and efforts to establish and uphold communication between them.

Ads and notes about forthcoming events were a key section of any anarchist paper, which remained equally important in situations of displacement. They served a dual function, which was to organize local groups and share information for potential attendees, and also for groups and individuals to manifest their existence by inscribing it in a paper.[30] The papers also functioned as a discussion space, a meeting point in print where important ideological debates unfolded transnationally. A classic example of these discussions regards terrorism, for instance with the discussion of terrorist attacks in *La Tribune Libre*, which rehearsed with a classic response to propaganda by the deed: 'while we deplore such attacks, we can repeat that the current system is entirely to blame and it is even surprising that there aren't more attacks'.[31]

This status of the press as a transnational discussion forum is exemplified in the 1890s by the protracted debates over labour organization and a possible anarchist permeation of trade unions, in which London's anarchist communist publications played a key role. *Le Rothschild*, which appeared before syndicalist ideas became established within the anarchist movement, was critical of newly established rituals such as the May Day demonstration and general strike in favour of the eight-hour workday, criticizing the reformist stance of these initiatives.[32] A leading early voice in favour of an anarchist infiltration of trade unions was the London-based, English-language anarchist paper *The Torch*, the English paper launched by the well-to-do adolescents Olivia, Helen and Arthur Rossetti, with strong Italian, Russian and French input. *The Torch* foregrounded organizational debates from 1892 onwards, reflecting the discussions which were taking place in London's international anarchist milieu, especially among British, Italian and French activists.[33] The influence of Italian exiles was especially important due to the centrality of organization as a theme within their movement.[34] These discussions were then relayed by French periodicals in London: *Le Père Peinard* was instrumental in disseminating pro-union views.[35] At the same time, a similar albeit vaguer message was promoted by Charles Malato in *Le Tocsin*, whose firebrand rhetoric gave way to an advocacy of organization in September 1894. Still in London, in 1902, *La Grève Générale/Lo Sciopero Generale* represented a much later stage of the same debates, when the anarchist permeation of trade union had become an institutional reality in France, with the Confédération Générale du Travail (CGT); this anarchist and anarcho-syndicalist paper tracked the progress of the general strike in France and called for the foundations of committees in other countries. In the US, despite Louis Goaziou's Francophone origins and the spread of syndicalist ideas, the pro-trade union discourse of his publications was rooted in different militant traditions, which were also favourable to labour organization as part of anarchism. A less drawn-out but still ambitious attempt at triggering a transnational discussion and develop practical organization was undertaken by *The Rebel*, where Charles Mowbray repeatedly encouraged and coordinated a transnational exchange of opinions to prepare for the 1896 London congress of the Second International. This started with a message advertising the London-based Freedom group, giving their contact details, with a view to sharing views ahead of the Congress.[36] A subsequent issue gave the address of James Tocchati (1852–1928), the editor of the London anarchist paper *Liberty* (1894–6) with the explicit goal of coordinating the anarchist pushback against a 'Marxist clique'.[37] The anarchist press thus served as a forum for transnational organization and strategic discussions, within a movement for which internationalism was both an ideological and a practical reality; conversely, engagement with these discussions informed the space and contents of the periodicals, in the form of feature articles and note sections, and was therefore a characteristic of its genre.

Finances were also paramount to the papers' activities, given their precarious existence. As pointed out by Nicolas Delalande in his study of internationalism within the socialist left, moreover, financial practices were not only guided by financial imperatives, but also imbued with symbolical and ethical dimensions.[38] Detailed accounts of donations were printed in papers, as a way of displaying accountability, but also manifesting these bonds of solidarity linking communities from all over the world. This dual role, both practical and ethical, applied to subscriptions, one-off collections for charity causes, and also fundraising done 'for the paper' (i.e. to contribute to the publication). As analysed by Christophe Charle in reference to French periodicals, militant papers in this period were increasingly marginalized due to the competition from 'the daily press and more ideologically neutral papers, with modern means of seduction and large capital', so that their survival depended either on patronage or, more likely for these papers, on 'dedicated militant networks'.[39] The papers examined here illustrate this funding model, through their relentless, multifaceted fundraising. Thus, within just a few months, *Le Père Peinard*'s acknowledged receipt of subscriptions 'to help with expanding *Le Père Peinard* pamphlets: From Spring Valley, D. Dubois, J. Libiez; S. Legat; A. Desaington; L. Dhesse; J. Legat [sic], Poulain: 25 sous each; Jeanquimarche, 20 fr; le vieux Savoyard, un des fondateurs du "*Révolté*", 5 fr'.[40] While such international fundraising was not specific to the anarchist press, the extent and range of these activities was another element of the genre. It was, however, closely correlated with the prestige of a given paper, which explains why *Le Père Peinard* received such generous and geographically spread-out donations. Another aspect of such finance-oriented network-building is illustrated by *La Tribune Libre*'s very proactive diffusion strategies, through the publication of lists of subscribers and encouragement for readers and subscribers to advertise the paper, from the very first issue ('if you have friends in this country who might be interested in this paper, send us their addresses and we will gladly send them a few copies'[41]). Comrades were also strongly encouraged to actively spread the paper in French-language areas.[42] The paper also fundraised towards planned US conference tour from London of the highly prominent French and Italian activists and writers Louise Michel and Pietro Gori; the tour was eventually cancelled, but had crystallized a transnational funding effort.[43] Another standard practice was the advertisement of other periodicals. However, this was primarily guided by the proactive effort to promote the movement itself and expand its readership. As such, it was integral to efforts to build a shared culture. Reciprocal advertisement was another community-building principle which blended organizing with the ethics of mutual aid. It was also a key way whereby the networks linking the various papers examined here were made visible, and the often impressive scale of their connections can be observed. Thus, when *Le Père Peinard* promoted Goaziou's papers: 'In the US, two issues of *L'Ami des Ouvriers*, a good monthly, have already appeared'. Address: Goaziou, Box 82, Hastings, Cambria'. The same issue advertised *La Questione Sociale* (Buenos Ayres).[44] Not long after, another issue acknowledged receipt of some material from 'A. G. Carleroi [sic] – P. St Louis'.[45] The paper also advertised other London publications, in French (*Le Tocsin*) and Italian (the manifesto 'La presa di porta Pia').[46] This publicity was mirrored in *Le Tocsin*, where the reappearance of *Le Père Peinard* in London was announced, and the same Italian manifesto was also warmly recommended.[47]

Lastly, the organizational role of the press included one function which was more specific to anarchism, as a movement facing all-pervasive repression, and especially so in situations of displacement: building networks of self-protection against censorship and repression. This epochal theme was central to the 'national' anarchist press but took on specific dimensions in exile, where the different modalities of surveillance and censorship prevailed, and required anarchists to adapt. This included, first and foremost, ensuring that censorship did not jeopardize the diffusion of periodicals. Thus, the first issue of *Le Tocsin* reassured potential subscribers that 'we hasten to warn those who hesitate to subscribe for fear that the paper might be banned from entering free France, that they can send us their money without fear: steps have been taken towards any possibility'.[48] *Le Père Peinard* shared information on the methods used by French authorities to police exile circles.[49] Its third issue documented the French authorities' efforts to get hold of the London *Père Peinard* – to no avail, due to the change of title with its issue – including with a circular being sent to all post offices in France and

Algeria. In the end, 'nothing is caught... except them!'.⁵⁰ In issue 4, Pouget very briefly discussed a bomb explosion in Mayfair, at the house of a judge involved in sentencing anarchists and Fenians, with the terse remark 'the English anarchos were not too pleased with the explosion: they say that since they're given plenty of leeway for propaganda, it is not in their interest to provoke the anger of rulers. Ditto for the refugees.'⁵¹ This was a very rare discussion of asylum politics by Pouget, prompted by the imperative of self-preservation. Similarly, the second issue of *Le Toscin* contained a long, multi-authored article documenting French policing methods in London and the French police's attempt to recruit spies in London.⁵² It narrated how, in the aftermath of the terrorist attack rue des Bons-Enfants in Paris, [agent] Fédée had approached a German comrade with an invitation to snitch for the French police; the individual in question, Victor Rabe, had accepted, and had become double agent X, 7. His work then allowed *Le Tocsin* to publish for the readers' sake the questions asked about the London anarchist groups, in a counter-blow to police surveillance. This was a striking example of the press's organizing and information-sharing role – this time in the highly sensitive area of (counter-)policing. All the French exile publications were under the close scrutiny of a complex intelligence hierarchy – from snitches to the French Embassy in London, as well as other countries involved in the surveillance of London-based anarchists, and this was one of several occurrences when the press exposed and detracted it, using mockery to further flag this small victory. The response of French and international authorities to such incidents consisted in escalating surveillance and international coordination – and trying to warn any infiltrated agents that they ought to be extremely cautious.⁵³

Building a shared culture

The very first issue of *The Rebel* proclaimed its intention of familiarizing its readers with key works on anarchism: 'We shall at all times endeavour to fill our columns with articles of the best-known writers on the subject of Anarchist Communism. The names of Kropotkine [sic], Reclus, Edelmann, Owen and Holmes should be sufficient guarantee of the literary character of *The Rebel*.'⁵⁴ Such highbrow cultural and theoretical aspirations had become a feature of the anarchist press in the 1880s, possibly in the wake of the highly influential cultural politics of the French anarchist paper *La Révolte*. The contents of such culture-focused sections were also shared, building an anarchist canon which transcended borders. *La Tribune Libre*'s bibliographic references were clearly located within the contemporary communist anarchist canon: Elisée Reclus, Kropotkin, Hamon.⁵⁵ *Germinal* strayed only very marginally, for instance, by serializing the book *La Folle d'Ostende*, by the communard Félix Pyat, alongside the anarchist classic by French novelist Octave Mirbeau, *La Grève des Electeurs* (the Voters' strike).⁵⁶ The London *Père Peinard* advertised many publications emanating from anarchist communist circles across languages, be it French classic Jean Grave's *La Société Mourante et l'Anarchie* (*Moribund Society and Anarchy*) or international publications. Only very occasionally did such bibliographies branch out into less familiar territory, for instance in December 1894,⁵⁷ when Pouget advertised 'Bombs', a book published by A. Wittick in Philadelphia, from an anarchist individualist perspective, yet recommended to comrades who can read English. Given the Frenchness of the publication, such a recommendation outside the canon can be read as a direct result of exile. *Le Toscin* included quotes from Goethe, Huxley and Karl Marx.[58]

Anarchist culture extended far beyond literary and social science references, and periodicals played an essential role in creating shared militant references, including by raising awareness of the difficulties faced by militants in other countries. Issue 4 of *The Rebel* thus contained a survey of social issues from France by Agnes Henry, writing from Pont-Aven (Brittany) about the strikes in Carmaux, but also opening with this telling statement:

> our movement is International. The interest of humanity in the march towards Freedom in every land is the same. Besides, the knowledge of how others are progressing is an incitement, often an encouragement, to those at home. Consequently, it occurred to me that I could not better testify to my pleasure in seeing *The Rebel* started, than by offering you some information for its columns, of proceedings here, in France.[59]

Germinal published a letter by French activist Achille Daudé-Bancel on the mining strikes in Le Creusot, castigating non-unionized workers, in a clear attempt to build transnational professional solidarity with the paper's own readers.[60] As noted by Klaus Weinhauer, the press played a major role in upholding the global consciousness of anarchism: 'Anarchists all over the world imagined themselves as being part of an international movement, a belief fuelled by the numerous anarchist papers that meticulously reported on activities of anarchists and syndicalists all over the world.'[61]

Variations in translations: culture, language and ideology

Discussing 'the International' of anarchist satirical periodicals with specific reference to the Czech press, Xavier Golmiche concluded that 'text and image borrowing was so common that the paper was mediating just as much as creating'.[62] The tension between repetition/virality and, on the other, creativity and invention is an important one; the anarchist press was famously pressed financially and precarious, but also extremely resourceful and inventive. The papers examined here were no exception, and can be noted for their formal/tonal innovation, largely as a result of the constraints imposed by censorship, and despite the increased precariousness imposed by displacement. Thus, *Le Rothschild* was largely based on the premise of censorship, and subverted it through the exclusive use of antiphrasis throughout the paper. It called itself 'the organ of the ruling class', opening with the rousing lead article 'Let's crush them', purportedly written from the perspective of the government and capitalists, which in fact charted the growing threat posed by anarchists.[63] It also included a spoof manifesto allegedly addressed to the soldiers by the 'Capitalists' union'[64] – thus aligning with anarchist antimilitarist propaganda. All sections were written in the same antiphrastic style: recommended readings came under the heading 'Ne pas lire' ('do not read'), and included Malato's *Révolution chrétienne et révolution sociale* ('Christian Revolution and Social Revolution') Kropotkin's *Les Paroles d'un révolté* ('Words of a Rebel') and Elisée Reclus's *Evolution et Révolution* ('Evolution and Revolution'). The recommendation was reinforced by the comment that 'these works written with remarkable science and talent are all the more dangerous since their authors, aiming only for the popularisation of their ideas have sought above all clarity and precision'.[65] Even the correspondence section, 'Petite poste', commented: '"Le Père Peinard" is all the more dangerous as it speaks a language which workers can understand effortlessly'.[66] Issue 3 amplified these strategies, with an article on 'the beauties of patriotism'.[67] Only a small insert at the end of each issue points to the strategy: 'Reproduced by an anarchist group.' The example of *Le Rothschild* demonstrates that mobility could multiply the formal innovation of the papers, rather than curtailing it. This may be one of the areas in which the difference between periodicals published in exilic and migratory contexts differ from the non-mobile anarchist press. The various sections and themes of the paper remained typical of the anarchist press, while the use of antiphrasis heightened the paper's bite.

Le Tocsin's first issue also carried a satirical correspondence section, and even included a satirical ad allegedly sent by war minister Charles de Freycinet: 'Engineer. Trous de c...hèques [untranslatable pun blending accusations of financial dodgy dealings with bodily humour]'.[68] This satirical vein also extended to the main content of the paper, for instance with the article 'Association de malfaiteurs' ('Criminal conspiracy') which claimed to have unmasked 'a ghastly conspiracy against the lives and liberty of 40 million individuals'.[69] The culprits included French president Jean Casimir-Périer, who was given a mock gangster name, as were earlier presidents, in a passage parodying the style of police informant reports: 'Casimir, aka le Mec des mecs [the ultimate bloke], aka la Mort-aux-gosses [death-to-the-kids], whose den is on faubourg Saint-Honoré, known as the Elysée [i.e. the French presidential palace], where the murderers Badingue, Foutriquet, Mac-Mac, Grevy and Concarnot lived previously'.

Innovation as a result of mobility also came in the guise of ideological hybridizations which would have been unlikely in national contexts. Thus, the individualist 'naturien' anarchist Henri Zisly was a close collaborator of Goaziou's in both *Tribune Libre* and *Germinal*, which represented a reframing of militant sociabilities in mobility. *Germinal* sold publications by Jean Grave and the presses des Temps Nouveaux, alongside those of the Etudiants Socialistes Révolutionnaires Internationalistes (ESRI) and Henri Zisly (1872–1945), and featured articles by anarchists from a broad ideological spectrum, for instance Emile Janvion (1866–1927).[70] Such blending of different anarchist tendencies represented a degree of ideological eclecticism that was extremely unlikely in a strictly French national context. As discussed above, thematic syntheses and widening perspectives also resulted from displacement and contact with local issues, as with issue I, 4 of *The Rebel*'s front-page article on 'The American Negro', written by 'a white Southerner';[71] this aspect was quite striking in Goaziou's periodicals in general.

Lastly, inventive linguistic strategies are also notable, most strikingly in the trilingual (French-Italian-English) London-based publication *La Grève Générale/Lo Sciopero Generale* (1902) inspired by Catalan paper *La Huelga General* (1901–3). This stood in contrast with other anarchist papers, which despite efforts to foster international solidarity often foregrounded the linguistic unity of the community to which they were addressed, and functioned along linguistic lines, deliberately or not. *Germinal* thus proclaimed that 'French-speaking exploited are numerous enough in the United States for our attempt to be understood and to receive the support of all those interested in the anarchist cause'.[72] As pointed out by Kenyon Zimmer, 'linguistic similarities provided the basis for cross-ethnic cohesion'.[73] Nonetheless, in the characteristic fashion of a movement deeply preoccupied with the practical construction of internationalism, steps were taken to address the exclusionary implications of monolingualism and ensure a wide readership, especially with the use of translated texts. International 'hubs' and global capitals of exile, such as London, were especially propitious to more creative explorations of the languages of militancy; an interesting initiative along these lines was the attempt at trilingual publishing by *La Grève Générale/Lo Sciopero Generale/The General Strike* (London, 1902), which flagged its internationalist intentions. As Pietro di Paola has pointed out, each version was created by different groups (usually in collaboration), and also reflected different ideological shades, with the Italian paper 'maintain[ing] a less vigorous stance on the general strike as a revolutionary tactic than the French version' – which showed variations in contents as well as languages.[74]

Conclusion

In the wider context of the global pre-1914 anarchist movement, the sample of papers examined here is a small one, in both its geographical and quantitative dimensions; however, given its connections with many of the anarchist hubs, leading periodicals and most prominent activists of the time, this exploration of transatlantic periodical entanglements highlights the remarkable reach and resilience of the ever-precarious anarchist press before 1914, and its effectiveness as a medium for transnational discussion. In return, the transnational elements of the papers were essential in establishing them as a distinctive genre, with considerable formal and thematic overlap despite the physical, linguistic and even ideological gaps separating each of these publications. These papers reflect the intense mobility of anarchists in this period, as well as the emphasis placed on internationalism; however, even more striking are the constant flows of information and material between various locations – that is to say, print rather than personal mobility. In sync with the diasporic organization of pre-1914 anarchism, it was papers that allowed the movement to function globally.

Pre-First World War anarchist periodicals can be regarded as a distinctive sub-genre within the radical press, but also part of the transnational flow of journalistic culture across global borders. This is true of the most internationalized 'national' anarchist papers, and even more so of those produced in contexts of displacement, such as exile and migration, as examined here Nonetheless, anarchist publications produced in situations of mobility reinforced the transnational and internationalist outlook which was integral to the most prominent anarchist periodicals, and led to instances of formal and ideological hybridization and innovation. These papers point to a spectacular individual and collective deftness in creating a shared language and identity even beyond physical and linguistic-cultural borders – but with variations that also pointed to variations in political allegiances and editorial positioning, which would have been clear to readers. So dense, but also intentional and explicit, were the webs of formal, textual, pictorial and ideological entanglements woven between these publications that it is appropriate to speak of an 'international' of anarchist journals.[75] Editors, collaborators and readers regarded themselves as part of a wide transnational movement, bound by links of solidarity and common enemies.

The sophistication of this press culture makes it a prime object of study for the emerging field of transnational periodical studies. In addition to the fact that the main anarchist periodicals were conceived as part of a transnational movement even when produced in a national context, the periodicals examined here exemplify an added layer of mobility, with implications with respect to both form and content. The anarchist press was a site of multiple cultural transfers, offering a prime example of how 'periodicals evolve in and through networks of people',[76] in legally and financially precarious publishing contexts, and how such barriers shaped and occasionally stimulated production.

Notes

1. I am extremely grateful to Ole Birk Laursen, whose customary generosity and collegiality made it possible for me to access one of the papers discussed here.
2. Jean Maitron, *Histoire du mouvement anarchiste en France* (Paris: Maspéro, 1975); Andrew Hoyt, *And They Called Them 'Galleanisti': The Rise of the* Cronaca Sovversiva *and the Formation of America's Most Infamous Anarchist Faction (1895–1912)*, unpublished PhD dissertation, University of Minnesota, 2018; James Yeoman, *Print Culture and the Formation of the Anarchist Movement in Spain, 1890–1915* (London, NY: Routledge, 2019).
3. Kenyon Zimmer, *Immigrants against the State. Yiddish and Italian anarchism in America* (Champaign, IL: University of Illinois Press, 2015), 4.
4. *La Tribune Libre* (London), I, 1, 15 November 1890.
5. Freeman Matthew, 'Branding consumerism: Cross-media characters and story-worlds at the turn of the 20th century', *International Journal of Cultural Studies* 18, no. 6 (2015). DOI: 10.1177/1367877913515868.
6. Michel Cordillot, *La Sociale en Amérique. Dictionnaire biographique du mouvement social francophone aux États-Unis, 1848–1922* (Paris: Editions de l'Atelier, 1997), 211.
7. *La Tribune Libre*, I, 1, 25 June 1896; Ronald Creagh, 'Socialism in America: The French-Speaking Coal-Miners in the Late Nineteenth Century', in *In the Shadow of the Statue of Liberty: Immigrants, Workers, and Citizens in the American Republic, 1880–1920*, ed. Marianne Debouzy (Champaign, IL: University of Illinois Press, 1992), 143–56.
8. *Le Tocsin*, I, 1, 31 December 1892.
9. René Bianco, 'La Grève Générale = Lo Sciopero Generale', in *Bianco: Presse Anarchiste*, https://bianco.ficedl.info/article1092.html, last accessed 4 January 2020.
10. See for instance Sylvie Aprile, *Le Siècle des Exilés. Bannis et proscrits de 1789 à la Commune* (Paris: CNRS Editions, 2010).

11 Pietro Di Paola, 'The Italian Anarchist Press in London: A Lens for Investigating a Transnational Movement', in C. Bantman and A. Suriani da Silva (eds.), *The Foreign Political Press in Nineteenth-Century London: Politics from a Distance* (New York: Bloomsbury Academic, 2018), 114.
12 All from *Le Père Peinard*, I, 2, October 1894. Unless otherwise stated, all translations are the author's own.
13 *Tribune Libre*, I, 14, 24 September 1896.
14 *Tribune Libre*, I, 13, 17 September 1896.
15 *Tribune Libre*, I, 32, 28 January 1897.
16 Bianco, 'La Tribune Libre', in https://bianco.ficedl.info, last accessed 4 January 2020.
17 *The Rebel*, I, 4, January 1896.
18 'Lucien Weil' in *Le Maitron. Dictionnaire biographique du mouvement ouvrier*, available at http://maitron-en-ligne.univ-paris1.fr/spip.php?article154235, last accessed 4 January 2020.
19 *Le Tocsin*, I, 1, 31 December 1892.
20 *Germinal*, I, 1, 1 October 1899.
21 *The Rebel*, I, 2, 20 October 1895; *Le Père Peinard* (November 1894, I, 4) has a long lead on Chicago.
22 *Tribune Libre*, I, 31, 21 January 1897.
23 *Germinal*, I, 6, 15 December 1899.
24 *Germinal*, I, 4, 15 November 1899.
25 *Tribune Libre*, I, 1, 25 June 1896.
26 *Tribune Libre*, I, 13, 17 September 1896.
27 *Tribune Libre*, I, 24, 3 December 1896; again in I, 31, 21 January 1897, with details about correspondence tracking.
28 *Tribune Libre*, ibid.
29 *Le Père Peinard*, I, 4, November 1894, 'Souscriptions'.
30 Hoyt, 'And they called them "Galleanisti"'.
31 *Tribune Libre*, I, 13, 17 September 1896; *Tribune Libre*, I, 31, 21 January 1897, by G. Jacques, 'A propos des actes de violence'.
32 *Le Rothschild*, 15 June 1891.
33 Constance Bantman and Pietro Di Paola, 'La presse militante transnationale: *The Torch* (1891–1896), journal anarchiste londonien', *Médias 19* [online], 2017; Guillaume Pinson and Marie-Ève Thérenty (eds.), 'Les journalistes: identités et modernités', available at http://www.medias19.org/index.php?id=23642 (last accessed 10 September 2020).
34 Pietro Di Paola, *The Knights Errant of Anarchy. London and the Italian Anarchist Diaspora, 1880–1917* (Liverpool: Liverpool University Press, 2013).
35 *Le Pere Peinard*, I, 1, September 1894; I, 2, October 1894.
36 *The Rebel*, I, 1, 20 September 1895.
37 *The Rebel*, I, 5, February 1896.
38 Nicolas Delalande, *La Lutte et l'entraide* (Paris: Seuil, 2019).
39 Christophe Charle, *Le Siècle de la presse, 1830–1939* (Paris: Seuil, 2004), 161.
40 *Père Peinard*, I, 8, January 1895, 'Débâcle bourgeoise'.
41 *La Tribune Libre*, I, 1, 25 June 1896.
42 *La Tribune Libre*, I, 24, 3 December 1896.
43 *La Tribune Libre*, I, 15, 1 October 1896.
44 *Père Peinard*, I, 3, October 1894.
45 *Père Peinard*, I, 5, December 1894.

46 *Père Peinard*, I, 2, 'Chouettes Flambeaux'.
47 *Le Tocsin*, I, 3, 23 September 1894.
48 *Le Toscin*, I, 1, 1 December 1892.
49 *Père Peinard*, I, 8, 'Le Mouchard Cotin'.
50 Ibid., I, 3, 3 October 1894.
51 *Père Peinard*, I, 4, November 1894.
52 *Le Tocsin*, I, 3, 23 September 1894, 'La Police prise à son piège'.
53 Constance Bantman, *The French Anarchists in London. Exile and Transnationalism in the First Globalisation* (Liverpool: Liverpool University Press, 2013), 116–42.
54 *The Rebel*, I, 1, 20 September 1895.
55 *La Tribune Libre*, I, 25, 10 December 1896.
56 *Germinal*, I, 3, 30 October 1899.
57 *Père Peinard*, I, 5, p. 12.
58 *Le Tocsin*, I, 1, 31 December 1892.
59 *The Rebel*, I, 4, January 1896.
60 *Germinal*, I, 4, 15 November 1899.
61 Klaus Weinhauer, 'Terrorism between Social Movements, the State and Media Societies', in Stefan Berger and Holger Nehring (eds.), *The History of Social Movements in Global Perspective. A Survey* (London: Palgrave Macmillan, 2017), 552.
62 Xavier Galmiche, 'Les *Šibeničky* [Petites Potences] et l'Internationale des revues satiriques anarchistes', in Evanghelia Stead and Hubert Védrine (eds.), *L'Europe des revues II (1860–1930). Réseaux et circulations de modèles* (Paris: PU Sorbonne, 2008), 487.
63 *Le Rothschild*, I, 2, 1 July 1891.
64 *Le Rothschild*, I, 1, 15 June 1891.
65 Ibid.
66 Ibid.
67 *Le Rothschild*, I, 3, 15 July 1891.
68 *Le Tocsin*, I, 2, 7 January 1893.
69 *Le Tocsin*, I, 8, 23 September 1894.
70 *Germinal*, II, 17, 30 May 1900. See also *La Tribune Libre*, I, 34, February 1897.
71 *The Rebel*, I, 4, January 1896.
72 *Germinal*, I, 1, 1 October 1899.
73 Kenyon Zimmer, 'A Golden Gate of Anarchy: Local and Transnational Dimensions of Anarchism in San Francisco, 1880s–1930s', in Constance Bantman and Bert Altena (eds.), *Reassessing the Transnational Turn: Scales of Analysis in Anarchist and Syndicalist Studies* (Oakland: PM Press, 2017).
74 Di Paola, 'The Italian Anarchist Press in London', 126.
75 Galmiche, 'Les *Šibeničky* [Petites Potences] et l'Internationale des revues satiriques anarchistes', 487.
76 'Forthcoming series: Studies in Periodical Culture', https://brill.com/page/1844?lang=en, last accessed 4 January 2020.

3

Collaborating across the Atlantic: Gigi Damiani and the Italian Anarchist Press in the United States (1909–45)

Isabelle Felici
University Paul-Valéry of Montpellier 3

Despite a turbulent life caused by the constant surveillance of police and diplomatic agents, Gigi Damiani, an Italian anarchist born in Rome (1876-1953), became a prominent exponent of the anarchist press, the main propaganda medium used by anarchists. Damiani spent most of his life in exile.[1] After more than twenty years in Brazil (1897-1919), where he became a pillar of the local anarchist press, he returned to Italy where he was very active in the anarchist movement. In 1926, he had to escape from fascist Italy. During this second exile, as he was being expelled from all the so-called democracies in Europe, he considered settling in the US, which he ironically described as 'the country of mass-produced cars and serial weddings'. In the end, however, he settled in Tunisia (1932–46).

During these years, he constantly wrote and, through his wandering life, he edited or collaborated with radical periodicals in Italian all over the world, including the US, despite never setting foot there. This chapter pays attention to the editorial production of Gigi Damiani while in exile and particularly to contributions to Italian-language anarchists periodicals in the US. My focus is on the frequency of his writing activity, the range of topics covered, and the context of his production. My intent is to contribute to a reflection on how anarchists thought and worked in spite of the censorship, exile and personal difficulties they faced as a result of the political climate. In this essay, I endeavour to illustrate how the Italian anarchist periodicals published in the US contributed to the circulation of ideas in the wider world of international Italian-speaking anarchists. The study also exemplifies the many dynamics between these interconnected newspapers.

Four American newspapers published Damiani's articles: *Cronaca sovversiva* (Barre, Vermont, later Lynn, Massachusetts), *Il Martello* (New York), *L'Adunata dei refrattari* (New York), and *Germinal* (Chicago, Illinois).[2] Even if they appeared in places where Italian immigration was massive,[3] the contributions and the readership were more global, and included Italian anarchists living both in Italy and all over the world, like

Damiani and many others. This study, which follows a chronological order of Damiani's articles, provides a new angle of interpretation on the so-called ethnic press in the US.

From São Paulo to Massachusetts: a transnational anarchist voice in the making

The first Italian periodical in the US to publish an article by Damiani was *Cronaca sovversiva* (Subversive Chronicle, 1903–19), an Italian-language anarchist paper founded in 1906 by a leading figure of the US labour movement: Luigi Galleani (1861–1931).[4] The latter arrived in the US in 1901, at the age of forty, after having been an anarchist activist in Italy, France, Switzerland and Egypt.

From 1906 to 1915, *Cronaca sovversiva* published only nine articles signed by Damiani. However, while quite limited in number, the texts expose his work process. When Damiani started sending material for publication to the paper in 1906, he was still a young activist, not well known outside of Brazil. By 1915, he had garnered the reputation of a self-made journalist. His first writings are characterized in a metaphorical style, dealing with some of Damiani's favourite topics such as anticlericalism, popular insurrection, and antimonarchism.[5] These writings commonly take the form of political tales,[6] a *genre* that Damiani developed during his journalistic experience in Brazil, and that typically offers an abundance of suggestive images that he embeds with a cold and ironic gaze. For instance, the quote below shows the articulation of his thought, while watching the rain: 'Will the modern sunshade, the silk umbrella with large lace swirls and curls, my ladies, be able to protect you when the great red rain comes, the blood rain?!'[7]

Most of these texts were previously released in the Brazilian anarchist press in Italian,[8] of which Damiani was a linchpin (only one was published first in *Cronaca sovversiva*). At the time, the Italian anarchists' main periodical in Brazil was the São Paulo-based *La Battaglia* (The Battle).[9] Once Damiani left São Paulo to spend a few years in Curitiba (Paraná), he established similar distant relations with the two newspapers, but his collaboration with *Cronaca sovversiva* ended when he returned to São Paulo at the end of 1908.

Figure 3.1 Masthead of *Cronaca sovversiva*, 19 August 1916. Author's personal collection.

The first direct link between Damiani and Galleani's weekly newspaper, *Cronaca sovversiva*, is not easy to reconstruct. Damiani was likely fond of Galleani's writings, as well as his ideas and personality. His admiration was evident on many occasions, even after Galleani's death, when Damiani defined him as 'one of our strongest forces', as a 'still relevant' intellectual whose 'thought has effectively contributed to raise strong barriers in defence of anarchism'.[10] Yet, beyond admiration, common ideological views united the two men: Galleani's periodical adopted an anti-organizationist stance, like most of the anarchist periodicals in Italian published in São Paulo. The subject of organization divided anarchism for decades and can be quickly summarized in a couple of questions: what are the best means to build an anarchist society? Should anarchists participate in the labour movement and according to which modalities?[11]

Cronaca sovversiva proved well-connected to the Italian anarchist press in Brazil, as elsewhere in the Western hemisphere. For instance, *Cronaca sovversiva* supported *Germinal*, an anarchist newspaper published in São Paulo (1902–4). Another Italian anarchist who had settled in São Paulo during the same time period, Oreste Ristori (1874–1943), also published an article in Galleani's *Cronaca sovversiva*, a few months before he created *La Battaglia* in June 1904. Such a collaboration was frequent and Damiani himself mentions 'about ten nations in America and Europe'[12] where Italian anarchists published the writings of *La Battaglia*'s editors – mainly himself and Ristori. Damiani's last four articles, published during the second phase of his collaboration with *Cronaca sovversiva*, vary in tone and themes, privileging current affairs. In 1912, Damiani thus defended Ristori who was then a victim of a discrimination campaign,[13] while his three articles of 1915 predictably dealt with the war in Europe, framing the conflict in the context of colonial wars fought in the name of civilization, patriotism and the interventionism of a few anarchists.[14]

Damiani's active involvement in the Italian anarchist press of Brazil is probably one of the reasons why he stopped writing for *Cronaca sovversiva*. Indeed, 1915 was also the year when Damiani created *Guerra Sociale* (Social War), as an answer to the void left in the Italian-Brazilian anarchist press by *La Battaglia*'s death.[15] Revealingly, the last piece Damiani published the same year in *Cronaca sovversiva* ends with an editor's note, maybe from Galleani himself, which expresses appreciation for *Guerra Sociale* and his fellow editor's 'wonderful work of frankness, courage and revolution'.[16]

The rise of fascism in Italy, Red Scare in the US: a new deal for the anarchist press

The next phase of Damiani's contribution coincided with the rise of fascism. Damiani had returned to his native country in 1919, and started to focus exclusively on the anarchist press in Italy. He became the editor-in-chief of the Milan (later Rome)-based *Umanità Nova* (New Humanity), directed by Errico Malatesta since its creation in 1920 and initially published daily, later weekly. Damiani's output for this newspaper – 'indispensable' and 'brilliant', according to some historians of anarchism[17] – remains to be examined and acknowledged. After *Umanità Nova* was shut down by the fascist regime, Damiani held on and began other publications.[18] He eventually fled from Italy, along with other radicals, to escape anti-anarchist repression especially following Gino Lucetti's (1926–43) assassination attempt of Mussolini in 1926.

At the same time, the Red Scare was raging in the United States. Radicals were arrested, anarchist newspapers were targeted by the police, and activists such as Luigi Galleani and Emma Goldman were expelled. The political climate grew staler with the Sacco-Vanzetti Case (1921–7), which exacerbated tensions in the country. These events significantly transformed the Italian-language anarchist press in the US and gave way to the birth of three new titles: *Il Martello*, *L'Adunata dei Refrattari* and *Germinal*, each having its specific character.

In 1917, *Il Martello* (The Hammer, 1916–43) became the property of Carlo Tresca (1879–1943),[19] whose political convictions evolved from socialism to anarchism shortly after his arrival in the United States in 1904. Tresca became a leader of radical unionism, active in the Industrial Workers of the World. Over the years, *Il Martello*'s subtitle changed from 'Popular journal of literature, science and art' to 'Weekly Combat Periodical directed by Carlo Tresca' in 1921. Only in February 1943, after Carlo Tresca was murdered for reasons that remain unknown, the newspaper became explicitly libertarian.

Carlo Tresca's periodical was a mouthpiece for anarchism at the international level. Its columns welcomed the signatures of all the leading figures of Italian anarchism, including Malatesta, Fabbri, Berneri and Damiani.[20] Yet, to some activists, Tresca was not a true anarchist:

> I knew Carlo Tresca when he was still a socialist and publishing *La Plebe* in Pittsburgh. It was at that time that someone cut his throat, so he grew a goatee.
>
> Tresca was no anarchist. To my way of thinking he was an opportunist, a jumping jack. There was nothing in common between the followers of Tresca and the followers of Galleani.[21]

From 1922 to 1971, another radical anarchist newspaper *L'Adunata dei Refrattari* (the title was self-translated as *The call of the Refractaries* or *The Refractaries' Adunation*[22]) was published in New York. Considered the heir of *Cronaca sovversiva*, since it was directed by Luigi Galleani's followers after he was deported to Europe, *L'Adunata* was *Il Martello*'s main adversary.

Figure 3.2 Masthead of *Il Martello*, 16 August 1924 (New York). Courtesy of Il Ministero della cultura – Pinacoteca di Brera – Biblioteca Braidense, Milano.[23]

Figure 3.3 Masthead of *L'Adunata dei refrattari* (New York), 26 June 1926. LC_FPR_0394_1926 « Collection La Contemporaine » (Nanterre, France).

Figure 3.4 Masthead of *L'Adunata dei refrattari* (New York), 31 January 1931. Source: gallica.bnf.fr/BnF.

Figure 3.5 Masthead of *Germinal* (Chicago), 15 May 1928. LC_GFP_5101_1936 « Collection La Contemporaine » (Nanterre, France).

Just as for the Chicago-based *Germinal*, it was initiated in 1926 and abruptly disappeared in 1930. This periodical is rarely mentioned,[24] probably because of the suspicion that one of its editors, Silvestro Spada, was a spy. According to the best specialists of fascist espionage, he might have been a double agent,[25] so the mystery remains. Damiani was not likely aware of Spada's possible police activities, similarly to other Italian anarchists who had given their articles for publication. The contributions from abroad by Damiani and other Italian anarchists are relevant to the discussion on the feud between *Il Martello* and *L'Adunata*.

This dispute is not easy to summarize or even to follow since it is frequently described from a partisan point of view. Damiani, Malatesta and others might have experienced similar difficulties as they resided outside the US and did not receive the issues on a regular basis. All too frequently, a cacophony of comments emerged in other periodicals, for instance in France or Switzerland, often with a delay. The two newspapers, *Il Martello* and *L'Adunata*, are generally presented with two opposing political themes: unionism versus anti-organization. Other reasons permeated the feud, including personal conflicts and personal choices. At stake were critical questions like: how to fight fascism, how to campaign for Sacco and Vanzetti and how to interact with the non-anarchist world. At that time, the fascist regime was in the process of deploying a 'strategy for infiltrating the workers and democratic forces in Italian-American communities'.[26] As the feud between the two newspapers began to 'weaken' the anarchists and 'the anti-fascist movement as a whole',[27] Italian anarchists endeavoured to stop it from abroad. One such anarchist was Luigi Fabbri who published an article that summarized the controversy, explaining the different perspectives of each newspaper and describing their circulation channels.[28]

There were ups and downs in the dispute, but in times of crisis, the various factions showed renewed solidarity as illustrated in a fundraising call in favour of *Il Martello*, published by *L'Adunata dei refrattari* on April 7 1923. The message of support was clear, as it invited readers to a meeting at Tammany Hall 'to testify our support and approval to the brave *Martello* and to provide it with good ammunition for the battles to come'.[29]

Crossing words: fighting fascism from within and without

Damiani's contribution to the Italian-American anarchist press resumed with *Il Martello* in September 1922, when *Umanità Nova* became a weekly. It intensified in 1923, after *Umanità Nova* stopped its publications. The volume of Damiani's contribution to each newspaper was different, as shown in Chart 3.1.

Damiani's choice to send his texts to *Il Martello* rather than to *L'Adunata* is perhaps surprising, because of his previous ties with the anti-organizationist press (ie. *Cronaca sovversiva*). However, the lack of a support from *L'Adunata* to *Umanità Nova* may be part of the explanation. In 1922, *L'Adunata* led a debate about how the newspaper should have evolved, giving space to all perspectives, including organizationist, anti-organizationist, and individualist.[30] By contrast, *Il Martello* did not question its Italian

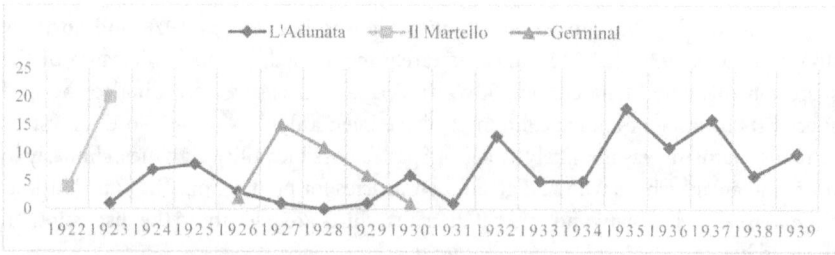

Chart 3.1 Number of articles published each year (1923–39) by Damiani in *L'Adunata dei refrattari*, *Il Martello* and *Germinal*.

colleague's choices and offered all the money from a fundraising event. Damiani, who wished to communicate about the atrocities of the fascist regime on the largest possible scale, may also have chosen the periodical with the widest circulation. Luigi Fabbri's appreciation for *Il Martello* might help to shed light on Damiani's choice: Fabbri explains that, despite disagreements, he found *Il Martello* a 'pleasant' newspaper 'for all the evil the fascist press said about it, for the hatred shown to it by our fiercest enemies, for its anti-fascist campaign, so ardent and tenacious'.[31]

All the articles he published in *Il Martello*, in his name or sometimes signed Simplicio or Ausonio Acrate, two of his pseudonyms, dealt with fascism. *Il Martello*'s editors warmly welcomed his first correspondence from across the Atlantic, praising his 'witty, subtle, pungent, sarcastic, good, strong and robust prose'. Historian Renzo De Felice writes a similar compliment about Damiani's keen analysis of mussolinism.[32] Damiani warned his readers that, since his articles were strongly rooted in current affairs, they might be obsolete by the time they were published. His purpose was to explain to readers outside of Italy how fascism was conquering the country. As he had done in all the newspapers he collaborated with, Damiani often quoted the major newspapers to point out their contradictions. One of his strategies was to ridicule Mussolini, showing the inconsistency of his deeds. Doing this, he also mocked Italians who supported him and encouraged the antifascist opposition that the fascist regime aimed to destroy.

Since Damiani wrote regularly for *Il Martello*, his contribution to the first issues of *L'Adunata* was very limited (only two articles in 1923). Yet, after October 1923, he signed no new article in *Il Martello* even though he continued to give texts to *L'Adunata*. He abruptly ended his collaboration with Carlo's Tresca periodical probably as a result of his Roman publication *Fede!* (Faith! 1923–6), which had first appeared in September 1923. This choice might also be related to the fact that Carlo Tresca was pragmatically prepared to soften some of his principles: 'He was, writes historian Gino Cerrito, a worker organizer, keen to compromise on principles'[33] and was preparing an anti-fascist alliance most anarchists disagreed with.[34]

From 1924 to 1926, although he was busy with his own periodicals, Damiani sent an average of six texts per year to *L'Adunata*, including a number of poems and political tales, particularly for the May Day issues. He also commented on the main political events, such as the 1924 Italian general elections and the so-called 'Aventine secession', when the opposition party withdrew from Italian Parliament following the assassination of Giacomo Matteotti.[35] His contribution intensified at the end of the 1920s, soaring further after 1935 (with eighteen articles), when he sojourned in Tunisia. Meanwhile, from 1926 to 1930, he favoured the newly born Chicago-based anarchist newspaper, *Germinal*, which offered him the possibility to continue publishing in the United States without having to take sides between *Il Martello* and *L'Adunata*.

During this period (1926–30), Damiani was unable to publish a newspaper of his own. However, in 1927, with the money left from his previous publications in Rome, he managed to publish three issues of a small sheet *Non molliamo* (Let's not give up!). The paper was allegedly published in Italy, but printed in Marseilles, where after illegally crossing the Alps, Damiani temporary settled with his family. He also sent articles to anarchist periodicals founded in Paris, like *Veglia* (Vigil 1926–7) and *La Diana* (1926–9).

The frequency of his contributions to *Germinal* matched the bureaucratic problems he faced. The last issue contained a letter sent by Damiani from 'Marianne's Republic' in which he narrated the many challenges he experienced in European democracies, mainly having to do with his incarcerations and expulsions.[36]

In spite of his tormented life, Damiani's contribution to *Germinal* is quite significant: thirty-two issues out of seventy-three feature one or two of his writings. In contrast to the articles he sent to *Il Martello*, the texts that appeared in *Germinal* were not only related to fascism, even if this remained his favourite topic, but also to topics like: fascism and monarchy, fascism and economy, fascism and emigration, fascism and journalism, fascism and spies, fascist violence against antifascists. Although more space would be necessary for a longer analysis, it clearly appears that this new series of antifascist propaganda articles was written from a different angle than his articles of 1923. This was the case in part because the regime was no longer in the embryonic stages of development, and in part, because Damiani was by now making observations from abroad.

Never give up: art as political propaganda

Among the plethora of topics addressed by Damiani, the range includes anticlericalism, one of his favourites, Russia and bolshevism, anarchism and free love, art and revolution. He started to develop the theme of art and revolution in a literary and political journal he founded in Rome, *Vita* (1925). *Germinal* also published a few of Damiani's poems, a drama (incomplete) and a longer text as a booklet: *Cristo e Bonnot* (Christ and Bonnot).[37] As we can observe studying Damiani's literary output, neither his personal difficulties nor political upheavals stopped him from writing. Rather, poetry, drama or playlets, even novels were genres that he considered as yet another type of propaganda. These accompanied and, in trying periods, replaced openly political writings.

While sending his texts to *Germinal* (1926–30), Damiani kept a correspondence with Osvaldo Maraviglia,[38] who was a member of the editorial team of *L'Adunata dei refrattari*. The letters they exchanged are helpful to advancing knowledge about Damiani's movements across Europe while he was fleeing fascist repression with no place to stay. Thus, there was no interruption in the relationship between *L'Adunata* and Damiani, or in the support he received from the American periodical. A careful examination of the newspaper from 1922 till 1945 confirms that over that long period of time, Damiani's collaboration fluctuated during different stages only as a result of remarkable occurrences in his personal life and international events.

At the beginning of the 1930s, after his administrative situation worsened, Damiani moved to Spain and then to Tunisia, and continued to send articles from North Africa exclusively to *L'Adunata*. Not surprisingly, the issues published at the outset of 1932 contained Damiani's insights on the Spanish political situation. Probably due to the impossibility of sending letters regularly – and also because some texts were written during the time he spent in jail – Damiani's articles became longer and were published in instalments. *L'Adunata* also borrowed from the French 'Non Molliamo' publishing house *Il re fascista* (The fascist King), a pamphlet that Damiani had printed in Marseilles denouncing King of Italy Victor Emmanuel's support of Mussolini. In 1933–4, the number of texts written by Damiani declined sharply following his wife's death in December 1932. It is likely that the dearth of articles written in 1933 were commissioned texts on topics that Damiani could not turn down. Among these, for instance, are an article and a poem respectively in commemoration of Malatesta and Virgilia D'Andrea on the first anniversary of their deaths.

Damiani's writing styles were usually tailored to the personality of the people he paid tribute to. For anarchist and poet Virgilia D'Andrea, who Damiani had collaborated with during the Paris years,[39] he composed a poem praising the courage of a woman who 'cut with her past and her family, to side with those who fight', was 'ever-present in front of risks', 'on the barricade', 'in prison', and was 'stronger than us, imperfect and plaintive men', 'smiling while we were swearing', 'sure, sharp, while we were hesitating'.[40] In the case of Malatesta, although it might seem paradoxical, he provided proof of sincerity and friendship by highlighting their dissent: 'In many details, of doctrine and method, our thought contrasted. Naturally, these contrasts never overshadowed our friendship: perhaps they strengthened it ... and increased my esteem for him, who had in high degree what many of us lacked: a sense of tolerance, and who shunned dogmatic sentencing.'[41]

While he was aware of his old friend's dislike for 'useless and anti-anarchist idolatry', Damiani had written texts using Malatesta's condition as a hostage of the regime, a prisoner in his own house, to recall all the other unknown, humble, modest hostages 'strong in their faith and proud of the martyrdom that tears them down'.[42] After Malatesta's death, Damiani emphasized how he epitomized willingness (*volontà*), 'a will that does not waver in the hour of defeat and faces defeat with the will to remain himself and not to despair'.[43] *Volontà* was also the title of a newspaper launched by Malatesta in Ancona (1913) and the same word is part of the title of the latter's last journal in Rome: *Pensiero e volontà* (Thought and will) (1924–6).

During the next years, Damiani's texts gained in density and visibility: they were rather long texts and placed on the front pages. Indeed, Damiani dealt with fundamental topics that deserved further exploration: libertarian education, State and freedom, racism and anarchism, fascist colonization, leninism and anarchism, mussolinism, anarchism and communism in Spain. Although the articles no longer dealt with the latest news, the connection with contemporary events remained obvious. Such was the case of the Italian colonial war – which was also the main subject of an antifascist newspaper *Domani* (Tomorrow) that Damiani published in Tunis in August and September 1935[44] – or again the topic of the Spanish war and the tensions between anarchists and communists. The year 1935 also signalled the highest number of Damiani's texts published in *L'Adunata*. In this period, Damiani also included literary contributions like tales and chronicles commonly entitled *Pagine di un libro inedito* ('Pages of an unpublished book').

The Second World War blocked the sending of mail overseas, thus interrupting Damiani's collaboration with *L'Adunata*. One of the last texts he submitted in 1939 is based on a topic Damiani had regularly dealt with: Anarchist organizationist and anti-organizationist positions. Showing no sign of slowing down, he reinitiated 'a discussion that reappears, under different pretexts, we may say at every decade and I do not remember since how many decades', 'a polemic that goes on especially among Italian anarchists'.[45] Damiani pointed out, once again, that individualism and antiorganizationism should not be confused, and that organization, or association, should exist without continuity, as a transitory event, with no commitment apart from the shared initiative. He provided a definition of affinity groups:

> I believe that autonomous groups, which live their lives as long as they have a reason to exist, are more than sufficient for the needs of our movement, for the various consecutive initiatives that demand the contribution of the majority. And I think that those groups will do useful work, all the more fruitful as they arise from elements and temperaments that go along well and tolerate each other.[46]

He endeavoured to act on his convictions with relentless faith following a return to Italy in 1946 until his death, as the poem 'Our muse' published in 1945, as the war was ending, tells us:

La nostra musa La Musa che c'ispira e a oprar ne sprona non usa il bistro e 'l labbro non insozza; le grazie sue al baccanal non dona ed i merli a cercar non va in carrozza.	Our muse[47] The Muse that inspires us and spurs us to action Does not paint her face nor profane her lips; she does not grace at the bacchanalia nor carouse in search of rich lovers.
E non la vedi pure in chiesa prona, preghiere mormora con voce mozza, chiedendo ai santi l'occasione buona che infin ti ripulisce e ti ringrazia.	And you won't see her prostrate at church, Whispering prays with a broken voice, Begging the saints to grant the happy moment, That cleanses and blesses at last.
La nostra musa non si chiama Bice, né Laura, né Eloisa, né Leonora; nobildonna non è, né meretrice.	Our muse's name is not Beatrice, Nor Laura, nor Héloïse, nor Leonora She is not a noblewoman, nor a prostitute.
È un'operaia che in fabbrica lavora; ha un bimbo senza padre, ed è felice di sentirlo gridar baciami ancora.	She works in a factory Her child has no father, and the sound of his voice demanding more kisses makes her happy.
Niente consente a chi d'amarla brama risponde non ho tempo: il bimbo chiama.	She does not allow anybody to love her and in response to their desires she replies: I'm running out of time, the child is calling.

When Damiani returned to Rome, after twenty complicated years abroad, his efforts focused on the rebirth of the Italian anarchist press. His relationship was with *L'Adunata* fairly intact, as he continued to receive 'from time to time a few dollars'.[48] The main obstacles to his writing and thinking went beyond financial challenges; they were related also to his health and eyesight. Italian anarchist propagandist Ugo Fedeli (1898–1964), who read *La mia bella Anarchia* (My Beautiful Anarchy), published in numerous instalments in *L'Adunata*, a few months before Damiani's death in 1953, described the text as 'brilliant' and unfortunately, 'succinct'.[49] Damiani's reply contained his usual sense of humour:

I agree with you that what was published by *L'Adunata* needed – as most of what I am writing – to be less concise. You should blame this on the fact that I am dictating and not writing by hand, and that I am not in the best conditions to do better. Please find for me a nice villa surrounded by a garden or on the Riviera and without the naggings of common needs and I assure you I will be able to do a better and more complete work.[50]

Needless to say, this never materialized, as Damiani died a few weeks later. To conclude and honour a lifelong collaboration between Damiani and the Italian-language anarchist press published in the United States, *L'Adunata* paid a lavish tribute to Damiani after his death, publishing his letters and poems as well as the testimonies of many anarchists he met all over the world.

All these years of collaboration from abroad are further evidence of 'how tightly the segments of the anarchist movement in Italy and abroad were ordinarily intertwined'.[51] Thanks to *Cronaca sovversiva*, Damiani gained esteem and recognition as a young anarchist and a young journalist on both sides of the Atlantic. His contributions to *Il Martello* attest to his eagerness to share as widely as possible his reflections and warnings about the political situation in Italy during the early fascism. His contributions to *Germinal*, which published his articles, poems, as well as a few of his booklets, were a way of distancing himself from the internal affairs of the Italian anarchist movement in the United States. During his exile, Tunisia became a physical refuge for Damiani and his family while *L'Adunata dei refrattari* signified refuge for his mind and his political reflections.

His collaborations with American newspapers marked not only a circulation between Italy and the US. It should also be considered in the larger, transnational context of the anarchist press, including other countries, beginning with Brazil, then France and Tunisia, where Damiani lived in exile, and Switzerland, where Italian-language anarchist newspapers published his articles. Damiani's articles should also be examined in the light of the writings of anarchists like Errico Malatesta, Luigi Fabbri and Camillo Berneri, all of whom collaborated from abroad as well. Much has been written about their wanderings and engagements with newspapers, which often moved with them, but the circulation of their texts – and ideas – and those of more obscure militants,[52] remains to be mapped.

Damiani's professional and personal life trajectories highlight the processes that led anarchists to collaborate with one periodical over another at specific moments in his live. Most of the time, his choices were driven by personal needs. Only in exceptional cases were his articles published in American newspapers as an alternative to newspapers that were not available in his local environment. No matter where he was, Damiani, like other anarchists in exile, spoke and wrote about what he knew best, in the language he knew best, with different purposes according to the time period. In this sense, the place of publication was less important, that is why it is inaccurate to label American radical periodicals as the newspapers of a 'colony in the colony'.[53] The role *L'Adunata dei refrattari* played on the rebirth of the anarchist movement in Italy in the post war period[54] – beyond the time limits of this study – is another argument to support this statement further.

Using Damiani and other anarchists' names from abroad was a guaranty of visibility for a global readership. This is one of the main reasons why we should exercise caution when referring to radical newspapers as part of the ethnic press.[55] If one insists on including the anarchist press in Italian inside this category, this does not necessarily imply that these periodicals were connected only with the local territory, as demonstrated by Damiani' contributions. This particular situation invites us to reconsider our thinking in transnational terms, that exceeds national borders and possibly obliterates those borders altogether.

Notes

1. As most of the Italian anarchists whose name appears in this article, Damiani has his entry in the *Dizionario biografico degli anarchici italiani* (Pisa, Biblioteca Franco Serantini 2003–5, vol. 1–2 and online: http://www.bfscollezionidigitali.org/collezioni/6-dizionario-biografico-online-degli-anarchici-italiani (accessed 14 February 2020). See also Isabelle Felici, *Poésie d'un rebelle. Gigi Damiani (1876–1953), poète, anarchiste, émigré* (Lyon: Atelier de Création Libertaire 2009).
2. Thanks to Alessia Bruni, Sonia Cancian, Ronald Creagh, Bénédicte Deschamps, Abdellah Diyari, Pascal Dupuy, Andrew Hoyt, Tomaso Marabini, Gilles Perez, Stéphanie Prévost, Franco Schirone, Davide Turcato, the staff of the Montpellier City Archives, the Montpellier University Library and the New York Public Library, who helped me manipulate microfilms, rolls, files, scans of the newspapers, and/or English language.
3. Leonardo Bettini, 'Appunti per una storia dell'anarchismo italiano negli Stati Uniti d'America', in Leonardo Bettini, *Bibliografia dell'anarchismo, vol.2, Periodici e numeri unici in lingua italiana pubblicati all'estero (1872–1971)* (Florence: Crescita politica editrice 1976), 289. Some nuances about the link between places of immigration and places of publication are given by Davide Turcato, 'The Other Nation. The Places of the Italian Anarchist Press in the USA', in Federico Ferretti, Gerónimo Barrera de la Torre, Anthony Ince and Francisco Toro (eds.), *Historical Geographies of Anarchism. Early Critical Geographers and Present-Day Scientific Challenges* (London: Routledge 2017), 41.
4. *Cronaca sovversiva* has been digitized and is available on the Library of Congress site: https://chroniclingamerica.loc.gov. On Luigi Galleani, see Antonio Senta, *Luigi Galleani: The Most Dangerous Anarchist in America* (Edinburgh Oakland Baltimore: AK Press 2020).
5. 'La tattica rivoluzionaria. Ai compagni d'Italia', *Cronaca sovversiva* no. 27 (7 July 1906) 2; 'I mandrilli!', *Cronaca sovversiva* no. 3 (1 January 1907) 1–2; 'Mentre piove', *Cronaca sovversiva* no. 8 (23 February 1908) 2; 'Una parola onesta', *Cronaca sovversiva* no. 1 (4 January 1908) 3; 'La bestia nera', *Cronaca sovversiva* no. 9 (27 February 1909) 2.
6. For one of those political tales see 'Viaggiando (La gente che s'incontra). *La Battaglia*, São Paulo (21 March 1908) in *Gli italiani all'estero* 4 (1996) Université de la Sorbonne Nouvelle-Paris 3, 163–9.
7. 'Mentre piove' *Cronaca sovversiva* 8, 23 February 1907, 2.
8. For instance 'La tattica rivoluzionaria', *La Battaglia*, 16 May 1907, 2; 'I mandrilli', *La Battaglia*, 2 December 1906, 1.
9. Isabelle Felici, *Les Italiens dans le mouvement anarchiste au Brésil (1890–1920)* (PhD, Université de la Sorbonne Nouvelle-Paris 3, 1994 https://hal.archives-ouvertes.fr/

tel-01359546). See also Isabelle Felici, 'La stampa anarchica in Brasile', in *Voci d'Italia fuori dall'Italia. Giornalismo e stampa dell'emigrazione*, ed. Bénédicte Deschamps and Pantaleone Sergi (Cosenza, Pellegrini editore, 2021). One issue of *La Battaglia* (no. 225, 1909) is now available online on the page dedicated to foreign-language newspapers published in Brazil by the Universidade Estadual Paulista (UNESP): https://bibdig.biblioteca.unesp.br/handle/10/26220.
10 'Parva favilla...', *L'Adunata dei refrattari* 48–9, 3 December 1932, 3.
11 For a synthesis in English of the different tendencies inside anarchism, see Davide Turcato, 'European anarchism in the 1890s: why labour matters in categorizing anarchism', *Journal of labour and society* 12, no. 3 (September 2009), 451–66: https://onlinelibrary.wiley.com/doi/abs/10.1111/j.1743-4580.2009.00248.x.
12 'Contro un'infamia', *Cronaca sovversiva* 33, 17 August 1912, 3.
13 Ibid.
14 'La barbarie tedesca' *Cronaca sovversiva* 1, 2 January 1915, 3; 'Gli anarchici e la guerra' *Cronaca sovversiva* 20, 15 May 1915, 1; 'L'ora dell'espiazione' *Cronaca sovversiva* 51, 18 December 1915, 1.
15 Some issues of *Guerra Sociale* are available at the UNESP digital Library: https://bibdig.biblioteca.unesp.br/handle/10/21.
16 'L'ora dell'espiazione', *Cronaca sovversiva*, 18 December 1915, 1.
17 Luigi Di Lembo, *Guerra di classe e lotta umana. L'anarchismo in Italia dal biennio rossa alla guerra di Spagna (1919–1939)* (Pisa: BFS 2001), 43; Ugo Fedeli, *Gigi Damiani. Note biografiche. Il suo posto nell'anarchismo* (Cesena: L'Antistato 1954). See also Ugo Fedeli, *Biografie di anarchici. Ciancabilla, Damiani, Gavilli* (Pescara: Samizdat 1997). On *Umanità Nova*, see *Cronache anarchiche. Il giornale Umanità Nova nell'Italia del Novecento* (Milano: Zero in condotta 2010). The whole collection is in the process of being fully digitalized.
18 *Fede!*, September 1923–October 1926.
19 Nunzio Pernicone, *Carlo Tresca. Portrait of a rebel* (Oakland, Edinburgh, Baltimore: AK Press 2010); Falcone Salvini, Concettina, Il Martello *di Carlo Tresca* (Casalvelino Scalo: Galzerano 2019).
20 Adriana Dadà, note to *Il Martello*, in Bettini, *Bibliografia dell'anarchismo*, 201–5. It is almost impossible to summarize in a few words the life and activities of these three important figures of Italian anarchism, all the more so as these names do not appear in publications for the general public. Only Errico Malatesta (1853–1932) has a notice in the *Encyclopedia Britannica*: advocate of 'propaganda of the deed', his encounter with Bakounine, his heroical *banda del matese*, spent almost thirty-five years in exile, a total of twelve years in prison, visited the US, France, Belgium, Argentina and Egypt, and lived many years in London. He returned permanently in Italy in 1919, welcomed as an Italian Lenin. Luigi Fabbri (1877–1935) was very young when he became an anarchist. As a school teacher, he refused to be loyal to the regime and had to escape to Switzerland, France, Belgium and finally Uruguay. Camillo Berneri (1897–1937) was called 'the most expelled anarchist in Europe'. A philosophy teacher in a high school and a fervent antifascist, he refused to be loyal to the regime and had to leave Italy in 1926. He started a wandering life, expelled and arrested in all the European democracies, while his wife Giovanna Caleffi took good care of their family. He joined the Spanish war and was very active until he died in jail a few days after he was arrested. The circumstances of this political assassination are still not clear.
21 Guy Liberti in Paul Avrich, *Anarchist Voices. An Oral History of Anarchism in America* (Princeton: Princeton University Press 1995), 157.

22 On the title, and for a brief presentation of *L'Adunata dei refrattari*, see Robert D'Attilio, 'L'Adunata dei Refrattari', in Mari Jo Buhle et al. (eds.), *Encyclopedia of the American Left* (Chicago: St. James Press 1990), 4.
23 http://emeroteca.braidense.it/epoca/full_screen.php?img=/export/epoca/617/ZZZI19240 81600001000000031000001.djvu&pageTitle=Testata%20Il%20Martello%20(1924-1944).
24 There is no mention of this newspaper by Ugo Fedeli, Gigi Damiani or Davide Turcato, 'The other nation'. There is a brief mention by Kenyon Zimmer, *Immigrants against the State. Yiddish and Italian anarchism* (Champaign: University of Illinois Press 2015), 178. The newspaper is indexed by Bettini, *Bibliografia dell'anarchismo*, 221 and by René Bianco, Ronald Creagh and Nicole Riffaut-Perrot, *Quand le coq rouge chantera. Anarchistes français et italiens aux États-Unis d'Amérique* (Marseille and Montpellier: Éditions Culture et Liberté et CIRCAN, [1986]), 60.
25 Mauro Canali, *Le spie del regime* (Bologna: Il Mulino 2004), 330–1. No mention of Silvestro Spada in Mimmo Franzinelli, *I tentacoli dell'Ovra: agenti, collaboratori e vitime della politiza politica fascista* (Torino: Bollati Borighieri 1999) and no entry in the *Dizionario biografico degli anarchici italiani*.
26 Adriana Dadà, 'I radicali italo-americani e la società italiana', *Italia contemporanea*, June 1982: 138.
27 Nunzio Pernicone, *Carlo Tresca*, 201.
28 Luigi Fabbri, 'Sul solito e doloroso argomento', *Germinal* 8, 15 May 1927, 3–4.
29 L'Adunata dei refrattari 9, 7 April 1923, 4.
30 B. Funa, 'Il quotidiano' *L'Adunata dei refrattari* 11, 15 September 1922, 4.
31 Luigi Fabbri, 'Sul solito e doloroso argomento', *Germinal* 8, 15 May 1927, 3.
32 Luigi Di Lembo quotes Renzo De Felice's praise of an article signed Ausonio Acrate, one of Damiani's pseudonyms, *Il Martello*, 20 October 1923. Luigi Di Lembo, *Guerra di classe e lotta umana. L'anarchismo in Italia dal biennio rossa alla guerra di Spagna (1919-1939)* (Pisa: Biblioteca Franco Serantini 2001), 147, note 166.
33 Gino Cerrito, 'Sull'emigrazione anarchica italiana negli stati uniti d'America', *Volontà* 22, no. 4 (July–August 1969): 272.
34 See, for instance, Luigi Fabbri, 'Sul solito e doloroso argomento'.
35 Giacomo Matteotti (1885–1924) was a Socialist member of Parliament. He denounced political violence perpetrated by the fascist Regime and especially during the 1924 general elections, which the fascist party won by two-thirds thanks to intimidation. As a consequence of this declaration held in the Chamber of Deputies, Matteotti was kidnapped and assassinated, presumably on Mussolini's orders. His corpse was found two months after the crime, in August 1924.
36 'Dalla Repubblica di Marianna 9-4-30', *Germinal* 5, 1 May 1930, 3.
37 This is only one of the twenty booklets Damiani published during the 1930s, most of them thanks to *L'Adunata dei refrattari*. Isabelle Felici, *Poésie d'un rebelle*, 175.
38 Osvaldo Maraviglia (1894–1966) arrived in the US at the age of seventeen. There he became an anarchist. He dedicated his life to his family, his work in a textile factory and to *L'Adunata dei Refrattari*, whom was one of the founders. As is the case for hundreds of Italian anarchists, he has a notice in the *Dizionario biografico degli anarchici italiani*, available online: https://www.bfscollezionidigitali.org/entita/14006-maraviglia-osvaldo?i=0 Maraviglia was in charge of the correspondence with the readers and contributors all over the world and also with Damiani. Ten letters from Damiani to Osvaldo Maraviglia, sent from 1924 to 1937, were published between June and December 1954 in *L'Adunata dei refrattari*.

39 Virgilia D'Andrea's (1888–1933) exile started in 1923: because of the publication of her collection of poems *Tormento* she was denounced for 'incitement to crime'. During her years in Paris, she published a journal *Veglia anarchica mensile (1926–1927) diretta da Virgilia D'Andrea*, which has just been re-edited in facsimile: Giorgio Sacchetti (ed.) (Rome: Nova Delphi 2020). She emigrated to the US in 1928, where she died of cancer. See her notice in the *Dizionario biografico degli anarchici italiani*, https://www.bfscollezionidigitali.org/entita/14022-dandrea-virgilia?i=2 and, for instance, Francesca Piccioli, *Virgilia D'Andrea: storia di un'anarchica* (Chieti: Centro studi libertari Camillo Di Sciullo 2002); Jennifer Guglielmo, *Living the Revolution: Italian Women's Resistance and Radicalism in New York City* (Chapel Hill: University of North Carolina Press 2010); Franca Iacovetta and Robert Ventresca, 'Virgilia D'Andrea: The Politics of Protest and the Poetry of Exile' in Donna R. Gabaccia and Franca Iacovetta (eds.), *Women, Gender, and Transnational Lives: Italian Workers of the World* (Toronto, ON: University of Toronto Press, 2002), 299–326; Franca Iacovetta and Lorenza Stradiotti, 'Betrayal, Vengeance, and the Anarchist Ideal: Virgilia D'Andrea's Radical Antifascism in (American) Exile, 1928–1933', *Journal of Women's History* 25, no. 1 (Spring 2013): 85–110.

40 'Ricordare necessita', *L'Adunata dei refrattari* 19, 12 May 1934, 3.

41 'Volontà', *L'Adunata dei refrattari* 29, 22 July 1933, 2.

42 Gigi Damiani, 'L'ostaggio', *Germinal* 3, 1 March 1927. This paper, which first appeared in a French anarchist newspaper, *Le Semeur contre tous les tyrans* (The Sower against all Tyrants) in February 1927, was dedicated to Errico Malatesta. It is a further illustration of how Damiani's rebel prose and poetry was widely requested and circulated in the larger network of anarchist papers in the world.

43 'Volontà', *L'Adunata dei refrattari* 29, 22 July 1933, 2.

44 Isabelle Felici, '*Domani* (1935), une publication antifasciste et anticolonialiste à l'initiative des anarchistes italiens de Tunisie', *Storie e testimonianze politiche degli italiani di Tunisia*, Silvia Finzi (ed.) (Tunis: Finzi 2016), 173–83. https://hal.archives-ouvertes.fr/hal-01381071.

45 Gigi Damiani, 'Cose nostre. Organizzazione e antiorganizzazione', *L'Adunata dei refrattari*, 32 and 33, 19 and 26 August 1939, respectively 1–2 and 1.

46 Ibid.

47 Gigi Damiani, 'La nostra musa', *L'Adunata dei refrattari* 4, 27 January 1945, 4. The poem was translated by the author.

48 From Gigi Damiani to Pio Turroni, 22 June 1953. Archives Pio Turroni, Centro Studi Libertari-Archivio Giuseppe Pinelli, Milano.

49 From Ugo Fedeli to Gigi Damiani, September 1953. *La mia bella anarchia*, was published as a booklet (Cesena: Edizioni l'Antistato 1953).

50 From Gigi Damiani to Ugo Fedeli, 8 September 1953.

51 Davide Turcato, 'Transnational Italian Anarchism, 1885–1915', *International Review of Social History* 52, no. 3 (2007): 433.

52 Pascal Dupuy, Folgorite. Parcours de Sante Ferrini, anarchiste, typographe, poète (1874–1939) (Lyon: Atelier de Création Libertaire 2020).

53 Augusta Molinari, 'I giornali delle comunità anarchiche italo-americane', *Movimento operaio e socialista* II, no. 1–2 (January–June 1981): 117. Even the most widely circulated Italian-language newspapers published abroad could not compete with the Italian anarchist newspapers: just a few weeks after circulating, *Umanità Nova* reached 50,000 copies. Luigi Di Lembo, 'Errico Malatesta e la nascita di *Umanità Nova*',

Cronache anarchiche. Il giornale Umanità Nova nell'Italia del Novecento (Milano: Zero in condotta 2010), 28.

54 Giorgio Sacchetti, *Sans frontière. Umberto Marzocchi 1900–1986* (Paris: Les Éditions libertaires 2020), 111.

55 Bénédicte Deschamps, *Histoire de la presse italo-américaine, Du Risorgimento à la Grande Guerre* (Paris: L'Harmattan 2020).

Section Two

Community Building and Transculturation: Allocating Foreign-Language Communities' Needs

4

French-Language Almanacs in the United States, from the Eighteenth Century to the Beginning of the Twentieth Century: Genres, Social Dimensions and Transcultural Adaptations[1]

Hans-Jürgen Lüsebrink
Universität des Saarlandes

Introducing the 'Colonial Weekday Bible': characteristics of French-language almanacs in Canada and the United States

An almanac is a periodical published once a year generally containing a calendar, ephemerides summarizing the important events of the past year and various information and texts (songs, riddles, short stories, advices) which were supposed to be of major interest for the reading public. Together with religious prints, it represented the most widespread and popular publications in all early modern societies. In Quebec, almanacs – especially the long-selling series with a very large diffusion, like the *Almanach du Peuple*, the *Almanach des Familles*, the *Almanach Rolland* and the *Almanach de la Langue Française* – were the most-widespread periodicals in Canada until the 1920s. With a circulation of more than 250,000 copies, the *Almanach du Peuple* edited by Beauchemin Publishing in Montreal was the most popular one among the more than 150 different almanacs published in French-speaking Canada between 1777 and the 1940s.[2]

In the British New-England colonies the first almanac, inspired by British models, was established in 1638 by Captain William Peirce (c. 1591–c. 1641) and published under the title *Almanack for 1639* by the editor Stephen Day in Cambridge, Massachusetts.[3] During the seventeenth, eighteenth and the first half of the nineteenth centuries, almanacs underwent a flourishing development which found its end only during the second half of the nineteenth century, because of the rise of daily and weekly newspapers. These print media had become far more affordable than before with the introduction of new printing technologies and rapidly increasing numbers of copies due to the spread of literacy and the expansion of the reading public. Milton Drake and other bibliographers of almanacs estimate that the total number of almanac-series published in the New England colonies and the early United States between the middle of the seventeenth century and the end of the nineteenth century reached more than 1,500 different titles. The most widespread almanacs were distributed in a considerable number of copies, comparable to those in Québec one and a half centuries later: the *Poor Richard's Almanack* published by Benjamin Franklin between 1732 and 1758 reached 10,000 copies a year; *The Astronomical Diary and Almanack for the Year...* published between 1725 and 1776 by Nathanael Ames in Dedham, Massachusetts, even attained 60,000 copies a year.[4] The *Ames* almanac was 'the most popular of the eighteenth century', states Louis Wechsel in his book on *The Common People of Colonial America,* 'to say nothing of the thousands of copies that were pirated'.[5] And whereas the most widespread newspapers at the time of the American Revolution, like the *Pennsylvania Chronicle*, barely reached a circulation of 2,000 copies in the 1770s, even less popular almanacs of obviously poor quality, such as the *Astronomical Diary* published by Stephen Row Bradley (1754–1830), succeeded in selling 2,000 copies the same year.

The 'New England' colonies, in the same way as the United States of the late eighteenth and the nineteenth centuries, were multilingual and multicultural societies where printing and publishing did not only take place in English, but also in other languages, especially in German and French. The earliest German-language almanac in North America, the *Teutsche Pilgrim, Mitbringende einen Sitten-Calender* (The German Pilgrim, with a moral calendar), appeared in 1731. The first printed sales list of German books was published as early as 1739 in another German-language almanac, *Der Hoch-Deutsche Amerikanische Calender* which was edited by Christoph Sauer in Germantown and Philadelphia, Pennsylvania and continued being published between 1739 and 1832.[6] The German literary historian York-Gothard Mix and his collaborators Bianca Weyers and Gabriele Krieg inventory and describe in detail in their pioneering commented bibliography on German-American almanacs of the eighteenth and nineteenth centuries no less than 113 different series published mainly in Pennsylvania, where more than 100,000 German-speaking immigrants lived in 1775, but also in Ohio (Cincinnati and Lancaster) and in Maryland (Hagerstown and Baltimore).[7]

In spite of these facts, the current studies and bibliographies on periodicals and their literary, cultural and intellectual history – and especially on almanacs published in the New England colonies and the United States – do not take into consideration the voluminous production of almanacs in other languages, notably in German and French, but also in Spanish and Dutch. Even the bibliography established by Milton Drake, *Almanacs of the United States* (1962), still the most complete bibliography from that perspective, is very incomplete with regard to almanacs published in languages other than English. The great variety of publications – books, periodicals, songbooks, broadsheets – in languages other than English began garnering increased scholarly attention by researchers in the late twentieth century in the wake of the increase in Hispanic immigration from the 1960s and the rise of the francophone cultural movement in Louisiana of the 1970s. Yet, publications in other languages than English never reached the same significance as in the eighteenth and the nineteenth centuries. Interest has henceforth concerned far more media like radio and television and, since the end of the 1990s, the Internet, than the printing press. On the whole, publications in languages other than English in the United States have generally not received adequate scholarly attention, in the fields of literary and cultural history or in print media studies. Important exceptions with regard to this neglect relate to publications in certain languages, especially German, in which important studies have been published over the last decades, notably on the production of almanacs.[8]

French-language almanacs in the United States: which models for transculturality?

Concerning French-language almanacs, their production and social diffusion had occurred at least since the last decade of the eighteenth century, first in the New England States and then in Louisiana, above all in Massachusetts and in New York City. California in the 1840s offers another ephemeral example where several almanacs like the *Almanach Franco-Californien. Petit Journal 'Directory' des Français de la Côte du Pacifique* appeared at the time of the so-called Gold Rush, and again in the 1920s, with the publication of the *Almanach des Français en Californie* published in San Francisco. In other American States, French-language almanacs were rare and were often not preserved in libraries, with some exceptions like the short-lived *Almanach illustré de Hostetter pour les États-Unis* published in Pittsburgh, Pennsylvania, in the late 1870s, of which the archives of the Historical New Orleans Collection held a copy.

The first French-language almanac in the United States is probably the *Étrennes historiques et intéressantes contenant l'Abrégé géographique du royaume de France, avec un mélange curieux d'anecdotes, d'événements remarquables, &c. &c. pour l'année de grâce 1786* (Historical and Interesting Annual Gifts, including a short geographical survey of the Kingdom of France, with a curious mix of anecdotes, remarkable events etc. etc. for the year of our God 1786). It was published in Boston, Massachusetts in 1786. With the exception of its place of publication, the indication that it had been edited by a publisher in the United States ('*imprimeur des États-Unis*') and of a section of two pages concerning local news, this almanac contained relatively few references to the New World. Its content was mainly limited to a calendar, to information on the history and the geography of France, on the French monarchy and on the members of the Royal Court of France. The ephemerides published in this almanac related to events which had occurred in France and Europe during the preceding year.

This pioneering, but probably short-lived almanac was followed in 1799 by the *Almanach chantant dédié aux Dames* ('Song almanac dedicated to women'), which began publication in New Orleans in 1809. Several other titles ensued. For instance, the *Almanach de la Louisiane* contained literary texts, including short stories and short theatrical pieces, such as the play *Les deux rivaux; ou un mariage au Bayou* (The Two Rivals; or A Marriage in the Bayou) which was published in the 1864 issue of the almanac. The *Almanach Chantant, dédié aux Dames* and the *Almanach Américain* published in Philadelphia in the early nineteenth century continued, in modified and adapted forms. The fashionable periodical genre of women's almanacs (*Almanachs des Dames*) had appeared in France and Germany, with such bestselling titles as the *Almanach des Graces* and the *Almanach des Dames*, which were co-edited for more than forty years (from 1801 on) by the French publisher Jean-George Treuttel in Paris and the German editor Johann Friedrich Cotta in Tübingen. The *Almanach des Dames* presented itself as an adaptation, specifically for female readers, of the *Almanach des Muses*, which had been created in 1765 in Paris by French journalist Claude Sixte Sautreau de Marsy (1740–1815). Marsy had directly inspired Friedrich Schiller's *Musenalmanach* published between 1796 and 1800.[9] The unknown director and editor of the *Almanach Américain* in Philadelphia referred explicitly to this European tradition when he addressed his readers as follows:

> Le succès qu'ont depuis plusieurs années, en France et en Allemagne, différents almanachs littéraires, nous a persuadé qu'un ouvrage de ce genre pourrait obtenir la même faveur auprès du public de l'Amérique.[10]
>
> (The success obtained over the last several years, in France and in Germany, by different literary almanacs has persuaded us to think that a similar periodical of this kind could gain the favour of the public in America).

The formal structure and the content of the American adaptations of the 'Almanacs for women' in Quebec, Pennsylvania and in Louisiana were largely similar to their French and German models, but they adapted their contents and also their structure to the expectations of their often bilingual and bicultural North American readers. They were also addressed to a largely female public of readers, publishing sentimental poems, but also philosophical reflections, for example on the Swiss physiognomist Johann Kaspar Lavater or on the evolution of post-revolutionary France, in an article intitled '*La France toujours la même*' ('France always the same'). They also integrated into their columns numerous elements referring explicitly to the American context, e.g. important dates of the calendar as well as historical dates and advertisements,

The specific case of Louisiana: French-language almanacs for the bourgeoisie

The almanacs edited during the nineteenth century in New Orleans – like the *l'Annuaire Louisianais*, published at the very beginning of the nineteenth century by the geographer and printer Barthélemy Lafon (1792–1820)[11] or the *Almanach, annonces de la librairie* published in the 1870s – were predominantly directories bound together with calendars and also containing numerous advertising pages. With its proud and traditional francophone bourgeoisie, New Orleans gave birth to quite sophisticated literary almanacs which strove for higher aesthetic quality. The *Almanach de la Renaissance* and the *Almanach Louisiane*, which were published from the 1860s to the end of the nineteenth century, are typical examples of this variety. In the preface to its very first issue of 1868, the editors of the *Almanach de la Renaissance* presented the new publication as the periodical of the '*grande famille louisianaise*' (the great Louisiana family) containing a significant 'choice of various and interesting themes, among which the local occupies an important part'.[12]

The *Almanach de la Louisiane* (launched in 1864) sought to represent one of the major voices of the French-speaking bourgeoisie in the public sphere in Louisiana. Beside the traditional elements of an almanac – the calendar with the seasons, the holidays, the names of the saints related to each day of the year and the lunar eclipses, followed by the ephemeris, to which was added, in the first years, a '*Revue rapide des principaux événements de la Guerre Américaine*' (a quick review of main events in the American Civil War) – it incorporated many literary texts (generally short anecdotes and poems), some of them translated from English or German, and programmatic articles concerning the identity and the situation of the French-speaking community in Louisiana.

François Tujague (1844–1924), the French-born and most influential journalist in New Orleans at the time, contributed a long article on the francophone literature of Louisiana, its present state and its future into the *Almanach de la Louisiane*'s second issue. Starting from the statement that the Civil War had suddenly ended the ancient order of things ('*l'ancien ordre des choses*') and that it could, despite the terrible bloodshed and violence, embody the chance of a new start, Tujague appealed to the writers and journalists in Louisiana to create a new, progressive literature in French. 'With their help,' concludes Tujague in the very last sentences of his article, 'New Orleans will occupy a first rank among the civilized cities and the dignity of the customs, the general prosperity and, finally, the progress, in its highest expression, will be the distinctive signs of this new era.'[13] But Tujague's very optimistic and even utopian vision was not confirmed by the economic, cultural and social development of New Orleans and Louisiana in the following decades. The francophone literature and culture of Louisiana underwent a constant decline after the Civil War, as well as French-language periodicals and almanacs, which gradually disappeared in the late nineteenth and early twentieth centuries. This decline was mainly caused by the very negative financial and economic legacy of the Civil War and the ongoing crisis in the French-speaking plantation economy in Louisiana. Despite the programmatic attempts to foster rebirth ('Renaissance') proclaimed by intellectuals, writers and journalists in post-civil-war Louisiana, decline could not be halted.

French-language almanacs in the New England States: rivalling with Canadian almanacs for readership

The most important production of French-language almanacs in the United States took place in the New England States and was closely related to the massive immigration of French-Canadians between the last decades of the nineteenth century and the 1920s. By the 1840s, these French-language almanacs faced competition from the popular French-Canadian almanacs edited in Montréal, like the *Almanach du Peuple*, which maintained offices in the New England States, in towns with an important French-Canadian population, for example in Lowell, Massachusetts or in Central Falls, Rhode Island. As almost half of the French-speaking population in North America migrated to the United States, the French-Canadian almanacs tried, with some success, to attract a readership especially in the New England States among the so-called *Franco-Américains* who lived mainly in Massachusetts, New York State, Connecticut, Rhode Island and Vermont.

There has been no systematic exploration of all French-language almanacs published in this area… This task represents a huge challenge, because of their very fragmentary conservation and their dispersion in numerous public libraries and private libraries and archives. As a result, their numbers and their social and cultural diffusion can only be approximated. Their total number can be estimated at forty to fifty different series for the period stretching the mid-nineteenth century to the late 1920s. In spite of their formal and structural differences, these French-language almanacs in the New England States shared four main functions that were determined by the fact that their reading public belonged to a linguistic minority whose literacy rate was significantly lower in comparison to the rate of the English-speaking majority of the country.

The French-language almanacs destined for the *Franco-Américains* were, like all almanacs in general, in the first place, genuine temporal guides which offered orientation to their readers by means of their calendars that indicated the seasons, the sacred holidays, the astrological signs and the weather forecast (generally for one year in advance). As Samuel Atkins, at the time student in mathematics and astrology and editor of one of the early American almanacs, the *Kalendarium Pennsilvaniense, or America's Messenger,* pointed out in his preface to the 1686 issue of the almanack, that the calendar and its supplements intended to meet above all the need of the popular reading public to improve its perception and its management of time:

> the People [were] generally complaining that they scarcely knew how the Time passed, and that they hardly knew the day of the Rest, or Lord's Day, when it was, for want of a Diary, or Day-Book, which we call an Almanack.[14]

The numerous blank pages inside the calendars served also as notebooks and sometimes even as rudimentary diaries for their holders and their families. One such precious testimony is to be found in the copy of the 1801 *Almanach Américain* (published in Philadelphia) currently held by the Library of the American Antiquarian Society in Worcester, Massachusetts. On those pages, handwritten notes by a female reader (and owner?) express her tender feelings for her husband, in sometimes quite clumsy French:

> La vertu est une chose qui est bien estimable/Les mauvais gens sont terribles./Mon mari est homme/comme il faut. Je voudrai[s] qu'il étoit toujours chez moi/parce que lui [sic!] aime plus que moi-même.
> (Virtue is a thing which is honourable/The bad people are terrible/My husband is a gentleman. I wish he could always be with me/Because I love him more than myself).[15]

Secondly, these almanacs also served as 'historical guides' ('*Guides dans l'histoire*'), indicating the most important events of French-Canadian history and the most relevant events of the past year. The *Almanach et Directorium Français des États-Unis*, à *l'usage des populations françaises de l'Amérique du Nord*, published in New York City from 1845 until the end of the nineteenth century, contained, for example, the 'Éphémérides de l'histoire américaine', a chronology of the major events of American history, which covered eight pages. The *Almanach Franco-Américain/French American Directory*, a bilingual almanac in English and French, published also in New York City until the end of the 1920s, was destined not only for French-Canadian immigrants, but also, and probably mainly, for immigrants from France. It included a history of the French colony in New York City ('La colonie française de New York') as well as detailed statistics on the French-speaking population in the United States according to geographical regions, states and main towns ('Population de Langue Française aux États-Unis par régions géographiques, par États et par villes principales'). According to the information provided in the almanac in its 1928 edition, this entailed 1,290,110 persons at the time.[16]

The third major function of the French-language almanacs was to respond to the need of their readers for practical and useful information. In almanacs like the *Almanach Franco-Américain*, readers could find statistics, a map of the United States, and indications of the distances between the different towns in the New England States. They also included information about the roads, the postal system and the railroads. They contained a *précis* about the American institutions, the administration, the judicial system and a digest of the most important American laws. At the end of the almanac, was added a voluminous 'Directorium général des noms', a general directory of all the subscribers of the almanac, with their names, their professions and their home addresses. In some almanacs, like the *Almanach et Directorium Français des États-Unis* of 1857, this practical information held the most important part of the periodical, which was divided into two major sections: the 'Directorium des Affaires à New York' (translated in the almanac itself by 'Business Directory'); and the 'Directorium général des noms' (translated as 'Name's Directory'), which included a 'Liste genérale des adresses des Français et autres nations répartis selon l'ordre des villes' ('A general list of the French and other nations divided into the different towns').

Finally, the French-language almanacs in the United States had a communitarian function; they provided significant information about the French-speaking communities, underlined the particularities of their cultural identity and their traditions, and promoted also their integration and progressive acculturation – not their assimilation – in the US-American society. In contrast to the French-Canadian almanacs, and also to several francophone almanacs in Louisiana, such literary texts as anecdotes, poems, songs or even short theatre plays – which represented an important element for the definition of the collective identity in Quebec, and more generally in French-speaking Canada (Lüsebrink 2014, 303–52) – did not play any significant role in the French-language almanacs in the New England States. Instead of that, practical advice and information, advertising in French, generally for American products or for services offered by members of the French-language community were regularly published. From this point of view, the French-language almanacs in the New England States represented an important means of inclusion and integration of the francophone population into and within the US consumer society; and also a major instrument of acculturation facilitating the access to new practices of health care, to professional activities and to adequate coping responses to the problems of everyday life, in short, to central elements of the US-American 'civilization' ('*civilisation*'). The *Almanach Américain, de Dr. Ayer, à l'usage des fermiers, planteurs, artisans, et des familles en général* published in Lowell, Massachusetts, an adapted French version of *Ayer's American Almanach* edited by the pharmaceutical company J. C. Ayer, defined its main objectives as follows in 1858 in its 'Editorial note':

> In this small handbook we provide to the public an exact calendar following the sequence of the seasons, and also some information of vital interest for the health of all. The remedies that we advertise have been created in order to heal the major illnesses which afflict us in these latitudes of the American States.... Do not refuse the assistance of a skillful doctor when you are sick; he represents one of the major benefits of civilization. There will still remain a place for our remedies to do incalculable good all over the world.[17]

Advertising pages could already be found in the very first French-language almanacs published in the New England States. The *Almanach Français de New York, composé principalement pour les populations françaises des États-Unis, pour 1848,* for example, published advertisements for boarding schools for young girls and for the services of lawyers' offices, but also for the subscription of books in French and the sale of coal by a supplier of French origin in New York City, who offered to supply coal at a special price to his '*compatriots*'.[18] Some Franco-American almanacs which were close to the British-American genre of the directories focused their contents on inventories of addresses which were completed by the compulsory calendar and an overview of historical events. This was the case in the *Guide Canadien-français ou Almanach des adresses de Fall River, et notes historiques sur les Canadiens de Falls River par H.A. Dubuque,* published with E. F. Lamoureux at Fall River, Rhode Island, as of 1888; or in the *Almanach du Commerce et de l'Industrie des États-Unis,* published as of 1872 in New York City which targeted primarily readers among the merchants and traders of French origin.

Seen from this perspective, the French-language almanacs in the United States often represented for their readers small pocket encyclopaedias which were revised, updated and completed at the end of every year. The older series of almanacs published between the end of the eighteenth and the mid-nineteenth century were based on European, especially French models like the *Almanach des Dames* or for the more popular ones, on the *Messager Boiteux*. Some French-language almanacs in the United States, like the *Almanach de Hostetter pour les États-Unis,* edited in Pittsburgh, Pennsylvania, even published until the end of the nineteenth century the 'Man of signs', a woodcut engraving surrounded by the twelve signs of the zodiac 'where lines pointed out the various combinations of celestial bodies with human anatomy'.[19] This figure, generally a 'hermaphroditic nude with female breasts and male genital', had a long popular tradition in the early-modern European cultures and had already appeared in the very first European almanacs of the sixteenth and seventeenth centuries.[20]

By the late nineteenth century, the two most successful French-Canadian almanacs, the *Almanach du Peuple* and the *Almanach Rolland*, had become the predominant models for the French-language almanacs in the New England States, together with the *Almanach Hachette* (1894–1972), a popular almanac in France which reached a circulation of 200,000 copies at the end of the nineteenth century. Like the *Almanach Hachette*, subtitled 'petite encyclopédie de la vie pratique' ('small encyclopaedia of practical life'), the most popular among the francophone almanacs in Canada and the French-language almanacs in the United States had in common the quality that they constituted, in fact, small pocket-encyclopaedias. They were published in general during the first week of December in order to be used throughout the whole following year. They were often collected – in contrast to newspapers and most other periodicals – and used for regular further consultations, precisely like popular encyclopaedias.

In order to meet the expectations of their readers concerning very practical advice, the almanacs inserted in their columns numerous useful and practical tips and information related to very different fields: for example, everyday medical remedies, body care, domestic economy, agriculture, the relations and the communication with institutions, especially administrations, extracts from US laws (concerning, for instance, the legislation on rentals, inheritances, financial debts, divorces, etc.) and problems related to the fact that Franco-Americans had to deal with their day to day business in a predominantly Anglophone society. The 1865 issue of the *Almanach et Directoire des États-Unis* contained for this purpose a 'Guide des États-Unis. Instruction adressée spécialement aux immigrants' (Guidebook of the United States. Instructions destined especially for immigrants). This guidebook of several pages in length included also a chapter entitled 'Étude de la langue anglaise' (Study of the English language) which was introduced as follows by the editor of the almanac:

> Knowledge of English is essential, if you do not want to run the risk of being cheated in half of your current affairs with the Americans, or exposed to the continuous expenses of translations or the help of translators.[21]

Even if the French-language almanacs in the New England States aimed at establishing strong cultural links between Québec and the new homeland of their readers and defended the French language and its use in the private sphere and in the cultural and religious institutions of the French-Canadian immigrants, they advocated at the same time for their extensive integration into US American society. In the chapter 'S'américaniser' ('How to americanize oneself') of the abovementioned '*Guide des États-Unis*' in the *Almanach et Directoire des États-Unis* intended for French-Canadian immigrants, the almanac gives the following advice:

> If you want to be successful among the Americans, you must follow their habits and respect their customs, even if these may not be compatible with ours; you should converse with them as much as possible, attend their meetings, and understand that we come to this country in order to get money from them, in working for them … The French should avoid withdrawing and *isolating* themselves, as some do it, as we could observe, and who remained consequently at the same degree of poverty, because they lacked commercial knowledge which

they could have taken from our almanac or in another handbook, and which they could also have tried to follow.[22]

The *Almanach et Directoire des États-Unis* sought to defend the culture, the language and the interests of the *Franco-Americains* and the immigrants who had come from France to the United States, thereby underlining the need for a certain integration in the American society.

By contrast, other almanacs – like the *Almanach des Adresses des Membres de l'Union Saint-Baptiste d'Amérique* published in Manchester, New Hampshire, as of 1904, or the *Almanach franco-américain et catholique* published in Fitchburg, Massachusetts, as of 1911 – stood for what could be termed the 'identity model' of the almanac. They dedicated an important part of the content of the almanac to the Catholic Church, to the clergymen and to the life of the French-language dioceses, but also to French-Canadian folklore and to popular literary forms. This type of almanac, instead of being oriented towards the surrounding anglophone society and the ways to integrate within it, were focused on the life and the institutions of the French-Canadian immigrant community.

These two antagonistic types of almanacs both reached a very large reading public among the French-speaking working classes in the New England States, in contrast with the literary almanacs mentioned in the beginning of this contribution. They co-existed and reflected different strategies regarding the integration of their readers within a predominantly anglophone society. They also catered for different needs. They illustrate the central cultural and political role of almanacs for communication networks and identity models of the French-speaking communities during the British colonial period and in the United States from the late eighteenth century to the early twentieth century. Like their readers, they evolved between two languages, two cultures and two social spaces which were fundamentally different.

French-language almanacs in broader perspective

Similarly to eighteenth- and nineteenth-century German-language almanacs, French-language almanacs of this period and of the early twentieth century reflected a dialectic relationship between traditional European models of the almanac genre and their creative adaptation, hovering between cultural transfer and increasing cultural autonomy. York-Gothard Mix's following statement, referring to the German-language almanacs, can be transposed to their French-language counterparts which borrowed/inherited from both French and British traditions and genre models (like the *Almanach des Dames*, the *Almanach Hachette* and the British *Directory Almanac*):

> Not only did the orientation towards North American life take place *within* the traditional almanac form inherited, above all, from Upper Germany and Switzerland, but it also avoided provocative breaks with tradition.... What at first sight appears to be a medium that steeped in tradition shows, at the same time, significant differences from its predecessor, despite parallels in format, conception, and content.[23]

A historical approach that combines textual analysis with a comparative dimension and that applies the methodological frame of cultural transfers thus allows for the identification of the cultural and social particularities of the French-language almanacs in the United States, but also for their transcultural origin and their numerous similarities with other almanacs produced and read by cultural minorities in a predominantly anglophone society and culture.

Notes

1 Parts of this chapter are based on an article that originally appeared in *Media19* in French under the following title: 'Les almanachs franco-américains des XIXe siècles et XX siècles: un média de communication et d'information populaire entre le Québéc et les communautés francophones aux États-Unis', in Micheline Cambron and Stéphanie Danaux (eds.), 'La recherche sur la presse: nouveaux bilans nationaux et internationaux' special issue, 2013, online: http://www.medias19.org/index.php?id=15554. Its content has been revised and enlarged. I am very grateful to Guillaume Pinson (Université Laval, Québec), editor of *Media19*, for allowing partial reproduction.
2 Hans-Jürgen Lüsebrink, 'Le livre aimé du peuple'. *Les almanachs québécois de 1777 à nos jours* (Québec: Les Presses de l'Université Laval (Coll. Cultures Québécoises), 2014).
3 Milton Drake, *Almanacs of the United States* (New York, The Scarecrow Press), vol. I, 272.
4 Numbers given by the detailed research conducted by Marion Barner Stowell in her book *Early American Almanacs: The Colonial Weekday Bible* (New York: Burt Franklin, 1977), 10.
5 Louis W. Wechsler, *The Common People of Colonial America* (New York: Vantage Press, 1978), xiv.
6 York-Gothart Mix, Bianca Weyers and Gabriele Krieg (eds.), *Deutsch-amerikanische Kalender des 18. und 19. Jahrhunderts/German-American Almanacs of the 18th and 19th centuries. Bibliography and Commentary* (Berlin/Boston: De Gruyter, 2012, 2 vols), 1; Robert E. Cazden, *A Social History of the German Book Trade in America to the Civil War* (Columbia, NC: Camden House, 1984), 8.
7 Mix, Weyers and Krieg (eds.), *Deutsch-amerikanische Kalender des 18. und 19. Jahrhunderts*, ibid., vol. I, 1.
8 See for example the detailed critical bibliographies published by Karl Ardt and John Richard (eds.), *The First Century of German Language Printing in the United States of America. A Bibliography Based on the Studies of Oswald Seidensticker and Wilbur H. Oda* (Göttingen, Universitätsverlag Göttingen, 1989), Coll. *Pennsylvania German Society* 21, vol. I (1728–1807); Mix, Weyers and Krieg (eds.), *Deutsch-amerikanische Kalender des 18. und 19. Jahrhunderts*, ibid.; Susanne Greilich and York-Gothart Mix (eds.), *Populäre Kalender im vorindustriellen Europa: Der 'Hinkende Bote'/'Messager boiteux'. Kulturwissenschaftliche Analysen und bibliographisches Repertorium* (Berlin and New York, 2006); and Hans-Jürgen Lüsebrink and York-Gothart Mix, 'Kulturtransfer und Autonomisierung. Populäre deutsch-amerikanische und frankokanadische Kalender des 18. und 19. Jahrhundertzs. Prämissen und Perspektiven der Forschung', *Gutenberg Jahrbuch* (2002), 188–200.

9 Hans-Jürgen Lüsebrink, 'Der Almanach des Muses und die französische Almanachkultur des 18. Jahrhunderts', in Paul Gerhard Klussmann and York-Gothart Mix (eds.), *Literarische Leitmedien. Almanach und Taschenbuch im kulturwissenschaftlichen Kontext* (Wiesbaden, Harrassowitz-Verlag, 1998), 3–15.
10 'Avertissement', *Almanach Américain pour 1801*. Philadelphie [1800], unpaginated.
11 Edward L. Tinker, *Les Écrits de langue française en Louisiane au XIXe siècle. Essais biographiques et bibliographiques* (Geneva: Slatkine Reprints, 1975), 276.
12 The French reads: 'choix de matières variées, intéressantes, et parmi lesquelles l'élément local a une large part'. 'Préface', *Almanach de la Renaissance, pour 1869* (New Orleans: Imprimerie de la Renaissance, [1868]), unpaginated.
13 F[rançois] Tujague, 'De l'avenir de la littérature à la Nouvelle Orléans', *Almanach de la Louisiane, 1866*, 121: 'Avec leur aide, la Nouvelle-Orléans prendra place au premier rang des villes civilisées, – et la dignité des mœurs, la prospérité générale, le progrès, enfin, dans sa plus haute expression, seront les signes distinctifs de l'ère nouvelle.'
14 'To the Reader', *Kalendarium Pennsylvaniense, or America's Messinger. Being an Almanack for the Year of Grace, 1686*. By Samuel Atkins. Philadelphia: William Bradford; and New York: Philip Richards [1685], 1.
15 *Almanach Américain pour 1801*. Philadelphie [1800], handwritten notes beside the inner title page.
16 *Almanach Franco-Américain*, 1928, 312–16, here 312.
17 'Les remèdes que nous annonçons ont été composés pour guérir les principales maladies qui nous affligent dans ces latitudes des États Américains.... Ne refusez pas l'assistance d'un habile médecin quand vous êtes malade, il est un des grands bienfaits de la civilisation, il restera encore à nos remèdes assez de place pour faire un bien incalculable dans le monde.' Quoted in 'Note de l'éditeur', *Almanach Américain, de Dr. Ayer, à l'usage des fermiers, planteurs, artisans, et des familles en général*, Lowell: Ayer & Company, 1858, 1. The thirty-six-page almanac was published in octavo format.
18 'Cour Française de Phénix, pour la vente des charbons de terre' [advertisement], *Almanach français de New York, composé principalement pour les populations françaises des États-Unis, pour 1848* (New York, Seth Williston Benedict [1847]), 39.
19 Timothy Feist, *The Stationers' Voice. The English Almanac Trade in the Early Eighteenth Century* (Philadelphia, American Philosophical Society, 2005), 101.
20 Ibid.
21 'La connaissance de l'anglais est indispensable, autrement vous risquerez d'être trompés dans la moitié de vos transactions avec les Américains, et vous vous exposez à faire des frais continuels de traductions ou d'aide d'interprètes.' Quoted in 'Guide des États-Unis. Instruction adressée spécialement aux immigrants', *Almanach et Directorium des États-Unis, à l'usage des populations françaises pour l'année 1861* (New York, 1860), 5.
22 'Si l'on veut réussir parmi les Américains, il faut suivre leurs habitudes, céder à leurs usages, même s'ils ne s'accordent pas avec les nôtres, converser avec eux autant que possible, assister à leurs assemblées, et comprendre que nous venons dans ce pays pour gagner de l'argent par eux, en travaillant pour eux.... aussi le Français doit-il éviter de s'*isoler*, comme nous en avons vus qui [le] faisaient, et qui par conséquent restaient au même degré de misère par défaut d'instructions commerciales qu'ils auraient pu puiser dans notre Almanach ou dans un Guide, et qu'ils auraient tâché d'observer' ('Guide des États-Unis', 'ibid.', 7). Translated by the author.
23 Mix, Weyers and Krieg (eds.), *Deutsch-amerikanische Kalender des 18. und 19. Jahrhunderts*, ibid., 9.

5

'A modest sentinel for German interests in England': The Anglo-German Press in the Long Nineteenth Century

Susan Reed
British Library

During the long nineteenth century, Germans grew to form one of the largest immigrant communities in Britain, reaching a peak of more than 50,000 in 1911.[1] It is therefore no surprise that various attempts were made throughout the period to establish newspapers for this community, with greater or lesser degrees of success. Between the first venture in 1810 and the outbreak of the First World War in 1914, which put an end to German publishing and German community activities in Britain, some fifty titles can be identified. Of these, only nine survived their first year, and only six ran for longer than five years. This chapter will provide an initial overview of the Anglo-German press during this period before moving on to look at the motivations of newspaper founders and editors, the challenges they faced in running a newspaper, the kinds of audiences targeted, and the reasons for success or failure.

Mapping the German-language press in Britain: overview and methodological considerations

Surveying the nineteenth-century Anglo-German press presents a number of practical challenges. Many newspapers survive only in a single copy, sometimes as an incomplete run, while some are known only from references (often partisan and tendentious) in contemporary articles or letters. Even with more successful titles, information about the circumstances of publication and the editors and contributors involved can be difficult to establish. Articles are generally unsigned, and in some newspapers no editor is named in print. Even where names are known, few were famous even in their own day.

It is also difficult to map the circulation and readership of these papers. All but one were published in London and, while distribution was by no means restricted to the capital, the lack of attempts to found regionally based titles, despite the existence of sizeable German communities in some northern English cities, suggests that there was not a large demand in the country as a whole for a home-grown German press. There is little evidence of readership in the published memoirs, letters and accounts of Germans living in or visiting Britain at the time.

While any detailed comparison with the nineteenth-century German press in the USA is beyond the scope of this chapter, some key contrasts deserve mention. German-American newspapers of the period were far more numerous, generally survived longer, and were more widely read and influential.[2] This reflects the far greater number of German immigrants in the USA,[3] their wider geographical distribution, including large rural populations, and their status as one of the largest and most prominent communities in a country significantly shaped by European immigration during the period. While Germans formed a large immigrant community in Britain, their press remained far smaller and never achieved anything approaching mainstream circulation or influence, raising questions about the role and self-image of the German community in Britain and its reach into wider society.

The first Anglo-German newspaper was the weekly *Der Treue Verkündiger* (The Faithful Messenger), printed by Johann Benjamin Vogel (d. 1832) and Gottfried Schulze (1772–1828),[4] which ran from January 1810 to June 1811, continuing as a fortnightly magazine, *Der Verkündiger*, until 1814. This was not a community-focused venture but a propaganda vehicle against Napoleonic rule in German-speaking territories. It has been suggested that the paper received financial support from the British government for this purpose.[5] Certainly a German newspaper of 1810 describes *Der Treue Verkündiger* as 'ganz im Sinne der Regierung geschrieben' ('written wholly in the spirit of the [British] government'),[6] and it is telling that its monthly successor ceased publication after Napoleon's first exile in 1814, and that the announcement of closure in the final issue explicitly attributes this to changed political circumstances on the continent.[7]

The next London German newspaper seems to have made a more genuine attempt to reach Germans in Britain. The *Londoner deutsches Wochenblatt* (London German Weekly) was launched in November 1819. Its editor, Karl Rakenius (c. 1778–1858),[8] was ambitious enough to write to Johann Wolfgang von Goethe in September of that year asking for a poem to christen the new venture, although he received no reply.[9] Nor was his initial optimism repaid with commercial success: the *Wochenblatt* closed after eight issues. There is no record of another German-language newspaper in Britain until 1841, when nine issues of *Die deutsche Presse* (The German Press) appeared.

The later 1840s and the 1850s, however, saw a rise in Anglo-German press ventures. It is no accident that this coincided with one of the peak periods of nineteenth-century German immigration and the arrival of exiled liberal writers and thinkers after the revolutions of 1848–9.[10] Most of the papers founded between 1845 and 1859 had some connection with liberal and radical exiles and their politics. The earliest of these was the *Deutsche Londoner Zeitung* (German London News), founded in 1845 and bought in 1847 by the former Duke Karl of Brunswick (1804–73),[11] who clearly saw no contradiction between his liberal politics and his desire to regain his hereditary dukedom. He hoped to use the paper as a means of promoting his cause and was willing to work with republican groups to this end, even establishing links with the

Communist League, founded in London as an international radical political party in 1847. Between March and July 1848, the *Deutsche Londoner Zeitung* serialized the Communist Manifesto, written for the League by Karl Marx and Friedrich Engels.

The Communists also had their own plans, although these enjoyed little success: a *Kommunistische Zeitschrift* (Communist Journal) did not go beyond a trial issue in 1847.[12] Six issues of Marx's *Neue Rheinische Zeitung* (New Rhenish News) bore a London imprint in 1850, although they were printed in Hamburg. This was presumably an attempt to escape German censorship restrictions, and in fact Marx could justly claim that the paper was edited from London as he had moved there permanently in June 1849 having been expelled from both Belgium and France and barred from returning to Germany.

Another group of radical exiles brought out *Der Kosmos* (The Cosmos), which lasted for only three issues in 1851.[13] An anonymous article about the German community in London published in 1855 in the popular German magazine *Der Gartenlaube* (The Bower)[14] mentions four other German newspapers which do not appear to survive: a German edition of the *Illustrated London News* edited by one Pokorny, *Der Telegraph* (The Telegraph) edited by a Professor Bartholdi (who, the author states, was not a professor but 'a swindler from Leipzig'), the bilingual English and German *The Confederate*, edited by Johannes Ronge (1813–87),[15] and the humorous weekly *How Do You Do* (despite its English title apparently a purely German-language publication), published by the tavern-owner and satirist Louis Drucker (c. 1801– c. 1860).[16]

Another title mentioned in the *Gartenlaube* article, the *Londoner deutsches Journal* (London German Journal), was more successful, running from August 1855 until mid-June 1858. Its first issue stated that it would be politically non-partisan, although it did in fact have a progressive liberal slant and was critical of the growing power of the Prussian state. In 1858, it began to take a more radical stance under the editorship of socialist journalist Bernhard Becker (1826–82), who sought to re-orient it towards a more working-class audience. However, Becker was soon dismissed, and the paper was relaunched in late June 1858 as the *Londoner deutsche Zeitung und allgemeiner Anzeiger* (London German News and General Advertiser), turning away from left-wing politics. In April 1859 it was renamed *Germania*, but ceased publication for good after five issues.

The years 1858–9 saw the foundation of other new titles, including what was to become the most successful German newspaper in London. This was *Hermann*, founded in 1859 by the prominent political émigré Gottfried Kinkel (1815–82), which survived until 1914 under the later title *Londoner Zeitung: Hermann* (London News: Hermann). *Hermann* owed its initial success in large part to Kinkel's respected position in the exile community and beyond. A former professor and established poet, he was seen as a revolutionary martyr following his imprisonment for armed insurrection in 1849, and as a hero for his dramatic escape the following year. To both German and British audiences, he was perhaps the most familiar of the German revolutionary exiles in Britain (far better known than Marx at the time). His name would have been for readers a guarantee both of the paper's liberal credentials and of its literary quality. In his early years in London, Kinkel had been associated with the Communist League, and toured America in the early 1850s to raise money for a revolutionary fighting fund. As one of the founders of *Der Kosmos*, his first plans for a newspaper were framed very much in the context of international revolutionary politics. However, by the time he founded *Hermann*, he was more concerned with the creation of a liberal and unified German state than with radical social change. He also believed strongly in the importance both of promoting German culture to British audiences and maintaining its importance in the lives of Germans living in Britain, and this was reflected in *Hermann*'s coverage of literature and the arts. By the end of 1859, *Hermann* allegedly had some 1,700 subscribers, and by 1866 it claimed a circulation of 3,000.[17] It even inspired a short-lived satirical rival, *Thusnelda*, in 1861.

More radical voices were behind *Die Neue Zeit* (The New Age), edited by Bernhard Becker, and its successor *Das Volk* (The People). The latter was, by the end of its run in August 1859, being effectively edited by Marx and funded by Friedrich Engels.[18] Although Engels had come to England as a political refugee in 1849, stable employment with his family's textile company enabled him to finance such projects such as *Das Volk*, but he could not save it from decline; under Marx's control both readership and profits fell, although Marx characteristically implied that this was the fault of readers not recognizing the quality of his work, claiming that 'as the paper improved, losses increased'.[19] Marx's correspondence is a fascinating and useful, if biased, source of information on the history of these papers and their shifting links to different radical groups and individuals in London. He is particularly vitriolic about Kinkel, whom he despised and accused, among other things, of deliberately sabotaging potential rivals to *Hermann*.[20] There was no doubt an element of truth in this, since eliminating competition to *Hermann* was certainly in Kinkel's interest.

The 1860s and 1870s saw further independent efforts: *Der Bote aus London* (The Messenger from London) ran to six issues in late 1860. The journalist Heinrich Dorgeel (pseudonym of Heinrich Geehl, c. 1843–1908), surveying the history of the London German press in 1881, refers to a *Deutsche Zeitung* (German News) published in 1864, which is not identifiable in any library catalogue.[21] In 1869, under new editorship and with Prussian government funding, *Hermann* had become politically a mouthpiece for the Prussian state.[22] In reaction to this shift, the *Londoner deutsche Post* (London German Post) was established in January 1870 with a more liberal agenda. However, on the outbreak of war between France and Prussia in July 1870, the *Post* also became an advocate of the Prussian cause and remained so until it ceased publication in 1871.

In the years after the unification of Germany under Prussian leadership, Anglo-German newspapers tended to reflect the self-confidence and national awareness of the new state, and to defend German interests against growing anti-German sentiment abroad. The patriotically titled *Das Vaterland* (Fatherland), which lasted for seven issues in 1876, claimed that its political tendency would be 'thoroughly liberal', but also in sympathy with Germany's new role as a nation state.[23]

The 1880s saw another rise in new Anglo-German newspapers, coinciding with another peak in German immigration to Britain, again including left-wing radicals oppressed by German anti-socialist laws from 1878 onwards.[24] An early example of this new radical press was *Freiheit* (Freedom), founded in London in 1879 by Johann Most (1846–1906). A former Social Democratic Party representative in the German Parliament, jailed for his support of the Paris Commune and for blasphemy, Most had sought refuge in London and quickly became active in radical circles there. Although British press laws were more tolerant than those of Germany, Most's celebration in *Freiheit* of the assassination of Tsar Alexander II of Russia in 1881 earned him a jail sentence. On his release the following year he moved to New York, taking *Freiheit* with him. The paper's masthead continued to bear the imprint 'London und New York', and to be read in London; in 1885 the Prussian police estimated that of 5,000 copies printed, 4,500 were circulated in Europe.[25] Josef Peukert (1855–1910), a former ally turned adversary of Most, established *Der Rebell* (The Rebel) in 1881 and *Die Autonomie* (Autonomy) in 1886 specifically to oppose *Freiheit*. *Der Rebell* appeared irregularly and in small print runs, moving between London and Geneva, and had comparatively little impact, but *Die Autonomie* lasted until 1893 and had some success in decreasing Most's influence.

Other radical foundations of the time included a 'free social-political paper' *Die Glocke* (The Bell), which enjoyed a short run in 1881. In 1886, the Communistische Arbeiter-Bildungs-Verein (Communist Workers' Education Association)[26] founded the *Londoner Arbeiter-Zeitung* (London Workers' News); in 1887 an independent cooperative took over the paper, which continued as the *Londoner Freie Presse* (London Free Press) until 1891. The left-wing *Der Sozialdemokrat* (The Social Democrat) moved from Zürich to London in October 1888 to take advantage of more liberal British press laws, and survived until September 1890.

There were also more mainstream ventures during this period. The *Londoner Journal* (London Journal) was founded in 1878 with the involvement of Heinrich Dorgeel. In 1884, a sister paper, the *Londoner Courier* (London Courier) started to appear on Tuesdays. This was intended to complement the *Journal*, which appeared on Fridays, although in fact there was regular duplication of material between the two. In July 1884 the *Courier* was succeeded by the *Londoner deutsches Tageblatt* (London German Daily), the first attempt at a daily Anglo-German paper. This only survived for four months; there was clearly no market for a daily German newspaper, especially one competing with an established weekly from the same editors. The *Londoner Journal* continued alone until 1891. These titles were not overtly political, but were decidedly conservative in tone, and the *Tageblatt* even reported examples of hate mail received from anonymous radicals.

A longer-lived foundation of the 1880s was *Der Landstreicher* (The Vagabond), which changed title twice in its first four years (to *Figaro's Chronik* (Figaro's Chronicle) in January 1891 and *Londoner Figaro-Chronik* (London Figaro Chronicle) in June 1893, before becoming the *Londoner General-Anzeiger* (London General Advertiser) in May 1894. Under this title it continued until 1914, the second-longest run of any Anglo-German newspaper. Initially intended as a humorous weekly, it gradually expanded its remit as it changed its name, eventually becoming a straightforward purveyor of news. An article celebrating its silver jubilee in early 1914 presents this as a natural evolution based on the changing interests and developing ambitions of the editor,[27] but it is more likely that there was no market for the paper as initially conceived and that financial necessity and reader demand drove the changes.

By the early twentieth century, Britain's German community was reaching its height in terms both of numbers and of activity. Nine newspapers began publication between

1900 and 1911, including the bilingual German and French *Rutli* for Swiss immigrants, and the *Manchester Nachrichten* (Manchester News), the only German title published outside London, although its subtitle 'eine deutsche Zeitung in England' ('a German newspaper in England') made clear that its intended scope was national rather than regional. The *Anglo-German Friendship Gazette*, published in 1911, was an attempt to counter the increasingly anti-German feeling in British public discourse; tellingly, it did not survive beyond its first issue. Another phenomenon of this late period was the publication of papers by and for particular professional groups. Some were finance- or business-focused, such as *Reuters Finanz-Chronik* (1896–1912), and some were bi- or trilingual with English and French. At least two were aimed at workers in the hotel and catering trades, which represented one of the largest areas of employment for German immigrants.[28] The *London Hotel & Restaurant Gazette* even briefly issued a German-language supplement, the *Illustrirte Familien-Zeitung* (Illustrated Family Newspaper), obviously aimed at the families of German workers in this sector and possibly at a wider Anglo-German audience.

The outbreak of the First World War put an abrupt end to all German publishing activity in Britain. Under the Government's fourth Aliens Restriction Order (20 August 1914), German-language publications were required to obtain a licence from the Home Secretary in order to continue. Of the two surviving newspapers, *Hermann* was denied a licence and ceased on 22 August, but the *Londoner General-Anzeiger* was allowed to continue, bearing above its masthead the words 'Permission for publication granted by the Home Secretary under the Alien Order (No.4) 1914'. Despite genuine fears of an 'enemy within' spreading anti-British propaganda or coded messages through their press, in the early weeks of the war a licensed German newspaper was a potentially useful tool to inform Germans in Britain of things that would affect their status, such as closures of institutions, the need to register with the police, and other restrictions brought in by the Aliens Registration Act of 5 August 1914 and subsequent Restriction Orders. However, in the febrile anti-German climate of the time, the Home Office came under pressure to revoke the *General-Anzeiger*'s licence, and it ceased publication on 16 September 1914. German civilian internees and, later, prisoners of war, would create a lively culture of camp newspapers in the course of the war[29] but, despite the post-war survival of a very few German institutions and the continued presence in Britain of citizens with a German background, a formally published German press in Britain would not re-emerge until the arrival of new political exiles from Nazi Germany in the 1930s.[30]

Connecting beyond the German-language readership in Britain: transcultural and translocal perspectives

In his study of the German-language press in America, Historian Carl Wittke describes immigrant press ventures as a means both of maintaining cultural ties with the old country and of introducing immigrants to their new home through the medium of their own language.[31] Looking back over nearly a century of attempts to create a

German press in London, we can see these ambitions reflected, and how the growth of German social and cultural institutions in Britain gave the papers a particular role as mouthpieces for a British-German community, while also looking beyond Germans in Britain.

In 1810, *Der Treue Verkündiger* had little to report from the community angle. This was largely because of its basic propagandist objective, but it is also true that the network of institutions for Germans in Britain that developed later in the century scarcely existed in its first two decades. The closest things to community institutions were German churches, but even those are never mentioned by the paper. Although *Der Treue Verkündiger* might have been a welcome source of information in their native language for some Germans in Britain, its mixture of British and international news, and somewhat eclectic coverage of literature and culture, has little to suggest deliberate outreach to a specific and self-identifying immigrant community.

In its first issue, *Der Treue Verkündiger* emphasizes the unique freedom of the British press.[32] Although this is part of its propagandist agenda, the importance of British press freedom is a factor repeated in other ventures and suggests that many editors and writers, especially in the first six decades of the century, remained as interested in reaching an audience back in Germany as in speaking to compatriots in Britain. This was particularly the case with the papers founded by political exiles in the 1840s and 1850s. In its first issue the *Deutsche Londoner Zeitung* explicitly states that 'eine in London erscheinende deutsche Zeitung nicht nur von den im Auslande lebenden Deutschen sondern auch in unserem Vaterlande selbst als eine erwünschte, einem dringenden Bedürfnisse erfüllende abhelfende Erscheinung begrüßt werden wird.'[33] The editors both solicited and received contributions from liberals in Germany as well as from émigrés in other countries. Its first editor, David Cahn,[34] expressed the hope that the paper would be 'die gelesenste und gefürchtestste aller deutschen Zeitungen' ('the most read and most feared of all German newspapers').[35] It was indeed officially banned in the states of the German Federation, and received a degree of publicity through attacks on it in the German press. The prospectus for *Der Kosmos* positions Germans in London as standing between continental Europe and America, and thus being best placed to maintain communication between exiles across the Atlantic and radicals still in Europe.[36] However, although there were close personal and institutional links between German political émigrés in Britain and the USA, it is unclear to what extent the Anglo-German press reached or influenced Germans in America, or vice versa, during this period.

A particular case in the context of Anglo-German political relations is the *Londoner Correspondenz* (London Correspondence), a daily digest of British news, reproduced by a lithographic process from handwriting. It was founded in 1850 by Max Schlesinger (1822–81), a journalist who settled in London after the failure of the Viennese revolution of 1848. Schlesinger worked as foreign correspondent for two major German newspapers, and produced the *Correspondenz* as an information sheet for smaller German papers that could not afford their own permanent London correspondent.[37] Although not strictly a newspaper, it was an interesting offshoot of Anglo-German relations in the press, and probably had more influence on German perceptions of Britain than any actual Anglo-German newspaper. The Prussian government felt threatened enough by its perceived anti-Prussian bias to set up a rival service. The future novelist Theodor Fontane (1819–98) was sent to London to carry out this plan but failed to win subscribers away from Schlesinger's established product; his *Deutsch-Englische Korrespondenz* (German-English Correspondence) lasted less than four months.[38]

'What is the role of a German Newspaper in London?': freedom of the press, free-mindedness and fact-checking

In an editorial heralding its third year, the *Londoner deutsches Journal* sets out some justifications for a German newspaper in England. The ability to discuss without censorship the political conditions in Germany is one of these, but, somewhat unusually for this period, it comes second to the perceived desire for a link to Germany and its language and culture to bring an echo of home to the immigrant. The editor makes the somewhat overwrought claim that poor German workers have told him they buy the paper from their meagre wages to bring news in German to their wives, who feel isolated and unhappy in London.[39] Back in 1855 the paper's opening editorial had also emphasized the potential usefulness of a locally published German-language newspaper for London German associations, and expressed the hope that it might be 'eine beschiedene Schildwache für deutsche Interessen in London' ('a modest sentinel for German interests in London').[40] True to its word, it covers and celebrates a range of German activities and institutions in London, including, unusually among nineteenth-century Anglo-German newspapers, those of the German Jewish community.[41]

Unlike many papers, *Hermann* carried no statement of editorial intent in its first issue, but in issue twelve, Kinkel set out his reasons for founding the paper in an open letter. Again, the ability of the British press to print what cannot be printed in Germany is emphasized, and readers in Germany as well as Britain are mentioned as a potential audience.[42] This ambition can be said to have succeeded insofar as *Hermann*, like the *Deutsche Londoner Zeitung*, was considered subversive and far-reaching enough to be banned in some German states in the early 1860s. In a later article, 'Was soll eine deutsche Zeitung in London?' ('What is the role of a German Newspaper in London?'), Kinkel celebrates the fact that the paper has had some success in Germany and mentions offers of articles from authors in Germany wishing to have an opportunity 'die wirklichen Zustände im Vaterlande treuer und schärfer zu beleuchten als irgend ein Blatt drüben es jetzt zu thun wagt' ('to throw a truer and sharper light on the real conditions in our fatherland than any paper there now dares to do').[43]

However, as the century progressed, the aspiration to reach an audience back in Germany with uncensored political news began to fade away, and papers began to look more towards the German community in Britain and to report on and encourage community activities and institutions. For the pragmatic newspaper editor churches, charities, and social, cultural or sporting associations had the potential to cut across political allegiances and attract a wider readership. Even the overtly radical papers *Die neue Zeit* and *Das Volk* mention not only political meetings, but also more social events, and a letter in the third issue of *Das Volk* laments the lack of a German gymnastic or shooting club in London. As well as its revolutionary aims, *Der Kosmos* promised to provide both cultural content and practical information for new immigrants.[44] An article in *Die Neue Zeit* in 1858 recognized that the majority of German immigrants were not political exiles but had come to Britain voluntarily in search of better-paid employment than they could find at home, and had no particular need or desire to agitate for political reform in Germany.[45] As such, they were as interested in their new home as their old one and, while they might enjoy social activities familiar from their native culture and shared with compatriots, they were less likely to consider themselves unofficial ambassadors for German culture as Kinkel hoped, or 'the embodiment of the real Germany'[46] in any political sense.

Beyond political exiles, German economic migrants: the German-language press in Britain and migrant integration

While David Cahn's introductory article in the first issue of the *Deutsche Londoner Zeitung* does not include any explicit mention of covering German life in London, a letter to the editors in the same issue describes the publication of a new German paper in London as a milestone for Germans in the city alongside the founding of a German club and a German hospital, proof that Germans in Britain are no longer mere economic migrants but are building a coherent community.[47] The number of Germans in London was a factor in Cahn's pitch to potential backers: he reckoned that there were 100,000 native German speakers in London, of whom at least 10 per cent would be interested in buying an uncensored newspaper in their native language.[48] This number was certainly an exaggeration, whether deliberate or not – the 1861 British Census listed 28,644 Germans in the whole of England and Wales, of whom 16,082 were resident in London[49] – but it showed an awareness of a sizeable immigrant community with potentially shared interests.

However, early attempts to reach that community still struggled and could be short-sighted in their view of the potential audience. Although early issues of *Das Volk* covered community institutions and activities, Christine Lattek describes the paper as 'distinctly parochial' in its narrow focus on East London's German community.[50] Newspapers published later in the century took an interest in the coverage of German community activities more for granted and embraced a wider range of Anglo-German activities. For example, as well as reports of German institutions and events in London, the *Londoner deutsches Tageblatt* in 1884 included an article about the German Church in Bradford, and listed the times of German church services in various cities. A note beneath the masthead in some later issues lists the London railway stations where the *Tageblatt* can be bought. Most are in or serve the east and south-east of London, popular areas for German immigrants to settle at the time. German newspapers and German community institutions existed in a symbiotic relationship: newspapers publicized and promoted institutions which then provided copy for the same newspapers' reports and reviews.

A more easily overlooked form of community engagement is advertising, which enabled businesses run by Germans or selling German-made products to reach out to potential customers, and Germans in London to seek employment or employees via personal advertisements. Advertising was also, of course, a source of much-needed revenue for publishers and editors. The *Londoner deutsche Zeitung* in 1859 regularly repeated David Cahn's exaggerated claim from a decade earlier about '100,000 Germans in London' in English on its masthead to appeal to paying advertisers. However, Theodor Fontane reported to the Prussian government in 1858 that the paper acquired part of its advertising revenue through a form of blackmail, requesting taverns frequented by Germans to advertise with them or become the subject of an unfavourable report.[51] Even if this was an extreme measure (or an exaggeration by Fontane), most newspapers tended to build their advertising sections slowly and with difficulty. Despite its connection with the pre-existing *Londoner Journal*, the *Londoner Courier* initially carried few advertisements, the only regular one being for the printing firm of its editor Johann Lachmann von Gamsenfels (1851–89). However, by its sixth month advertisements were taking up three of the four columns on the back page. (The fact that one is repeatedly printed upside down suggests that the type was not reset between issues once advertisers had been secured.) The *Courier* also emphasized that its regular publication day of Tuesday made it the only German newspaper to publish advertisements and requests for lodgings, jobs or servants close to the beginning of the working week.

Early advertisers in many papers were booksellers, publishers and printers. This was in part because they had connections with the papers' production and distribution, but a desire to promote literature and culture was also important to the London German papers from the start. A few brief announcements of new books are among the closest things to advertisements found in *Der Treue Verkündiger* which, despite its political agenda, featured some cultural content in all but a few issues, often in the form of serialized non-fiction works. Serializations remained popular – Gottfried Kinkel, for example, first published his late wife Johanna's autobiographical novel *Hans Ibeles in London* in *Hermann*. Later in the century, *Hermann* was one of various papers to publish illustrated supplements containing short stories or serialized novels, poetry, and sometimes pictures, puzzles, cartoons and riddles. Even the politically motivated *Londoner Freie Presse* published such a supplement during its last year, and the marketing of the *Londoner Journal* and its sister-papers emphasized this kind of content as much as their news coverage. Theatre criticism appeared early on, with three issues of the *Londoner deutsches Wochenblatt* in 1820 devoting considerable space to the first English production of Friedrich Schiller's *Maria Stuart* and the reasons for its failure. Cultural coverage could also be used to support a paper's political agenda or criticize conditions in Germany. The *Deutsche Londoner Zeitung*'s long statement of intent in its first issue boasts that its book reviews will be independent, unlike the allegedly more tendentious 'reviewers' nonsense' typical of the German press,[52] while *Die Neue Zeit*, reviewing an amateur German theatre production in London, claims that, as with the free press, only London has a truly free theatre.[53] Although German arts and literature were of particular interest to the Anglo-German press, cultural coverage was not restricted to these. Translated novels were serialized in several papers, and there are examples of advertisements for books and newspapers produced by other immigrant communities.

Struggling to retain readers over the long term: resisting or embracing Anglicization?

For all their efforts, London German newspapers often struggled to reach and retain their intended audience, as evidenced by the short duration of so many titles. Although the German community in Britain was comparatively large, it could not support a wide-ranging press, and the success of a very few titles made it even harder for new ventures to succeed. In an article published in *The Northern Whig* in 1882, German-born writer Helen Zimmern (1846–1934) describes 'four principal as well as several minor German newspapers ... published weekly in London', but continues:

> We fear it can hardly be said that the colony supports these, and it is questioned whether the account-books of these papers would show a satisfactory balance. Moreover, it is calculated that about 12,500 journals arrive daily by post from the Fatherland, of which, no doubt, the largest proportion are absorbed by the resident Germans, thus keeping them mentally linked with their country.[54]

As well as buying German newspapers from Germany, many Germans who settled in Britain for the long term simply bought British ones as they and their British-born and -educated children assimilated into British society. As Carl Wittke points out, 'the foreign-language press does not keep its monopoly over the minds of its immigrant readers very long',[55] especially once the second generation starts to grow up. Second-generation Germans in Britain, even if they retained an interest in or attachment to German language or culture, would not necessarily have felt a need for a German-language newspaper, especially one printed outside Germany itself.

If the German community in Britain was hard to reach, there is evidence of other potential audiences for German-language newspapers. Lists of the sights of London and details of German churches both in and outside the capital published in some papers suggest that not only settled immigrants, who would presumably be familiar with these things, but also German visitors to Britain were a potential target.[56] However, tourists alone would not have been sufficient to give major support to a paper, and it is impossible to ascertain whether they read the papers in any numbers. Outside of a few specific studies of London's German community, Germans writing about Britain in the nineteenth century generally show no interest in the Anglo-German press. Theodor Fontane's 1860 collection of essays *Aus England*, based on his stay in London in the 1850s, does not list any German (or indeed any other foreign-language) titles in a long section on the British press.[57] Likewise Max Schlesinger, editor of the *Londoner Correspondenz*, makes no mention of foreign-language titles in a similar survey in his *Wanderungen durch London*.[58] Both men were certainly aware of the London German press, but did not bother even to mention its existence.

A more significant audience comprised learners and non-native speakers of German. The appeal of a newspaper to language learners as a cheap and regular way to acquire foreign reading matter is obvious, and more advanced students and Germanophones no doubt found the newspapers a welcome source of information on

German politics and culture. While it is unlikely that any paper was founded with such an audience uppermost in the editor's mind, the fact that some new German newspaper ventures were announced and advertised in the English-language press implies an awareness of potential interest among British readers and a desire to act as a form of intermediary between immigrants and the host country. *Die deutsche Presse* of 1841 was even reviewed in the London newspaper *The Atlas*, which described the paper's appearance as 'an event of some interest in the literary world' because of the growth in the study of German in Britain.[59] The statement of intent in the first issue of the *Deutsche Londoner Zeitung* in 1845 specifies that its literary coverage will pay particular attention to material from journals readily available in Germany but less familiar in Britain.[60] This chimes with the desire of editors like Kinkel to promote German culture among the British, and seems to have succeeded to a large extent. In 1857, the editor of the *Londoner deutsches Journal* claimed that two-thirds of the paper's support came from English readers,[61] and an advertisement (in English) in the London *Times* of 16 June 1857 describes the *Journal* as 'highly to be recommended to students of German'. Almost two decades later, a German-language teacher writing to *Das Vaterland* praises the paper's use of a roman rather than German typeface precisely because it makes the paper easier to read for foreign learners of German.[62] After the outbreak of the Franco-Prussian War in July 1870, the *Londoner deutsche Post* began to publish regular pieces in English arguing for the Prussian side. For there to be any logic in doing this, the editor must have been aware of the paper's potential to find its way into native English-speaking circles.

Even with potential readers outside the German community, the difficulty of finding and retaining a paying audience was the primary reason for the failure of most Anglo-German newspaper ventures. Several mention the lack of income as a threat to survival, such as *Die Neue Zeit* of 9 April 1859, which begins with an emotional appeal for financial support if the paper is to survive for another week. Although a brief note on 16 April claims that the paper has been rescued from 'the brink of the grave',[63] the support received was clearly too little and too late as this was the final issue. A brief editorial published in *Der Treue Verkündiger* as it moved into its second year explained that because of the small number of subscribers, 'jeder Gedanke von Gewinn wegfallen muß' ('any thought of profit must be set aside').[64] The same piece also mentions other difficulties, notably that of printing and spelling errors caused by a lack of typesetters in London familiar with the German language and Fraktur type. These problems would remain a constant for all German publishing ventures in London, but were a particular issue for newspaper editors who were constrained by regular deadlines and, unlike book publishers, did not have the option of sending copy for printing abroad. The editor of the *Londoner deutsche Post* felt obliged in its second issue to apologize for the many printing errors in its first, which he blamed on the extra effort required to prepare the paper for publication on New Year's Day.[65]

In a somewhat rueful note in its closing issue the editor of the *Londoner deutsches Tageblatt* describes the experience of publishing a German newspaper abroad as 'unliebsam...im großen Ganzen' ('disagreeable...on the whole').[66] Others in the same position would no doubt have agreed with him, given the financial and practical difficulties of the task, yet many made the attempt, even if they lacked the capital or copy to look far beyond their first issue. Like the newspapers published by immigrant communities around the world, the Anglo-German press of the nineteenth century attests to the continued vitality of a society of immigrants, despite their difficult circumstances, committed to serving the nation even beyond its national borders. These newspapers also provide evidence of the formation and development of a community in a foreign cultural sphere through political and literary activities, and shed interesting light on the real and perceived interests and priorities of German immigrants to Britain and the shifting currents of Anglo-German cultural and political relations in the period, not only in their content but in the very history of their publication.

Setting aside the earliest attempts, from the 1840s onwards there is a pattern of politically motivated ventures giving way to a focus on German community interests. Outreach to audiences back in Germany and political émigrés in other countries had some limited success, but overseas sales could not sustain any paper for long, and a paper pushing a narrow political agenda would never reach more than a limited audience of supporters, most already committed to the cause. The fact that a community focus was key to survival is exemplified by the fates of *Das Volk* and *Hermann* in 1859. While *Das Volk* lost readers by replacing material of general and community interest with more ideologically focused content, *Hermann* made direct appeals to Germans in Britain as a group, and shrewdly foregrounded the mass celebrations by Germans in London and other British cities of Friedrich Schiller's centenary that year, which transcended political allegiances, and to some extent social divisions, and offered German immigrants a chance to show public pride in their culture and identity. While *Das Volk* failed, *Hermann* survived.

Nonetheless, the lack of a lasting rival to *Hermann* until the late 1880s is a reminder that Germans, although one of the largest immigrant groups in Britain, did not necessarily identify as a single group with sufficient shared interests or views, or enough strength, cohesion or political influence to sustain a varied press. The development towards the end of the period of papers aimed at specific groups of workers or particular nationalities suggests that, as the community grew larger, individual interest groups began to take precedence over any general sense of Germanness.

In terms of wider reach, although some papers overtly sought an audience of non-native speakers in Britain, and most probably had some British readership, they never exercised a major influence in the national discourse; the majority of British readers would have been primarily interested in culture, literature and general information about Germany, and in practising their own German reading skills. Nonetheless, some may also have wanted insights into the doings of a foreign community and into German views of Britain, especially as the relationship between the two countries deteriorated in the decades before 1914.

Despite its small scale and comparative lack of influence, the Anglo-German press of the nineteenth century is an invaluable source for research into Britain's German community of the period, reflecting, like any immigrant press, the development, activities and interests of a community, and that community's interactions – cultural, political, commercial and social – with its host nation.

Notes

1. Panikos Panayi, *German Immigrants in Britain during the Nineteenth Century, 1815–1914* (Oxford: Berg, 1995), 91.
2. The US National Endowment for the Humanities 'Chronicling America' project states that 'in the 1880s the 800 German-language newspapers accounted for about 4/5 of non-English publications, and by 1890, more than 1,000 German newspapers were being published in the United States'. https://www.neh.gov/divisions/preservation/featured-project/chronicling-americas-historic-german-newspapers-and-the-grow (retrieved 28 November 2020).
3. In 1900 the German population of New York alone was larger than the entire German population of Britain at its height.
4. On Vogel and Schulze and their partnership see Graham Jefcoate, *Deutsche Drucker und Buchhändler in London, 1680–1811: Strukturen und Bedeutung des Deutschen Anteils am englischen Buchhandel*. Archiv für Geschichte des Buchwesens. Studien; Band 12 (Berlin: de Gruyter, 2015), 379–99.
5. Ibid., 394–5.
6. 'England', *Baierische National-Zeitung*, no. 143, 19 June 1810, 575.
7. Untitled announcement, *Der Verkündiger*, no. LXXII, 30 June 1814, 321.
8. Rakenius (1777–1858) was born near Braunschweig. How long he lived in London is unknown, but by 1838 he had settled in Hamburg.
9. Regestenausgabe 'Briefe an Goethe', Klassik Stiftung Weimar, Goethe- und Schiller-Archiv, Online, Nr. 8/1031: https://ores.klassik-stiftung.de/ords/f?p=403:2:::::P2_ID:12466 (retrieved 28 November 2020).
10. Christine Lattek, *Revolutionary Refugees: German Socialism in Britain, 1840–1860* (London: Routledge, 2006), gives a thorough account of the individuals and groups in the radical socialist milieu of 1840s and 50s London and their various schisms. This is particular area where comparison with the USA is interesting. The papers founded by American 'forty-eighters' were more successful, and the exiles involved tended to be (or became in their new homeland) better-known figures.
11. Karl was deposed in 1830 following protests against his rule, and his close ties to the ruling British House of Hanover made Britain a logical destination for his exile, although he later spent time in Paris and Madrid.
12. Reprinted in *Die Londoner 'Kommunistische Zeitschrift' und andere Urkunden aus den Jahren 1847/1848, mit einer einleitenden Abhandlung über 'Die Entstehungsgeschichte des Kommunistischen* Manifests', ed. Carl Grünberg. Hauptwerke des Sozialismus und die Sozialpolitik; neue Folge, Bd. 5 (Leipzig: Hirschfeld, 1921), 35–81.
13. Julius H. Schoeps, '*Der Kosmos*: ein Wochenblatt der bürgerlich-demokratischen Emigration in London im Frühjahr 1851', *Jahrbuch des Instituts für Deutsche Geschichte* [Tel Aviv], Bd. 5 (1976), 212–26.
14. 'Wanderung durch Deutschland in London', *Die Gartenlaube*, Heft 34, 1855, 449–51. *Die Gartenlaube* (Leipzig and Berlin, 1853–1944) was one of the earliest mass-circulation magazines aimed at a middle-class family audience, and was influential in promoting ideas of German national identity. Articles on German emigrant communities were a frequent feature: see Kirsten Belgum, *Popularizing the Nation: Audience, Representation and the Production of Identity in* Die Gartenlaube *1853–1900* (Lincoln: University of Nebraska Press, 1998) 49–54.
15. Ronge, a priest, writer and educator, fled to Britain after the revolutions of 1848, and lived in London, Manchester and Leeds before returning his native Silesia (then part of Prussia) under an amnesty in 1861.

16 For the comparatively few details known about Drucker see Hans-Jürgen Paech, *Zum Leben und Wirken des vergnügten Weinhändlers Louis Drucker* (Potsdam, 2016) https://opus4.kobv.de/opus4-slbp/files/9338/Paech_2016_04_Drucker.pdf (retrieved 25 November 2020).
17 Christine Lattek, *Revolutionary Refugees*, 194.
18 Ibid., 204–6.
19 Ibid., 206.
20 Letter from Marx to Engels, 18 May 1859, Marx/Engels, *Collected Works*, volume 40, Letters 1856–9, 437–9. Online at http://www.hekmatist.com/Marx%20Engles/Marx%20&%20Engels%20Collected%20Works%20Volume%2040_%20Ka%20-%20Karl%20Marx.pdf (retrieved 25 November 2020).
21 Heinrich Dorgeel, *Die deutsche Colonie in London* (London: August Siegle, 1881), 87.
22 This change had an adverse effect on circulation, and after a decade *Hermann* returned to its older moderate liberal stance.
23 'Unser Programm', *Das Vaterland*, 25 March 1876, 1.
24 For a detailed survey of the Socialist and Anarchist groups and their newspapers of this period see Daniel Laqua, 'Political Contestation and Internal Strife: Socialist and Anarchist Newspapers in London, 1878–1910', in *The Foreign Political Press in Nineteenth-Century London: Politics from a Distance*, ed. Constance Bantman and Ana Cláudia Suriani da Silva (London: Bloomsbury Academic, 2019), 135–54.
25 Ibid., 136.
26 A long-established radical group, founded in the early 1840s as the Deutsche Arbeiterbildungsverein (German Workers' Educational Association).
27 '25 Jahre Londoner General-Anzeiger', *Londoner General-Anzeiger*, 3 January 1914, 1.
28 See Panikos Panayi and Stefan Manz, *The Rise and Fall of Germans in the British Hospitality Industry, c1880–1920* https://publications.aston.ac.uk/id/eprint/27202/1/Germans_in_the_British_hospitality_industry.pdf (retrieved 25 November 2020).
29 For a full list, see Rainer Pöppinghege, *Im Lager unbesiegt: deutsche, englische und französische Kriegsgefangenen-Zeitungen im Ersten Weltkrieg* (Essen: Klartext, 2006), 319–21. A well-documented example is *Die Stobsiade*, produced at Stobs Camp in the Scottish Borders (later moved to Knockaloe, Isle of Man), available in full transcription at http://www.stobsiade.org/index.html (retrieved 28 November 2020).
30 Although it could also be applied to the political nineteenth-century Anglo-German papers, the German term 'Exilpresse' ('Exile Press') tends to be reserved for this later anti-Nazi press.
31 Carl Wittke, *The German-Language Press in America* (Lexington: University of Kentucky Press, 1957), 3–6.
32 Untitled editorial, *Der Treue Verkündiger*, 2 January 1810, 1.
33 'A German newspaper appearing in London will be welcomed not only by Germans living abroad but also in our Fatherland itself as a longed-for phenomenon, helping to fulfil an urgent need.' 'An die Leser', *Deutsche Londoner Zeitung*, 4 April 1845, 1.
34 Presumably the David Cahn (1811–64) listed in the 1861 British census as a 'Stationer and Printer', a naturalized British subject born in Germany.
35 Quoted in Tibor Dénes, 'Lehr- und Wanderjahre eines jungen Schweizers (1845–1848): Jakob Lukas Schabelitz, Herzog Karl II von Braunschweig und die *Deutsche Londoner Zeitung*', *Schweizerische Zeitschrift für Geschichte = Revue suisse d'histoire = Rivista storica svizzera* 16 (1966): 55.
36 *Der Kosmos – Deutsche Zeitung aus London*, 10 April 1851, signed by Ernst Haug, Gottfried Kinkel, Johannes Ronge and Arnold Ruge, Gottfried Kinkel papers,

University of Bonn https://digitale-sammlungen.ulb.uni-bonn.de/ulbbnhans/content/pageview/4545771 (retrieved 28 November 2010).
37 Rudolf Muhs, 'Max Schlesinger und Jakob Kaufmann: Gegenspieler und Freunde Fontanes' in *Exilanten und andere Deutsche in Fontanes London*, ed. Peter Alter and Rudolf Muhs. Stuttgarter Arbeiten zur Germanistik; Bd. 331 (Stuttgart: Hans-Dieter Heinz, 1996), 305.
38 Ibid., 314.
39 'An unsere Leser', *Londoner deutsches Journal*, no. 74, 27 December 1857, 1.
40 'An unsere Leser', ibid., 4 August 1855, 1.
41 Lattek, *Revolutionary Refugees*, 163–4.
42 'Brief des Herausgebers an einen Freund in Amerika', *Hermann*, 26 March 1859, 2–3. The article's title suggests that an American readership for *Hermann* was at least an aspiration.
43 'Was soll eine deutsche Zeitung in London?', *Hermann*, 26 November 1859, 1.
44 Prospectus for *Der Kosmos*, 1851 (see note 36).
45 'Die Aufgabe eines deutschen Blattes in London', *Die Neue Zeit*, 24 July 1858, quoted in Rudolf Muhs, 'Theodor Fontane und die Londoner deutsche Presse', *Jahrbuch der Deutschen Schillergesellschaft* 45 (2000), 55.
46 *Londoner deutsches Journal*, 15 November 1856, quoted in Lattek, *Revolutionary Refugees*, 188.
47 Letter from Dr Sutro, *Deutsche Londoner Zeitung*, 4 April 1845, 7.
48 Dénes, 'Lehr- und Wanderjahre', 54.
49 Panayi, *German Immigrants*, 92.
50 Lattek, *Revolutionary Refugees*, 206.
51 Letter from Fontane to Ludwig Metzel, 13 October 1858, quoted in Rudolf Muhs, 'Theodor Fontane und die Londoner deutsche Presse', 50.
52 'An die Leser', *Deutsche Londoner Zeitung*, 4 April 1845, 1.
53 *Die Neue Zeit*, 12 March 1859, 3.
54 Helen Zimmern, 'The German Colony in London', *The Northern Whig*, 11 April 1882, 8.
55 Wittke, *German-Language Press*, 4.
56 This information would of course have been of use to new immigrants, but only for a short time before they became familiar with their new home, although it might have been a means of winning regular readers among new arrivals.
57 Theodor Fontane, *Aus England: Studien und Briefe über Londoner Theater, Kunst und Presse* (Stuttgart: Ebner & Seubert, 1860), 245–325.
58 Max Schlesinger, *Wanderungen durch London*, vol. 2 (Berlin: Franz Duncker, 1853), 252–314.
59 'Die Deutsche Presse', *The Atlas*, 31 July 1841, 496.
60 'An die Leser', *Deutsche Londoner Zeitung*, 4 April 1845, 1.
61 'In Sachen des Londoner deutschen Journales', *Londoner deutsches Journal*, 7 November 1857, 2.
62 Letter from Conrad Führer, *Das Vaterland*, 6 May 1876, 3.
63 A. Scherzer, 'An unsere Leser', *Die Neue Zeit*, 16 April 1859, 1.
64 'An unsre Leser', *Der Treue Verkündiger*, 1 January 1811, 1.
65 'Zur Neujahrs-Nummer', *Londoner deutsche Post*, 8 January 1870, 1.
66 'An Freund und Feind', Londoner deutsches Tageblatt', 8 October 1884, 1.

6

The Soul of the Colony: Origins and Cultural Imaginary of the Portuguese-Language Press in the United States (1877–2019)[1]

Alberto Pena-Rodríguez
University of Vigo

The American ethnic press in a foreign-language is a phenomenon taking place among immigrant communities established throughout history in the United States.[2] Those immigrants, originating from different parts of the world, created a truly unique journalistic ecosystem, producing written communication media in dozens of different languages.[3] Their informative goal was to satisfy their readers by conveying news, and to connect them spiritually and culturally through a shared imaginary.[4] Simultaneously, this press supported the business goals of their creators, immigrants searching for the American dream through journalism. In a mosaic of colonies from diverse origins and established in different places, the first newspapers in Portuguese appeared by the late nineteenth century.[5]

The Portuguese-language ethnic press in the United States emerged in 1877, with the foundation of the weekly newspaper *O Jornal de Notícias* (News Journal) in Erie (Pennsylvania). This newspaper was edited by the typographer João Maria Vicente, whose son took the newspaper business to San Francisco, California, where he moved to establish the weekly newspapers *O Progresso Californiense* (The Californian Progress, 1885) and *A União Portugueza* (The Portuguese Union, 1887).[6] Between 1880 and 1930, there was a massive surge of Portuguese immigrants in United States ports. According to the *Yearbook of Immigration Statistics* (2012),[7] 233,532 Portuguese arrived in the country during that period. The edition of newspapers in Portuguese extended to several States, especially Massachusetts, California and Hawaii, which were the main destinations of Portuguese emigrants by the end of the nineteenth century.[8] In Massachusetts or California, Portuguese immigrants thrived in the whaling industry,[9] textiles, agriculture or livestock.[10] The Portuguese arriving in Hawaii since 1870 mainly worked in sugarcane plantations.[11] Between 1880 and 1927, they published up to twelve newspapers, including *O Luso-Hawaiano* (The Luso-Hawaiian, 1885–90), *Aurora Hawaiana* (Hawaiian Aurora, 1888–91), *A União Lusitana-Hawaiana* (The Lusitanian Hawaiian Union, 1891–6) or *O Facho* (The Mogul, 1906–27). The latter was the last newspaper published in Portuguese in Hawaii.[12]

The massive influx of immigrants into the United States drove the emergence of Portuguese journalism, a phenomenon that would be consolidated as the years went on. The population dispersion of Portuguese immigrants led to the progressive appearance of new newspapers in the states of Rhode Island, New York, New Jersey, Florida, Connecticut and Virginia. This developing expansion originated at least 167 periodical publications in Portuguese since 1877 until our days. Although many were short-lived (forty-three lasted less than a year), five of them lasted longer than half a century. Of those periodicals, 119 emerged in the period 1890–1929, especially in the early years, which corresponds to the most productive period in terms of the number of new newspapers and magazines founded, coinciding with the peak of Portuguese immigration to the United States. The cities concentrating the largest number of serials were New Bedford (MA), the epicentre of Portuguese immigration in New England, with thirty-eight, Oakland (CA) with sixteen, Newark (NJ) with fifteen, Fall River (MA) with twelve, and New York (NY) with eleven.[13]

To understand the dimension of Portuguese journalism in the context of the American ethnic press, it is necessary to analyse quantitative data.[14] Statistics published by different authors provide revealing information to comprehend the evolution of the non-English language press in the United States.[15] Around 1910, there were more than 1,100 non-English language newspapers, published in about thirty different languages, according to the *N.W. Ayer & Son's American newspaper annual and directory* (1909). Several hundred titles were in German, nearly ninety in Spanish, seventy-eight in Swedish and seventy-five in Italian.[16] Although this source does not provide detailed information about the Portuguese press, research for this contribution retrieved that at least eighteen newspapers were published in Portuguese in 1910. At that time, ethnic publications as a whole reached an estimated circulation of 2.6 million copies, and about 150 were daily papers.[17]

The phenomenon of the Portuguese-language press in the United States is directly related to the evolution of migratory flows. The appearance or disappearance of newspapers founded by Portuguese settlers there depended on migratory currents, on the arrival of new immigrants and economic and social changes affecting the Portuguese-American community, forcing many of the members to change residence to another city or state in the country.[18] Domestic migration within the American territory also affected newspapers, accounting for new headquarters or even new names.

According to the Observatory of Portuguese Emigration,[19] the flow of emigration from Portugal to the United States can be divided into five historical periods. The first took place during the latter part of the eighteenth century, from the Azores to New England; the second occurred in the second half of the nineteenth century, also from the Azores, with California as the main destination; the third happened at the turn of the twentieth century, and involved primarily the movement of families from Madeira to Hawaii; the fourth took place in the first decades of the twentieth century, when more than 147,000 Portuguese entered the United States; and the fifth and last was the great wave that occurred between 1960 and 1980, and comprised around 175,000 migrants. Since then, as data from the *Yearbook of Immigration Statistics 2012* suggests, there has been a considerable decline in migratory flows from Portugal.[20] The decline is a result of the adoption of restrictive policies by the United States and the entrance of Portugal into the European Union in 1986, which encouraged greater migration within Europe.

The push factors for their emigration to the United States were poverty, lack of ploughable land and, especially in the case of the Azores islands (where most of immigrants come from), overpopulation in the late nineteenth and early twentieth centuries or the eruption of the Capelinhos volcano in 1957.[21] The shipping companies also had an advertising role, trying to increase their business through publicity in the European press.[22] The ads promised all sorts of comforts and advantages. In the early 1900s, the competing Portuguese and American companies even promoted the sale of railroad tickets to reach the Western states.[23] In 1934, the Portuguese colony was estimated at 376,893 people, with about 150,000 residing in Massachusetts and Rhode Island, 20,000 in New York and surrounding areas, and 100,000 in California.[24] The Portuguese-American community currently totals 1.2 million, with more than half living in Massachusetts and California.[25]

The press in the diaspora has historically served to promote the Portuguese language and culture, while developing a role as an instrument of civic education. It also promoted and supported social cohesion, political consensus and associative projects. Through its press, the Portuguese-American community succeeded in creating a public opinion expressed in its own voice that resisted the dominant mainstream discourse in English. The dissemination and duration of some of these newspapers, as well as the dialogue they maintained with their readers, show that the immigrant press contributed significantly both to the development of a sense of belonging among the group and increased their visibility within the American social context by promoting Portuguese traditions and culture. More than this, editing serials in Portuguese in the USA had many consequences. This type of press facilitated a true sense of community among the members of each immigrant colony. It fostered economic and cultural revitalization, and increased political influence and participation. It also promoted the development of community projects and was an important agent towards education, orientation and social integration in the USA.[26]

This chapter analyses some of the most paradigmatic symbolic representations in the Portuguese American journalistic discourse. Within each community, a struggle for leadership was commonplace, and the press was the most effective means of promoting ideological positions. For the Portuguese press, issues such as republicanism vs monarchism or clericalism vs anti-clericalism, or the support of, or opposition to, certain policies in fraternal societies, were sources of controversy in the late nineteenth and much of the twentieth centuries. In some cases, ideological intolerance caused personal confrontations to assume a public dimension because of the amplifying effect of newspapers.[27] Over time, the latter helped shape long-lasting features in the cultural imaginary of Lusophone immigrants.

This chapter explores how the American press in Portuguese has both reflected and contributed to an epic narrative wrapped in a mythology of its own and cementing the community. In particular, this contribution will highlight how the Portuguese-language press is heavily influenced by cultural identity markers of the immigrants, and in particular of immigrants from the Azores and Madeira islands who have made up the bulk of the Portuguese emigration to the United States over the years. Though speaking to the Portuguese-language American reading community at large (including readers not from Portugal), the Portuguese-language press in the United States reflects a particular perception of reality.[28] Not incidentally, the close discursive analysis of the corpus also reveals its shaping role as Portuguese immigrants adapted to their new linguistic environment, even leading to the emergence of what is sometimes regarded as a Portuguese-North American dialect.

The methodology used in this approach is mainly qualitative, within a model of analysis integrated in the history of immigrant journalism and will especially focus on the *Diario de Noticias* (Daily News, New Bedford, MA, 1927–73) and the weekly *Jornal Português* (Portuguese Newspaper, Oakland, CA, 1932–97). The main goal is to characterize this type of press and to identify and analyse from a historical perspective, the most representative symbolical discourse elements in the production and towards the dissemination of Portuguese-language newspapers.

A 'business of poets': the immigrant press as a cultural instrument

For many immigrants, newspapers allowed a powerful triangulation between their community, the country of origin and the United States. One of the key tasks of the ethnic press has been historically to educate immigrants in their different roles as American citizens, providing information about their countries of origin and also promoting political views. They adapted to the evolving needs of the populations, even linguistically. As immigrants raised new families with descendants schooled in English, the increase of readers in the local language translated into many ethnic newspapers offering contents in both languages. Since the onset, the ethnic press tried to find a market niche complementary to that of the American local press. This was achieved by publishing different news, namely related to the immigrants' countries of origin, to immigration or nationalization policies, or public events in the colony. Some were simply spokespersons for corporate or religious institutions,[29] but others were a means of survival and an opportunity for professional development.[30]

Most of the Portuguese immigrant editors, like Manuel F. Martins Trigueiro, Pedro L. C. da Silveira or Artur Vieira Ávila who respectively founded in California *A União Portuguesa* (The Portuguese Union, 1887–1942), *O Arauto* (The Herald, 1896–1919) and *A Colónia Portuguesa* (The Portuguese Colony, 1924–32) believed their vocation of public service towards their countrymen was implicit in their entrepreneurial initiative. Both the editorialists and the readers needed the spiritual encouragement provided by a headline in Portuguese, which could mean an affective bond that gave social cohesion to the community and become a symbol of patriotic affirmation. Some editors thus faced their profession as a mission and a public good. The weekly newspaper *A Luta* [The Struggle], founded in 1936 in New York by Monsignor Joseph Cacella, thus highlighted its role in the personal and collective development of immigrants:

The Portuguese press is the soul of the colony! It announces our parties, defends the interests of our compatriots, advertises collectivities, publishes news from our Homeland, revives patriotism, ventilates local issues and brings the sad news of the Portuguese who gave their last breath in this country, far from our land that served as their cradle.[31]

Portuguese newspapers from the end of the nineteenth century upheld this commitment through slogans of cultural or patriotic affirmation adorning their front pages, such as: 'Honesty is the aim of Portuguese colony' (*O Lavrador Portuguez* The [Portuguese Farmer], Leemore, 1912–27); 'For the Country and for the People' (*A Tribuna* [The Tribune], Newark, 1931–4); and 'For the Good of Portugal, for the Good of the Colony' (*A Pátria* [The Homeland], New Bedford, 1935–6), among others. Each newspaper published by Portuguese immigrants throughout history represented a business project with commercial implications. In addition, they had a symbolic significance, making them an essential public reference within the community. In fact, to a greater or lesser extent they helped affirm shared cultural values and the eagerness to progress economically and socially without losing touch with their national origins.[32] According to August Mark Vaz, 'they encouraged, they scolded, sometimes they quarreled and gossiped – but it was in the familiar tongue and with the familiar phrases and in the quiet of evening they brought some comfort, encouragement, and above all remembrance to their readers'.[33] The feeling of belonging to the Portuguese community that fed the Portuguese press was an element that reinforced their ability to uphold their interests. This was understood by the Portuguese ambassador to the United States between 1933 and 1947, João António de Bianchi, who after visiting the Portuguese colony in California in September 1935, stated he was impressed by the great value of newspapers to instruct and contribute to the progress of the Portuguese community.[34]

Like other immigrant periodicals, most of the newspapers published by the Portuguese in the United States during the first half of the twentieth century were short-lived and produced in an almost artisanal fashion. The readership was limited, publicity was sporadic, and the subsidies through institutional advertising from the Portuguese or American governments were scarce. Despite these limitations, the quality of Portuguese-language publications was similar to that of other ethnic newspapers and sometimes even close to that of the press published in Portugal. Some titles exerted a great influence over the immigrant community, such as the *Diario de Noticias* (Daily News) from New Bedford (MA), whose circulation on many occasions exceeded 10,000 daily copies.[35] However, each of them had a story to tell: a story of struggle, success and dignity, starring Portuguese citizens who chose to found a periodical for the purpose of serving their ethnic community. Nonetheless, according to João P. Brum, one of the most popular newspaper businessmen in the Californian Portuguese community, journalism was a ruinous business: 'To make newspapers was a business of poets, of idealists, of broke people without a penny in their pocket'.[36] In fact, Portuguese newspapers were often published by immigrants with previous typographical experience who were unaware of journalistic routines and professional news writing. Many took up the challenge of self-learning the trade, turning their small businesses into genuine journalism schools, such as the aforementioned *Diario de*

Noticias (Daily News), the weekly *Jornal Português* (Portuguese Newspaper) from Oakland (1932–97), or the bi-weekly *Portuguese Times*, founded in Newark in 1971, and the weekly *O Jornal* (The Newspaper), edited in Fall River (MA) from 1970 and from New Bedford since 1973. Generally, editors worked with a small team of fellow countrymen who cumulated different tasks: journalistic, administrative and commercial. Nevertheless, newspapers attracted directors or editors for four reasons: it provided some power, it allowed visibility within the community, it offered prestige, and if reasonably managed it could produce enough profit to make a living based on advertising income.

The most characteristic features of the Portuguese-American press are the following: it resulted from private initiative, initially linked to typographers who saw an opportunity to do business through commercial advertising. Most of the editors were from the Azores Islands; it was generally an irregular press, whose readership varied depending on the arrival of new immigrants; and due to migrant concentrations in Massachusetts and California, many were published in these two states. Throughout their history, some titles competed strongly for readership and influence within the Portuguese community. Quite emblematic is the rivalry between the *Diario de Noticias* and *Jornal Português*. While the first was liberal and opposed the Portuguese Autocratic Regime, the second was conservative and campaigned in favour of the Corporatist Regime of the Estado Novo (New State). After the establishment of António de Oliveira Salazar's dictatorship in 1933, through pressure from their consular agents and the embassy, the Portuguese government tried to influence the editorial line of the most important newspapers in order to legitimize itself among the immigrants.[37] During the period from the Spanish Civil War to the Second World War (1936–45), the Secretariat of National Propaganda pressured some media to censor information critical of the regime that was published by the former Republican Minister of Education João Camoesas in newspapers such as *O Colonial* or *Diario de Noticias*. Not surprisingly, the ethnic press provided a most effective means of propagating ideological postulates. In the Portuguese case, at stake were the traditional debates opposing republicanism against monarchism, clericalism against anti-clericalism. In some cases, ideological intolerance produced personal confrontation, gaining momentum and public dimension due to the amplifying effect of newspaper diffusion. This was the case with Mário Bettencourt da Câmara and Father Guilherme Silveira da Gloria. The Catholic criticism heralded by Mário Bettencourt da Câmara when he was editor-in-chief of the San Francisco weekly *A União Portuguesa* (The Portuguese Union, 1887–1942) was harshly criticized by da Gloria in the Irvington weekly *O Amigo dos Cathólicos* (The Friend of the Catholics, 1888–96), stemming a sharp debate that would last as long as the latter was published.

Since its emergence, the Portuguese-language press has allowed the immigrants to read information in Portuguese about their community, related to the activities of their associative organizations, commercial life, traditions, festive celebrations, community agenda and events sharing a common sociocultural imaginary. They also commented on American life, labour or legal matters, made recommendations on community life, disseminated commercial messages, helped learning English and Portuguese, taught to look for work and offered ideas to start new businesses. Yet the transcription of news from other newspapers sometimes made up for lack of talent, a situation which incited the most educated members of the community to collaborate to the newspapers, in order to shape a greater vision for the future of their countrymen. It is not easy to measure the real impact of those periodicals on the Portuguese immigrants. Nonetheless, considering the length and wide dissemination of some newspapers, one can assume that the readers were certainly receptive to their informative and instructive value.[38]

Such an influence is clear in the case of the *Diario de Noticias* (Daily News), which was published between 1927 and 1973 and replaced *A Alvorada* (The Dawn, 1919–26), which ceased publication when the *Diario de Noticias* began. Both titles were founded by the same businessman, Guilherme Machado Luiz, who originated from Terceira Island (Azores) and went to the US as a young man without knowing how to read or write. The *Diario de Noticias* (Daily News) published, almost without interruption, abundant and varied articles on the Portuguese-American community,[39] with a clear and patent defence of the Portuguese language, identity and culture. This was the fraternal commitment with its readers, held high as a flag during its long-lasting existence. In 1966, as it struggled for survival, it appealed to the patriotic sense of the Portuguese, publishing advertisements with the following message: 'If you are Portuguese and want the "Diario de Noticias" to endure, get us new subscribers.'

The issue of the use of vernacular by immigrants is very complex, since it should be analysed not only from the dichotomic perspective of English opposing Portuguese, but also taking into account the existing dialect variants between some Azorean and continental immigrants. In addition, the use of anglicisms among themselves was frequently the result of their adaptation to a new idiomatic context.[40] Reading the Luso-American press reveals that the Portuguese language used in those pages includes English-language neologisms and borrowings, but also grammar errors, mainly during the first mass emigration period. During this stage, training publishers and copywriters were also more precarious and had lower levels of literacy, including in Portuguese.

In *A Língua Portuguesa nos Estados Unidos* (The Portuguese Language in the United States, 1925), the former Portuguese consul in Boston, Eduardo de Carvalho, argues that the systematic modification of words and use of anglicisms in spoken and written Portuguese by immigrants could be considered a dialect *per se*.[41] According to him, this new idiom had four main characteristics: English terms and anglicisms were applied to things and objects that the immigrants did not know in Portuguese; Portuguese words were used with a different meaning; English sentences and American idiomatic expressions were literally translated to Portuguese, and English syntax was applied to Portuguese sentences.[42] Carvalho credits the press with a key role in the creation and dissemination of Portuguese-American neologisms. According to the diplomat, the lack of preparation and professional expertise of editors to translate information from English and to write accurately in Portuguese was one of the main reasons for the emergence of the new vocabulary.[43] Besides, some Portuguese immigrants anglicized their names to make them easier to spell, pronounce and understand in English. As they wished to belong and to avoid prejudice, they replaced João with John, Maria with Mary, António with Tony and Pereira with Perry, to mention just a few examples. This was highlighted by several Portuguese newspapers, which were worried about the 'cultural shyness' of immigrants and the widespread increase of this 'Englishing' phenomenon. The *Diario de Noticias* (Daily News) interpreted this phenomenon as a lack of sensitivity towards the values of Portuguese culture.[44] Aware of the problem that the Portuguese language was facing in the United States, the *A Alvorada* argued in the editorial of 6 December 1926 that only newspapers and churches could help save the Portuguese language.[45] When dealing with the issue of linguistic and cultural preservation, the editorials of many Portuguese newspapers employed a patriotic, ethnic-centred rhetoric, often interspersed with melancholy. The popular Portuguese-American poet Josefina do Canto e Castro (1907–2008) described this commitment as a 'brotherly embrace' meant to educate immigrants emotionally.[46] To her, newspaper workers such as those working for the *Diario de Noticias* were 'a bunch of poets', writing daily 'from the US the most beautiful love poems dedicated to Portuguese Homeland'.[47] This view is shared by the Portuguese journalist and poet Joaquim de Oliveira, editor of the Danbury (CT) monthly *O Trabalho* (The Work, 1939–40), who published a lyrical article entitled 'Salutations, *Diario de Noticias* from New Bedford'.[48] The nationalistic appeal was a recurring feature in the editorials of the Portuguese press, especially in the *Diario de Noticias*, which played the part of a protector and beacon of the Portuguese language and traditions in the United States.

The symbolic imaginary of Portuguese journalism in the United States

Portuguese-American newspapers were quite instrumental in maintaining social cohesion among immigrants and also emotional links with their places of origin. Additionally, they were pedagogical resources creating spaces of cultural intersection between their own idiosyncrasies and the dominant cultural brands of American society through their media and lifestyle or other immigrant communities. Over time, they developed a mythological narrative about those most outstanding aspects of the Portuguese presence in the US territory that contributed to create a common imaginary among citizens from Portugal.

The journalistic discourse of the Portuguese-language press presents a revised vision of history from an ethnic perspective that highlights or reaffirms the traces of Portuguese presence dating back to epic moments of the past with great symbolic relevance for Portuguese-American immigrants. This ethnic-centred narrative claims the Portuguese participation in the origin of the United States, essentially through three stepping stones: the discovery of the east coast by explorer João Rodrigues Cabrilho (1499–1543), the connection to Portugal of the Dighton Rock archaeological finding, and the heroic contribution of patriot Peter Francisco (1760–1831) to the War of American Independence.

It is common knowledge that the Portuguese presence in America can be traced back to before the first migratory flows in the seventeenth century. This early presence is mentioned in the symbolical account of the arrival of the first Portuguese in North America by the time of the Golden Age of the Portuguese Discoveries, as endorsed by the historian Manuel S. Cardozo.[49] This is the predominant argument of a common narrative in the Portuguese-American press, emphasizing the Portuguese contribution to the cultural foundation of North America. Such accounts mirror a sense of a collective experience, shared beliefs and ethnic pride. According to them, the Portuguese arrival on American soil dates back to the pre-Columbian era and includes the participation of Portuguese sailors and soldiers in American expeditions under the flag of Spain after the conquest of Mexico by Hernán Cortés (1485–1547), between 1519 and 1521. The Portuguese navigator João Rodrigues Cabrilho stood out as the first European to reach the coast of California. Setting sail from the west coast of Mexico, he reached San Diego Bay on 28 September 1542.[50] This historical episode is portrayed as an epic achievement by the Portuguese-American press, highlighting the Portuguese contribution to the discovery of American territories and the subsequent formation of the United States of America.[51] An extensive network of social clubs was founded in Californian cities in the 1930s, with several thousand associates, to vindicate this 'special' connection, and a magazine entitled *Cabrillo Commentator, Discoverer of California* (1937–8) was then published to celebrate the Portuguese involvement in the discovery of California. In addition, the two most influential and long-lived newspapers of the American-Californian press, the *Jornal Português* (Portuguese Newspaper) and the *A União Portuguesa* (The Portuguese Union), issued two large memorial editions in 1942, commemorating the fourth centenary of the Portuguese discovery of California.[52] Joaquim Rodrigues da Silva Leite, former editor of *Portugália, Cabrilho Comentator* and *A Revista Portuguêsa* (The Portuguese Magazine, 1914–25), synthetized in the following eulogy, the spirit of the Portuguese immigrant pride, diaspora, and past deeds in racial terms: 'it is difficult to find another name in History incorporating so many assertions of the best qualities of the Portuguese race'.[53]

Another episode of the self-celebrating journalistic narrative was the historical record of another Portuguese navigator, João Vaz Corte Real (1420–96). From the Azores, he explored the Labrador and Newfoundland regions in the early sixteenth century, although there is no reliable data on whether or not he landed in the territory that is now the United States. His ship is supposed to have sunk at some unknown point on the East Coast of Northern America. However, the study of the petroglyphs of the Dighton Stone in Berkeley (MA), whose existence has been known since the seventeenth century, carried out by Brown University professor Edmund B. Delabarre (1863–1945) who, in 1918, believed to have found inscriptions related to the Portuguese explorer. One of the inscriptions was said to date back to 1511, triggering an extensive controversial debate with significant echo in the Portuguese-American press.[54] According to Delabarre, the American East Coast had also been discovered by a Portuguese navigator.[55] The Portuguese-language newspapers fuelled the debate on the Portuguese discovery of North America, publishing its own reports and articles on the subject. This increased curiosity about Portugal as one of the primary players in the European age of discovery and exploration. This magnified the feeling of Portuguese-American patriotism and promoted the foundation of the

Dighton Rock State Park and Museum in the State of Massachusetts. A replica of the rock is kept in the Maritime Museum in Lisbon, in Portugal, as a symbol of unity between both countries.

The Portuguese-American newspapers used regularly a third argument for the cultural affirmation of the Portuguese in the US territory. Among numerous reports and accounts of Portuguese nationals deserving eulogy at some point in the US history, Portuguese newspapers highlighted Peter Francisco, born Pedro Francisco. He was a heroic soldier in the American Revolutionary War and won the nickname of the 'Giant of the Revolution' in American historical literature.[56] Not much is known about his early life, but according to legend and tradition, he was born in Porto Judeu, Terceira Island, in the Azores, was brought onto a ship bound for America, eventually to be abandoned on the port of City Point, Virginia. The boy would later be adopted by the local judge and in 1777, Francisco enlisted in the 10th Virginia Regiment and joined the Continental Army. His courage earned him the public recognition of General George Washington, commander-in-chief of the army. The merit of his exploits rendered him one of the most famous private soldiers of the Revolutionary War.[57] In spite of the fact that there is little documentary evidence to support much of Francisco's wartime deeds, the Portuguese ethnic press heralded his outstanding contribution as a Portuguese soldier in an American war.[58] Portuguese leaders promoted public relations events honouring the memory of his exploits and crediting his merit, thereby ensuring that he would remain a compelling figure in American history. In 1926, the Portuguese journalist Vasco de Sousa Jardim, who had been director and owner of the *Luso-Americano* (1928–), organized a campaign with the help of the priest Augusto Furtado to publicize the Portuguese origin of Peter Francisco among Portuguese immigrants.[59] With the support of the *American Legion* magazine and the Portuguese Continental Union, fraternal society, created the 'Peter Francisco Award' to distinguish individuals or institutions who bring prestige to people of Portuguese heritage in the United States and to the Portuguese language and culture. Among the recipients, one can mention John F. Kennedy, at the time a United States senator from Massachusetts and later president of the United States, Basil Brewer, editor and owner of the Journal *Standard Times* of New Bedford (MA), John dos Passos, classic American novelist and poet of Madeiran descent, João R. Rocha owner and managing editor of *Diário de Notícias*, from New Bedford (MA), and Anibal Branco, editor of *O Independente* (*The Independent*).

Although several monuments were erected in Peter Francisco's honour in Newark, the capital of New Jersey, the *Luso-Americano* newspaper and the Portuguese-American Scholarship Foundation lobbied for the creation of the Peter Francisco Park in the urban triangle between the Ferry Street, Edison Place and Railroad Avenue. It still stands today in an area where many Portuguese resided. The work was completed in 1976 with the inauguration of an obelisk in honour of the hero in the homonymous square. In 1953, the governor of the State of Massachusetts, Christian A. Herter, proclaimed 15 March as Peter Francisco Day. This day (anniversary of the Battle of Guilford Court House in 1781) is officially recognized as Peter Francisco Day in Massachusetts, Rhode Island, Virginia and Maryland. The mayor of New Bedford, Arthur R. Harriman, made an official proclamation in 12 March 1954, published in the Portuguese press, so that the flag of Portugal would be placed next to the American flag in the town hall building, to honour Peter Francisco and the Portuguese community in the United States.[60]

Hence, like other immigrant communities settling in the United States throughout history, the Portuguese-Language press has developed a narrative and a model of representation of reality that has reinforced the idiosyncrasies of the imagined Portuguese community's cultural values and that has dignified its presence and role in the host society. This press has been using a symbolic imaginary and a discursive structure with ethnic codes of interpretation to celebrate foreign heritage and identity in a sought-after nation of immigrants: the United States of America.

Conclusion

From an identity, cultural and ethnic perspective, this narrative legitimized the Portuguese presence in the US and simultaneously fuelled pride and patriotism, relating the immigrants to a formerly imperial nation whose language and cultural traits they were bound to assimilate. The foreign-language press discourse introduced the immigrants to the national values of American society, encouraging behaviours and attitudes as active agents participating in a glorified US history. The identification with outstanding figures, events or milestones, galvanized the Portuguese identity in the US society. Endorsing historical and ethnic benchmarks, the Portuguese press conveyed new normative beliefs and values, presented an ideal way of life in the new society, and symbolically bridged the two cultural moments and worlds: the old Portuguese and the new American.

The continual migration of readers to digital media, however, is making the profitability of print newspapers increasingly difficult, especially those with small audiences. In the Internet era, immigrants have various sources of free information through networks that reduce the prominence and relevance of traditional media. The great cyber showcase and the phenomenon of digital applications has created a virtual universe that presents great challenges to the survival of the paper-based press, forcing it to adapt to this new disruptive environment. Faced with these challenges, Portuguese-American newspapers have adapted in a variety of ways. In general, coverage regarding activities of the community increased as news from Portugal decreased, since digital and television media already provided extensive information on continental Portugal and the islands. Some of them also decided to create digital editions, both free and paid. The *Luso-Americano*, for example, offers a paid digital edition, while the only Portuguese newspaper published today in California, *A Tribuna Portuguesa*, which turned forty in 2019, offers a free digital edition that allows it to increase its media projection and reach a greater number of readers. The future of the Portuguese press in the United States will therefore depend on its ability to remain a useful source of information for immigrants in this new communications context in which achieving the American dream by publishing newspapers is becoming more and more difficult.

Notes

1. This work was produced in the scope of the research project PTDC/COM-JOR/28144/2017 – *Towards a history of journalism in Portugal*, funded by the FCT (Portuguese Foundation for Science and Technology).
2. K. Vismanath and P. Arora, 'Ethnic Media in the United States: An Essay on Their Role in Integration, Assimilation, and Social Control', *Mass Communication & Society* 3, no. 3 (1997): 39–56.
3. Sally M. Miller, ed. *The Ethnic Press in the United States. A Historical Analysis and Handbook* (New York-West Port-Connecticut-London: Greenwood Press, 1987).
4. Melissa A. Johnson, 'How Ethnic Are U.S. Ethnic Media: The Case of Latina Magazines', *Mass Communication & Society* 3, no. 2–3 (2000): 229–48.
5. Alberto Pena-Rodríguez, 'El periodismo portugués en California. Notas históricas sobre el *Jornal Português* de Oakland (1932–1997)', *Estudios sobre el Mensaje Periodístico* 25, no. 1 (2019): 443–57; and Alberto Pena-Rodríguez, 'Los inicios de la prensa portuguesa en los Estados Unidos de América', *Revista Famecos. Mídia, Cultura e Tecnologia* 24, no. 2 (2017).
6. Geoffrey L. Gomes, 'The Portuguese-Language Press in California: The Response to American Politics, 1880–1928', *Gávea-Brown. A Bilingual Journal of Portuguese American Letters and Studies* 15–18 (1995): 5–90; Leo Pap, 'The Portuguese Press', in *The Ethnic Press in the United States. A Historical Analysis and Handbook*, ed. Sally Miller.
7. Yearbook of Immigration Statistics: https://www.dhs.gov/immigration-statistics/yearbook/2012.
8. Maria I. Baganha, 'The Lusophone Migratory System: Patterns and Trends', *International Migration* 47 no. 3 (2009): 5–20; J. Williams, *In Pursuit of Their Dreams. A History of Azorean Immigration to the United States* (North Dartmouth: Tagus Press, Center for Portuguese Studies and Culture-University of Massachusetts Dartmouth, 2007); and Christian Bannick, *Portuguese Immigration to the United States: its Distribution and Status* (San Francisco: R&E Research Associates, 1971).
9. Donald Warrin, *So Ends This Day. The Portuguese in American Whaling, 1765–1927* (North Dartmouth: Tagus Press, Center for Portuguese Studies and Culture-UMass Dartmouth, 2010); and David Bertão, *The Portuguese Shore Whalers of California, 1854–1904* (San Jose, CA: Portuguese Heritage Publications of California, 2006).
10. Eduardo Mayone Dias, *A Presença Portuguesa na California* (San Jose, CA: Portuguese Heritage Publications, 2009); Donald Warrin and Geoffrey L. Gomes, *Land as Far as the Eye Can See. Portuguese in the Old West* (Washington: The Arthur H. Clark Company, 2001); and August Mark Vaz, *The Portuguese in California* (San Francisco: IDES Supreme Council, 1965).
11. Genevieve B. Correa, and Edgar W. Knowlton, 'The Portuguese in Hawaii', in *Ethnic Sources in Hawai'i. A Special Issue for The University of Hawai'i's Seventy-Fifth Year* (Honolulu: The United Press of Hawaii, 1982).
12. Edgar C. Knowlton, 'The Portuguese Language Press in Hawaii', *Social Process in Hawaii* 24 (1960): 89–99.
13. Pena-Rodríguez, 'Los inicios de la prensa portuguesa'.
14. Robert E. Park, *The Immigrant Press and its Control* (New York: Harper & Brothers, 1922).
15. Sandra L. Jones Ireland, *Ethnic Periodicals in Contemporary America: an Annotated Guide* (New York: Greenwood Press, 1990).

16 'Publications in Foreign Languages', *N.W. Ayer & Son's American Newspaper Annual and Directory* (Philadelphia: N.W. Ayer & Son, 1909), 1135–47.
17 Margaret A. Blanchard, ed. *History of the Mass Media in the United States. An Encyclopedia* (Chicago-London: Fitzroy Dearborn Publishers, 1998).
18 Clyde W. Barrow, ed. *Portuguese Americans and Contemporary Civil Culture in Massachusetts* (North Dartmouth: Tagus Press, Center for Portuguese Studies and Culture-University of Massachusetts Dartmouth, 2002); Leo Pap, *The Portuguese-Americans* (Boston: Twayne Publishers, 1981); and Bannick, *Portuguese Immigration to the United States*.
19 Observatório da Emigração Portuguesa: http://www.observatorioemigracao.secomunidades.pt.
20 *Yearbook of Immigration Statistics*: https://www.dhs.gov/immigration-statistics/yearbook/2012.
21 In 1921, a quota system was implemented to drastically reduce the influx of immigrants from the east and the south-east of Europe in favour of northern Europe. The access was reduced to 440 Portuguese per year. The great depression of 1929 worsened the scenario, and the economic recovery after the Second World War didnt change too much this restrictive trend. See Baganha, 'The Lusophone Migratory System'; and Gilberta Rocha, *Dinâmica Populacional dos Açores no Século XX: Unidade. Permanência. Diversidade* (Ponta Delgada: Universidade dos Açores, 1991).
22 Gustavo Luca de Tena, *Noticias de América* (Vigo: Nigra, 1993).
23 Williams, *In Pursuit of Their Dreams*.
24 Diplomatic-Historical Archive of Lisbon (DHA). Portuguese Embassy in Washington (PEW). Note no. 117, process 9/34, from Embassy Secretary of Portugal in Washington, João de Deus Ramos, to the Minister of Foreign Affairs, box no. 18, 1934.
25 António Luís Vicente, *Os Portugueses nos Estados Unidos de América. Política de Comunidades e Comunidade Política* (Lisbon: Fundação Luso-Americana, 1998).
26 Leara D. Rhodes, *The Ethnic Press: Shaping the American Dream* (New York: Peter Lang, 2010); and Jerzy Zubrzycki, 'The role of the foreign-language press in migrant integration', *Population Studies* 12 no. 1 (1958): 73–82.
27 Pena-Rodríguez, 'Los inicios de la prensa portuguesa'.
28 Due to an increase in the number of Brazilians in the US from the 1980s and 1990s to the present, some newspapers like the historical bi-weekly *Luso-Americano* (Luso-American) of Newark (NJ) has been devoting more attention to issues related to this community. Possibly the first newspaper that tried to make Brazilian immigrants visible and pay attention to them was the ephemeral weekly O Luso-Brazileiro, emerged in New York City in 1918. Clémence Jouët-Pastré, and Leticia J. Braga (eds.), *Becoming Bazuca. Brazilian Immigration to the United States* (Cambridge: Harvard University Press, 2008).
29 Dolores Ann Liptack, *Immigrants and Their Church. Makers of the Catholic Community* (New York-London: McMillan, 1989).
30 Rhodes, *The Ethnic Press*.
31 'A imprensa portuguesa é a alma da colónia! É ela que anuncia as nossas festas, defende os interesses dos nosso compatriotas, faz propaganda das colectividades, publica noticias da nossa Pátria, aviva o patriotismo, ventila questões locais e leva a travez dos nucleos portugueses as noticias tristes dos que exalaram neste pais o último sopro de vida, longe da nossa terra que lhes serviu de berço'. *A Luta*, weekly, 2 February 1938, 1.
32 Joe Machado et al. *Power of the Spirit. A Portuguese journey of building faith and churches in California* (San Jose, CA: Portuguese Heritage Publications of California,

2012); and Holton, Kimberly Dacosta and Andrea Klimt (eds.), *Community, Culture and the Makings of Identity. Portuguese-Americans along Eastern Seabord* (North Dartmouth: Tagus Press, Center for Portuguese Studies and Culture-University of Massachusetts Dartmouth, 2009).
33 August Mark Vaz, *The Portuguese in California*, 65.
34 João António Bianchi, 'Interview', *A Liberdade* (The Freedom, Sacramento, CA), weekly, 7 September 1935, 1.
35 Rui Antunes Correia, 'Salazar em New Bedford. Leituras Luso-Americanas do Estado Novo nos Anos Trinta' (MA diss., Universidade Aberta, Lisbon, 2004), 43.
36 João P. Brum, 'Um negócio de poetas', *Notícia* (New, San José, CA), weekly, 5 December 1984, 1.
37 Torre do Tombo National Archives, Oliveira Salazar Archive, SGPCM-GPM, Box 5, PC-156, 3, n° 4. Report no. 1273 from the Director of the Secretariado de Propaganda Nacional, António Eça de Queiroz, to the President of the Council of Ministers, 19 September 1938.
38 August Mark Vaz, *The Portuguese in California*, 139–40.
39 Only in the final section of its existence, it stopped publishing some days, specifically on Saturdays and Sundays between 27 November 1971 and 19 October 1973.
40 George Monteiro, *Caldo Verde is not Stone Soup: Persons, Names, Words and Proverbs In Portuguese America* (New York-Oxford-Berne: Peter Lang, 2017).
41 Eduardo Carvalho, *A Língua Portuguesa nos Estados Unidos (extracto do relatório de Boston, de 9 de abril de 1924)* (Boston: Editora Emprêsa de Propaganda Patriótica, 1925).
42 Ibid.
43 Ibid.
44 'O português dos imigrantes', *Diario de Noticias* (New Bedford), 16 January 1928, 2.
45 'A defesa da nossa lingua', *A Alvorada* (The Dawn) (New Bedford), 6 December 1926, 2.
46 Josefina Canto e Castro, 'Um punhado de poetas', *Diario de Noticias*, Special Issue 50th Birthday, 12 May 1969, n. p.
47 Ibid.
48 Joaquim de Oliveira, 'Salve Diario de Noticias de New Bedford', *Diario de Noticias*, 31 December 1935, 2.
49 Manuel da Silveira Cardozo, *The Portuguese in America (590 B.C.–1974)* (New York: Oceana Publications, 1976).
50 Mayone Dias, *A Presença Portuguesa na California*.
51 Jim Cullen, *The American dream: A short history of an idea that shaped a nation* (Oxford-New York: Oxford University Press, 2003).
52 *Jornal Português* (Portuguese Newspaper, Oakland), 3 July 1942; and *A União Portuguesa 1887–1937* (Portuguese Union, San Francisco), 28 March 1937.
53 J. Rodrigues da Silva Leite, 'Rodrigues Cabrilho', *A União Portuguesa*, 28 March 1937, 23.
54 M. L. Silva, 'Is the name of a Portuguese navigator engraved in the Dighton Rock?', *A Alvorada*, 3 September 1926, 3.
55 Following his research on the rock in 1918, Brown University professor Edmund Delabarre found the inscription '1511' and carved shapes similar to the crosses and shield of Portugal. The finding stirred the Portuguese nationalist movement both inside and outside the US, culminating in the decoration of the American professor in 1926 by the Portuguese Government.

56 Renee Critcher Lyons, *Foreign-Born American Patriots: Sixteen Volunteer Leaders in the Revolutionary War* (North Carolina: McFarland & Company Inc., Publishers Jefferson, 2014).
57 Harry M. Ward, *For Virginia and for Independence: Twenty-Eight Revolutionary War Soldiers from the Old Dominion* (North Carolina: McFarland & Company Inc., Publishers Jefferson, 2011).
58 'The Portuguese in the American Revolutionary War', *Jornal Português* (Portuguese Newspaper, Oakland), 22 September 1950, 19.
59 Vasco Sousa Jardim, 'Medalha Peter Francisco', *Luso-Americano* (Luso-American, Newark), 18 November 1989, 33.
60 A. R. Harriman, 'Official proclamation', *Diario de Noticias*, 12 March 1954, 2.

7

'Spotlight on Jim Crow': Radical Slovak and Polish Immigrant Newspapers in Solidarity with Black Civil Rights

Robert M. Zecker
St Francis Xavier University

As scholars such as David Roediger and Mathew Frye Jacobson have noted, European immigrants to the US[2] 'became' White in large measure through learning to distance themselves spatially and cognitively from African Americans, their new country's permanent pariahs. The immigrant press was complicit in creating this anti-Black animus, often printing dismissive accounts of Blacks as impermissible outsiders to the 'white man's republic'.[1] Lurid accounts of ritualized lynchings of Blacks were designed, historian Grace Hale argues, to solidify the unity of the White race threatened by industrialization and modernity. But even Slavic immigrants, who in other contexts alarmed native-born Whites, read macabre lynching accounts dismissing blacks as sexualized, criminal threats in papers such as the Slovak-language *New Yorský denník* (New York Daily).[2] Minstrel-show performances were frequently advertised in such papers, where humour at Blacks' expense was a staple. By 1921, readers wrote to *New Yorský denník* contributing their own jokes slighting African Americans, indicating many immigrants internalized the Black-White binary as a natural, vital component of New World acculturation.[3]

Yet, not all immigrants embraced race thinking; a forgotten road to interracial, working-class solidarity was articulated for Slavic newcomers in newspapers such as Slovak *Rovnosť ľudu* (Equality for the People), published from 1906 until around 1950, and Polish *Głos Ludowy* (The People's Voice), published from 1901 to 1979. These leftist papers offered unequivocal dissent from White-ethnic hostility to blacks and America's segregated *status quo*. While support for civil rights was often couched in self-interest, as immigrants, especially leftists, knew how readily they were stigmatized as un-American by the same conservatives segregating blacks, it seems to have been no less heartfelt. A brief survey of the coverage of civil-rights campaigns in *Rovnosť ľudu* and *Głos Ludowy* suggests not all Slavic Americans embraced White privilege. Many leftists favoured equality for Americans across the colour line and worked with people of all races to achieve these goals.

The roots of White-ethnic interracial activism were deep. *Rovnosť ľudu*, published in Chicago, was started by the Slovak-language branch of the Socialist Party, the Slovak

Workers Society (SWS), in 1906. After 1919, the SWS affiliated with the Communists, and from 1930 the paper became the Slovak organ of the International Workers Order (IWO), an interracial insurance fraternal that vigorously lobbied for racial equality. The SWS, as well as its newspaper (which went through several name changes)[4] were placed on the Attorney General's List of Subversive Organizations during the post-Second World War Red Scare, and the paper ceased printing around 1950. One of the bills of indictment the House Un-American Activities Committee (HUAC), attorney general and other red-baiters levelled at the SWS was its steadfast commitment to racial equality, not, for conservatives, a badge of honour. The paper gave its enemies plenty of ammunition in this regard, for thirty years forcefully championing Black Civil Rights.[5]

Głos Ludowy was edited by Detroit state Senator Stanley Nowak (1903–94) and comrades from 1942 until 1979, reviving an earlier paper. *Głos Ludowy* offered similar, spirited advocacy of 'nothing less than full freedom'[6] for Black fellow citizens, in contrast to other Polish-language newspapers' indifference or hostility to the status of African Americans. Support for Blacks' equality continued to be expressed vigorously in Nowak's paper, even as he faced government deportation campaigns because of his alleged Communist past.[7] *Rovnosť ľudu* reached 26,550 readers by 1938, and *Głos Ludowy*, according to Dirk Hoerder, topped out at 10,000 circulation, although both papers were often purchased by International Workers Order lodges and other leftist sites, so readership was almost certainly larger.[8] Both papers supported interracial campaigns for racial equality by Communist-led organizations such as the IWO and the Civil Rights Congress, providing extensive coverage of progressive White ethnics who joined black comrades in battling racial as well as class oppression.[9]

While most Slavic and other White-ethnic leftist organizations were felled by anti-communism (the IWO and SWS were disbanded in 1954, for example), the Polish paper avoided destruction, continuing to publish left-wing views on civil rights through the 1970s. The case of this paper suggests that we must question the periodization of radicalism's demise and look to strands connecting progressive White ethnics of the Old Left to the New. Even as other Whites became the building blocks of anti-civil rights coalitions backing conservative politicians, *Głos Ludowy* continued a fifty-year tradition of progressive Slavic American journalism, championing Black-White unity. An analysis of the Slovak and Polish leftist papers suggests not all Slavic Americans so readily embraced Whiteness or were indifferent to African American fellow workers.

Slovak-language *Rovnosť ľudu* campaigning for early Black-White solidarity

As early as 1919, *Rovnosť ľudu* embraced the cause of black fellow workers, lamenting Chicago's race war in which Whites murdered blacks regarded as usurpers of neighbourhoods and job sites. 'In the giant Civil War,' the paper noted, '400,000 whites lay down their lives for the liberation of black people from slavery and today they murder each other ... [I]t is a very sad phenomenon that these race wars lead poor people from both sides to battle each other.' *Rovnosť ľudu* foregrounded class analysis, and, like the Socialist Party that it still supported, was confident race problems would evaporate with better workers' organization to remove racism and other capitalist discontents. Still, the paper said 'we mourn the lives that fell there' – a far cry from mainstream Slovak papers. *New Yorkský denník* was more alarmed by the fact some black Chicagoans were military veterans stockpiling weapons after Whites assaulted blacks for swimming too near Whites-only beaches or straying into White neighbourhoods. This black threat, the New York paper alleged, necessitated the mayor's calling in the Army to 'occupy every Negro quarter'. While some Polish priests calmed parishioners' racial anxieties, *Národ Polski* (Polish Nation) suggested attacks were justified due to Blacks' alleged sexual promiscuity.[10]

While other Slavic newspapers only noticed anti-black assaults in exceptional moments of crisis, and with sparing sympathy, *Rovnosť ľudu* continued to decry White attacks on blacks throughout the 1920s–40s, and demanded readers work to bring justice to African Americans. In 1935, when a black teenager was 'shamefully beaten' by a Harlem storekeeper for allegedly 'stealing a ten-cent pen knife', the paper reported black women activists affiliated with the left-wing International Labor Defense (ILD) sprang to his aid, only to have police rush in and beat them. The paper reported 'One black woman was seriously hurt and dragged to the police station'. This culminated in a police riot against demonstrating Harlem residents, a scene reminiscent of recent police assaults on blacks angered by police brutality in Ferguson, Missouri, Minneapolis and Baltimore. The paper cried that Harlem's '400,000 black citizens are being terrorized by the police, who are armed with tear-gas bombs, revolvers, rifles and machine guns. One man was killed, more than 100 wounded and 120 arrested after yesterday's police-orchestrated riot, which began in Tuesday night's attack on a meeting of people protesting in the streets'. The 'swirling riot' was blamed by the conservative Hearst press on Communists, who 'were inciting the latest riots against public safety, reports whose example was followed by all the other capitalist newspapers'. The Slovak paper, though, called on readers to come to the aid of Black victims of this 'fascist police assault'. When the mayor's committee investigating the riot was slow to release its findings, *Denník Rovnosť ľudu* republished a report in the Communist *Daily Worker*, saying the mayor's report 'was suppressed ... because even capitalist investigators had to conclude that "black citizens still live in a state of poverty, ... and in general everything is against them by a very special discrimination ... this is what caused the explosion"'. The Slovak paper further detailed the employment discrimination and 'police barbarism' facing blacks in Harlem and elsewhere.[11]

Ľudový denník, the new name for the paper, in 1935 also presciently warned of 'the latest method of spreading the poison of race discrimination' when a chain letter was disseminated in Detroit calling for preservation of segregated neighbourhoods and schools. The paper denounced the campaign 'by cowardly fascists who undoubtedly get their inspiration from the Hearst press'. While historian Thomas Sugrue notes the majority of Detroit's neighbourhoods were covered by racially restrictive covenants, the article in the English-language section of *Ľudový denník* indicates some Slavic Americans resisted the attractions of White privilege by battling segregation. Moreover,

Ľudový denník cited an article in the African-American *Tribune Independent* of Detroit, suggesting interracial cooperation by leftists in opposing educational and residential apartheid. The black weekly was approvingly quoted as declaring, 'Prejudice is a disease, and those who deliberately seek to inject this poison into the hearts and lives of their fellow citizens, are enemies of society and should be branded as traitors to the nation.'[12]

The poison proved lethal seven years later in Detroit, when a White mob stormed Sojourner Truth Houses, a public-housing project designed for black workers. *Ľudový denník* reported on 'white mobs' that 'swarmed blacks'. The paper noted in spite of the White mob's violence, all but three of the 101 arrests were of blacks defending themselves. 'The property owners, who had been sitting on the stairs [of Sojourner Truth] with 200 guns, were not arrested.' The paper noted the African American *Michigan Chronicle* telegrammed President Roosevelt to decry police inaction in allowing Whites to attack Black defence workers.[13]

On the edge of community: Polish *Głos Ludowy* fighting Nazism and segregation

On this point, the Slovak daily was joined by Polish *Głos Ludowy*, which likewise found much to condemn in Jim Crow America. The riot at Sojourner Truth occurred because 'Poles ... and other rowdy elements' joined in 'preventing Negro families ... from moving in'. While *Głos Ludowy*'s columnist neglected to mention a Polish priest had sermonized it was parishioners' duty to keep the 'niggers' out of the neighbourhood,[14] he did condemn the 'skulldugging support' 'Polish hoodlums' at Sojourner Truth received from 'certain sections of the Polish press'. The widely circulated *Ameryka-Echo* (American Echo) – by the 1920s, it already reached 120,000 readers – praised Polish homeowners as 'rising in Paul-Revere attitude of gallantry to protect their homes ... from being devalued by having coloured families moving into the neighborhood'. Other Polish papers ran letters to the editor defending the White rioters. Patriotic imagery was appropriated by both left and right during the Second World War and many Poles began to see racially segregated neighbourhoods as their birthright.[15]

To be sure, some White-ethnic Detroiters enrolled in the IWO and the leftist American Slav Congress supported open housing and other civil-rights initiatives, and Stanley Nowak, editor of *Głos Ludowy*, was elected in a heavily Slavic Detroit district, even as he prominently featured his support of a state Fair Employment Practices Bill and work to integrate local drugstores in his campaign brochures.[16] Still, the Polish paper acknowledged fractures within Slavic Detroit, demanding to know 'How United is Polonia?' when denouncing community leaders such as Congressman Rudolph Tenerowicz who had abetted the mob. It argued that Tenerowicz had to be defeated for re-election as 'unrepresentative of the strongly anti-fascist community he comes from'. The paper failed to consider that Tenerowicz might have been all too representative of the anti-Black animus at least some Poles expressed.[17]

A Detroit hate strike at Packard, where White auto workers downed tools rather than work alongside newly hired blacks, was blamed on the Klan, like at Sojourner

Truth Houses. Perhaps acknowledging the implausibility of Catholic Slavs taking direction from the virulently anti-Catholic Klan, *Głos Ludowy* also blamed the strike on 'fascist work among the ethnic groups', especially conservatives within the Polish lobbying society KNAPP (*Komitet Narodowy Amerykanów Polskiego Pochodzenia* – National Committee of Americans of Polish Extraction.) In opposition to this anti-black attitude, the paper praised two Polish American union officials, an IWO member and other 'progressive, patriotic workers, who did not lightly submit to the terrorism and threats of the KKK and worked to break the wildcat strike'. The Slovak paper likewise condemned a hate strike by Philadelphia trolley motormen.[18]

In labelling 'anti-black action' the work of Fifth Columnists intent on foiling the war effort, *Głos Ludowy* failed to consider that some Polish Americans saw no conflict between battling Nazis in Europe while defending all-White work sites in America.[19] Still, *Głos Ludowy* relentlessly condemned racism. A similar mob action to keep blacks out of public housing in the heavily Polish city of Hamtramck was denounced, with the paper noting Nazi occupiers of Poland similarly marked public spaces with signs '*nur für Deutsche*' (Only for Germans.) The Sojourner Truth riots were condemned as providing ammunition to the Axis, as Japan aired broadcasts about the riots to India, the Philippines and elsewhere. 'It was a scoop for our enemies.'[20]

More violent race riots occurred the following year as Whites attacked Blacks throughout Detroit after rumours of an interracial fight in a park spun out of control. Blacks were pulled from streetcars and their cars overturned. Twenty African Americans were killed in the melee on 'Bloody Monday in Detroit'; *Głos Ludowy* noted the IWO, which the paper supported, 'issued a special statement condemning the anti-black riots', but that the city's mainstream Polish paper, *Dziennik Polski* (Polish Daily), 'was the only newspaper not to condemn these riots'. The more leftist *Głos Ludowy*, however, was unequivocal in condemning the White racism fuelling 'Detroit's Shame', warning, 'Social progress in America depends upon the continued cohesion and mutual confidence among all groups and races who make up this nation.' The racism that erupted in June 1943, the paper warned, was 'potential dynamite to blast the very foundations upon which our democracy has been founded'. The paper also worried 'the monstrous mob spirit' unleashed against blacks 'can as readily be turned against the foreign-born'.[21]

The Slovak paper, while equally condemnatory of racism among its ethnic cohort and other Americans, placed its faith in education and the Popular Front progressive coalition. In 1935, it devoted a long article to debunking the pseudo-scientific question, 'Are Blacks the Lowest Race of People?' The paper said 'growing nationalism and the fascist question of "higher and lower" races' compelled it to publish scientific refutation of 'the speeches of capitalist exploiters ... While we have to listen to the speeches of the capitalists, we have to believe in science. And science says something quite different from the capitalists and their apologists.' *Ľudový denník* detailed the early civilizations in Egypt and China far in advance of Europeans. 'History teaches us that long before any civilization started among the Whites, coloured nations had highly developed civilizations,' the Slovak paper argued, belittling the forebears of supposedly superior Nordic Europeans. 'A thousand years ago the Germans were half-savage tribes ... Likewise, in England, where the Roman legions found people living in caves indulging in cannibalism.' Nor did *Ľudový denník* spare its own Slavic culture. 'At the time, the Slavs obviously lived in a savage way. It is quite obvious that if in the past the coloured races exceeded the White race in intelligence, this would prove that there is no reason to believe that their levels of intelligence are lower than those of white people.' The paper also recommended to its readers books that 'will help rebut the myths of white supremacy'. In the 1930s, when other Slavic newspapers were asserting their cultural (and racial) bona fides to gain acceptance in race-besotted America, this leftist paper defended the intellectual and cultural primacy of African and Asian cultures, as a counter to White race-thinking.[22]

Polish *Głos Ludowy* and Slovak *Ľudový denník* fighting to make lynching a federal crime

Ľudový denník's commitment to racial equality flowered during the wartime Popular Front, when it offered a 'Reply to those who are anti-black' addressed to the many American Slovaks 'who are prejudiced against blacks and consider black people to be inferior'. The leftist paper noted: 'The editor of a Slovak fraternal newspaper recently wrote that blacks are an internal threat to the U.S., against which all forces must defend us.' To counter this calumny, *Ľudový denník* offered the example of an African-American man named Jackson who had invented a better rifle helping in the fight against Nazi Germany and stressed, 'prejudice against blacks is just as un-American and undemocratic as Hitler's racism and cannibalism against the Jews. America has evolved into a powerful country, because of the different races and nationalities that live here in harmony.' Five months later the paper noted: 'Mrs. Roosevelt Hopes the War Will End Race Discrimination.' In 1944, the paper again highlighted Detroit, with a photo of a mock funeral featuring a coffin. 'Here Lies Jim Crow,' the marchers announced in celebrating segregation's imminent demise.[23]

Both papers were not always so sanguine on 'harmony' between Blacks and Whites. Lynchings were reported in condemnatory accounts and Slavic readers were urged to become involved in anti-lynching campaigns the papers publicized. Lynchings in South Carolina and Mississippi pointed to the need, *Rovnosť ľudu* argued, for a Communist newspaper in the South. 'Only in this way will it be possible to make the Southern White and Black workers a united force, not enemies.' Such a paper 'not only will protect the life of the Black workers, but will contribute to the solidarity of White and Black workers and hasten the time of winning the working class in America'. The article ignored the fact many working-class Whites embraced racialized privileges rather than abstract worker solidarity. The article noted 'hundreds' of Whites had fired gunshots at one of the lynch victims on even a suspicion he 'wanted to rape a white woman'. It was unclear how a Communist newspaper would overcome such racial phobias. Still, as historians Robin Kelley and Michael Honey have noted, Communist and socialist organizers did build interracial social movements in the 1930s South, at great bodily peril. The Slovak paper publicized these efforts, too, with frequent coverage of the Southern Tenant Farmers Union and the violence White terrorists deployed against sharecropper organizers. In 1935, the paper noted sixteen recent lynchings included sharecroppers' union organizers. The tenor of these articles suggests radical Slovaks' commitment to interracial campaigns for racial and class justice.[24]

The Slovak paper frequently ran articles detailing macabre torture-spectacle lynchings, as when it sardonically announced 'open season for hunting' after a Mississippi Black man's lynching. A particularly brutal torture-murder in Arkansas caused the paper to declare, 'Lynchings of blacks is the entertainment of 100-percent patriotic banditry in America.' In 1929 the paper reported, 'Black Woman Lynched in "Civilized" America!' A Tennessee lynching was called 'the recent lynching of democracy'. A long article wanted to know, 'Can Lynching be Ended?' Four years later, following the macabre Sherman, Texas lynching of George Hughes, an editorial called for a national campaign against the 'Wholesale Lynching of Blacks in South' and the paper covered protest meetings against the Sherman atrocity, where 'the brutality of lynchers bordered on the pagan'.[25]

The complicity of mass media in publicizing lynching spectacles was dramatically revealed in the mob murder of Claude Neal in October 1934. 'Lynchers Announced Murder Plan in Capitalist Newspapers,' *Denník Rovnosť ľudu* cried. As with several other sensational lynchings, Neal's torture-murder was publicized ahead of time, and 'officials failed to lift a finger against the planners of this lynching, even though it was announced 24 hours in advance in reports in the capitalist press, and broadcast throughout the area: "All white people, come out to the comedy!"' Neal, on the run after being accused of murdering a White woman in Marianna, Florida, was captured but delivered by the sheriff into the hands of a 'lynch committee'. Newspapers reported a lynching would occur the following day; such notifications had occurred in several earlier cases so enough White spectators and participants could travel to the 'lynch dance'. While the ILD begged authorities to prevent the publicized lynching, Neal's torture-murder proceeded. Only after armed Blacks tried to defend their homes from the un-satiated mob did the National Guard intervene – to arrest several Blacks. The mainstream press facilitated lynching; the Communist Slovak paper condemned it.[26]

The frequent lynching accounts in the radical paper indicate the severity of White terrorism against African Americans. Such accounts were often published in mainstream Slovak papers, too, albeit without the Communists' outrage.[27] And unlike the mainstream immigrant press, Communist papers not only reported grisly lynchings, they publicized anti-lynching campaigns they told their White-ethnic readers it was their duty to join. In 1936, *Ľudový denník* publicized efforts by the young African-American community organizer Ella Baker and other activists to make lynching a federal crime; the following year, the paper reported on a Harlem march to pressure Congress to enact such a bill. A photo showed Black and White marchers with signs demanding the measure, necessary since southern juries invariably exonerated lynchers. The paper later reported success in getting the bill through the House, but called on readers to pressure the Senate to act.[28]

Congress never succeeded in making lynching a federal crime. As late as 1946, *Ľudový denník* again publicized anti-lynching picketers, Black women from several states who demonstrated at the White House for federal protection. 'How is Lynching Democratic?' the paper wanted to know. The paper applauded the collaboration with

Black activists by Whites in left-wing groups such as the IWO, which in its own, multilingual *Fraternal Outlook* often turned a 'spotlight on Jim Crow'.[29]

The Slovak paper reported on various efforts to smash Jim Crow. *Denník Rovnosť ľudu* exposed racial disparities in benefits extended by New Deal programmes.[30] Fortunately, Slavic leftists relied on more than the government to achieve justice, working in tandem with African Americans for progress. 'The IWO Stands for Racial Equality!' *Denník Rovnosť ľudu*'s English-language 'Voice of the Youth' page declared. To counter the assaults Black swimmers endured on Chicago's segregated beaches, the IWO joined the Communist League of Struggle for Negro Rights in organizing an integrated swim-in at Jackson Park. Although the article did not mention it, Chicago's 1919 race riot began when White swimmers fatally attacked a Black teen who drifted too near a Whites-only beach. The IWO anticipated by more than twenty-five years integrated swim-ins civil-rights activists orchestrated to break segregation at beaches and amusement parks. Similarly, *Głos Ludowy* later celebrated Black bowlers in leftist union leagues who challenged the segregated American Bowling Association.[31]

Głos Ludowy and *Ľudový denník*: with a single voice for racial equality in unions

Enduring Black-White alliances were built in the labour movement, too. In 1937, a Slovak in the Workers Alliance wrote *Ľudový denník* about an interracial march on Washington that encountered segregated restaurants and hotels. 'Is this not worthy of condemnation?' he asked his Slovak readers. 'And then they tell us that only in this land is there freedom and democracy, in this supposed home of the brave.' Within left-wing unions, it was Jim Crow that was shown the door. The paper praised interracial packinghouse worker meetings, where Black and White unionists were addressed in Polish and English. The paper also hailed the decision by Pittsburgh-area Black churches to endorse the Steel Workers Organizing Committee's unionization drive, as well as SWOC President Philip Murray's pledge of racial equality in the union.[32]

During and after the Second World War, both papers editorialized in favour of banning the racially exclusionary poll tax, making lynching a federal crime and extending permanent status to the wartime Fair Employment Practices Committee (FEPC), tasked with investigating racial discrimination in war industries. *Ľudový denník* reported that the FEPC chairman declared persistent racial discrimination hurt the war effort. He outlined 'the horrible consequences that employment discrimination would cause to the nation's destiny, not just to the ostracized individuals'. 'We need every pair of hands' for war work, he added.[33] At war's end the paper publicized the IWO campaign for a permanent FEPC. An interracial delegation, including Charles Musil of the Slovak Workers Society, lobbied 'every Senator and Congressman in Washington to fulfil his pledge of office and uphold the right of every American, regardless of race or religion, to work and equal opportunity'. Enactment of a full-time civil-rights agency was called 'the acid test of honest patriotism'.[34]

A cartoon ran in both papers demanding 'Relief from the Poll Tax Hydra' that barred millions from voting and also made it easier for lynchers to evade justice when they were invariably exonerated by all-White juries.³⁵ Two years later the Polish paper still urged, 'Strike Down the Poll Tax!'³⁶ A spate of lynchings in 1942 caused the paper to equate Mississippi with Nazi Germany, and declare, 'Time to remove this terrible stain from American soil'; the Slovak paper reported a Saint Louis meeting where 5,000 people condemned a Missouri lynching.³⁷

When, shortly after the Second World War, two Black veterans and their wives were lynched in Georgia, the Polish paper declared this 'The Lynching of Democracy'. The paper decried not just the 'bestial' murders, but the fact that 'local authorities, devoted to Hitlerist ideology, are in no hurry to prosecute the murderers. They need time to hide their tracks. Even the U.S. attorney has to make sure that "civil rights have been violated." Human corpses don't mean much to him as evidence.' In 1946, *Głos Ludowy* doubled down on its denunciation of the segregationist South, criticizing President Harry Truman's attorney general, Tom Clark of Texas. 'There's no hurrying Clark, who has the "most snakelike" tasks to perform, namely, lobbing the most venomous propaganda at progressive elements, including those who are honestly struggling against lynching.' The paper publicized the IWO's telegram campaign, which tried in vain to get Clark and Truman to bring federal charges against the Georgia lynchers. *Głos Ludowy* published a cartoon showing '1,000,000 U.S. Negroes who fought fascism' facing the 'KKK Lynchings' and wanted to know, 'Have we Really Defeated Fascism?' The paper indicted Clark along with the lynchers he failed to prosecute, saying, 'These snakes are closely associated with the growing number of assassins of the American people, who are attempting to lynch them through their organized work.' Sure enough, while the following year New York's Black Communist Councilman Benjamin Davis congratulated the paper and its Polish IWO society for its anti-lynching campaign, Clark put the IWO on his list of subversive organizations, and deportation proceedings were reopened against editor Nowak.³⁸

In the face of red-baiting investigations, *Głos Ludowy* remained defiant in demanding full equality for Black citizens. In the eyes of many congressmen such as HUAC Chair John Rankin of Mississippi, this may have been the ultimate act of subversion, but still the papers carried on. The Slovak paper publicized efforts by Representative Vito Marcantonio to get Mississippi segregationists expelled from Congress, and both papers derided Rankin as a bloody-minded fool.³⁹

The Polish paper publicized a petition campaign calling for an effective, permanent FEPC. The paper reminded readers, 'Almost all working people, especially those of Polish origin, belong to minority groups. They, too, have experienced discrimination. Let us hurry and add our signatures to the petition.' The paper publicized activities sponsored by the IWO during the then-labelled 'Negro History Week' (forerunner to the 'Black History Month' in 1969), and used the occasion to editorialize in favour of an anti-lynching bill, permanent FEPC and an end to HUAC. It decried the filibuster by which a handful of southern segregationist senators hamstrung the FEPC; a cartoon showed a windbag senator blocking the road 'to vital legislation'. The paper declared, 'This Fascist Racism Must be Defeated.'⁴⁰

White-supremacist violence waged against Black civil-rights activists was aptly labelled 'terrorism', as when the paper wrote of the Civil Rights Congress' campaign in 1950 to get the president to support an anti-lynching bill after five mob massacres in the year's first ten days. The fire-bombing murder of African-American Florida activist Harry Moore and his wife was denounced as terror, and the IWO, already under a legal cloud as a suspected subversive organization, lobbied Truman to act on the murders, 'a shame and blot against America'. 'The prevalent anti-Negro violence has the earmarks of genocide', the unrepentant IWO added.[41]

Defiance of the defenders of the segregated status quo took principled bravery and commitment to racial equality. But such attacks on the terrorist defenders of segregation may have also stemmed from self-interest. Readers of *Głos Ludowy* learned the same people defending segregation also expressed anti-immigrant xenophobia, anti-Semitism and contempt for working people. Nowhere was this more apparent than in the ravings of Mississippi Democratic Senator Theodore Bilbo. The arch-segregationist lawmaker often read into the record diatribes on Black inferiority, but also shrieked that Italians, Slavs and Jews were 'mongrelizing' America. His speeches were derided by the paper as 'just so much fascist gas'. 'When Senator Bilbo addresses opposition to the FEPC, he expels from his mouth a stream of every fascist filth,' the paper derided the toad-like senator. The Slovak paper called him 'an enemy of democracy' for blocking repeal of the poll tax.[42]

When an Italian-American IWO member wrote to Bilbo urging him to support the FEPC, he sent her a letter beginning 'Dear Dago'. This letter was publicized by well-connected IWO members such as Congressman Marcantonio, who demanded an apology. Others tried to take their beef directly to the senator. Edward Bykowski, a disabled Polish-American Navy veteran, picketed the senator's hotel with a placard featuring an image of his Purple Heart awarded for combat wounds. 'Was this in vain? Tell it to me, Bilbo. I fought for democracy.' Bykowski was joined on the picket line by other progressive Americans, who decried Bilbo for similar insults to Jewish and African Americans. The veteran unsuccessfully sought a meeting with the senator, then decided to honour him for his commendable service – to the Nazis. 'Senator Theodore Bilbo of Mississippi has been given the Nazi Iron Cross for his meritorious fascism,' the paper reported. Bykowski sent this war trophy to Bilbo along with a letter, explaining, 'Of course, I would like to pin this Cross on you personally, but my past experience convinces me that you are a dishonorable man, who I can never seem to pin down'. Bykowski promised to continue the 'oust Bilbo' campaign 'until the Washington airs are cleansed of this Bilbo poison'.[43]

Głos Ludowy lauded Bykowski as 'the pride of Polonia and America', and supported a petition campaign by the IWO and other organizations to get Bilbo expelled from the Senate. The Slovak paper also backed the IWO's effort. Bilbo was now portrayed in cartoon not as a Nazi toad, but puppet master of the KKK, whose resurgence the Polish paper warily noted. The paper published in Polish excerpts from an article, 'Hitler in the Senate', written by Dashiell Hammett for the IWO's magazine, *Fraternal Outlook*. 'Hitler Lives!' the author of *The Maltese Falcon* declared in exposing Bilbo's racist mind. 'I heard him as he spoke on a tub-thumping day in the U.S. Senate.' *Ľudový denník* had beaten the novelist to the metaphor; in August 1945, it ran a cartoon of the sclerotic senator standing on a copy of *Mein Kampf* while spewing racial and ethnic epithets. His defiance of the federal government in calling on supporters to bar Black voters from the polls merited, the paper argued, expulsion from the Senate.[44]

Not every Slavic American saw eye to eye with the paper, and racism was not confined to below the Mason-Dixon Line.[45] In 1951, when a Black veteran and his family rented an apartment in the virtually all-White and heavily Slavic city of Cicero, west of Chicago, a mob of thousands, abetted by police failure to curb them, trashed the Black family's apartment and gutted the entire building. *Głos Ludowy* demanded to know why Police Chief Ervin Konofsky and his force 'twiddled their thumbs' as the mob wreaked havoc. Citing an investigation by the *Chicago Daily News*, the Polish paper said a witness to the riots related a mob leader had shouted in an 'inflamed' voice, 'This is a neighborhood inhabited by decent white people.' 'I'd never seen this speaker before,' the paper quoted the witness. 'He looked like a madman,' adding, 'this witness was right when he said the mob's leaders were "madmen". Similar madmen followed the Nazis, who managed to murder Jews, Poles and Russians.' The paper warned in Cicero and elsewhere Blacks were the target of looming fascism. A columnist cautioned that 'Polonia cannot accept racism', for 'whatever form it assumes, it is a poison, destructive of democracy, and a divisive force which weakens the struggle of the people for peace, security and democracy'.[46]

As historian Arnold Hirsch has noted, by 1951 far more Polish Americans joined other White ethnics in resisting integration than shared these sentiments.[47] The paper called racism 'the shame of America', while noting the Confederate flag had recently emerged as a badge of honour of segregationists, North and South. When Cicero's grand jury convened, it exonerated Konofsky, other city officials and White mob leaders, instead charging 'the blacks and those who defended them from the attack' had 'organized a conspiracy aiming to lower real-estate prices'. While the paper condemned this as the behaviour of fascist outliers, in Chicago and other cities plagued by housing battles, such acts by Poles and other White ethnics were not isolated events. The paper's attempts to maintain the wartime interracial Popular Front coalition dissented from the more dominant embrace of Whiteness and a virulent, conservative anti-communism.[48]

Głos Ludowy could take some solace, though, that even mainstream Polish papers such as *Nowy Świat* (New World) of New York and *Dziennik Chicagoski* (Daily Chicagoan) now grudgingly concluded that 'the same forces which act this way toward the Negroes, tomorrow will use the same approach toward Catholics, non-citizens, "foreigners"'. Still, *Głos Ludowy* couldn't help questioning the Chicago paper's commitment to racial equality, noting that it carried a news item the following day which reflected the racist thinking of the United Press. The left-wing paper, labelled Communist by its rivals, was alone in its unequivocal support for Black equality on residential and other matters.[49]

Surviving as dissident foreign-language newspapers: the Red Scare and beyond

Głos Ludowy and editor Nowak survived the Red Scare – the federal government's last attempt to deport him as a subversive was thrown out by the Supreme Court in

1957 – and his paper continued forcefully advocating full equality for African Americans – a lonely voice in Polonia into the modern civil-rights era and beyond.[50] The paper was delighted when the Supreme Court 'ruled that the segregation of children in black and white schools was unconstitutional'. Still, the paper was prescient in noting the court 'has not taken any practical action for the implementation of this decision ... [D]iscrimination will continue.' The paper reported the venomous 'massive resistance' rhetoric segregationist officials such as Georgia Democratic Gov. Herman Talmadge expressed. The paper reported that already in September 1954, Mississippi acted to abolish public schools rather than integrate them, a move quickly followed in other jurisdictions. Whites-only, private Christian academies circumvented the ruling. White Citizens Councils – the Klan by any other name – rapidly developed to terrorize Blacks into not pushing for educational or voting rights. 'Time After Time,' the paper commented, 'Racist Terror Confronts Blacks.' Southern congressmen urging 'massive resistance' to the Brown decision were working 'with all their renowned fierceness to excite the revolt against the Supreme Court decision ending racial segregation in public schools'. The paper noted calls to defy the high court and the Constitution went unpunished, even though 'such a speech by a unionist or a liberal would be deplored by the attorney general and an FBI agent would snatch them in his paws'. A *Głos Ludowy* columnist pointed out segregationist politicians such as Democratic Senator James Eastland of Mississippi and Alabama Judge Tom Brady were active in the White Citizens Councils; the latter luminary was 'like the Goebbels of the WCC, also author of the idea that the United States should buy (or seize) the Mexican region of Baja California and deport to that peninsula several millions of its Negroes'. The columnist asked, 'Will racists cause fratricidal slaughter in the USA?'[51]

Sadly, the answer came with the brutal lynching, in 1955, of Emmett Till, a Black teenager from Chicago visiting family in rural Mississippi. On a dare, he whistled at a White woman and in retaliation, her husband and his half-brother kidnaped, tortured and murdered the teen. *Głos Ludowy* ran the excruciating details of Till's murder, first outlined in a *LOOK* magazine article, as well as a photo of Till's mother sobbing by his casket and poems in Polish and English commemorating the teen. When an all-White jury exonerated the accused, in spite of their bragging of their deed, the Polish paper declared, 'There are, in fact, eminent Americans who have decided not to stand down in this fight until the black stain of shame has been scrubbed from the Star Spangled Banner.'[52]

While the paper tirelessly exposed the depths of White racist resistance to equality, it celebrated, too, the agency of African Americans who battled for their liberation. 'Solidarity Walk of Blacks in Montgomery' cheered the 1955 bus boycott begun by NAACP activist Rosa Parks, saying, 'The eyes of the world are fixed today on Montgomery, Alabama.' The paper lauded Martin Luther King and other leaders who went to jail in the seminal Black freedom campaigns. And when in early 1960, Black students politely sat in at lunch counters demanding equal service, the paper applauded their courage and commitment. Nowak approvingly editorialized on 'this historic week for the black people'. 'Freedom and human dignity is the issue in the sit-ins.'[53]

Głos Ludowy contrasted its stance with other Polish papers such as *Nowy Świat*, which argued that 'not so long ago ... in the U.S.A. "persecution of blacks does not exist" and that "it is the invention of Communist propaganda".⁵⁴ And when Washington hesitated to guarantee freedom to Black Mississippians facing 'wild anti-black terror', it declared that 'the whole civilized world' demanded to know 'how long this astonishing savagery will last'. In 1963, the paper noted, Attorney General Robert Kennedy 'cannot find any free time to come to the aid of persecuted citizens of the South'. Into the 1960s, *Głos Ludowy* was determined to turn a spotlight on American racism.⁵⁵

Głos Ludowy's advocacy of racial justice outlasted the McCarthy Era, offering a counterhegemonic voice to the rise of White-ethnic hostility to Blacks and embrace of law-and-order conservatism. Left-wing Polish and Slovak papers nuance our understanding of conservative White ethnics as the building blocks of the New Right. *Głos Ludowy* and *Ľudový denník* demonstrate that another, dissenting world was possible. As other Slavs embraced race privilege, fashioning a valorizing immigrant narrative marginalizing Blacks from worthy Americanism, these papers were dissenting voices representing a missed opportunity for intersectional commitment to working-class justice *and* racial equality, and Black-White alliances on the left. Such editorial voice is still much needed.

Notes

1 David Roediger, *The Wages of Whiteness* (New York: Verso, 1991); James Barrett and Roediger, 'Whiteness and the Inbetween Peoples of Europe', *Journal of American Ethnic History* 16, no. 3 (Summer 1997): 3–44; Mathew Frye Jacobson, *Roots Too* (Cambridge, Massachusetts: Harvard University Press, 2006); Jacobson, *Whiteness of a Different Colour* (Cambridge, Massachusetts: Harvard University Press, 1998); Robert Zecker, *Race and America's Immigrant Press* (New York: Continuum, 2011).
2 Grace Hale, *Making Whiteness* (New York: Vintage, 1999); Zecker, *Race and America's Immigrant Press*, 12–49; *New Yorský denník*, 14 June 1921, 1.
3 *New Yorský denník*, 4 June 1921, 6; 18 June 1921, 6.
4 In January 1934, the name was changed to *Denník Rovnosť ludu* (Daily Equality for the People) and in June 1935, it was rechristened *Ľudový denník* (People's Daily).
5 Robert Goldstein, *American Blacklist (*Lawrence: University Press of Kansas, 2008).
6 *Głos Ludowy*, 27 October 1951, 1, second section, 'National Negro Labor Council to Hold Convention in Cincinnati'.
7 Margaret Nowak, *Two Who Were There* (Detroit: Wayne State University Press, 1989) discusses Nowak's career. On government deportation of radicals, Rachel Buff, *Against the Deportation Terror* (Philadelphia: Temple University Press, 2018).
8 *N.W. Ayer and Son's Directory of Newspapers and Periodicals* (Philadelphia: Ayer and Son, 1938), 208; Dirk Hoerder, ed., *The Immigrant Labor Press in North America, 1840s–1970s: An Annotated Bibliography, Volume 2: Migrants from Eastern and Southeastern Europe* (New York: Greenwood Press, 1987), 71.
9 Robert M. Zecker, *'A Road to Peace and Freedom'* (Philadelphia: Temple University Press, 2018).
10 *Rovnosť ludu*, 6 August 1919, 1, 'Plemenné boje'; *New Yorský denník*, all 1: 30 July 1919, 31 July 1919, 1 August 1919, 2 August 1919. Translations of Slovak articles by the author. On the Polish press and the 1919 riots, cf. Dominic Pacyga, *Polish Immigrants*

and Industrial Chicago (Columbus: Ohio State University Press, 1991), 214–27; Pacyga, 'To Live Among Others: Poles and Their Neighbors in Industrial Chicago, 1865–1930', *Journal of American Ethnic History* 16, no. 1 (1996): 55–73. Jan Voogd, *Race Riots and Resistance* (New York: Peter Lang, 2008).

11 *Denník Rovnosť ľudu*, 23 March 1935, 1, 'Černošský ľud v Harlem terorizovaný policiou'; *Ľudový denník*, 6 July 1936, 1, 'Zprávu o Černochoch v New Yorku Objavili' and 15 August 1935, 1, 'Výbor Mayora La Guardia Viní Mesto za Marcový Výbuch v Harleme'. Mark Naison, *Communists in Harlem during the Depression* (Urbana: University of Illinois Press, 1983).

12 *Ľudový denník*, 9 August 1935, 6, 'Anti-Negro Chain Letter Sent in Detroit'; Thomas Sugrue, *The Origins of the Urban Crisis* (Princeton, New Jersey: Princeton University Press, 1996).

13 *Ľudový denník*, 3 March 1942, 6, 'Detroitská lúza sa oborila na černochov'.

14 John McGreevy, *Parish Boundaries* (Chicago: University of Chicago Press, 1996).

15 *Głos Ludowy*, 11 April 1942, 5, Ed Falkowski, 'How United is Polonia?' For Popular Front-era Communist embrace of American icons, Library of Congress, Communist Party USA collection, Reel 303, Delo 3983, pamphlet, Earl Browder, 'Who are the Americans?' (1936). For *Ameryka-Echo*, see Anna D. Jaroszyńska-Kirchmann. *The Polish Hearst: Ameryka-Echo and the Public Role of the Immigrant Press* (Urbana: University of Illinois Press, 2017).

16 Wayne State University, Reuther Library, Stanley and Margaret Nowak collection, Box 4, Folder 4-6, flyer, 'Nowak is the Man! Help Blast Jim Crow – Loveland's' (no date, 1940s).

17 *Głos Ludowy*, 11 April 1942, 5, Falkowski, 'How United is Polonia?'; 13 June 1942, 5, 'Stop Discrimination!'; 18 July 1942, 6, Thomas X. Dombrowski, 'Congressional Elections – Friends of Dies Must Be Defeated'; 1 August 1942, 5, Dombrowski, 'Tenerowicz Befriends Fifth Column Elements'.

18 *Głos Ludowy*, 12 June 1943, 1, 'Ku-Klux-Klan Odpowiedzialny Za Strajku Packarda'. Translation of Polish articles by the author. *Ľudový denník*, 26 August 1944, 4, 'Keď ruka vlády zasiahla'; 16 March 1942, 3.

19 *Głos Ludowy*, 4 July 1942, 2, 'Żadanie Federalnej Inwestygacji Piątej Kolumny w Detroit'.

20 *Głos Ludowy*, 13 June 1942, 5, 'Stop Discrimination!'; 1 August 1942, 5, Dombrowski, 'Tenerowicz Befriends Fifth Column Elements'.

21 *Głos Ludowy*, 26 June 1943, 1, '"Krwawy Pondelok" w Detroit'; 26 June 1943, 1, second section, 'A Nazi Conspiracy!'; 3 July 1943, 1 and 2, 'Tydzień Organiczonego Stanu Wojennego w Detroit'; 3 July 1943, 1, second section, Falkowski, 'The Negro and the Poles'.

22 *Ľudový denník*, 26 June 1935, 4, 'Zo sveta vedy a techniky – Sú Černoši nižším plemenom ľudstva?'.

23 *Ľudový denník*, 3 January 1942, 4, 'Odpoveď tým, čo štvú proti Černochom'; 25 June 1942, 2, 'Pani Rooseveltá dúfa, že vojna skončí rasovú diskrimináciu'; 6 July 1944, 5. The 3 January 1942 article refers to Hitler's *'židožrútstvo'* (cannibalism of the Jews).

24 *Rovnosť ľudu*, 26 April 1930, 1, 'Lynčovanie černochov priam kričí za Komunistickým časopisom'; Robin Kelley, *Hammer and Hoe* (Chapel Hill: University of North Carolina Press, 2016); Michael Honey, *Sharecroppers' Troubadour* (New York: Palgrave Macmillan, 2013). On the STFU, *Denník Rovnosť ľudu*, 27 May 1935, 1, 'Poprava odsúdených na smrť odložená'; *Ľudový denník*, 3 October 1935, 4, 'Šestnásť lynčov na deväť mesiacov tohoto roku'; 25 June 1936, 1, 'Farmerovi hrozí lynčovanie jestlie bude

vydaný do rúk Arkansaským úradom'; 30 June 1936, 5, 'Vydá Horner Bennetta Južným Lynčerom?'; 8 November 1937, 1, 'Plantážnici mučili černocha, aby verboval sbieračov'.

25 *Rovnosť ľudu*, 14 May 1929, 1, 'Otvorená sezona sa započala; jedon černoch lynčovaný'; 18 March 1929, 1, 'Lúza Lynčovala zase černocha v Georgii'; 21 March 1929, 1, 'Dvaja černoši lynčovaní'; 23 March 1929, 1, 'Dvaja černošsi postrelaní'; 5 May 1926, 1, 'Či lynčom bud učinený koniec?'; 1 June 1929, 1; 'Lynčovanie toť demokracia'; 12 May 1930, 1, 'Luža spálila súdnu budovu spolu s černošskom väze'; 14 May 1930, 1 and 2, 'Stanné právo v Sherman'; 19 May 1930, 6; 21 May 1930, 5, 'Bosses Increase Lynching – Workers Increase Organizing'; 22 May 1930, 6; 24 May 1930, 2, 'Lynčovanie černochov bielymi otročitélmi'; 29 May 1930, 1, 'Surovosť lynčovníkov nezná medzí'; 2 June 1930, 1.

26 *Denník Rovnosť ľudu*, 1 November 1934, 1, 'Lynčovníci hlásili plán vraždy v kapitalistických časopisoch'. Hale, *Making Whiteness*.

27 *Rovnosť ľudu*, 6 March 1923, 1, 'Lynčeri boli Zatknuti'; 29 May 1923, 1, 'Kratké americké Zprávy'; 20 February 1925, 3; 8 June 1926, 1, 'Bičováni obnoveno v Delaware'; 7 January 1928, 1, 'Lynčuju ubylo v r. 1927'; 4 June 1928, 1, 'Po 13-ročnom väzení bol oslobodený'; 22 June 1928, 1; 'Demokratická konvencia v meste najnovšieho lynču'; 3 January 1929, 1, 'Černoch lynčovaný a Spálený'; 19 January 1929, 1, 'Lynčovali nevinného černocha'; 27 June 1929, 1, 'Biela ľúza postrielala zbila černošského robotníka'; 11 April 1930, 1, 'Černošský posluhovač lynčovaný'; 25 April 1930, 1, 'Dvaja černoši lynčovaní'; 3 June 1930, 1, 'Zase jeden černoch lynčovaná; 20 June 1930, 1, 'Černoch zastřelen pro láhev pomáslí'; 23 June 1930, 1, 'Černoch lynčovany zas!'; *Denník Rovnosť ľudu*, 6 April 1934, 6, 'Zabil černocha a je volný'; 23 June 1934, 1, 'V Texase Lynčovali Černocha lebo sa priatelil s bielou dievčinou'; 11 July 1934, 1, 'Černoch lynčovaný na juhu'; *Ľudový denník*, 10 September 1936, 1, 'Dotknul sa ženy, lynčovaný'; 30 September 1936, 1, 'Černoch lynčovaný'; 26 July 1937, 2, 'Černoch lynčovaný'; 14 October 1937, 1, 'Černoch lynčovaný v Alabame'; 30 August 1946, 1, 'Ozbrojení do Boja Proti Černochom'. Zecker, *Race and America's Immigrant Press*, 12–49.

28 *Ľudový denník*, 6 March 1936, 6, 'Harlem Asks Federal Penalty for Lynching'; 26 February 1937, 6, 'Zastavte Lynče'; 5 April 1937, 2, 'Nástup proti lynčovaniu'; 17 April 1937, 'Dom Zástupcov Prijal Gavanovu Predloho Proti Lynčom'; 24 July 1937, 2, 'Bandera Lynčerov na Práci'.

29 *Ľudový denník*, 14 August 1946, 1, 'Piketujú Biely Dom Proti Lynčovaniu'; 20 November 1946, 4, 'Či aj lynčovanie je demokratické?' *Fraternal Outlook*, October–November 1949, 4–5, Sam Milgrom, 'Spotlight on Jim Crow'. The magazine published sections in English and ten other languages, including Slovak and Carpatho-Rusyn. Many articles dealt with civil rights.

30 *Denník Rovnosť ľudu*, 7 April 1934, 4, 'N.R.A. nepomahá mnoho délnikom a černyšským nič'; *Ľudový denník*, 5 April 1937, 5, 'HOLC vyházdala na ulicu tri ďalšie nezamestnané rodiny'. George Lipsitz, *The Possessive Investment in Whiteness* (Philadelphia: Temple University Press, 1998).

31 *Denník Rovnosť ľudu*, 27 July 1934, 4, 'The IWO Stands for Racial Equality!'; *Głos Ludowy*, 15 January 1949, 7, 'Barred from Bowling Tourney'. For segregated recreation, Victoria Wolcott, *Race, Riots, and Roller Coasters* (Philadelphia: University of Pennsylvania Press, 2014); Voogd, *Race Riots and Resistance*.

32 *Ľudový denník*, 17 February 1937, 5, 'Zatracuje predpojatosť proti černošským rob.'; 6 November 1937, 4, 'Černošski a polski robotníci sa v jatkách organizujú'; 11 February 1937, 1, 'Černoši pomôžu budovať uniu AA'.

33 *Ľudový denník*, 13 March 1942, 6, 'Diskrimináciou možno zmariť vojnove úsilie Ameriky'.
34 *Ľudový denník*, 13 July 1945, 6, 'I.W.O. Delegation in Washington for F.E.P.C.'
35 *Ľudový denník*, 23 March 1942, 4, 'Volebná daň otravuje život Ameriky'; *Głos Ludowy*, 28 March 1942, 2, 'Odciac Łeb Hydrze'.
36 *Głos Ludowy*, 25 March 1944, 2, 'Ubíc Poll-Tax'. *Ľudový denník* also denounced the poll tax. 24 July 1945, 6, 'Pepper Heads Group to Abolish Poll Tax'.
37 *Głos Ludowy*, 7 November 1942, 2, 'Straszne Owoce Rasowej Nienawiści'; *Ľudový denník*, 10 February 1942, 3, '5,000 Ľudi zatratilo lynčovanie'.
38 *Głos Ludowy*, 3 August 1946, 4, 'Lynczowa Demokracja'; 10 August 1946, 1, 'Żadają Oskarżenia Rasistów Bilbo, Rankina a Talmadge'; 10 August 1946, 7, 'MZR Żąda Ujęcia i Ukarania Winnych Zbrodni w Georgia'; 10 August 1946, 1, second section, 'IWO Calls for Action against Georgia Lynchers'. Cornell University, Kheel Center, International Workers Order collection, Box 4, Folder 2, letter, 29 May 1947, Councilman Benjamin Davis (New York) to Boleslaw Gebert, Polonia Society, IWO. *Detroit Times*, 6 October 1949, 12-C, 'Nowak Linked to Red Affair'; Wayne State University, Reuther Library, Don Binkowski Papers, Box 7, Folder 7-48, pamphlet, 'An American Family Faces Separation or Exile' (no date, 1956?).
39 *Ľudový denník*, 16 March 1946, 4, 'Americkí vyslúžilci proti Rankinovi', 1 June 1946, 1, 'Pokrokárov vyšetrovať, to áno – ale nie Ku Klux Klancov'; 8 August 1946, 1, 'Marcantonio žiada vylúčenie Rankina a Bilba z kongresu'; *Głos Ludowy*, 16 February 1946, 13; 6 September 1952, 3, 'Fanatyk Supremacji Bialej Rasy Przegał Wybory w Mississippi'.
40 *Głos Ludowy*, 30 November 1946, 2, 'Akcija Petycyjna Za Stanowym FEPC'; 8 February 1947, 6, 'Tydźień Historji Murzynów'; 9 February 1946, 8, 'Ten Faszystowski Rasista Musi Być Pokonany'.
41 *Głos Ludowy*, 21 January 1950, 1, 'Protest Przeciw Lynczowi'; 5 January 1952, 2, second section, 'Halt Lynch Terror!'; 12 January 1952, 1, second section, 'IWO Groups Tell Truman to Act on Florida Murders'.
42 *Głos Ludowy*, 21 July 1945, 4, 'Jadowite Przemówienie'; *Ľudový denník*, 1 April 1944, 3, 'Nepriateľ demokracie'.
43 *Głos Ludowy*, 11 August 1945, 5, 'Sprawy Krajowe: Beczelny Sen. Bilbo Pisze Władisław Kucharski'; 18 August 1945, 3; 8 September 1945, 4, 'Chluba Polonji i Ameryki'; 8 September 1945, 1, second section, 'Polish American Veteran Protests Bilbo's Fascist Raving in Senate'; 6 October 1945, 2, 'Weteran Edward Bykowski – Masową Pikietę'; 13 October 1945, 1, 'Nazistowski Żelazny Krzyż Dla Sen. Bilbo'.
44 *Głos Ludowy*, 8 September 1945, 4, 'Chluba Polonji i Ameryki'; 13 October 1945, 1, 'Nazistowski Żelazny Krzyż Dla Sen. Bilbo'; 24 November 1945, 6, 'Polecamy Broszurę "Impeach Bilbo"'; 17 August 1946, 3, 'Egzekutywa UAW-CIO Potępia Senatora Bilbo i Ku-Klux-Klan'; 16 November 1946, 6, 'Apel do Group MZR o Poparcie Akcji Za Usunięciem Senatora Bilbo'; 7 December 1946, 6, 'Kongres Obrony Praw Obywatelskich Wzywa do Usunięcia Bilbo z Senatu'; *Ľudový denník*, 13 December 1946, 3, 'Akcia IWO-za odstránenie Bilboa'; 18 August 1945, 4, 'Bilbo a nesnášanlivosť – dvaja bratia'; 18 October 1945, 4, 'Prefašista Bilbo sa skryl pred vyslúžilcami'; 30 August 1945, 6; 28 June 1946, 6, 'Bilbo sa protiví federálnej vláde'.
45 Sugrue, *The Origins of the Urban Crisis*; Sugrue, 'Crabgrass-Roots Politics: Race, Rights, and the Reaction Against Liberalism in the Urban North, 1940–1964', *The Journal of American History* 82, no. 2 (September 1995): 551–78.
46 *Głos Ludowy*, 21 July 1951, 1, second section, 'Lynch Mob Storms Building in Fascist-Like Act in Chicago'; 21 July 1951, 4, second section, 'Anti-Negro DP Hoodlums on

Rampage in Fascist Outbreak in Chicago'; 28 July 1951, 2; 28 July 1951, 3, 'Troops Face Anti-Negro Rioters'; 11 August 1951, 6, 'Rozpoczęto Inwestygację Rasowych Rozruchów w Mieście Cicero, Illinois'; 18 August 1951, 6, 'Walka z Rasistami w Cicero'; 20 October 1951, 2, second section, Casimir T. Nowacki, 'Polonia Cannot Accept Racism'.

47 Arnold Hirsch, *Making the Second Ghetto* (Chicago: University of Chicago Press, 1998).

48 *Głos Ludowy*, 6 October 1951, 5, 'Fikcyjny "Dobrobyt" Robotników w USA'; 13 October 1951, 2, second section, Nowacki, 'Racism a Threat to All'; 20 October 1951, 2, second section, Nowacki, 'Polonia Cannot Accept Racism'; 17 November 1951, 9, 'Sprawy Krajowe – Dyskyminacja Rasowa Hańbi Amerykę'. Hirsch, *Making the Second Ghetto*; Sugrue, *Origins of the Urban Crisis*; Andrew Diamond, *Mean Streets* (Berkeley: University of California Press, 2009).

49 *Głos Ludowy*, 16 February 1952, 1, second section, Dombrowski, 'Attacks on Negro People Also Hit on the Foreign Born'.

50 'An American Family Faces Separation or Exile'.

51 *Głos Ludowy*, 22 May 1954, 1, 'Najwyższy Trybunał Swą Decyzją Zniósł Segregację w Szkołach'; 25 September 1954, 15, 'No Bias in Baltimore Schools'; 24 December 1955, 2, 'Ząb za Ząb – Rasistowski Terror Woberc Murzynów'; 11 February 1956, 9, 'Sprawy Krajowe: Dixiecraci Wzywają Do Buntu'; 18 February 1956, 11, Józef G-cky, 'Czy Rasiści do bratobójczej rzezy w USA?'.

52 *Głos Ludowy*, 10 September 1955, 1, 'Czternastoletni Chłopiec Zlinczowany w Mississippi; 17 September 1955, 2, 'Bolejąca Matka Płacze Przy Trumnie Syna'; 24 September 1955, 14, 'Dwaj Bracia Oskarżeni o Morderstwo'; 1 October 1955, 1, 'Zlyncowania Sprawiedliwość'; 1 October 1955, 2, 'Główni Świadkowie w Procesie Tilla'; 8 October 1955, 7, 'Oświadczenie Matki Tilla'; 21 January 1956, 12, Adam Kujtkowski, 'Jak Emmett Till Został Zamordowany'. A Polish poem to till, as well as an English poem by Langston Hughes commemorating him, were published. 8 October 1955, 5, Kujtowski, 'Do Matki Emmetta Louisa Tilla'; 12 November 1955, 6, Langston Hughes, 'Mississippi – 1955'.

53 *Głos Ludowy*, 10 March 1956, 3, 'Aresztowani Przywódcy Murzyńscy w Montgomery, Ala.'; 7 April 1956, 16, 'Negro Pastor Continues Fight'; 27 February 1960, 1, Stanley Nowak, 'Tydzień Historii Ludu Murzyńskiego'; 26 March 1960, 1; 26 March 1960, 12, 'Freedom and Human Dignity is the Issue in "Sit-Ins"'.

54 *Głos Ludowy*, 10 March 1956, 7, 'Sprawa Autherine Lucy – Jawny Bunt Rasistów w Alabama'.

55 *Głos Ludowy*, 13 April 1963, 3, 'Wild Anti-Black Terror Continues in Mississippi'.

8

Manufacturing Identities of Poles in the UK in Polish-Language Online Media Following the Brexit Campaign

Katarzyna Molek-Kozakowska
University of Opole

Introduction: historical and demographic context

With Poland's admission to the European Union in 2004, the number of Polish residents in the UK has been steadily increasing. Since 2008, Polish has been the most common non-British nationality with various estimates of Polish-origin residents and temporary workers reaching one million. The trend was not reversed during the years of the economic downturn, even though fewer Poles tended to arrive in the UK. However, 2018 saw the largest annual decrease in the Polish-born population in the UK, dropping by 90,000 to 832,000, according to data from the Office for National Statistics.[1] Emigration from the UK is likely to be the result of economic and status uncertainty for British Poles brought by the Brexit referendum and the subsequent political instabilities, as well as a steady growth of the economy back in Poland,[2] which created a demand for workers in most professions.

Together with the post-Second World War Polish diaspora in Britain (e.g. military personnel that did not return to communist-controlled Poland after 1945, their families and other political exiles),[3] the current Polish community has morphed into a distinct, yet heterogeneous, ethnic minority,[4] whose cultural needs have been taken care of by a large number of Polish organizations[5] over the timespan of the last seven decades. There is a selection of long-standing Polish-language media designed for British Poles, from print political and lifestyle magazines (notably *Dziennik Polski/Tydzień Polski, Goniec Polski, Panorama Magazine, Cooltura*)[6] to online news and announcement portals, from local radio stations to online multimedia channels.[7] These ethnic outlets have also been instrumental in helping the most recent Polish migrants to accommodate to the British economic and social context, to keep in touch with the news from Poland, and to integrate better as a community.

It is generally accepted that if ethnic groups are to become 'imagined communities', they require the rituals of their collective identity to be repeatedly performed in order to forge and confirm the sense of belonging together.[8] The literature on minority collective identities in multicultural societies stresses the fact that native-language media, currently often online (glocal)[9] outlets, are essential to maintaining and reproducing a sense of identity of diasporic communities.[10] Nevertheless, the process of identification or construction of a 'new self' in the context of European migratory experience has been demonstrated as laced with insecurity and alienation with respect to some less integrated communities whose 'modes of belonging'[11] do not comply with economic goals, cultural mores or social expectations of host countries. Although the sense of culture shock and anomie tends to be most intense with migrants from culturally distant locations, it can also be noticed when it comes to some ethnic Central/Eastern Europeans migrating to Western Europe.[12]

Polish migrants were first warmly welcomed in the UK workforce after Poland's admission to the EU,[13] yet since the 2008 economic slump they started to be perceived as possible 'job stealers' and 'benefit tourists'.[14] Unable or unwilling to shed their Polishness despite their relative cultural proximity, they have been seen as unintegrated outsiders (with their Polish shops, restaurants or churches), which was often exaggerated by British tabloids[15] or other popular media productions.[16] Some studies indicate that, despite having ventured abroad to seize the opportunity to change their lives for the better, Poles have been branded as opportunistic or materialistic both at home and in their host countries. This had to breed a sense of anomie and the perpetuation of imagined boundaries between 'us' and 'them' – British Poles as opposed to Poles in Poland and the British.[17] The sense of undeserved stigmatization was magnified with a spike in Eurosceptic attitudes fostered by vociferous LEAVE campaigners prior to the Brexit referendum planned for 2016. Increasingly hostile attacks on Poles, who were scapegoated for anything from the collapse of the British welfare state, to the economic crisis and a rising crime rate, were reported throughout 2016 and 2017.[18] Incidentally, it was the British Poles, among other minorities, that had to bear the brunt of hate attacks motivated by the angry and divisive anti-immigrant rhetoric of the LEAVE campaign.[19]

This study takes a discursive perspective to elaborate on how Polish-language online media respond to community-building and ethnic identification needs in the dynamic economic, political and cultural contexts of life in the UK. In particular, it looks at how collective identities of British Poles are 'manufactured' following the outcome of the Brexit referendum and the ensuing prospect of a hard Brexit. It analyses the main strategies Polish-language media outlets used to mitigate the threats to Poles' sense of stability and as a community in Britain. This analysis is an extension on two previous case studies that investigated the changing mediated discursive representations of the collective identities of Polish immigrants to the UK, first in the period of 2014 post-crisis political and economic reforms and the general election campaign won by the incumbent Prime Minister David Cameron[20] and then in the period of 2016 Brexit referendum campaign (more on this below).[21] Both investigated how the political and economic tensions impinged on the volatility of 'modes of belonging' of Polish immigrants, and showed the discursive strategies that ethnic media used to offer support to overcome anomie and foster a willingness for migrants to re-imagine themselves as British Poles. The ethnic media texts analysed both then and here have been collected from MojaWyspa.co.uk (MyIsland), which is one of the largest Polish-language glocal media portals targeting all generations of Poles on the British Isles.[22] It is owned privately by DMA Partners Ltd and financed through carrying online advertising. Its partners include other Polish media outlets whose materials are reprinted, online service providers and Polish organizations in the UK.[23] Its popularity stems from its non-politicized, aggregative character and diversity of publishing and networking services. As the portal is focused on practical issues of migrants' lives, rather than promoting an ideology, it is interesting to trace the major themes, sources, stances and strategies that cumulatively project a specific imagined identity of British Poles – a community still characterized by a sense of 'in-betweenness'.

MojaWyspa.co.uk, or the pulse of Polish collective identity in post-Brexit Britain

MojaWyspa ('My Island') started in 2003 as an informal network that provided information to the Polish people who were planning to move to Britain. As explained on its anonymous 'about us' page, initially it based on the personal experience of the founders of a simple advice webpage, who, having lived in the UK for some time, decided which announcements and instructions were relevant, useful, current and authoritative enough to be aggregated and published online.

Over the last decade the portal grew to encompass new areas: news (both British and Polish), guide sections, classified ads, frequently asked questions, a review of Polish presses, a family advice section, and, more recently, a Brexit section. Now the portal also offers a discussion forum and a gallery allowing registered users to share information and photos and to interact. The unassuming web design, the regularity of updates, and the continuity and trust of the community of contributors and moderators made *MojaWyspa* develop into a prime Polish-language information outlet and a networking site attracting British Poles, as well as Poles in the US, and their families back in Poland. The editorial office consisting of half a dozen Polish-born men and women now based in Sussex have shown the awareness of the target audience and highlighted the community-building function of their portal:

> In the beginning it was mainly young Poles coming to the UK for a short time to work and to make some money. In recent years this has changed and a very large part of the regular users are families who are planning to stay in the UK for a much longer time. Although the English-speaking skills of these people are growing rapidly, the complex process of integration into a new culture is easier in their native language. Even as time goes by and the language problems dissipate, there will still be a strong cultural and linguistic bond within the group.[24]

In the two previous case studies, representative samples of media texts analysed were garnered from a dedicated news and feature column called 'Polak na wyspie' ('The Pole on the Isle'). Both studies focused on the discursive construction of collective identity and revealed internal tensions in the Polish migrants' self-presentations in the collected material. They were also timed for 2014 (a decade after EU access) and 2016 (Brexit referendum) to prove that the Polish identity forged within *MojaWyspa* was in the process of renegotiation: it was neither an extension of Polish national collective identity, nor yet an assimilated or cosmopolitan sense of community. While the earlier study focused on the discursive strategies of representing various stages of Poles' sense of 'in-betweenness' in accommodating to British social reality and cultural mores, the latter revealed that with the consequences of Brexit becoming apparent for Polish residents, and with more instances of hate and racial attacks (e.g. the Harlow murder[25]), the Polish-language media became overlaid with the sense of collective insecurity and victimization.

Given the fact that online media that aggregate information and carry readers' commentary, such as *MojaWyspa*, will inevitably transmit a polyphony of voices representing various modes of belonging, studies that reveal contesting collective identities are not uncommon. For example, even if laden with initial anomie, the gradual processes of acculturation of Polish diaspora's collective identity prior to Brexit left space for resisting dominant, nationalistic and stereotypical identifications and allowed migrant Poles to negotiate their new self-reflective positions as British Poles, Londoners or Europeans. After Brexit, the mediated collective identifications seem to have settled more along ethnic (tribal) lines and attention-gathering victimhood scenarios.[26] Apart from adding the latest chapter to British Poles' grasp of the consequences of the UK government's negotiations of the terms of EU leave, the current study additionally traces the trajectory of these contested identities diachronically.

The present study is designed to include the available material published on MojaWyspa.co.uk between 1 March and 31 October 2019 (one of the official former deadlines for Brexit), to match the sampling in the previous studies, and to identify the current strategies in the discursive construction of the Polish identity, particularly with the aim of examining any possible 'retribalization' techniques. It is hypothesized that, in view of the intense political pressure of a hard Brexit, status insecurity and continued tabloid media scapegoating, British Poles would rally around a more conservative, patriotic and officially endorsed identity that would be mustered to counteract the previous labelling as 'Polish scum' or 'second-class citizens' in order to mitigate the 'threats' to the community's collective 'face'.

Ethnic press and its role in identity manufacturing

The conceptual framework adopted here is compatible with the *MojaWyspa* research it aims to continue, but at the same time it shifts the focus from the discursive strategies of identity formation to the discursive 'manufacturing' of a new imagined community of British Poles. The difference between the construction of identities and their manufacturing, as postulated here, lies in a more purposeful and strategic coordination of textual materials, more institutional 'top-down' inputs, and more mitigation in the context of reacting to external pressures (i.e. other mediated discourses purporting to represent the community). First, the current study maps the textual resources that seem to be directed at positioning the self ('us') against significant others ('them') – Poles in Poland, the British, also some other minorities in the UK – and at contesting the position of an undeservedly 'othered' community.[27] Second, it analyses how content choices and linguistic representations of issues taken up by *MojaWyspa* have been mitigating a continuous threat to their face.[28] It shows how the Polish-language media mobilize the sense of coherent collective identity in view of a social, even existential, threat, which has important implications for the recreations of a stronger version of ethnic 'Polishness', referred to as retribalization here.

Allophone presses have always had a specific interest in enabling particular ethnic, cultural or language minorities to self-express, to promote their culture and (if necessary) to contest their mainstream-media representations. In this vein, it can be claimed that ethnic media produced by minority groups in a host country are spaces for resident non-native individuals, or 'insider-outsiders',[29] to anchor their sense of belonging through flexible processes of discursive construction of a new imagined community. In addition, glocal media technologies provide a set of resources for hypertextual and interactive identification processes that involve negotiations and polemics in below-the-line comment sections (as was previously done through published letters to editors). Although the news and feature sections are compiled and provided by a group of local editors and reporters, they aggregate a wider range of voices that add alternative narratives. As a result, such media enable counterhegemonic imaginaries to exist along with dominant representations.[30] Additionally, ethnic glocal media may quickly expose the underlying discriminatory discourses and stereotyping processes in the mainstream media, and provide venues for identity expressions that are more compatible with the sensibilities and cultural needs of the community.[31]

It is assumed here that collective identities are formed in ongoing social interactions and negotiations. They are 'malleable, fragile, and, frequently, ambivalent and diffuse'.[32] With regard to ethnic identities, apart from material symbols and performed rituals, media discourse is the main domain where the construction of self-knowledge and social hierarchies takes place. The discursive constructions of migrant identities can draw on and reinforce existing identity schemas related to a nation's founding myths, history, collective memory, heritage culture, religious practices, language and literature. The claim made here is that a glocal outlet does much more of diverse discursive work, often by helping navigate between competing collective memories and personal narratives, as well as by mitigating issues that position the ethnic group in conflict or clash with other significant groups.[33]

To operationalize the discursive mitigation of threats to collective identity of *MojaWyspa* readership, the study applies the concept of 'face'. In his classical work on interactional rituals in face-to-face encounters, the prominent Canadian-born sociologist and social psychologist Erving Goffman mentions that individuals (just as collectives here) feel the need to have their wants recognized (pride), their emotions acknowledged (dignity), and their decisions and achievements affirmed (honour).[34] These feelings are desired and (verbal) behaviours that help uphold them are referred to as 'face-work' as they are helping one to 'keep [a] positive face', or preventing one from 'losing face'. However, in the situations of conflict or clash of cultures, numerous cases of 'threats to face' (self-worth) may occur, which can be mitigated through linguistic face-work or, in other words, a range of interactional and discursive strategies. Goffman discusses some examples of avoidance strategies that are resorted to in order to diminish the likelihood of a clash, and some corrective processes aimed at reconciliation. Some of the strategies that are sought in the analytic material here include those that *MojaWyspa* applies to mitigate the threats to the collective face of British Poles, such as preventive acts (e.g. announcements or warnings to forestall awkward situations), protective strategies (e.g. euphemistic styles or descriptive formulations to report on face-threatening developments), and defensive strategies (e.g. denial or suppression of some types of information or emotion).

Sourcing and content analysis: the impact of institutional voices in *MojaWyspa*

Relatively few articles (forty-three) were published by *MojaWyspa* in the section devoted to the life of Poles in the UK over the period of eight months between March and October 2019, as compared to 104 articles published within the ten months between June 2016 (Brexit referendum) and March 2017 (when article 50 was invoked).[35] As regards the sourcing of the material, it can be seen that one-third of the articles are based on Polish-language official sources, notably the Polish embassy and some registered Polish organizations in the UK. A number of articles is based on press releases from various institutional sources, including translations of statements from the police or the courts and reprints of reports posted on webpages of Polish organizations. A few articles are related to recent scholarly publications or personal narratives and human-interest stories that were collected, compiled or translated by the editorial office. Table 8.1 illustrates the sourcing in the material.

Table 8.1 Main sources of *MojaWyspa* articles.

Source	No. of articles (n=43)	% of articles	Genre of articles
MojaWyspa	18	41	Features or interviews provided by editorial office
Polish embassy	10	23	Open letters, announcements, invitations
News agencies and other media outlets	7	16	Press releases, news media reports translated into Polish by editorial office
Police, court	4	10	Reports on missing persons, convictions
Polish institutions and organizations: National Memory Institute (IPN), Ministry of Technology, British Poles, Polish Street	4	10	Announcements about festivals or contests, alerts and calls
		100	

Table 8.2 Main thematic categories in *MojaWyspa* articles.

Thematic category	% of articles	Examples
Criminal incidents involving Polish victims and/or perpetrators	15	Investigations, convictions, missing persons
Brexit negotiations and legal status of Poles	12	Residency, voting in elections (European, Polish)
Official (embassy-sponsored) celebrations of historical occasions and tributes to Polish heroes in the UK	12	Outbreak of Second World War, Independence day, Polish Enigma engineers
Announcements and appeals to Polish communities in the UK	12	Coming forward with information, witnesses, registering for elections
Discrimination and racism experienced by Poles	9	Cases of hate attacks and racist acts, studies and statistics of hate crime against Poles
Actions representing British-Polish solidarity	7	Joint publications, community projects, parliamentary debate
Polish heritage and cultural events in the UK	7	Polish days/festivals, Polish culture exhibitions, contests
Information about the prospects and support for Poles returning to Poland	7	Open letters, reports from Poland, an official portal about returns
Human interest stories related to Poles	7	Travelling, interesting people, hobbies
Charity events organized by Polish communities and associations	7	Blood donations, Polish schools, centres, monuments, cemetery maintenance.
Poles and the UK economy and labour market	5	Employment opportunities, Polish start-ups
	100	

Through a content analysis of articles' major themes (often encapsulated in titles and lead-ins), it is possible to determine the distribution of types of topics and measure the frequency of prominent content categories. With one content category being attributed to one article, and through generalization of content categories into larger thematic categories, it can be induced which dominant themes feature in the material. Table 8.2 illustrates the hierarchy of thematic categories.

Given the thematic categories that dominate this batch of articles (the baseline of 5 per cent was used to eliminate miscellaneous categories), one can notice that although negative reports about incidents of crime and discrimination, and the stories on post-Brexit uncertainty of Polish residents tend to be relatively frequent, many positive developments are reported as well. In fact, while the coverage immediately following the Brexit referendum was much more focused on the frustrations and victimization (hate attacks, the Harlow murder), this sample illustrates a significant reversal in topics and sentiments.[36] Admittedly, this is due to a number of anniversaries and occasions that were used to celebrate Polish historical achievements and were meticulously covered by *MojaWyspa* (the fifteenth anniversary of Poland's joining the EU, the centenary of Poland's Independence, the outbreak of WW2 and the Battle of England).

Sentiment and need analysis: fostering pride and dignity and defending Polish immigrants' honour

In the previous study on Brexit referendum articles in *MojaWyspa*,[37] automated sentiment analysis (a software-based classification of lexical units as exponents of emotional and attitudinal categories) revealed the scores for positive emotions (joy, trust) and for positive values (utility, happiness) outnumbering the scores for negative emotions (sadness, anger) and negative values (harm, uselessness).[38] Although this was contrary to initial expectations, the result could be explained with the increasing number of support-giving and community-building articles on Polish charity actions, or of announcements about community initiatives, such as 'Polish days', and 'success stories' of individual British Poles. However, automated sentiment analysis is particularly useful for large corpora. Given the smaller sample collected here, it was not resorted to. Rather, the small corpus under study lends itself to an in-depth manual analysis and interpretation. In addition, this study aims to follow Goffman's idea that in face-saving interactions, communicators tend to project (or protect) their basic psychological needs, which may be discursively constructed with various linguistic resources and whole discursive strategies, not just individual words.

In the sample material, it is relatively easy to find excerpts that are representative of textual strategies that cater to specific community needs of British Poles to elevate their position in the British society and to mitigate the negativity of the mainstream UK presses. For example, the excerpts reproduced below[39] can be interpreted as articulations of *pride* in Polish entrepreneurial and cultural innovativeness. Example (1) presents a statement by Wojciech Szaniawski, a member of a committee responsible for awarding the annual prize for the best Polish start-up in London, whereas example (2) announces a Polish festival as a contribution to Shakespearian studies:[40]

> (1) I'm *positively surprised* with the *quality* and *maturity* of the start-ups. Their leaders not only presented their prospective business in an *interesting* way, but also have already *benefited* from their *clearly articulated* aims. I *liked* the *innovations*, but also the way that *competences* and tasks were shared and how the *vision of growth* was presented... Both the main *prize* and the public's vote went to Comixify – a startup that was *awarded* for its *pro-social* character, as it will help autistic children. 14 March 2019. *Polish start-ups in London.*[41]
>
> (2) The festival is aimed at *celebrating* the *variety* and *novelty* of Polish productions, poetry and translations. The *central* points of the audition will be the *first ever* translations into English of Wyspiański's 'The Study of Hamlet' and 'The Death of Ophelia'. 27 June 2019. *London: Shakespeare and Poland.*[42]

Both of these examples foreground thematically the creative potential of British Poles and celebrate the successful outcomes of their innovative enterprises. The sentiment is unequivocally positive (see italics) and *MojaWyspa* readers' sense of pride can be triggered. The emphatic and superlative lexis used ('already benefited', 'main prize', 'first ever', 'central point'), as well as contextualizing the Polish achievements as a 'festival' or a 'contest' have elevated the status and publicity of these contributions. Such coverage is likely to mitigate the stereotypical images of Polish manual workers (plumbers, builders or cleaners), who, no matter how hardworking, are not likely to be educated or creative enough to contribute significantly to the British society. The outlet invites British Poles to identify as professionals, entrepreneurs, creators and innovators as well.

As regards textual articulations of *dignity*, which may consist in the acknowledgement of emotional and existential needs of the community, the sample offers many examples of reports on Polish communities' civic engagements and solidarity-building initiatives. Examples (3) and (4) highlight the community spirit of British Poles and reverse the stereotype of migrants being a 'burden' to the British welfare system.

(3) Hundreds of photos are posted every day in social media showing Poles giving blood in local hospitals and blood stations marked by #polishblood logo ... Thousands of Poles living in the UK decided to donate blood this year to the British NHS. They aimed to promote the ideals of Polish-British solidarity, and to prove the valuable input of our community to the United Kingdom. 13 August 2019. *Poles will donate blood for the fifth time.*[43]

(4) Six enthusiasts from Manchester decided to clean up Ashworth Woods – a park popular with people of Rochdale ... The river Naden Brook that crosses the park is littered with plastic waste, cans and even old tires. The group of six Poles decided to change that. 12 June 2019. *Polish Squadron 606 fighting plastic waste.*[44]

Such reports on community actions either implicitly or explicitly indicate the social value of the Polish diaspora's activities. They also show that Poles feel at home in Britain and that they do not see themselves as second-class citizens or just temporary migrant workers. Poles are quite likely to advance the common good and to confront local problems in solidarity with other ethnic groups that inhabit British towns and cities. *MojaWyspa* also indicates that Poles are not just individuals who settled in Britain, but have managed to transform into highly committed and easily mobilized local communities. For instance, example (3) stresses the high numbers of Poles donating blood, whereas example (4) presents the clean-up action as extraordinary in character and likely to be taken up only by true environmental 'enthusiasts'. Both excerpts seem to represent Poles as capable of sacrifice and thus as worthy of respect, which is to dignify the community's position in the wider society.

The third type of Goffman's basic need is related to *honour*, which, as regards an ethnic group, is often manifested in the attempt to rearticulate the group's significance in the context of historical events, notably the war effort, the fight for independence or the resistance to totalitarian ideologies. All the above can be traced in the articles that report on political initiatives or on official celebrations of historical occasions. For example, some of *MojaWyspa*'s articles involve paying tribute to Polish cryptologists who deciphered Enigma's code and allowed the allies to intercept Nazi military communications and to Polish troops fighting in Europe during the Second World War.[45] Other texts praise the part Polish cavalry officer and intelligence agent Witold Pilecki (1901–48) played in the resistance at Auschwitz, and celebrate the founder of the first female police department in Poland, Stanisława Paleolog (1892–1968), who repatriated to the UK to escape communist persecution. Others celebrate the sixtieth anniversary of the Polish cultural institution Dom Polski in Manchester. There is also a call to propose nominations for the honorary title of 'History's Witness', and to get involved in the various actions related to the Polish sailing ship *Dar Młodzieży* visiting London as part of its Polish Independence centenary cruise.[46] However, the most politically significant event covered by *MojaWyspa* was a special debate in the British Parliament:

> (5) On 2 July, British Parliament saw an exceptional debate. Daniel Kawczynski, the only British MP born in Poland, decided once again to fight to restore Poland's good reputation and remind the British about the ways Polish armed forces contributed to the WW2 effort... Over twenty British MPs and lords gave speeches and honored the sacrifice and heroism of the Polish soldiers who fought alongside the British to restore freedom and independence. 9 July 2019. *British MPs honoring Polish soldiers who fought during WW2.*[47]

The lengthy article, of which example (5) is a lead-in, meticulously summarizes each debater's contribution and focuses on the praise imparted on the Polish soldiers, fighter pilots, military commanders, intelligence agents, resistance movement leaders, civilian staff, scientists and engineers, as well as the general populace that never yielded to Nazi occupiers and the individuals who risked their lives hiding and saving their Jewish neighbours during the Holocaust. The article bases on prominent public speakers' ethos to make an appeal to recognize the heroism and devotion of Poles during the Second World War, and particularly in the Battle of England (1940). It implies that, due to their contribution to Britain's freedom and world peace, British Poles should be honoured by the society, not treated as unwanted 'scum that should go home'. It may also function to rally the Polish community to overcome current artificial divisions between Western and Eastern/Central Europeans and indicate the sense of common purpose and shared values. As the debate was widely covered in other Polish-language media in a similarly pathetic tone, it may be representative of a larger top-down strategy of manufacturing Polish identity as characterized by highly patriotic, but not nationalist attitudes.[48]

Mitigation strategies: the art of preventing, protecting and denying

Goffman's essay on face-work can be used as an inspiration to seek out textual strategies that indicate the communicators' attempts at mitigating conflicts and preventing negative outcomes that go beyond simple politeness strategies. They include preventive acts, protective strategies and defensive strategies (e.g. warnings, euphemisms and suppression of some types of information or emotion, respectively).

Preventive acts allow communicators to signal troublesome areas and be alerted to the possibility of preventing conflict by withdrawing from discussion on sensitive issues. They might also include warnings that sensitize one to possible confrontation and loss of face. The announcement by the Polish ambassador Arkady Rzegocki, reproduced by *MojaWyspa* in example (6) can be classified as Goffman's preventive act, as it is an appeal to the Polish community members to take precautions to ensure their residency in the UK and make sure that their status is confirmed before Brexit. The ambassador even asks them to consider returning to Poland:

(6) I want to encourage you to seriously consider returning to the Fatherland and to get acquainted with information available on the website powroty.gov.pl[49] ... Our country's economy is developing fast and this creates ever better conditions and prospects for our citizens. Wishing you all the best, I appeal to you to take good care of your future. 18 September 2019. *A letter from the ambassador to Poles in the UK*.[50]

As was shown in Table 8.2, 7 per cent of *MojaWyspa*'s current coverage is exclusively devoted to persuading British Poles to consider returning to Poland. The arguments in the articles encouraging Poles to return to the country include such issues as low unemployment, increase in wages, new child benefits, intense economic growth, government investments in innovative sectors of the economy and foreign investments in Poland. Such analyses aim to bridge the identity split between British Poles and Poles in Poland, which was relatively stark in some previous studies, where Poles migrating to the UK claimed to be escaping the stagnant, ineffective and corrupt economic arrangements in post-communist Poland in order to prosper financially and professionally and to enjoy an 'easier' and 'fairer' life.[51] As no-deal Brexit loomed and economic slump in the UK was being predicted, Poles were to prevent misfortune and disappointment if they considered returning.

Protective strategies could be conceived of as uses of euphemistic and emotionless language to report on possible conflicts of interests. They can also include using factual information that builds the argument instead of anecdotal or emotional appeals. Example (7) below, despite its slightly sensationalist headline style – 'Polish youths in the UK are victims of racism' – uses a scientific study and its findings and a descriptive style to publicize information on the wide scope of harassment that Polish students' undergo at schools.

(7) Scientists from Strathclyde University in Glasgow have published research that finds that over three fourths of students from East Europe experienced some form of racism, xenophobia and bullying. Studies show that these situations spiked after the Brexit referendum in 2016 and were often masked as jokes. 23 August 2019. *Polish youths in the UK are victims of racism.*[52]

Another example of using scientific jargon to present a profile of the Polish migrant in the UK is an article based a commissioned study of the demographic and professional layout of the Polish migrant diaspora in Western Europe:

(8) Great Britain is chosen as a destination by people who are better educated and who come from mid-sized and big cities of Poland ... In general, Polish migrants

are professionally very active, which results from their average age (20–45 years) and their motivation for migration (to earn money)... The improving situation on the Polish labour market has caused many informants to declare much less often that they would stay in Britain for ever. They mostly intend to work abroad for 3 years or more and then come back. This trend has been strengthened in the case of the Poles in Great Britain as they are not sure what will happen after Brexit. 29 July 2019. *What are Polish migrants in the UK like?*[53]

If defensive strategies include suppression of some types of information or reversal of sentiment, then one could find example (9) to be illustrative of that. This is a concluding statement following a series of articles that cast doubt on the validity of British criminal proceedings related to a sexual assault allegedly perpetrated by a Polish man.[54] After finding faults with the ways the investigation and trial were conducted, *MojaWyspa* reports on the case as a classical 'trial by media':

(9) While the British media made the Polish law student, who came to the Isles to get an additional job, look like a cruel pervert and assailant, the majority of Polish journalists voiced the opinion that the boy is a likely victim of a legal error. 20 February 2019. *A Pole who was convicted of rape tries to regain his reputation.*[55]

The outlet conveys an impression that Poles get harsher sentences and are often blamed for various misdeeds because the British media have been persistently branding Eastern and Central Europeans as criminals.

Conclusion

More than fifteen years after Poland's accession to the EU, some Polish residents in the UK tend to flag their ethnic and linguistic difference, which often positions them in an ambiguous place if 'in-betweenness', as 'insider-outsiders'. Even if economic surveys indicate Poles' continuing positive contribution to the British society, they, as is the case with other Central/Eastern Europeans, are misrepresented in mainstream British media as a largely unintegrated minority consisting of job stealers, benefit tourists or criminals escaping justice in their home country. As a result, the Polish migrant self-identifications in Polish language ethnic media have been contested and polarized. This case study has shown that although the Polish diaspora has been taunted as economically productive, historically heroic and politically democratic, as well as culturally sophisticated, it has been left to fend for itself by rallying around more conservative, tribal identities and celebrating its distinct Polishness rather than its cosmopolitanism, or its sense of belonging to the UK's multicultural society.

From the studies of British newspapers after the Brexit referendum, it emerges that immediately after the implications of the LEAVE win became apparent, the press spent about six months to contemplate not on what was to be gained, but on what was to be lost after the UK was no longer to take advantage of regulations ensuring the free movement of people, goods and capital.[56] However, the pro-migrant articles focused mostly on the unsure future of some sectors of the UK economy that relied on migrant workers (from Polish plumbers to tech engineers to investment bankers) and on the lamentable loss of British competitive advantage. Unfortunately, the negative framing of free movement and migrants as invaders plundering jobs and exploiting the welfare state returned after the initial shock of the referendum outcome was absorbed by the media elites.[57]

Without taking for granted the idea that ethnic media always endorse and sustain the homeland identity,[58] this study has demonstrated discursive constructions of British Poles' ethnic identities leaning towards national/tribal projections and highlighting patriotic and communitarian characteristics of the imagined diaspora. In particular, by reviewing Polish-language media's dominant patterns of self-presentations, sentiments and face-saving techniques, it was possible to map the relations between British Poles and their significant others, particularly the Poles in Poland, and the British (neighbours, employers, public officials, law-enforcement institutions). To highlight the constructed nature of such self-representations, this study suggests calling this phenomenon the 'discursive manufacturing' of imagined community, with its strong focus on ethnic cohesion and a predominantly positive sentiment regarding the projection of 'us' and our values. The use of official institutional sources and intense efforts at mitigating and contesting the negative representations of Poles in British media feature prominently in the repertoire of discursive strategies applied here to foreground pride, dignity and honour. Although there is no evidence of the portal being subsidized by Polish organizations or homeland institutions, its close cooperation with institutional partners and reproduction of official stances of British Poles' organizations (only 41 per cent of material is attributed to *MojaWyspa* editors) inevitably shapes the discursive representation of Poles as an ethnic minority and citizen interest group. This is not to claim that the portal has been completely hijacked by some sort of state propaganda, or that it lost its complexity and polyphony of voices, but to indicate the subtle shift towards strengthening the sense of Polishness as a primary 'mode of belonging' in the context of pressures related to the status as a community and the insecurity related to the consequences of hard Brexit.

Indeed, while in the previous studies of *MojaWyspa* of which this one is an extension there was a sense of media promoting assimilation, distancing from native Polishness and championing a willingness to participate in a pan-European society, this has changed after the Brexit referendum and during the protracted negotiations over the terms of Britain's deal with the EU. Poland has been increasingly 'proximized' as homeland and 'idealized' as a place of possible return. This is because glocal ethnic media (of which *MojaWyspa* is a prominent example) have started reproducing official institutional discourses that imply that Poles would be better off in Poland while continuing to illustrate with community-generated stories how hard individual British Poles have had to 'fight' to prosper in the UK now. It may be ventured that Polish-language online media have crystallized attitudes that more opinionated organs of the Polish organizations in the UK have been demonstrating all along. Instead of 'just' helping Polish migrants to prosper materially and accommodate to conditions and regulations in Britain, online portals have also started providing them with the sense of belonging to a community that prides itself on self-representing as British Poles rather than Polish(-origin) Brits.

Notes

1. Overview of the UK population: August 2019, available at https://www.ons.gov.uk/peoplepopulationandcommunity/populationandmigration/populationestimates/articles/overviewoftheukpopulation/august2019.
2. The International Monetary Fund's references for GDP, available at https://www.imf.org/external/datamapper/NGDP_RPCH@WEO/OEMDC/ADVEC/WEOWORLD.
3. Krystyna Iglicka, *Poland's Post-war Dynamic of Migration* (Aldershot: Ashgate, 2001); Keith Sword, Norman Davies and Jan Ciechanowski, *The Formation of the Polish Community in Britain: 1939–1950* (London: University of London Press, 1989).
4. Kelly Burrell (ed.), *Polish Migration to the UK in the 'New' European Union: After 2004* (Aldershot: Ashgate, 2009); Anne White, *Polish Families and Migration since EU Accession* (Bristol: Policy Press, 2011).
5. Some of them associated in the Federation of Poles in Great Britain CIO, as available at http://zpwb.org.uk/index.php/default/category/member_organizations.
6. *Dziennik Polski* [trans. as 'Polish daily'] published since 1940, and now *Tydzień Polski* [trans. as 'Polish weekly'] published since 1959, have been official organs of the Polish Cultural Organization (PSOK) representing the interests of Polish diasporas around the UK, both have historically been involved in covering Polish politics, notably in critiquing the communist regime, now closely cooperate with Polish consulates, more online at http://www.tydzien.co.uk/o-dzienniku; *Goniec Polski* [trans. as 'Polish runner/page' – ambiguous meaning] published since 2002, is a monthly political, opinion and lifestyle magazine owned by 1MM Media Ltd giving ample space to announcements for Polish companies and advice columns, often involved in correcting stereotypes about Poles in Britain; *Panorama Magazine,* published since 2006, in 2016 renamed as *LAJT Magazine,* a monthly glossy lifestyle magazine owned by Polish Express Media Group that publishes summaries of international press coverage relevant to Poland and Britain and, increasingly, lifestyle and celebrity information, more online at https://issuu.com/panoramamagazine; *Cooltura* [a blend of 'cool' and 'culture'] published since 2004, owned by Polish Media Group based in London, is a weekly cultural magazine that prospered through an influx of Polish migrants in the UK in the late 2000s, which publishes news, entertainment (reports and announcements about Polish-language events), features and classifieds.
7. More listed, e.g. at https://medianaemigracji.wordpress.com/polskie-media-w-wielkiej-brytanii-katalog/, cf. Katarzyna Molek-Kozakowska 'Media polonijne w Londynie a kształtowanie tożsamości polskich emigrantów po 2004 roku [Polish media in London and the shaping of Polish emigre identities after 2004]' *Rocznik Biblioteki Głównej Uniwersytetu Opolskiego* (Opole: Wydawnictwo Uniwersytetu Opolskiego, 2014), 91–100.
8. Benedict Anderson, *Imagined Communities: Reflections on the Origin and Spread of Nationalism* (London: Verso, 1991), 46.
9. In the media studies context, 'glocal' means having both local and global characteristics, e.g. local coverage that is available worldwide, similar to business practices outlined e.g. by Roland Robertson, *European Glocalization in Global Context* (Basingstoke: Palgrave, 2014).

10 Ola Ogunyemi, 'Introduction: Conceptualizing the Media of Diaspora', in *Journalism, Audiences and Diaspora*, ed. Ola Ogunyemi (Basingstoke: Palgrave Macmillan, 2015), 1–14.
11 Michał Krzyżanowski, *The Discursive Construction of European Identities. A Multilevel Approach to Discourse and Identity in the Transforming European Union* (Frankfurt am Main: Peter Lang, 2010).
12 For an overview of various ethnic cases of experiencing 'othering', cf. Jan Chovanec and Katarzyna Molek-Kozakowska (eds.), *Representing the Other in European Media Discourses* (Amsterdam: John Benjamins, 2017).
13 Aleksandra Grzymala-Kazlowska, 'From Connecting to Social Anchoring: Adaptation and 'Settlement' of Polish Migrants in the UK', *Journal of Ethnic and Migration Studies* 44, no. 2 (2018): 252–69.
14 Ian Fitzgerald and Rafal Smoczynski, 'Anti-Polish Migrant Moral Panic in the UK: Rethinking Employment Insecurities and Moral Regulation', *Czech Sociological Review* 51, no. 3 (2015): 339–61.
15 Joanna Fomina and Justyna Frelak, *Next Stopski London. Public Perceptions of Labour Migration within the EU. The Case of Polish Labour Migrants in the British Press* (Warsaw: Institute of Public Affairs, 2008); Ariel Spigelman, 'The Depiction of Polish Migrants in the United Kingdom by the British Press after Poland's Accession to the European Union', *International Journal of Sociology and Social Policy* 3 no. 1–2 (2013): 98–113.
16 Notably documentaries, such as Timothy Samuels's 'The Poles are Coming!' made by Tonic Productions for BBC TV and broadcast on 17 October 2013, now available at https://vimeo.com/77151640, as analysed by Alicja Portas, 'Representations of Polish Migrants in British Media from the Perspective of "Moral Panic" Theory', *Polish Journal of English Studies* 4, no. 1 (2018): 113–42.
17 Przemysław Wilk, 'Construing the Other: On Some Ideology-laden Construals of Europeans in *The Guardian*', in Jan Chovanec and Katarzyna Molek-Kozakowska (eds.), *Representing the Other in European Media Discourses* (Amsterdam: John Benjamins, 2017), 121–34.
18 Alina Rzepnikowska, 'Racism and Xenophobia Experienced by Polish Migrants in the UK before and after Brexit Vote', *Journal of Ethnic and Migration Studies* 45, no. 1 (2019): 61–77.
19 Home Office, 'Hate crime, England and Wales, 2017 to 2018' *Home Office Statistical Bulletin* 20 (2018) available at https://www.gov.uk/government/statistics/hate-crime-england-and-wales-2017-to-2018, Ref: ISBN 978-1-78655-706-3; see also Matthew Weaver, 'Hate Crime Surge Linked to Brexit and 2017 Terrorist Attacks', *The Guardian*, 16 October 2018, available at https://www.theguardian.com/society/2018/oct/16/hate-crime-brexit-terrorist-attacks-england-wales.
20 Katarzyna Molek-Kozakowska, 'Negotiating an Identity: The Mediated Discursive Self-Representation of the Polish Immigrant Community in the UK', in *Representing the Other in European Media Discourses*, ed. Jan Chovanec and Katarzyna Molek-Kozakowska (Amsterdam: John Benjamins Publishing, 2017), 158–81.
21 Katarzyna Molek-Kozakowska, 'Fuzzy Identities in (Dis)Integrating Europe: Discursive Identifications of Poles in Britain Following Brexit', in Péter B. Furkó, Ildikó Vaskó, Csilla Ilona Dér and Dorte Madsen (eds.), *Fuzzy Boundaries in Discourse Studies: Theoretical, Methodological, and Lexico-Grammatical Fuzziness* (Basingstoke: Palgrave Macmillan, 2019), 55–76.
22 According to its own estimate, the portal has a potential audience of 2 million people (70 per cent in the UK and 30 per cent in Poland and the US) http://www.mojawyspa.co.uk/english (accessed 12 November 2019).

23 http://www.mojawyspa.co.uk/pages.php?name=partnerzy (accessed 12 November 2019).
24 http://www.mojawyspa.co.uk/english (accessed 12 November 2019).
25 This was a well-publicized incident of six Essex teenagers attacking a Polish man, Arkadiusz Jóźwik, 39, who died in hospital from head injuries. This prompted Polish diplomatic actions and sending Polish police officers to help on the case. More: 'Harlow Murder: Inquest Hears Head Injury Caused Death', *BBC News* (5 September 2016) available at https://www.bbc.com/news/uk-england-essex-37275724; 'Harlow Murder: Arek Jozwik "killed by single punch"', *BBC News* (6 September 2016) available at https://www.bbc.com/news/uk-england-essex-37291524.
26 Molek-Kozakowska, 'Fuzzy Identities', 57.
27 Chovanec and Molek-Kozakowska (eds.), *Representing the Other*.
28 Erving Goffman, 'On Face-Work. An Analysis of Ritual Elements in Social Interaction', in *Interaction Ritual: Essays on Face-to-Face Behavior* (New York: Doubleday, 1967), 5–45.
29 A phrase used by Myria Georgiou in 'Crossing the Boundaries of the Ethnic Home: Media Consumption and Ethnic Identity Construction in Public Space' *Gazette: International Journal for Communication Studies* 63, no. 4 (2001): 311–29.
30 This idea has been explored in Nick Couldry and James Curran, *Contesting Media Power: Alternative Media in a Networked World* (Lanham, MD: Rowman and Littlefield, 2013).
31 Sebastian M. Rasinger, '"Lithuanian Migrants Send Crime Rocketing": Representation of "New" Migrants in Regional Print Media', *Media, Culture & Society* 32, no. 6 (2010): 1021–30; Hun-Yul Lee, 'At the Crossroads of Migrant Workers, Class, and Media: A Case Study of a Migrant Workers' Television Project', *Media, Culture & Society* 34, no. 3 (2012): 312–27; Isabelle Rigoni and Eugénie Saitta, *Mediating Cultural Diversity in a Globalised Public Space* (New York: Palgrave Macmillan, 2012).
32 Ruth Wodak, Rudolf de Cillia, Martin Reisigl and Karin Liebhart, *The Discursive Construction of National Identity* (Edinburgh: Edinburgh University Press, 2009), 4.
33 The online practices of members of diasporas were discussed by Monika Metykova 'Only a Mouse Click away from Home: Transnational Practices of Eastern European Migrants in the United Kingdom' *Social Identities* 16, no. 3 (2010): 325–38; or Eugenia Siapera, 'Digital News Media and Ethnic Minorities', in *The SAGE Handbook of Digital Journalism,* ed. Tamara Witschge, C. W. Anderson, David Domingo and Alfred Hermida (London: SAGE, 2012), 35–50.
34 Goffman, 'On Face-Work', 5–10.
35 Molek-Kozakowska, 'Fuzzy Identities', 64.
36 Incidentally, a title used in the 2019 study (Molek-Kozakowska, 'Fuzzy Identities', 62) for one of the analytic sections – 'From "the heroes that fought the Nazis" to "the scum that should go home"' – which illustrated the anti-Polish sentiment in the previous corpus could well be reversed now to read 'From "the scum that should go home" to "the heroes that fought the Nazis"'.
37 Molek-Kozakowska, 'Fuzzy Identities', 60.
38 See Molek-Kozakowska, 'Fuzzy Identities', 63–4, for sentiment analysis assisted by free CLARIN-PL tool WoSeDon accessible online. This operation consists in automated classification of lemmas into the categories of primary emotions: positive (joy, trust, excitement) vs negative (sadness, anger, fear, disgust, surprise), and basic values: positive (utility, truth, knowledge, beauty, happiness) vs negative (uselessness, harm, ignorance, error, ugliness, unhappiness) and is explained by Paweł Kędzia, Maciej

Piasecki and Marlena J. Orlińska in 'Word Sense Disambiguation Based on a Large Scale Polish CLARIN Heterogeneous Lexical Resources', *Cognitive Studies* 15 (2015): 269–92.

39 Interestingly, the same or similar wordings of fragments of press releases and quotes from prominent interviewees can be found in other Polish-language media covering the same events, which testifies to minimal re-working of the material provided by partners by *MojaWyspa*'s editors.

40 In all subsequent excerpts, translations from Polish-language texts are mine and italics are inserted to highlight the textual feature discussed.

41 The original reads: 'Jestem pozytywnie zaskoczony poziomem dojrzałości start-upów. Ich liderzy nie tylko ciekawie prezentowali swoje biznesy, ale osiągają w nich już pierwsze sukcesy i mają jasno wytyczone cele. Podobały mi się pomysły, ale także podział kompetencji w zespołach i wizja skalowania ... Zarówno nagrodę główną, jak i nagrodę publiczności zdobył start-up Comixify, który został również wyróżniony za prospołeczny charakter, bo jednym z jego założeń jest pomoc dzieciom chorym na autyzm. 14 marca 2019. Polskie start-upy w Londynie.'

42 'Festiwal ma na celu uczczenie zarazem bogactwa jak i surowości polskich produkcji, poezji i tłumaczeń. Punktem centralnym przeglądu będą pierwsze w historii tłumaczenia na język angielski "Studium Hamleta" i "Śmierci Ofelii" Wyspiańskiego.' 27 czerwca 2019. Londyn: Szekspir i Polska.

43 The original reads: 'Setki zdjęć z brytyjskich szpitali i stacji krwiodawstwa Polaków oddających krew z logiem #polishblood co roku zalewają media społecznościowe ... Tysiące Polaków zamieszkałych w Wielkiej Brytanii zdecydowało się oddawać krew w brytyjskich placówkach NHS. Ich celem było promowanie szczytnej idei, budowanie polsko-brytyjskiej solidarności, a także kolejny raz udowodnienie, jak cenny jest wkład naszej społeczności do Zjednoczonego Królestwa.' 13 sierpnia 2019. Polacy po raz piaty oddadzą krew.

44 In the original language: 'Sześciu entuzjastów z Manchester postanowiło posprzątać znany mieszkańcom Rochdale Ashworth Woods ... Przepływająca przez park rzeka Naden Brook zaśmiecona jest dużą ilością głównie plastikowych odpadów, puszek a otoczenie rzeki straszy porzuconymi oponami. Grupa sześciu Polaków postanowiło to zmienić.' 12 czerwca 2019. Dywizjon 606 w walce z plastikowymi odpadami.

45 *Remembering Polish cryptologists during the WWII*, 27 July 2019, http://www.mojawyspa.co.uk/artykuly/37371/Ku-pamieci-polskich-kryptologow-z-II-wojny-swiatowej or *British MPs honoured Polish soldiers who fought during WW2*, 9 July 2019. http://www.mojawyspa.co.uk/artykuly/37293/Brytyjscy-poslowie-uhonorowali-wklad-Polakow-w-II-ws,2.

46 '*Dar Młodzieży' finished its voyage in London*, 20 March 2019. http://www.mojawyspa.co.uk/artykuly/36833/8222Dar-Mlodziezy-zakonczyl-wizyte-w-Londynie.

47 '2 lipca w brytyjskim Parlamencie miała miejsce wyjątkowa debata. Daniel Kawczynski, jedyny brytyjski poseł urodzony w Polsce, po raz kolejny postanowił zawalczyć o dobre imię Polski i przypomnieć Brytyjczykom o wkładzie Polskich Sił Zbrojnych w wysiłki wojenne w czasie II wojny światowej ... Na debatę przybyło ponad 20 brytyjskich posłów i lordów, którym nie jest obce poświęcenie i bohaterstwo polskich żołnierzy walczących o wolność i niezależność ramię w ramię z Brytyjczykami.' 9 lipca 2019. Brytyjscy posłowie uhonorowali wkład Polaków II wś.

48 See https://www.britishpoles.uk/brytyjscy-poslowie-wreszcie-uhonorowali-wklad-polakow-w-ii-wojne-swiatowa; https://londynek.net/wiadomosci/article?jdnews_id=60529; https://hansard.parliament.uk/commons/2019-07-02/debates/0194C6A5-4403-42D0-BDEF-86FBE0CC110E/WorldWarTwoPolishContribution.

49 'powroty' is a noun and means 'return' in plural; the site supports any British Poles who would like to relocate back to Poland with administrative, financial and psychological advice.
50 The original reads: 'Zachęcam też Państwa do poważnego rozważenia możliwości powrotu do Ojczyzny i do zaznajomienia się z informacjami na portalu powroty.gov.pl ... Szybko rozwijająca się gospodarka naszego kraju stwarza obywatelom coraz większe możliwości na rozwój i dobre warunki do życia. Życząc Państwu wszystkiego, co najlepsze, apeluję o zadbanie o swoją przyszłość.' 18 września 2019. List ambasadora do Polaków w UK.
51 Molek-Kozakowska, 'Negotiating an Identity', 178.
52 'Naukowcy z Uniwersytetu Strathclyde w Glasgow opublikowali badania, z których wynika, że ponad trzy czwarte uczniów z krajów Europy Wschodniej doświadczyło ze strony kolegów zachowań rasistowskich, ksenofobicznych oraz zastraszania. Badania wskazują, że takie sytuacje nasiliły się po referendum w sprawie brexitu w 2016 roku i często były maskowane jako żart.' 23 sierpnia 2019. Młodzi Polacy w UK są ofiarami rasizmu.
53 From the original: 'Wielką Brytanię jako cel wyjazdu zarobkowego najczęściej wybierają osoby lepiej wykształcone, pochodzące ze średnich i największych miast Polski ... Polscy emigranci są przeciętnie bardzo aktywni zawodowo, co wynika zarówno ze struktury ich wieku (20–45 lat), jak i z motywacji wyjazdu (cele zarobkowe) ... Poprawiająca się sytuacja na polskim rynku pracy powoduje, że emigranci wyraźnie rzadziej niż dwa lata wcześniej deklarowali chęć pozostania za granicą na stałe, natomiast częściej pobyt powyżej 3 lat, ale z perspektywą powrotu. W Wielkiej Brytanii trend ten był prawdopodobnie wzmocniony niepewnością związaną z brexitem.' 29 lipca 2019. Jacy są polscy emigranci w UK.
54 http://www.mojawyspa.co.uk/artykuly/36695/Polak-skazany-za-gwalt-walczy-o-dobre-imie; http://www.mojawyspa.co.uk/modules.php?name=News&file=notes&keyword=Jakub_Tomczak.
55 'I tak jak brytyjskie media zrobiły z polskiego studenta prawa, który przyjechał na Wyspy by dorobić, okrutnego zboczeńca i bandytę, to przeważającą większość polskich dziennikarzy przychylała się do opinii, że chłopak jest ofiarą pomyłki wymiaru sprawiedliwości.' 20 lutego 2019. Polak skazany za gwałt walczy o dobre imię.
56 James Morrison, 'Re-framing Free Movement in the Countdown to Brexit? Shifting UK Press Portrayals of EU Migrants in the Wake of the Referendum', *The British Journal of Politics and International Relations* 21, no. 3 (2019): 594–611.
57 Morrison, 'Re-framing', 594.
58 Mirca Madianou, 'Beyond the Presumption of Identity? Ethnicities, Cultures and Transnational Audiences', in *The Handbook of Media Audiences,* ed. Virginia Nightingale (Malden, MA: Wiley-Blackwell, 2012), 444–58.

Section Three

Betwixt Local Politics and the Home Country's Politics: Extraterritorial Media Staging of Political Conflicts

9

Betwixt Spain and England: The Spanish Liberals' Spanish-Language Media Strategies in London (1810–50)

María José Ruiz Acosta
University of Seville

Political exile is one of the most regrettable chapters of contemporary history. The exodus of those who were forced to leave their country to avoid political persecution became far too commonplace in Spain as from the beginning of the nineteenth century. In 1823, England became the preferred country of asylum for Spanish liberals, namely those who had to flee the peninsula to escape the persecution of the absolutist King Ferdinand VII. After having settled in London, these political refugees plied different trades to make ends meet. The lucky ones, in addition to scraping enough money together to cover their most urgent needs, had the time and courage to persevere in their political struggle. For a large group of these Spaniards, there were opportunities in education, translation and, specially, journalism.

As a result, exiled liberals ended up writing a lot, publishing a lot and forging links with some thirty editor-printers in the English capital. Making the most of the freedom of expression that they enjoyed there, several of these emigrants collaborated with a number of English magazines. Furthermore, they published a considerable number of weekly and monthly Spanish-language newspapers.

In light of the foregoing, the aim of this chapter is to analyse the career paths of the Spanish liberals in exile, paying special attention to the role played by those who dedicated their time to writing or journalism. This aspect has been previously addressed by prominent researchers such as Daniel Muñoz Sempere and Barry Taylor, both of whom have focused on the evolution of the Hispanic publishing world in nineteenth-century London. Likewise, scholars of the stature of Fernando Durán López and his team continue to strive to gain a better understanding of Spanish intellectual émigrés in the British capital.

Based on the aforementioned research, the intention here is to offer an overview of the main actors in that publishing world and the works that they produced. To this end, they have been divided into groups following different criteria, with an eye to offering further insights into the role played by Spanish-language publications produced in England in the history of journalism, in general, and in the history of Hispanic liberalism, in particular, during the nineteenth century.

Background

In 1814, at the end of the war in which the Spaniards had confronted Napoleon Bonaparte,[1] a pamphlet published in Seville warned King Ferdinand VII that, although the French invaders had been finally expelled, he should not drop his guard, insofar as the war was not over yet. In the opinion of the pamphleteer, it was still necessary to wage a last battle that was more dangerous than the previous ones, since it was not a question now of fighting against foreign invaders, but against domestic enemies, traitors who were trying to assassinate the king, destroy his throne and put an end to the Catholic religion, by all imaginable means possible. The author of the document was referring to the liberals, that is, those Spaniards who, taking advantage of the military situation, had managed to establish the first Spanish constitution in 1812.

In fact, the Peninsula War (1808–14) was the ideal occasion for a group of thinkers to initiate a particular struggle, whose ultimate goal was not only to overthrow Napoleon Bonaparte, but also to exploit the war scenario to bring the absolutist regime prevailing hitherto to an end. This led to another conflict, in this case not between different nations but between the Spaniards themselves. During the six years that the war lasted, both factions had remained united insofar as they opposed a common enemy (France). Nevertheless, they participated in heated discussions in which they attempted to impose their particular vision of the political system that should prevail in post-war Spain: while the absolutists advocated for maintaining the existing status quo, the liberals were in favour of constitutionalism, an ideal that finally began to gain the upper hand after the promulgation of the 1812 Constitution of Cadiz. The latter's victory, however, was marred by the constitution's very short life, as it was repealed by King Ferdinand VII, but two years after its proclamation. In 1814, a civil conflict broke out between two warring factions: the proponents of the old regime and the advocates of a constitutional system. While supporting the former, Ferdinand VII took a hard line against the latter.

Thus, the liberals, who shortly before had been willing to lay down their lives for their king, began to fill the mainland prisons or were sent to the presidiums of North Africa. To avoid further complications, others had to go into exile. As of 1814, the return to the Old Regime would entail, among other aspects, the political repression of those who had supported constitutionalism. Manuel Moreno Alonso called them 'the men of 1808', conferring on them a leading role in the founding of the Spanish liberal state.[2] Enlightened and educated, they owned books that enabled them to become familiar with new ideas (those of Voltaire, Rousseau and Montesquieu) and helped them to design the new political system that they longed for in Spain. At the end of the Peninsula War, these men were forced to leave their homeland. But in their flight, they did not forget their ideas.

Aiming for London and connecting with British anti-absolutist circles (1823–50)

Versus the repression unleashed by Ferdinand VII in Spain, London offered the exiled liberals political asylum, as well as the opportunity to develop a cultural programme with which to demolish the pillars of the absolutist regime. Although Spanish writer, theologian, journalist, secularized Catholic priest José María Blanco White[3] had sought refuge in England in 1810, the exodus to London of most of the liberals began in 1824. By the end of the nineteenth century, the Spanish community had taken up residence in Euston (where the train station is today), an area that was regarded as peripheral, or in Somers Town, a little further to the north. This new neighbourhood would become a touchstone for Spanish expatriates.

By the end of the eighteenth century, during its incipient and not altogether successful urban development, Somers Town had already been home to the feminist pioneer Mary Wollstonecraft, at a time when the French Revolution was in full swing. Years later, around 1823, when still a child, Charles Dickens would become an exceptional witness to the growing presence of the Spanish liberal diaspora in Somers Town, named after the Somers family who had once owned the land on which the neighbourhood was developed. Not only the Spanish refugees escaping from Ferdinand's repression settled in this new neighbourhood, but also others, like Wollstonecraft, fleeing from the unrest and persecution resulting from different revolutions and conflicts, had previously sought protection there, thus making Somers Town a natural destination for expatriates of all kinds and one of the city's poorest suburbs.

Owing to his frequent encounters with liberal refugees in the streets of his childhood, years later Dickens would evoke the image of the Spaniards who used to walk wrapped in their cloaks, smoking their 'little paper cigars'.[4] But Somers Town also had a special allure for those Spaniards who, in many cases and despite their liberal ideology, continued to believe in Catholicism, which, however, did not prevent them from criticizing the control that the Church authorities exerted through their traditional alliance with the Crown. The presence of St Aloysius, a recently built Catholic chapel with its respective cemetery, might have been one of the reasons behind the Spanish émigrés' preference for Somers Town as a place to settle and to make their new *home*, which, nonetheless, was a temporary one while they waited for their long-desired return to their homeland. Thus, in their London refuge where they received financial aid from the Government and the support of personalities such as Lord and Lady Holland, and imbued with English liberalism, they continued their unrelenting struggle against absolutism, using different instruments, such as the press. As Vicente Llorens already noted in the mid-1950s in his pioneering work *Liberales y románticos. Una emigración española en Inglaterra* (Liberals and Romantics. A Spanish Emigration in England), addressing the phenomenon of the Spanish liberal exile in the nineteenth century entails speaking of a *geografía de la emigración* (emigration geography) with two major milestones.[5] The first would be the abolition of the Constitution of Cadiz and the restoration of absolutism in the period between the return of Ferdinand VII in 1814, after the Peninsula War, and the beginning of the Liberal Triennium in 1820 with the Riego uprising.[6] During this period, France was still the main option for Spanish émigrés. While the second, when the British capital assumed a more important role, would be determined by the intervention of the Holy Alliance and 'The Hundred Thousand Sons of Saint Louis', to wit, the French army that enabled Ferdinand VII to re-establish absolutism in 1823 until his death in 1833.

During this so-called 'Ominous Decade', England became the preferred European destination for Spanish liberals, since France, which hitherto had attracted the largest number of refugees, treated most of them as prisoners of war. This was especially true during the first six years of the absolutist decade, for in 1830 a considerable number of refugees in England moved to France as a result of the July Revolution. But London would become the émigrés' true political and intellectual centre, giving rise to a series of Anglo-Hispanic synergies that allowed numerous entrepreneurial projects of a cultural, literary or journalistic nature to be undertaken.[7] Regarding the latter, it should be noted that they were hugely important for the future development of Hispanic liberalism. Despite the sporadic nature of the magazines and newspapers that they published, their authors were highly successful in engaging their fellow exiles and the British intelligentsia and political class with their principles.

Nor was the situation favourable for Spanish political refugees on the other side of the Atlantic, insofar as it was a difficult time for the former Spanish colonies struggling to place their independence on firmer footing. Nonetheless, some of the most eminent émigrés in England and France ended up in South America or the United States due to their professional worth, especially those working in the field of journalism, literature or education. This was the case with José Joaquín de Mora.[8] In London, he left his stamp on some of the leading newspapers and publishing houses at the time, before travelling to Argentina, Chile – whose 1828 Constitution he drafted, as well as participating in journalistic and educational initiatives – Peru and Bolivia. Besides Europe and America, Spanish liberals even settled in Africa, primarily Morocco, where the emperor gave them a cordial welcome and refused Ferdinand VII's repeated requests for their extradition.

Figuras de la emigración and Spanish cultural politics in England: José María Blanco White's *El Español* (1810–14)

As already noted, for a large group of these Spaniards there were opportunities in education, translation and journalism. Specifically, this last profession was one of the most popular because writing satisfied their need to keep hope alive. The written word was also used to campaign against the absolute monarchy that had forced them into exile.

Exiled liberals thus wrote abundantly when in Britain and stroke durable friendships with editor printers in London, where they enjoyed extensive freedom of expression. *The European Review* and the *New Monthly Magazine* were prime sites where Spanish liberalism was fully voiced at the time.

The *New Monthly Magazine* published the contributions of famous exiles, such as Blanco White (from a more political perspective, with his critiques *Cartas de España* [Letters from Spain], published under the pen name 'Leocadio Doblado'), and Manuel Eduardo de Gorostiza[9] (from a more literary point of view, focusing on theatre).

In addition to the aforementioned Blanco White and José Joaquín de Mora, there were other intellectuals who also stood out in the journalistic and literary fields, such as Alcalá Galiano[10] and Pablo de Mendíbil[11] whose name regularly appeared in Spanish and English magazines. As with Blanco and Mora, Mendíbil also participated as an author in the ambitious business projects of the German publisher Rudolph Ackermann. To these should be added Espronceda[12] who, together with other liberals such as Patricio de la Escosura,[13] had founded the secret society *Los Numantinos* (to avenge the death of Rafael del Riego, after witnessing his torture in 1823) and for whose activity they were forced to emigrate. There were many Spaniards who participated in the journalistic activities of the London exile and who took advantage of this as a useful way of disseminating their tolerant ideology from several perspectives.

Furthermore, they published a considerable number of weekly and monthly Spanish-language newspapers. Not all these periodicals had the same impact. In fact, they can be divided into different groups according to their intentions.

The most relevant publications were those whose aim was to become mouthpieces for persecuted liberalism, to continue the struggle against absolutism and to keep the émigré community united and informed. It was an exile press, written in exile and for exiles. It also catered to the peninsular Spaniards, to the limited extent that such publications were introduced clandestinely.

The worth of this press lay in the fact that this émigré community facilitated the exchange of ideas between the Spanish, the English and refugees of different nationalities and ideological bents, who were then living in the British capital, an authentic haven for political exiles.

The most relevant publication was *El Español* (The Spaniard), a Spanish newspaper published in London by José Maria Blanco Crespo or Blanco White between 1810 and 1814. Blanco made a splash in the London press with the launching of this magazine, the pacesetter of Spanish exile journalism, paving the way for other publications that would promote liberal thinking in its many facets – political, religious, cultural and educational – aimed especially at the new Latin American nations. *El Español*'s importance in contemporary Spanish history was owing to the fact that it was the first to criticize government policy openly and to its obsessive desire to raise public awareness in Spain and America. It should be recalled that, in Spain, Blanco White had previously launched another political publication that was also scathingly critical with the powers that be. Called *Semanario Patriótico* (Patriotic Weekly),[14] this magazine can very well be considered as the germ of what would later become *El Español*.

Although it had been founded in Madrid in 1808, when the French troops entered the Spanish capital, the *Semanario Patriótico* had to continue to be published in Seville. During this time (from May to August 1809), it was run by Blanco White (Blanco Crespo at the time) and Isidoro Antillón. Although the Seville edition maintained the same tone (serious, doctrinal and without concessions to mockery or satire) and objective of engaging a literate public with progressive ideas, it was more direct and impetuous 'because the circumstances were more pressing'.[15]

At that time, Blanco had continued to believe firmly in the constituent potential of the Cortes, in its legitimacy to change things and in its mandate to build a nation on new political foundations. But now, in 1809, he sensed that the revolution that had just broken out in Spain was going to fail; something that, in his opinion, was down to the indolence of those making up the Junta Central (Central Board). It was in this context that Blanco came into his own, becoming one of the best political journalists in the country.

With that professional baggage, Blanco Crespo-Blanco White (he changed his surname after settling in England) undertook the task of founding *El Español*. This newspaper was an excellent source of information not only on current affairs in Spain and in its American colonies, but also on Westminster politics. In short, it was unmatched by any other Spanish newspaper at the time.

Throughout its history, the newspaper strove to apply the English political model – British 'political wisdom' – in Spain. Its objective was to modernize the country by spreading English political ideas, especially 'practical politics'. Such a vision was palpable at very specific moments, as in the numbers devoted to discussing one of the burning issues of the moment: the approval of the 1812 Constitution.[16] This perspective was directly associated with the idea that the Spanish liberals believed that, besides the country's tradition of offering refuge to all kinds of political exiles, England was some paradise. Indeed, the relations between both groups (the Spanish exiles and the British political class) went back to before the Peninsula War. For instance, the Hollands, who financially supported Blanco White in his English exile and journalistic enterprises, had spent time in Spain between 1803 and 1805. After the outbreak of the conflict in 1808, the British aristocracy were convinced than ever that they had something to say in Spanish politics. Wielding their influence through the patronizing of the Spanish-language periodicals published in England and distributed throughout Spanish-speaking areas was a way of doing so.

Monthly periodicals, or why opt for the review format?

Although the number of Spaniards living in exile in London during the first years of the 'Ominous Decade' has led to a certain amount of controversy, there is a greater consensus on the political and cultural momentum that it gave to the subsequent rise of the liberal movement in Spain. While for Menéndez Pelayo there were between 500 and 600 Spanish refugees living in Somers Town, Llorens claims that without any great error it can be estimated that by 1824 there would have been a little over 1,000 families from all walks of life, including people such as the quaint *banderillero* Muselina. Drawing on an anecdote appearing in *Recuerdos* (Memories) by Alcalá Galiano, one of the most notable political exiles, Menéndez Pelayo claims that even though Muselina did not know how to read or write, he received a subsidy as a writer. Although Llorens is of the mind that the middle-classes and self-employed predominated (military, lawyers, priests, merchants, writers, physicians, etc.), to these should be added other prestigious men of science, letters and the arts who, in the words of Alcalá Galiano, are those who form the backbone of the liberal party in any country.

Most of them formed a distinguished group who remained in London for more than two decades. In spite of the harsh living conditions that they had to endure, they did not go unnoticed by contemporary English society. In fact, the Government tolerated them and a part of that society showed some sympathy for the exiles who they helped both materially and symbolically. The majority of them lived in the hope of returning home (some of them always had their bags packed) and, disheartened, not a few of them Hispanicized it to a certain extent, instead of adapting to their new environment. Be that as it may, the Spanish liberal exile in London also gave rise to the work of those men who Llorens called *figuras de la emigración* (outstanding émigrés), a large group of intellectuals who organized gatherings at home, in bookshops and cafes (the British Coffee House is iconic in this respect) with journalists and writers, and who fraternized with other mainly Italian and Portuguese émigrés, as well as with English liberals. In addition to the famous gatherings at Holland House, which outstanding journalists and writers like Blanco White attended, the director of the *New Monthly Magazine* Thomas Campbell, who during those years had fervently embraced the Spanish émigrés' cause, organized lively soirees at home in which the Spanish refugees sang the 'Spanish Patriots' Song', composed by him in their honour.[17] It was published in his magazine, along with 'Stanzas to the Memory of the Spanish Patriots', a poem that he also dedicated to them.

In the meantime, some of them, as has been seen in the case of Blanco White, became involved in a number of flagship publications. First and foremost, *El Español Constitucional* (The Constitutional Spaniard), which was published in two stages: from 1818 to 1820 and from 1824 to 1825. Although it was envisaged as a weekly, high running costs soon led it to being published on a monthly basis.[18] This revolutionary newspaper was largely the brainchild of the military physician and former guerrilla fighter Pedro Pascasio Fernandez Sardino. In a line similar to that of the press that had already developed in Spain, *El Español Constitucional* even went so far as to demand the elimination of the royal family and the clergy. According to Llorens, Sardino also launched *El Telescopio* (The Telescope), although scant information in this respect has come down to us.

The men responsible for *El Español Constitucional*, Fernández Sandino and Manuel M. Acevedo, were considered as radicals in their day, insofar as they belonged to one of the two groups into which Spanish liberalism was divided during the first decades of the nineteenth century. In favour of abolishing absolutism, they wanted to convert Spain into a democratic republic where suffrage was more representative. In the first issue, it claimed that its mission was to present the essential facts about the Spanish and American revolutions by airing the issues that had remained concealed from the public eye.

To these should be added *Ocios de españoles emigrados* (Pastimes of Spanish Émigrés). An advocate of moderate liberalism, this magazine was known for its high quality and prestige. After the good reception of Spanish literature in England, its promoters launched this new project for the purpose of increasing its readership's knowledge of Spain. Canga Argüelles and the Villanueva brothers undertook the task of enlightening without tiring, by means of articles covering a variety of topics which were neither too long nor too short; viz. historical anecdotes, literary pieces and financial columns, in addition to features on Spanish politics and bibliography, ecclesiastical history and statistical releases. In short, *Ocios*' main aim was to discuss Spanish history, literature, economy and politics, thus highlighting what the country had to offer Europe.

Along with the aforementioned magazines, the émigré community also produced other types of publications that could be described as being philo-Protestant. Their *raison d'être* had to do with the fact that Spanish liberalism, since its inception, had always accepted all freedoms, except the religious kind. From the 1812 Constitution to those enacted during the reign of Isabel II, Catholicism was the faith of the Spanish liberals. Even when they finally came to power, the different constitutional bodies agreed that Protestant propaganda would only exacerbate the differences of opinion in the country. Whereby the religious status quo was maintained throughout the nineteenth century: the nascent liberal bourgeoisie was ignorant of or refused to accept religious pluralism and only made a tardy and half-hearted attempt at addressing the issue in the Democratic Manifesto of 1849 and in the 1869 Constitution.

In any case, although religious debate was taboo for liberalism in Spain, this was not the case abroad. Spanish émigrés made an important contribution to the production of religious propaganda that sooner or later reached Spain and Latin America. The most relevant of them was *Catolicismo Neto* (Pure Catholicism), the first Protestant Spanish-language newspaper. Published from 1849 to 1851, it was read in England and Spain, as evidenced by the fact that the Spanish authorities tried to ban it. *El Examen Libre* (The Free Examination) followed on from *El Catolicismo Neto*. To avoid the governmental and ecclesiastical persecution to which the latter had been subject, Juan Calderón, its promoter, was obliged to publish another magazine that upheld identical principles and objectives, but under a different title. Published between 1851 and 1854, it achieved a greater circulation than its forerunner, being distributed in Madrid, Valencia and part of Andalusia. *El Alba* (The Dawn) was the initiative of different British evangelization societies, which launched it after the death of Juan Calderón. As of 1855, *El Alba* became the most influential Protestant Spanish-language publication in Spain and Latin America.

Collaborating with the London publishing scene: British and foreign connections

There was another expatriate press of a remarkably different character, even though many of its authors also wrote for the aforementioned publications. This was directly promoted by British publishers who took advantage of the émigré community to print Spanish-language magazines offering culture and entertainment to readers in Latin America. After achieving independence, the Spanish colonies in America began to open up to British trade and investment, and publishers devised a strategy to introduce their products into that market, where a complex network of contacts and interests was established.

The most relevant magazines were those produced by Rudolf Ackermann. Of German extraction, this publisher unleashed his enterprising spirit in London by specializing in the field of graphic arts. After settling in England in around 1786, Ackermann had begun his professional career designing carriages that he would later reproduce for advertising purposes. He supplemented his earnings by selling art supplies, as well as opening an art gallery, with paintings, drawings and engravings, on the Strand.

As an entrepreneur, Ackermann experimented with many technical and commercial innovations, such as lithography, of which he was one of the pioneers. To his mind, this procedure could serve to mass produce, among other things, illustrations for the emerging middle classes. To this end, he engaged European workers, engravers and writers who had emigrated to London fleeing from war, political turmoil or economic crisis in their countries of origin. At that time, London became a refuge for thinkers and a place from which to disseminate their thoughts and which, in the early nineteenth century, offered the Spanish liberal diaspora the wherewithal to carry forward their demands. Not only was there individual and religious freedom involving all aspects of social life, but journalism was also a feasible activity as evidenced by the fact that in the first decades of that century there was an extraordinary large number of publications: from weeklies on politics and literature to biweeklies and monthlies on all types of subjects. In fact, during those decades numerous publishing houses had been established in the country, some of which ended up supporting the journalistic initiatives of the Spanish liberals.

Ackermann's business acumen led him to commission Spanish exiles to edit printed materials that were then distributed in Latin America, a market he had long wanted to penetrate and which was now possible thanks to the wave of independence movements sweeping over the continent at the time. According to Fernando Durán, as of 1820 Ackermann's publishing house implemented an ambitious plan for printing and distributing books in Spanish in Latin America, subsequently accounting for 72 per cent of British book exports to the continent.[19]

In this American campaign, which included books on a large variety of subjects, Ackermann also promoted Spanish-language newspapers. The first of these was *Variedades o El Mensajero de Londres* (Varieties or The London Messenger), a quarterly that was in circulation from 1823 to 1825. The English entrepreneur knew how to make the most of the technical developments of the period to satisfy the instructional and entertainment needs of the Latin American bourgeoisie, a sector that independence had opened up to the British market. The potential readers in these new republics wanted to catch up on European fashions and customs, a thirst for news that their own publishing houses did little to slake.

Ackermann entrusted the undertaking to Blanco White who produced a magazine that was conceived as a miscellany encompassing a broad variety of topics intended for an audience unaccustomed to reading long books. Likewise, the magazine kept to the middle ground as regards politics and religion in order not to alienate its Latin American readership.

Other publications included *Museo Universal de Ciencias y Artes* (Universal Science and Arts Museum), a quarterly that was intended to be a supplement to *Variedades*, which hitherto had focused mainly on literary themes. It covered scientific and artistic topics, which in London, a city regarded as the capital of the world, was entirely possible. Moreover, since 1834 many Spanish scientists had sought refuge in the city. Illustrated with numerous prints, the magazine was very practical. And, lastly, mention should also go to *El Instructor o Repertorio de historia, bellas artes y letras* (The Instructor or Repertoire of History, Fine Arts and Letters).

While many exiles returned to Spain after the amnesties decreed as of 1834, some remained in London. Ackermann employed them to produce a magazine between 1834 and 1841, which followed in the wake of the illustrated publications that had begun to appear in Europe. *El Instructor* (The Instructor) would become the first illustrated magazine in Spanish, to the extent that it was not a mere translation of an original in another language. Although it was published in London, it was conspicuously tailored to the Spanish-speaking world. This monthly was presented as an encyclopaedic newspaper whose main purpose was instruction, followed by entertainment. It not only included literary texts, ancient and modern history, descriptions of monuments, miscellaneous issues relating to different countries, customs, art and geography, but also matters pertaining to agriculture, trade, the stock market and even technical or industrial developments.

La Colmena, periódico trimestre de Ciencias, Artes, Historia y Literatura (The Beehive, Quarterly Newspaper of Sciences, Arts, History and Literature) was a project with which Ackermann entrusted Ángel de Villalobos. As of 1842, it was published as a sequel to *El Instructor* (The Instructor), although with less scientific content and a more entertaining editorial line. Admittedly, the objectives remained the same, although reinforced by the quest for 'pictorial beauty and typographic clarity', which could be achieved by using wood blocks and some steel engravings. This resulted in a periodical publication similar to a general encyclopaedia or a collection of independent treatises on different branches of knowledge, whose main aim was to keep its readers informed about all new developments.

Doing politics twice remotely: Spanish-language periodicals in the Latin American colonies

Lastly, other Spanish-language magazines, covering current affairs in Spain and in its former American colonies, were also published in London at the time. They are called 'the American publications' here because they attempted to create a new Latin American information space during the independence process.

Before the diaspora began, most liberals did not accept the independence of the colonies that Spain retained in America. But once in London, they arrived at the conclusion that the ousting of Ferdinand VII would not only mean their return to Spain and, therefore, the start of a constitutional process, but would also imply a change in policy as regards Latin America in which independence was the only possible scenario. Hence the need to resort to various means (meetings, publications, etc.) in order to forge a common identity for all, since the political unity between the metropolis and its colonies was in its death throes.

To understand the change in attitude of these thinkers it is necessary to bear in mind that during the first decades of the nineteenth century, in addition to the Spanish liberal contingent, a group of Americans also travelled to England seeking help to place the process of independence from Spain on a firmer footing. These included Francisco de Miranda, Simón Bolivar, Andrés Bello, José de San Martín, Vicente Rocafuerte and José Joaquín de Olmedo, who all discovered that there was no better city than London to learn about the best type of government to be established in the former Spanish colonies. For them, London was the ideal place to become familiar with good governance practices that could then be implemented in the new Latin American republics.

Politicians, diplomats and men of letters arrived in the British capital encouraged by the spirit of freedom prevailing in the country. For all of them and the fledgling American nations, newly constituted as states or in the process of formation, the trip was fundamental to drum up political and military support for their cause in Europe, to acquire first-hand knowledge of the Old World and to gain experience in the management of public affairs, something that would have been impossible in America.

And it was in this way that the Spanish liberals and the Americans became acquainted, fostering a spirit of fellowship and active cooperation. In the modest neighbourhood of Somers Town, where most resided, they entered into a fruitful dialogue, precisely when their respective governments were at war. At first exclusively political – the Spanish refugees learned that the causes that had forced the nations of the New World to seek freedom were the same as those that had led them into exile – their discussions soon veered towards cultural issues, leading to intellectual cooperation and, in some cases, open friendship. English soil became a refuge for both groups. There, the Spaniards and the Americans could not be enemies because they were all pursuing the same goal. In Pedro Grases' words, the affinity between desires and ideals merged in one of the most beautiful embraces ever to be seen in history. As a result, the publications produced during those years were in Spanish and focused on Latin America.[20]

During their sojourn in London, these politicians and intellectuals became involved in publishing periodicals for Latin American audiences. These included *La Biblioteca Americana* (The American Library) and *El Repertorio Americano* (The American Repertoire), both designed to promote the recognition of the new republics and to disseminate in the New World the cultural, scientific and practical news circulating in Europe.

Both aimed to popularize the idea that Spain had kept America isolated from the rest of the world, thus preventing it from broadening its horizons and even creating its own identity. All of which had made it impossible to develop its own thought, which, at the beginning of the nineteenth century, was now an urgent matter. Aware of the need to shape new citizens who knew themselves and their history, they envisaged these magazines as windows to the outside world that would provide their fellow countrymen with a much broader worldview than they had had before.

Published during 1823, the chief aim of *La Biblioteca American* was to raise the cultural level of the Americans to prepare them for the new situation deriving from the independence process. Distributed in the New World, it contributed to the emancipatory cause with the written word, shaping and consolidating a more moral and ideological reality. It represented the first and most ambitious American cultural initiative launched in Europe. The magazine, the work of men educated in America, would offer a much broader worldview by focusing on several ideals tending towards achieving independence. It provided an overview in which America was seen as a whole and its inhabitants as members of a community and not of a particular nation.

The fostering of such ideals required a careful selection of articles, a filtering process whose intention was to establish a content structure that promoted the construction and development of that 'one nation' concept. And although this objective was never met, the publication contributed to sow the seeds of integration among its readership.

For its part, *El Repertorio Americano*, published from 1826 to 1827, picked up from where its predecessor had left off. Its purpose was identical to that of *La Biblioteca Americana*, namely, to cover a variety of topics that might contribute to progress in America in such different fields as the arts, the sciences, civilization and inventions. Its aim was to educate the inhabitants of that continent in order that they might lay the foundations of enlightened institutions on par with the most hallowed in Europe.

Conclusion

As has been seen throughout this study, for the Spanish liberal émigrés London became a safe haven from which to combat the absolutism of Ferdinand VII at the beginning of the nineteenth century. This was largely possible thanks to the role played by the press. Later on, those same Spaniards who had been forced into exile made the acquaintance of some of the leading figures in the embryonic Latin American independent movements. Both groups received help from their British hosts and established alliances that led to the launching of periodical publications essential to their struggle for freedom. In this context, the Spanish liberal exile became much more than a political emigration, since it was also a cultural and entrepreneurial phenomenon.

Notes

1 The Peninsula War was waged from 1808 to 1814 in the context of the Napoleonic Wars, pitting the allied powers of Spain, the United Kingdom and Portugal against the First French Empire, whose intention was to place José Bonaparte, Napoleon's brother, on the Spanish throne.
2 Manuel Moreno Alonso, *La generación española de 1808* (Madrid: Alianza Editorial, 1989).
3 José María Blanco y Crespo (Seville, 11 July 1775–Liverpool, 20 May 1841), better known as José María Blanco White, was a Spanish writer, theologian, journalist, secularized Catholic priest and literary critic. He collaborated with Isidoro de Antillón in running the *Semanario Patriótico* (1808–9), one of the most relevant newspapers edited in Spain during the Peninsula War. On 29 January 1810, he moved to Cadiz and on 23 February he embarked for England, arriving in London on 3 March 1810. He would never return to Spain.
4 Charles Dickens, *Bleak House* (Peterborough, ONT: Broadview Editions, 2010).
5 See Juan Francisco Fuentes, 'Geografía del liberalismo español en la Década Ominosa: emigración política y exilio interior', in Armando Alberola, and Elisabel Larriba (eds.), *Las élites y la Revolución de España (1808–1814). Estudios en homenaje al profesor Gérard Dufour* [The elites and the Spanish Revolution (1808–14). Studies in tribute to Professor Gérard Dufour], 309–31 (Alicante: Universidad de Alicante-Université de Provence-Casa de Velázquez, 2010).
6 The period of contemporary Spanish history running from 1820 to 1823 is known as the Liberal Triennium or Constitutional Triennium. It began with the uprising of Colonel Rafael del Riego, who re-established the 1812 Constitution. This period ended when France helped to restore the absolute monarchy of Fernando VII.

7   See Vicente Llorens, *Liberales y románticos. Una emigración española en Inglaterra (1823-1834)* (Madrid: Castalia, 1979).
8   José Joaquín de Mora y Sánchez (Cádiz, 10 January 1783–Madrid, 3 October 1864) was a Spanish writer, educator, journalist, poet, jurist and politician. After the invasion of the Hundred Thousand Sons of San Luis in 1823, he emigrated to London like other Spanish liberals and remained in England until the end of 1826. With the help of the publisher Ackermann, he founded *Don't Forget Me*, a kind of prose and verse almanac of which six volumes were published between 1824 and 1829. He was the director and sole editor of the *Museo Universal de Ciencias y Artes* (1824–6) and of the *Correo político y literario de Londres* (London Political and Literary Mail), all of which were aimed above all at Latin Americans. He continued to collaborate with Ackermann in writing and disseminating the famous *Catecismos* (Catechisms), a series of manuals on various scientific subjects and disciplines, which served as textbooks in countries that lacked works of this type in recently emancipated Spanish America.
9   Manuel María del Pilar Eduardo de Gorostiza y Cepeda (Veracruz, Viceroyalty of New Spain, 13 October 1789–Tacubaya, Mexico, 23 October 1851) was a Spanish-Mexican playwright, journalist and diplomat.
10 Antonio Alcalá Galiano y Fernández de Villavicencio (Cadiz, 22 July 1789–Madrid, 11 April 1865) was a Spanish politician and writer. He was named Minister of the Navy in 1836 and Minister of Development in April 1865. Elected as a deputy for Cadiz in 1822, he was considered to be a great orator who defended liberalism during the Liberal Triennium, in which he was active in the secret society Confederation of Communal Knights. He then became involved in Freemasonry and in the moderate party and, after voting in favour of the motion tabled to declare King Ferdinand VII incapable in 1823, was forced into exile. In London, he survived teaching Spanish language and literature. Until then, he had been fundamentally an avid reader of Montesquieu's oeuvre. Thenceforth, he became imbued with the spirit of English political thought and, in keeping with Edmund Burke's moderate liberalism, rejected politics based on abstract principles and started to endorse utilitarianism, until converting to the doctrinaire liberalism of Alexis de Tocqueville and Benjamin Constant.
11 Pablo León José Mendibil Grao (Dulantzi, Alava, 11 April 1788–London, 1832) was a well-known liberal writer, teacher and journalist who died in exile in England. During the Liberal Triennium (1820–3), he was a member of the association 'Tertulia Constitucional' of San Sebastián. In 1823, when Ferdinand VII established absolutism, he fled to London where he taught Spanish and French. He also wrote for the magazine *Ocios de Españoles Emigrados* and in 1824, when Jaime Villanueva died, took over running it.
12 José de Espronceda y Delgado (Almendralejo, 25 March 1808–Madrid, 23 May 1842) was a Spanish writer who was regarded as the most representative poet of early Romanticism in Spain. In 1825, after being reported to the absolutist police for his intellectual activities, he was sentenced to exile from Madrid for five years, although his sentence was finally reduced to three months which he spent in the monastery of Guadalajara where his father was living. In the summer of 1827, he travelled to Portugal and later to England, where he arrived on 15 September. He came into contact there with the circle of Spanish liberal émigrés residing in Somers Town, more specifically with that of General Torrijos, who conspired to overthrow the absolutist regime. From there he established himself in Brussels as the general's emissary, before finally settling in Paris as a liberal exile, from where he travelled again to London to

receive orders. He returned to Spain after the amnesty was granted on the death of the king in 1833, where he devoted his time to politics and journalism.
13 Patricio de la Escosura Morrogh (Madrid, 1807–Madrid, 1878) was a Spanish politician, journalist, playwright, mythographer, critic and romantic writer. He was a senator for the province of Cordova (1872–3) and for the Spanish Academy (1877–8).
14 http://hemerotecadigital.bne.es/details.vm?q=id:0004036221&lang=en. As already noted, some authors contend that the *Semanario Patriótico* was the germ of *El Español*, as did some contemporaries such as Lady Holland. See https://archive.org/details/spanishjournalof00holl/page/328/mode/2up?q=white.
15 See Mª Cruz Seoane, *Historia del periodismo en España. 2. El siglo XIX* (History of journalism in Spain. Vol. 2. The 19th century) (Alianza Editorial, Madrid, 1983), 32.
16 See http://hemerotecadigital.bne.es/issue.vm?id=0004341075&search=&lang=fr and https://core.ac.uk/reader/71837114.
17 See https://babel.hathitrust.org/cgi/pt?id=hvd.32044092691203&view=1up&seq=529 Blanco White also wrote for *The New Monthly Magazine*, but the Spanish liberal revolution of 1820 made him take a new interest in his country of origin. Commissioned by Thomas Campbell, the magazine's director, he began to write *Cartas desde España* in Spanish in 1820, before translating them into English. In 1821, he published his letters in *The New Monthly Magazine* under the pseudonym 'Leocadio Doblado', after which they were compiled in a book in 1822. Besides covering quotidian topics, such as the descriptions of Holy Week, bullfighting and plays, he bitterly criticized the intolerance and backwardness of Spain. He also offered a comprehensive critique of Catholicism, which made him one of the pioneers of contemporary Spanish anticlericalism.
18 The choice of the magazine's format should probably be understood as being a political and financial strategy, for at the time printed monthlies could elude British political censorship more easily. Furthermore, it should be borne in mind that the monthly format was less associated with the political press.
19 Fernando Durán, *Versiones de un exilio: los traductores españoles de la casa Ackermann (Londres, 1823–1830)* (Madrid: Escolar y Mayo Editores, 2015).
20 Pedro Grases, *Tiempo de Bello en Londres y otros ensayos* (Caracas: Ediciones del Ministerio de Educación, 1962).

10

The *Megali Idea* in New York's Greek-Language Press (1915–22): Doing Greek Politics from a Distance?

Nicolas Pitsos
Inalco/CREE, Paris

In his 1964 book *The Greeks in the United States*, historian Theodore Saloutos described a phenomenon already apparent to nineteenth-century visitors to Greece: that Greeks were among the world's most insatiable newspaper-readers.[1] Even an illiterate Greek would, he said, always find someone learned enough to read it to him in the nearest café. With such avid consumers, the first newspapers in Greek were quick to emerge following the settlement of Greek-language migrants in the United States, as can be seen in the selection below.[2]

They addressed the need of a population that did not yet fully master English and that consequently sought information in its own language, on both what was going on

Table 10.1 Greek-language newspapers published in the United States of America from the late nineteenth century to the first half of the twentieth century (non-exhaustive list).[3]

Press titles	Place and year of first issue
Νέος Κόσμος (The New World)	Boston, 1892
Αστήρ (Star) bilingual	Chicago, 1904
Ελλάς (Greece)	Chicago, 1902
Ελληνικός Αστηρ (The Greek Star) bilingual	Chicago, 1904
Ελληνικός Τύπος (Greek Press) bilingual	Chicago, 1929
Πατρίς (Patria)	Massachusetts, 1905
Αργοναύτης (Argonaut), bilingual	New York, 1959
Ατλαντίς (Atlantis)	New York, 1894
Δωδεκανήσιος (Dodecanese) bilingual	New York, 1934
Εθνικός Κήρυξ (The National Herald)	New York, 1915
Ελεύθερος Τύπος (Free Press) bilingual	New York, 1943
Ελληνικά Νέα (Greek News) bilingual	New York, 1963
Ελληνισμός Αμερικής (Hellenism in/from America) bilingual	New York, 1951
Ελληνο-Αμερικανικό Βήμα (The Greco-American Tribune)	New York, 1941
Εμπρός (Forward)	New York, Chicago, 1927
Εστία (Hearth) bilingual	New York, Montreal, 1929

in their regions of origin, particularly Greece and Ottoman territories, and within American society. According to statistics published in 1929, around half a million Greek-language migrants were estimated to have settled in the United States between 1899 and 1924.[4] Those numbers are also reflected in what the French Consul in Washington said to the French President of the Council of Ministers, Alexandre Millerand, in January 1920:

> There are many Greeks in the United States of America; and many have been naturalized which gives them influence through voting. They are very active and do not allow their Representatives and Senators to ignore the aspirations of their former homeland, and sometimes, they manage to make Congress take them into account, for whatever it is worth. There was an example yesterday in the Senate, where a resolution in favour of attributing Thrace to Greece was adopted.[5]

From the 1912–13 Balkan Wars to the military expedition to Ottoman Asia Minor (*Mikrasia* in Greek) in the wake of the 1919 Versailles Treaty – not to mention the division of the country between interventionists and neutralists during the First World War – territorial expansion projects (aka the *Megali Idea*, 'the Great Idea)' guided the external politics of the Greek State at the turn of the century.[6] From 1919 to 1922, the Greek army occupied the Ottoman provinces (*vilayets*) of Thrace and Smyrna, before launching a campaign of territorial conquest towards the city of Ankara. Faced with a counter-offensive led by Ottoman officers/Young Turks behind Mustafa Kemal, this operation would end in defeat.[7] These events, which sealed the end of what is commonly known as the Eastern Question,[8] led to the mass displacement of populations fleeing the devastating effects of conflict.[9] Some of these war refugees emigrated to the United States, or the 'New World', to use the title of the first Greek American newspaper, *Νέος Κόσμος*, and contributed to a greater circulation of the Greek-language press.

This chapter primarily looks at two key, rival Greek-language newspapers published in those years, 1915–22. Founded in New York in 1894, *Ατλαντίς* (Atlantis) was a pioneer of the Greek-American press. Its advent was closely followed by that of *Εθνικός Κήρυξ* (*Ethnikos Kyrix*, i.e. the National Herald) a few years later in the same Manhattan neighbourhood. This chapter aims to analyse the two newspapers' discourse on military confrontations and political tensions involving Greece between 1919 and 1922. More specifically, it focuses on how events involving Greek expansionist policy at the time were seen by these two American Greek-language newspapers that targeted a Greek-language audience from different regions of South-East Europe and the Eastern Mediterranean, wherever they found themselves.[10] Beyond the immediate perception of these events, these newspapers shed light on the US policy as to these conflicts. They also give valuable information about how other communities in the United States who had emigrated from countries involved in the last phase of the Eastern Question positioned themselves.

This contribution argues that *Atlantis* and *Ethnikos Kyrix* did Greek politics on the *Megali Idea* from a distance, from the United States and functioned as informal propagandist vectors of Greek parties. The reasoning is three-fold. First, a brief presentation of the two newspapers will be given, with a focus on actors of that press.

Then, the two newspapers will be appraised for what they have in common. Put differently, what will be at stake here is how *Atlantis* and *Ethnikos Kyrix* supported the Greek dimension of the Eastern Question and contributed to disseminating the *Megali Idea* in the United States. The last section of this chapter will show how, despite a common objective – advocating the *Megali Idea* – internal political divisions in the contemporary Greek society were translated to the United States, thereby leading to a fierce media battle between the two titles, which resounded well beyond the American sphere. These divisions will lead us to reflect on a Greek 'imagined community' (to borrow the words of Benedict Anderson) in America.

Portraying *Atlantis* and *Ethnikos Kyrix*: origins, actors, financing

Atlantis was launched in New York on 1 March 1894, by Solon J. Vlasto (1852–1927). He had arrived two decades earlier from his native island of Syros and initially formed an import-export partnership with his brother, Demetrius J. Vlasto (1869–1944). The newspaper was first published as a weekly, before becoming a daily in 1905. It had a circulation of 30,000 on the eve of the First World War, and was then the most influential paper within the Greek-language community. *Atlantis* boasted of having high-performance technical equipment including four Monotype machines and high-speed printing presses, which contributed to its renown.[11]

Who were the Vlasto brothers and why did they set up *Ατλαντίς*? The Vlastos were active in New York City's Greek-American community. In 1891, Solon founded the Greek Society of Athena, serving as its president from until 1895. Athena members sought to help Greek-speaking immigrants adapt to social and political conditions in the United States – for instance, by setting up the first Greek Orthodox church, the Holy Trinity, in New York City, in 1892. Still enthused with that idea of reaching out to the Greek American community, the two brothers founded the weekly *Atlantis*. The title comes from the name given by the Ancient Greeks to land beyond the Atlantic Ocean – which the history of the United States published in Greek by the *Atlantis* printing house in 1919 makes clear.[12] Solon J. served as its publisher until he died in 1927. The first editor-in-chief of *Atlantis* was Socrates A. Xanthaky, but he left to found the rival newspaper *Panhellinios* in 1907. Adamantios T. Polyzoidis succeeded him from 1907 to 1933 and was also a correspondent for *The New York Times* in Greece. *Atlantis* also operated a Greek-language book department, which published a calendar and several titles.[13] Overall, they tried to introduce Greek-speaking immigrants to American politics, but had their own biases – the Vlasto brothers were staunch supporters of Theodore Roosevelt for example.[14] As naturalization became more popular after the First World War, *Atlantis* advocated American citizenship for Greek immigrants, all the while remaining a firm supporter of King Constantine.

Ethnikos Kyrix was established in 1915 by Petros Tatanis to support the interventionist line defended by Greek Prime Minister Eleftherios Venizelos during the First World War and propagate it among Greek-language immigrants who had settled in the United States. It presented itself as 'the progressive Greek daily newspaper' (subtitle in 1917). In 1926, its circulation was 35,000. Petros Tatanis was born in

Amaliada (Peloponnese) and moved to the United States in 1905. He was well-known in the banking, commercial and industrial circles of New York,[15] and acquired the famous firm Caracanda Bros, pioneers in import-export with Yemen. With its good network of branches in the United States, Egypt and France, and its offices throughout Arabia and Abyssinia, the Caracanda Bros practically controlled the most part of Yemen's Mocha coffee trade and a large portion of that of Abyssinia. Tatanis was a successful businessman.

Beside his commercial activities, Petros Tatanis was also a close friend of Venizelos. The latter's policy found a positive echo among middle-class citizens in Greece and especially Greek merchants and businessmen in cities such as Alexandria, Constantinople, Smyrna and New York. *Ethnikos Kyrix* reflected this. Its title and logo were inspired by Venizelos's newspaper, published in Chania, Crete, as *Kyrix*. The word 'national' was added to show that the newspaper did not address only Greeks based in New York, but rather Greek-speaking American citizens all over the country. Just like *Atlantis*, *Ethnikos Kyrix* had its own printing house.

The *Megali Idea* in the New York Greek-language press: a patriotic swansong

In April 1922, a Greek-American soldier and long-standing subscriber to *Atlantis* wrote to the newspaper's director from the Asia Minor front, asking him to send them the paper more regularly, as well as novels to break up the monotony of the battlefield.[16] A few days earlier, *Atlantis* had published the calendar of Greater Greece,[17] illustrating its conception of the settling of the Eastern Question, which was in total synergy and harmony with official Greek foreign policy aims: expanding the borders of the Hellenic state towards Ottoman Anatolia. Above and beyond a strategy of self-promotion – that is, instrumentalizing the representation of the Eastern Question in order to highlight and celebrate their own popularity – the two newspapers also published stories from war correspondents on the supposed qualities of the Greek army, in order to galvanize the population at the rear. In this respect, in March 1922, *Ethnikos Kyrix* translated the flattering report of an Italian correspondent travelling on the Orient Express for its readers, concerning the Greek army stationed in Thrace.[18] A few days later, the same newspaper published the glowing praise of Herbert Adams Gibbons, an American journalist and correspondent for several New York papers in Greece, concerning the strong position of the Greek army in Asia Minor.

Moreover, the two newspapers sought to influence and guide American public opinion in favour of the Kingdom of Greece's expansionist cause. To do so, they worked to identify how Greek foreign policy stakes in the Eastern Question could intersect American interests and the *Atlantis* even chose to publish editorials in English to reach a wider audience than the Greek-language community. In one such editorial, the director of *Atlantis* called on its readers to imagine the Pacific Ocean in place of the Aegean and what the policy of an aggressive Japan could achieve against the United States.[19] While *Atlantis* brandished the spectre of the 'yellow peril',[20] a widespread element of language in early twentieth-century US society, it sought to associate it with the 'Ottoman peril', exploiting the amalgamation of the unsettling and intimidating representations of Asia and the Asiatic in the public opinion of the time. Meanwhile, *Ethnikos Kyrix* played on references in the collective media memory, which had cast the 'Turk' as the epitome of barbarism and brutality since the advent of the Eastern Question (that is from the fight for Greek independence a century earlier).[21] From that Orientalist perspective, a cartoon was published in June 1922 of the 'bloodthirsty Turk', lamenting the fact that Turkey was 'the only nation to have succeeded, with the support of the great powers, in regaining its pre-war status'.[22] In times unconducive to the continuation of the Greek army's military operations in Asia Minor, the two newspapers sought to alarm American public opinion by discrediting any adversary of the *Megali Idea* in Anatolia. With this in mind, they also tried to raise American awareness of the atrocities committed by Kemalist troops, publishing reports by philanthropic associations (like the Relief Committee for Greeks of Asia Minor) that aided victims within the Greek Orthodox population of Anatolia.[23]

With the same aim, *Atlantis* revived the issue of the Middle East and American opinion in its 4 April 1922 edition about a debate at the American League for Foreign Affairs. It mentioned the contributions of Stephen Duggan,[24] Director of the Institute for International Education;[25] Adamantios Polyzoidis, editor-in-chief of *Atlantis*; and the Philhellenic journalist Paxton Hibben.[26] Despite his commitment to bringing peoples together through educational exchanges, Duggan reproduced a constant element of turn-of-the-century anti-Turkish discourse, whereby the Eastern Question could not be resolved so long as the Turks remained in Europe and had not been pushed back towards inner Asia Minor. Duggan thus condemned the indulgence and self-interest of the Great European powers with regard to Turkey. In that debate, Polyzoidis once again focused on the fight of Greek civilization against Asian regression, this time adding arguments about the supposed 'Greekness' of the regions claimed in Asia Minor under the *Megali Idea*. The newspaper also mentioned the statement by a Turkish student at Columbia University, who was described as a Kemalist agent and who seemingly blamed massacres in Turkey on the multiple foreign interventions.

For his part, Greek diplomat Ioannis Gennadios, Ambassador to London and Special Envoy to Washington, answered the Montreal Greek community's invitation to take part in the national Greek Independence Day celebrations on 25 March. Addressing them via *Atlantis*, he called on them to remind their countrymen that 'the struggle to free our still enslaved brethren has not ceased during the past century, but that the flower of our race, unwearied by the hardships and unexhausted by the sacrifices of nine years' continual campaigning, are still fighting in the highlands of Asia Minor – that most ancient cradle of Hellenism – fighting for Christianity, freedom and civilisation.'[27] He wrote his letter in English, in order to encourage members of the Greek-language community of Montreal to spread his message among their English-speaking countrymen.

Apart from Greece's relations with the nascent Republic of Turkey, Albania's territorial claims were another parameter of the Eastern Question of concern to the American Greek-language press post-First World War. *Atlantis* and *Ethnikos Kyrix* did not fail to remind their readers that Albanians in America claimed 'with lyricism and arrogance, the region of Northern Epirus, as if it belonged to them, under the name of *Tosqueria*' through articles in American Albanian-language papers – such as *Dielli* (The Sun).[28] Today's Southern Albania was incorporated into the irredentist projects of Greek nationalists during the last phase of the Eastern Question: Greek-language and Orthodox Christian communities were in the majority there, particularly in the region of Korçe, Himara and Saranda.[29] The *Atlantis* edition of 7 April 1922 made space for Georgios Christakis-Zografos, the President of the provisional Government of the Autonomous Republic of Northern Epirus – Northern Epirus being the label for the part of Southern Albania claimed by Greek irredentists. Christakis-Zografos denounced anti-Greek acts by the Albanian political leader Fan Noli against the Orthodox community in the region. More specifically, Christakis-Zografos was worried about Fan Noli's desire to introduce Albanian as the liturgical language, in lieu and place of Greek. Such antagonisms for linguistic hegemony between the various Christian communities of the Balkans were the main feature of the Balkan dimension of the Eastern Question. Fan Noli was essential to the promotion of teaching in Albanian in Ottoman Albania, funding the *Shkolla Normale* teacher training institution in Elbasan – the first high school to teach in Albanian – from its onset. He also established Besa-Besën, the Albanian diaspora's cultural and political association in the United States of America, which merged with other Albanian American associations in 1912 to form Vatra, the Pan-Albanian Federation of America. The newspaper *Dielli* would later become the association's official mouthpiece.

'Divide and rule': the 'National Schism' as media feud

In reality, the cult of the *Megali Idea* observed in *Atlantis* and the dissonance between *Atlantis* and *Ethnikos Kyrix* were vehemently expressed between 1919 and 1922, but their roots were much older. The question of participation in the First World War revived latent pre-First World War socio-political tensions, which crystallized splits in the conception of the Kingdom's foreign policy between King Constantine and Prime Minister Eleftherios Venizelos. The division between these two embodiments of political authority was initially rhetorical, before gradually shifting towards a dogged battle with reciprocal challenges and accusations, in what Greek historiography calls the 'National Schism' (*Ethnikos Dichasmos*).[30]

Frictions between the two sides culminated in an armed dispute in early December 1916. The Allies feared a secret pact between the Greek royalist government, led by a supposedly Germanophile King, and the Central Powers. Such an alliance would have jeopardized the Allied forces stationed in Macedonia since the end of 1915. Throughout the summer of 1916, intense negotiations took place between King Constantine and Allied diplomats. The king wanted Greece to maintain its neutrality, a position that would favour the plans of the Central Powers in the Balkans, while the Allies required the demobilization of the Greek army and the surrender of war equipment. The political confrontation in Greece between interventionists (represented by the party of Venizelos) and the neutralists (behind King Constantine) peaked in November 1916 when, with the support of the Allies, Venizelos established a Provisional Government of National Defence in Thessaloniki, with the aim of overthrowing the authorities in Athens. The Government in Athens did not recognize its authority. Fighting soon broke out between the different Greek forces, while an Allied contingent landed in Athens on 1 December 1916 to restore order. The Allies evacuated Athens as soon as skirmishes ended (following a compromise between partisans of Venizelos and of the king).

Tensions between the two camps also rose within the Greek-language communities of the United States, leading to rowdy meetings, such as one in San Francisco where 500 people met in Stanley Palace. The event did not go unnoticed, and even aroused the interest of the newspapers of the city's other communities, such as *L'Italia*, which wrote on 21 November 1916:

> among the local Greeks, there is great admiration and enthusiasm for Venizelos. He is considered by Greeks across the United States as a national hero ... it should also be added that among the local Greeks, there is great admiration and sympathy for the Allied Nations and that Venizelos is admired and liked in his representation and interpretation of the ideals of the Allied Nations in the face of Germany.[31]

L'Italia informed its readers that, during this meeting, 'the revolutionary faction soon proved dominant, even though the royalists, the partisans of King Constantine's pro-German policy, were also numerous and influential. The meeting was very agitated.'[32] The newspaper highlighted that the Greek community in San Francisco was riven with 'internal strife more vivid than even we Italians, who pass for excitable people – could imagine'.[33] Speaking to the stereotypes on the different communities in American public life at the time, the comment also evidences the violence of the confrontations within the Greek American community.

Atlantis (supporting the neutral stance of King Constantine) and *Ethnikos Kyrix* (backing Venizelos) were fully engaged in this debate. Both newspapers spurred on the development of organizations to facilitate public expressions of support for their respective leaders. Rallies and proclamations increased from the autumn of 1916 and caught the attention of the American press. Their editors were quick to develop their views in the English-speaking press to reach English-speaking compatriots and gain wider exposure and support. They fought pitilessly, with no second thoughts about filing libel proceedings against their competitors, which were also an opportunity to show off the contacts the two editors-in-chief had in American politics. *The Washington Herald* of 7 December 1915 brings this into sharp relief, reporting that William Jennings Bryan (1860–1925), US Secretary of State between 1913 and 1915, was summoned to court for examination concerning the transaction by which the US government sold two American battleships to the Greek Government. Bryan would testify in a libel suit brought by Petros Tatanis of *Ethnikos Kyrix* against *Atlantis*, which had accused Tatanis of 'trying to block the transaction by creating ill feeling between Bryan and the Greek Premier'.[34] In May 1916, *Ethnikos Kyrix* announced that Tatanis had won the libel suit against *Atlantis* and Solon J. Vlasto.[35]

As the United States entered the war alongside the Allies in 1917 and the Espionage Act was adopted on homeland security grounds, their confrontation took on a new turn. *Atlantis* found itself under scrutiny, suspected of pro-German propaganda because of its royalist political leanings. While the investigation under the Espionage Act into the content and editorial line of the newspaper did not conclude that the law had been broken, it is interesting that, following the return of Venizelos as head of the Provisional Government in June 1917, *Atlantis* was banned from sale in Greece.[36] Denying the accusations against his newspaper, Vlasto went on with his apology, aiming accusations of propaganda at his opponents. Following this strategy, he highlighted in the *Evening Star* that:

> the revolutionary junta of Venizelos by paid advertisements printed in several American newspapers was simply wasting money in a vain effort to obtain recognition by the USA government and to influence public opinion here. This revolutionary committee after six months of hard work, travelling all over the USA, organising mass meetings all over, urging every Greek to support Venizelos, printing and distributing circulars, giving interviews and spending freely many thousands of dollars in propaganda for Venizelos, was finally forced two weeks ago to disband and return to Saloniki. Their mission failed completely and hopelessly when they realised that 90 per cent of the Greeks in the USA are in favour of the constitutional government in Greece.[37]

Petros Tatanis claimed the exact opposite when it came to Greek American political affinities, saying that 'there are 400,000 Greeks in the USA, fully 80 per cent of whom are followers of Venizelos'.[38]

This was not the only dispute between Greek-language newspapers during that period. In June 1917, *Ethnikos Kyrix* accused *Loxias*, the Chicago Greek-language newspaper, of unfairness and selfishness in its effort to expose the Greco-German propaganda of *Atlantis* and Solon Vlasto. The editor of *Loxias* protested that he did his utmost to capture what he regarded as the double-faced propaganda of the Loyalist (royalist) camp and insisted that he had immediately delivered whatever evidence he had to the American authorities, after taking photostatic copies, which *Loxias* published. In reality, *Ethnikos Kyrix* blamed *Loxias* for refusing to forward the original letter and telegram it had transferred to the authorities and merely forwarding the photostatic copies and cuts to its sister newspaper in New York. Finding the grounds for division unfair, *Loxias* was questioned the ultimate motivations both – patriotism and self-interest – and concluded that *Atlantis* and *Ethnikos Kyrix* followed the tactics of 'divide and rule': 'They have divided the Greeks in America into Venizelists and Royalists for their own interest, not through patriotism. If *Atlantis* was pro-Venizelos, the *National Herald* would be pro-Royalist and vice versa'.[39]

For years, the two newspapers had made no secret of their role as propaganda outlets for the two main parties in the Greek political landscape. They now sought to influence the course of the electoral campaign of November 1920, where the main issue at stake was the future of the *Megali Idea*. The mouthpiece of the supporters of Venizelos in the New York media encouraged its readers to vote against the candidates of the 'Little Greece' policy[40] – an allusion to the position of the pro-Constantine party which called for the demobilization of the Greek soldiers in Asia Minor and exploited

Greek society's fatigue following a long, practically uninterrupted period of mobilization from 1912 (First Balkan War) to the aftermath of the First World War. Meanwhile, *Atlantis*, the key pro-Constantine organ in New York, announced on 1 November 1920 that 20,000 workers had attended an anti-Venizelos demonstration in Athens.

In addition to covering politics in Greece, the two newspapers also looked at the political activities of their fellow citizens in America. *Ethnikos Kyrix* reported on the rally in Chicago supporting Venizelos in November 1920, while *Atlantis* drew its readers' attention to 'the grandiose rally of the "omogenis" [expatriates]'[41] in support of the king and Prime Minister Gounaris and against Venizelos in Pocatello, Idaho.[42] *Atlantis* also published a telegram from the Greeks of Philadelphia to the Greeks of Greece in the Athens newspaper *Athinaikin*, in the hope of encouraging them to vote against the Venizelist party in the elections of 20 November 1920:

> Obeying the voice of the *Atlantis* newspaper, one of Greek conscience keen to contribute in turn, to the extent of our capacities, to ridding our country of the band in the pay of foreign powers, we have decided to wire the following to the *Athinaikin* newspaper ... polling stations are in churches, churches that have been profaned by the Dictator's Senegalese. Examine your conscience and vote. A vote to sanction the Tyrant and terrible Dictator! Signed by your brothers across the Atlantic, the Greeks of Philadelphia, faithful to the constitution.[43]

First and foremost, this call translates how Venizelists were perceived by their opponents: as a party subject to the interests of the Great Powers, particularly those of the Entente, which were accused of conducting a policy hostile to Greece's interests. Secondly, the telegram plays on the bad memories among the local population of the French occupation of part of Greece's territory during the First World War.[44] In October 1917, the commander of the 'Eastern army', Maurice Sarrail, imposed the creation of a buffer zone between the 'national defence' government proclaimed by Venizelos in Salonika that summer with French and British support, and the Athens government under the influence of King Constantine. In the buffer zone, which covered part of Central Greece, General Sarrail had the Greek authorities replaced with French officers, who relied largely on regiments of soldiers from the French colonial troops from Africa, widely known as 'Senegalese Tirailleurs'. In his memoirs, Sarrail compared his mission to France's earlier colonial expeditions. In his memoirs, he recalled that one of his officers wished to behave as he had seen done in Madagascar, China and elsewhere.[45]

Tensions between the two newspapers regarding their support for the two main post-First World War political formations in Greece gradually took the form of a media battle. In April 1922, *Atlantis* condemned *Ethnikos Kyrix*'s mismanagement of the money collected in fundraising campaigns for the widows and orphans of the Greek Orthodox community in Anatolia. A genuine war of words[46] had even broken out the month before, when a reader of *Atlantis* discredited the information published by *Ethnikos Kyrix* on the state of the Greek army in Asia Minor as being defeatist and dishonest. A month later, *Ethnikos Kyrix* pictured Venizelos as a threat, on the ground that he called for the Greek army's withdrawal from the territories it occupied in Asia Minor. Meanwhile, *Ethnikos Kyrix* responded to the *Atlantis* reader's accusations by condemning the Greek government's pre-campaign announcement (against the Ottoman capital) as 'Athenian Quixotism'.[47] In April 1922, as the Greek army became bogged down in Asia Minor, *Ethnikos Kyrix* offered a screening to its readers of the film *Greater Greece in the Time of Venizelos* at the new Metropolitan Auditorium.[48] This was first and foremost a film recounting the main events in the Greek state's territorial expansion from the Treaty of Versailles through to the defeat of Venizelos in the November 1920 elections, from the point of view of the prodigal Cretan. In contrast to that nostalgic representation, *Atlantis* promoted a screening of a film on the battle of Eskişehir on 6 April 1922, produced by its local correspondent: it chose an event corresponding to the continuation of the Asia Minor campaign by the government close to King Constantine, which was supposed to do away with the policies of the Venizelos era.[49]

The most sensitive issue was that of the displaced Greeks of Asia Minor, and the fate of Greek Orthodox Christians there, the *Mikrasiates*. The latter were mostly gathered in the Ottoman *vilayet* of Smyrna, occupied for a time by Greek troops, and were considered close to the party of Venizelos. They were therefore ill-looked-upon by Constantine's supporters, who feared that upon arrival in Greece they would form a reserve of potential voters for the other party. The pro-Venizelos *Ethnikos Kyrix* newspaper therefore defended the *Mikrasiates* while *Atlantis* criticized their lack of patriotism, as they had demanded only autonomy and not union with Greece.[50] The 1920 Sèvres Treaty provided for a referendum to be organized in the *vilayet* after five years and outlined three scenarios: the reunion of the region to the Greek state; autonomy; or its remaining part of the Ottoman state. *Ethnikos Kyrix* reminded its readers in turn that the Greek government of Dimitrios Gounaris, close to King Constantine, described the *Mikrasiates* as a sort of colony that he wanted to see attached to Greece. In so doing, *Ethnikos Kyrix*'s treatment sought to go beyond the National Schism binaries.

Ethnikos Kyrix was sensitive to the fate of refugees following the defeat and withdrawal of the Greek army in August 1922. It also became a medium for communication between the refugees of Asia Minor in Greece and their family members who settled in the United States before the war. Its page on refugee news – for they were now recognized as refugees under the Treaty of Lausanne of 1923 – on 24 July 1924 read: 'Ioannis Lagos, from the town of Ayvali in Asia Minor, thirty years old, a cobbler by trade, settled for fifteen years in the United States, is sought by Miss Eleni Lagos, his sister, currently living in Athens.'[51] Another advertisement asked anyone who '[knew] the address of Georgios Sotiropoulos, from the town of Smyrna, who had stayed a few years earlier in California and who had been recruited by the US Army, to send him to his refugee sisters, Magdalini and Vasilia Sotiropoulou, who [were] in the Kokkinia refugee camp'.[52] The newspaper became a platform and a bridge to restore ties and renew family contact broken by the brutal, forced displacements.

Conclusion

Although transformed into a transatlantic media battleground between the supporters of Constantine and Venizelos and opposed in their approach to the realization of the

Megali Idea, *Atlantis* and *Ethnikos Kyrix* both served as vectors in promoting this irredentist project within American society. But that was not the be-all and end-all of their political line. Keen to identify publications discussing the Eastern Question in newspapers founded by other immigrants from the countries involved, they helped create a forum for discussion between the different linguistic communities that made up the US media landscape in the aftermath of the Great War. While dedicating much space to the Eastern Question, the two newspapers also used it for self-promotion, given the central role of the subject in the European and American media landscape of the time. Lastly, and while they were aimed primarily at a Greek-language readership on both sides of the Atlantic, these newspapers were also US-oriented: while their editorial lines reflected the 'National Schism' seen both in the Greek population in Greece and new Greek arrivals in the US, both sought to influence political opinions. The two newspapers had two main target audiences: on the one hand, Greek-language readers settled in the United States, relaying socio-political news from Greece and their neighbouring countries of origin; and on the other, readers in these countries, echoing the events held by representatives of Greek-language communities in the United States. Of course, both sought to consolidate a position on the US media stage through their contacts within the editorial committees of the major English-language newspapers. However, the most significant aspect of the period following the signature of the Treaty of Lausanne in 1923 and the forced population displacements between Greece and Turkey is perhaps the forum that these two newspapers offered for the exchange of information between family members separated against their will and scattered across Greece, the United States and other countries around the world. They were essential anchors for the diaspora, and as such fully deserve their place in Greek refugee history.

Notes

1. Theodore Saloutos, *The Greeks in the United States* (Cambridge: Cambridge University Press, 1964), 19. For an overview of the Greek press, see Loukia Droulia and Gioula Koutsopanagou (eds.), *Εγκυκλοπαίδεια του Ελληνικού τύπου 1784–1974: εφημερίδες, περιοδικά, δημοσιογράφοι, εκδότες* (Athens: Institute of Neohellenic Research, 2008). This collective work in four volumes (Encyclopaedia of the Greek Press 1784–1974: Newspapers, Periodicals, Journalists and Editors) covers the majority of newspapers published in Greece (in several languages) or in Greek worldwide from the eighteenth through to the late twentieth century. It contains information on certain Greek-language journalists and editors in the United States. *Atlantis* and *Ethnikos Kyrix* have been digitized and are available in the database of the Hellenic Parliament Library (Βιβλιοθήκη της Βουλής) at https://library.parliament.gr/Portals/6/pdf/digitalmicrofilms.pdf.
2. There are few works solely dedicated to the history of the press of Greek-language communities. Among most representative examples: Viktor Papacosma, 'The Greek Press in America', *Journal of the Hellenic Diaspora* 5/4 (Winter 1979), 45–61; Alexander Kitroeff, 'The Transformation of the Greek American Press: the *National Herald* 1915–1939', *Etudes Helléniques* 25/2 (Autumn 2015), 125–38.
3. Titles of newspapers listed in Droulia and Koutsopanagou (eds.), *Encyclopaedia of the Greek Press*.

4   On Greek-language immigration to the USA, see Dimitris Tziovas, *Greek Diaspora and Migration since 1700: Society, Politics and Culture* (Surrey: Ashgate, 2009) and George Kaloudis, *Modern Greece and the Diaspora Greeks in the United States* (Lanham: Lexington Books, 2020).
5   'Les Grecs sont nombreux aux Etats Unis d'Amérique, beaucoup sont naturalisés, ce qui, avec le vote, leur assure l'influence. Très actifs ils ne laissent pas leurs députés et sénateurs ignorer les aspirations de leur ancienne patrie et ils obtiennent de temps en temps, pour servir et valoir ce que de droit, le Congrès en tienne compte. On a pu en voir hier un exemple au Sénat où fut votée une résolution favorable à l'attribution de la Thrace à la Grèce.' *French Diplomatic Archives*, Thrace, vol. 5, Washington, 21 January 1920, no. 44.
6   The *Megali Idea* refers to the expansionist project that governed Greek foreign policy throughout the Eastern Question period. It was about extending the borders initially awarded to the Greek State in 1830, in order to restore the medieval range of the Byzantine Empire in the Balkans and Asia Minor. These irredentist ambitions were expressed officially for the first time by Prime Minister Ioannis Kolettis in his speech to Parliament on 14 January 1844, outlining the *Megali Idea*. On this project, see Anastasia Stouraiti, Alexander Kazamias, Nikiforos Diamantouros, Thalia Dragonas, Caglar Keyder, *The Imaginary Topographies of the Megali Idea: National territory as utopia* (London: I.B. Tauris), 2010.
7   The Greek-Ottoman War of 1919–22 resulted from the occupation by the Greek army of Ottoman territories in Anatolia, following the Treaty of Sèvres.
8   In historiography in general and this study in particular, the Eastern Question is associated with the sequence in international relations concerning the destiny of the Ottoman Empire throughout the nineteenth century, through to its dissolution in 1923. In reality, several Eastern Questions could be identified during that period, sketching out the borders of a multiple geography in the Ottoman territories, of course, but also in Central Asia, the Caucasus and the Far East. What links these questions is their resulting in several conflicts between the different countries or different communities domestically, in a struggle for political, economic and cultural hegemony between the period's great powers, in these world regions dubbed 'Eastern' by great powers' geographers and diplomats. For an overview of the Eastern Question, see Stéphane Yerasimos, *Questions d'Orient: frontières et minorités des Balkans au Caucase* (Eastern Questions: Borders and Minorities of the Balkans in the Caucasus), Paris, La Découverte, 1993. On the East as a mental construction serving geopolitical interests, see Thierry Hentsch, *L'Orient imaginaire. La vision politique occidentale de l'Est méditerranéen* (The Imaginary East. the Western Political Vision of the Mediterranean East), Paris, Minuit, 1988.
9   The Treaty of Lausanne, signed in 1923, engendered massive population displacements between Greece and Turkey. Those concerned were Muslim citizens of Greece and Greek Orthodox citizens of Turkey. In total, around two million people had to migrate across the Aegean in one direction or another.
10 On the press in Greek and other languages, see https://bulac.hypotheses.org/7695.
11 In the Monotype advertisement that appeared in *The Washington Herald* on 28 August 1915, *Atlantis* was mentioned among the newspapers using the machines.
12 Ιστορία των Ηνωμένων Πολιτειών της Αμερικής (History of the United States of America) (New York: Atlantis, 1919), 29.
13 See Judith Felsten, *Atlantis, National Daily Newspaper, 1894–1973* (Philadelphia: The Research Library of the Balch Institute for Ethnic Studies, 1982).

14 See Yannis Papadopoulos, 'The Role of Nationalism, Ethnicity, and Class, in Shaping Greek American Identity, 1890–1927: an Historical Analysis', in *Identity and Participation in Culturally Diverse Societies: A Multi-Disciplinary Perspective,* ed. A. Azzi, X. Chryssochoou, B. Klandermans, B.Simon (New Jersey: Wiley-Blackwell, 2010), 16.
15 See *Simmon's Spice Mill: Devoted to the Interests of the Coffee, Tea and Spice Trades.* Vol. 41, 1918, 868.
16 *Atlantis,* 2 April 1922.
17 *Atlantis,* 3 April 1922.
18 *Ethnikos Kyrix,* 26 March 1922.
19 'America's place in the Near Eastern settlement', *Atlantis,* 9 April 1922, 2.
20 In the United States, where immigrants from China and Japan settled at the turn of the twentieth century, the 'yellow danger/peril' was widespread in the popular imagination. According to Jacques Decornoy, the 'yellow peril' was an invention of European and American imperialists and colonialists, building on the myth of the Barbarians and tying in with another obsession of Western societies during the Belle Époque and the interwar period: the fear of decadence. See Jacques Decornoy, *Péril jaune, peur blanche* (Yellow Peril, White Fear) (Paris, Grasset, 1970).
21 On that representational heritage, see Serhat Uluagli, *L'image de l'Orient turc dans la littérature française: les idées, les stéréotypes et les stratégies* (The Image of the Turkish Orient in French Literature: Ideas, Stereotypes and Strategies) (Istanbul: Isis, 2007). Meanwhile, Mark Mazower places the turning point in representations of the Ottoman regime in the imagination of Western European societies in the second half of the seventeenth century. From then on, and under the influence of authors including Montesquieu, the Sultan's reign was seen as tyrannical and despotic. See Mark Mazower, *The Balkans: a Short History* (The Modern Library, 2007).
22 'το μονο εθνος που με τη συνδρομη των δυναμεων καταφερε να επανελθη εις το προπολεμικο καθεστως', *Ethnikos Kyrix,* 25 June 1922.
23 See 'Υπερ των θυμάτων της κεμαλικής θηριωδίας' (In Support of the Victims of Kemalist Atrocities), *Atlantis,* 1 November 1920.
24 Stephen Pierce Hayden Duggan (1870–1950) was a United States scholar and educator known as the 'apostle of internationalism'. He was a professor of diplomatic history and later the history of education at College of the City of New York (CCNY), becoming head of the education department in 1906.
25 The institute was established in 1919 following the First World War by Nobel Peace Prize winners Nicholas Murray Butler, president of Columbia University, and Elihu Root, former US Secretary of State, and Stephen Duggan, Professor of Political Science at CCNY.
26 When the First World War broke out, Hibben turned to journalism and became a war correspondent, first for *Collier's Weekly* and later for the Associated Press. The AP sent him to Athens in 1915 to cover Greek politics, where he became an ally of King Constantine in the latter's struggle to keep Greece neutral in the war.
27 'Διά τον πανηγυρισμόν της εθνικής εορτής εν Μόντρεαλ.' (Around the Commemoration of the National Day in Montreal), *Atlantis,* 6 April 1922, 4.
28 See 'με αλαζονεια και λυρισμο για την δηθεν αναγνωριση του αλβανικου κρατους και την ενσωματωση της Βορειας Ηπειρου ως Τοσκερια', *Ethnikos Kyrix,* 11 June 1920, 1. Of note, the first Albanian-language newspaper in the USA, *Kombi* (The Nation), was founded in Boston in 1905 by Sotir Peçi (1873–1932), but it was the *Dielli* that became the most important and longest-lasting organ in the country's Albanian-language

press. In the aftermath of the First World War, its editor-in-chief was Faik Bey Konica (1875–1942). Konica was born in the town of Koniçe (now Konitsa in Greece) and learned Turkish at the primary school there, before continuing his studies at the Jesuit school in Scutari (Shkodra) and then at the Galatasaray French imperial school in Istanbul. After continuing his studies in France, he had the opportunity to study at Harvard. He launched the periodical *Albania* in 1897, while staying in Brussels, and it was published until 1909, when Konica left for the United States of America. In its time, it was one of the most prominent mouthpieces of the Albanian National Awakening movement.

29 The delimitation of the southern borders of the Albanian state envisaged in the 1912 Conference of London was challenged by the Greek Government. On the eve of the First World War, the Greek army occupied the region around the city of Korçë (Koritsa). From summer 1916, as relations between Greece and France deteriorated, the French staff also stationed in Southern Albania, in place of the Greek army. See Stefan Popescu, 'Les Français et la république de Kortcha' (The French and the Republic of Korçë), in *Guerres mondiales et conflits contemporains*, 2004/1, no. 213, 77–87.

30 For a detailed reconstruction of the events that led to the official involvement of Greece in the conflict, see George B. Leon, *Greece and the Great Powers, 1914–1917* (Thessaloniki, Institute for Balkan Studies, 1974) and Yannis Mourelos, *L'intervention de la Grèce dans la Grande Guerre* (Greece's Intervention in the Great War) (Athens: EFA, 1983).

31 '…fra i greci locali, grande è l'ammirazione e l'entusiasmo per Venizelos, che è considerato dai greci di tutti gli Stati Uniti come un eroe nazionale… si deve aggiungere che fra i greci locali grandi sono l'ammirazione e la simpatia per le Nazioni Alleate e che Venizelos è ammirato ed amato in quanto che esso rappresenta e interpreta gli ideali delle Nazioni Alleate contro la Germania…' 'Un importante meeting di greci di San Francisco', *L'Italia*, 21 November 1916, 4.

32 'la fazione rivoluzionaria si mostrò subito in prevalenza benché anche i monarchici, i fautori cioè della politica tedescofila di re Constantino mostrassero d'essere abbastanza numerosi e influenti. La riunione fu assai agitata..', idem.

33 'lotte intestine cosi vivaci che noi italiani – che pure passiamo per gente eccitabile … – non potremmo neppure immaginare.' 'Le lotte della colonia greca', *L'Italia*, 15 June 1916.

34 'Calls Bryan as witness', *The Washington Herald*, 7 December 1915, 4. See also 'W. J. Bryan makes deposition in libel suit against Greek paper *Atlantis*', *The New York Times*, 5 January 1916, 8.

35 *Ethnikos Kyrix*, 27 May 1916, and *The New York Times*, 28 May 1916.

36 Papacosma, 'The Greek Press in America', 51.

37 'New Chapter in Greek Dispute', *Evening Star*, 6 June 1917, 9.

38 Idem.

39 'Patriotism or Self-Interest?', *Loxias*, 13 June 1917.

40 'του μικροελλαδισμου', *Ethnikos Kyrix*, 11 November 1920, 4.

41 'μεγιστη συγκεντρωση ομογενων', *Atlantis*, 9 April 1922. In the Greek-language press, and more specifically in the two newspapers studied here, the terms used to refer to the readership are '*omoethnis*' and '*omogenis*'. Under this conceptualization of the category of 'Greeks', any person of Greek language and Christian Orthodox religion, from Greece or a country other than Greece and who did not necessarily have Greek nationality when they emigrated, is considered to be Greek. In other words, the

newspapers studied use an ethnicist definition of the immigrant-reader. This approach was also used by the American authorities for the classification, identification and categorization of incoming migrants. The creation and construction of an ethnic identity was behind the advent of the Greek nationalist movement from the end of the eighteenth century, and of other nationalist movements in Europe and elsewhere throughout the nineteenth. The *ethnos*, now the driver of the creation of the nation state, was in the Greek case a product of the antagonisms within *millets*, religious communities of the Ottoman Empire, during their ethnicization and nationalization, in the wake of the ideas of the French Revolution and in the context of rivalries between the European Great Powers which sought to instrumentalize and manipulate each linguistic and/or religious community's demands for autonomy.

42 Idem.
43 'Υπείκοντες εις την φωνήν της φιλτάτης Ατλαντίδος, φωνήν Ελληνικής συνειδήσεως, και θέλοντες ίνα και ημείς συντελέσωμεν εν τω μέτρω των δυνάμεών μας υπέρ της απαλλαγής της πατρίδας μας από την ξενόδουλον σπείραν, απεφασίσαμεν όπως τηλεγραφήσωμεν εις Αθήνας τα εξής/ Εφημερίδα Αθηναικήν/ . . . Τα εκλογικά τμήματα θα είναι εντός των εκκλησιών . . ., των εκκλησιών τας οποίας εβεβήλωσαν οι Σενεγαλέζοι του Δικτάτορος. Εξετάσατε την συνείδησίν σας και ψηφίσατε. Μαύρο στον Τύραννον και απαίσιον Δικτάτορα !/Οι πέραν του Ατλαντικού αδελφοί σας συνταγματικοί Έλληνες Φιλαδέλφειας'. 'Το τηλεγράφημα των Ελλήνων της Φιλαδέλφειας προς τον ελληνικό λαό' (Telegram of the Greeks of Philadelphia to the Greek People), *Atlantis*, 1 November 1920, 4.
44 On the French presence in this region, see Christos Vittos, *Ο εθνικός διχασμός και η γαλλική κατοχή, 1915–1920* (National Division and the French Occupation, 1915–1920) (Thessaloniki: Olympos, 2008).
45 See Maurice Sarrail, *Mon commandement en Orient* (My Command in the East), Paris, 1920, 18.
46 On the phenomenon of media battles, see Nicolas Pitsos, *Marianne face aux Balkans en feu: Perceptions françaises de la question d'Orient à la veille de la Grande Guerre* (Marianne and the Balkans in Flames: French Perceptions of the Eastern Question on the Eve of the Great War) (Paris: L'Harmattan, 2017).
47 'αθηναικος δονκιχωτισμος', *Ethnikos Kyrix*, 12 August 1922, 1.
48 *Ethnikos Kyrix*, 12 March 1922.
49 The party close to King Constantine won the elections of November 1920. Contrary to its position during the election campaign, i.e. the termination of the Asia Minor expedition launched by the Venizelos government, King Constantine's party continued military operations in Anatolia once it came to power. The screening was organized by the Daniel Webster Memorial Committee to raise funds for the edification of a statue in Greece dedicated to the Philhellenic American statesman.
50 *Ethnikos Kyrix*, 14 August 1922, 4.
51 'Λαγός Ιωάννης, εξ Αϊβαλί της Μ.Ασίας, ετών 30, υποδηματοποιός, ευρισκόμενος εν ταις Ηνωμέναις Πολιτείαις από 15ετίας, ζητείται υπό Δίδος Ελένης Λάγου, αδελφής του, ήδη ευρισκόμενης εν Αθήναις. . .', *Ethnikos Kyrix*, 24 July 1924.
52 'παρακαλείται ο γνωρίζων την διεύθυνσιν του κ. Γεωργίου Σωτηροπούλου, εκ Κασαμπά Σμύρνης, διαμένοντος προ ετών εν Καλιφορνία και υπηρετήσαντος εις τον Αμερικανικόν Στρατόν, να την αποστείλη προς τας πρόσφυγας αδελφάς του Μαγδαληνήν και Βασιλείαν Σωτηροπούλου, καταυλισμός Προσφύγων Κοκκινιάς. . .', *Ethnikos Kyrix*, 24 July 1924.

11

Barzini Overseas: The *Corriere d'America*, from Promoting Italianità to Fascist Propaganda

Lorenzo Benadusi
Roma Tre University

In the early 1920s there were around two hundred Italian-language newspapers published regularly in the United States; and they sold a total of about 800,000 copies daily.[1] Among these, *Il Progresso Italo-Americano* was the oldest (founded in 1879) and the most widespread, with a circulation of more than 100,000 copies. Also in New York, there was the monthly nationalist magazine *Il Carroccio*, e *Il Grido della stirpe*, which was described as the 'most faithful voice of Fascism in America'. *Il Popolo Italiano*, *L'Opinione* and *La Libera Parola* in Philadelphia, *Gazzetta del Massachusetts* and *La Notizia* in Boston, *L'Araldo* and *La Voce del Popolo Italiano* in Cleveland, *La Tribuna d'America* in Detroit, *La Capitale* in Sacramento, and *L'Italia* in San Francisco had a more restricted circulation.

These newspapers served as an intermediary between Italian immigrants and American society and, given the lack of interest of the national press in Italian news, they were the only way for emigrants to get news about what was happening back home. Bénédicte Deschamps called them the 'echoes of Italy', emphasizing their important role as a sounding board and source of information for Italians living abroad.[2] It was therefore quite natural for the fascist regime to consider Italian-American newspapers its main propaganda tool in the United States, as they provided easy access to both the middle class and the working class. Fascism's swift penetration of the Italian press abroad was also due to the ease of mistaking 'the political interference of the consulates for the manifestation of the genuine interest of a government that had until then been indifferent to the problems of immigration'.[3]

The regime exercised control over these publications mainly by offering subsidies, economic incentives and help selling advertising space and with discounts on telegraphic services and on the rates to receive news from the Stefani Agency, which had been increasingly dependent on the government since 1881 and even more so since 1923.[4] As a result, the Italian-language press was in danger of losing its independence and originality. The problems those newspapers faced arose not only from the degree of uniformity imposed by the fascist regime. They were almost all united in their aim of carrying forward the 'apostolate of Italianness'[5] in the guise of nostalgia and conservatism, and wanted to promote and safeguard the motherland, without upsetting the host country.

Another problem was how to distribute these publications around the country, given the fragmented nature of the closed, highly regionalist local communities. Because of controls on migratory flows and the low level of literacy of Italian emigrants, there was also little likelihood of increasing readership. In the early 1920s, however, there still appeared to be a chance of creating an authoritative newspaper, that would challenge *Il Progresso Italo-Americano* and the other existing periodicals of the 'Little Italies', thanks to the collaboration of leading Italian journalists. Such was the dream of a well-known figure of Italian journalism: Luigi Barzini (1874–1947).

This chapter investigates Luigi Barzini's trajectory of promoting Italianità in the United States at the time of Mussolinian Italy (1922–43), shortly after his arrival in New York in 1921. Prior to his crossing, Barzini was one of the most important and well-known Italian journalists throughout the world, particularly for his foreign correspondences and reportages from war fronts.[6] His evocative and impressive descriptions of the Boxer Rebellion in China (1899) and the 1905 Russo-Japanese War for the *Corriere della Sera* (Milan), as well as his victory in the Peking-Paris motor race (1907) won him international recognition. It looks at how in the immediate post-war period, Barzini drifted away from *Corriere della Sera*, and distinguished himself by his intense nationalism and irredentism, which led him to move closer to the fascist movement. A first section of this chapter presents the quixotic choices Barzini was faced with when he wanted to make a durable imprint on the American Italian-language press in the United States. The second section discusses Barzini's *Il Corriere d'America* (1922–43?) very much as a one-man journalistic venture, that he strove to maintain afloat. The last section discusses Barzini's embracing a profascist editorial line both in terms of the promotion of Italianità and pragmatic editorial choices.

Starting an editor's career in the United States: Barzini's dream

The latter, who had a long experience as a war correspondent, went to the United States in November 1921 to accompany Luigi Albertini (1871–1941), the owner of the Milan-based *Corriere della Sera*, who was part of the Italian delegation to the naval conference in Washington.[7] He hoped that his stay in America would help him bolster his professional career and make the contacts he needed to carry out his ambitious plan: managing an Italian-American newspaper. Barzini faced a dilemma: should he create a brand new newspaper or try to purchase an existing one? One option was to buy *Il Progresso Italo-Americano*, the most influential Italian newspaper in the United States, which generated an annual profit of around 300,000 dollars. The idea of picking up such a well-established newspaper was appealing, but the negotiations proved difficult.[8] The owner, Carlo Barsotti (1850–1927), was a powerful figure in New York City's Little Italy, a banker suspected of having mafia connections and of being involved in patronage. After considerable hesitation, Barzini managed to find financial backing from Pio Crespi (1881-1969), a rich, Texan cotton industrialist related to the Crespi brothers, the owners of the *Corriere della Sera*.

He wanted to create a new newspaper for the many Italian emigrants. The project was launched with a great deal of enthusiasm but did not get the fundamental economic and political support of the *Corriere della Sera* company. The business of founding and running a paper immediately proved to be a very difficult undertaking. There were the organizational aspects relating to production and distribution as well as the financial and purely editorial ones. In order to manage what was to become the *Corriere d'America*, the Tiber Publishing Company was founded in September 1922, with an initial capital of 500,000 dollars. Crespi was president and Barzini vice president. The new daily had its headquarters in the Puck Building in New York, between Lafayette Street and Mulberry Street.

All aspects relating to equipment and facilities were handled by the engineer Charley Hart, the mechanical superintendent of *The New York Times*, who decided to start publishing with two Hoe rotary presses and twelve intertypes. Anthony Crocco was the business manager and Francesco Panciatichi the managing editor, with a salary of 8,000 dollars a year and 2.5 per cent of the profits. The latter was responsible for selecting the editorial staff; and he quickly hired several journalists, most of them from *Il Progresso* and the *Corriere della Sera*, including the vice director Beniamino De Ritis, Frank Cantelmo, Luigi Roversi (1859-1927), Luigi Giovanola, Egidio Grella, Andrea Luotto and Mario De Cellis. The editorials were written by Barzini, Felice Ferrero, correspondent in New York City for the *Corriere della Sera*, Ercole Cantelmo, editor of the New York based *La Vita Internazionale* and sometimes by the Italian politician Luigi Luzzatti (1841-1927).[9]

The first issue of the *Corriere d'America* was published on 27 December 1922 at a cost of 3 cents and expressly paid a tribute to the Genoese-born Christopher Columbus, with the title: *Seguendo il sol lasciammo il vecchio mondo* (*Following the sun, we left the old world*). Columbus was then the perfect symbol of Italian-American identity: the dual identity reflecting the ambiguous relationship between Italians and their adoptive country. The openly stated aim of the newspaper was 'to bring the lessons of American civilization home to the Italians living here, to urge them not to set themselves apart and nourish feelings of foreignness, but rather to identify with the life around them'.[10] Safeguarding Italian tradition allowed emigrants to better adapt to their new country without losing their original identity. Historian Pellegrino Nazzaro explained that 'according to Barzini, a primary objective of the newspaper was to correct the misunderstanding that existed 'among Italians about Americans and among Americans about Italians'. Barzini advocated a new spirit: 'both Italy and the United States needed love and will to do good'.[11] Following in the footsteps of other newspapers, *Il Corriere d'America* thus invited its readers to accept 'soft' Americanization by taking the best from both countries.

The importance of defending Italianness powerfully emerged with the Sacco and Vanzetti case.[12] In 1921 these two Italian anarchists were charged with murder; and in March 1923 Barzini used his paper in their defence, noting that even though he did not share their ideals, he believed they were innocent. He thought that these two Italians had to be saved at all costs in spite of their political leanings, and that for this purpose they should distance themselves from the defence committee, accused of only being interested in subversive propaganda. Therefore, he formed 'a committee of his own – the Comitato Pro Sacco-Vanzetti – run by a group of conservative Italians and Americans *prominenti*'.[13]

Italians anxiously followed the battle and this new American-style Dreyfus case fostered the rapid growth of the *Corriere d'America*. In many ways, the newspaper was also successful because it was innovative. The format was smaller, like a tabloid, and a large amount of space was dedicated to photographs, which occupied two thirds of the first page, leaving only one column for the editorial. This solution was probably adopted to reduce the huge costs involved in running the paper (75,000 dollars a month).

Striving to keep *Il Corriere d'America* afloat

In June 1923 in a letter to Luigi Albertini, Barzini took stock of the newspaper's initial evolution, pointing out the difficulties they had come up against, particularly due to the fierce competition of *Il Progresso*. He described the newspaper's development in the following way:

> It was like trying to survive a knife fight. *Il Progresso* had organized its retail sales in a way that prevented the *Corriere* from reaching readers. It paid retailers, distributors and railroad employees to suppress it. The bundles of papers were not even opened. Whoever managed to buy it once, by chance, could not find it anymore. By January 18 sales had dropped from 40,000 to 18,000. Naturally, I battened down the hatches. I created ten retail inspectors, I had people I trusted monitor distribution – a revolver in their pockets – the stuff of adventure novels. I immediately got through the crisis. From then on, the rise in sales was continuous. Today 62,000 copies of the *Corriere d'America* are printed and only 15% is given back. I am organizing two initiatives that will bump effective circulation up to at least 65,000 copies. Advertising is going well … and revenues now hit 40,000 dollars a month. I hope to bring this up to 50 or 55,000 by the end of the year. Soon the paper will be making a profit. It still is not.[14]

This was an optimistic outlook. However, Barzini was less confident than he showed, and shared his concerns with his wife Mantica Pesavento, whom he asked not to mention to the Milanese investors the economic difficulties they had come up against. In fact, losses were still very high and in July 1923 amounted to 26,000 dollars.[15]

Even by October, when more than 80,000 copies were being sold, the business was unable to break even. It was not easy to attract new readers: the number of readers who had switched over from *Il Progresso* were not high enough for the *Corriere* to topple its rival's supremacy. In short, there did not appear to be a demand among Italian-Americans for two rather similar newspapers. At Crespi's request, Barzini had no choice but to downsize the business. He fired some of the staff and reduced the number of pages and resellers, focusing distribution on New York and reorganizing work.[16] Yet it was still not enough. Barzini was forced to seek a loan of 2.5 million lire, granted by the Banca Commerciale Italiana. This was the beginning of the end, as the great journalist turned out to be a rather modest businessman. Debts were so high that they gobbled up what little profit was generated, making the newspaper 'a rickety cart, which sold a few copies to emigrants and was always on the verge of folding'.[17]

Barzini found himself more and more alone and debt-laden. His American dream of using the newspaper to climb the social ladder had vanished. He had gone to the US to seek his fortune mostly for economic reasons; yet he actually felt as if he had not gotten nearly as much from the *Corriere della Sera* as he had given to the daily. His expectations were entirely reasonable, as shown in the recollections of his son, Luigi Barzini Junior:

> Father, to be sure, did not expect to become a millionaire in the United States. All he wanted was a little more independence for himself, a house of his own, a car, a little more comfort and ease for us all, luxuries like an extra pair of shoes for his children, an occasional good dress for his wife, a few more books, a trip or two for the family, and possibly to set aside some safe investments for his old age. The decision to change continents was, as usual, a last resort.[18]

The entire family was very disappointed, especially his wife Mantica, who had always found it difficult to get used to their new life in the US:

> For some reason, she never felt happy in the United States. She had few friends and it was difficult for her to meet the well-travelled, well-read, well-mannered Americans with whom she could have exchanged *mots d'esprit*, obscure quotations, rare kitchen recipes, reminiscences, and anecdotes. She thought such Americans did not exist.... She lived in the United States eight months a year (she went back to Italy every summer) as resignedly and courageously as the wife of a missionary in an incomprehensible and practically uninhabitable country.[19]

Indulging the Duce: playing the card of pragmatism?

Mantica herself confessed to her husband that she could no longer bear a life of 'material hardship, monotonous and sad solitude ... made up of regrettable duties without having anything, nothing except boredom, hardship, sacrifice'.[20] In order to overcome these difficulties, it was essential to maintain excellent relations with fascism by pandering to the Duce, the only card left to play to survive.

Initially the *Corriere*'s editorial line differed from that of *Il Progresso*. It was more lukewarm towards the regime. In an interview for *The New York Times*, Barzini attributed the success of fascism to Italians' instinct that had long sought the leadership of a man with determination. As if due to a fatal anthropological defect, the Italians needed strong, authoritarian government. 'The reason why the *fascisti* had such wonderful success was because they offered the Italian people not only the realization of their higher ideals but also the attraction of a powerful organization'.[21] Hence, despite the deleterious aspects of *squadrismo* ('action squads' of the fascist regime) and the unbearable influence of the Italian Fasci Abroad,[22] fascism seemed first to be the lesser evil and then the best remedy for the country's problems. Barzini's letter to Mussolini of 28 October 1923 for the anniversary of the March on Rome underscores this even more clearly:

> No one like the Italians abroad can fully feel the greatness of Italy's national Risorgimento, due to Your government because from afar we clearly see its enormous, sound transformation and we can measure Your magnificent rise in Italy's growing authority. The prestige of Italy is increasingly affirmed before this public opinion... In my twenty-five years of life as a journalist abroad I have never felt more like the son of my fatherland than I do now.[23]

National prestige above all else. From an American perspective, the successes of fascism were clear because 'here you can see the surplus budget, you can see the railroads working, you can see the treaties, you see stable currency, you see an Italy that never existed in the appreciation from abroad'.[24] Following Italian deputy Giacomo Matteotti's murder in 1924 and Albertini's departure from the *Corriere della Sera*, the *Corriere d'America* increasingly turned into a pro-fascist newspaper.[25] Fascism was lauded for having restored order in the country and a sense of prestige to the nation. However, above all, the *Corriere* was pro-Mussolini: almost every day it praised the Duce as 'a serene, powerful and thoughtful giant'. Its intention was to commend the work of the regime, enhance Italy's image overseas and reinforce emigrants' national pride. The criticism expressed in American newspapers as to fascism's dictatorial nature was countered by praise for the 'Man of Providence'. Barzini believed it was inconceivable to 'denigrate Italy overseas, and among Italians, with anti-government campaigns'.[26] This was a clear criticism of *The Times*, which had called fascism a form of tyranny. 'It is time that certain newspapers realise that their idea of the Italian tyrant, like something out of a movie, is ridiculous. Italy and its government are as one.... "Duce" is the name that the people have given to Mussolini. The word does not mean dictator, but guide.'[27] This sort of patriotism, based on the regime's identification of the homeland with fascism, led the *Corriere* to orchestrate a press campaign against declared antifascist exiles, in particular against historian Gaetano Salvemini (1973–57), who was very active in the anti-Duce propaganda the United States.[28] The response to the 'angry, hateful lies' about the regime of this 'sad refugee' was harsh:

> The giant, prodigious figure of Mussolini and the constructive works of Fascism may now be seen with such concrete accuracy in the American public opinion that the verbal attacks of a traitor seem like nothing more than the yapping of an irritated little dog at a moving train.[29]

However, it was mainly the spectre of bolshevism that gave rise to 'the era of anxiety' and fuelled the fears of Americans – and also of many Italians from America who superimposed the Red Scare and the red biennium.[30] People liked the idea of a strong, determined government; and this seemed to spread a positive image of Italy abroad: the successes of fascism intensified nationalism and strengthened the pride of Italians abroad. In the so-called 'Italian colonies', prominent men strongly influenced Italian-American public opinion through their mainstream newspapers. Their voice strengthened patriotism against the 'anti-Italian' forces that were hostile to the regime. It was in this struggle against radical Italian immigrant culture that Barzini was on the frontlines. Due to his accusations of betrayal against the subversive press and his zealous attitude towards Mussolini, Barzini was often criticized by antifascist Italian-American newspapers. In particular, anarchist Carlo Tresca's paper *Il Martello* – discussed in this volume by Isabelle Felici – and *Il Nuovo Mondo*, a daily sponsored by the International Ladies' Garment Union and the Amalgamated Clothing workers of America, addressed a series of hard-hitting attacks against him and his newspaper. For instance, *Il Proletario* rhetorically asked: 'Why do Italian-boorish newspapers vie to prostitute themselves to Fascism?',[31] and in the cartoon, Barzini was featured poised to receive a little bag of dollars from the hand of fascism. In another cartoon, socialist artist Fort Velona (1886–1965) portrayed Barzini 'pushing an unwilling donkey toward a big bowl from which an ugly animal, resembling a dog, is already avidly munching. The donkey represented the 'affectionate readers' of the *Corriere d'America* while the other animal symbolized fascism'.[32]

At the same time, Barzini understood the risks of overly rhetorical propaganda. Most of the American press and the public opinion adopted an attitude to fascism that historian John Diggins rightly termed one of 'benevolent expectation'.[33] Therefore, the most important thing was to highlight actions rather than words. On this matter, Barzini wrote:

> In Italy there is a misconception about the sort of propaganda that should be directed towards Italians and Italian-Americans in North America. The only useful propaganda comes from Italy's situation. It can come from Rome, with a government that gives the real impression of governing properly, of having prestige, and continuously improving the country's economic and financial situation. That is the only sort of propaganda that can reinforce the sense of Italianness and give Italians living in America a sense of pride in their origins. All rhetoric is detrimental, and may produce results that are totally contrary to those hoped for, no matter how noble the aim. The logic of actions over words is the best possible form of propaganda.[34]

These may have been fine intentions, which were unfortunately often not acted upon. There was no lack of flattery directed at the regime. For instance, Barzini was constantly demanding economic contributions in order to host the representatives of government and the fascist hierarchies that were visiting New York.[35] He even became an unofficial advisor to Mussolini on the Italian-American press.[36]

The *Corriere* also tended to force parallels between Italy and the United States, trying to make the Mussolini regime seem similar to the American political system. It was necessary to 'translate into American' ('into Yankee') the aims and values of fascism and depict it as an adaptation of American ideals to the practical needs of Italians.[37] Ample use was made of the concept of relativism to justify the anti-liberal nature of the dictatorship, arguing that there was no perfect form of government. Every country had to come up with the most suitable systems for the specific nature of its population. As has been widely documented, 'thus Fascism was no longer a political party, but an authentic expression of the Italian spirit'.[38]

Barzini tried in every way to promote his efforts to spread propaganda before the eyes of Mussolini, as shown in this flattering letter attached to a series of articles sent to the Duce's secretary:

> I hope you do not mind my sending you this collection of my articles ... They are an extremely remote, modest, final echo of the enormous efforts you have given rise to. Should you happen to read just a few lines, you would feel the loyalty, passion, conviction and love of the everyday struggle to steer all Italian and American consciences towards the fascist truth, to elevate Italy's prestige and most effectively defend its interests. That you might notice this brings me comfort.[39]

Barzini's late days at *Il Corriere d'America*

Despite its service to the regime and the support of leading figures, the economic state of the *Corriere d'America* failed to improve. The differences between Barzini and Crespi were increasingly evident because while Barzini strove towards new development, Crespi was trying to free himself of this investment as soon as possible. As early as 1926, Barzini had thought of expanding by acquiring the New York-based *Bollettino della Sera*. Then in 1927, with the death of Carlo Barsotti, he tried to convince Crespi to offer a takeover bid for *Il Progresso Italo-Americano*. However, Crespi responded by starting negotiations to withdraw from the *Corriere* by selling it to the highest bidder.[40] In January 1928 pro-fascist Italian-American businessman Generoso Pope (1891–1950),[41] after acquiring *Il Progresso*, made a deal with Crespi to acquire the *Corriere*, but at that point the Italian government contacted the embassy requesting that the transaction be stopped to prevent the two main Italian-American newspapers from being concentrated in the hands of a single owner.[42] This was also meant to stifle any possible rivalry between newspaper owners right from the start and to avoid giving the impression that one was being favoured over the other. After all, the friction between Barzini and Pope had long been known in Rome. However, Barzini's efforts to discredit Pope due to his connections to the mafia fell flat. By that time, the debts Barzini had been accumulating ended up making him a prisoner of his own creation. He remained at the helm of the *Corriere d'America* until September 1931, when it was eventually bought by Pope.[43] A few years later, he shut it down for good.

Notes

1 See Pietro Russo, *La stampa periodica italo-americana*, in *Gli italiani negli Stati Uniti. L'emigrazione e l'opera degli italiani negli Stati Uniti d'America* (Florence: Istituto di Studi Americani, 1972), 494–8; Pietro Russo, *Catalogo collettivo della stampa periodica italo-americana, 1836–1980* (Rome: Centro Studi Emigrazione, 1983).

2   Bénédicte Deschamps, 'Echi d'Italia. La stampa dell'emigrazione', in *Storia dell'emigrazione italiana. Arrivi*, ed. Piero Bevilacqua, Andreina De Clementi, Emilio Franzina (Rome: Donzelli, 2002), 313–34.
3   Deschamps, 'Echi d'Italia', 328. See also Stefano Luconi, *La diplomazia parallela. Il regime fascista e la mobilitazione politica degli italo-americani* (Milan: Franco Angeli, 2000); Stefano Luconi and Guido Tintori (eds.), *L'ombra lunga del fascio. Canali di propaganda fascista degli italoamericani* (Milan: M&B Publishing, 2004); Matteo Pretelli, *Propaganda fascista negli Stati Uniti: gli anni Venti. Un quadro d'insieme*, in *L'Italia fascista tra Europa e Stati Uniti d'America*, ed. Michele Abbate (Orte: Centro Falisco di Studi Storici, 2002), 93–131; João Fabio Bertonha, 'Emigrazione e politica estera: la "diplomazia sovversiva" di Mussolini e la questione degli italiani all'estero, 1922–1945', *Altreitalie* 23 (2001): 39–60.
4   The Italian agency Stefani had been set up as a family business in 1853. From 1881 it became more dependent upon the government. Since 1923, the new director Manilo Morgagni changed the agency to better respond to needs of the fascist state and turn into the main outlet for the regime's propaganda. See Philip V. Cannistraro, *La fabbrica del consenso. Mass media e fascismo* (Rome-Bari: Laterza, 1975); Romano Canosa, *La voce del Duce. L'agenzia Stefani: l'arma segreta di Mussolini* (Milan: Mondadori, 2002).
5   *Per la mostra del Lavoro degli italiani all'estero, Esposizione Internazionale di Torino per il cinquantenario dell'Unità nazionale*, in *Il Progresso Italo-Americano* (1911). Quoted in Bénédicte Deschamps, *La stampa etnica negli Stati Uniti, tra nostalgia nazionale, ricostruzione dell'identità e alternativa culturale*, in *La società di tutti. Multiculturalismo e politiche dell'identità*, ed. Francesco Pompeo (Rome: Meltemi, 2007), 151–68.
6   Simona Colarizi, *Luigi Barzini. Una storia italiana* (Venice: Marsilio, 2017); Andrea Barzini, *Una famiglia complicata* (Florence: Giunti, 1996); Enzo Magrì, *Luigi Barzini: una vita da inviato* (Florence: Pagliai, 2008); Ludina Barzini, *I Barzini. Tre generazioni di giornalisti, una storia del Novecento* (Milan: Mondadori, 2010).
7   See Paola Magnarelli (ed.), *Il ricordo di viaggio. Un carteggio familiare di Luigi Albertini, 1921–1922* (Macerata: Eum, 2007).
8   Barzini started the negotiations by offering 1 million dollars, with the possibility of raising the offer to 1,250,000 dollars. In the end, Barsotti refused the offer.
9   Some interesting information on the organization of the editorial staff of the *Corriere d'America* may be found in the recollections of Francesco Panciatichi given to the FBI before his interrogation on 9 May 1942 in order to be released from internment on Ellis Island.
10 Pellegrino Nazzaro, *Fascist and Anti-fascist Propaganda in America. The Dispatches of Italian Ambassador Gelasio Caetani* (New York: Cambria Press, 2008), 28.
11 Nazzaro, *Fascist and Anti-fascist Propaganda in America*, 28.
12 On the long tradition in the Italian-American press of defending Italian-Americans against nativist and racist attacks, see Peter G. Vellon, *A Great Conspiracy Against Our Race. Italian Immigrant Newspapers and the Construction of Whiteness in the Early 20th Century* (New York: New York University Press, 2014); Rudolph J. Vecoli, 'The Italian Immigrant Press and the Construction of Social Reality, 1850–1920', in *Print Culture in a Diverse America*, ed. James Philip Danky, Wayne A. Wiegand (Urbana: University of Illinois Press, 1998), 17–33; Mark I. Choate, *Emigrant Nation. The Making of Italy Abroad* (Cambridge: Harvard University Press, 2008).
13 Philip V. Cannistraro, 'Mussolini, Sacco-Vanzetti, and the Anarchists: The Transatlantic Context', in *The Journal of Modern History* 68, no. 1 (March 1996), 51. See also Michael M. Topp, 'The Sacco and Vanzetti Case and the Psychology of Political Violence', in *The*

Routledge History of Italian Americans, ed. William J. Connell, Stanislao G. Pugliese (New York-London: Routledge, 2018), 286–304.
14 Letter of Barzini to Luigi Albertini, New York, 4 June 1923, in Luigi Albertini, *Epistolario, 1911–1926*, vol. III, ed. Ottavio Barié (Milan: Mondadori, 1968), 1727.
15 Letters of Barzini to Mantica, 5 May 1923; 2 July 1923, quoted in Colarizi, *Luigi Barzini*, 86.
16 With this downsizing, the number of copies sold was roughly 50,000–60,000.
17 In a letter to Luigi Federzoni, Ugo Ojetti argued that one of reasons why the Crespi brothers decided against letting Barzini direct the *Corriere della Sera* was because they thought he had 'frittered money away' in the investment in the US (letter of 30 November 1925, quoted in Daniele D'Alterio, *Tre capitoli su politica e cultura nell'Italia del Novecento*, Trento: Tangram 2017, 577). Barzini complained expressly to Mario Crespi because he had believed Pio Crespi's accusations against him.
18 Luigi Barzini Jr., *O America when you and I were Young* (New York: Harper & Row, 1977), 39.
19 Barzini Jr., *O America*, 58.
20 Letter of Mantica to Luigi Barzini, 20 March 1926, quoted in Colarizi, *Luigi Barzini*, 151.
21 Luigi Barzini, 'Fascismo and Its Future as Seen by Leading Italian Journalist', *The New York Times*, 14 January 1923.
22 Matteo Pretelli, 'Fasci italiani e comunità italo-americane: un rapporto difficile (1921–1929)', in *Giornale di Storia Contemporanea* 4, no. 1 (2001): 112–40. See also Luca De Caprariis, 'Fascism for Export? The Rise and Eclipse of the Fasci Italiani all'Estero', in *Journal of Contemporary History* 35, no. 2 (April 2000): 151–83; Emilio Franzina, Matteo Sanfilippo (eds.), *Il fascismo e gli emigrati. La parabola dei Fasci italiani all'estero (1920–1943)* (Rome-Bari: Laterza, 2003).
23 Telegram of Luigi Barzini to Benito Mussolini, in *Il Popolo d'Italia*, 28 October 1923.
24 Letter of Luigi Barzini to Mantica, New York, 23 December 1924, quoted in Domenico Corucci, *Luigi Barzini (1874–1947)* (Orvieto: Fondazione Cassa di Risparmio di Orvieto, 2000), 133.
25 On 1 July 1924, Barzini himself enrolled in the National Fascist Party and a few years later was one of the people who signed the manifesto of fascist intellectuals (see Magrì, *Luigi Barzini*, 250, 253).
26 Letter of Barzini to Mantica, New York, 23 July 1925, quoted in Colarizi, *Luigi Barzini*, 94.
27 Luigi Barzini, 'Il Pilota', in *Corriere d'America*, 14 September 1926. Barzini had already orchestrated a press campaign against the *World*, for some articles in which the violence of fascist dictature was denounced. See Mauro Canali, *La scoperta dell'Italia. Il fascismo raccontato dai corrispondenti americani* (Venice: Marsilio, 2017).
28 Gaetano Salvemini, *Dai ricordi di un fuoriuscito, 1922–1933*, ed. Mimmo Franzinelli (Turin: Bollati Boringhieri, 2002), 53.
29 Luigi Barzini, 'Foreign Policy Ass.', in *Corriere d'America*, 25 January 1927. It was perhaps due to this campaign against anti-fascism that Vincenzo Capuana, collaborating with the newspaper *Il Martello*, tried to attack the *Corriere d'America* in early 1926.
30 Michael. E. Parrish, *Anxious Decades. America in Prosperity and Depression, 1920–1941* (New York: Norton, 1992); David J. Goldberg, *Discontent America. The United States in the 1920s* (Baltimore: Johns Hopkins University Press, 1999); Lorenzo Benadusi, 'Addio alle armi: la smobilitazione e gli effetti della Grande Guerra in Italia e negli Stati Uniti', in *1917. L'inizio del secolo americano. Politica, propaganda e cultura in Italia tra guerra e dopoguerra*, ed. Daniela Rossini, Anna Villari (Rome: Viella, 2018), 253–76.

31 *Il Proletario*, 25 June 1927, quoted in Marcella Bencivenni, *Italian Immigrant Radical Culture. The Idealism of the Sovversivi in the United States, 1890–1940* (New York: New York University Press, 2011), 203.
32 Bencivenni, *Italian Immigrant Radical Culture*, 203.
33 John Patrick Diggins, *Mussolini and Fascism. The View from America* (Princeton: Princeton University Press, 2015 [1st edn. 1972]).
34 'L'Italia come la vedono gli americani (intervista con Luigi Barzini', in *I Fasci Italiani all'Estero*, 11 April 1925.
35 See letter of Antonio Demo to Luigi Barzini, 19 November 1926, in Center for Migration Studies, box 5, folder 35.
36 Barzini to Mussolini, New York, 28 November 1930, in National Archive, Washington, DC, Personal Papers of Benito Mussolini, Together with Some Official Records of the Italian Foreign Office and Ministry of Culture T586, doc. n. 015112/1.
37 Letter of Barzini to Arnaldo Mussolini, 24 August 1927, in Archivio Centrale dello Stato [ACS], Segreteria Particolare del Duce [SPD], Carteggio Riservato [CR], box 25, folder 241/R.
38 Francesco Di Legge, *L'Aquila e il Littorio: Direttive, Strutture e Strumenti della Propaganda Fascista negli Stati Uniti d'America, 1922–1941*, PhD dissertation, Università degli Studi del Molise, 2014, 90. On some reflections on these topics, see Stefano Luconi, *The Ethnic Press and the Translation of the U.S. Political System for Italian Immigrants in the United States, 1924–1941*, in Marina Camboni, Andrea Carosso, Sonia Di Loreto and Marco Mariano (eds.), *Translating America: The Circulation of Narratives, Commodities, and Ideas Between Italy, Europe and the United States* (New York: Peter Lang, 2011), 317–31.
39 Letter from Luigi Barzini to Alessandro Chiavolini (the personal secretary of Benito Mussolini), New York, 5 February 1927, in ACS, SPD, CR, box 25, folder 241/R.
40 At the same time, Barzini was invited to take over management of the illustrated newspapers published by the *Corriere della Sera*; but he rejected the proposal for economic reasons. See Renata Broggini, *Eugenio Balzan, 1874–1953. Una vita per il 'Corriere', un progetto per l'umanità* (Milan: Rizzoli, 2001, 197); Katy Hull, *The Machine as a Soul. American Sympathy with Italian Fascism* (Princeton: Princeton University Press, 2021).
41 Generoso Pope was supervisor and then president of Colonial Sand & Stone Company, which was the largest sand and gravel company in the world. He was part of a network of business interests and labour union affairs, and thanks to his ability to operate 'in the grey area between legitimate enterprise and machine politics', Pope would eventually become the owner of the four major Italian-language daily newspapers: *Il Progresso Italo-Americano, Il Bollettino della Sera, L'Opinione*, and precisely *Il Corriere d'America*. Philip V. Cannistraro, 'Generoso Pope and the Rise of Italian American Politics, 1925–1936', in *Italian Americans. New Perspectives in Italian Immigration and Ethnicity*, ed. Lydio F. Tomasi (New York: Center for Migration Studies, 1985), 264–88; Philip V. Cannistraro and Elena Aga Rossi, 'La politica etnica e il dilemma dell'antifascismo negli Stati Uniti: il caso di Generoso Pope', in *Storia Contemporanea* 17, no. 2 (1986): 217–43.
42 Ambassador Giacomo De Martino was therefore very worried about the sales of the *Corriere d'America*, as may be seen in his correspondence with the Minister of Foreign Affairs of November 1928. See John Patrick Diggins, *Mussolini and Fascism. The view from America*, 86.
43 'To Buy Corriere d'America', in *The New York Times*, 5 September 1931.

Section Four

Monolingualism, Plurilingualism and Rivalling Languages: Language Choice and Identity Framing

12

Why French? The Multiple Uses of French-Language Periodicals in London (UK) and Sydney (Australia) during the Nineteenth Century and Beyond

Dr Valentina Gosetti
University of New England, Australia

During the long nineteenth century, more than a hundred French-language periodicals were produced and circulated in London and throughout the United Kingdom.[1] A preliminary analysis of these papers has shown the astonishing breadth of their typology, functions, and multiple possible readerships.[2] Especially if surveyed in their rich variety, these publications, albeit often short-lived, were not aimed solely at the closed circle of the French émigré community, but they were intended for – and open to – a much larger local and cosmopolitan readership for whom French had a privileged role as international *lingua franca*.[3] The present chapter builds on this UK-based preliminary research to inaugurate a novel comparison between contemporaneous nineteenth-century French-language periodicals published in London (UK) and in Sydney (Australia). The main aim here is thus to understand whether the French-language press performed similar functions in such different English-speaking contexts at the two ends of the globe, during the century of the press.[4] It is indeed undeniable that, at that time, the press was the prominent media and source of information for the literate population of these two faraway, yet somewhat co-dependent, geopolitical contexts. In other words, studying the press in the nineteenth century is not dissimilar to studying social media today, or television in the 1980s and 1990s.

When thinking of Australian colonial history, what usually comes to mind is its indissoluble link to the British Empire, more specifically, the uncomfortable history of a British invasion to the detriment of the Aboriginal population, the oldest continuing living culture in the world.[5] Thinking of colonial New South Wales in particular, it is hard to forget its chief role as an overseas penal colony, a police state populated by convicts, who will go on to form the first generations of so-called 'Australians'.[6] Suffice it to say that present-day Australians, with considerable pride, still measure their Australian claim by how closely their lineage approaches 1788 when the first fleet arrived (but not earlier). Having (British) 'convict blood' is in fact called 'Australian

Royalty'. Yet French presence is embedded in the history of colonial Australia, from early expeditions and explorations[7] to vivid trans-colonial Franco-British – and later Franco-Australian – relations and interactions.[8] The exchange has continued ever since, in varying forms.

The *Courrier Australien*: then and now

Since its first appearance on 30 April 1892, the Sydney-based French-language periodical *Le Courrier Australien* (The Australian Courier – hereafter *CA*) has played a prominent role in such transcontinental and trans-colonial relations[9] in general and for the French-speaking community in the southern hemisphere in particular, an importance clearly reflected in the amount of research attention this paper has received by Australia-based French studies scholars, and even by students studying French in Australian universities, *CA* being a favourite subject for Honours dissertations in the field.[10] For instance, *CA* receives an extensive mention in the pioneering 1967 study *The Foreign-Language Press in Australia, 1848–1964*,[11] which also includes references to other Sydney-based French-language papers, such as the monthly *Revue Australienne* (Australian Review, 1873–4), and *L'Océanien* (The Oceanian, 1874)[12] – both rather short-lived attempts due to lack of funding, just like the very first French-language periodical down under, published, this time, outside of Sydney, *Le Journal de Melbourne* (The Melbourne Journal), which, as Ivan Barko and Alexis Bergantz have recalled, was founded in 1858 and only lasted three issues.[13] *CA* is rightly defined as 'Australia's oldest surviving foreign-language newspaper', a title which it would uninterruptedly hold until 2011, as Bergantz outlines in his forthcoming ground-breaking chapter 'Remembering *Australasie*: European Settlers and Trans-Imperial Thinking in the Cosmopolitan *Le Courrier Australien* (1892–1896)'.[14] Miriam Gilson and Jerzy Zubrzycki, the authors of the 1967 study, also stress the importance of trans-imperial relations in the very foundation of these periodicals:

> The origin of the French-language press can be traced to the activities of French traders in Sydney and the close commercial ties between New South Wales and the French colony in New Caledonia. French interests in New Caledonia were prominent in the pages of the monthly *Revue Australienne* published in Sydney in 1873–4 as well as its successors, the short-lived *Océanien* (1874) and *Le Courrier Australien*.[15]

As convincingly argued in subsequent studies and as shall be discussed below, however, since its foundation, *CA* has performed many different functions and has aimed to satisfy the needs of different audiences, beyond covering French interests in New Caledonia and targeting French traders in Sydney. Bergantz has recently summarized it in these terms:

> It [*CA*] enjoyed an uninterrupted 109-year run, from 1892 until 2011, gradually changing from a weekly publication with global ambitions to a niche monthly

local periodical focused on French affairs for French expatriates. It was revived in 2016 as an online bi-lingual edition once again with eyes turned to the world.[16]

Before moving on to the main topic of the present chapter, which proposes to set the basis for a novel and more specific comparison between some of the French-language periodicals[17] published in London and Sydney in the nineteenth century, it might be interesting to briefly explore the unusual recent destiny of *CA*, which, as mentioned by Bergantz, was revived in 2016 after a five-year gap, as an outward-looking online publication.

As Belgian journalist François Vantomme and French businessman Bernard Le Bouriscot, the current co-owners of *CA,* explain in a recent message, the Sourdin family, who had managed the periodical for more than fifty years, sold the business to Bernard Elatri in 1999. Tragically, Elatri died prematurely of cancer in 2012 and *CA* ended with him.[18] Saddened by this event and by the disappearance of the oldest surviving foreign-language periodical in Australia, some scholars started advocating on behalf of this publishing enterprise by appealing to the French Ambassador to Australia and the Consul General in Sydney. One of the main advocates was Ivan Barko, who had also been instrumental in the digitization of all the existing copies of *CA*, from April 1892 to December 1892 and then from March 1896 to the end of 2011.[19] In 2016, Bernard Le Bouriscot became the new owner of *CA*, by purchasing its name, rights and archives. In the same year journalist François Vantomme, who, in the meantime, had launched *VoilaSydney*, another French-language online publication, joined Le Bouriscot as co-owner and decided to amalgamate *VoilaSydney* with the online *CA*. Their joint aim was to 'make the savoir-faire of France, Europe and Australia known'.[20] In November 2016 the two relaunched the periodical at 'a great celebration held at the Consulate General of France in the presence of French, Belgian, Swiss and Canadian diplomats'.[21]

Since then, *CA* has been published online and now enjoys an important social media presence (on Facebook and Twitter in particular), reflecting the widespread worldwide transition from paper to web, which is particularly relevant to under-funded foreign-language periodicals. This process is not specific to Australia, as historian Michel Rapoport has shown in his study of the French-language press in London today.[22] According to its present-day website, *CA* is still aiming to perform some of the same functions that it fulfilled back at the time of its launch on 30 April 1892 when it claimed to be a 'Cosmopolitan Saturday Paper' dealing with 'Politics, Literature, Science, Fine Arts, Trade, Fashion, etc.'. These cosmopolitan aspirations were idealistically promoted by the founder of *CA*, who, perhaps surprisingly, was not a French expat, but a Francophile Polish migrant named Charles Wroblewski (1855–1936). The latter was an analytical chemist posted to New South Wales in 1885, who went on to marry 'Daisy Marie Consolation, only daughter of Jean Emile Serisier, a French-born storekeeper and vigneron'.[23] Wroblewski himself could be defined as a 'cosmopolite', a representative of the well-travelled, well-educated nineteenth-century European multilingual community.[24]

This initial outward-looking, cosmopolitan, attitude, however, was destined to change throughout the history of *CA*. As recalled by Ivan Barko, among others, the cosmopolitan aspirations of this periodical, which are so evident in its explicit original subtitle, were somewhat short-lived:

> Wroblewski sold the paper to a group of Sydney French 'notables' who formed a public company in 1898. The new owners thought . . . that time had come to revert to the basics, i.e. the 'idée nationale'. This was a reflection not so much on the cosmopolitan tendencies of Wroblewski's paper in the early years but rather on the ten-month directorship of F.O. Cailliau, who in October 1897 took the *Courrier* off at an aggressively nationalistic and often anti-Australian tangent.[25]

After fluctuating between the two ends of the spectrum – cosmopolitanism and nationalism – post-1898 *CA* thus took a much more moderate and diplomatic turn, promoting bilateral relations with Australia, while defending French interests and reputation. These efforts towards a mediating role between the two cultures are evidenced, for instance, by the publication of 'a 2-page English-language supplement' to attract an Australian audience between January 1899 and April 1900.[26] In the same years the ties between *CA* and official bodies of the French Government (namely the Alliance française, the French Consulate-General, and the French Chamber of Commerce) were becoming stronger and stronger, culminating in the new September 1899 subtitle 'Organe de la Chambre de commerce et du Comité de l'Alliance française de Sydney' (Organ of the Chamber of Commerce and the Committee of the Alliance française).

The current online iteration of *CA* is extremely proud of these historic official diplomatic ties as well as its 'cosmopolitan' ('international' in today's terms) origins as 'the oldest foreign newspaper in Australia'. The online *CA* in fact claims the continuity of such legacy, despite the five-year gap (2011–16), subsequent change of management, and larger presence of Australia-related content published in English. This said, articles in French regarding Australia also continue to feature prominently, as well as on a range of broader topics, including international news, business, sport, culture, life style, portraits, which makes *CA* similar to other local newspapers.[27] On the other hand, the rubrics 'learn French' and 'French market' remind us of the supplementary niche target audiences of this originally French-language publication, which, as we shall see below, had also offered French lessons and advertised Sydney-based French business. As testimony of the online *CA* pride in its historical legacy, a richly illustrated collector's bilingual edition, anthologizing a selection of 'the most emblematic covers & articles of the oldest foreign newspaper in Australia' to uncover 'the French-Australian relationship since 1892', was advertised as the perfect 2019 Christmas gift for the Australian Francophile.[28] In such definition, the idea of 'foreign' – rather than 'foreign-language' – could nonetheless be challenged. The online *CA* is indeed a product of twenty-first-century 'multilingual Sydney';[29] as a comparison, one cannot avoid to wonder whether a Chinese-Australian publication in Sydney, or a Greek-Australian periodical in Melbourne would be considered foreign in these two cities with prominent Chinese and Greek communities, respectively.

Lastly, the readers' social media reviews on the *CA* Facebook page also betray some continuity, showcasing some of the diverse uses and functions of the original nineteenth-century *CA* (as well as other French-language publications in both London and Sydney) that will be explored in the next sections of the present chapter. Here is a small sample:

> A quality daily newspaper that flies the French colours and those of French-speaking world in Australia!
> Nice opening onto the world, very interesting!
> A good source for the latest news.
> Very interesting for showcasing the relationships between France and Australia due to the diversity of the editorial team.
> Professional, curious, comprehensive, interesting, historical (oldest {>130 years}foreign-language media of Australia)... in short essential.[30]

From a reliable and diverse source of news to a key organ in Franco-Australian relations, from a source of national pride to an international player with a long history, it is clear that the uses of the *CA* go beyond serving the sole interests and needs of the French-speaking émigré community. This is true now and has been true throughout the *CA* history.

Building Cosmopolis? The pedagogical uses of French-language periodicals

As discussed thus far, attention has been devoted to the role of *CA* within the Australian and trans-colonial Pacific context during the nineteenth and early twentieth century, with excellent contributions of such researcher as Colin Nettelbeck, Wallace Kirsop, Gilson and Zubrzycki, Barko and Bergantz, among others. The ambition of the present chapter is to build on this research in order to set out the preliminary basis for a novel comparison between the French-language press of two contemporaneous English-speaking contexts, London and Sydney. The overall aim is to nuance the reflection on the scope and purpose(s) of these periodicals in the two cities by highlighting the peculiar privileged role of the French language in the long nineteenth century as a 'cosmopolitan' means of communication. The cosmopolitan ambitions of foreign-language periodicals were not uncommon: other highly influential papers around Europe were indeed founded, similarly to *CA*, by well-travelled, multilingual cosmopolites. In her research work devoted to the best-known nineteenth-century Paris-based English-language periodical, *Galignani's Messenger*, for instance, Diana Cooper-Richet recalls that this paper was founded in 1814 by Giovanni Antonio Galignani (1757–1821), born in Brescia (Italy), whose aim was to spread news via the medium of the English language, even across the Channel, in the continent.[31] Galignani, who had lived in London before Paris and was fluent in at least Italian, English and French, founded a newspaper whose ambition was to go beyond the needs of British tourists in Paris. His paper was a truly international publication conveying news from all around the world for an English-speaking audience, effectively acting as a mediation tool between the host country and other countries in the world and translating the main French and Parisian news items for an English-speaking readership.[32] Decades later, across the oceans, and this time, through the medium of French, Wroblewski had similar international plans for *CA*.

In his recent chapter on *CA*, Bergantz has lucidly and innovatively discussed the complex meaning of 'cosmopolitanism', a deeply European concept, with specific reference to the 'Australasian' trans-colonial context. Bergantz's essay has filled an important gap by taking 'a step back from the link between the *Courrier* and the French and Francophone community to flesh out the deployment of the ideal of cosmopolitanism under the directorship of the paper's creator', arguing that "French" and "Cosmopolitan" 'could often be amalgamated'.[33] In fact, critics agree on the fact that for many cosmopolites like Wroblewski, French often had a privileged role as *lingua franca*, the language of culture, international diplomacy, of sciences and trade etc., a language worth spreading and learning. It is thus not surprising that one of Wroblewski's chief aims was, in the words of Gilson and Zubrzycki, not only to 'serve the needs of the French residents in Australia, New Zealand, and Oceania', but also 'to appeal to the Australians interested in the study of the French language and in French affairs'. This is an excerpt from the *CA* very first editorial:

> We are less exclusive [than the Oceanian] and we aim to address not only our compatriots, but also all the Australian youth and all those who want to learn our beautiful French language, the language of Diplomacy, which is increasingly becoming the international language of trade.[34]

Precisely because of this particular role of French as the *lingua franca* of the international community, many of the nineteenth-century French-language London-based periodicals published during the nineteenth-century were also conceived with the specific pedagogical function of spreading the use and knowledge this language.[35] The aspirational English-speaking middle class of the host country felt a certain social pressure to be part of this worldly club, thus, French-language periodicals were seen as a further learning tool by those seeking to be part of the cosmopolitan French-speaking milieu. Within the purely pedagogical category, there are papers devoted specifically to children, such as *Aux Enfants* (To the Children), also *Aux Petits* (To the Little Ones) published in London and Paris (1812); and *Le Petit étranger* (The Little Foreigner) appearing in Birmingham, Leicester, London and Paris (1890–2), or periodicals for a more general audience of learners, such as *Hugo's French Journal,* London, 1896–1932, subtitled 'an illustrated weekly for those who know French, and those who want to'. Although *CA* had a much broader scope than solely serving this function, it also featured a dedicated column entitled 'French Course' by 'PARISIS', which proposed an innovative – albeit quite unsuccessful – 'European' method for language learning and opened with some lengthy instructions and considerations in English. Here is a short excerpt that clearly evidences how *CA* was designed to be read well beyond the French émigré community:

> *A Few Words of Advice to Intending Students.*
>
> Before entering upon the course of lessons we propose to publish in this paper for the benefit of the Australian student, we have thought it quite necessary to preface

our lessons with a few remarks ... It is almost a truism to say that in Australia, the study of French and German, considered in its results, is, on the whole a failure. So much so that an Australian student writing or speaking with any degree of readiness or fluency, without having resided in France or Germany, may be considered a prodigy.

These remarks ended with a somewhat polemic statement in defence of the European (read French) presence in Australia:

> And we hope you will realise that those who earnestly work towards the advancement of Australia, and whose endeavours are to bring you acquainted with the progress made in Europe in the method of treating languages, deserve your sympathy and regard, instead of being pointed out to you as the enemies of your country.[36]

Continuing the comparison with nineteenth-century London-based publications, the (somewhat incorrect and rather simplistic) general assumption that virtually all French-language periodicals should have pedagogical end was much broader. As argued elsewhere:

> Apart from these specific cases ... within the English-speaking community, it was sometimes assumed that the majority of French-language publications published in the UK were devoted to language acquisition or, at least, language advancement. Take, for instance, the perception of *L'Observateur français* (London, 1845–8), a rather conventional weekly publication covering news of all sorts from both sides of the Channel. In Mitchell's *Newspaper Press Directory* for the year 1846, this periodical was defined as 'a very well arranged and entertaining Journal' that was 'well adapted for circulation in English families, as a means of facilitating the acquirement of the French language'. The ... *Furet de Londres* too, a typical nineteenth-century literary and cultural periodical not dissimilar to its contemporary literary papers circulating in Paris, was seen, in the English press, as 'very well calculated for the purpose, which ... such publications might be well made to serve, namely, that of facilitating the acquisition of the French language' (*The London Magazine*, March 1829).[37]

But obviously, for papers like *L'Observateur français* (The French Observer) in London or the original *CA* in Sydney, it was not a matter of pedagogy in itself. Learning French was a ticket to Cosmopolis and a means to fully embrace and understand its values.

From Cosmopolis to bilateral relations[38]

According to the *Online Etymology Dictionary*, the noun 'cosmopolite' is defined as:

> 'man of the world; citizen of the world, one who is cosmopolitan in ideas or life,' 1610s, from Latinized form of Greek kosmopolites 'citizen of the world,' from

kosmos 'world' (see cosmos) + polites 'citizen,' from polis 'city' (see polis). In common use 17c. in a neutral sense; it faded in 18c. but was revived from c. 1800 with a tinge of reproachfulness (opposed to patriot).[39]

From 1833, the adjective 'cosmopolitan', which, in 1815 had meant 'free from local, provincial, or national prejudices and attachments', took up a more specific meaning, as 'belonging to all parts of the world, limited to no place or society' and in 1840 'composed of people of all nations, multi-ethnic'.[40] The definition of this term can thus fluctuate with meanings from worldly, well-travelled and cultivated to international, multiracial, and global. What emerges is that in the nineteenth century there was a perceived stark dichotomy between cosmopolitanism and nationalism (or the less negative 'patriotism', depending on the viewpoint).

To illustrate this, take for instance the highly influential European, radically multilingual,[41] monthly periodical *Cosmopolis*, subtitled *An International Review*, published between January 1896 and November 1898, a publication that could pride itself with contributors of the calibre of Paul Bourget, Anatole France, Stéphane Mallarmé, Somerset Maugham, Jean Moreas, Friedrich Nietzsche, and Robert Louis Stevenson among many others. *Cosmopolis* was distributed all around Europe and indeed beyond from Amsterdam, Netherlands (1898) to Berlin, Germany (1898), from London, England (1896) to New York, USA (1896), from Paris, France (1898) to St Petersburg, Russia (1898) and Vienna, Austria (1898). According to the *Waterloo directory of English Newspapers and Periodicals*, *Cosmopolis: An International Review* was created in 1896 to help protect the intellectual life of Europe from the destructive forces of nationalism'. *Cosmopolis* published in each issue contributions in English, French, and German. In a Europe still recovering from the Franco-Prussian War, this paper looked forward to the time when 'all the chief tongues of Europe and all the leading minds of both continents may one day find in [*Cosmopolis*] a common ground for interchange of thought'. *Cosmopolis* undoubtedly had a crucial role in fostering cosmopolitan exchange, in the sense that it provided the true 'cosmopolite' with a common ground of readings and a shared cultural heritage.

There is a tendency to think that this kind of cosmopolitan ideals reach their apex with the fin-de-siècle, when both *Cosmopolis* and *CA* were founded, while, conversely, the early nineteenth century coincides with the consolidation of the idea of the Nation-state, with some European nations (Italy and Germany in particular) working towards unification. Broadly speaking, this is partly true. Yet, throughout the century, and indeed even earlier, in the late eighteenth century, foreign-language periodicals, particularly French-language ones, fostered and promoted the ideals of a shared cosmopolitan identity, in all of the acceptations of this term, a cultural community without borders.

In his important study *French Exile Journalism and European Politics 1792–1814*, Simon Burrows had already identified that foreign-language papers in French were indeed the preferred media of a wider cosmopolitan élite:

> The journals were received regularly by an international, cosmopolitan, Francophone élite world-wide. It included men in or close to positions of executive

power, the very people taking or advising diplomatic decisions, in Germany, Russia, Sweden, Haiti, Portugal, Brazil, and Spain.[42]

Further evidence of the existence of a cosmopolitan readership, well beyond the expat community, is often found when researching in the archives. In the *British Library*, for instance, it is not unusual to find a multilingual and international bundle of periodicals, all probably belonging to the same original owner. For example, *Molière and Shakespeare, an international review of stage* (London, 1858), is bundled with *Canadian News*, and *Jacques Bonhomme*, a French-language satirical periodical published in London between March 1857 and June 1858. A brief comparison with the UK and European context thus further reinforces the argument that French-language publications, such as Wroblewski's cosmopolitan early *CA*, were certainly not merely aiming to serve the interests of a closed circle of émigrés, but rather, a multicultural, multilingual community. Regarding multilingualism, commenting on the introduction of a Polish-language column in *CA* (on 31 July 1931), Gilson and Zubrzycki have noted that '[t]he publication of a foreign-language section ... was not an isolated instance of this practice' within foreign-language journalism.[43]

As mentioned above, after a brief chauvinistic hiatus under the editorship of F. O. Cailliau, post-1898 *CA* became the official Organ of the Chamber of Commerce and the Committee of the Alliance française, clearly taking on a sort of diplomatic role specifically representing and defending French interests and culture in Australia. At this stage, it may thus seem that, by the end of the nineteenth century, *CA* was (finally) mainly, or even solely, serving the needs of the French expat community. The contention of the present essay, however, is that even during this particular phase, this was not the case. Its embeddedness in the Australian context inevitably invites a mediating role, one which *CA* never lost in its numerous iterations and one that continues today in its post-2016 online version. A final comparison with the aforementioned *L'Observateur français* (The French Observer), a slightly earlier London-based counterpart of *CA*, supports this view. *L'Observateur*'s first editorial contains this statement of purpose:

> We shall continue the conciliatory mission that the *Courrier de l'Europe* started: like this paper, we believe that the greatest interests of humanity (whether moral or material) rely on this Anglo-French alliance.[44]

Even without the European label, *L'Observateur français*'s editor, Jean Baptiste Desplace, was well aware of the important in-between status of his publication and, as argued here, this awareness was not uncommon in French-language periodicals published in the nineteenth century in London and Sydney, at the two ends of the world.

In fact, even the short-lived Australia-based periodical *L'Océanien*, which was perceived by Wroblewski as too narrowly focused on the French community, had had broader multicultural ambitions. According to the *Daily Telegraph* (6 November 1886, Sydney NSW), this would be 'a journal which will be read with interest, not only by our French neighbours, but also by the English people, with whom they gladly assimilate under the generic name of "Australians".⁴⁵ On Wednesday 10 November 1886, *The Telegraph* (Brisbane Qld.) welcomed in these terms the French-language publication:

> A French Newspaper.
>
> We are in receipt of the first number of a newspaper entitled *L'Océanien*, published in French, in Sydney ... In the course of a whimsically written and lively leading article entitled 'Nouveau Programme', the editor ... says, 'There are several thousand Frenchmen in Australia occupying diverse positions, but all impregnated uniformly with profound sentiments towards our common mother-country. ... These virgin countries which we inhabit, and which the English genius had colonised for itself ... have offered us cordial hospitality, and the privilege of enjoying absolutely all the liberties conferred by the constitutions of their several Governments, and we certainly esteem it one of our first and most elementary duties to *assimilate ourselves* to as great a measure as possible to the life and manners of these young peoples; to study their language so as to be able ... to take part in the development of their prosperity' ... The editors further ... state that in entering upon the publication of a French journal in Sydney they hope to fulfil a double end – that is, to satisfy a want long experienced by all the Frenchmen who are in the colonies, and at the same time the desire which they have often seen manifested by English persons, to become familiar with the French language and literature. 'We do not present ourselves', the editors continue, 'to the public as French-men, Swiss, Belgians, or such others, *but as citizens of this free and hospitable country called Australia.*⁴⁶

Perhaps surprisingly, French-language periodicals published in Sydney in the nineteenth century were also seen to have this additional important ambition: the building of a shared multicultural and multilingual Australian identity, one that would include the French-speaking community in its diversity and one that continues today. Key to achieving this was the building of a multicultural and multilingual common ground, or at least a platform to facilitate exchange and debate beyond the English medium.⁴⁷

Conclusion

The overall objective of this chapter has been to add to existing scholarship related to CA by initiating a comparative reflection related to some of the (stated and perceived) uses and purposes of nineteenth-century French-language periodicals in London and Sydney in order to uncover features which may be more difficult to tease out without such comparanda. It is hoped that this starting point may invite future transcontinental comparisons extending beyond the long nineteenth century and beyond French-language periodicals to cover present-day foreign-language e-publications in these multilingual and multicultural contexts at the two ends of the globe.⁴⁸

Notes

1 This figure comprises both long- and short-lived periodical as well as multilingual press that includes French as one of its main languages, such as, for instance *The Stranger in London* (1866).
2 Valentina Gosetti, 'Nineteenth-Century French-Language Press in the UK: Readership, Typology, and Cultural Integration', in *Los medios en lengua extranjera. Diversidad cultural e integración*, ed. Juan Antonio García Galindo and Laura López Romero (Granada: Editorial Comares, 2018), 95–103.
3 'Le français au XIXème ... occupe une place particulière, celle d'une langue de culture, d'une langue de distinction', in Diana Cooper-Richet, 'Avant-Propos', in *Los medios en lengua extranjera*, xii.
4 See, for instance, Marie-Ève Thérenty and Alain Vaillant (eds.), *Presse, nations et mondialisation au XIXe siècle* (Paris: Nouveau Monde, 2010); Dominique Kalifa, Philippe Régnier, Marie-Ève Thérenty and Alain Vaillant (eds.), *La Civilisation du journal: histoire culturelle et littéraire de la presse française au XIXe siècle* (Paris: Nouveau Monde, 2011), and Edmund Birch, 'Literature and the Press in France', *Dix-Neuf* 21, no. 4 (2017), 223–30, DOI: 10.1080/14787318.2018.1446290.
5 See, for instance, Henry Reynolds, *An Indelible Stain?: The Question of Genocide in Australia's History* (Melbourne: Penguin Books Australia, 2001); Martin Nakata, *Disciplining the Savages Savaging the Disciplines* (Canberra: Aboriginal Studies Press, 2007); Bill Gammage, *The Biggest Estate on Earth. How Aborigines made Australia* (Sydney: Allen & Unwin, 2012); Heather Goodall, *Invasion to Embassy. Land in aboriginal Politics in New South Wales, 1770–1972* (Sydney: Sydney University Press, 2008); Stan Grant, *Talking to my Country* (Sydney: HarperCollins Publishers, 2016), Steven and Evan Strong, *Out of Australia: Aborigines, the Dreamtime, and the Dawn of the Human Race* (Newburyport, MA: Hampton Roads Publishing Co, 2017). See also Larissa Behrendt's *Guardian* article 'Indigenous Australians know we're the oldest living culture – it's in our Dreamtime', 22 September 2016, https://www.theguardian.com/commentisfree/2016/sep/22/indigenous-australians-know-were-the-oldest-living-culture-its-in-our-dreamtime (accessed 23 February 2021). Larissa Behrendt, who is Distinguished Professor at the University of Technology Sydney and Director of Research and Academic Programs at the Jumbunna Institute of Indigenous Education and Research has authored various textbooks on indigenous legal issues, including, for a more general audience: *Indigenous Australia for Dummies* (Milton, QLD: Wiley Publishing Australia Pty Ltd, 2012).
6 See, for instance, Robert Hughes, *The Fatal Shore: The Epic of Australia's Founding* (New York: Knopf, 1987), Grace Karskens, *The Colony. A History of Early Sydney* (Sydney: Allen & Unwin, 2009).
7 To discover more about French explorations and voyages, refer to the extensive work of Australia-based French studies scholars such as John West-Sooby and Jean Fornasiero on Nicolas Baudin's expeditions to Australia. To name but a few studies by these prolific academics see, for instance, John West-Sooby and Jean Fornasiero 'Matthew Flinders through French Eyes: Nicolas Baudin's Lessons from Encounter Bay', *The Journal of Pacific History* 52, no. 1 (2017): 1–14, DOI: 10.1080/00223344.2017.1316756; Jean Fornasiero, John West-Sooby, 'The Narrative Interruptions of Science: The Baudin Expedition to Australia (1800–1804)', *Forum for Modern Language Studies* 49, no 4 (2013): 457–71, DOI: https://doi.org/10.1093/fmls/cqt036; John West-Sooby West-Sooby, Jean Fornasiero, and Lindl Lawton, eds., *The Art*

of *Science: Nicolas Baudin's Voyagers 1800–1804* (Mile End: Wakefield Press, 2016); John West-Sooby, ed., *Discovery and Empire: the French in the South Seas* (Adelaide, Australia: University of Adelaide Press, 2013). For a general survey of the French presence in Australia see, for instance, Anny P. L. Stuer, *The French in Australia* (Canberra: Department of Demography, Institute of Advanced Studies, Australian National University, 1982); Jean Rosemberg, *Studies in the French Presence in Australia*. Unpublished typescript c. 1985, accessed 15 December 2019, https://www.isfar.org.au/resources/jean-rosemberg.

8 Different aspects of French-Australia relations in the long nineteenth century have been studied by Colin Nettelbeck, Wallace Kirsop, Ivan Barko, and, more recently Paul Gibbard, Alexis Bergantz, among others. See, for instance, Colin Nettelbeck, ed., *The Alliance Française in Australia 1890–1990 – an Historical Perspective* (Melbourne: Fédération des Alliances Françaises en Australie Inc. in association with the Institute or the Study of French-Australian relations, 1990); Wallace Kirsop, 'Some notes on Georges Biard d'Aunet (1844–1934)', *Explorations* 19 (1995) [issued December 1997], 31–6; Ivan Barko, 'The *Courrier Australien* and French-Australian Relations during the Biard d'Aunet Years (1892–1905)', in *The Culture of the Book: Essays from Two Hemispheres in Honour of Wallace Kirsop* (Melbourne: Bibliographical Society of Australia and New Zealand, 1999); Paul Gibbard, 'Empiricism and Sensibility in the Australian Journal of Théodore Leschenault de la Tour', in R. Garrod and P. J. Smith (eds.), *Natural History in Early Modern France: The Poetics of an Epistemic Genre* (Netherlands: Brill, 2018), 263–90; Alexis Bergantz, 'French Connection: The Culture and Politics of Frenchness in Australia, 1890–1914' (PhD thesis, The Australian National University, 2016). For an account of more recent Franco-Australian relations, see Paul Soyez, *Australia and France's Mutual Empowerment. Middle Powers' Strategies for Pacific and Global Challenges* (Cham: Palgrave Macmillan, 2019).

9 Some advertisements appearing in *CA* can be taken as further evidence of these trans-colonial networks, for instance: '*The France Australe*. The oldest and most widely read daily in New-Caledonia receives by cable the principal news of the World. The only independent Newspaper in Noumea. The best advertising medium in the Colony.'

10 Further surveys of the history and role of the *CA* have been undertaken by Ivan Barko in the aforementioned chapter, 'The *Courrier australien* and French-Australian Relations'. Ivan Barko also very generously shared with the author of the present chapter a brief history of the *CA* as well as some of his personal correspondence. Barko's 'Bref historique du *Courrier Australien/Le Courrier Australien*: a short history', can now be found in a recent richly illustrated bilingual collector's edition edited by François Vantomme and others, *Le Courrier Australien 1892–1945. Creating the French-Australian Connection since 1892* (Sydney: Le Courrier Australien Pty Ltd, 2019), 14–16.

11 Miriam Gilson and Jerzy Zubrzycki, *The Foreign-Language Press in Australia, 1848–1964* (Canberra: Australian National University Press, 1967). Examples of undergraduate dissertations related to *CA* include, Naomi Forwood, 'Les Français en Australie – A travers *le Courrier Australien* 1892–1901 – Analyse sociologique' (Honours diss., University of Sydney, Australia, 1983); the Honours dissertation of Jillian Elizabeth Donohoo resulted in the publication 'Feeding 'the sacred fire': *Le Courrier Australien* and France Libre', *History in the Making* 1, no. 2 (2013): 8–20. https://historyitm.files.wordpress.com/2013/08/donohoo.pdf.

12 No copies of this publications can be found on the Australian Trove online database: https://trove.nla.gov.au nor in the local archives of the State Library of New South

Wales, which holds copies of *CA*. References to *L'Océanien* are nonetheless present in some local English-language publications as it will be shown below.

13 See Ivan Barko, 'and French-Australian Relations', and Alexis Bergantz, 'Remembering *Australasie*'. As Rosemberg outlines, other French-language periodicals published in Australia in the early twentieth century include *Le Français à l'Université de Melbourne* (French at the University of Melbourne) 1903–6, *Trident* 1906–8, *Le Petit Français* (The Little French) 1907–12, *Le Français Classique* (Classic French) 1908–10, *Le Français en Australia, Journal de la Jeunesse Australienne* (French in Australia, Journal of Australian Youth) 1913–21, all monthly publications founded by Maurice Carton, see Jean Rosemberg, 'Chapter nine' in *Studies in the French Presence in Australia*.

14 Alexis Bergantz, 'Remembering *Australasie*: European Settlers and Trans-imperial Thinking in the Cosmopolitan *Le Courrier Australien* (1892–1896)', *Voices of Challenge in Australia's Migrant and Minority Press*, ed. Catherine Dewhirst and Richard Scully (Basingstoke, Palgrave Macmillan, forthcoming). This will be the second volume of a project on the Australian foreign-language press led by Dewhirst and Scully. By the same editors, see vol. 1: *The Transnational Voices of Australia's Migrant and Minority Press* (Basingstoke, Palgrave Macmillan, 2020).

15 Gilson and Zubrzycki, *The Foreign-Language Press in Australia*, 15.

16 Alexis Bergantz, 'Remembering *Australasie*', forthcoming.

17 Diana Cooper Richet uses the French definition 'presse allophone' to refer to press published in a language other than the official national language(s), see 'Avant-Propos' in *Los medios en lengua extranjera*, xiii. Cooper-Richet is one of the founders of TRANSFOPRESS (Transnational Network for the Study of Foreign Language Press), whose aim is to study the press in languages other than the national language(s): http://transfopresschcsc.wixsite.com/transfopress/copie-de-prsentation.

18 François Vantomme and Bernard Le Bouriscot, 'Message des propriétaires/Message from the owners', in *Le Courrier Australien 1892–1945. Creating the French-Australian Connection since 1892*, 12–13. See also, Ivan Barko, 'Bref historique du *Courrier Australien*/*Le Courrier Australien*: a short history', 16.

19 There is a gap in the records between December 1892 and March 1896 with issues yet to be found.

20 Vantomme and Le Bouriscot, 'Message des propriétaires/Message from the owners', 13.

21 Vantomme and Le Bouriscot, 'Message des propriétaires/Message from the owners', 13.

22 Michel Rapoport. 'Du journal papier à l'e-journal: La presse francophone de Londres aujourd'hui', in *Los medios en lengua extranjera*, 88–93.

23 See the entry 'Wroblewski, Charles Adam Marie (1855–1936)', in the online *Australian Dictionary of Biography*, http://adb.anu.edu.au/biography/wroblewski-charles-adam-marie-13258 (accessed 28 December 2019).

24 It might be surprising to discover that 'on 20 March 1893 he launched another newspaper in Sydney, the Deutsch-Australische Post, for the German-speaking public'; he was thus instrumental in the creation of at least two Sydney-based French-language periodicals. See 'Wroblewski, Charles Adam Marie (1855–1936)', http://adb.anu.edu.au/biography/wroblewski-charles-adam-marie-13258 (accessed 28 December 2019).

25 Ivan Barko, The *Courrier australien* and French-Australian relations.

26 Ibid.

27 See, for instance, 'Incendies: Comment réagir aux différents niveaux d'alerte', https://www.lecourrieraustralien.com/did-you-know-incendies (accessed 22 February 2021).

28 A review on the *CA* Facebook page reads: 'I received *Le Courrier Australien* book 1892–1945 (Collector Edition) for Christmas and the news stories from the late 19th

and early 20th century are absolutely fascinating. It must have been a daunting job to put all this together so kudos to the LCA team for this very insightful book. I highly recommend it to anyone interested in learning and understanding the relationship between Australia and France. The photos are also amazing! The LCA book is on my bedside table and I'll definitely enjoy every single page throughout 2020!' https://www.facebook.com/pg/lecourrieraustralien/reviews/?ref=page_internal (accessed 30 December 2019).

29 See the ongoing multidisciplinary project on Multilingual Sydney spearheaded by Alice Chik and Phil Benson at Macquarie University Australia, resulting in publications such as Alice Chik, Phil Benson, Robyn Moloney eds., *Multilingual Sydney* (London; New York, NY: Routledge, 2019). The project's very active and informative Twitter page can be found at @MultilingualSy1.

30 https://www.facebook.com/pg/lecourrieraustralien/reviews/?ref=page_internal (accessed 27 January 2020). All translations from French are by the author.

31 Diana Cooper-Richet. 'La Presse pour "touristes", un marché de niche inventé au XIXe siècle: L'exemple des journaux en anglais publiés en France', in *Los medios en lengua extranjera*, 81.

32 For further evidence of this mediating function performed by foreign-language press in different geographical contexts see Isabelle Richet, 'The English-Language Press in Italy as Community Builder and Bridge Toward the Host Society', in *Los medios en lengua extranjera*, 105–12.

33 Alexis Bergantz, 'Remembering *Australasie*', forthcoming.

34 *CA*, 30 April 1892. Translation from French by the author. *L'Océanien* (The Oceanian), of which we do not have any surviving copies, was indeed welcomed by some the Australian English-speaking press as targeting the émigré French community. According to the *Daily Telegraph* (Sydney NSW) on 6 November 1886, for instance, 'A FRENCH NEWSPAPER. The first number of a newspaper to be published in French on the 1st and 15th of every month, has just been issued in Sydney, under the title of 'L'Océanien', and as it promises to be a literary success, such as might be justly expected from the culture and esprit of our French residents, we may express the confident hope that it will meet with every financial support. In a witty article in which the object of the new enterprise is explained, the editorial management disclaim management disclaim any intention of formulating a cut and dried programme … They thus half in jest, half in earnest, deny any political intention, and confine their object to the social union of their French readers and to the discussion of all that concerns France and the civilisation of which they are the sons. Every department of literature, politics, philosophy and art criticism will receive the attention of the new journal.' https://trove.nla.gov.au/newspaper/article/239328110?searchTerm=l%27oc%C3%A9anien&searchLimits (accessed 25 January 2020).

35 Gosetti, 'Nineteenth-Century French-Language Press in the UK', 98–100.

36 *CA*, 14 May 1892.

37 Gosetti, 'Nineteenth-Century French-Language Press in the UK', 99.

38 This reflection is indebted to all the discussions sparked by the two-day international conference 'Cosmopolis and Beyond: Literary Cosmopolitanism after the Republic of Letters' organized by Stefano Evangelista at Trinity College, Oxford from 18–19 March 2016: https://cosmopolisandbeyond.wordpress.com.

39 https://www.etymonline.com/search?q=cosmopolite&source=ds_search (accessed 29 January 2020).

40 https://www.etymonline.com/search?q=cosmopolitan (accessed 29 January 2020).

41 For a recent analysis of the value of its multilingualism see Frederik Van Dam, 'An Outpost of Modernism: The Diplomatic Design of *Cosmopolis*', *Victoriographies* 8, no. 2 (2018): 170–86, DOI: 10.3366/vic.2018.0304.
42 Simon Burrows, *French Exile Journalism and European Politics 1792–1814* (Suffolk (UK), Rochester (NY): Royal Historical Society, 2000), 78.
43 Miriam Gilson and Jerzy Zubrzycki, 17.
44 Cited in Gosetti, 102. Translation from the original French by the author.
45 https://trove.nla.gov.au/newspaper/article/239328110?searchTerm=l%27oc%C3%A9anien (accessed 22 February 2021).
46 Emphasis added. https://trove.nla.gov.au/newspaper/article/185513343?searchTerm=l%27oc%C3%A9anien&searchLimits= (accessed 20 January 2020).
47 The founder of *L'Océanien*, Albin Villeval, former 'Communard' sent to New Caledonia, was the author of a biographical study on Victor Hugo published in Sydney in 1895, which he concluded with this statement: 'To unfold the phases of the life of such a man before the eyes of a young country which is fast developing into a nation ... appeared to me to be a work possessive of some usefulness', https://nla.gov.au/nla.obj-405579096/view?partId=nla.obj-405579602 (accessed 20 January 2020), 46. On the phenomenon of French convicts – including 'Communards' – relocating from New Caledonia to Australia, see Alexis Bergantz, '"The Scum of France": Australian Anxieties towards French Convicts in the Nineteenth Century', *Australian Historical Studies* 49, no. 2 (2018): 150–66, DOI: 10.1080/1031461X.2018.1452951.
48 I would like to express my gratitude to Ivan Barko and Alexis Bergantz for their generous help and feedback and to Michael Brogan for his bibliographical advice on Indigenous Studies.

13

Revolutionizing Women's Roles in the Late Nineteenth-Century US-Based Spanish-Language Press

Kelley Kreitz
Pace University

This chapter brings the US-based Spanish-language press of the nineteenth century into this book's investigation of immigrant and exile communities of print. The topic is an ambitious one to represent in a single chapter, as the Spanish-language press in the United States during that century was certainly not monolithic. The first newspapers in Spanish in the United States appeared just after the turn of the nineteenth century.[1] By the latter half of that century, centres of Spanish-language publishing thrived across the country – in major east coast and southern cities, including New York, Philadelphia and New Orleans, and throughout the vast territory in the west and southwest that belonged to Mexico until its transition to the United States following the Mexican-American War. The topics, genres, writing styles, visual features and missions of the publications produced in these communities varied over the decades and across the wide range of experiences that their writers, editors, and readers encountered. Those included the struggles of the former Mexican citizens who found themselves after the Treaty of Guadalupe Hidalgo (1848), through which Mexico lost nearly half its territory to the United States, as foreigners needing to defend their property and human rights without ever having moved from their land. Others who became active in nineteenth-century US-based Spanish-language publishing had immigrated (or in many cases fled) to the United States; they sought press freedom and models of democracy not available in Cuba and Puerto Rico, which remained Spanish colonies until 1898, or in some of the newly independent nations of Latin America that had shifted towards increasingly autocratic regimes. The United States appeared varyingly in these publications – sometimes even within the same article – as a nation actively engaged in the hypocrisy and injustice of carrying out political oppression of its own citizens, an imperialist threat to the newly independent and aspiring nations of Latin America, a site of press freedom unavailable in most of Latin America, and a desperately needed symbol of the promise of true (if also far from fully realized) democracy.

From today's perspective, one of the greatest commonalities shared by the publications produced by this expansive and diverse print culture is the way that history has treated them. For most of the twentieth century, scholars and archivists of US literary and cultural history failed to recognize US-based Spanish-language communities of print. The scholarly attention that publications from those communities did receive came from Latin American studies, where scholars have understood them (and collected them) as minor venues for leading Latin American writers of the period.[2] The archive of nineteenth-century US-based Spanish-language texts thus ended up, as Rodrigo Lazo has noted, 'dispersed . . . and incomplete'.[3] It was not until the final decades of the twentieth century, especially as a result of the ambitious indexing project led by the University of Houston's Recovering the US Hispanic Literary Heritage Project, that those publications that did survive began to regain visibility to researchers interested in understanding the long history of people of Latin American descent in the United States. In the early 2000s, scholars working in US literary studies, including Anna Brickhouse, Kirsten Silva Gruesz, and Rodrigo Lazo, argued for the relevance of these archival materials to US literary, cultural, and political history – especially to situate that history in a broader hemispheric context and to explore 'the possibility of a meaningful commonality of the idea of Latino expression, even before the term was invented'.[4] More recently, Marissa López, Raúl Coronado and Jesse Alemán, among others, have expanded the historical focus of Latinx Studies to elucidate the nineteenth-century origins of later forms of US-based Latinx culture and identity and bring into focus 'a lost Latino public sphere'.[5] How might the presence of this understudied part of print history in the United States help to advance understanding of immigrant and exile publishing communities that this collection pursues? How did its writers and editors make use of language and notions of community to form and mobilize their audiences? And what insights into the formation of notions of *latinidad* do their formulations of community, identity, and the possibilities for social and political change provide?

To take up these questions, this chapter centres its analysis on a rare example of a women-led publication from the nineteenth-century US-based Spanish-language press: the Tampa, Florida-based *La Revista de Cuba Libre* (Free Cuba Magazine), a bi-weekly periodical published from December 1897 to August 1898 by the Club de Justo Carrillo (Justo Carrillo Club), one of the many women's clubs formed in the final decades of the century to support organizing for Cuban and Puerto Rican independence. *La Revista de Cuba Libre*'s editorial team led by the club's president, Maria Teresa de la Torriente, drew on and fashioned its own brand of two overlapping types of late nineteenth-century Spanish-language periodicals.[6] First and foremost, the magazine entered into conversation with an already robust community of newspapers dedicated to advancing Cuban and Puerto Rican independence, especially *Patria* (Fatherland) launched in 1892 by Cuban writer and revolutionary José Martí (1853–95) and *Doctrina de Martí* (Martí's Doctrine) founded in 1896 by Afro-Cuban writer and educator Rafael Serra (1858–1909). In addition, the editors evoked an earlier tradition of US-based Spanish-language illustrated magazines that thrived in New York City, including Enrique Piñeyro's *El Mundo Nuevo* (The New World, 1871–75), *La América* (America, 1873–?) and Elías de Losada's *La Revista Ilustrada de Nueva York* (New York Illustrated Magazine, 1885–90), which mediated a hemispheric, Spanish-speaking publishing community.[7] By giving their magazine its own unique identity in conversation with all of these predecessors, *La Revista de Cuba Libre*'s editors constructed their own vision of a future Cuban democracy that situated women more centrally as actors rather than auxiliary supporters. The magazine shows women making use of publishing to support what ended up being the final year of the war effort – from the increased press censorship in Havana at the outset of 1898, to the arrival of the *Maine* and the building tension between the United States and Spain in aftermath of its destruction, to arrival of US troops and the beginning of their withdrawal by August 1898.

Ultimately, this unique and rarely studied publication proves illuminating in two main ways for the purposes of this collection.[8] First, as one of the few periodicals from the period with an editorial team made up almost entirely of women, it provides an unusual opportunity to locate the revolutionary work of Cuban women, who typically found few opportunities within the movement to leave lasting, public evidence of their roles. Second, the publication provides a window on the broader Spanish-language publishing network in which its editors thoughtfully and strategically situated *La Revista de Cuba Libre*.

Locating *La Revista de Cuba Libre*

La Revista de Cuba Libre's story participates in a broader history of hemispheric Spanish-language print culture and revolutionary politics that scholars drawing on Latinx Studies and Latin American Studies have recently elucidated.[9] Well before *La Revista de Cuba Libre*'s debut in December 1897, the ambitions and worldviews of Spanish-language illustrated magazines and Cuban revolutionary newspapers intersected. This was especially the case in the thriving Spanish-language publishing community of New York City, where many of the same writers and editors participated in both types of publications. In 1891, the New York-based *La Revista Ilustrada de Nueva York* was the first to publish José Martí's influential essay 'Nuestra América' (Our America). The idea that Martí articulates there of a unified hemispheric community made up of the people of former and then still-struggling Spanish colonies builds on the foundations of earlier illustrated magazines, including another New York-based magazine, *El Mundo Nuevo* (The New World), which was affiliated for about a year after its founding in 1871 with Frank Leslie's enterprise before continuing independently as *La América Ilustrada* in 1872. As Kirsten Silva Gruesz has shown, '*El Mundo Nuevo/ La América Ilustrada* ... brings together in its pages many of the essential components of his foundational thought, anticipating Martí's vision of *Nuestra América* as a linguistically based print community'.[10] Building on Gruesz's observations, Laura Lomas has argued that Martí's early writings for another New York-based illustrated magazine, *La América,* where he served as a staff writer and then an editor from 1883 to 1884, updated and revised what was a largely commercial vision of hemispheric unity in the earlier magazines: 'In contrast to *El Mundo Nuevo*'s scant sympathy with revolutionary remedies for working-class miseries, *La América* under Martí anticipates Cuba's subsequent revolutionary projects by defining a North-South grid of power in the hemisphere.'[11] His writing and editing for *La América*, and later for *La Revista*

Ilustrada de Nueva York, show Martí beginning to articulate the possibilities of hemispheric unity. In the context of an expanding and increasingly interconnected world of print, he saw possibility in these magazines not simply for selling products, as many of these magazines were first created to achieve, but for advancing democracy and social justice.

By the early 1890s, those earlier efforts to mediate change through illustrated magazines informed a new wave of periodicals founded to support the growing momentum from a new coalition of supporters, which Martí played a leading role in building, for organizing another attempt at independence from Spain.[12] The constituents included workers from the growing cigar industry in the United States, as well as artisans and intellectuals. Among these contributors to the movement were printers, editors, and writers of African descent, including Rafael Serra and Sotero Figueroa (1851–1923), who helped to update earlier independence efforts that promoted the interests (and often the prejudices) of white elites.[13] In partnership with Figueroa, who had also served as a contributing editor for *La Revista Ilustrada de Nueva York*, Martí worked to create *Patria* newspaper as a vehicle for constructing what Jesse Hoffnung-Garskof has called 'a careful balance ... between profiles of wealthy, white patriots and profiles of exemplary black soldiers, poets, and teachers'.[14] When that balance within *Patria* toppled following Martí's death in Cuba in an early battle of the war in 1895, Figueroa helped Serra to found *Doctrina de Martí*, which debuted in 1896 as another space in which the future of democracy in Cuba might be debated and circulated. Indeed, by this point, as the revolutionary community began to look ahead to the work of building a Cuban democracy, periodicals dedicated to the war effort and to envisioning its aftermath proliferated. In New York alone, at least four new periodicals dedicated to Cuban independence appeared in 1897, including *Cacara Jícara*, which was founded by poet Enrique Hernández Miyares (1859–1914), who had previously edited the illustrated magazine *La Habana Elegante* (Elegant Havana) in Havana.[15] In Tampa, *La Revista de Cuba Libre* debuted in 1897 alongside three other new periodicals: *La Nueva República* (The New Republic), *El Oriente* (The East), and *El Eco de Martí* (Martí's Echo).[16] *La Revista de Cuba Libre*'s careful positioning took shape at that moment – when publishing a newspaper provided a primary vehicle for entering into the debate about what the future of Cuban democracy might look like.

By the time *La Revista de Cuba Libre*'s first issue appeared in 1897, as everyone involved in the revolutionary community knew all too well at this stage in Cuba's long struggle for independence, what was at stake was not just Cuba's liberation from Spain; it was also a question what kind of democracy a newly independent Cuba would pursue. Even as a growing network of Spanish-language newspapers agreed on the dire need for Cuban independence, debate raged over who would get to participate in the resulting democracy, especially in recognition of the struggles to escape elitism and authoritarianism in already established nations throughout Latin America. In that context, print provided a primary means for supporters who all agreed on the dire need for Cuban independence from Spain to articulate and circulate multiple, often competing, views of what the future of democracy in the Caribbean might look like. In *La Revista de Cuba Libre*, the primary concern was how to define a role for women at a time when dominant narratives of women's roles in the Cuban cause – including those circulated by Martí and many of his allies – cast them as auxiliary supporters rather than as their own political actors. The editorial team of *La Revista de Cuba Libre* revised women's roles by invoking *Patria* and other revolutionary newspapers as its most direct interlocutors, while exhibiting the influence of illustrated magazines.

Printing revolution

When *La Revista de Cuba Libre* first appeared in print in December 1897 to pursue 'our object or purpose [which] is the most honorable currency ever conceived by humankind: to help the Fatherland', its editors recognized that they were joining a well-populated field.[17] A note on the front page of the first issue extends 'to the separatist press ... our sincere greeting at the same time as we ask for your support in our task'.[18] In subsequent issues, *La Revista de Cuba Libre* brings its revolutionary community of print into view through a mix of news on the war in Cuba written by members of the Cuban Revolutionary Party, poetry by male and female supporters of the Cuban cause, updates on the political and cultural situation in Cuba from correspondence in Havana, and profiles of leading figures in the Cuban revolutionary movement. A note in the 18 February 1898 issue makes use of the common practice of listing the newspapers that the editorial office had recently received, in order to show their participation in a network of revolutionary newspapers that stretched from the east coast of the United States into Mexico and included '*Patria, Porvenir, Doctrina de Martí*, de New York; *El Yara, El Vigia*, de Key West; *Cuba* de Tampa y *El Grito de Baire* de Veracruz'.[19] While these titles, especially those from New York appear most frequently throughout *La Revista de Cuba Libre*, another class of Spanish-language magazines, the illustrated magazines which also thrived in New York City, also entered into the magazine's earliest descriptions of its character and purpose.

Throughout *La Revista de Cuba Libre*'s run, the editorial team emphasizes its commitment to using the latest print technologies, especially the photoengraving techniques employed by illustrated magazines. In a note 'To our readers' in the first issue, the editors refer to 'our humble newspaper' for which 'a complete success awaits us'.[20] That future success, the note goes on to suggest, will come in subsequent issues of the magazine if:

> as has been our desire, we would improve the Magazine by publishing engravings and portraits at the level of other interesting publications; and Tampa would be better represented in the Cuban cause and what is more ... we would give more to the Fatherland.[21]

The note links increased capacity to produce high-quality illustrations directly to their ability to support the Cuban cause. Improving their illustrations, the editors suggest, provides an essential means of contributing to the independence effort. A later note 'To our subscribers' in the 19 March 1898 issue proudly announce the magazine's first photo engravings, which 'we will continue increasing and soon, very soon, we will introduce improvements that, without increasing its price, will make the REVISTA DE

CUBA LIBRE without a doubt a worthy representative of the cause that it represents'.[22] By making public their goals and achievements relating to improved print quality and capacity, the editors employed a practice also used by the best-known illustrated Spanish-language magazines from the period.

Throughout *La Revista Ilustrada de Nueva York*, increased print capacity – including the use of photoengraving to bring the magazine 'to the height at which one arrives at the level of exquisite art' – offers a primary means of achieving the magazine's mission of advancing culture and democracy in Latin America.[23] When publisher Elías de Losada (1848–96) took over as the magazine's owner and editor in 1885, at first as part of his job running a Latin American export division for Thurber-Whyland, he fashioned the magazine into a vehicle for pursuing 'the purpose of establishing in this great center of civilization a newspaper that worthily represents our language and our race'.[24] From the beginning, Losada saw print technology as a primary lever for achieving his ambitious goals.[25] According to a January 1890 announcement of the establishment of a new publishing house following the opening of an in-house print shop links this 'new field' of the magazine's work directly to its mission to 'serve in various ways the cause of the intellectual and moral progress of the Latin American people'.[26] Increased print capacity here powers increased ability to support the Cuban cause.

In *La Revista Ilustrada de Nueva York*, as in many of the illustrated magazines that preceded *La Revista de Cuba Libre*, that power made possible by access to print belonged almost exclusively to men. While illustrated magazines often appealed to an imagined female readership, advocated for women's education and included some women writers, their management, contributor lists, and visions of the future of print were dominated by men.[27] That male-dominated vision became even more prevalent as the interests of those involved in such publications turned towards the Cuban Revolutionary Party and its organizing for war. According to Jesse Hoffnung-Garskof, 'No variant of liberal or nationalist politics in this period offered a visible role as active citizens – soldiers, voters, or writers – to women, although women were actually present in many forms of political mobilization.'[28] Even among the Cuban Revolutionary Party leaders who worked the hardest to move away from elitist and racist visions of the future of Cuban democracy – including Figueroa and Martí – 'They wrote hardly at all about women. Their vision of racial unity was heavily invested in a shared experience of manhood.'[29] In that context, *La Revista de Cuba Libre* offered a revolutionary revision of this view of the independence movement – by positioning of women as major contributors to the world of print.

In the pages of *La Revista de Cuba Libre*, the women-led editorial team shifts the work of the auxiliary club, meant to provide support from the sidelines, to centre stage. On the front page of every issue, a list of the editorial leadership boasts an entirely female team, with the exception of Justo Carrillo, the club's namesake and honorary president. Each issue includes a mix of articles, poetry and correspondence that situated the publication's female editors and contributors alongside leading male military leaders and organizers of the war effort. In addition, in many of its articles by and about women, the periodical engages directly with typical characterizations from the period of women in the war effort, reproducing while also revising the most familiar roles available to women – that of wives, mothers and daughters.

A series published in *La Revista de Cuba Libre* honouring heroes of the independence movement illustrates the publication's approach. The first article of the series features a young Cuban woman named Rosario Sigarroa (1860?–1925), who was a contributing editor to the publication known for her 'good taste and the elegance and correctness of her style' and for her support of the Cuban Revolutionary Party.[30] While later instalments of the series feature men who played leading roles in the Cuban Revolutionary Party, the choice of Sigarroa, 'with whom the REVISTA DE CUBA LIBRE today inaugurates its gallery of honor', signals the magazine's commitment to positioning women as key contributors.[31] The article begins by showcasing familiar characterizations of women's roles in support of Cuban independence, casting Sigarroa, as a 'victim, like so many others, during the Ten Years War, of Spanish cruelty' because her father died in the war.[32] Along with her mother who, 'with that sublime denial, so common in Cuban mothers, devoted herself to the education of the unfortunate orphan', Sigarroa appears here as having suffered the ultimate sacrifice. Yet, the loss of her father is not ultimately what qualifies Sigarroa, according to the narrative, as exemplary in 'her faith in the triumph of freedom and the future of her Cuba'.[33]

The feature explains that the choice of Sigarroa – referred to by her nickname, Charito – is the result of her own actions: 'The moment when Charito manifested herself with all the greatness of her soul and with all the qualities of her exceptional character, was at the outbreak of Baire's revolution'.[34] Referencing the *grito de Baire* that marked the outbreak of Cuba's insurrection on 24 February 1895, the article places Sigarroa at the centre of Cuba's revolutionary action: 'Without fearing the anger of the tyrant she was consistently the most active and trusted aid of all the delegations of the Revolutionary Party'.[35] Moreover, the narrative suggests that being a woman proves key to her success: 'Her sex, discretion, tact, and reserve allowed her to perform the most difficult and dangerous commissions, for which she was always happy to volunteer'.[36] Here, Sigarroa's refinement – the same quality touted earlier in reference to her prose – enables her to face danger readily and courageously. In print and on the battlefield, Sigarroa epitomizes *La Revista de Cuba Libre*'s revision of women's contributions to the war effort, which both affirms many of the period's notions of womanhood while also assigning women new leadership roles.

Indeed, the issues of the magazine that followed her feature in *La Revista de Cuba Libre*'s series of photo-engravings of heroes of the war effort portrayed her consistently as one of its leaders. In keeping with the custom of printing letters addressed to editors by designated correspondents, she was often the editor to whom writers addressed their updates for the magazine. Her byline also appeared on a series of articles entitled 'Crónica' ('Chronicle'), another regular feature of illustrated magazines that highlighted cultural and community news – in this case from Key West. Another article entitled 'Siempre en su puesto' in the 6 August 1898 issue features Sigarroa again on her way to Santiago de Cuba as a member of the Red Cross: 'Charito has been a great paladin for our magazine; her work, her chronicles always gave to our newspaper real momentum'.[37] The knightly heroism achieved by her editorial work, the article suggests, will be carried on in Santiago de Cuba, as she helps 'those who shed their noble blood in sacrifice to our just cause', and serves as 'our agent in that Cuban town'.[38] Her work aiding the wounded on the battlefield appears here as a continuation of her heroism in the editorial office.

A note included in the first issue of *La Revista de Cuba Libre* further elucidates the way in which the periodical repositioned women within the illustrated and revolutionary press. Addressed to the 'Club Revolucionario Justo Carrillo', the announcement written by the club's secretary Maria Broderman issues a call from 'la Sra. Presidenta' (Madam President) to 'las socias de este Club' (the female members of this club), urging them to attend their upcoming meeting 'since important issues will be discussed regarding the newspaper and accounting for its outcomes, the attendance of all is recommended'.[39] The message does more than remind club members of an important meeting. It revises the very purpose of auxiliary women's clubs like El Club de Justo Carrillo to include, centrally, the work of publishing a newspaper. Within the long tradition of Spanish-language publishing in which *La Revista de Cuba Libre* participated, there was no more fundamental activity than producing a publication. As de la Torriente and her team knew well, print provided a powerful platform for envisioning and mobilizing for Cuban independence – a platform that *La Revista de Cuba Libre* provided to women.

Fashioning a female editorial voice

Throughout the magazine's run, the representation of women in editing roles is one of *La Revista de Cuba Libre*'s most striking features. When male military leaders contributed updates to the magazine, they often addressed them to its female leaders, including Sigarroa and de la Torriente who, as president of the club, served as the magazine's director and editor in chief. When the magazine's regular correspondent from Havana, who signed the pen name Aurora, sent her updates on the state of the war in that city, she addressed them to 'mi querida directora' (my dear woman director).[40] Every issue provided multiple opportunities to witness women engaged in leadership roles to produce their publication and advance the Cuban cause.

Aurora's updates from Havana show the degree to which both sides treated newspapers as essentially another theatre of the war. In this tense environment, where 'on the streets, in the parks and theaters, you see nothing but military officers who offend, even with their eyes', military officers and supporters of the autonomist movement that was loyal to Spain often targeted newspaper offices.[41] Her instalment in the 22 January 1898 issue recounts how 'a group of about 60 military members, mostly officers' attacked the editorial offices of two newspapers, *El Reconcentrado* (Brought Together) and *La Discusión* (The Discussion), for their views on independence.[42] The violence, as a result of which 'nothing was left standing in *The Discussion*', led to another wave of censorship efforts by Spanish colonial authorities.[43]

In the midst of that censorship crisis, Aurora uses her platform to show the power of her own voice. She mocks as hopeless and ridiculous a new edict from Captain General Ramón Blanco y Erenas, which required that 'all work be sent to the print *12 hours prior to publication!*'.[44] Aurora's claim at the outset of her letter already demonstrates the inefficacy of this edict: 'Since I don't have a censor I will give my readers the pleasure of knowing the truth.'[45] Empowered by her position as a Havana correspondent with a Tampa-based periodical, Aurora demonstrates her ability to be a defiant advocate for Cuba's independence who operates outside of the Spanish state's authority.

It is from this type of empowered editorial voice that the magazine also launches its critique of the US press. On the front page of the 6 August 1898 issue, the lead editorial article reflects on 'The American fourth estate'. The editors criticize 'that babbling and jingoistic press' in the United States that 'has said all the bad things that can be said these days about Cubans'.[46] The unsigned article indicates that the editors had been watching the US press closely, concluding: 'We have assigned little importance to certain newspapers in their efforts to fuss and talk about even what they know nothing about.'[47] The observation is especially interesting in light of the fact that Clemencia Arango (1860–1920) served as a contributor and distribution agent in New York for *La Revista de Cuba Libre*. Undoubtedly, the editors were familiar with the series of articles by North American reporter Richard Harding Davis that appeared in *The New York Journal* in February 1897, which made sensational and unfounded suggestions that Arango had been sexually harassed by Spanish soldiers when she was taken into custody by them on board a US-bound steamer called the Olivette. Without naming this incident specifically, the article indicates the degree to which the Cuban revolutionary community had been paying attention the Anglophone press in the United States – and also turning a blind eye to stories such as the ones associated with the Olivette incident that ultimately supported the Cuban cause, however misguidedly. In contrast to that story, *La Revista de Cuba Libre*'s editors exhibit their power to critique and undermine the US press, while also showing Arango herself in an active role that starkly contrasts with her victimization in the US press.

Perhaps the most illustrative example of the magazine's efforts to revolutionize women's roles in print comes in the final issue, whose cover boasts the words 'Hasta Luego' (see you later). An editorial note explains:

> *La Revista de Cuba Libre* bids farewell to its usual readers, and says goodbye with a *see you later* because it intends to continue in Cuba, not the anti-Spanish company that we have held so far, because the vanquished only deserve compassion, but the campaign of the regeneration of the Cuban people... the campaign for order, morality and justice.[48]

At this moment following the signing of the Protocol of Peace between Spain and the United States, anticipating the Treaty of Paris that would follow in December 1898, the writers turn their attention hopefully from the independence effort to the cause of building a just Cuban democracy. They do so by making the point that, although they may be shutting down their presses in Tampa, they will be setting them up again in Cuba. As another editorial note in the same issue explains, 'As our readers will have read in the editorial article of this issue, we are going to Cuba and for this reason we suspend the "Magazine" until later.'[49] Looking ahead to Cuba's future, the editors confidently pack up their paper with the promise that there will be more to come: 'Since most of the married and unmarried ladies who make up our club are leaving for Havana, it is almost certain or at least, it is our intention, to form the club in that Capital.'[50] Just as the opening issue showed its editorial team organizing to start their editorial work, this note assures readers that they will be resuming their effort back at home.

Futures of media and democracy

La Revista de Cuba Libre thus ends on a hopeful note at a crossroads in Cuba's history. The editors were not naive about the challenges that lay ahead. Increasingly, the last few issues of the publication considered with concern the significant challenges to Cuba's future posed by the views circulating widely in the US press of Cubans as unfit to rule themselves – and by the divisions among Cubans themselves that were the legacy of long-entrenched views of the autonomist, annexationist and separatist parties. At the same time, the final issue of *La Revista de Cuba Libre* sounds a note of hopefulness that shows the editors planning for a Cuban democracy in which a print culture that made more room for women would continue to play a leading role.

Some of those hopes became realities. Sigarroa went on to found a magazine called *Cuba Libre* in Cuba in 1899. Its 20 May 1902 issue triumphantly celebrated the start of Cuban independence as the island transitioned from US rule. But, in hindsight, there is also much more to that story – from the limits to Cuban sovereignty left by the Platt Amendment; to the increasing breakdown before and after 1902 of efforts to realize the vision of racial unity that powered the most hopeful visions of Cuban democracy from the organizing efforts led by Martí, Serra, Figueroa, and others in the 1890s in New York City; to the dictatorship of the US-backed Fulgencio Batista that would ultimately lead to the 1959 revolution.

Looking back to the hemispheric Spanish-language publishing community of the nineteenth century, *La Revista de Cuba Libre*'s abrupt ending helps to explain why that magazine and so many others like it disappeared from view in the twentieth century. In the political and media context of that century, the possibility of an expanding world of print – and of a hemispheric, Spanish-language community that could come together to promote democracy in Cuban and throughout Latin America – seemed farther from reach than it must have for *La Revista de Cuba Libre*'s editor team. By the end of the century, too, notions of *latinidad*, which in the nineteenth century did not draw the same line between those in Latin America and those in the US, began to separate into today's more familiar formations.

From today's perspective, as scholars seek to understand nineteenth-century US-based print culture, this magazine that tells an important Cuban story also tells another one. That less-familiar story elucidates the way in which nineteenth-century US-based Spanish-language print culture circulated revolutionary notions of identity, community, and the possibilities of social and political change throughout the hemisphere. It's a story that promises to shed light on the relationship between media and democracy of the past at a time when its lessons are urgently relevant to the present.

Notes

1   Scholars typically cite *El Misisipí*, founded in New Orleans in 1808, as the first Spanish-language newspaper to be published in the United States. For a foundational history on US-based Spanish-language publishing, see Nicolás Kanellos and Helvetia Martell, *Hispanic Periodicals in the United States, Origins to 1960: A Brief History and Comprehensive Bibliography* (Houston: Arte Público Press, 2000).

2   Much of this research resides in studies of the Latin American literary movement known as *modernismo*. For an influential consideration of the literary magazines of *modernismo* see Chapter five of Gerard Aching, *The Politics of Spanish American 'Modernismo': By Exquisite Design* (Cambridge: Cambridge University Press, 1997). See also Vernon A. Chamberlin and Ivan Schulman's account of the process of recovering one such periodical, *La Revista Ilustrada de Nueva York* in their *La Revista Ilustrada de Nueva York: History, Anthology, and Index of Literary Selections* (Columbia: University of Missouri Press, 1976).

3   Rodrigo Lazo, 'Introduction: Historical Latinidades and Archival Encounters', in Rodrigo Lazo and Jesse Alemán (eds.), *The Latino Nineteenth Century* (New York: New York University Press, 2016), 9.

4   Kirsten Silva Gruesz, *Ambassadors of Culture: The Transnational Origins of Latino Writing* (Princeton: Princeton University Press, 2002), xi. Influential studies from this wave of scholarship also include Anna Brickhouse, *Transamerican Literary Relations and the Nineteenth-Century Public Sphere* (Cambridge: Cambridge University Press, 2004) and Rodrigo Lazo, *Writing to Cuba: Filibustering and Cuban Exiles in the United States* (Chapel Hill: University of North Carolina Press, 2005).

5   Anna Brickhouse, 'The Black Legend of Texas', *PMLA* 131, no. 3 (2016): 735. See, for example, Marissa López, *Chicano Nations: The Hemispheric Origins of Mexican American Literature* (New York: New York University Press, 2011), Raúl Coronado, *A World Not to Come: A History of Latino Writing and Print Culture* (Cambridge: Harvard University Press, 2013), and Jesse Alemán and Rodrigo Lazo, eds., *The Latino Nineteenth Century* (New York: New York University Press, 2016).

6   More research is needed to recover biographical details about Maria Teresa de la Torriente.

7   See Schulman and Chamberlin, *La Revista Ilustrada de Nueva York*.

8   I have not been able to locate any extensive studies on *La Revista de Cuba Libre,* which is somewhat surprising given recent emphasis on locating Latina voices within nineteenth-century print culture. Nancy A. Hewitt mentions the magazine in *Southern Discomfort: Women's Activism in Tampa, Florida, 1880s – 1920s* (Urbana: University of Illinois Press, 2001). On the challenges of and archival approaches to locating Latina voices, I have found especially helpful Jesse Hoffnung-Garskof, *Racial Migrations: New York City and the Revolutionary Politics of the Spanish Caribbean* (Princeton: Princeton University Press, 2019) and Nancy Mirabel, *Suspect Freedoms: The Racial and Sexual Politics of Cubanidad in New York, 1823–1957* (New York: New York University Press, 2017).

9   See, for example, Chapter five of Gruesz's *Ambassadors of Culture*; Laura Lomas, *Translating Empire: José Martí, Migrant Latino Subjects, and American Modernities* (Durham: Duke University Press: 2008); Hoffnung-Garskof, *Racial Migrations*; and Mirabel, *Suspect Freedoms*.

10 Gruesz, *Ambassadors of Culture*, 192.

11 Lomas, *Translating Empire*, 97.

12 On this topic, foundational texts include Gerald Poyo's *With All, and For the Good of All: The Emergence of Popular Nationalism in the Cuban Communities of the United States, 1848–1898* (Durham: Duke University Press, 1989); James Winston, *Holding Aloft the Banner of Ethiopia: Caribbean Radicalism in Early Twentieth Century America* (London: Verso, 1999); Aline Helg, *Our Rightful Share: The Afro-Cuban Struggle for Equality, 1886–1912* (Chapel Hill: University of North Carolina Press, 1995); and Ada Ferrer, *Insurgent Cuba: Race, Nation, and Revolution, 1868–1898* (Chapel Hill: University of North Carolina Press, 1999).

13 Recent studies that elucidate the roles played by Afro-Cubans and Afro-Puerto Ricans, including Figueroa and Serra, in the Cuban revolutionary movement include Hoffnung-Garskof, *Racial Migrations*; Mirabel, *Suspect Freedoms*; and Nicolas Kanellos, 'Sotero Figueroa: Writing Afro-Carribbenas into History in the Late Nineteenth Century', in Rodrigo Lazo and Jesse Alemán (eds.), *The Latino Nineteenth Century* (New York: New York University Press, 2016).
14 Hoffnung-Garskof, *Racial Migrations*, 223.
15 This is another periodical on which few scholars have written, although I have found through my own research on the Havana-based *La Habana Elegante* that *Cácara Jícara* provides a fascinating window on Enrique Hernández Miyares's journey from supporter of Cuban independence as an editor in Cuba to exile in New York. I have written about *La Habana Elegante*'s and its participation in hemispheric print culture at the end of the nineteenth century in my 'Telephonic *Modernismo*: *Latinidad* and Hemispheric Print Culture in the Age of Electricity', *English Language Notes* 56, no. 2 (2018): 90–103.
16 Dates and titles are from the index provided in Kanellos and Martell, *Hispanic Periodicals in the United States, Origins to 1960*.
17 'Nuestro Propósito', *La Revista de Cuba Libre*, 25 December 1897, 1. Updates throughout the periodical's run suggest that a primary form of such help was by making the magazine another means of raising funds for the Cuban Revolutionary Party. Translations from this and other articles cited throughout this chapter are mine. Unfortunately, space in this volume did not allow for the inclusion of the original Spanish.
18 'Saludo', *La Revista de Cuba Libre*, 25 December 1897, 1.
19 'Gacetillas', *La Revista de Cuba Libre*, 18 February 1898, 8.
20 'A nuestros lectores', *La Revista de Cuba Libre*, 25 December 1897, 5.
21 Ibid.
22 'A nuestros suscriptores', *La Revista de Cuba Libre*, 19 March 1898, 7.
23 'Trabajos en nuestra imprenta', *La Revista Ilustrada de Nueva York*, March 1890, 6.
24 'La Revista Ilustrada a sus lectores', *La Revista Ilustrada de Nueva York*, December 1890, 4.
25 I have discussed *La Revista Ilustrada de Nueva York*'s unique approach to pursuing the possibilities that Losada and his editorial team saw in their changing world of print in my 'American Alternatives: Participatory Futures of Print from New York City's Nineteenth-Century Spanish-Language Press', *American Literary History* 30, no. 4 (2018): 677–702. There, I argued that the magazine and Martí's 'Nuestra America' (Our America), debuted there in January 1891 envisioned an emergent participatory form of modern media. Here, my purpose is to show how *La Revista Ilustrada*'s emphasis on increased print capacity as a lever for pursuing its goals for Latin America echo in *La Revista de Cuba Libre*'s editorial approach.
26 'Lo que ofrecemos a lectores', *La Revista Ilustrada de Nueva York,* January 1890, 13.
27 *La Revista Ilustrada de Nueva York* provides an example of this. As I noted in my 'American Alternatives', the magazine published a statement of its commitment to women's education when introduced Amalia Puga (who would later marry the magazine's editor to become Amalia Puga de Losada).
28 Hoffnung-Garskoff, *Racial Migrations*, 55.
29 Hoffnung-Garskoff, *Racial Migrations*, 12.
30 'Rosario Sigarroa', *La Revista de Cuba Libre*, 19 March 1898, 1.
31 Ibid.

32 Ibid.
33 Ibid.
34 Ibid.
35 Ibid.
36 Ibid.
37 'Siempre en su puesto', *La Revista de Cuba Libre,* 6 August 1898, 2.
38 'Siempre en su puesto', *La Revista de Cuba Libre,* 6 August 1898, 2, 3.
39 Maria Broderman, 'Club Revolucionario Justo Carrillo', *La Revista de Cuba Libre,* 25 December 1897, 7.
40 Aurora, 'Interesante carta de la Habana', *La Revista de Cuba Libre,* 22 January 1898, 5.
41 Aurora, 'Carta de la Habana', *La Revista de Cuba Libre,* 8 January 1898, 6.
42 Aurora, 'Interesante carta de la Habana', *La Revista de Cuba Libre,* 22 January 1898, 6.
43 Ibid.
44 Ibid.
45 Aurora, 'Interesante carta de la Habana', *La Revista de Cuba Libre,* 22 January 1898, 6.
46 'El cuarto poder . . . americano', *La Revista de Cuba Libre,* 6 August 1898, 1.
47 Ibid.
48 'Hasta luego', *La Revista de Cuba Libre,* 27 August 1898, 1.
49 'Nos vamos a Cuba', *La Revista de Cuba Libre,* 27 August 1898, 8.
50 Ibid.

14

Divergency in Russian Emigré Publishing in Late Victorian Britain: The Case of the *Narodovolets* and *The Anglo-Russian*[1]

Robert Henderson
Queen Mary, University of London

In his definitive bibliography of the Russian émigré press in Britain in the sixty-year period leading up to the 1917 revolution, historian John Slatter listed no fewer than forty nine periodical and newspaper titles.[2] And, as the author mentioned in his introduction, these journals made a considerable and often unacknowledged contribution to the movement against tsarism both among Russians and among their British hosts.[3] The current contribution takes the form of a case study of two of these titles, the *Narodovolets* (1897–1901) and *The Anglo-Russian* (1897–1914). It examines the lives and publishing activities of their respective editors: Vladimir L'vovich Burtsev (1862–1942) and Jaakoff Moiseevich Prelooker (1860–1935) and attempts to evaluate their impact on both their Russian and British audiences. These two journalists, although appearing to have much in common, and although striving for the same goal – namely, the liberation of the Russian people – chose to set out on very different paths on their way to achieving that ultimate objective. However, as a result of certain events which played out in Britain in the final years of the nineteenth century and the first few years of the twentieth, the paths of these two diverse individuals would converge dramatically and unexpectedly. At least superficially the two appeared to have much in common: both arrived in emigration in London in the same year, 1891 and six years later, in 1897, both saw their respective journals appear in print for the first time. This contribution will centre on the role of language (English vs Russian) and will more specifically reflect on the choice of language to express divergency. This first presupposes exposing some background details on editors' lives prior to their arrival in Britain.

Setting Russian scenes and exilic trajectories

Vladimir Burtsev was born on 17 November 1862 in Fort Alexandrovsky on the eastern shores of the Caspian Sea (now Fort Shevchenko in Kazakhstan). His revolutionary life began when he enrolled as a student at St Petersburg University at the age of nineteen.

Figure 14.1 V. L. Burtsev. *The Anglo-Russian*, vol. 8, no. 11 (November 1904), 859. Courtesy of the British Library Board. Shelfmark General Reference Collection 1904 LOU. LON 744 [1898].

Shortly thereafter, he took part in a student protest meeting and was arrested and imprisoned without trial for a month. Then, two years later in Kazan, he was again arrested under suspicion of involvement in revolutionary activity. This resulted in a lengthy prison spell followed by exile to Siberia. In July 1888, having completed only a few months of his four-year sentence he set out on his escape and arrived in Geneva in the autumn of that year. It was there that Burtsev embarked on his journalistic career taking over the production of the revolutionary journal *Samoupravlenie* (Self-government). While working on issues 3 and 4 of that title (February and April 1889), he started up his own journal, *Svobodnaia Rossiia* (Free Russia), which he co-edited with V. K. Debagory-Mokrievich (1848–1926) and M. P. Dragomanov (1841–95).[4] It was at this point that he showed the first signs of a remarkable flair for investigative journalism, bringing to the public's attention news of tsarist atrocities in the Siberian prison camps. It was thanks to Burtsev that the west first came to hear of the shocking massacre of political prisoners in Yakutsk in 1889 and of the flogging and suicide of female political prisoners on the Kara Peninsula later that year. Unfortunately, *Free Russia* folded after only three issues due to editorial disagreements. Soon afterwards, Burtsev moved to Paris where he began making plans for a new journal. In order to secure funding for the project he set off for Russia, but quickly realized that the Russian Department of Police was aware of his intentions. There followed a dramatic pursuit through much of Western Europe and the Balkans, which ended with his safe and triumphant arrival in London on board an English merchant ship in January 1891.

Figure 14.2 J. M. Prelooker. Frontispiece from his *Russian Flashlights*. London: Chapman and Hall, 1911.

Jaakoff Prelooker was two years Burtsev's senior having been born in Pinsk, Belorussia in 1860 into a family of orthodox Jews – his grandfather was a celebrated Rabbi. In 1880, having successfully completed secondary education, Prelooker took up the position of assistant master of the Second Government School for Jews at Odessa and followed that educational calling for the next ten years. Alongside his teaching duties, he wrote a number of philosophical and religious works and was also involved in journalism from an early age working for various Russian, Ukrainian and German periodicals such as *Nedelia* (The Week), *Odesskii listok* (The Odessa Leaflet), and *Zeitung*.[5] In 1882, he founded a reformist Jewish sect under the name of New Israel, whose objective was to introduce reforms into the Jewish religion which would reconcile it with Christianity. For his troubles, that same year he was excommunicated as a heretic by the Jewish Assembly in Odessa. New Israel's attempts to win over Christian members also led to its suppression by the Russian authorities and to its founder being forbidden from delivering lectures which, in due course, led to Prelooker's self-imposed exile. On his arrival in London in July 1891, he was received warmly by a number of important social figures such as the pacifist William Evans Derby (1821–92).

Ecumenical reconciliation vs the destruction of autocracy: *The Anglo-Russian* vs *Narodovolets*

Over the years, Prelooker's initial idea of the reconciliation of Jew and Christian developed and widened into a desire to bring together into one universal family all religious creeds. Furthermore, he set himself the ambitious task of unifying the nations in the spirit of brotherly love and decided to begin by working towards a strengthening of ties between Russia and Britain. He embarked on a series of lecture tours around Britain to rally support for his beliefs. In 1895, he established The Russian Reformation Society (*Obshchestvo sodeistviia rossiiskim reformam*) and, two years later, having gathered sufficient funding – primarily from two elderly sisters who held 'advanced' pacifist and suffragist views – was able to found a monthly English-language journal for the Society.[6]

The first issue of *The Anglo-Russian* appeared in June 1897 and included a personal commendation from none other than the famous English novelist and playwright Jerome K. Jerome (1859–1927), who declared that he entirely sympathized with the journal's aims. The chief of these, as described by its editor, was:

> to endeavour to remove those misunderstandings which at present divide two such great nations as the English and the Russians into antagonistic camps, suspicious of one another, to the detriment of their mutual interests, and the interests of the world at large. We are firmly convinced that there is no real cause for antagonism – that the natural conditions under which both nations exist and labour are such as to make them natural allies. Each could supply the wants of the other – Russia with the inexhaustible wealth of her natural resources, England with the abundance of her industries and manufactures.[7]

Figure 14.3 *Anglo-Russian*, vol. 7, no. 1, 1898, 1. Courtesy of the British Library Board. Shelfmark General Reference Collection 1898 LOU.LON 744 [1898].

The programme, content and intended audience of Prelooker's journal stood in sharp contrast to Burtsev's *Narodovolets* which had first appeared two months earlier, in April 1897. However, Burtsev's path towards publication had proved to be considerably more difficult than that of Prelooker.

Tsar Alexander III had taken a personal interest in the Balkans pursuit of the escaped exile and had shown his displeasure at the failure to recapture him. The Paris-based section of the Russian political police, the so-called Foreign Agency (*Zagranichaia agentura*), were thus obliged to step up their efforts and, during Burtsev's occasional trips from London to the continent in the early 1890s, made several attempts to effect an arrest. The elusive revolutionary, however, always managed to slip through their grasp. He felt secure in Britain where, although obliged to lead a frugal life, he was, nonetheless, able to enjoy the riches of the British Museum Library, to indulge in various literary pursuits and to make plans for his next journalistic venture. He was by no means the only émigré journalist to make use of the unparalleled collections of the Library which, from the early years of the nineteenth century, had served as a sanctuary for a variety of intellectuals and others who had been forced to flee their homeland due to persecution whether it be of a political or religious nature.

Meanwhile, far from giving up on his pursuit of the fugitive, the head of the Foreign Agency, P. I. Rachkovsky, had infiltrated agents into the London Russian émigré community, including a certain Lev Beitner who succeeded in gaining entry to Burtsev's closest circle.[8] Rachkovsky had also had the good fortune to strike up a relationship with Chief inspector William Melville of Scotland Yard, who was more than willing to offer up his services and those of his staff. Together they kept a close watch on every move of Burtsev and his associates and thus in 1896 were the first to learn of his intention to set up a new radical journal.[9] Indeed, there is evidence to suggest that Rachkovsky did more than simply follow the progress of the journal towards publication for, when it looked as if the venture was about to fail for lack of money, he apparently stepped in and, via Beitner, provided Burtsev with the necessary finances to complete the project. Bearing in mind the value of the information that his agent was already supplying from the editorial offices of the newspaper, Rachkovsky may well have considered it worthwhile to provide the monies that would ensure its survival.[10] Burtsev had decided to call his journal the *Narodovolets*, which literally translated as 'Member of the Party of the People's Will'. His intention was to use it as a vehicle to advocate a return to the revolutionary traditions and terrorist methods of that party.[11]

When the first issue of the journal appeared, it created, perhaps, more of a stir than the editor had expected. Its radical programme was clearly laid out in a twelve-page leader in which Burtsev called for the revival of the Party of the People's Will and laid out the credo of this proposed new party:

> Our first task is the destruction of the autocracy, the transfer of all state business out of the hands of the present bureaucracy into the hands of legally elected people's representatives, the creation of a federal state, with regional and local self-government, with guaranteed rights for all freedoms: of speech, of the press, of the individual, of nationality, etc. In the field of economics, we shall defend and uphold everything that will help us attain the final socialist ideal.
>
> To attain these ends we shall recognize all means which are realistic and effective in the struggle with the current Russian government – from the most moderate to the most extreme and revolutionary, depending on time and place. We may say, in the words of the late Stepniak: 'We are revolutionists, not only to the extent of a direct rising of the people, but to the extent of military conspiracies, to the extent of nocturnal invasions of the Palace, to the extent of bombs and dynamite.[12]

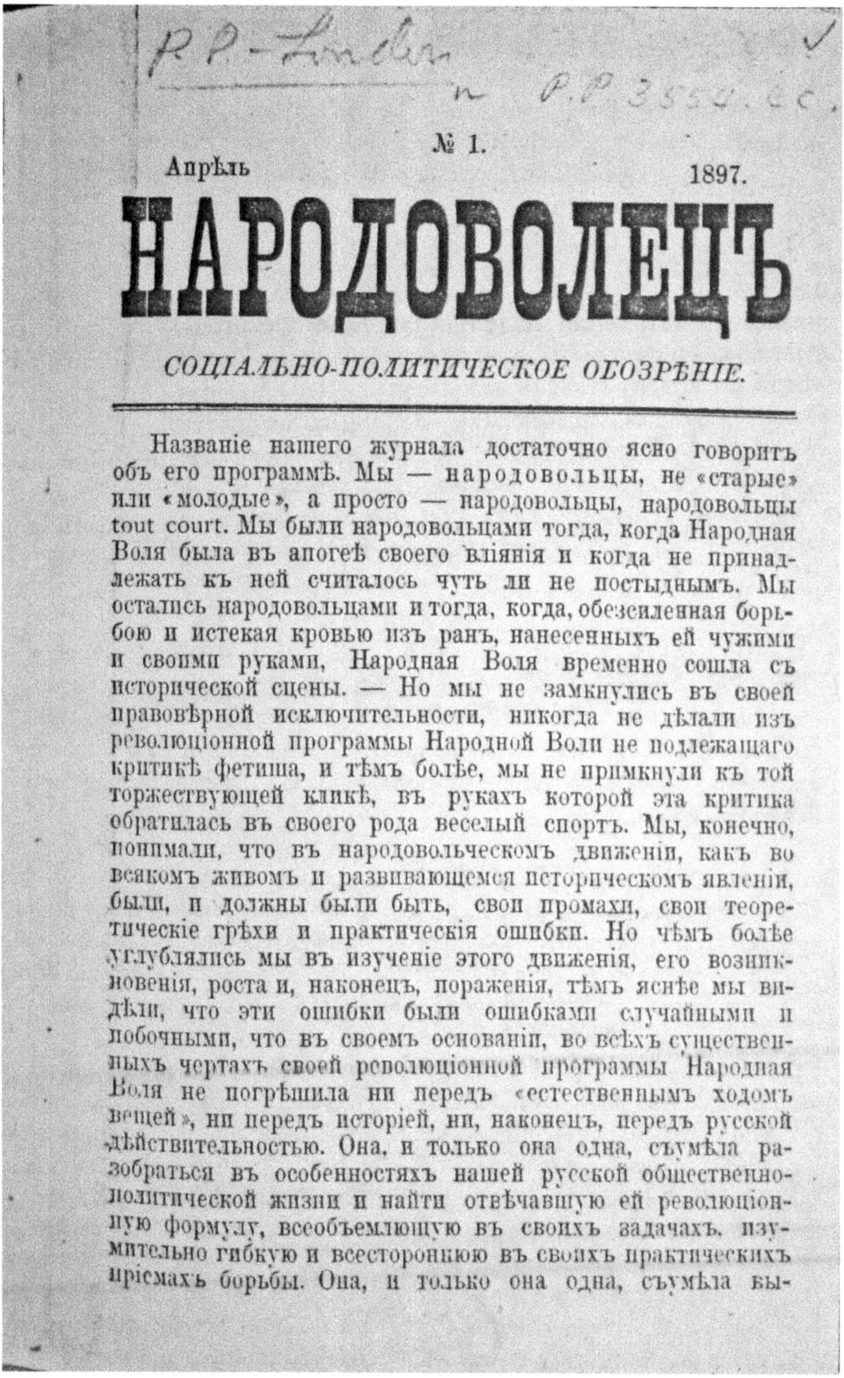

№ 1.

Апрѣль 1897.

НАРОДОВОЛЕЦЪ

СОЦІАЛЬНО-ПОЛИТИЧЕСКОЕ ОБОЗРѢНІЕ.

Названіе нашего журнала достаточно ясно говоритъ объ его программѣ. Мы — народовольцы, не «старые» или «молодые», а просто — народовольцы, народовольцы tout court. Мы были народовольцами тогда, когда Народная Воля была въ апогеѣ своего вліянія и когда не принадлежать къ ней считалось чуть ли не постыднымъ. Мы остались народовольцами и тогда, когда, обезсиленная борьбою и истекая кровью изъ ранъ, нанесенныхъ ей чужими и своими руками, Народная Воля временно сошла съ исторической сцены. — Но мы не замкнулись въ своей правовѣрной исключительности, никогда не дѣлали изъ революціонной программы Народной Воли не подлежащаго критикѣ фетиша, и тѣмъ болѣе, мы не примкнули къ той торжествующей кликѣ, въ рукахъ которой эта критика обратилась въ своего рода веселый спортъ. Мы, конечно, понимали, что въ народовольческомъ движеніи, какъ во всякомъ живомъ и развивающемся историческомъ явленіи, были, и должны были быть, свои промахи, свои теоретическіе грѣхи и практическія ошибки. Но чѣмъ болѣе углублялись мы въ изученіе этого движенія, его возникновенія, роста и, наконецъ, пораженія, тѣмъ яснѣе мы видѣли, что эти ошибки были ошибками случайными и побочными, что въ своемъ основаніи, во всѣхъ существенныхъ чертахъ своей революціонной программы Народная Воля не погрѣшила ни передъ «естественнымъ ходомъ вещей», ни передъ исторіей, ни, наконецъ, передъ русской дѣйствительностью. Она, и только она одна, съумѣла разобраться въ особенностяхъ нашей русской общественно-политической жизни и найти отвѣчавшую ей революціонную формулу, всеобъемлющую въ своихъ задачахъ, изумительно гибкую и всестороннюю въ своихъ практическихъ пріемахъ борьбы. Она, и только она одна, съумѣла вы-

Figure 14.4 *Narodovolets* no. 1, April 1897, 1. Courtesy of the British Library Board. Shelfmark General Reference Collection P.P.3554.ec.[13]

The editor made it clear, however, that the call to enter the fray was directed only at revolutionaries *within* Russia, whom he exhorted 'boldly to follow in the footsteps of the Zheliabovs, the Perovskys, the Khalturins and their friends, and to pay heed to the testament which they have bequeathed us. In their testament lies our programme'.[14] Another article was even more incendiary, summarizing the programme of the journal as 'in one word – regicide and, if necessary, then a whole series of regicides and a programme of systematic terror'.[15]

Where language matters: Russian-language serials and censorship

Not unexpectedly, the journal caused great consternation in Russia where the government claimed it called openly for the murder of Tsar Nicholas II and demanded that Burtsev be brought to book. The Conservative Prime Minister of the day, Robert Gascoyne-Cecil, 3rd Marquess of Salisbury (1830–1903), who was keen at that time to improve Anglo-Russian relations, needed little persuasion.[16] Burtsev was later to describe what happened next:

> At about 2 o'clock on the afternoon of the 16th December 1897 a few English detectives together with Chief Inspector Melville of Scotland Yard appeared in the Reading Room of the British Museum. Under some pretext they called me outside into the corridor, read me a warrant for my arrest charging me with a violation of the 'Offences against the Person Act', and asked me to accompany them to Bow Street Police Station.[17]

Burtsev appeared before the magistrate that same afternoon and was charged with having 'solicited, encouraged, persuaded, and endeavoured to persuade divers persons to murder his Imperial Majesty the Emperor Nicholas II of Russia'. The speed with which the press got hold of the story is remarkable, with reports appearing in the evening papers that same day. Questions were also asked in the House of Commons, reflecting the great public interest in the affair.[18]

The Russian government was naturally cock-a-hoop and was determined that this time Burtsev should not escape punishment. To this end, Rachkovsky was despatched to London to organize a cell of *provocateurs* and to make contact with the English police. They then worked out a detailed plan on how to 'prepare' the case for trial.[19] Beitner had been in regular contact both with Melville and Rachkovsky and had even been able to make the latter aware of the contents of Burtsev's journal before publication. The spy, of course, had made sure he was out of the country when the arrest took place. At the trial, on 11 February 1898, it was reported that, when arrested, Burtsev had in his possession a parcel of books addressed to a 'Monsieur Baitner, of Geneva' which raises the suspicion that Rachkovsky, Beitner and Melville had contrived to make the arrest at a time when they knew Burtsev would have this incendiary material in his possession. In the event, however, such machinations were not needed. Burtsev's defence team stressed that the articles in the journal had been written in Russian by a Russian for the exclusive use of Russians, and it was a nonsense therefore that he should be tried in an English court. The defendant's strategy revealed how exiled foreign editors and journalists tried to navigate political press surveillance rules and practices. It further showed that *Narodovolets* was published in Russian also, because it was meant to travel back to Burtsev's home country in the hope of influencing local politics there. Indeed, it was not by accident that the journal had been published on thin paper and in small octavo format but rather, it was to make it easier to transport into Russia for illicit distribution. And of course, the Russian Department of Police was well aware of Burtsev's intentions in this regard.[20] Moreover, the most offensive passages were not the editor's own but merely quotations from a work by Stepniak-Kravchinsky – a stratagem which aimed to shield Burtsev against murder charges. These objections, however, were quickly overruled. Inspector Melville himself was then called and was happy to perjure himself on not one but two occasions in order to ensure that the defendant would be found guilty. First, he denied knowing that, since his escape from Siberia, Burtsev had been pursued throughout Europe by agents of the Russian government and secondly, when, asked, 'Have you heard that he has been the object of Russian spies and informers in this country?', the Chief Inspector again answered in the negative.[21] In any event, long before the arrest, legal opinion on the likelihood of a successful prosecution had already been sought and, no one expected there to be much chance of acquittal. It came as little surprise therefore, when the defendant was handed down the maximum sentence permissible by law of eighteen months hard labour with solitary confinement.

Thus, it was that Burtsev became the first Russian revolutionary to be imprisoned in Britain. Clearly, much had changed in the country in the last decade of the nineteenth century. Whereas the fugitive Burtsev had been feted as a persecuted hero upon his arrival in London in 1891, there was no major public outcry at his trial a mere seven years later.[22] On the contrary, *The Times*, making no mention of the lawfulness or otherwise of the proceedings, thundered out its own verdict on the outcome:

> The justification of the jury in finding him guilty and of the judge in sentencing him to eighteen months imprisonment is that no one is to be excused for publishing as to a foreign sovereign that which would be highly criminal in regard to a private person. The prisoner pleads for one law for all in his own country: this equality of treatment is meted out to him here.[23]

During his time in London, Burtsev had ploughed a solitary furrow, having little contact with any member of the émigré political community outside his closest circle of friends. In this instance, however, he did attract their support. On the whole, the London émigrés and many in the British liberal establishment were appalled by the judge's severity. Prince Kropotkin's anarchist journal *Freedom* devoted an editorial to the case, commenting acidly that the trial and sentence was 'to our mind one of the worst judicial scandals that has happened in many a year'.[24] Members of the Russian Free Press Fund were likewise convinced that it had been a purely political trial, directed by a biased and unreliable judge.[25] It was Felix Volkhovsky's judgment that 'The whole affair from beginning to end was not one of justice, nor was it even one of a necessity to enforce law, but merely a matter of political convenience of the moment. It was thought imperatively necessary to pay a visible compliment to one of "our neighbours" at the lowest possible cost'.²⁶

The wider implication of the court's verdict was clear for all to see. Burtsev's main line of defence had failed. The claim that his newspaper had been published in a foreign language and was therefore evidently intended for a non-British readership had been roundly dismissed as irrelevant by judge and jury. The law courts had in effect delivered a stark warning to all publishers and editors of foreign-language journals based in Britain.

Public outcry at censoring Burtsev and *Narodovolets*: beyond community sympathy?

A month after sentence had been passed, demonstrations were held in Trafalgar Square and Clerkenwell Green where speeches were made calling for a complete amnesty for Burtsev and all other 'political prisoners'.²⁷ Extracts were read from Stepniak's 'Nihilism as It Is', with the speaker reminding the audience that, whereas Burtsev had been sentenced for simply quoting from this work, neither the author nor publisher of the book had ever been prosecuted. While the crowd was certainly in agreement with this sentiment, a newspaper reporter present felt obliged to point out that public interest in the case was 'not of an overwhelming character', as evidenced by the fact that a collection on the day could raise no more than a paltry fifteen shillings and tenpence ha'penny.²⁸

However, prior to the trial, not all in the Russian émigré community had been sympathetic to Burtsev's plight. Indeed, there were those who behaved in an openly antagonistic manner towards him. One such was Jaakoff Prelooker who, by his own admission, had been:

> a humble schoolmaster, never inciting anyone to revolutionary actions against the government, even opposing, when opportunity presented itself, terrorist enterprises as useless, and harmful to the cause itself, preaching only a religious reformation to my people, disseminating ideas of reconciliation between creed and creed, class and class, man and man.²⁹

He stood, in other words, at the opposite end of the political spectrum from Burtsev and yet, the Russian authorities had made life 'too hot' even for him. Since his arrival in Britain, he had continued to preach his gospel and to 'point out the dangers of all ill-calculated attempts at violent revolution'.³⁰ It is not surprising, therefore, that in January 1898, as Burtsev awaited trial, far from coming out in support of him, Prelooker published a vicious attack:

> We have to oppose strongly the policy by which the party of Russians, represented by Mr Bourtzeff, believes to be able to attain the ends it has in view ... Leaving ethics and speculative theories aside, we ask Mr Bourtzeff's sympathisers and

supporters, what practical ends do they hope to attain by preaching a reign of terror in Russia and inciting to regicide? In our conviction the propaganda of terror does certainly only harm and no good whatever and is defeating its own ends.[31]

That said, the following month, Prelooker, at least, had the decency to publish a circular from the Society of Friends of Russian Freedom (SFRF) announcing the establishment of the Burtsev Defence Fund and to agree, grudgingly, that the accused at least deserved a fair trial.[32] But then, suddenly, in the March issue of his journal, Prelooker changed tack completely. Taking advantage of the fact his paper was published in English, he addressed his British readership and, in a lengthy article, highly critical of the sentence passed on the accused, he proclaimed:

> Bourtzeff is no enemy of society but wants to see society controlled by equal laws of justice and humanity. He is himself guided by no murderous instincts, but on the contrary by the highest motives of humanity, by that spirit of self-abnegation which was bequeathed to the world on Golgotha. He is exposing himself to greatest personal danger that others may be raised from the terrible slavery and suffering.[33]

What had caused this sudden change in attitude remains a mystery. As far as is known, at no later point did Prelooker attempt to explain his sudden Damascene conversion. It is doubtful whether the confirmed atheist Burtsev would have welcomed the comparison to Christ but, be that as it may, he would have been glad to have found a new devoted follower in Prelooker. The latter felt Burtsev's defence should have raised the case of the revolutionary Vera Zasulich whom, in 1878, a Russian jury had acquitted of attempted murder and who, fearing re-arrest, had later sought refuge in London.[34] Prelooker wondered whether a British jury would now be asked to prosecute *her* on behalf of the tsar. He continued:

> As the British government cannot or will not plead on behalf of the oppressed people of Russia, it ought not to interfere on behalf of the oppressors. We cannot help feeling that, under a Liberal government in England, Russian autocracy would not have ventured the experiment.[35]

This further conversion of the proselyte Prelooker to Burtsev's cause serves as proof of the strength of support that the hapless refugee's imprisonment had engendered among the émigré community. What, Prelooker wondered, would be the practical consequences of Burtsev's eighteen months' hard labour?

> If Siberia has not shaken his faith in the righteousness of his cause, an English prison will not do it, and on leaving it he will be only a still more determined and more skilful conspirator. Having been known to a few only before, he will now be admired by millions with hearts beating for oppressed and downtrodden humanity. The prosecution and punishment have not weakened, but decidedly strengthened, the cause both in Russia and even in England.[36]

Prelooker was correct in every respect, including his prediction of an increase in support from the British public. He returned to the case in the April issue of his journal but, this time, confined himself to publishing extracts from the March number of *Free Russia*, the English-language journal of the SFRF, including the opinion of a reader from Manchester, that 'it would be a sad day for liberty generally should England descend to the level of France and become a servant of the secret police of the tsar'.[37] This correspondent was by no means the only Englishman to come out in support of Burtsev and to berate the British Conservative government for its act of betrayal.

Burtsev's friends redoubled their efforts to get him out of prison. Numerous interpellations were addressed to Lord Salisbury with Liberal politicians like Charles Dilke (1843–1911) and John Morley (1838–1923) interceding personally with the ministers on his behalf both individually and in parliament but to no avail.[38] Undaunted, his friends persevered. A year into his sentence, a number of Burtsev's supporters, including the English Liberal politician and President of the SFRF Robert Spence Watson (1837–1911), other members of the SFRF and such notables as C. P. Scott, the Liberal-Radical editor of the *Manchester Guardian*, petitioned Home Secretary Sir Matthew White Ridley (1842–1904), pleading once more for the remainder of the prisoner's sentence to be remitted. But again the Secretary of State rejected the plea out of hand.[39] Tsar Nicholas, it would appear, had stipulated that Burtsev should serve his sentence to the last day.

When *The Anglo-Russian* and *Narodovolets* converge: serving the cause of unity in different languages

Although it is not entirely clear what had caused Prelooker's conversion, it would appear that, following Burtsev's release from prison in the summer of 1899 and his departure thereafter for Paris, their association lapsed temporarily. By January 1904, however, the two had renewed contact.[40] What the exact subject of their correspondence was is unknown, although, based on the contents of the February edition of *The Anglo-Russian*, one can assume that Burtsev had forwarded Prelooker some of his publications. They received the following brief but not entirely unsympathetic review:

> 'Down with the Tsar', 'From the Past', and 'The Will of the People' are three collections of various articles by extreme Russian revolutionists, chiefly by Mr Vladimir Bourtzeff. What is the strength at present of this Russian Party numerically we do not know, but it is clear that Russian terrorists are quite active and form no very small section of the Russian opposition. Of this we can judge by the number of publications they are able to issue, and by the financial contributions to their funds published in these periodicals.[41]

The 'party of terrorists' was certainly gaining in popularity, helped in no small measure by the continuing successful political assassinations carried out by the Combat Organization of the Party of Socialists-Revolutionaries (SRs). Burtsev was, as ever, critical of some SR policies but, nevertheless, continued to call on the opposition to unite. Prelooker, too, had published an appeal for unity and asked for comments from his fellow émigrés, which he duly received.[42] In the March 1904 issue, among other responses published was a letter from Burtsev, whose attitude was generally supportive, though critical of the author for putting the idea forward as if it had never been advocated before. The criticism was humbly accepted.[43]

Russian, a revolutionary language standing for liberty?

But, as well as having opened up a public debate, the two had also been in private communication. A few months earlier, in an attempt to widen the readership of his journal, Prelooker had even started to include a few pages in Russian, which may have positioned him closer to Burtsev in the eyes of British and Russian authorities, as well as Russian émigré readers in Britain. Regarding language, Burtsev's personal file at the Russian State Archive of Social and Political History (RGASPI) contains a fascinating letter from Prelooker dated 14 February 1904.[44] One section reads as follows:

> With regard to an English publication of episodes from your life – escape from Siberia, attempted arrest in Constantinople, experiences in an English prison – I doubt you will find an English publisher, thanks to your reputation as a dangerous man, and I am almost sure they would not give you an advance but I, personally, would very much like to give you the possibility of continuing your literary works in peace and here is what I propose: that you write a plain narrative of the above episodes without getting argumentative and defending terrorist methods; I will then translate them into English and try to get them published; if I do not succeed then I will publish them in my own paper. I will pay you £25 for an article and advance you £4 per month which will allow you to work quietly for six months in the country.

Interestingly, along with the English translation, what was suggested here was the necessary softening of Burtsev's revolutionary past. Having made this most generous offer, Prelooker then continued with the following intriguing observation:

> I agree that all possible forceful means should be used to deal with a strong enemy, but I recommend you be practical and wise as a snake. I think Volkhovsky was right to try to defend you in the way he did: *keeping quiet about certain undertakings. There will be time enough to talk about these when you are no longer amongst the living.*[45]

What did Prelooker mean by these 'certain undertakings'? It is tempting to conclude that he knew some dark secret of Burtsev's. Was the latter, indeed, a practising terrorist as the Russian police had always claimed rather than a merely theoretical one? It was certainly the belief of Rachkovsky's successor in Paris, Leonid Rataev that Burtsev was not only mixed up in terrorist plotting but was one of the key organizers of these conspiracies.⁴⁶ This, stands in stark contrast to the view of other commentators who believed that, although he was 'venerated by the younger generation of insurgents for his past achievements and his present propaganda services, Burtsev was considered too meek and gentle to mix into current terrorist plotting. He was never a member of any of the revolutionary committees nor admitted to the inner councils. He was, above all, not privy to the dead secrecy of assassination conspiracies'.⁴⁷

Based on available archival documents, it is impossible to say with certainty which of these two opinions is correct, although one can, of course, speculate. From the moment of Burtsev's arrival in Paris, Foreign Agency chief Rataev and the Russian Ambassador had been keen to impress on the French government that this was not just any revolutionary they were dealing with, but a terrorist of the most dangerous sort. Their main contact in Paris at that time, Maurice Paléologue, then Deputy Director of Political Affairs at the Foreign Ministry, recalled Rataev claiming that, in December 1901, Burtsev had actually been one of the founders of the Combat Organization, an allegation he would repeat at a later date. Bearing in mind that one of the other co-founders named was the arch provocateur Evno Azef and that Rataev had inherited the services of the latter as an informer, one may conclude that his assertion concerning Burtsev's involvement might carry some weight.⁴⁸ On the other hand, it is difficult to conceive of Burtsev as some kind of secret member of the Party of Socialists-Revolutionaries and, consequently, almost impossible to imagine him as a member of such a clandestine subgroup. Further, not a single reference is made to Burtsev's membership of the Combat Organization in the memoirs of those most intimately associated with it such as Gershuni, Savinkov, Chernov and Nikolaevsky.⁴⁹ However that may be, the Russian government continued to exert pressure and demand the revolutionary's expulsion. Burtsev was obliged, therefore, to leave Paris for his own safety and duly arrived back in London in June 1904.

The Britain that Burtsev found that summer may, initially, have appeared more welcoming than it had for some time past. Prelooker, for one, thought he detected a decrease in Russophobia from when he had first started publication of his journal in 1897, writing that:

> newspapers notorious hitherto for their strong anti-Russian sentiments now begin to explain that for the Russian people they cherish but the kindliest feelings and best wishes and their Russophobia is directed exclusively against the iniquitous system of Russian autocratic and bureaucratic government for which the people are not responsible in the least.⁵⁰

In the recent past, there had been no shortage of examples of the Russian government's excesses for the British press to report on, for instance, the appalling massacres of Jews at Kishinev in April 1903.⁵¹ An interesting illustration of how far the tsarist regime had fallen out of favour with the British public was to be found in how the press chose to report the departure from public life of one of Nicholas's most loyal British servants.

News of the retirement of Chief Inspector William Melville, the 'most celebrated detective of the day', first appeared in *The Times* in November 1903.⁵² While mentioning Melville's duties as bodyguard to visiting dignitaries such as the German emperor and the French president, the newspaper correspondent carefully avoided any reference to his past services to the tsars of Russia. Then, some six months later, in May 1904, Melville received a most impressive testimonial at City Hall Westminster.[53] If press reports are to be believed, almost every foreign embassy in the land either was present at the ceremony or was a signatory to the address presented to him, again, with the notable exception of that of Russia.[54]

Whether, in fact, there was a Russian presence and the press simply chose not to report it in order to avoid any awkwardness for Melville is not recorded but two years later the *Daily Express* was not a bit concerned at the possibility of causing embarrassment when it reported 'on Russian authority' that the ex-Superintendent had joined the tsar's police, following an approach from his old friend 'Ratshkovsky'.[55] This 'scoop' was retracted a few days later when they received Melville's rebuttal in which he stated that he was still in London enjoying his retirement and was, 'content to follow revolutionary movements through the medium of his daily paper. He found the assertion that he had entered the service of another government, which service might at any moment bring him into conflict with his own country, both unfair and offensive'.[56]

Hostile though the British press may have been to the Russian tsar and his secret police, and sympathetic to those of his subjects who were forced into exile, this could not disguise the fact that xenophobia in general was on the increase in the country and that calls for immigration controls were now attracting more popular support than at any time. As early as 1900, the 'rapidly recurring murders of kings and presidents' on the continent had given rise to calls not only for further legislation to deal with the anarchist problem but for increased international police cooperation and surveillance.[57] At the same time, interest had been renewed in proposals for an Aliens Bill. Following the return of Salisbury's government to power in November 1900, Conservative MP for Stepney, Major W. E. Evans-Gordon, set up a Parliamentary Committee on Alien Immigration that, within the year, had reported on its fears of a rise in anti-Semitic feeling in the country and had contacted the prime minister with the recommendation that the reintroduction of his 1894 Bill would go a long way to checking the rise of such a movement.[58]

Evans-Gordon and his followers in the proto-fascist 'British Brothers' League' (slogan: 'England for the English') playing on fears of unemployment, housing shortages and an increase in crime, attracted much support in London's East End (and, indeed, elsewhere in the country) with their demands for the restriction of immigration of destitute foreigners and, in particular, East European Jews.[59] Salisbury himself gave the proposal his backing but did not live to see the legislation come into force. In poor health, he resigned as Prime Minister in July 1902 and was succeeded by his nephew, Arthur James Balfour, who set about guiding his uncle's Bill through parliament.[60] The Bill, however, would not have a smooth passage.

Among its opponents were, of course, the SFRF and Jaakoff Prelooker. The May 1904 issue of *The Anglo-Russian* carried a letter calling for a protest to be drawn up, 'signed by such men and women of England who love their country'. The journalist gladly restated his opposition to the proposed Bill and his willingness to support such a protest.[61] On this occasion, the Liberal opposition in parliament proved strong enough and the Bill was eventually talked out at Committee stage.[62] The SFRF would later express the view that the success of such a Bill would constitute 'a reversal of the old traditions of offering asylum to the victims of political or religious persecution which has been one of the chief glories of our country in times past'.[63] In the summer of 1904, Burtsev, having again had cause to give thanks to Britain in its role as the sole European refuge for the politically oppressed, would, doubtless, have concurred.

Appraising Burtsev: 'The Nestor of the Russian Revolutionary Movement'

In August, following the reopening of the French parliament, Burtsev was advised that it was now safe for him to return to Paris.[64] He duly said his farewells to his London comrades and set off back across the Channel. Shortly after his departure, Prelooker considered it appropriate to publish an appreciation of his good friend – a valedictory of sorts – for the benefit of his British readers. The November issue of *The Anglo-Russian* duly appeared carrying a photographic half-portrait of the revolutionary on its front page over the caption: 'M. Vladimir Bourtzeff. The Nestor of the Russian Revolutionary Movement'. A positively glowing biographical sketch of the man was contained within. Having described Burtsev's great political and literary achievements, Prelooker ended with the following effusive tribute:

> Nothing can break his determination and devotion to the cause. Extremely gentle, humane, unassuming, and industrious in his private life, conscientious to a scrupulous degree, and sacrificing his whole life to the work for the amelioration of the condition of the Russian people, he is at the same time the most irreconcilable foe of Russian autocracy, for the destruction of which he believes all means are permissible. In the eyes of the Russian government he is one of the most dangerous Nihilists, in those of the revolutionists he is a saint and martyr for the national cause.[65]

Prelooker, however, had overestimated the degree of danger to the autocracy which his friend now posed. Owing to ill-health and lack of funds, Burtsev's journalistic activities had now ceased and, by the end of the year, the Russian Department of Police had all but lost interest in him as a serious terrorist threat. The Sûreté, also, had ceased to file anything of importance concerning him for some time and as for Scotland Yard, from available files, it would appear they too had lost interest in this 'dangerous Nihilist' long before his departure from London in August 1904. The Okhrana had long since refocused its attentions on what it had identified as the real threat to the person of his majesty and his empire: namely, the emergence of a unified political opposition coupled with the growth in strength and popularity of the Party of Socialists-Revolutionaries and its Combat Organization. Following the assassination of Plehve, A. L. von Aehrenthal (1854–1912, the Austrian ambassador to St Petersburg, summarized the prevailing mood in the country thus:

> The most striking aspect of the present situation is the total indifference of society to an event which constituted a heavy blow to the principles of the government. I

have found only totally indifferent people or people so cynical that they say no other outcome was to be expected. People are prepared to say that further catastrophes similar to Plehve's murder will be necessary in order to bring about a change of mind on part of the highest authority.[66]

And further catastrophes there were, such as the assassination of the tsar's own uncle, Grand Duke Sergei.[67] It is interesting to note that, when recording this murder in his diary, Paléologue, while condemning the Combat Organization, at the same time admitted the brutality of the Russian regime.[68] Many, who had previously been firmly opposed to violent political action, were now in the process of re-evaluating their position. One such was Prelooker, who later wrote:

> Who can wonder that as the Russian persecutors make a law unto themselves and slay their victims in their thousands, so also amongst the millions of persecuted Russians there will always be found groups or even individuals who, too, will take the law into their own hands and avenge their slaughtered brothers and sisters?[69]

Prelooker, that former confirmed law-abiding pacifist, had come full circle and had now apparently fallen completely under Burtsev's spell. At the same time, he continued to do his best on the pages of his journal to fight the rise in anti-alienism but could not prevent the Aliens Bill passing into law on 1 January 1906. As it would transpire, the new legislation was of little concern to the Russian émigré community since most of them (including Burtsev in Paris) had rushed back to their homeland at the end of 1905 to continue the fight after Tsar Nicholas had been forced by impending revolution to offer a number of concessions. Prelooker, however, decided to stay behind in his adopted country and actually took up British nationality a few years later. He simply did not have the staying power to maintain the struggle against the tsar and instead began to devote more time to his other favoured causes – such as women's rights and pacifism, but after a few years he seemed to have tired even of these. In March 1913, when his journal was obliged to change from a monthly to a quarterly due to a fall in circulation, he wrote, 'I feel as if I had practically said all I had to say of interest both to Russian and to Englishmen', and indeed *The Anglo-Russian* would cease publication the following year.[70]

Burtsev, on the other hand, was made of stronger stuff and would see the fight through to the end. Before setting out on his escape from Siberian exile, the young revolutionary had left behind a letter addressed to the Russian government which concluded with the following defiant challenge:

> I am making my escape to fight against you to the death. If you succeed in catching me, so much the better for you. For I give you warning that if I get free I shall arouse the vengeance of the oppressed against you![71]

He would remain true to his word and it is fair to say that the name of the religious pacifist Jaakoff Prelooker could also be included, at least for a short while, in the long list of those he inspired into action.

Notes

1. This contribution contains edited extracts from the author's unpublished PhD thesis (*Vladimir Burtsev and the Russian Revolutionary Emigration: Surveillance of Foreign Political Refugees in London, 1891–1905*. Queen Mary, University of London, 2008), parts of which were later incorporated in R. Henderson's *Vladimir Burtsev and the Struggle for a Free Russia: A Revolutionary in the Time of Tsarism and Bolshevism* (London: Bloomsbury Academic, 2017).
2. John Slatter, 'The Russian Émigré Press in Britain, 1853–1917', *Slavonic and East European Review* 73, no. 4 (1995): 716–47. For an overview of some of the major titles published during this period, see Charlotte Alston, 'News of the Struggle: The Russian Political Press in London 1853–1921', in *The Foreign Political Press in Nineteenth-Century London: Politics from a Distance*, ed. Constance Bantman and Ana Claudia Suriani da Silva (London: Bloomsbury Academic, 2018), 155–74.
3. Slatter, 'Russian émigré press': 719.
4. *Svobodnaia Rossiia*, nos. 1–3 (February–May 1889).
5. *Nedelia* (St. Petersburg, 1866–1903); *Odesskii listok* (Odessa, 1880–1920); *Allgemeine Zeitung* (Munich, 1798–1925).
6. John Slatter, 'Among British Liberals. Jaakoff Prelooker and the Anglo-Russian', *Immigrants and Minorities* 2, no. 3 (November 1983): 53.
7. *The Anglo-Russian* 1, no. 1, 1897, 1.
8. Little is known of Beitner other than a brief biographical note in L. P. Men´shchikov (ed.), *Russkii politicheskii sysk za granitsei. Chast´ 1 (Sekretnye doneseniia departamentu politsii Rachkovskago, Rataeva, i Gartinga, zavedyvaiushchikh rozysknoi agenturoi)* (Paris: L. Menstschikoff, 1914), 203, 213, note 130. For a detailed account of Burtsev's struggles with the Russian imperial police during his first years in emigration, see the author's PhD thesis, *Vladimir Burtsev and the Russian Revolutionary Emigration: Surveillance of Foreign Political Refugees in London, 1891–1905*. Queen Mary, University of London, 2008.
9. Documents concerning the relationship between the two senior policemen are held at the Hoover Institution on War Revolution and Peace, Russia, Departament Politsii, Zagranichnaia Agentura, Paris (Okhrana) Collection. 35/V/c/Folders 1–4, 'Relations with Scotland Yard'.
10. Gosudarstvennyi arkhiv Rossiiskoi Federatsii (State Archive of Russian Federation), Moscow, f. 102. D. 3. op. 88 (1890 g.) Del 569, T. 4. Burtsev to Gringmut, 21 December 1896, 226–7. Also, T. L. Panteleeva, 'Obshchestvenno-politicheskaia i izdatel´skaia deiatel´nost´ V. L. Burtseva, 1882–1907 gg', Moskovskii Gosudarstvennyi Universitet, Kandidatskaia Dissertatsiia, 1998, 121–2.
11. The *Partiia narodnoi voli* had come into existence in 1879 when the populist revolutionary society *Zemlia i volia* (Land and Freedom) split in two. The other faction *Chernyi peredel* (Black Partition) eschewed terror in favour of increased propaganda among the peasants and workers.
12. *Narodovolets*, no. 1 (April 1897), 11. S. M. Kravchinsky (pseud. Stepniak, 1851–1895) was a Russian revolutionary, writer and leading figure in the emigration until his untimely death. (The term 'revolutionist' was a commonly used synonym of 'revolutionary' throughout the nineteenth century.)
13. In total, four issues of the journal were published. Nos 1–3 in London in 1897 and a fourth in Geneva in 1903.

14 *Narodovolets*, no. 1 (April 1897), 12. A. I. Zheliabov (1851–1881) and S. L. Perovskaia (1853–1881) were founder members of the Executive Committee of the People's Will. They were sentenced to death for their role in the assassination of Alexander II. S. N. Khalturin (1856–1882) was responsible for an earlier attempt on the tsar's life. He too received a death sentence the following year for the murder of procurator V. S. Strel´nikov.
15 Ibid., 14–15.
16 Robert Gascoyne-Cecil, 3rd Marquess of Salisbury (1830–1903), served three terms as Prime Minister: from 1885 to 1886, from 1886 to 1892 and from 1895 to 1902. A few months before the Burtsev trial, France had made public its hitherto secret alliance with Russia which had been signed in 1894. It was in part due to the threat posed by this new and powerful partnership that Salisbury had been obliged to review his policy towards Russia and adopt one of appeasement.
17 V. Burtsev, *Doloi tsaria!* (London, 1905), 43.
18 The arrest was reported throughout the British and European press and also in America. See for example, 'Police Courts', *The Times*, 17 December 1897, 11; 'Nihilist Editors in London', *The New York Times*, 23 December 1897, 9. The affair was raised in the House of Commons by concerned MPs on a number of occasions both before and after the trial. See for example *Hansard*, House of Commons Debate, 'The Bourtzev Case', 21 February 1898, vol. 53.
19 V. Burtsev, *Bor'ba za svobodnuiu rossiiu* (Berlin, 1923), 133.
20 Some years earlier, telegrams had been sent to all Russian ports warning of Burtsev's possible return and giving detailed instructions on how to conduct a search – looking out for false-bottomed cases and, in particular, making sure to search under collars. See Gosudarstvennyi arkhiv Rossiiskoi Federatsii f. 102. D. 3. op. 88 (1890 g.) Del 569, T. 1. ll. 14–16, 21 November 1890.
21 Treasury Solicitor and Director of Public Prosecutions Office, The National Archives (TNA), Kew, London, DPP 4/32 ff. 175, 176.
22 'English Sympathy for Russian Refugees', *The Times*, 13 January 1891, 3. Also Tribute to Captain Rees, of the Steamship Ashlands', *The Times*, 19 January 1891, 7.
23 'Editorial', *The Times*, 14 February 1898, 7.
24 'A Condemnation for Opinion: The case of Vladimir Bourtzev', *Freedom*, March 1898, 12.
25 'Delo Burtseva', *Letuchie Listki* no. 42 (23 March 1898), 7.
26 Quoted in 'Bourtzeff's Case Again', *The Anglo-Russian* 1, no. 10 (April 1898), 112. F. V. Volkhovsky (1846–1914) was an influential London émigré and a close friend of Stepniak whom he succeeded as editor of the SFRF's journal *Free Russia*
27 'Socialism', *Reynolds's Newspaper*, 27 March 1898, 1.
28 Ibid., also 3; 'Socialism', *Reynolds's Newspaper*, 10 April 1898, 1.
29 Prelooker, J. *Under the Czar and Queen Victoria* (London: Nisbet, 1895), 160.
30 *The Anglo-Russian* 1, no. 7 (January 1898), 78.
31 Ibid., 79–80: 'Foolish Schemes of Russian Revolutionists'. There are no hard and fast rules as to how to transliterate words from the Cyrillic to the Latin alphabet. Other variations of the name encountered include 'Burcev', 'Bourtzev' and 'Bortsoff'.
32 'For Justice and Liberty', *The Anglo-Russian* 1, no. 8 (February 1898), 86.
33 'Tsar and Man: Russian v. English Juries', *The Anglo-Russian* 1, no. 9 (March 1898), 99–100.
34 V. I. Zasulich (1851–1919). In 1878, she had been acquitted by the jury at her trial for the attempted assassination of the Governor of St Petersburg.

35 *The Anglo-Russian*, vol. I, no. 7 (January 1898), 78.
36 Ibid.
37 'Bourtzeff's Case Again', *The Anglo-Russian*, vol. 1. no. 10 (April 1898), 112.
38 *The New York Times*, 5 September 1909, SM4: 'The Man Who Unmasked the Spies of the Czar'.
39 TNA, PRO HO 144/A59222B/23: R. S. Watson to M. White Ridley, 27 January 1899.
40 Rossiiskii gosudarstvennyi arkhiv sotsial'no-poiticheskoi istorii (RGASPI), f. 328, op. 1, ed. khr. 58: Prelooker to Burtsev c/o P. Akselrod, 13 January 1904.
41 *The Anglo-Russian* 7, no. 8 (February 1904), 796.
42 Ibid., 793–5. 'There is a need for an anti-governmental government and a non-party party: Russians, Poles, Jews, Finns, Armenians, Latvians, Lithuanians and others, unite!'
43 The *Anglo-Russian* 7, no. 9 (March 1904), 806–7.
44 RGASPI, f. 328, op. 1, ed. khr. 59.
45 Ibid., emphasis added.
46 Maurice Paléologue, *The Turning Point. Three Critical Years, 1904–1906* (London: Hutchinson and Co, 1935), 102.
47 Rita T. Kronenbitter, 'The Sherlock Holmes of the Revolution', in *Okhrana: The Paris Operations of the Russian Imperial Police*, ed. Ben B. Fischer (Washington: History Staff of the Center for the Study of Intelligence, CIA, DIANE Publishing, 1999), 47.
48 Paléologue, *The Turning Point*, 60–1.
49 G. A. Gershuni (1870–1908), B. V. Savinkov (1879–1925), V. M. Chernov and B. I. Nikolaevsky (1887–1966) were senior members of the Party of Socialists-Revolutionaries.
50 'Our Seventh Anniversary', *The Anglo-Russian* 7, no. 12 (June–July 1904), 844–5.
51 For a detailed examination of the events, see E. H. Judge, *Easter in Kishinev: Anatomy of a Pogrom* (New York: New York University Press, 1992).
52 'Retirement of Superintendent Melville', *The Times*, 10 November 1903, 9. For a description of Melville's later role as the founding father of MI5, see Andrew Cook, *MI5's First Spymaster* (Stroud: Tempus, 2004).
53 An Executive Committee set up to organize his testimonial included among its members Sir Arthur Conan Doyle. See 'Testimonial to Superintendent Melville', *The Times*, 1 January 1904, 5.
54 'Court Circular', *The Times*, 18 May 1904, 5.
55 'To Spy on Russia's Enemies – Ex-Superintendent Melville Joins the Czar's Police Force', *The Daily Express*, 28 February 1906, 2.
56 'Superintendent Melville', *The Daily Express*, 2 March 1906, 5.
57 See, for example, *The Birmingham Daily Post*, 7 August 1900, 5. Attempts had already been made on the lives of, among others, the Prince of Wales and on the Shah of Persia, while in July, Italian anarchists had succeeded in murdering King Umberto I.
58 'Alien Immigration', *The Times*, 28 August 1901, 5.
59 'The Unwanted, the Unfed, and the Unemployed', *The Manchester Evening Chronicle*, 19 April 1905, 2.
60 Salisbury died a year after his resignation, on 22 August 1903.
61 *The Anglo-Russian* 7, no. 11 (May 1904), 834.
62 'House of Commons. Monday, July 11', *The Times*, 12 July 1904, 6. So many amendments were being tabled that the Bill was estimated to be making progress at the rate of half a line a day.
63 *The Anglo-Russian* 9, no. 5 (June 1905), 946.

64 RGASPI f. 328, op. 1, ed. khr. 66: I. Rubanovich to Burtsev c/o Teplov, 12 August 1904, l. 2.
65 *The Anglo-Russian* 8, no. 11 (November 1904), 859 and 863.
66 Quoted in Abraham Ascher, *The Revolution of 1905: Russia in Disarray* (Stanford: Stanford University Press, 1988), 54.
67 Grand Duke Sergei Aleksandrovich (1857–1905) was killed on 4 (17) February by the SR Ivan Kaliaev.
68 Paléologue, *The Turning Point*, 191. Diary entry for 19 February 1905. He expanded on this theme in his entry for 30 March 1905, in which he also repeated his belief that Burtsev was one of the leaders of the Combat Organization. Ibid., 213–14.
69 Jaakoff, Prelooker, *Under the Russian and British Flags. A Story of True Experience* (London: Spriggs Publishing Agency, 1912), 147–8.
70 *The Anglo-Russian*, New Series, 1 (March 1913), 6. Quoted in Slatter, 'Among British Liberals', 61.
71 'The Man Who Unmasked The Spies Of The Czar', *The New York Times*, 29 August 1909, 1.

15

Le Haïasdan, L'Arménie, Armenia and *Hnch'ak*: Language Choice and the Construction of a Cosmopolitan Armenian Diasporic Identity in London and Paris (1888–1905)

Stéphanie Prévost
Université Paris Cité/Institut Universitaire de France

The history of the Armenian-language press has always largely been transnational and exogenous to Armenia as a political region/space, a trend which was tragically accelerated by the Armenian Genocide of 1915 and the dispersion of the Armenian diaspora. For instance, the first-ever Armenian-language periodical *Azdarar* (The Monitor) was published in British-controlled Madras in 1794, under the editorship of Harutyun Shmavonian. *Azdarar* only ran for eighteen monthly issues (1794–6), with only about forty subscribers and a fierce local opposition from part of the Armenian Madras community. Despite its short life, *Azdarar* has been central in the history of Armenian-language publishing as it articulated questions of language and national identity. The last issue of *Azdarar* included an engraving of an air-balloon, which metaphorically sketched the forthcoming historical journey of the Armenian-language press.[1] By making the Armenian-language press a vector for the development of an Armenian identity, the engraving presented *Azdarar* as a forerunner both for Armenians in the Ottoman Empire (where most Armenians lived at the time) and in the diaspora.

Yet having a press organ in the language of an immigrant/exile community is often less straightforward than is assumed, as this volume shows. Armenian editors based in London at the turn of the twentieth century pondered over the issue of having organs in Armenian there. In so doing, they fuelled the debate over which language to use in their organs. This contribution will thus further probe into the bond between the Armenian language and Armenianness at a time when Armenian nationalism entered a new phase and when some European theories of nationalism – like that of Ernest Renan in France – looked to language as the cement of nations, including of nations in the making. In combining local and more global perspectives, this chapter will take the example of the three main Armenian periodicals published in London at the time – namely *Le Haïasdan*/ՀԱՅԱՍՏԱՆ (bilingual French-Armenian, 1888–92), *Armenia*

(English version of *L'Arménie*, 1889–1905) and *Hnch'ak* (The Bell, Armenian, 1894–1905) – to reflect on the attraction of London as a hotbed for Armenian political publishing, whereas the size of the community over the period remained small (a few hundred at the most). After a brief review of how diasporic periodicals contributed to fostering Armenianness and the Armenian nation during the nineteenth century, the second section will pay attention to debates within those London-based papers over language use for serials that embraced cosmopolitanism. Focusing more specifically on *Le Haïasdan*, the third section will address the technical constraints to publishing in Armenian, as more or less inherent to non-Latin script periodical printing. Finally, the last section of this contribution will discuss the benefits and setbacks of publishing an Armenian-language periodical in London in that high time of Armenian nationalism. It will position editors and organs within the broader context of Ottoman-British surveillance of the foreign political press and against the backdrop of late-nineteenth-century British Armenophilia.

Articulating Armenianness through diasporic periodicals

After the unfulfilled promises of a representative Ottoman polity, the development of a more exclusive form of Ottoman nationalism under the reign of Ottoman Sultan Abdul Hamid II from 1876 strengthened a burning feeling for an all-Armenian nationalism on the part of a younger generation of Armenian nationalists in the 1880s. This was particularly strong in the diaspora, so that the 1880s saw urges for an Armenian nation not only in Ottoman Armenia, but also in Persia, Russia, as well as elsewhere, especially in Britain and in the United States. As historian Aram Arkun contended, 'within each of the three empires [Ottoman, Persian, Russian], a standard [Armenian] written language, schooling, books and newspapers created a new type of unity'.[2] The Armenian periodical press published across the three historical empires that had an Armenian population and in the larger world played a crucial role in that process, as Lisa Khachaturian's *Cultivating Nationhood in Imperial Russia* (2009) demonstrates for Armenian-language serials appearing in Tsarist Russia.[3]

Born out of Armenian political activity and of intellectual exchanges between Armenian nationalists and sympathetic networks throughout the world, Armenian nationalist periodicals flourished in Russia, Georgia, Austria. This was also the case to a lesser extent in the United States, France and Britain in the 1880s, where leaders of political formations eventually found refuge. Most well-known is Mkrtitch Portugalian (1848–1921), founder of the Armenakan party in Van in 1885, whom the Ottoman government exiled to Marseilles the same year, where he published an irregular weekly *Armenia: lragir azgayin qalaqakan arevtrakan ew ayln* (Armenia: Journal in Armenian Language, 1885–1923). The paper was secretly distributed in Ottoman Armenia and actually gave the party its name. It advocated the liberation of Armenia by force, as well as the return of migrant Armenians (including economic migrants to Constantinople) to provinces of Ottoman Armenia (Van, Sivas, Bitlis, Harput, Diyarbekir, Erzurum) conceptualized as 'homeland' and which are currently in Eastern Turkey. Portugalian's hesitation in forming a revolutionary party drove certain of *Armenia*'s contributors, especially Armenian poet and political activist Avetis Nazarbekian (1866–1939), to quit what they perceived as the too moderate Armenakan and found the Marxist-leaning Hunchakian party in Geneva in 1887.[4] By late 1894, Nazarbekian relocated the seat of the party to East London, where he lived and from where he published several organs of the party, especially *Hnch'ak* (The Bell).

Whereas the diasporic space facilitated the formation of an Armenian national identity – because it could be easier to vent such ideas outside the Ottoman Empire and bypass Sultan Abdul Hamid's censorship – lack of consensus over the political project for Armenia (*Hayastan*), as well as over strategies to secure autonomy or independence for Armenia (through propaganda, or armed struggle in particular) nonetheless came to be recurrent features of turn-of-the-century Armenian nationalism and the Armenian-language press. In such a context, the preservation of Armenianness (*hayapahpanum*) and the preservation of a nation (*azgapahpanum*) fuelled imaginations of Armenia, especially for editors in exile, who also found themselves reflecting on what the exile country could represent for them and their readerships. As in the case of the rife debate between *Le Haïasdan* and *Armenia*, such conjectures implied reflecting on which language to publish in and which readership(s) to address.

Armenianness in cosmopolitan periodicals: which language for which identity?

Language choice was thus central to the construction of an Armenian diasporic identity in the late nineteenth-early twentieth centuries, but did not only revolve over which variety of Armenian to use – increasingly, diasporic titles had given up on Grabar (Classical Armenian, used especially in liturgy) for Ashkharhabar (New Armenian) which seemed more appropriate for fostering the political project of an Armenian nation. Exchanges between editorial teams of *Le Haïasdan* and *L'Arménie/Armenia* powerfully bring this to life, showing how they endeavoured to construct a distinct Armenian national identity in languages other than Armenian, while still ensuring that Armenia was mapped out as part of an imagined cosmopolitan Christian Europe, especially through the choice of literary references. The question always remained of when to use Armenian – the two serials differing in their approaches, reflecting divergent political options.

Le Haïasdan ('Armenia') ran as a bilingual French-Armenian periodical (originally bi-monthly, then monthly) between 1888 and 1892.[5] It was the organ of the Armenian Patriotic Committee, a structure formed to defend Armenian interests in the margins of the 1878 Treaty of Berlin, which ended the Russo-Turkish war. In April 1891, *Le Haïasdan* became the organ of the Anglo-Armenian Association (AAA), which had been formed in 1879 by British Liberal jurist James Bryce to highlight the plight of fellow Ottoman Armenian Christians, especially in contexts of violence. Printed in Paris for its first two issues, *Le Haïasdan* was always produced in London, where Garabed Hagopian (1850–1926), the president of the Armenian Patriotic Committee, resided and where he and *Le Haïasdan*'s editor Mihran Sevasly (1863–1935), an Armenian jurist who had left the United States for Britain, could benefit from the

Figure 15.1a and 15.1b *Le Haiasdan*, issue 1, 1 November 1888, 1 (Armenian and French versions). Courtesy of the AGBU Nubar Library, Paris.

1ʳᵉ ANNÉE — N° 1.   Paraissant le 1ᵉʳ et le 15 de chaque Mois.   1ᵉʳ NOVEMBRE 1888 (11 SAHMI 4360).

Le Haïasdan

DIRECTEUR POLITIQUE : **Jean Broussali**

RÉDACTEUR EN CHEF : **M. Sévasly**

PRIX DE L'ABONNEMENT
Grande-Bretagne et Union post.ᵉ (un an) .. 12 50
Un Numéro 0 20
Vingt-cinq Exemplaires 6 25
Annonces : la Ligne 2 50

Sous-chef de la Rédaction : **James Malcolm**

ORGANE DE L'ASSOCIATION PATRIOTIQUE ARMÉNIENNE
(Comité central : LONDRES — Président : G. HAGOPIAN)

BULLETIN

Depuis longtemps la nécessité, pour la nation arménienne, d'avoir en Europe un organe indépendant, s'étant manifestée, pour défendre efficacement sa cause, nous avons cru aujourd'hui devoir assumer cette responsabilité. Pour combler cette lacune, nous avons entrepris, au milieu de l'agitation qui règne en Arménie et dans nos sphères patriarcales de Constantinople, la publication du *Haïasdan*, qui, entouré de nos insignes nationaux, sera l'organe officiel de l'Association patriotique arménienne et de ses comités.

Nous savons combien la tâche présente de difficultés, mais nous sommes néanmoins résolus de lutter fermement contre tous les obstacles et de consacrer tous nos efforts, pour faire triompher les droits sacrés de notre patrie oubliée. Nous ne reculerons donc devant aucun sacrifice, et rien ne saura nous décourager dans cette campagne; car nous avons eu et nous aurons pour devise : *En avant toujours*.

Nous avons aussi foi dans l'appui et le concours dévoués que tous les hommes de cœur, dans le monde entier, s'empresseront de nous assurer pour faciliter notre mission.

Notre principal rôle sera de servir d'interprète entre l'Arménie et l'Europe, entre les hommes d'État, les publicistes et les organes européens, pour éclairer l'opinion publique sur les souffrances et sur les aspirations du malheureux peuple arménien, afin de lui gagner les sympathies du monde civilisé.

Nous aurons en même temps, et autant que les rigueurs de la censure nous le permettront en Turquie, à renseigner le peuple arménien, lui-même, sur la vérité des sentiments de l'Europe à son égard, et à lui inspirer les moyens pacifiques, mais fermes, par lesquels il doit revendiquer l'exécution des réformes qui lui ont été promises au Congrès de Berlin.

Pour remplir ce double but, nous publierons le *Haïasdan* dans les deux langues : française et arménienne ; la langue française étant la langue internationale de la diplomatie. Un organe simplement en arménien n'aurait pu remplir ni l'une ni l'autre de ces conditions. Inaccessible à l'Europe par son idiome et ne pouvant pénétrer dans la masse des Arméniens, par suite des mesures d'interdiction qui l'attendent aux frontières, il serait demeuré dépourvu d'autorité et de crédit. Quant aux articles détachés, publiés de temps en temps dans les journaux européens, ils ne pouvaient constituer un système régulier de défense, ne pouvant entretenir l'opinion d'une façon suivie. L'organe aura au contraire l'avantage de nous mettre à *l'évidence* ; ayant un caractère national, il sera favorablement accueilli par tous ceux qui s'intéressent à la question arménienne, et ses informations seront périodiquement reproduites par la presse européenne.

Notre politique sera à la fois ferme et conciliante. Nous nous efforcerons de revendiquer devant l'Europe, par les moyens pacifiques, d'un ton digne et loyal, la prompte réalisation de l'autonomie administrative et locale, qui a été promise à l'*Arménie turque*, par l'article 61 du traité de Berlin de 1878. Mais si nous nous engageons à ne point critiquer systématiquement la Turquie, nous n'hésiterons jamais à dénoncer la vérité, dans l'intérêt même de celle-ci. Car, tant qu'il y aura une question arménienne en suspens, la voie sera ouverte à toutes les convoitises qui gravitent autour de Constantinople. Et l'inexécution de l'article 61 constituera une menace perpétuelle pour le maintien de la paix et du *statu quo* en Orient.

En un mot, c'est pour préparer l'opinion en faveur de la question arménienne, que nous convions la nation à s'agiter et à travailler, comme en 1878 ; une crise en pouvant comme on 1878 ; une crise en pourvu pouvant éclater d'un moment à l'autre, peut-être demain.

Que tout ce qu'il y a donc d'hommes éclairés et de patriotes dans la nation, laissant l'esprit de parti et les questions de personnes de côté, se rallie autour de notre drapeau, afin que nous puissions tous, la main dans la main, travailler pour la régénération et l'émancipation de notre patrie souffrante, nous montrant ainsi dignes de notre passé et de nos glorieux ancêtres.

NOS AMIS

Plusieurs lettres d'adhésion et de sympathie nous parviennent de nos éminents amis en Europe. Nous nous empressons d'en publier deux dans le présent numéro :

JAMES BRYCE
MEMBRE DE LA CHAMBRE DES COMMUNES,
Ancien sous-secrétaire d'État aux affaires étrangères,
35, Bryanston Square, W.
London, October 9ᵗʰ 1888.

Dear Sirs,

I hear with great satisfaction that you are starting a journal devoted to the interests of the Armenian nation. The powers which signed the treaty of Berlin, after virtually engaging to deliver the Armenians from the sufferings which they have borne with unexampled constancy have until now done little or nothing to redeem the engagements formed in 1878; and it becomes necessary to call the attention of Western Europe to the most emphatic manner possible to the oppressions exercised by the Turks, the impossibility of obtaining redress against them unless by the intervention of Europe, and the dangers to the peace of the east which a continuance of the present situation will assuredly involve.

I earnestly hope that your journal may be the means of stimulating the patriotism of the Armenians every where, and of rousing the attention of Western statesmen to the duty and interest which Europe has in the prompt settlement of the Armenian question and I wish you all success in your laudable efforts.

Faithfully yours,

J. Bryce.

TRADUCTION

Chers Messieurs,

J'apprends, avec beaucoup de satisfaction, que vous allez entreprendre la publication d'un journal consacré aux intérêts friendly support of the AAA from the onset. As a matter of fact, the very existence of the AAA made London a particularly welcoming resort for Armenian political exiles and their publications in the 1880s.

By contrast to *Le Haïasdan*, *L'Arménie* and *Armenia* were one-man journalistic ventures, those of Ottoman Armenian publicist Minas Tchéraz (1852–1929), who used to teach French in Constantinople before settling in London, apparently in 1889.⁶ It is precisely the year in which *L'Arménie, journal politique et littéraire* started appearing in London on a monthly basis. An English version was added in November 1890 and with both versions appearing twice a month for a few years. *Armenia* appeared until 1898, on and off though (only two issues in 1893), mostly due to the lack of funding.⁷ Content-wise, it was more and less a translation of the French edition – with the former being distributed in English-speaking countries (Britain; the British Empire including India, Egypt and Cyprus; the United States) and the French edition being primarily circulated elsewhere (Belgium, France, Germany, Switzerland, Austria-Hungary, Italy, Russia, Servia, Bulgaria, Rumania, Turkey, Barbary, Massowah, Persia and Oceania).⁸ In the meantime, the French version sometimes included article titles in English to catch the eye of those interested in the lot of Armenians, who might not yet have been completely fluent in French.⁹ In 1898, editor-in-chief Minas Tchéraz decided to relocate his publication to Paris. Only the French edition was published there, until 1905.

Reading *Le Haïasdan/L'Arménie/Armenia* alongside reveals the centrality of cosmopolitanism for these journalistic ventures. In the minds of editors, this comes with a choice of priority languages – French and English, rather than Armenian – and of main targeted readerships, who were cast as readers of these *lingua francas/*diplomatic languages (including educated Armenians). On the surface, the cosmopolitan option might seem incompatible with the defence of Armenianness, but these two papers tell us otherwise. They surfed on the vibrant cosmopolitanism of fin-de-siècle Britain, whereby intellectual figures in Liberal and progressive circles frequented invited 'individual[s] to imagine themselves as part of a community that reache[d] beyond the geographical, political and linguistic boundaries of the nation'.¹⁰ Beyond a common goal – the implementation of article 61 of the 1878 Berlin Treaty, which promised reforms to guarantee the security of Ottoman Armenians – *Le Haïasdan* and *L'Arménie/Armenia* offer different varieties of cosmopolitanism that translated their political projects and in turn, justified their language policy.

Le Haïasdan upholds moral cosmopolitanism and frontstages an ethical cosmopolitan doctrine that 'entails first and foremost the equal and fundamental moral status of individuals and obliges us to consider the good of all humankind in our actions'.¹¹ Put differently, *Le Haïasdan* resorted to moral cosmopolitanism to remind readers that 'all persons stand in certain moral relations to one another' and that everyone, as 'citizens of the world', had a responsibility in international treaty provisions being fulfilled.¹² Such citizens needed to be 'enlightened' on Ottoman Armenians' plight. This was *Le Haïasdan*'s role, as the first issue on 1 December 1888 made clear: 'it sought to act as an intermediary between Armenia and Europe, between statesmen, publicists and European bodies, in order to enlighten public opinion about the sufferings and aspirations of the poor Armenian people and eventually win over the sympathies of the civilised world'.¹³ *Le Haïasdan* projected that the security of Ottoman

Armenians would be best guaranteed by the political and local autonomy of Ottoman Armenia, which the organ advocated and for which the Armenian Patriotic Committee banked on a cosmopolitan, transnational solidarity. The first issue published the Committee's charter, which invited to set up an international Armenian association gathering Armenian writers, as well as learned people and publicists throughout Europe who would regularly meet up in neutral cities such as Brussels or Geneva and would do their utmost to win autonomy for Armenia. By stressing that all shared a common humanity – and that in the name of humanity, violence against Armenians was intolerable – *Le Haïasdan* tapped into the global citizenship register: the lot of Ottoman Armenians was to be improved through the mobilization of individual citizens, who in turn would force governments to act.

The editorial team's cosmopolitan strategy gave *Le Haïasdan* its format. Each issue was composed of two editions presented together and sold as one issue, with the edition in French coming before the edition in Armenian. The bilingual presentation in two separate editions, rather than the juxtaposition of dual-language columns in a single edition made the separate circulation of one or the other edition easier – for instance, when free issues were distributed to sympathetic parties for propaganda purposes (for instance, the British Liberal daily *The Daily News*). The taking over of *Le Haïasdan* by the Anglo-Armenian Association in April 1891 confirms that the targeted readership was meant to be fluent in reading French, rather than Armenian. From 1891 on, the periodical mostly covered British Liberal endeavours towards securing a solution for Ottoman Armenia in keeping with the terms of aforementioned article 61 (1878 Berlin Treaty) and tended to eschew references to Armenian nationalists' activities throughout the world, as before. Among others, disagreements between the Anglo-Armenian Association and former editorial members over means to achieve an autonomous Armenia – especially over physical force as a legitimate political means – led to *Le Haïasdan*'s closing down in 1892.

Indeed, *Le Haïasdan*'s rather vindictive moral cosmopolitanism and open attacks against Ottoman governance split the Anglo-Armenian movement and community. In particular, the older generation of Ottoman Armenian merchants established in Manchester thought that *Le Haïasdan* did more harm than helped the cause. As a case in point, they quoted the embarrassment the circulation of the paper inflicted to the Armenian patriarch with Ottoman authorities in Constantinople and urged Bryce to use the AAA's influence to tone down *Le Haïasdan*'s virulence – in vain.[14] The older generation proposed a different mediatic strategy resting on cultural cosmopolitanism, as that sported by Tchéraz in *L'Arménie/Armenia* and which supporters of Tchéraz suggested was missing in *Le Haïasdan*. A fairer assessment may be that the latter privileged moral cosmopolitanism – i.e. humanitarian and legal arguments (common humanity) – over a more classical cultural cosmopolitanism that would stress common cultural heritage.

By contrast, *L'Arménie/Armenia* systematically tried to infuse readers with a better knowledge of Armenian literature, in particular poetry, and folklore. The quasi absence of Armenian (none up to issue 17 of *L'Arménie* in 1891) and the selection of French and English indicate that he targeted 'friends of Armenia', rather than Armenian readers. Tchéraz's new appointment as chair of Armenian at King's College, London, from 1891 enabled him to pursue his objective of diffusing and mediating Armenian culture to a broader audience, through conferences organized in Britain, like at the Royal Asiatic Society. To Tchéraz, the promotion of Armenian culture as of foundational importance to Europe's Christian history was to bring home that the European signatories of the 1878 Berlin Treaty (France, Britain, Russia, Germany, Austria-Hungary, Italy) could not let down Armenia – or they were letting themselves down. To secure support from fellow Christians, Tchéraz constantly sought to make a rapprochement between Armenian and European literature. 'The Unpublished East' series section served this purpose: classics of Armenian literature were discussed side by side with European classics – showing how there could be recuperation, cross-contamination, etc. and how most Armenian classics had been sources of inspiration for Renaissance/Enlightenment European productions.[15]

Tchéraz was not just passing on traditions to a largely non-Armenian readership who might not have been familiar with Armenian culture – *L'Arménie* had a circulation of 2,000 issues and was almost immediately banned from the Ottoman Empire and Russia. Rather Tchéraz intended to show that despite the 'Asiatic' location of Armenia, 'Armenians belonged in the wider world'.[16] On several occasions – as with Tchéraz's 1896 paper on 'Homer and the Armenians' in which he argued that Armenians were Greeks, including in manners – Tchéraz made reference to comparative philology and anthropology to demonstrate that Armenians were Indo-Europeans, who thus shared linguistic, if not ethnological origins with Europeans, especially the British.[17] As historian Joan Laycock in *Imagining Armenia* (2009) reminds us: 'The Indo-European connection thus strengthened the claim that Armenia was culturally, if not territorially, part of Europe, a claim – she insists – fully exploited in Armenophile and diaspora propaganda.'[18]

Awaiting the report of an international investigation by France-Russia-Britain into the Sasun massacre that killed several thousands of Armenians following the brutal repression of a tax protest (August 1894)[19] – Tchéraz reverted to the association of Armenia as Eden in the 1 May 1895 edition of *L'Arménie*, to arouse sympathy in Britain.[20] In a formulation that resonated with James Bryce's 1877 travelogue statement that Armenia was 'the cradle of the human race',[21] Tchéraz voiced a poignant appeal to British politicians to take action and prevent the furtherance of massacres. At the time, a mass campaign (mostly in Liberal newspapers) had been ongoing since November 1894 and now resulted in many public petitions to Parliament and the Foreign on behalf of Ottoman Armenians. As a former delegate for Armenia at the 1878 Berlin Congress, Tchéraz had always had high hopes that his stance would help him foster the Armenian cause with the British government fighting for the implementation of article 61.

Conversely to *Le Haïasdan*, which had moral and financial support from the AAA and Liberal politicians (especially the family of long-standing Liberal Premier W. E. Gladstone), Tchéraz had always maintained an independent course and banked on cultural cosmopolitanism as the means to secure his political objective. Nonetheless, the return of a Conservative government in late July 1895 was a source of disappointment for Tchéraz – one which accrued as the Conservative Premier, the 3rd Marquess of Salisbury, declared that not even the British navy could protect the Armenians. Against the backdrop of the 1894-6 Armenian massacres (eventually causing about 250,000-300,000 victims), Britain's avowed powerlessness in the European diplomatic game left Tchéraz bitter. A close study of *Armenia* betrays Tchéraz's complete disarray with British Liberals and Conservatives alike. Over the course of a few months, reports about British parliamentary sessions on what was known as 'the Armenian Question' gave way to a sharper focus on the French Armenophile movement, with which Tchéraz now placed his hopes. As a consequence, he relocated the paper to Paris in 1898. By then, the paper only appeared in French and Tchéraz moved closer to French Armenophile circles, especially figures involved with the Paris-based *Pro-Armenia* monthly (1900-). The cosmopolitan ambitions of *Le Haïasdan*, *L'Arménie* and *Armenia* implied privileging diplomatic languages (French/English) over Armenian. To a certain extent, all three serials managed to meet their targeted readerships – friends of Armenia – and get some representation in European newspapers. Nonetheless, *Le Haïasdan*'s recurrent financial difficulties (due to the AAA's diminished supported and limited subscriptions) remind us that *L'Arménie/Armenia* owed their longevity to Tchéraz's affluence. Realizing this, Tchéraz thought more economically viable to keep Armenian to a congruous portion of *L'Arménie/Armenia*, as he believed that educated Armenians would have been taught French, and possibly English (in French, British and American missionary colleges in Asia Minor) and thus could still be reached in a French-language only organ. One could ask: Why did *Le Haïasdan* stick to its bilingualism and pursue with the Armenian edition despite difficulties?

Meeting the challenges of composing in Armenian in late nineteenth-century London

A competitor in the field, Ottoman Armenian publicist Minas Tchéraz was bewildered at the language strategy of *Le Haïasdan*. For him, Armenians wanting to read Armenian would turn to good quality periodicals in Armenian rather than opt out for a bilingual serial whose Armenian section was poorly composed. While upfront and severe, Tchéraz's remark addressed a sensitive issue: the complex linguistic articulation of identity in exile and technical difficulties of composing texts in non-Latin scripts. Put differently, the question raised here is whether the language(s) of diplomacy could be reconciled with the languages of the homeland – Armenian, which itself was one of the languages of the Ottoman Empire, but not the official one (Osmanli) – and the host country? Tchéraz and *Le Haïasdan*'s editorial team held divergent views. Tchéraz would argue that single-issue periodicals with a diplomatic plank should use the *lingua franca(s)*. Sévasly and others at *Le Haïasdan* intended to contribute to strengthening the Armenian national awakening by adding the Armenian-language section: publishing in Armenian was therefore central to their own political agenda. No surprise then that *Le Haïasdan*'s editorial team refused merging with Tchéraz's ventures in 1890-1 to form a single pro-Armenian paper in London.[22] The Armenian-language edition is not only telling of the difficulties at composing in a non-Latin alphabet, but also of the ideological anchorage of *Le Haïasdan* as a radical paper, which Armenian served to inscribe in a dense network of Armenian(-language) serials published within and without the Ottoman Empire.

Le Haïasdan celebrated Armenian from its very title, which literally translates as 'the country of Haïk', Haïk being the mythical patriarch and founder of the Armenian nation. Everything across the two editions spoke to the pride and development of Armenianness, starting with the choice of calendar in Armenian. Indeed, the first issue was published on 1 November 1888, which was surprisingly translated as '11 Sahmi 4380'. Rather than select the Armenian calendar, *Le Haïasdan* followed the ancient Armenian calendar of the pagan period (known as *Haïka-schirtchan*, or 'cycle of Haïk'), which retained 11 August 2492 BC as the founding date of the Armenian nation. The year 2492 BC was meant to refer to Haïk's victory over giant Belus (*Dyutsaznamart* in Armenian, 'the battle of giants') around the Lake Van region, then located in Ottoman Armenia.[23] Systematically printed across the French and Armenian editions of *Le Haïasdan*, the choice of the ancient Armenian calendar was very unusual. Not even the Armenian-language periodical *Haik* published in New York from 1891 and distributed in England made any reference to the Haïk calendar whatsoever.[24] Turned into a key component of *Le Haïasdan*'s nationalist repertory, *Haïka-schirtchan* served to remind Armenians throughout the world of the antiquity of the Armenian nation and to demonstrate the righteousness of *Le Haïasdan*'s pressing for the autonomy of Ottoman Armenia, where ancient Armenians had long preceded Turks.

Armenianness was more fully extolled in the Armenian-language edition of *Le Haïasdan*. Although the two editions (French/Armenian) were usually overall similar – with letters of friends of Armenia (British, French, Italian, Belgian, Swiss, German mostly), articles about the general situation of Armenia and discussions of treaty obligations (often with reference to international legal scholars), a digest of Armenian news in European newspapers, a digest of Armenian newspapers throughout the world and local news of Ottoman Armenia – the Armenian text regularly included extra elements. For instance, while the French-language edition reproduced Armenophiles' letters in their original language and published a translation in French, the Armenian edition only included a translation in Armenian. It freed space in the Armenian edition, which was taken up by poems and signatures of Armenian nationalist figures, as ways of emboldening readers' faith in *Le Haïasdan*'s political programme.[25] This forced competitor Tchéraz to include Armenian script in both *L'Arménie* and *Armenia* from 1891 to celebrate major contemporary Armenian poets who chanted a free Armenia (like Sayat-Nova, 1712–95) and to insert poems specifically written for the review, such as 'To Gladstone' by Russian-born contemporary Armenian poet Raphael Patkanian (1830–92). Nonetheless, Tchéraz's inclusion of passages in Armenian failed to overturn the preference given to *Le Haïasdan* by Armenian diasporic newspapers. In the end, *L'Arménie* and *Armenia* still read too moderate.[26]

Out of political convictions, *Le Haïasdan*'s editorial team stuck to printing in Armenian, whereas they experienced practical difficulties from the onset (by contrast to the immaculate French edition). After the first two issues were printed in Paris (for the director jurist Jean Broussali lived in France), printing was taken to London as early as December 1888. It was entrusted to Gilbert and Rivington, who were then the only London printers with Armenian types. Although there had been a tradition of scholarly, philological publishing in England (at Oxford and Cambridge) since 1736, Armenian printing was extremely limited in that country. Only thirty-five titles in Armenian were printed there until 1914 – versus about ninety published in Paris in between 1812 and 1866.[27] This rarity placed *Le Haïasdan*'s editorial team at the mercy of Gilbert and Rivington. Collaboration with that printing house ceased in February 1890, due to exorbitant rises in printing costs. The exceptional issue of December 1889, which had culminated at twenty pages and included the sole illustration ever (a coloured folding map of the administration divisions of Ottoman Armenian provinces), caused the fallout between *Le Haïasdan*'s editorial team and Gilbert and Rivington. The latter charged £30 for printing, including £10 solely for the map, which were costs that *Le Haïasdan* could not really meet, especially on account of many late subscription payments and a stable subscription price. The first issue had originally been four pages altogether and the second issue totalled eight pages (with separate numbering for the French and Armenian sections, each four pages long), before the number of pages more or less stabilized at twelve (with both sections equal in length). The augmented number of pages (to sixteen for the June, August and October 1889 issues, and to twenty for the December 1889 serial), together with the lack of sufficient Armenian types at Gilbert and Rivington, and the difficulty in having a composer proficient enough in Armenian at hand forced *Le Haïasdan*'s editorial team to drop the fortnightly publication and opt out for a monthly one in December 1888. The sizeable increase in content/pages meant spiralling expenditure for the serial, with a swollen budget for production and despatch, as well as salary costs.

This resulted in quixotic choices for the editorial team, such as reducing the font of the printed text to keep costs manageable (as with the August 1889 issue), or devolving the task of composing the French section on another printer (like Ranken, Ellis & Co.), despite the fact that only about 100 copies seemed to have been printed of the Armenian edition (meant for the Ottoman Empire) and about 1,000 in English.[28] With tensions irremediably escalating between *Le Haïasdan*'s editorial team and Gilbert and Rivington from late 1889, the former actively sought to buy enough Armenian and French characters to compose the serial itself, in vain. Because of that situation, the editorial board recurrently found itself apologizing for the poor quality of the text in Armenian. In the February 1890 issue, the editorial committee eventually announced that it was resorting to stereotyping as a durable solution and promised that delivery to subscribers would be made to date. Switching to this particular process enabled the editors to reuse their own characters to compose one page after the other, once perfect facsimiles in type-metal of the previous page had been made. It even permitted the new printer, Ranken, Ellis & Co., who was later asked to produce the whole periodical, to print longer issues and still meet the delivery schedule.

For *Le Haïasdan*'s editorial team, publishing in Armenian was a political statement that was perfectly compatible with (their) cosmopolitanism. But it was not the case of Ottoman authorities, which increasingly kept an eye on Ottoman Armenian publishing within and without the Ottoman Empire and always regarded the use of an Ottoman community language in overseas publishing as under the purview of national censorship. Put differently, *Le Haïasdan*'s bilingual strategy should also be considered as a way to navigate Ottoman censorship and transnational Ottoman surveillance.

The cosmopolitan political Armenian-language press and state surveillance

Often described as 'the asylum of nations', Britain had a long tradition of welcoming political exiles. Throughout the nineteenth century, Britain saw many launching political newspapers as means of expressing political dissent and of formulating political projects for the countries they had left behind. Some of these titles are evoked in this volume. Directly relevant here is Russian political exile Alexander Herzen (1812–70)'s *Kolokol* (The Bell). His serial appeared in London from 1857 to 1867 and then in Geneva (1868–70), where it formed a source of inspiration for Armenian Hunchakians like Avetis Nazarbekian, who in their turn would transfer their *Hnch'ak* (Bell) to London in the 1890s, as discussed below.[29]

The radicalism of these publications was a source of worry – and surveillance – for foreign governments that underwent attacks, but sometimes also feared for their lives. Such was the concern voiced by the Ottoman ambassador at St James' Court, Musurus Pasha, in January 1870 when a political newspaper published in London in Osmanli (Ottoman Turkish written in a version of the Arabic alphabet) under the title *Hürriyet* (Freedom, 1868–70) called Ottoman Muslims to sedition and even encouraged them to assassinate members of the Ottoman government to end misgovernance. Musurus Pacha seized on the British Home Office for them to take legal action against *Hürriyet*, for copies to be seized, figures behind the newspaper to be arrested and sentenced, and for *Hürriyet* to be stopped altogether. To justify his intervention and to placate possible accusations of foreign interference in British politics, Musurus Pasha pressed that '*Hürriyet* being printed in Turkish, it was withdrawn from the sanction of British public opinion'.[30] Musurus Pasha legitimized his undertaking on the grounds that what mattered was the language in which the newspaper was circulated – and the nationality of figures behind the paper – not the country of publication. The Ottoman ambassador's argument was that *Hürriyet* was meant to be circulated in the Ottoman Empire – not so much in Britain – and that as such, the Ottoman government's demand about *Hürriyet* was grounded. The Home Office paused as such a step contravened free speech, which had vehemently upheld by British reformers in the preceding years, resulting in 'taxes on knowledge' (stamp, advertising and paper duties placed on British newspapers since 1712) coming to an end in 1861. Before settling on the case, the Home Office brought up the Orsini Affair (1858) as a parallel. The latter had led to the downfall of the Palmerston government in late February 1858 after it considered revising British Criminal Law (Conspiracy to Murder Bill) to facilitate the arrests and prosecutions of contacts of Italian revolutionary Felice Orsini (1819–58) as the assassination attempt on Napoleon III in Paris ('the Orsini plot') had been prepared in England and as Napoleon III threatened to break diplomatic ties with Britain. Finally, after inquiries – and a more or less independent translation of recent copies of *Hürriyet* – the Home Office decided that *Hürriyet* should be prosecuted on two grounds: that the anti-Sultan, pro-constitutional tone of the reforming Young Ottomans had become more aggressive since the previous *Mukhbir* (The Informer, 1867–8) and that it could pose a threat to British safety, as Musurus Pasha had intimated. To avoid a repetition of the Orsini affair, the case was nonetheless passed on to a libel court, rather than be treated as a diplomatic affair. It seemed that for the time being, the British government was favouring a prudent course with such cases.

Successive Ottoman governments took cue, although Musurus Pasha – on behalf of Sultan Abdul Hamid II (reigning since 1876) – did try to have *Le Haïasdan* offices close, citing a threat to the Ottoman Empire. Eventually, this did briefly happen in 1889 as the Prime Minister/Foreign Secretary, the 3rd Marquess of Salisbury, was eventually convinced by Musurus Pasha that the offices harboured revolutionary, possibly terrorist activities, which did not only jeopardize Ottoman governance, but threatened British security. The case was taken to Parliament by James Bryce, who denounced false accusations – as he himself was blamed for partaking in such revolutionary activities.[31] He made a strong case that this was an unacceptable interference of a foreign power on British soil and an intolerable attack on the freedom of the press in Britain. He recounted how, after weeks of harassment by the Ottoman Embassy, Scotland Yard was eventually allowed by Salisbury to search the paper's premises, asking whether 'the Metropolitan Police [was] at the disposal of a foreign Government'.[32] Bryce surfed on the memory the House had of the Orsini affair to press his point, while insisting that *Le Haïasdan* was only seeking to expose the Musa Bey affair, which appeared in the British press in just as crude terms.[33] He quoted passages of the French edition to show that *Le Haïasdan* merely sought to record instances of violence against Armenians for Europe to act and have Ottoman governance fulfil international treaty obligations. In early 1889, near Mush in eastern Anatolia, a local Kurdish warlord named Musa Bey had kidnapped, raped and forcefully married Gulizar, a teenage Armenian girl, whom he forced to convert to Islam.[34] Protests in the local community arose and rapidly were voiced in diasporic newspapers, especially in Marseilles and London, as Musa Bey was acquitted.[35] In Britain, Gladstone himself led a media-savvy campaign on behalf of Gulizar and Ottoman Armenians for immediate justice and the implementation of article 61.

The intensity of the Armenophile campaign in Britain forced Salisbury to backtrack and to allow the publication of *Le Haïasdan* anew. From that moment, a patronage committee including Anglo-Armenian Association members and chaired by Bryce, was formed and was to serve as some form of moral warranty, but also as a legal buttress against future Ottoman censorship (as it strengthened the Englishness of *Le Haïasdan*). Pressures built up again in 1892 when the Ottoman embassy in Britain crusaded against all radical London based printed press by former Ottoman subjects.[36] In that context, *Le Haïasdan* quickly ceased publication, only to be resurrected as *The Anglo-Armenian Gazette* a few months later (it seems to have lasted until 1895). By then, it was as the AAA's organ and its editorial line was much more moderate in wording. Although former London members of *Le Haïasdan*'s editorial team were part of the AAA, their input in the *Gazette* was now contained and no Armenian edition was produced.

The Ottoman government's political intimidation was not limited to pressures on the British government in London. Rather, it made use of its worldwide surveillance network to collect information about publications and try to stop their distribution. Even a few months before *Le Haïasdan* appeared, there was fidgeting at the Ottoman Interior Ministry concerning the Armenian Patriotic Committee's alarming representations to the British Premier Salisbury about the situation in Ottoman Armenia. Consequently, as soon as the first issue was out in November 1888, the following communication was sent to the Ottoman Ministry of the Interior:

> The translation of the telegram, which came in response to the notification made to the London Embassy, was presented in a letter dated November 29, 1888, as required by the Sultan's will to make an effort to ban the publication of the newspaper called *Haïasdan*, which is published by the Armenian Patriotic Association founded in London under the chairmanship of a person named Agopyan [sic]. A translation of letter n° 275, dated 15 November 1888, from the Vienna ambassador, mentions that the first issue of the *Haïasdan* newspaper posted to him was sent for information. According to its contents, it was published in Paris, but its administrative office is in London. Necessary recommendations to the Ottoman Embassy in Paris have been given for sound attempts before the French Ministry of Foreign Affairs to ban the printing and publication of this newspaper. It is supplied.[37]

There had indeed been an attempt by the Ottoman ambassador in France for some months already to have Jean Broussali, the paper's director, sued for sedition under Ottoman law, as the Ottoman Empire didn't recognize Broussali's French citizenship as valid.[38] Though early attempts at ending *Le Haïasdan* failed, the Ottoman Ministry of Interior also tried to act on the Ottoman soil. Indeed, the 1864 Ottoman Press Code had proscribed the import of 'foreign' newspapers published by Ottoman dissenters abroad, and controls had been reinforced under the reign of Sultan Abdul Hamid II within a few months of his arrival to the throne in 1876, through the Ottoman Press Bureau. Publications often surreptitiously made their way into the Empire nonetheless – and the British Embassy's postal service was often incriminated for letting through Ottoman dissidents' publications, which caused recrimination. Ottoman censors could check on parcels, including those coming through foreign embassies. If, in the early years of the Ottoman Press Bureau, printing in another language than those used in the Ottoman Empire could be an asset, inspectors acquired notions of French/English and were provided with a list of banned titles, so that censorship could not be so easily circumvented. Still, when there was contest over a periodical sent through the British Embassy and the periodical was either printed in English and/or published in Britain, ambassadors could play on extraterritorial jurisdiction to at least negotiate for publications to be available in social resorts frequently by the Anglo-American community. In the case of *Le Haïasdan*, *L'Arménie* and *Armenia*, however, British ambassador at Constantinople William A. White (1885–91) did not wield extraterritoriality to defend London-based Armenian papers and contest the distribution ban. But they still circulated in the Ottoman Empire, well beyond the number of print-out issues, as oral reading of key passages *Le Haïasdan* was often given – much to the alarm of local Ottoman administrators who feared that it would incite Armenians in the Ottoman Empire to rebel.[39]

Ottoman surveillance spared no publication and editors knew it. *Hnch'ak*, the organ of the Hunchakian party, was another case in point. Avetis Nazarbek and the team behind *Hnch'ak* frequently relocated publication of the paper over the years, to escape Ottoman censorship (Geneva 1887–92, Athens 1893, London 1894–1904, Paris 1905–14).[40] To cover their traces, but still reach out to their readers, they often used pseudonyms – for instance, the correspondent of *Hnch'ak* in Geneva was named Beniard, a bare play-on-words on the newspaper's title 'The Bell' and a reference to Big Ben.[41] They also avoided clearly indicating where the administration offices of the paper were. Rather, they mentioned a series of *poste restante* addresses using pseudonyms, as well as a place of publication thought safe, but not necessarily squaring with reality. This was a way to buy time, during which editors sought protection of international powers. So was the strategy used by *Hnch'ak* for a couple of years. In 1888, issues of the paper mention London, sometimes Montpellier beguiling Ottoman authorities into believing the administration of the paper was there, though it was probably not the case till the early 1890s, when Nazarbek settled in London – at least temporarily – before the headquarters of the Hunchakian party officially moved there in 1894.[42] By then, London was the seat of the main two party's periodicals *Hnch'ak* and the satirical journal *Aptak* (The Slap), which had originally appeared in Athens. In moving to London, *Aptak* changed styles several times as its calls for the advent of 'Armenia' through revolution (as the European concert had failed them) became more pressing.[43] The editorial teams took with them to London a printing press and Armenian fonts, thereby making sure they would elude difficulties met by *Le Haïasdan*'s team.

While Hunchakians tried to alert European powers of the deteriorated situation in Ottoman Armenia – sometimes resorting to violence to do so, especially in the context of the 1894–6 Armenian massacres – British governments of those years stood aloof to pressure from the Ottoman embassy to have these serials suppressed. The mass agitation in Britain on behalf of Ottoman Armenians in those years – about 5,000 petitions had been sent to the Foreign Office to denounce the massacres and to a certain extent, call for British action[44] – had made revolutionary Hunchakians less suspect – even to British authorities.

Indeed, just as Ottoman authorities were seeking to suppress *Hnch'ak*, the Hunchakian party underwent internecine, inter-personal and ideological tensions in 1896 leading the anti-Nazarbek faction to establish its own paper, also entitled *Hnch'ak*. Nazarbek then took the case to a London court over title ownership and British Liberal friends tried to use their influence for Nazarbek to retain the paper – arguing over ownership, but also over the fact that though revolutionary, the paper was not advocating terror.[45] After a few months of litigation, Nazarbek won the case *Nazarbek v. Sevasly*, forcing dissidents to find another title for their paper. *Mart* (March) was chosen, after the paper illegally appeared without a title for the few months of the legal contest. The coverage the case got in the British press highlighted Nazarbek's rights as a newspaper proprietor, treating the case as it had done with other similar affairs. In a way, 'the gentle art of revolution' mocked by *The Sheffield Daily Telegraph* in 1894 then seemed sufficiently mainstream for Nazarbek to be part of the cosmopolitan London scene, which characterized that fin-de-siècle.[46] To the Liberals and Radicals at least, *Hnch'ak* and *Aptak* embodied the legitimate expression of revolutionary ideas and action in the face of the situation in the Ottoman Empire.

Conclusion

This study of British-Armenian serials emphasizes the role of language in the construction of a cosmopolitan diasporic Armenian identity in the heyday of Armenian nationalism. Armenian is given a heightened role in more radical papers (*Le Haïasdan/Hnch'ak*), for which a cosmopolitan Armenian paper cannot do without that language – thereby recalling how modern Armenian was central to the articulation of Armenianness. The proportion of Armenian used depended on the main targeted readership and on the political vision of Armenia they proposed. Despite contrasting strategies, *Le Haïasdan, Hnch'ak* and Tchéraz's *L'Arménie/Armenia* shared a common ambition of making Armenia European in the minds of readers, especially of non-Armenian friends of Armenia. Even *L'Arménie/Armenia*, which infrequently resorted to Armenia on the ground that educated Armenians could read French or English, did not go the whole way of producing a cultural review for a diasporic cosmopolitan Armenian elite – i.e. 'cosmopolitan' in the sense of at ease, outside of their country – and had to include discussions of Armenia's future, despite its claims of not being strictly political.

When Nazarbek won the ownership suit, Tchéraz used *Armenia* to express regret that beyond ideological differences, Armenian exiles failed to unite and speak in a single voice to find pragmatic solutions for Armenia and transform their periodicals in a fundraising platform for survivors of the massacres and reconstruction.[47] In that Tchéraz followed *Mart*, which also called for reunion between all Armenian political parties in the name of an autonomous, if not independent Armenia. Notwithstanding Tchéraz's rather harsh words for *Le Haïasdan* and *Hnch'ak*, all serials studied here suffered the same pressures from the Ottoman State and wielded their cosmopolitanism (especially in the context of extraterritorial jurisdiction) to continue living on. Again, beyond their different understandings of cosmopolitanism (moral/cultural), *Le Haïasdan, Hnch'ak* and Tchéraz's *L'Arménie/Armenia* all engaged with the creation of a supra-European identity of which Armenia was part and parcel and which envisaged cosmopolitanism in a constructionist perspective.

Put differently, all attempted the *tour de force* of reconciling Armenian nationalism and cosmopolitanism, not merely in the domain of ideas, but also of praxis as they argued for a fairer governance for Armenia –and by extension, for humanity. Ultimately, these periodicals were a laboratory for re-creating their nation, but also for rethinking stalemated European governance, which is quite visible in the double-page high quality *Aptak* engravings. While such an ambition placed Armenian periodicals on the margins of the British political, but also mediatic spheres in the 1880s, this was not the case any more after the Armenian massacres – at least, until 1903.

In the autumn of that year, the rivalries between the two Hunchakian factions culminated in the assassination of an Armenian Nazarbekian leader, Sagatiel Sagouni, by members of the other group (the Alfaris) in Nunhead, an area of East London. Both out of support for the Nazarbekians, but also baffled by the extreme violence within Armenian revolutionary circles in London, the tabloid daily *The Daily Express* printed an excerpt of the *Hnch'ak*'s front page news coverage of the Sagouni murder as part of its own article on the *fait divers*.[48] This inclusion of an Armenian periodical snapshot within a mainstream English-language daily is extraordinary in itself and attests to the cosmopolitanism discussed here. Less candidly however, it should also serve to remind us that the foreign-language element was at the time, and perhaps still is, always at the risk of being appraised and downgraded as 'foreign' and seditious – a risk that the turn-of-the-century Home Office sought to contain by keeping a record of most, if not all foreign-language serials published in Britain.

Notes

1. 'Untitled', *Azdarar*, 1796 (issue 18), 47. National Library of Armenia Periodical Collections, Erevan.
2. Aram Arkun, 'Into the Modern Age', in Edmund Herzig and Marina Kurkchiyan (eds.), *The Armenians: Past and Present in the Making of National Identity* (London: Routledge, 2004), 73.
3. Lisa Khachaturian, *Cultivating Nationhood in Imperial Russia: The Periodical Press and the Formation of a Modern Armenian Identity* (New Brunswick, NJ: Transaction Publishers, 2009), 3.
4. Ronald G. Suny, *Looking Toward Ararat: Armenia in Modern History* (Bloomington: Indiana University Press, 1993), 73.
5. Several complete collections survive at the Bibliothèque universitaire des Langues et Civilisations (Paris), the AGBU Nubarian Library (Paris), the British Library (London) and the National Library of Armenian (Erevan).
6. The most complete collection seems to be that of the Bibliothèque nationale de France (Paris).
7. 'A nos Compatriotes', *L'Arménie*, 1 October 1893, 1.
8. 'Avis', *Armenia*, 1 November 1890 (issue 13), 2.
9. For instance: 'Struggles for Life', *L'Arménie*, 15 June 1890, 1.
10. Stefano Evangelista, *Literary Cosmopolitanism in the English Fin de Siècle: Citizens of Nowhere* (Oxford: OUP, 2021), 1.
11. Adam E. Etinson, 'Cosmopolitanism: Cultural, Moral and Political', in Diogo Pires Aurélio, Gabriele De Angelis and Regina Queiroz (eds.), *Sovereign Justice: Global Justice in a World of Nations* (Berlin: De Gruyter, 2011), 27.
12. Thomas W. Pogge, 'Cosmopolitanism and Sovereignty', *Ethics* 103, no. 1 (1992): 49.
13. Translated by the author of this article. The original reads: 'Notre principal rôle sera de servir d'intermédiaire entre l'Arménie et l'Europe, entre les hommes d'Etat, les publicistes, et les organes européens, pour élciarer l'opinion publique sur les souffrances et les aspirations du malheureux peuple arménien, afin de lui gagner les sympathies du monde civilisé.' 'Bulletin', *Haiasdan*, 1 November 1888, 1.
14. Joan George, *Merchants in Exile: The Armenians in Manchester, England, 1835–1935* (London: Gomidas Institute, 2002), 56.
15. The series was later published in book form as: Minas Tchéraz, *L'Orient inédit: légendes et traditions arméniennes, grecques et turques* (Paris: Leroux, 1912).
16. Joan Laycock, *Imagining Armenia: Orientalism, Ambiguity and Intervention* (Manchester: MUP, 2009), 55.
17. This point was only hinted at by scholars whom Tchéraz presents as Armenologists, especially Friedrich Max Müller and Angelo de Gubernatis, whereas Armenian was but one element in their comparative philology.

18 Laycock, *Imagining Armenia*, 58.
19 For a broader historical perspective, see Owen Miller, 'Rethinking the Violence in the Sasun Mountains (1893–1894)', *Études arméniennes contemporaines* 10 (2018): 97–123.
20 'Au Très Hon. W.E. Gladstone', *L'Arménie*, 1 May 1895, 1; 'To the Right Hon. W.E. Gladstone', *Armenia*, 1 May 1895, 1.
21 James Bryce, *Transcaucasia and Ararat: Being Notes of a Vacation Tour in the Autumn of 1876* (London: Macmillan & Co., 1877), 281.
22 'To our countrymen', *Armenia*, 15 October 1892 (issue 46), 1.
23 Cesare Tondini de Quarenghi, 'Étude sur le calendrier liturgique de la nation arménienne', *Bessarione – Rivista di Studi Orientali* 90–2 (1906): 5.
24 Cf. *Haik* (New York), 1 January 1891 (issue 1).
25 See for instance p. 2 of the Armenian edition of *Haiasdan*, 1–15 January 1889.
26 *Ara: A Journal of Literature, and of Armenian Politics and History*, Dacca. Copies in the Gladstone Papers, Hawarden Library, 11C/16-21. This consultation was made possible thanks to the Drew Scholarship awarded by the Gladstone Library (2019).
27 Ara Sanjian, *Celebrating the Legacy of Five Centuries of Armenian-Language Book Printing, 1512–2012*, Exhibit Booklet (University of Michigan: Dearborn, 2012), 5.
28 Print run in secret letter from the Ottoman Embassy in London to the Ministry of Foreign Affairs, 23 March 1889, BOA, Y. A. HUS, 224/44. Quoted in Quoted in *Osmanlı Belgelerinde Ermeni-İngiliz İlişkileri, Volume 1 (1845–1890)*, Osmanlı Arşivi Daire Başkanlığı. Yayın Nu: 58, Ankara, 2002, 159.
29 Suny, *Looking Toward Ararat*, 72.
30 Musurus Pacha to Home Office, 19 January 1870, quoted in 'Case', Home Office Papers, The National Archives, Kew, London, HO 45/94721/A38025, unnumbered folio. The original is in French and reads: 'cette publication écrite en langue turque et par conséquent soustraite au contrôle de l'opinion publique en Angleterre'. The rest of this paragraph builds on the whole dossier (folios unnumbered).
31 James Bryce, 'Armenian Christians', House of Commons Debate, 3 March 1896, vol. 38, § 111.
32 James Bryce, 'Foreign Journalists', House of Commons Debate, 21 March 1889, vol. 334 § 408–9.
33 'New in Brief: The Turkish Armenians', *The Times*, 7 May 1889, 5; 'Turkey', *The Times*, 27 May 1889, 5.
34 Arménouhie Kévonian, *Les noces noires de Gulizar*, Paris: Editions Parenthèses, 2005.
35 Owen R. Miller, '"Back to the Homeland" (Tebi Yergir): Or, How Peasants Became Revolutionaries in Muş', *Journal of the Ottoman and Turkish Studies Association* 4, no. 2 (2017): 287.
36 The whole volume FO 78/4591 (Foreign Office Papers, The National Archives, Kew, London) is about such pressures, against *La Turquie Libre*, *Armenia*, *Haiasdan* and *H'nchak*.
37 Letter to the Grand Vizir, 1 December 1888, Ottoman State Archives (Başbakanlık Osmanlı Arşivi, BOA) BOA, Y.A. HUS, 219/61. Quoted in *Osmanlı Belgelerinde Ermeni-İngiliz İlişkileri*, 22.
38 Said Pasha to Esad Pasha, 14 August 1888, BOA. HR. SYS. 2781-1/12, 13. Quoted in *Osmanli Belgelerine Göre Ermeni-Fransiz İlişkileri, Volume 1*, Osmanlı Arşivi Daire Başkanlığı. Yayın Nu: 67, Ankara, 2004, 150–1.
39 Fehti (from St Petersburg) to Said Pasha, 9 August 1889 and enclosure of the Ottoman Consul at Batum of 30 July 1889, BOA, HR. SYS, 2761/13. Quoted in *Osmanlı Belgelerinde Ermeni-İngiliz İlişkileri*, 190–1.

40 Louise Nalbandian, *The Armenian Revolutionary Movement: The Development of Armenian Political Parties* (Berkeley and Los Angeles: University of California Press, 1963), 211.
41 Publication information, *H'nchak*, n° 3 (1888), 8.
42 FO to Sir Clare Ford, Confidential, 'Print_Asiatic Turkey', 23 May 1892, FO 78/4591, folio not numbered.
43 Claire Mouradian, 'La Caricature dans la presse arménienne du Caucase, d'un Empire l'autre', in M. Quarez, *Russie, URSS, 1914-1991, Changements de Regards* (Nanterre: BDIC, 1991), 40-7.
44 Stéphanie Prévost, 'L'opinion publique britannique et la Question arménienne (1889-96) Quelles archives pour quel récit ?', *Études arméniennes contemporaines* 8 (2016), DOI: https://doi.org/10.4000/eac.1170.
45 Henry Sidgwick to James Bryce, 4 December 1896, Bryce Papers, Bodleian Library, Oxford, f. 168-9.
46 'The Armenian Exposure', *The Sheffield Daily Telegraph*, 9 September 1896, 5.
47 'Le Scandale Hentchakiste', *Armenia*, 1 January 1897, 4.
48 'The Assassination in a London Suburb', *The Daily Express*, 29 October 1903, 6. Quoted in Gagik Stepan-Sarkissian, 'The Peckham Armenian Martyrs', *The Armenian Institute News* 7 (2009), 10.

16

The Power of the Transnational Native Tongue in Exile: Belgian Refugees during the First World War, Their Exile Press and Their Fragmented Identity

Christophe Declercq
Utrecht University/CenTraS, University College London

In a dynamic view, culture is both transnational and translational.[1] This approach, which points to 'the increasing importance of developing transnational cultural studies explicitly from the perspective of translation and displacement'[2] aims at understanding cultures primarily as a blurring of boundaries and a focus on intercultural differences that break away from the enclosed mental worlds of nation-specific traditions[3]). Scholar of forced migration Laura Rubio Díaz-Leal uses the term de-territorialization to refer to 'the ways in which displaced people feel they belong to various communities despite the fact that they do not share a common territory with all the other members'.[4] This fragmented translation of a refugee identity was indeed visible from the daily lives of the different Belgian refugee communities during the First World War and was represented by the several geographically bound operations of a hugely varied Belgian exile press.[5] With sizeable exile communities in the Netherlands, France and the United Kingdom, and respective exile press operations collaborating or borrowing from one another, any notion of a Belgian press in exile, based in any of those three nations, transcends geographical constraints. Therefore, the history of the Belgian refugees in Britain during the First World War is posited in its context of transnational displacement and translation – and by extension code switching and replication. Code switching takes place when information communicated in one language is characterized by infrequent additional use of another language, usually isolated words, phrases or short sentences. Replication is when one newspaper replicates information from another source, it quotes, borrows and references the secondary source. The chapter uses the Belgian press in Britain as a key to extending findings that are nation- or refugee community-specific into the transnational history of wartime Belgian press. A context emerges on how the refugee communities in exile were catered for by their exile newspapers, most notably along specific ideological and linguistic divides. How the power of the native tongue marked the sojourn in exile, a truly multilingual and transnational temporary diaspora can be seen through an analysis of the publishing context of Belgian exile newspapers such as the francophone *L'Indépendance Belge* (Independent Belgium) and *La Métropole d'Anvers* (The Metropolis of Antwerp) and the Dutch *De Stem Uit België* (The Voice From Belgium).[6]

German atrocities, anti-German sentiments and British sympathy

As soon as Germany violated Belgium's territorial neutrality, which was agreed in the 1839 Treaty of London through which Britain acted as guarantor to Belgium, and Britain declared war on Germany, several developments provided a setting in which Belgian voices in exile could be heard: the atrocities perpetrated by German troops caused a mass movement of displacement, and anti-German sentiments drove British sympathy towards the reception of tens of thousands Belgian refugees.

In less than three weeks in August 1914, German troops had advanced through Belgium, entering the most northern parts of France. Leuven had fallen on 19 August, Brussels the next day. By the end of 23 August, a line from Namur over Charleroi to Mons had been broken. Atrocities by Germans in the initial weeks of the conflict as well as stories of atrocities had triggered a mass movement. Hundreds of thousands of Belgians were first internally displaced, mainly heading for the port city of Antwerp, deemed a safe haven. A city of more than 400,000 inhabitants already, the urban area became host to probably twice as many Belgians on the run.[7] Antwerp fell on 9 October and most of the internally displaced people became international refugees as they headed for safer grounds.[8] A large part went to the Netherlands, which received over a million of refugees in a matter of days – figures that dwarf more contemporary humanitarian crises in Europe. On 15 October 1914, the Germans captured Ostend and the next day the First Battle of Ypres started. Four years of attrition ensued. Ultimately, more than 1.5 million Belgians spent large parts of the war period in exile. Focus lies with Britain, where more than 250,000 Belgians stayed at one point during the war, and how the varied exile press there supported, claimed or created which sense of identity for the Belgian community in exile there.[9] Belgian refugeedom in Britain thus developed within an intricate setting of sympathy and support, which was ultimately shaped by the British press.[10]

On 12 August 1914, the British satirical and popular journal *Punch* printed a cartoon by the famous illustrator Frederick Henry Townsend (1868–1920). Belgium is portrayed as a young boy, threatened by a stereotypical German figure. The cartoon worked on several levels, it responded to anti-German sentiments in Britain by producing an unfriendly depiction of Germany as well as by constructing an early victimization of friendly Belgium.

By the time the cartoon was published German troops had entered Belgium little over a week earlier. Because of the violation of Belgium's territorial neutrality – to which Britain acted as its guarantor through the 1839 Treaty of London – Britain declared war on Germany.

Already prevalent as a dominant perspective on Germany in the years – decades even – prior to the outbreak of the First World War, anti-German sentiments in Britain soared when the First World War commenced and the image of the proud but stubborn boy Belgium withholding a no-good German bully channelled those sentiments.[11] The mockery would soon shift to more grim realities – the first British soldier died ten days after the cartoon was published – but for now the foolishly simplistic patriotism prevailed. The sausages pulling out of the German character's jacket were connecting to wider concerns: between 1850 and 1914, the German sausage had become a metaphor for the German nation, linking a cultural and gastronomic stereotype to German national diet as well as to their (perceived) aggressive nature.[12] The other part of the imagery from the cartoon, the Belgian boy, addressed a whole different idea, that of a vulnerable but friendly nation. The call for empathy was clear.

Early public discourse in Britain in terms of support for the war was very patriotic; soon *Poor Little Belgium* became an additional element in the narrative and imagery put before the British people by their national press.[13] Whether they were internally displaced in the early stages of the war or arrived in Britain in trickles, the Belgian refugees soon became an important part of the narrative driving the war effort.[14] This proto-propaganda not only mobilized volunteers to join the army, but also galvanized support for Belgian refugees.

On 24 August 1914, a War Refugees Committee (WRC) was founded by three proponents of late Victorian and Imperial Britain. Instrumental in its inception was journalist Flora Shaw (1852–1929), then Lady Lugard, the wife of Sir Frederick Lugard (1858–1945), a former Governor of Hong Kong and by the time of the First World War the Governor-General of Nigeria. Also involved were novelist and activist Edith Balfour (1865–1948), who had become Alfred Lyttelton's second wife, and Viscount Herbert John Gladstone (1854–1930), son of the former Prime Minister William Ewart Gladstone, and himself former Home Secretary and Governor-General of South Africa. In order to get the WRC widely known, a letter was published in the British press, appealing for help and support.[15] The appeal reverberated across the nation. With the emergence of the WRC, other relief funds for Belgian refugees mushroomed and many hundreds of charitable organizations emerged, all in support of the war refugees, the overall majority of which were Belgian.

Relief fund organization was supported through a practice established very early on in the war. British newspapers provided a platform for Belgians who had already established themselves in Britain, such as the author Emile Cammaerts (1878–1953) or the consul in Edinburgh, Charles Sarolea (1870–1953), as well as for less well-known voices describing or bearing witness to atrocities. Atrocity stories, which appeared in the British press through interpreters or even members of the general public who spoke French, added to the national sentiment of empowerment in terms of the war effort. However, the accounts often related to second hand testimonies, or hearsay even, communicated whilst in transfer across the Channel.[16] Other than the complicated and contested nature of witness testimonies, what emerges from the numerous articles is an institutionalized empathy. The accounts of German atrocities in the British press translated into the physical presence of Belgians seeking refuge in Britain. Belgian refugees, who were represented by accounts in the British press or in real life through their accommodation proper, embodied the reason why Britain had gone to war in the first place. As long as the conflict continued and Belgians remained a visible presence in British cities, towns and villages, Belgian voices only seemed to become stronger.

Paving the way for a foreign-language press: translation as a transitional tool for Belgian refugees

Prior to the First World War, translation had played an important part in shaping late nineteenth-century art and literature, such as the Decadent movement, for instance. Not only did Decadent writers – who advocated the idea of art for art's sake – devote much of their time to translating literary works, but they also put 'translation at the heart of their creative practices. Translation was seen as a way of entering into dialogue with their counterparts abroad – a practical necessity that became a theoretical concern'.[17] This practice continued well beyond the Decadent movement, even though its creative value was much more vigorously contested. From the onset of the First World War, translation in Britain was used in several ways, but typically served the purpose of supporting the war effort. Witness reports by refugees, statements by allies, all of whom were not native English people, were translated to instigate as well as extend the sentiments of indignation and revenge towards the German enemy. The most notorious act of translation was the Bryce report,[18] which, upon publication early in 1915, gave a seemingly official stamp to stories of atrocities because the report was in part based on translated German diaries and letters. Here translation was no longer a manner of entering into dialogue, but also served a propaganda purpose, enabling the British people themselves to gauge the vile nature of the Germans. However, already during the war it transpired that both the witnesses providing the testimonies and the witness reports could not be found, they had been the fabrication of the Masterman propaganda machine.[19] Yet the report itself was translated into several languages so that the Allies could share in the empathy the report was devised to engender.

From the start of the First World War, interlingual translation acted as a means both of vilifying the enemy and of engaging home audiences as well as allied ones, and Belgian civilians were the protagonists of the many translations. British newspapers – national ones such as *The Times* and *The Manchester Guardian* but equally so more regional newspapers and journals – played a pivotal part in creating the image of Belgium and its inhabitants as either *gallant* or *poor*. Ten days into the war, *The Times* included a translation into English of the *Brabançonne*, the Belgian anthem, a 'stirring chant' that was little known in England.[20] Towards the end of August 1914, the same week the War Refugees Committee was established, the anthem was performed at the Promenade concert, immediately after the English national anthem. Throughout the war, including the Belgian national anthem was institutionalized further through versions of it at charity events in support of Belgian relief, through cultural events organized by Belgians themselves, and through persistent attention by the British press, especially the local newspapers.

Including the Belgian anthem in British journals at the start of the First World War was a stroke of propagandist genius as well as an early representation of the attention to Belgian culture – in exile or not – by the British press. This consideration also assumed a different dimension when notices in other languages spoken in Belgium were printed in the British press, usually French ones, but sometimes also Dutch ones.[21] An advertisement by the Belgian Consul-General was printed in both English and French on 16 September and as a trilingual notice one week later.[22] Regional and local newspapers followed. The *Hull Daily Mail* printed 'Avis aux réfugiés Belges', elsewhere this became 'Aux réfugiés Belges' ('To the Belgian refugees'), 'Avis Aux Belges' ('Advice for the Belgians'), 'Les Dernières Nouvelles en Français' ('The latest news, in French') and 'Colonne des réfugiés Belges' ('Section for the Belgian refugees').[23] The *Surrey Mirror* included the 'Colonne' section once or twice a week from early November 1914 until the end of May 1915, after which the section was renamed 'Colonne en Français' ('Section in French'). The latter appeared until end of January 1916. Although fewer in occurrence, Dutch-speaking refugees were also accommodated. However, other than the unique 'Nieuws voor Belgen' ('News for Belgians') in the *Evening Despatch* (West Midlands),[24] Dutch text was part of a section with a French heading such as 'Réfugiés de Belgique' ('Belgian refugees') or even with an English heading such as the frequent 'For Belgian readers' in the *Yorkshire Evening Post*.[25]

Peculiarly, this attention to Belgian refugees in Britain in the British press itself occurred alongside a gradual decrease of British newspaper articles on Belgian refugees. The mentions of the phrase 'Belgian refugees' in the British Library Newspaper Archive between August 1914 and November 1918 total 46,730.[26] Nearly three quarters of these mentions (74 per cent) were published in the first year of the war (14 August–15 July), 16 per cent in the second year (15 August–16 July), and 10 per cent between August 1916 and November 1918. This disappearance from view in the press also created a gradual but notable decline of sections in the British press in one of the two languages spoken by the Belgians.[27] Although these two modes of disappearance largely co-occurred, another factor most certainly resulted in much less attention being paid to Belgian sections in British journals by the Belgians themselves: the establishment of an intricate Belgian press in exile in Britain.

Walloon vs Flemish: what language for the Belgian refugee press in Britain?

The predominant impression in Britain was that most, if not all, Belgians spoke French.[28] Moreover, Belgian prominent people were easily put on a par with the French, or sometimes even categorized as French.[29] Even references to Flemish history and their historical mottos were not put into an explanatory context and appeared detached from the linguistic reality of – in part perceived – dominant francophone spheres in Belgium.[30] Infrequent early references to the fact that two languages were spoken in Belgium, applied to Belgium itself, or its troops, rather than the Belgian refugees in Britain. Although awareness of language differences among Belgian refugees in Britain had started to appear in the British press by the end of September,[31] misconceptions about linguistic intricacies and related socio-political sensitivities remained in place long after.

The native language of nearly three quarters of the Belgian refugees in Britain was Flemish, or Dutch, even though a census in 1910 had found that 54 per cent of the Belgian population used Flemish as their first language.[32] Attributing an appropriate qualifier for the language spoken in Flanders is not easily done. On the one hand, the language can be described as Dutch proper but, on the other hand, it can also be labelled Flemish, a southern and distinct variant of Dutch. However, how to label the Dutch language spoken in Flanders is not a matter of either/or. In fact, then as now, regional variation within Flanders has often been perceived as greater than the differences between Dutch and Flemish.[33] In the Belgian exile community in Britain, 62.7 per cent of the Belgian refugees had come from the on the whole Flemish-speaking provinces of Antwerp (41.7 per cent), Limburg, West Flanders and East Flanders. Another 19 per cent of the Belgian refugees had come from the province of Brabant, which was a bilingual province. Adding half the people from that province to the above-mentioned figure of Flemish-speaking people, around 75 per cent of Belgians in Britain spoke Flemish.[34] Therefore, the majority of people who spoke Dutch/Flemish, or a variant of it, was even bigger in exile than in the home nation prior to the war.

The linguistic boundaries between the French-speaking and the Dutch-speaking Belgians in Britain did not only go back to a geographical one in the home nation, but also one of social stratification. A sample mapping of the addresses of Belgian refugees in Glasgow added to the acknowledged statistical figures. For instance, most refugees from Antwerp, roughly one in four Belgians in Britain, were working-class labourers from poorer urban areas.[35] As well, like English in Wales, French was the language of advancement throughout Belgium. It can therefore be argued that a considerable proportion of the Flemish refugees in Britain were to some extent bilingual, whereas most Francophone Walloon refugees would not have been bilingual at all. Both language communities, be it in Belgium or in exile, knew very well what a language of social advantage entailed. This linguistic perpetuation of pre-war times can also be seen in the relocation of Belgian newspapers and journals to a place of publication abroad. For the Belgian exile press in Britain *L'Indépendance Belge* ('The Independent Belgium') or *La Métropole d'Anvers* ('The Metropolis of Antwerp') are clear examples of benchmark continuation publications there. The use of the new reality of displacement as an opportunity is evidenced by the emergence of many journals, especially *De Stem Uit België* ('The Voice From Belgium'), but most did not manage to provide such a powerful alternative to the established entities that they actually managed to survive.

The intricate network of Belgian exile newspapers and journals in Britain is characterized by issues limited in time and geographical spread. Several newspapers appeared for several years, sometimes even for the entire duration of the conflict, whereas others did not. A representation of the periods when Belgian exile newspapers appeared in Britain is included in table 1. So far, twenty-four Belgian exile publications have come to light. The mere idea that French was the language of social advancement in exile is also supported by the fact that nearly all journals and newspapers (twenty) were in French, whereas Dutch (nine) was included nearly as often as English (six). Twelve publications on the list were in either French or Dutch, and these included the main newspapers such as *L'Indépendance Belge*, *La Métropole d'Anvers* and *De Stem Uit*

België. Nine publications were bilingual, but these did not include translations into one language of articles in another. Nearly all bilingualism related to different content in different languages. However, *Anglo-Belgian Exports* did have English and French in parallel columns. As the issue printed contributions in several languages *Le Courrier Belge* (The Belgian Courier), which was arguably the most trilingual of all. *The Birtley Echo* can also be considered trilingual, but was one of the publications that also relied on substantial code switching, where words and phrases of one language entered texts that were written in another language. *Le Franco-Belge* (The Franco-Belge) switched codes much less and therefore cannot be regarded as trilingual. From the overview it becomes clear that London was the capital of the Belgian exile community in Britain. Even though roughly only one in three Belgians resided there during the war, the overall majority of newspapers and journals were published in London. Issuing an exile press took place in many ways. *La Métropole d'Anvers* for instance initially appeared as an insert in the *London Standard*. More intricacies were at play. Minor journals like *L'Avant Garde* (The Avant-Garde), *Ons Blad* (Our Journal) and *Souvenir d'Exil* (Souvenirs of Exile) were even handwritten, so circulation must have been very limited or covered only a very small area.

A few publications have not been included because information about them was incomplete, or no copy has been found so far. One example, the *Maandelijksche Katholieke Brieven* (Monthly Catholic Letters) was published in London by the British Catholic Information Society[36] and is currently only available from the Hoover Library. No immediate reference has been found in *De Stem Uit België*, of an equally Catholic imprint. It is noteworthy, however, that *De Paaschklok* (The Easter Bells) is sometimes categorized as Belgian exile press in Britain,[37] whereas in fact it was published in Calais. Some of the Belgian soldiers' press, such as *'t Gazetje van Tongerloo* (The Tongerloo Gazette) *and De Leijegalm voor Bisseghem en Omliggende* (The Lys Echo for Bisseghem and Surrounding), was issued in England and then sent on to the front. This partly blurred identity of specific publications can also be seen in the appearance of the much overlooked *Le Neptune (d'Anvers)* (The Neptune of Antwerp)? This was an English-French journal that already had offices in London prior to the war, which facilitated the relocation there of the entire wartime editorial effort.[38]

To make matters more complicated, *Le Courrier Belge*, which was published in Derby, had the same name as a bilingual pamphlet published in occupied Brussels in 1915. The *De Stem Uit België* appeared as a bilingual newspaper for the first two years of exile, after which it became a solely Dutch and Flemish issue. Its francophone half continued to be published but soon vanished. When *De Stem Uit België* had become a Dutch-only newspaper, code switching still took place in that words and phrases from another language still appeared in the issues, only this time it was English, the language of the host society. *La Métropole d'Anvers* sometimes also included brief sections in English, as in the case of the memorial service of Lord Rothschild in the Aldgate Synagogue.[39] If using English was a clear sign that the Belgian refugee community related to its host country, then advertising each other's issues was proof that the intricate network of the Belgian exile press in Britain was mutually supportive. This support continued throughout the war: *La Métropole d'Anvers* supported the *Anglo-Belgian Trade Review* as an interesting and well-documented publication[40] and

Table 16.1 Year by year periods for the publication of the Belgian exile press in Britain, ordered alphabetically.[41]

Newspaper/journal	1914	1915	1916	1917	1918	1919	location	Language
Anglo-Belgian Exports							London	ENG/FRE
The Anglo-Belgian Trade Review							London	ENG/FRE
L'Avant Garde: journal des boy-scouts belges en exil							London	DUT/FRE
Le Belge Indépendant							London	FRE
La Belgique Nouvelle							London	FRE
The Birtley Echo							Birtley	DUT/ENG/FRE
Le Courrier Belge/De Belgische Koerier							Derby	DUT/ENG/FRE
Le Cri de Londres							London	FRE
De Dageraad							London	DUT
La Dépêche							London	FRE
Le Franco-Belge							Folkestone	DUT/FRE
L'Indépendance Belge							London	FRE
De Belgische metaalbewerker/La métallurgiste belge							London	DUT/FRE
La Métropole (d'Anvers)							London	FRE
Le Neptune							London	ENG/FRE
Ons blad							Sheffield	DUT
Ons Fulhamsch Volk							London	DUT
Questions (La Revue Belge/The Belgian Review)							London	ENG/FRE
La Renaissance							Sheffield	FRE
Souvenir d'Exil							Barmouth	FRE
De Stem Uit België							London	DUT
(De Stem Uit België /) L'Echo de Belgique							London	DUT/FRE
La Tribune Congolaise (d'Anvers)							London	FRE
Turnhout: St Jozef's college/Turnhout: collège Saint Joseph							London	DUT/FRE

L'Indépendance Belge promoted the readership of *Anglo-Belgian Exports*.[42] Many such examples abound.

The readership of the Belgian exile press was not limited to refugee communities, authorities in exile, respective host nations or non-occupied Belgium. Germans also scanned the many publications, in support of counter publications that served propaganda purposes as well as to undermine enemy authority. In 1918, it was concluded from *Anglo-Belgian Exports* issues and the multitude of Belgian companies, which had moved to London and were subscribed to the business journal, that London had become the centre of Belgian economic policy, much more so even than Sainte-Adresse, where the Belgian government was in exile.[43]

Another example of the way in which the Germans picked up on the Belgian exile press in Britain was *Le Cri de Londres* (The Cry from London), which appeared from London early on in the war. In June 1915, *Le Cri de Londres* concluded a contribution by Belgian writer Hubert Colleye (1883–1972),[44] one of the post-war editors of *La Métropole d'Anvers*, with the sentence 'La Belgique de demain sera Latine ou elle ne sera pas' ('The Belgian nation state of the future will be Latin or will not be at all'), which sent waves of support round Belgicist circles and even round Walloon activists. However, it created such profound indignation among Flemish nationalists that even the more moderate nationalists felt offended. The German newspaper the *Kölnische Zeitung* (The Cologne Courier) reported on the increasing linguistic friction in the Belgian community, even while in exile, which did not help Colleye's reputation. Nonetheless, in 1916, Colleye started *L'Opinion Wallonne* (The Walloon Opinion), an exile journal for Walloon separatists, which operated from Paris.[45] The distribution of the Belgian exile press and its socio-cultural, linguistic and political tendencies across the boundaries of reception countries was rather elaborate and is clear proof of the transnational history of the Belgian refugees during the First World War: the Belgian exile press in Britain sat within a larger assembly of exile publications.

Adaptive replication: model circulations in a transnational multilingual refugee press network

If the exile in Britain, France and the Netherlands extended socio-cultural and political fault lines that troubled Belgium prior to the war, then the conflict aggravated the fragmented nature of the Belgian nation. During the First World War, Belgium not only consisted of a home nation, a large part of which was occupied by Germans, and a small part that wasn't, but there were also different exile communities, scattered authorities, even forced labour communities... all in all more than a dozen part nations.[46] The exile communities soon felt the need to liaise with one another so as to transcend the boundaries of the respective country of reception: from a sense of supranational community identity, it only made sense for the Belgian exile press in Britain to liaise with the exile press in the Netherlands and in France, but also to relate to Belgian authorities in non-occupied Belgium as well as to the daily life of the civilians living in occupied territory.[47] This need could therefore only be met by replicating the socio-cultural structures in place prior to the war or by using exile to add to specific political, social or cultural tendencies.

While the focus here is not the exile press in the Netherlands and France, even a more succinct assembly of the most representative journals provides a clear view of the intricate network in place, whether through daily or weekly newspapers or through more regional or more limited publications. After the overview, an equally limited but representative sample is given as to how these publications borrowed from one another within a network of adaptive replication, re-using information printed elsewhere for the purpose of their own issues.

Although what is included in Table 16.2 is not an exhaustive list for France and the Netherlands, additions to the overview will be brief for two parts of the Belgian wartime press that need to be mentioned. First, a small community of a few thousand Belgians resided in Switzerland, most of them children, and arguably *Les Tablettes* (The Columns) was the main journal of note, issued from Geneva between 1916 and 1919. However, no immediate replication of note in other exile newspapers has been retrieved so far. A second journal that needs to be added was not strictly speaking an exile newspaper as such. *De Belgische Standaard* (The Belgian Standard) appeared in the small unoccupied part of Belgium. However, in order to obtain a relatively substantial readership, it had to be circulated elsewhere. Most sources agree that only *De Belgische*

Table 16.2 List of Belgian exile press in France and the Netherlands (not exhaustive).[48]

France	• *Informations Belges* (Le Havre), *L'Écho Sportif* (Calais), *L'Idéal Sous Les Armes* (Lyon), *L'Opinion Wallonne* (Paris), *La Nation Belge* (Paris), *La Nouvelle Belgique* (Paris), *La Nouvelle Revue Wallonne* (Paris), *La Patrie Belge* (Paris), *La Tribune Belge* (Paris), *Le XXième Siècle : journal d'union et d'action catholique* (Le Havre), *Les Annales* (Paris), *Notre Avenir: hebdomadaire social, chrétien belge* (Le Havre), *Notre Belgique* (Calais)
	• *Le Courrier de l'Armée/De Legerbode* (Le Havre), *l'Universitaire/De Hoogstudent* (Le Havre)
	• *Het Belgisch volk: orgaan der in Frankrijk verblijvende Belgische socialisten* (Paris), *Het Vaderland* (Le Havre), *Ons Limburg* (Le Havre), *Ons Sinjorenblad* (Sainte-Adresse), *Ons Vaderland* (Calais),[49] *Ons Vlaanderen* (Paris), *Onze Samenwerking* (Le Havre), *Onze Toekomst* (Le Havre), *Oorlogsklokje* (Paris), *Pitthem in 't leger en in den vreemde* (Pau), *Uit 't Land van Aelst* (Calais)
The Netherlands	• *Amon Nos Autes: nosse gazette veut l'djoû totes les samainnes* (Amersfoort), *Belgisch Dagblad* (The Hague), *De Klok Uit België/La Cloche de Belgique* (Maastricht), *Journal des Réfugiés* (Bergen-Op-Zoom), *L'Écho Belge* (The Hague/Amsterdam), *L'Écho d'Anvers* (Bergen-op-Zoom), *La Belgique* (Rotterdam), *La Vesdre* (Maastricht), *Le Courrier de la Meuse* (Maastricht),
	• *Le Socialiste Belge/De Belgische Socialist* (Rotterdam), *Les Nouvelles* (Maastricht)
	• *Bulletin der Belgische comités en der Belgische instellingen in Nederland* (The Hague), *De Beiaard* (Amersfoort), *De Vlaamsche Stem* (Amsterdam), *Het Vlaamsche land: Vlaamsch orgaan voor België en Nederland* (Rotterdam), *Hoop in de Toekomst* (Amsterdam), *Vlaamsch-Belgisch Verbond* (The Hague), *Vrij België* (The Hague/Scheveningen)

Standaard – which was published from De Panne – can be considered as press published in 'free' Belgium. Others add *Ons Vaderland* (Our Native Land), even though it was published from nearby Calais most of the time. Resistance press such as *Droogstoppels* (Boring But Funny)[50] and *Het Nachtlichtje* (The Light at Night), or soldiers' press and trench journals (*frontblaadjes*) such as *Gazetje van Thielt* (The Thielt Courier) constitute an entirely different category and are not included in this study.

De Stem Uit België had been established in Britain early on in the war – Antwerp had not fallen yet – and among its initial key aims was providing information on whereabouts of individual refugees or families and to act as a framework through which the mainly Catholic refugees could be guided in a mainly Protestant country. The newspaper was backed by Alfons van de Perre (1872–1925), a Belgian Christian-democratic MP. In the weeks before the war, he wanted to start the first Dutch newspaper in Belgium, *De Standaard* (The Standard), which he aimed to further along with Frans Van Cauwelaert (1880–1961) – another Christian-democratic MP – and Arnold Hendrix (1866–1946), a Catholic and a notable Flemish entrepreneur.[51] If van de Perre had been a driving force behind a Catholic newspaper in the United Kingdom, then Van Cauwelaert was so in The Netherlands with *Vrij België* (Free Belgium). Both *De Stem Uit België* and *Vrij België* were moderately pro Flemish causes and were broadly aligned with the sole newspaper appearing in occupied Belgium, *De Belgische Standaard*. However, throughout the war, nuances between editorial stances increasingly became shifts along the line of moderate to more outspoken Flemish nationalism. The core arguments here were the position of Dutch as a language among common soldiers while French was used by officers, the cultural disposition of Flanders (within Belgium but also in relation to the German occupier) and the future of Flanders within Belgium after the war. If early on in the war *De Stem Uit België* was relatively moderate still – joining Belgian national and pro-Royal voices from other journals – then this changed gradually whereby its positions became less nuanced compared to *Vrij België* and *De Belgische Standaard*. Flemish nationalism played on the pages of three different journals in three different countries. For some contributors, more ardent Flemish nationalism was needed and editorial staff moved on to the radical journal *Ons Vaderland*, Juul Callewaert (1886–1964) – a Catholic priest who increasingly supported Flemish nationalism during the war – moved there from *De Stem Uit België* and Frans Daels from *De Belgische Standaard*. This also happened at *De Vlaamsche Stem* (The Flemish Voice). Initially along moderate lines and with the support of Van Cauwelaert, the journal changed course in the summer of 1915, no longer allowing the Belgian model of Flanders alongside Wallonia but in favour of a bigger unified The Low Countries, an ideology supported by the Germans.

With nationalism emerging from the pages of the exile press during the First World War, it can be argued that, although they were not separate entities at such, the socio-cultural and political developments in Belgium and its constituent regions continued abroad. The transnational Belgian exile press therefore assumes a pivotal role in the history of Belgium during the First World War.

Table 16.3 Selected overview of transnational networks of Belgian exile press in France, Britain and The Netherlands and their nationalist affiliation.

Title	Established	main support	Contributors (o.a.)	Other
De Stem Uit België	London (UK), 25.09.1914	Alfons van de Perre (1872–1925), Mgr Dewachter	Floris Prims (1882–1954), Juul Callewaert (1886–1964), Alfons van de Perre (1855–1932)	• Also *L'Echo de Belgique* until 10 February 1916. The French journal ceased publication in August 1916.
Ons Vaderland	Calais (FR), 31.12.1914	J. Baeckelandt (n.d.), also father Augustin De Groeve (n.d.) and A. Tempere (n.d.)	Juul Callewaert, Frans Daels (1882–1974), Jozef Simons (1888–1948), Alfons van de Perre, Adiel Debeuckelaere (1888–1979)	• Became more radical Flemish nationalist in May 1915. • Quite a few of the contributors formed the Front Movement, the ultimate Flemish nationalist association during the war.
De Belgische Standaard	De Panne (BEL), 10.01.1915	Marie Belpaire (1853–1948), Ildefons Peeters (1886–1926)	Frans Daels, Harry Baels (1878–1951), Omer Wattez (1857–1935), Juul Filliaert (1890–1948)	• Filliaert was the editorial secretary of *De Belgische Standaard*, but also published in exile journals in France and the Netherlands. • Encountered opposition from Belgian military authorities and *Le XXe Siècle*.
De Vlaamsche Stem	Bussum (NL), 01.02.1915	Albéric Deswarte (1875–1928)	René De Clercq (1877–1932), Johan Eggen (1883–1952)	• Initially loyal to Belgium but in favour of cultural emancipation of Flanders. • More radical from the summer of 1915 onwards, aiming for as much devolution as possible and confederalism • Early contributions by Cyriel Buysse (1859–1932), André De Ridder (1888–1961), Frans Van Cauwelaert and Julius Hoste who all left by the summer of 1915.
Vrij België	The Hague (NL), 27.08.1915	Frans Van Cauwelaert (1880–1961), Julius Hoste (1884–1954)	Frans Van Cauwelaert, Alfons van de Perre, Ernest Claes (1885–1968), August Van Cauwelaert (1885–1945)	• Founded in response to the radicalization of *De Vlaamsche Stem*.
Le XXe Siècle	Brussels (1895), Le Havre (FR) in WW1	Joris Helleputte (1852–1925), Charles de Broqueville (1860–1940), Fernand Neuray (1874–1934)	Fernand Neuray, Norbert Wallez (1882–1952)	• Belgian nationalist, pro-royal, anti-Flemish movement. • Heavily opposed *De Belgische Standaard*, *De Stem Uit België* and *Ons Vaderland*.

Conclusion

The majority of Belgian refugees moved across geographical borders and between humanitarian spheres. Wartime Belgian exile was characterized by two main features. First, Belgians who sought refuge elsewhere were dispersed across several host countries such as France, the Netherlands and the United Kingdom, and enjoyed the relative liberty to move from one country and resettle in another. This transnational aspect of displacement lines up well with a profound sense of the de-territorialization of Belgian culture in exile: identification spheres extended well beyond the boundaries of national borders as well as the temporal delineations of the exile. In the case of the First World War, Belgians extended these relational spaces of 'refugeedom' and called as well for comparing several languages of representation.

The study of the Belgian exile press in Britain must therefore not only extend its geographical reach to include the spheres of other host nations, more particularly the Netherlands and France, but must also reach out to the split personality of the home nation, which consisted of a non-occupied part where the exile press related to the limited 'free' press, and an occupied part. These diverse senses of becoming and multiple directions for fluidity existed in different language realities. Belgian refugees were provided with an operative sense of becoming that they were allowed to encourage. In Britain, the humanitarian borders in which refugee agencies developed by means of an exile press were not only shaped by the post-Victorian and post-Edwardian voluntary and statutory relief and support practices, but were also defined by the relational spaces in which the Belgian refugees moved, i.e. beyond the traditional borders of a single host nation.

If the history of the Belgian refugees, more in particular their exile press, is a case of 'refugeedom' on behalf of the reception country – allowing the space for refugees to develop their community – then the marked continuation of a representation of national identity through an exile press supports the transnational aspect of this temporary refugee history. Moving across different language spheres in different ways – through code switching, borrowing, translation or in parallel – Belgian exile newspapers have indeed been the means through which the transnational history of Belgian refugees extended the sense of identity and community and, therefore, also superseded the spatial delineations of displacement. Belgian national identity in exile is a clear case of a transnational community through the various exile press relations: in exile, Belgian newspapers still represented socio-cultural, linguistic and political realities as still being rooted in the homeland.

List of newspaper and journal titles discussed and an approximate translation equivalent

(*De Stem Uit België* /) *L'Echo de Belgique* ('The Voice from Belgium'), later simply *De Stem Uit België*
't Gazetje van Tongerloo ('The Tongerloo Gazette')
Amon Nos Autes (strong Walloon dialect, difficult to translate, ed.)

Anglo-Belgian Exports
Belgisch Dagblad ('Belgian Daily')
Bulletin der Belgische comités en der Belgische instellingen in Nederland ('Bulletin of Belgian committees and Belgian institutions in the Netherlands')
De Beiaard ('The Chimes')
De Belgische metaalbewerker/La métallurgiste belge ('The Belgian Metalworker')
De Belgische Standaard ('The Belgian Standard')
De Dageraad ('The Dawn')
De Klok Uit België/La Cloche de Belgique ('The Belgian Tower Bell')
De Leijegalm voor Bisseghem en Omliggende ('The Lys Echo for Bisseghem and Surrounding')
De Paaschklok ('The Easter Bells')
De Vlaamsche Stem ('The Flemish Voice')
Droogstoppels ('Boring But Funny')
Gazetje van Thielt ('The Thielt Courrier')
Het Belgisch volk ('The Belgian People')
Het Nachtlichtje ('The Light at Night')
Het Vaderland ('The Fatherland')
Het Vlaamsche land ('The Flemish Land')
Hoop in de Toekomst ('Hope for the Future')
Informations Belges ('Belgian Informations')
Journal des Réfugiés ('Refugees' Journal')
Kölnische Zeitung ('The Cologne Courrier')
L'Indépendance Belge ('The Independent Belgian')
L'Avant Garde ('The Avant-Garde')
L'Écho Belge ('The Belgian Echo')
L'Écho d'Anvers ('The Echo from Antwerp')
L'Écho Sportif ('The Sports Echo')
L'Idéal Sous Les Armes ('The Armed Ideal')
L'Opinion Wallonne ('The Walloon Opinion')
l'Universitaire/De Hoogstudent ('The University Student')
La Belgique ('Belgium')
La Belgique Nouvelle ('The New Belgium')
La Dépêche ('The Report')
La Métropole d'Anvers ('The Metropolis of Antwerp')
La Nation Belge ('The Belgian Nation')
La Nouvelle Belgique ('The New Belgium')
La Nouvelle Revue Wallonne ('The New Walloon Tiding')
La Patrie Belge ('The Belgian Fatherland')
La Renaissance ('The Renaissance')
La Tribune Belge ('The Belgian Tribune')
La Tribune Congolaise (d'Anvers) ('The Congo Tribune')
La Vesdre ('The River Vesdre')
Le Belge Indépendant ('The Independant Belgian')
Le Courrier Belge/De Belgische Koerier ('The Belgian Courrier')
Le Courrier de l'Armée/De Legerbode ('The Army Messenger')
Le Courrier de la Meuse ('The Meuse Courrier')
Le Cri de Londres ('The Cry from London')
Le Franco-Belge ('The Franco-Belge')
Le Neptune (d'Anvers) ('The Neptune of Antwerp')

Le Socialiste Belge/De Belgische Socialist ('The Belgian Socialist')
Le XXième Siècle ('The 20th Century')
Les Annales ('The Annals')
Les Nouvelles ('The News')
Les Tablettes ('The Columns')
Maandelijksche Katholieke Brieven ('Monthly Catholic Letters')
Notre Avenir ('Our Future')
Notre Belgique ('Our Belgium')
Ons Blad ('Our Journal')
Ons Fulhamsch Volk ('Our People in Fulham')
Ons Limburg ('Our Limburg')
Ons Sinjorenblad ('Journal for Antwerp')
Ons Vaderland ('Our Native Land')
Ons Vlaanderen ('Our Flanders')
Onze Samenwerking ('Our Collaboration')
Onze Toekomst ('Our Future')
Oorlogsklokje ('War clock')
Pitthem in 't leger en in den vreemde ('Pittem in the Army and Abroad')
Questions ('La Revue Belge/The Belgian Review')
Souvenir d'Exil ('Souvenirs of Exile')
The Anglo-Belgian Trade Review
The Birtley Echo
Turnhout: St Jozef's college/Turnhout: collège Saint Joseph
Uit 't Land van Aelst ('From the Aalst Region')
Vlaamsch-Belgisch Verbond ('Flemish-Belgian Alliance')
Vrij België ('Free Belgium')

Notes

1   Homi K. Bhabha, *The Location of Culture* (London/New York: Routledge, 1994), 247.
2   Doris Bachmann-Medick, 'The Transnational Study of Culture: A Plea for Translation', in Birgit Mersmann and Hans G. Kippenberg (eds.), *The Humanities between Global Integration and Cultural Diversity* (Berlin/Boston: De Gruyter, 2016), 29–49.
3   Maria Tymozcko, 'Trajectories of Research in Translation Studies', *Meta* 50, no.4 (2005): 1082–97.
4   Laura G. Rubio, 'Displacement, Territoriality and Exile: The Construction of Ethnic and National Identities in Tibetan Refugee Communities', Manchester University, unpublished PhD dissertation, 2004, 13–14.
5   The Belgian exile press, most notably the one in Britain, was mainly provided by VIAA and its online newspaper database hetarchief.be. Both data sets were sampled from through the use of simple but effective search techniques and topic tracking. In terms of the formal features of the Belgian exile press, details were obtained from many sources, historical ones as well as more contemporary digital databases. Other than site visits to archives and libraries (The British Library, Ghent University Library, Antwerp City Library (Conscience Library), Antwerp University Library, the Belgian National Archives), details have been retrieved from hard copy and online catalogue databases such as the following:

Abraham. *Catalogus van Belgische kranten* (no date), online (krantencatalogus.be and shorturl.at/eLO25, accessed 31 January 2020).

Belgian War Press (CEGESOMA, no date), online (https://warpress.cegesoma.be/en/newspaper-list?field_war_number_target_id=1, accessed 31 January 2020).

Bibliographie de Belgique (Brussels: Bibliothèque Royal/G. Van Oest, 1919).

British Library Newspaper Archive (London: British Library, no date), online (https://www.britishnewspaperarchive.co.uk, accessed 31 January 2020).

British Library online catalogue (London: British Library, no date), online (http://explore.bl.uk/primo_library/libweb/action/search.do?vid=BLVU1, accessed 31 January 2020).

An Callens, 'Het weekblad *De Stem Uit Belgie* (1914–1919)' (KU Leuven: Unpublished MA dissertation, 1980).

Jean Massart, *La Presse Clandestine dans la Belgique Occupée* (Paris: Berger-Levrault, 1917).

Nieuws van de Groote Oorlog (2018), Gent: Viaaa, online (https://nieuwsvandegrooteoorlog.hetarchief.be/, accessed 31 January 2020).

Stanford Libraries SearchWorks catalog (no date), online (https://searchworks.stanford.edu/, accessed 31 January 2020).

The Belgian Press from The Great War (no date), online (https://belgianpressfromthegreatwar.be/en/, accessed 31 January 2020).

The Newspaper Press Directory and Advertisers' Guide (London: C. Mitchell, 1917).

The Newspaper Press Directory and Advertisers' Guide (London: C. Mitchell, 1918).

6 Translations of Belgian exile newspaper or journal titles appearing in the text itself are provided with a translation between inverted commas upon their first occurrence. Titles appearing in tables are included in the full overview of titles, with translations, in the reference section.

7 For a more general history on Belgium and the First World War see Sophie De Schaepdryver, *De Groote Oorlog: Het Koninkrijk België Tijdens de Eerste Wereldoorlog* (Amsterdam/Antwerpen: Atlas, 1997).

8 Christophe Declercq, *Belgian Refugees in Britain 1914–1919: A Cross-Cultural Study of Belgian Identity in Exile* (London: Imperial College London, 2015), 88–93.

9 Peter Cahalan, *Belgian Refugee Relief in England During the Great War* (New York: Garland Publishing, 1982). Michaël Amara, *Des Belges à l'épreuve de l'exil. Les réfugiés de la Première Guerre mondiale en France, en Angleterre et aux Pays-Bas* (Brussels: Presse Universitaire de Bruxelles, 2008). Christophe Declercq, ibid.

10 First, the corpus of British wartime press was provided by the British Library Newspaper Archive as well as by the digital archives of national newspapers such as *The Times* and *The Manchester Guardian*.

11 Anti-German sentiment, mockery depictions and negative framing had emerged on the back of the Prussian victory after the Franco-Prussian war (1870–1). For more on anti-German sentiments in Britain, please see Panikos Panayi, *The Enemy in Our Midst: Germans in Britain during the First World War* (Providence/Oxford: Berg Publishers, 1991).

12 Keir Waddington, '"We Don't Want Any German Sausages Here!" Food, Fear, and the German Nation in Victorian and Edwardian Britain', *Journal of British Studies* 52 (2013):1017–42.

13 Christophe Declercq, 'From Antwerp to Britain and Back Again: The Language of the Belgian Refugee in Britain During the First World War', in Christophe Declercq and Julian Walker (eds.), *Languages and the First World War: Representation and Memory* (London: Palgrave-MacMillan, 2016), 97–9.

14 Cahalan, *Belgian Refugee Relief in England During the Great War*; Amara, *Des Belges à l'épreuve de l'exil*; Declercq, *Belgian refugees in Britain 1914–1919*.
15 *The Times*, 24 August 1914, 9.
16 Declercq, *Belgian refugees in Britain 1914–1919*, 118.
17 Matthew Creasy, *Decadence and Translation* (University of Glasgow: School of Critical Studies, 2018), online https://gtr.ukri.org/project/48C3809C-06F3-4DA1-B862-08C4BE46988C.
18 *Report of the Committee on Alleged German Outrages appointed by His Britannic Majesty's government and presided over by the Right Hon. Viscount Bryce* (Bryce Report) (London, HMSO, 1915).
19 For the ultimate study of the veracity of these atrocity stories, see John Horne and Alan Kramer, *German Atrocities, 1914: A History of Denial* (New Haven: Yale University Press, 2001).
20 *The Times*, 15 August 1914, 5. The Belgian national anthem, the *Brabançonne*, created by a Frenchman during the Belgian revolution of 1830, was entirely in French, and underwent various substantial changes until 1921. Its Dutch translation was only made official in 1938. Despite claims that the Belgian national anthem had been little-known, it had appeared in the British press before the First World War, quite frequently even in the 1850s and 1860s – to the extent where it hardly needed an explanatory label (*Heywood Advertiser* 6 June 1857, *Manchester Courier and Lancashire General Advertiser* 20 October 1866, 11, and *Kentish Chronicle* 27 October 1866, 7) – but its use had decreased from well over 400 mentions in the 1860s to barely twenty in the 1890s and a mere forty in the 1900s. Intriguingly, the attention in the 1910s – the majority of which was triggered by the outbreak of the First World War and the ensuing empathy towards the Belgians – was on a par with that of the 1860s. Figures British Library Newspaper online, 31 January 2020.
21 The subsequent part of this paragraph draws from Christophe Declercq, 'Belgian Exile Press in Britain', in Felicity Rash and Christophe Declercq (eds.), *The Great War in Belgium and The Netherlands* (London: Palgrave-MacMillan, 2018), 121–41.
22 *The Times*, 16 September 1914, 11.
23 *Hull Daily Mail*, 14 September 1914, 3. *Hull Daily Mail*, 15 September 1914, 3. *Western Daily Express*, 29 October 1914, 2. *Western Daily Express*, 30 October 1914, 2. *Aberdeen Journal*, 9 November 1914, 4. *Derby Daily Telegraph*, 6 November 1914, 3. *Surrey Mirror*, 10 November 1914, 2.
24 *Evening Despatch* (West Midlands), 22 January 1915, 2.
25 *Derby Daily Telegraph*, 15 December 1914, 3. *Derby Daily Telegraph*, 28 December 1914, 3. *Western Daily Press*, 9 November 1914, 4. *Yorkshire Evening Post*, 10 October 1914, 5. After that date, the newspaper included the section several times a week until early April 1915.
26 Date of search phrase snapshot 31 January 2020.
27 Declercq, *Belgian refugees in Britain 1914–1919*, 177–8; Lorna Hughes, 'Finding Belgian Refugees in Cymru1914.org: Using Digital Resources for Uncovering the Hidden Histories of the First World War in Wales', *Immigrants & Minorities: Historical Studies in Ethnicity, Migration and Diaspora* 34, no.2 (2016): 210–31.
28 Declercq, *Belgian Refugees in Britain 1914–1919*, 161.
29 Edmund Gosse, *French Profiles* (New York: Dodd, Mead and Company, 1915).
30 In one of the first reports about the fierce fighting near Liège in August 1914, there was a reference to 'schild en vriend', the motto of Flemish craftsmen when they fought the French in 1302 and to the fact that the motto was deemed still valid at the time of the

early battles in 1914, and this despite the fact that hardly anyone in the Liège region spoke Dutch. *The Times*, 10 August 1914, 7.
31 In the Edmonton Refuge and in Alexandra Palace, the first two major dispersal centres for Belgians, 'notices throughout the building are printed both in French and Flemish. Some know both languages, but, as a rule, the refugees speak but one or the other'. *The Times*, 22 September 1914, 12.
32 De Schaepdryver, *De Groote Oorlog*, 27.
33 Declercq, *Belgian refugees in Britain 1914–1919*, 162.
34 Figures are based on de T.T.S. Jastrzebski, 'The Register of Belgian Refugees', *Journal of the Royal Statistical Society* 79, no.2 (1916): 142–4.
35 *Glasgow Register of Belgian Refugees*, 1914–20, online (https://www.glasgowfamilyhistory.org.uk/ExploreRecords/Documents/Belgian%20refugees%20-%20online%20version.pdf, accessed 31 January 2020).
36 Alexis August Verbouwe, *De Vlaamsche pers buiten bezet België en de Vlaamsche Sluikbladen in 1914–1918* (Baasrode: Drukkerij Bracke-Van Geert, 1920).
37 Verbouwe, *De Vlaamsche pers buiten bezet België*.
38 In the years before the Second World War, *L'Indépendance Belge* – one of the Belgian newspapers appearing already before the First World War and in exile in Britain during that conflict – would lead a consortium of journals to which *Le Neptune* also belonged, another First World War exile journal.
39 *La Métropole d'Anvers*, 20 April 1915, 2.
40 *La Métropole d'Anvers*, 20 June 1915, 1.
41 Declercq, *Belgian refugees in Britain 1914–1919*, 183–4.
42 *L'Indépendance Belge*, 30 October 1917, 4.
43 Karl Bittmann, Jozef von Grassmann, Georg Max Jahn, Karl Rathgen and Friedrich Schulte, *Belgiens Volkswirtschaft* (Leipzig/ Berlin: Verlag von B.G. Tuebner, 1918), 311–12.
44 An alias for Raymond De Weerdt.
45 Declercq, *Belgian Refugees in Britain 1914–1919*, 201.
46 Declercq, 'Belgian Exile Press in Britain', 122.
47 Ibid.
48 Based on Declercq, *Belgian Refugees in Britain 1914–1919*, 172–3, with additions.
49 *Ons Vaderland* did not provide an address for a distribution point in Britain, but it was available there. Based on Declercq, *Belgian refugees in Britain 1914–1919*, ibid.
50 The translation of the title is not straightforward. A 'droogstoppel' has many meanings. An appropriate translation would be a seemingly boring person with a sense of dry and wry humour.
51 The three had already established a Flemish journal in 1911, *Ons Volk Ontwaakt* (*Our Nation Awakens*).

Selected Bibliography

Primary sources

Archives

Archives nationales, Paris. Ministère de l'Intérieur, Direction de la Presse. Presse parisienne et agences de presse: dossiers, des journaux (1820–94) F/18/377, Dossier 58, LIBANON (LE) 1864–7.
Gosudarstvennyi arkhiv Rossiiskoi Federatsii (GARF), State Archive of Russian Federation, Moscow.
Osmanlı Belgelerinde Ermeni-İngiliz İlişkileri, Volume 1 (1845–90), Osmanlı Arşivi Daire Başkanlığı. Yayın Nu: 58, Ankara, 2002.
Osmanli Belgelerine Göre Ermeni-Fransiz İlişkileri, Volume 1, Osmanlı Arşivi Daire Başkanlığı. Yayın Nu: 67, Ankara, 2004.
Rossiiskii gosudarstvennyi arkhiv sotsial′no-poiticheskoi istorii (RGASPI), The Russian State Archive of Socio-Political History, Moscow.
The National Archives (TNA), Kew, London.
* Foreign Office Papers, FO 78/4591 (Stoppage of Newspapers and Turkey).
* Home Office Papers, HO 45/94721/A38025, Hurriyet Case.
* Treasury of Solicitor and Director of Public Prosecutions Office, Burtzeff Case, DPP 4/32.
The National Archives. Washington DC.

Legislation

Council of Europe, *European Charter for Regional or Minority Languages*, ETS 148 – Regional or Minority Languages, 5.XI.1992.
Universal Declaration of Linguistic Rights Follow-Up Committee, *Universal Declaration of Linguistic Rights*, Barcelona, 1998. https://culturalrights.net/descargas/drets_culturals389.pdf (accessed 2 August 2022).
US House of Representatives Bill. H.R.997 – English Language Unity Act of 2017 https://www.congress.gov/bill/115th-congress/house-bill/997/text (accessed 2 August 2022).

Serials

Please note that only titles that get more than a brief mention in the volume are listed.

- Albanian-language press titles in the US

Dielli (The Sun), New York (New York), 1909–2006, 2011–.
Kombi (The Nation), Boston (Massachusetts), 1906–9.

- Armenian-language press titles in Britain and the US

Aptak, Athens, 1894, then London, 1894–7.

Haik, New York (New York), 1891.

Hnch'ak, Geneva, 1887–92; Athens 1893; London, 1894–1904; finally, Paris, 1905–14.

Le Haïsdan, London, 1888–92, bilingual French/Armenian. Then *The Anglo-Armenian Gazette*, London, 1892–9?.

Mart, London, 1897–1901.

- Dutch-language press titles in Britain

't Gazetje van Tongerloo, ?, 1915–16.

De Belgische metaalbewerker/La métallurgiste belge, London, 1915–18. Dutch/French.

De Dageraad, London, 1918–19.

De Leijegalm voor Bisseghem en Omliggende, London, then Belgium, 1917–?.

De Stem Uit België, London, 1914–19. Originally entitled *De Stem Uit België/L'Echo de Belgique* (September 1914–August 1916) and bilingual Dutch/French. From August 1916, in Dutch only.

L'Avant Garde: journal des boy-scouts belges en exil, London, 1918. Dutch/French.

Le Courrier Belge/De Belgische Koerier, London, 1914–15. Trilingal Dutch/French/English.

Maandelijksche Katholieke Brieven, London, 1916–17.

Ons Blad, Sheffield, 1917–18.

Ons Fulhamsch Volk, London, 1917–18.

The Birtley Echo, London, 1917. Trilingal Dutch/French/English.

Turnhout: St Jozef's college/Turnhout: collège Saint Joseph, London, 19?. Dutch/French.

- French-language press titles (mostly in Britain, the US and Australia)

Almanach Américain pour 1801. Philadelphia (Pennsylvania), [1800].

Almanach Américain, de Dr. Ayer, à l'usage des fermiers, planteurs, artisans, et des familles en général. Lowell: Ayer & Company, 1858.

Almanach chantant, le Chansonnier des grâces, pour l'année 1809, dédié aux Dames, rédigé par Alexis Daudet. New Orleans (Louisiana): Imprimerie de Th. Lamberte, 1809.

Almanach de la Louisiane, 1866. New Orleans (Louisiana): Francis Bouvin, [1865].

Almanach de la Renaissance, pour 1869. New Orleans (Louisiana): Imprimerie de la Renaissance, [1868].

Almanach des Adresses des Membres de l'Union Saint-Baptiste d'Amérique. Manchester (New Hampshire): Union Saint-Jean-Baptiste, 1904–.

Almanach des Français en Californie. San Francisco (California): George Lanson, 1920–5.

Almanach du Commerce et de l'Industrie des États-Unis. New York (New York): H. de Mareil, 1872.

Almanach et Directoire Français des États-Unis pour 1866, à l'usage des populations françaises de l'Amérique du Nord. New York (New York): Docteur J. D. L. Zender [1864].

Almanach et Directorium Français des États-Unis pour l'année 1857. À l'usage des populations françaises. New York (New York), 1856.

Almanach français de New York, composé principalement pour les populations françaises des États-Unis, pour 1848. New York (New York): Seth Williston Benedict [1847].

Almanach franco-américain et catholique. Fitchburg (Massachusetts): L.H. Bourguignon, 1911–13.

Almanach Franco-Californien. Petit Journal 'Directory' des Français de la Côte du Pacifique. San Francisco (California): L. Grégoire et Cie., 1876.

Almanach illustré de Hostetter pour les États-Unis 1876. Pittsburgh, Pa.: Hostetter and Smith [1864].

Annuaire Louisianais: commençant à l'équinoxe de mars 1808 et se terminant à celui de Mars 1809 [By Bartholomé Lafon]. New Orleans (Louisiana): Bartholomé Lafon, 1808.
Aux Enfants, London and Paris, 1812.
Aux Petits, London and Paris, 1812.
Étrennes historiques et intéressantes contenant l'Abrégé géographique du royaume de France, avec un mélange curieux d'anecdotes, d'événements remarquables, &c. &c. pour l'année de grace 1786, Boston (Massachusetts), 1786 (annual).
Germinal. Organe Libertaire. Paterson, New Jersey, 1899–1903 (?).
Hugo's French Journal, An illustrated weekly for those who know French, and those who want to, London, 1896–1932.
La Belgique Nouvelle, London, 1915–16.
La Dépêche, London, 1914–15.
L'Almanach Franco-Américain/French American Directory, New York, 1928 (published by *Le Moniteur franco-américain*).
La Métropole d'Anvers, Antwerp, 1894–1914 and 1919–74; London, 1914–19.
La Renaissance, Sheffield, 1916.
La Tribune congolaise (d'Anvers), Antwerp, 1902–14; London, 1915–19; Brussels, 1919–41.
La Tribune Libre, London, 1890–1.
Le Belge Indépendant, London, 1918–19.
Le Courrier Australien, Sydney (Australia), 1892–.
Le Cri de Londres, London, 1914–16.
Le Furet de Londres, Journal littéraire et d'avertissemens, London, 1826–31.
Le Journal de Melbourne, Melbourne (Australia), 1858.
Le Neptune (d'Anvers), in Antwerp 1906–36 (French/Dutch), but for the period February 1917–February 1919 when it was published in London (French/English).
Le Père Peinard, London, 1894–5.
Le Petit étranger, Birmingham, Leicester, London and Paris, 1890–2.
Le Rothschild, London, 1891.
Le Tocsin, London, 1892–4.
L'Indépendance Belge, London, 1914–18.
L'Observateur français, London, 1845–8.
L'Océanien, Sydney (Australia), 1874.
Questions (La Revue Belge/The Belgian Review), London, 1915–16. English/French.
Revue Australienne, Sydney (Australia), 1873–4.
Souvenir d'Exil, Bournemouth, 1916–17.
The Rebel. Chicago, 1895.
VoilaSydney, Sydney (Australia), 2016–. Online.

- German-language press titles in Britain and the US

Das Vaterland. London, 1876.
Das Volk. London, 1859.
Der Bote aus London. London, 1860.
Der Hoch-Deutsche Amerikanische Calender, Germantown and Philadelphia, Pennsylvania, 1739–1832 (annual).
Der Kosmos. London, 1851.
Der Landstreicher. London, 1889–1914. (1891–3 as *Figaro's Chronik*, 1893–4 as *Londoner Figaro-Chronik*, 1894–1914 as *Londoner General-Anzeiger*.)
Der Rebell. London, 1881–6. (Place of publication varies, some issues published in Geneva.)
Der Sozialdemokrat. London, 1886–90.

Der Treue Verkündiger. London, 1810–11.
Deutsche Londoner Zeitung: Blätter für Politik, Literatur und Kunst. London, 1845–51.
Deutsche Zeitung. London, 1864.
Die Autonomie: Anarchistisch-communistisches Organ. London, 1886–93.
Die deutsche Presse: Zeitung für Politik, Literatur, Handel und Gewerbe. London, 1841.
Die Glocke: Ein freies sozial-politisches Blatt. London, 1881.
Die Neue Zeit: Organ der Demokratie. London, 1858–9.
Die Philadelphische Zeitung, Philadelphia, Penns., 1732.
Englische Correspondenz. London, 1850–81.
Freiheit: Socialdemokratisches Organ. London, 1879–81. (Continued in New York, 1882–1910 as *Freiheit: Internationales Organ der Anarchisten deutscher Sprache*.)
Germania: Deutsche Londoner Zeitung und Anzeigeblatt für In- und Ausland. London, 1859.
Hermann: Deutsches Wochenblatt aus London. London, 1859–1914. (From 1870 as *Londoner Zeitung: Hermann*.)
Illustrirte Familien-Zeitung: Beilage zur London Hotel & Restaurant Gazette. London, 1890–1.
Kalendarium Pennsilvaniense, or America's Messinger. Being an Almanack for the Year of Grace, 1686. By Samuel Atkins. Philadelphia (Pennsylvania): William Bradford; and New York: Philip Richards [1685] (annual).
Kommunistische Zeitschrift. London, 1847.
Londoner Arbeiter-Zeitung. London, 1886–90. (From 1887 as *Londoner Freie Presse*.)
Londoner Courier. London, 1884.
Londoner Deutsche Post. London, 1870–1.
Londoner Deutsche Zeitung und allgemeiner Anzeiger. London, 1858–9.
Londoner Deutsches Journal. London, 1855–8.
Londoner deutsches Tageblatt. London, 1884.
Londoner deutsches Wochenblatt. London, 1819–20.
Londoner Journal: Deutsches Organ für Politik, Finanzwesen, Handel, Assecuranzen, Kunst und Literatur. London, 1878–91.
Manchester Nachrichten: eine deutsche Zeitung in England. Manchester, 1910–12.
Reuters Finanz-Chronik. London, 1896–1912.
Rutli: Organ der Schweizer in Grossbritannien. London, 1900–3.
Telegraph: Londoner Anzieiger. London, 1864–67.
Teutsche Pilgrim, Mitbringende einen Sitten-Calender, Philadelphia (Pennsylvania), 1731–? (annual).
Thusnelda, teutonisch-satyrisch-humoristisches Klatschblatt. London, 1861.

- Greek-language press in the US

Atlantis, New York (New York), 1894–1973.
Ethnikos Kyrix, New York (New York), 1915–.
Loxias, Chicago (Illinois), 1908–21.

- Hebrew-language press

Halbanon/Ha-Levanon, Jerusalem, 1863; as *Le Libanon*, Paris 1864–71; as Supplement to *Der Israelit*, 1871–82; as *The Levanon*, London, 1886.
Ha-Maggid, originally first in Lyck, Prussia, and after 1890 successively in Berlin, Cracow, and finally Vienna, 1856–1903.
Ha-Melitz, St Petersburg, 1860–1904.
Havatzelet, Jerusalem, 1863, 1870–1911.

Ha-Yom, St Petersburg, 1886–8.
Ha-Zefira, Warsaw, later Berlin, 1862–1931.

- Italian-language press (mostly in the US)

Cronaca sovversiva, Barre, Vermont, 1908–18.
Germinal, Chicago, 1926–30.
Il Corriere d'America, New York, 1923-1931.
Il Martello, New York, 1917–40.
Il Progresso Italo-Americano, New York, 1880-1988.
L'Adunata dei refrattari, Newark, 1922–45.
La Battaglia, São Paulo, 1904–11.

- Polish and Polish-language press in the UK and the US

Ameryka-Echo, Toledo (Ohio), 1902–71.
Cooltura, The Polish Weekly Magazine, London, 2004–.
Dziennik Chicagoski, Chicago (Illinois), 1890–1971.
Dziennik Polski, Detroit (Michigan), 1904–.
Dziennik Polski, London, 1940–. Renamed *Tydzień Polski*, London, 1959–.
Głos Ludowy, Detroit (Michigan), 1901–79.
Goniec Polski, London, 2002–.
MojaWyspa, MojaWyspa.co.uk, Online, 2003–.
Národ Polski, Chicago (Illinois), later Detroit (Michigan), 1897–.
Nowy Świat, New York, 1932–99?.
Panorama Magazine, London, 2006. Renamed as *LAJT Magazine* in 2016 (ongoing).

- Portuguese-language press in the US

A Alvorada, New Bedford (Massachusetts), 1919–26.
A Pátria, New Bedford (MA), 1935–6.
A Tribuna, Newark (NJ), 1931–4.
A União Lusitana-Hawaiana, Hawaïi, 1891–6.
A União Portuguesa, San Francisco, 1887–1942.
Aurora Hawaiana, Hawaïi, 1888–91.
Diario de Noticias, New Bedford (Massachusetts), 1927–73.
Jornal Português, Oakland, 1932–97.
Luso-Americano, Newark (New Jersey), 1928–.
O Amigo dos Cathólicos, Irvington, 1888–96.
O Facho, Hawaïi, 1906–27.
O Independente, New Bedford (Massachusetts), 1895–1945.
O Jornal (The Newspaper), Fall River (MA) from 1970 and from New Bedford since 1973.
O Jornal de Noticias, Erie, Pennsylvania, 1877–84.
O Lavrador Portuguez (The Portuguese Farmer), Leemore, 1912–27.
O Luso-Hawaiano, Hawaïi, 1885–90.
O Progresso Californiense, San Francisco (California), 1885–7.
O Trabalho, Danbury, CT, 1939–40.

- Russian-language periodicals in the UK

Kolokol, London 1857–65, and then Geneva, 1865–7.
Letuchie Listki, London, 1893–9.
Narodovolets, Sotsial'no-politicheskoe obozrenie, London, 1897, and then Geneva in 1903.

- Slovak-language press in the US

Denník Rovnosť ľudu/Rovnosť ľudu, Chicago, 1906–c. 1950. Rebranded *Ľudový denník* in 1935.
New Yorkský denník, New York, 1913–62.

- Spanish-language press in Britain and the US

Doctrina de Martí, New York, 1896–8, then Havana, Cuba, 1899–1901.
El Alba. Periodico de instruccion y recreo, London, 1854–?.
El Catolicismo Neto, London, 1849–51. Then *El Examen Libre; periódico religioso, de indeterminado periodo, destinado á propagar el conocimiento de la pura religion del Evangelio*, London [1851–4].
El Eco de Martí, Tampa (Florida), 189?.
El Español, London, 1810–14.
El Español Constitucional, London, 1818–20 and 1824–5.
El Ibérico Gratuito, London, 2010–, digital since 2018.
El Instructor o Repertorio de historia, bellas artes y letras, London, 1834–?.
El Misisipí, New Orleans (Louisiana), 1808.
El Mundo Nuevo, New York (New York), 1871–5.
El Oriente, Tampa (Florida), 189?.
El Porvenir, New York (New York), 18??–18??.
El Repertorio Americano, London, 1826–7.
El Telescopio, London, n.d.?
El Vigia, Key West (Florida), 1897.
El Yara, Key West (Florida), 1878–98?.
La América, New York? (New York), 1873–?.
La Biblioteca Americana, London, 1823.
La Colmena, periódico trimestre de Ciencias, Artes, Historia y Literatura, London, 1842–5.
La Doctrina de Martí, New York (New York), 1896–9?.
La Nueva República, Tampa (Florida), 189?.
La Revista Ilustrada de Nueva York, New York, 1889–92.
Museo Universal de Ciencias y Artes. Supplement to *Variedades o El Mensajero de Londres*, London, 1825–6.
Ocios de españoles emigrados, London, 1824–7.
Patria, New York (New York), 1892–8.
Revista de Cuba Libre, Tampa (Florida), 1897–8?.
Variedades o El Mensajero de Londres, London, 1823–5.

- Turkish-language serials in the UK

Hürriyet, London: Imprimerie Centrale de la Jeune Turquie, 1868–70.

- Other periodical titles (in English)

Anglo-Belgian Exports, London, 1917–18. Bilingual English/French.
Anglo-German Friendship Gazette, London, 1911.
Ara: A Journal of Literature, and of Armenian Politics and History, Dacca, 1892–5.
Armenia, London, 1890–8 (irregular). English version of *L'Arménie, journal politique et littéraire*, London, 1889–1905, later published in Paris.
Cosmopolis, An International Review, Paris, 1896–8 (In French, English and German).
Freedom, London, 1886–2014. Short interruption in the 1830s. Irregular since 2016. (Originally issued by the Russian community.)
How do you do. London, 1851–? (partly for the German community).

Reynolds's Newspaper, London.
The Anglo-Belgian Trade Review, London, 1915–16. Bilingual English/French.
The Anglo-Russian, London, 1897.
The Confederate. London, c. 1851. (Partly for the German community.)
The Galignani Messenger, Paris, 1814–95.
The Times, London.

Other printed primary material

Bibliographie de Belgique. Brussels: Bibliothèque Royal/G. Van Oest, 1919.
Bittmann, Karl, Jozef von Grassmann, Georg Max Jahn, Karl Rathgen and Friedrich Schulte. *Belgiens Volkswirtschaft*. Leipzig/Berlin: Verlag von B. G. Tuebner, 1918.
[Bril, Yehiel]. 'Qol mevasser. Perah Levanon', prospectus, November 1864. Bibliothèque nationale de France, Paris.
Bril, Yehiel. 'The Publisher Discourses with his Readers', in *Ketab al-Rasil* (tr. From Hebrew: *Sefer Iggrot*), edited by Todros Halevi Abulafia. Paris, 1871: 3.
Bril, Yehiel. *Yessod Hama'ala*. Mainz, 1883.
Burtsev, Vladimir L. *Bor'ba za svobodnuiu rossiiu*. Berlin: Gamaiun, 1923.
Burtsev, Vladimir L. *Doloi tsaria!* London: [privately published], 1905.
De Jastrzebski, T. T. S. 'The Register of Belgian Refugees'. *Journal of the Royal Statistical Society* 79, no. 2 (1916): 142–4.
Die Londoner 'Kommunistische Zeitschrift' und andere Urkunden aus den Jahren 1847/1848, mit einer einleitenden Abhandlung über 'Die Entstehungsgeschichte des Kommunistischen Manifests', edited by Carl Grünberg. Hauptwerke des Sozialismus und die Sozialpolitik, neue Folge 5, 35–81. Leipzig: Hirschfeld, 1921.
Guide Canadien-français ou Almanach des adresses de Fall River, et notes historiques sur les Canadiens de Falls River par H.A. Dubuque, published with E. F. Lamoureux at Fall River, Rhode Island, 1888–.
Marx, Karl and Friedrich Engels. *Collected Works, Volume 24: Marx and Engels 1874–83*. Lawrence & Wishart: Electric Book, 2001.
Massart, Jean. *La Presse Clandestine dans la Belgique Occupée*. Paris: Berger-Levrault, 1917.
Mitchell, Charles. *Newspaper Press Directory. Containing Full Particulars Relative to Each Journal Published in the United Kingdom and the British Isles*. London: Mitchell, 1846.
'Notes on the history of Hebrew Press', *Haolam* 30, 1912: 13.
N. W. Ayer and Son's *Directory of Newspapers and Periodicals*. Philadelphia: Ayer and Son, 1930.
Prelooker, Jaakoff M. *Russian Flushlights*. London: Chapman and Hall, 1911.
Prelooker, Jaakoff M. *Under the Czar and Queen Victoria*. London: Nisbet, 1895.
Prelooker, Jaakoff M. *Under the Russian and British Flags. A Story of True Experience*. London: Spriggs Publishing Agency, 1912.
Stepniak-Kravchinsky, Sergey M. *Nihilism as it is. Being Stepniak's Pamphlets*. London: T. Fisher Unwin, [1895].
The Newspaper Press Directory and Advertisers' Guide. London: C. Mitchell, 1917.
The Newspaper Press Directory and Advertisers' Guide. London: C. Mitchell, 1918.
Tujague, F[rançois]. 'De l'avenir de la littérature à la New Orleans'. *Almanach de la Louisiane, 1866*. New Orleans: Francis Bouvin, [1865], 119–21.
Verbouwe, Alexis August. *De Vlaamsche pers buiten bezet België en de Vlaamsche Sluikbladen in 1914-1918*. Baasrode: Drukkerij Bracke-Van Geert, 1920.

Secondary sources

(NB. All links to webpages active at the date of last consultation, 15 March 2023.)

Abraham. *Catalogus van Belgische kranten*. Online. krantencatalogus.be.

Adedeji, A. O. 'Analysis of Use of English and Indigenous Languages by the Press in Selected African Countries', *Arabian Journal of Business and Management Review* 4, no. 8 (2015), 35–45.

Albertini, Luigi. *Epistolario, 1911–1926*, vol. III, edited by Ottavio Barié, Milan: Mondadori, 1968.

Alston, Charlotte. 'News of the Struggle: The Russian Political Press in London 1853–1921', in *The Foreign Political Press in Nineteenth-Century London: Politics from a Distance*, edited by Constance Bantman and Ana Claudia Suriani da Silva, 155–74. London: Bloomsbury Academic, 2018.

Amara, Michaël. *Des Belges à l'épreuve de l'exil. Les réfugiés de la Première Guerre mondiale en France, en Angleterre et aux Pays-Bas*. Brussels: Presse Universitaire de Bruxelles, 2008.

Anderson, Benedict. *Imagined Communities: Reflections on the Origin and Spread of Nationalism*. London: Verso, 1991.

Aprile, Sylvie. *Le Siècle des Exilés. Bannis et proscrits de 1789 à la Commune*. Paris: CNRS Editions, 2010.

Aprile, Sylvie. '"Translations" politiques et culturelles: les proscrits français et l'Angleterre', *Genèses. Sciences sociales et histoire* 38 (2000): 33–55.

Arndt, Karl John Richard and Reimer Eck, eds. *The First Century of German-Language Printing in the United States of America. A Bibliography Based on the Studies of Oswald Seidensticker and Wilbur H. Oda*. Göttingen, Universitätsverlag Göttingen (Coll. Pennsylvania German Society 21), 1989. vol. I (1728–1807).

Avrich, Paul. *Anarchist Voices. An Oral History of Anarchism in America* (Princeton: Princeton University Press, 1995).

Bachmann-Medick, Doris. 'The Transnational Study of Culture: A Plea for Translation', in *The Humanities between Global Integration and Cultural Diversity*, edited by Birgit Mersmann and Hans G. Kippenberg, 29–49. Berlin/Boston: De Gruyter, 2016.

Baganha, Maria I. 'The Lusophone Migratory System: Patterns and Trends'. *International Migration* 47, no. 3 (2009): 5–20.

Ban, Oscar. 'Death Comes to the Foreign Press', *New Outlook*, July 1933, 44–8.

Bannick, Christopher. *Portuguese Immigration to the United States: its Distribution and Status*. San Francisco: R&E Research Associates, 1971.

Bantman, Constance and Ana Cláudia Suriani da Silva, eds. *The Foreign Political Press in Nineteenth-Century London: Politics from a Distance*. London: Bloomsbury, 2017.

Bantman, Constance and Pietro Di Paola. 'La presse militante transnationale: *The Torch* (1891–1896), journal anarchiste londonien', in *Médias 19* [online], 2017, 'Les journalistes: identités et modernités', edited by Guillaume Pinson and Marie-Ève Thérenty. http://www.medias19.org/index.php?id=23642.

Bantman, Constance. *The French Anarchists in London. Exile and Transnationalism in the First Globalisation*. Liverpool: Liverpool University Press, 2013.

Barbour, Stephen. 'Nationalism, Language and Europe', in *Language and Nationalism in Europe*, edited by Stephen Barbour and Cathie Carmichael, 1–17. Oxford: OUP, 2000.

Barko, Ivan. 'The *Courrier australien* and French-Australian Relations during the Biard d'Aunet Years (1892–1905)', in *The Culture of the Book: Essays from Two Hemispheres in Honour of Wallace Kirsop*, edited by David Garrioch, Harold H R Love, Brian J

McMullin and Meredith Sherlock, 430–45. Melbourne: Bibliographical Society of Australia and New Zealand, 1999.

Barrett, James, and David Roediger. 'Whiteness and the Inbetween Peoples of Europe'. *Journal of American Ethnic History* 16, no. 3 (Summer 1997): 3–44.

Barrow, Clyde W. ed. *Portuguese Americans and Contemporary Civil Culture in Massachusetts*. North Dartmouth: Tagus Press, Center for Portuguese Studies and Culture-University of Massachusetts Dartmouth, 2002.

Barzini Jr., Luigi. *O America when you and I were Young*. New York: Harper & Row, 1977.

Barzini, Andrea. *Una famiglia complicata*. Florence: Giunti, 1996.

Barzini, Ludina. *I Barzini. Tre generazioni di giornalisti, una storia del Novecento*. Milan: Mondadori, 2010.

Belgian War Press (CEGESOMA, no date). https://warpress.cegesoma.be/en/newspaper-list?field_war_number_target_id=1.

Benadusi, Lorenzo. 'Addio alle armi: la smobilitazione e gli effetti della Grande Guerra in Italia e negli Stati Uniti', in *1917. L'inizio del secolo americano. Politica, propaganda e cultura in Italia tra guerra e dopoguerra*, edited by Lorenzo Benadusi, Daniela Rossini and Anna Villari, 253–76. Rome: Viella, 2018.

Bencivenni, Marcella. *Italian Immigrant Radical Culture. The Idealism of the Sovversivi in the United States, 1890–1940*. New York: New York University Press, 2011.

Bergantz, Alexis. *French Connection: The Culture and Politics of Frenchness in Australia, 1890–1914*, unpublished PhD thesis, Australian National University, Canberra, Australia, 2016.

Bergantz, Alexis. '"The Scum of France": Australian Anxieties towards French Convicts in the Nineteenth Century', *Australian Historical Studies* 49, no. 2 (2018): 150–66.

Bergantz, Alexis. 'Remembering *Australasie*: European Settlers and Trans-imperial Thinking in the Cosmopolitan *Le Courrier Australien* (1892–1896)', in *Voices of Challenge in Australia's Migrant and Minority Press*, vol. 2, edited by Catherine Dewhirst and Richard Scully, 43–61. Basingstoke: Palgrave Macmillan.

Bertão, David. *The Portuguese Shore Whalers of California, 1854–1904*. San Jose, CA: Portuguese Heritage Publications of California, 2006.

Bertonha, João Fabio. 'Emigrazione e politica estera: la "diplomazia sovversiva" di Mussolini e la questione degli italiani all'estero, 1922–1945', *Altreitalie*, no. 23 (2001): 39–60.

Bettini Leonardo, *Bibliografia dell'anarchismo, vol.2, Periodici e numeri unici in lingua italiana pubblicati all'estero (1872–1971)*. Florence: Crescita politica editrice, 1976.

Bhabha, Homi K. *The Location of Culture*, London/New York: Routledge, 1994.

Bianco, René. *Bianco: Presse Anarchiste*, https://bianco.ficedl.info/article1092.html.

Birch, Edmund. 'Literature and the Press in France', *Dix-Neuf* 21, no. 4 (2017), 223–30. DOI: 10.1080/14787318.2018.1446290.

Blanchard, Margaret A., ed. *History of the Mass Media in the United States. An Encyclopedia*. Chicago-London: Fitzroy Dearborn Publishers, 1998.

Blavatskyy, Serhiy. 'Constructing Victimization Grand-Narrative in the Ukrainian Foreign-Language Press (1901–1926)' (in French and English), *Media History* (2022). DOI: 10.1080/13688804.2022.2057284.

Boulard Jouslin, Claire. 'Du *Mercure Anglois* au *Paris Monthly Review*: Quelques réflexions sur les phénomènes de transfert et d'influence dans les presses anglaise et française du long XVIIIe siècle', *Études Épistémè* 26 (2014). https://doi.org/10.4000/episteme.295.

Bourne, Jill. 'Languages in the School Systems of England and Wales', *Linguistics and Education* 3, n°1 (1991): 81–102.

Brake, Laurel. 'Writing the Contemporary in the Periodical Press: Art and News 1893–1906', *Journal of European Periodical Studies* 4, no 2 (2019): 27–47. DOI: https://doi.org/10.21825/jeps.v4i2.10725.

Brake, Laurel and Marysa Demoor, eds. *DNCJ. Dictionary of Nineteenth-Century Journalism*. Ghent: Academia Press, 2009.

Brickhouse, Anna. 'The Black Legend of Texas'. *PMLA* 131, no. 3 (May 2016): 735–42.

Brickhouse, Anna. *Transamerican Literary Relations and the Nineteenth-Century Public Sphere*. New York: Cambridge University Press, 2004.

Broggini, Renata. *Eugenio Balzan, 1874–1953. Una vita per il 'Corriere', un progetto per l'umanità*. Milan: Rizzoli, 2001.

Budarick, John. *Ethnic Media and Democracy, From Liberalism to Agonism*. New York: Palgrave MacMillan, 2019.

Burrell, Kelly, ed. *Polish Migration to the UK in the 'New' European Union: After 2004*. Aldershot: Ashgate, 2009.

Burrows, Simon. *French Exile Journalism and European Politics 1792–1814*. Suffolk (UK), Rochester (NY): Royal Historical Society, 2000.

Burrows, Simon. 'Les journaux des émigrés et la communauté française des exilés, 1792–1814', in *Arrachés et Déplacés: Réfugiés Politiques, Prisonniers de Guerre, Déportés, 1789–1918*, edited by Nicolas Beaupré and Karine Rance, 241–57. Clermont-Ferrand: PUBP, 2016.

Byford, Andy and Olga Bronnikova, 'Introduction. Transnational Exopolities. Politics in Post-Soviet Migration', *Revue d'études comparatives Est-Ouest* 4, no. 4 (2018): 10–25.

Cahalan, Peter. *Belgian Refugee Relief in England during the Great War*. New York: Garland Publishing, 1982.

Calleja, Juan. 'No me veo con la misma ilusión por quedarme en Reino Unido que hace cinco años', CEXT, 22 July 2016, https://www.cext.es/posts/experiencias/no-me-veo-con-la-misma-ilusion-de-quedarme-en-londres-que-hace-cinco-anos.

Callens, An. *Het weekblad 'De Stem Uit Belgie' (1914–1919)*. KU Leuven: Unpublished MA dissertation, 1980.

Canadian Ethnic Media Association website, https://canadianethnicmedia.com.

Canali, Mauro. *La scoperta dell'Italia. Il fascismo raccontato dai corrispondenti americani*. Venice: Marsilio, 2017.

Cannistraro, Philip and Aga Rossi, Elena. 'La politica etnica e il dilemma dell'antifascismo negli Stati Uniti: il caso di Generoso Pope', *Storia Contemporanea*, no. 2 (1986): 217–43.

Cannistraro, Philip. 'Generoso Pope and the Rise of *Italian American* Politics, 1925–1936', in *Italian Americans. New Perspectives in Italian Immigration and Ethnicity*, edited by Lydio F. Tomasi, 264–88. New York: Center for Migration Studies, 1985.

Cannistraro, Philip. 'Mussolini, Sacco-Vanzetti, and the Anarchists: The Transatlantic Context'. *The Journal of Modern History*, no. 1 (March 1996): 31–62.

Carvalho, Eduardo. *A Língua Portuguesa nos Estados Unidos (extracto do relatório de Boston, de 9 de abril de 1924)*. Boston: Editora Emprêsa de Propaganda Patriótica, 1925.

Cazden, Robert E. *A Social History of the German Book Trade in America to the Civil War*. Columbia, NC: Camden House, 1984.

Cerrito, Gino, 'Sull'emigrazione anarchica italiana negli Stati Uniti d'America' (Italian anarchist emigrationin the United States of America), *Volontà*, XXII, 4, July–August 1969, 269–76.

Chadova, Elena. *Between the Eagle and the Bear: Coverage of U.S.-Russian Foreign Policy Disputes in Russian Ethnic Media in the United States*. Sarrebruck: VDM Verlag, 2010.

Chamberlin, Vernon A. and Ivan Schulman. *La Revista Ilustrada de Nueva York : History,*

Anthology, and Index of Literary Selections. Columbia: University of Missouri Press, 1976.

Charle, Christophe, *Le Siècle de la presse, 1830–1939.* Paris: Seuil, 2004.

Chik, Alice, Phil Benson, Robyn Moloney. Eds. *Multilingual Sydney.* London; New York, NY: Routledge, 2019.

Choate, Mark. *Emigrant Nation. The Making of Italy Abroad.* Cambridge: Harvard University Press, 2008.

Chovanec, Jan, and Katarzyna Molek-Kozakowska, eds. *Representing the Other in European Media Discourses.* Amsterdam: John Benjamins, 2017.

Clough, Eric A. and Jacqueline Quarmby. *A Public Library Service for Ethnic Minorities in Great Britain.* London: Library Association, 1978.

Cobbing, Andrew. *The Japanese Discovery of Victorian Britain: Early Travel Encounters in the Far West.* Richmond, UK: Japan Press, 1998.

Colarizi, Simona. *Luigi Barzini. Una storia italiana.* Venice: Marsilio, 2017.

Conolly-Smith, Peter. *Translating America: an Ethnic Press and Popular Culture, 1890–1920.* Washington, DC: Smithsonian Books, 2004.

Cooper-Richt, Diana. 'Les imprimés de langue anglaise en France au XIX° siècle: rayonnement intellectuel, circulation et modes de pénétration', in *Les mutations du livre et de l'édition dans le monde du XVIII° siècle à l'an 2000,* edited by Jean-Yves Mollier and Jacques Michon, 122–40. Paris: L'Harmattan, 2001.

Cooper-Richt, Diana. 'Presse en anglais et littérature, à Paris, dans la première moitié du XIXe siècle', in *Presse et plumes. Journalisme et littérature au XIXe siècle,* edited by Marie-Ève Thérenty and Alain Vaillant, 153–68. Paris: Nouveau Monde, 2004.

Cooper-Richt, Diana. 'Diffusion du modèle victorien à travers le monde. Le rôle de la presse anglaise publiée en France au XIXe siècle', in *Presse, nations et mondialisation au XIXe siècle,* edited by Marie-Ève Thérenty et Alain Vaillant, 17–31. Paris: Nouveau monde, 2010.

Cooper-Richt, Diana. 'Aux marges de l'histoire de la presse nationale: les périodiques en langue étrangère publiés en France (XIXe-XXe siècles)'. *Le Temps des médias* 16, no. 1 (2011), 175–87. DOI: http://10.3917/tdm.016.0175.

Cooper-Richt, Diana. 'La presse en langue étrangère', in *La Civilisation du journal: histoire culturelle et littéraire de la presse française au XIXe siècle,* edited by Dominique Kalifa, Philippe Régnier, Marie-Ève Thérenty and Alain Vaillant, 583–604. Paris: Nouveau Monde, 2011.

Cooper-Richt, Diana, 'Distribution, diffusion et circulation du *Galignani's Messenger* (1814–1890), premier quotidien parisien en anglais', in *La distribution et la diffusion de la presse du XVIII° siècle au 3° millénaire,* edited by Gilles Feyel, 121–39. Paris: Éditions Panthéon-Assas, 2002.

Cooper-Richt, Diana. '*París y los ambos mundos*: une capitale au cœur du dispositif de production et de mise en circulation de livres et de journaux, en espagnol, au XIXe siècle', *Cahiers des Amériques latines* 72-3 (2013), 201–20. DOI: 10.4000/cal.2895.

Cooper-Richt, Diana. 'Avant-Propos', in *Los medios en lengua extranjera. Diversidad cultural e integración,* edited by Juan Antonio García Galindo and Laura López Romero, xi-xiii. Granada: Editorial Comares, 2018.

Cooper-Richt, Diana. 'La Presse pour "touristes", un marché de niche inventé au XIXe siècle: L'exemple des journaux en anglais publiés en France', in *Los medios en lengua extranjera. Diversidad cultural e integración,* edited by Juan Antonio García Galindo and Laura López Romero, 78–88. Granada: Editorial Comares, 2018.

Cordillot, Michel. *La Sociale en Amérique. Dictionnaire biographique du mouvement social francophone aux États-Unis, 1848–1922*. Paris: Editions de l'Atelier, 1997.

Coronado, Raúl. *A World Not to Come: A History of Latino Writing and Print Culture*. Cambridge, Massachusetts: Harvard University Press, 2013.

Correa, Geneviene B. and Edgar W. Knowlton. 'The Portuguese in Hawaii', in *Ethnic Sources in Hawai'i. A Special Issue for The University of Hawai'i's Seventy-Fith Year*, 70–7. Honolulu: The United Press of Hawaii, 1982.

Correia, Rui Antunes. 'Salazar em New Bedford. Leituras Luso-Americanas do Estado Novo nos Anos Trinta'. MA diss., Universidade Aberta, Lisbon, 2004.

Corucci, Domenico. *Luigi Barzini (1874–1947)*. Orvieto: Fondazione Cassa di Risparmio di Orvieto, 2000.

Couldry, Nick, and James Curran. *Contesting Media Power: Alternative Media in a Networked World*. Lanham, MD: Rowman and Littlefield, 2003.

Creagh, Ronald. 'Socialism in America: The French-Speaking Coal-Miners in the Late Nineteenth Century', in *In the Shadow of the Statue of Liberty: Immigrants, Workers, and Citizens in the American Republic, 1880–1920*, edited by Marianne Debouzy, 143–56. Champaign, Ill.: University of Illinois Press, 1992.

Creasy, Matthew. *Decadence and Translation*, University of Glasgow: School of Critical Studies, UK Research and Innovation project description, 2018. https://gtr.ukri.org/project/48C3809C-06F3-4DA1-B862-08C4BE46988C.

D'alterio, Daniele. *Tre capitoli su politica e cultura nell'Italia del Novecento*. Trento: Tangram, 2017.

Daniel, Dominique. 'Elusive Stories: Collecting and Preserving the Foreign-Language Ethnic Press in the United States', *Serials Review* 45, no. 1–2 (2019): 7–25.

Danky, James P. and Wayne A. Wiegand, eds. *Print Culture in a Diverse America*. Chicago: University of Illinois Press, 1998.

Darieva, Tsypylma. *Russkij Berlin. Migranten und Medien in Berlin und London*. Münster: Lit, 2004.

De Caprariis, Luca. 'Fascism for Export? The Rise and Eclipse of the Fasci Italiani all'Estero', *Journal of Contemporary History*, no. 2 (April 2000): 151–83.

De Schaepdryver Sophie. *De Groote Oorlog: Het Koninkrijk België Tijdens de Eerste Wereldoorlog*. Amsterdam/Antwerpen: Atlas, 1997.

Declercq, Christophe. *Belgian Refugees in Britain 1914–1919: A Cross-Cultural Study of Belgian Identity in Exile*, unpublished PhD dissertation, London: Imperial College London, 2015.

Declercq, Christophe. 'From Antwerp to Britain and Back Again: The Language of the Belgian Refugee in Britain during the First World War', in *Languages and the First World War: Representation and Memory*, edited by Christophe Declercq and Julian Walker, 94–107. London: Palgrave-MacMillan, 2016.

Declercq, Christophe. 'Belgian Exile Press in Britain', in *Beyond Flanders Fields: the Great War in Belgium and the Netherlands*, edited by Felicity Rash and Christophe Declercq, 121–41. London: Palgrave MacMillan, 2018.

Declercq, Christophe. 'Making home in limbo: Belgian refugees in Britain during the First World War', in *Refuge in a Moving World: Refugee and Migrant Journeys across Disciplines*, edited by Elena Fiddian-Qasmiyeh. London: UCL Press, 2020.

Dénes, Tibor. 'Lehr- und Wanderjahre eines jungen Schweizers (1845–1848): Jakob Lukas Schabelitz, Herzog Karl II von Braunschweig und die Deutsche Londoner Zeitung', *Schweizerische Zeitschrift für Geschichte = Revue suisse d'histoire = Rivista storica svizzera*, 16 (1966): 34–79.

Deschamps, Bénédicte. 'Echi d'Italia. La stampa dell'emigrazione', in *Storia dell'emigrazione italiana. Arrivi*, edited by Piero Bevilacqua, Andreina De Clementi and Emilio Franzina, 313–34. Rome: Donzelli, 2002.

Deschamps, Bénédicte. *Histoire de la presse italo-américaine, du Risorgimento à la Grande Guerre*. Paris: L'Harmattan, 2020.

Deschamps, Bénédicte and Pantaleone Sergi, eds. *Voci d'Italia fuori dall'Italia. Giornalismo e stampa dell'emigrazione*. Cosenza: Pellegrini editore, 2021.

Deschamps, Bénédicte. 'La stampa etnica negli Stati Uniti, tra nostalgia nazionale, ricostruzione dell'identità e alternativa culturale', in *La società di tutti. Multiculturalismo e politiche dell'identità*, edited by Francesco Pompeo, 151–68. Rome: Meltemi, 2007.

Deschamps, Bénédicte and Stéphanie Prévost. 'Language Matters: Presse anglophone en France/Presses d'exil et d'immigration aux Etats-Unis'. Exhibition, Grands Moulins Library, Paris, 2017–18. [Virtual exhibition at www.language-matters.fr, website created by Karl Gosselet, forthcoming 2023].

Dewhirst, Catherine and Richard Scully, eds. *The Transnational Voices of Australia's Migrant and Minority Press*. Cham, Switzerland: Palgrave Macmillan, 2020.

Dias, Eduardo Mayone. *A Presença Portuguesa na California*. San Jose, CA: Portuguese Heritage Publications, 2009.

Diggins, John Patrick. *Mussolini and Fascism. The View from America*, first edn. 1972. Reprint. Princeton: Princeton University Press, 2015.

Di Lembo, Luigi, 'Errico Malatesta e la nascita di Umanità Nova', *Cronache anarchiche. Il giornale* Umanità Nova *nell'Italia del Novecento*. Milano: Zero in condotta, 2009, 17–39.

Di Legge, Francesco. *L'Aquila e il Littorio: Direttive, Strutture e Strumenti della Propaganda Fascista negli Stati Uniti d'America, 1922–1941*, PhD dissertation, Università degli Studi del Molise, 2014.

Di Paola, Pietro. 'The Italian Anarchist Press in London: A Lens for Investigating a Transnational Movement', in *The Foreign Political Press in Nineteenth-Century London: Politics from a Distance*, edited by Constance Bantman and Ana Cláudia Suriani da Silva, 113–34. New York: Bloomsbury Academic, 2018.

Di Paola, Pietro. *The Knights Errant of Anarchy. London and the Italian Anarchist Diaspora, 1880–1917*. Liverpool: Liverpool University Press, 2013.

Donohoo, Jillian Elizabeth. 'Feeding "the sacred fire": *Le Courrier Australien* and France Libre', *History in the Making* 1, no. 2 (2013): 8–20. https://historyitm.files.wordpress.com/2013/08/donohoo.pdf.

Dorgeel, Heinrich. *Die deutsche Colonie in London*. London: August Siegle, 1881.

Drake, William. *Almanacs of the United States*. New York: The Scarecrow Press, 2 vols, 1962.

Droulia, Loukia and Gioula Koutsopanagou, eds. *Εγκυκλοπαίδεια του Ελληνικού τύπου 1784–1974: εφημερίδες, περιοδικά, δημοσιογράφοι, εκδότες*. Athens: Institute of Neohellenic Research, 2008.

Drummond, Rob et al. *Manchester Voices*. Exhibition, Manchester Central Library, 2022.

Dufoix, Stéphane. *Politiques d'exil. Hongrois, Polonais et Tchécoslovaques en France après 1945*. Paris: PUF, 2002.

Durán López, Fernando. 'Blanco White aconseja a los americanos. Variedades o el Mensajero de Londres', in *Blanco White, El rebelde ilustrado*, edited by Antonio Cascales Ramos, 53–92. Sevilla: Centro de Estudios Andaluces-Facultad de Comunicación de la Universidad de Sevilla, 2009.

Durán López, Fernando. 'Rudolph Ackermann (1764–1834)', in *Editores y Editoriales Iberoamericanos, siglos XIX–XXI* (EDI-RED, Alicante: Biblioteca Virtual Miguel de

Cervantes, 2015), http://www.cervantesvirtual.com/obra/rudolph-ackermann-1764-1834.

Durán López, Fernando. *Versiones de un exilio: los traductores españoles de la casa Ackermann. Londres, 1823–1830.* Madrid: Escolar y Mayo Editores, 2015.

Durán López, Fernando, and Muñoz Sempere, Daniel. 'Periódicos españoles en Londres: prensa "en" y "desde" el exilio', in *La prensa hispánica en el exilio de Londres, 1810–1850*, edited by María José Ruiz Acosta, 45–78. Salamanca: Comunicación Social Ediciones y Publicaciones, 2016.

Edwards, Viv. 'New Minority Languages in the United Kingdom', in *Multilingual Europe: Facts and Policies*, edited by in Guus Extra and Durk Porter (eds.), 253–4. Berlin and New York: Mouton de Gruyter, 2008.

Etinson, Adam E. 'Cosmopolitanism: Cultural, Moral and Political', in *Sovereign Justice: Global Justice in a World of Nations*, edited by Diogo Pires Aurélio, Gabriele De Angelis, Regina Queiroz, 25–46. Berlin: De Gruyter, 2011.

European Association of Daily Newspapers in Minority and Regional Languages. *Midas*. Website. https://www.midas-press.org.

Evangelista, Stefano. *Literary Cosmopolitanism in the English Fin de Siècle: Citizens of Nowhere*. Oxford: OUP, 2021.

Extra, Guus and Durk Gorter, eds. *The Other Languages of Europe: Demographic, Sociolinguistic and Educational Perspectives*. Clevedon, Multilingual Matters, 2001.

Faingold, Eduardo D. *Language Rights and the Law in the United States and Its Territories*, New York: Lexington Books, 2018.

Fedeli, Ugo. *Biografie di anarchici. Ciancabilla, Damiani, Gavilli*. Pescara: Samizdat, 1997.

Fedeli, Ugo. *Gigi Damiani. Note biografiche. Il suo posto nell'anarchismo*. Cesena: L'Antistato, 1954.

Feist, Timothy. *The Stationers' Voice. The English Almanac Trade in the Early Eighteenth Century*. Philadelphia: The American Philosophical Society, 2005.

Felici, Isabelle. *Poésie d'un rebelle. Gigi Damiani (1876–1953), poète, anarchiste, émigré* (Lyon: Atelier de Création Libertaire, 2009).

Felici, Isabelle. '*Domani* (1935), une publication antifasciste et anticolonialiste à l'initiative des anarchistes italiens de Tunisie', *Storie e testimonianze politiche degli italiani di Tunisia*, edited by Silvia Finzi, 173–83. Tunis: Finzi, 2016. https://hal.archives-ouvertes.fr/hal-01381071.

Felsten, Judith. *Atlantis, National Daily Newspaper, 1894–1973*. Philadelphia: The Research Library of the Balch Institute for Ethnic Studies, 1982.

Ferrer, Ada. *Insurgent Cuba: Race, Nation, and Revolution, 1868–1898*. Chapel Hill: University of North Carolina Press, 1999.

Ferretti, Federico. 'Publishing Anarchism: Pyotr Kropotkin and British Print Cultures, 1876–1917', *Journal of Historical Geography* 57 (2017): 17–27.

Finkelstein, David, ed. *The Edinburgh History of the British and Irish Press, Volume 2. Expansion and Evolution, 1800–1900*. Edinburgh: EUP, 2020.

Fitzgerald, Ian, and Rafal Smoczynski. 'Anti-Polish Migrant Moral Panic in the UK: Rethinking Employment Insecurities and Moral Regulation'. *Czech Sociological Review* 51, no. 3 (2015): 339–61.

Fomina, Joanna, and Justyna Frelak. *Next Stopski London. Public Perceptions of Labour Migration within the EU. The Case of Polish Labour Migrants in the British Press*. Warsaw: Institute of Public Affairs, 2008.

Fornasiero, Jean and John West-Sooby. 'The Narrative Interruptions of Science: The Baudin Expedition to Australia (1800–1804)'. *Forum for Modern Language Studies* 49, no. 4 (2013), 457–71.

Forwood, Naomi. 'Les Français en Australie – A travers *Le Courrier Australien* 1892–1901 – Analyse sociologique'. Honours diss. University of Sydney, Australia, 1983.
Fraenkel, Josef. *Exhibition of the Jewish Press in Great Britain*. London: World Jewish Congress, 1963.
Franzina, Emilio and Sanfilippo Matteo, eds. *Il fascismo e gli emigrati. La parabola dei Fasci italiani all'estero (1920–1943)*. Rome-Bari: Laterza 2003.
Freeman, Matthew. 'Branding consumerism: Cross-media characters and story-worlds at the turn of the 20th century'. *International Journal of Cultural Studies* 18, n°6 (2015): 629–44.
Fuentes, Juan Francisco. 'Geografía del liberalismo español en la Década Ominosa: emigración política y exilio interior', in *Las élites y la 'Revolución de España' (1808–1814). Estudios en homenaje al profesor Gérard Dufour*, edited by Armando Alberola and Elisabel Larriba, 309–31. Alicante: Universidad de Alicante-Université de Provence-Casa de Velázquez, 2010.
Galmiche, Xavier. 'Les *Šibeničky* [Petites Potences] et l'Internationale des revues satiriques anarchistes', in Evanghelia Stead and Hélène Védrine (eds/), *L'Europe des revues II (1860–1930). Réseaux et circulations de modèles*, 487–503. Paris: PU Sorbonne, 2008.
Georgiou, Myria. 'Crossing the Boundaries of the Ethnic Home: Media Consumption and Ethnic Identity Construction in Public Space'. *Gazette: International Journal for Communication Studies* 63, no. 4 (2001): 311–29.
Georgiou, Myria. 'Mapping Minorities and Their Media: The National Context – The UK', 2002 [European Media, Technology and Everyday Life Network] https://www.thinkethnic.com/wp-content/uploads/2017/09/Ethnic-media-in-EU.pdf.
Gibbard, Paul. 'Empiricism and Sensibility in the Australian Journal of Théodore Leschenault de la Tour', in *Natural History in Early Modern France: The Poetics of an Epistemic Genre*, edited by Raphaele Garrod and Paul J. Smith, 263–90. Netherlands: Brill, 2018.
Gilson, Miriam and Jerzy Zubrzycki. *The Foreign-Language Press in Australia, 1848–1964*. Canberra: Australian National University Press, 1967.
Glasgow Register of Belgian Refugees, 1914–1920. Accessed 31 January 2020, https://www.glasgowfamilyhistory.org.uk/ExploreRecords/Documents/Belgian%20refugees%20-%20online%20version.pdf.
Goldstein, Robert J. *Political Repression in 19th Century Europe*. Abingdon: Routlege, 2010; first edition 1983.
Gomes, Geoffrey L. 'The Portuguese Language Press in California: The Response to American Politics, 1880–1928'. *Gávea-Brown. A Bilingual Journal of Portuguese American Letters and Studies* 15–18 (1995): 5–90.
Gosetti, Valentina. 'Nineteenth-Century French-Language Press in the UK: Readership, Typology, and Cultural Integration', in *Los medios en lengua extranjera. Diversidad cultural e integración*, edited by Juan Antonio García Galindo and Laura López Romero, 95–103. Granada: Editorial Comares, 2018.
Goulart, Tony, ed. *Capelinhos. A Volcano of Synergies: Azorean Emigration to America*. San José, CA: Furtado Imports, 2007.
Grant, Stan. *Talking to my Country*. Sydney: HarperCollins Publishers, 2016.
Grases, Pedro. *Tiempo de Bello en Londres y otros ensayos*. Caracas: Ediciones del Ministerio de Educación, 1962.
Green, Nancy L. *The Limits of Transnationalism*. Chicago: Chicago University Press, 2019.
Greilich, Susanne, and York-Gothart Mix, eds. *Populäre Kalender im vorindustriellen Europa: Der 'Hinkende Bote'/'Messager boiteux'. Kulturwissenschaftliche Analysen und bibliographisches Repertorium*. Berlin/New York: De Gruyter, 2006.

Gruesz, Kirsten Silva. *Ambassadors of Culture: The Transamerican Origins of Latino Writing*. Princeton: Princeton University Press, 2002.

Grzymala-Kazlowska, Aleksandra. 'From Connecting to Social Anchoring: Adaptation and 'Settlement' of Polish Migrants in the UK'. *Journal of Ethnic and Migration Studies* 44, no. 2 (2018): 252–69.

Hampton, Mark. 'Transatlantic Exchanges', in *The Edinburgh History of the British and Irish Press, Volume 3: Competition and Disruption, 1900–2017*, edited by Martin Conboy and Adrian Bingham, 151–70. Edinburgh: EUP, 2020.

Harzig, Christiane and Dirk Hoerder, eds. *The Press of Labor Migrants in Europe and North America 1880s–1980*. Lexington: Lexington Books, 1985.

Helg, Aline. *Our Rightful Share: The Afro-Cuban Struggle for Equality, 1886–1912*. Chapel Hill: University of North Carolina Press, 1995.

Hewitt, Martin. *The Dawn of the Cheap Press in Victorian Britain: The End of the 'Taxes on Knowledge', 1849–1869*. London: Bloomsbury, 2015.

Hewitt, Martin. 'The Press and the Law', in *Journalism and the Periodical Press in Nineteenth Century Britain*, edited by Joanne Shattock, 147–64. Cambridge: Cambridge University Press, 2017.

Hewitt, Nancy A. *Southern Discomfort: Women's Activism in Tampa, Florida, 1880s–1920s*. Urbana, Champaign: University of Illinois Press, 2001.

'Historical Background', *Stobsiade*. http://www.stobsiade.org/introduction/historicalBackground.html.

Hoerder, Dirk, ed. *The Immigrant Labor Press in North America, 1840s–1970s: An Annotated Bibliography, Volume 2: Migrants from Eastern and Southeastern Europe*. New York: Greenwood Press, 1987.

Hoffnung-Garskof, Jesse. *Racial Migrations*. Princeton: Princeton University Press, 2019.

Holt, Sally and John Packer. 'OSCE Developments and Linguistic Minorities'. *International Journal on Multicultural Societies* 3, no. 2 (2001). https://unesdoc.unesco.org/ark:/48223/pf0000138776.

Holton, Kimberly Dacosta and Andrea Klimt, eds. *Community, Culture and the Makings of Identity. Portuguese-Americans along Eastern Seabord*. North Dartmouth: Tagus Press, Center for Portuguese Studies and Culture-University of Massachusetts Dartmouth, 2009.

Hoyt, Andrew. *And They Called Them 'Galleanisti': The Rise of the* Cronaca Sovversiva *and the Formation of America's Most Infamous Anarchist Faction (1895–1912)*, PhD dissertation, University of Minnesota, 2018.

Hunter, Edward. *In Many Voices: Our Fabulous Foreign-Language Press*. Norman Park: Norman College, 1960.

Hutton, Frankie and Barbara S. Reed, eds. *Outsiders in 19th-Century Press History: Multicultural Perspectives*. Bowling Green: Bowling Green State University Popular Press, 1995.

Iglicka, Krystyna. *Poland's Post-war Dynamic of Migration*. Aldershot: Ashgate, 2001.

Ireland, Sandra L. Jones. *Ethnic Periodicals in Contemporary America: an Annotated Guide*. New York: Greenwood Press, 1990.

James, Winston. *Holding Aloft the Banner of Ethiopia: Caribbean Radicalism in Early Twentieth Century America*. Reprint, Edition. London; New York: Verso, 1999.

Jaroszyńska-Kirchmann, Anna D. *The Polish Hearst*. Urbana: University of Illinois Press, 2017.

Jefcoate, Graham. *Deutsche Drucker und Buchhändler in London, 1680–1811: Strukturen und Bedeutung des Deutschen Anteils am englischen Buchhandel*. Archiv für Geschichte des Buchwesens. Studien 12. Berlin: de Gruyter, 2015.

Johnson, Melissa A. 'How Ethnic Are U.S. Ethnic Media: The Case of Latina Magazines'. *Mass Communication & Society* 3 no. 2–3 (2000): 229–48.
Jones, Thomas C. and Constance Bantman. 'From Republicanism to Anarchism: 50 Years of French Exilic Newspaper Publishing', in *The Foreign Political Press in Nineteenth-Century London: Politics from a Distance*, edited by Constance Bantman and Ana Cláudia Suriani da Silva, 91–112. London: Bloomsbury, 2017.
Jouët-Pastré, Clémence and Leticia J. Braga, eds. *Becoming Bazuca. Brazilian Immigration to the United States*. Cambridge, MA: Harvard University Press, 2008.
Kaloudis, George. *Modern Greece and the Diaspora Greeks in the United States*. Lanham, Lexington Books, 2020.
Kanellos, Nicolás. 'Sotero Figueroa: Writing Afro-Carribbeans into History in the Late Ninteenth Century', in *The Latino Nineteenth Century*, edited by Rodrigo Lazo and Jesse Alemán, 323–40. New York: New York University Press, 2016.
Kanellos, Nicolás, and Helvetia Martell. *Hispanic Periodicals in the United States, Origins to 1960: A Brief History and Comprehensive Bibliography*. Houston: Arte Público Press, 2000.
Karlowich, Robert A. *We Fall and Rise: Russian-Language Newspapers in New York City, 1889–1914*. Metuchen, NJ and London: Scarecrow Press, 1991.
Karskens, Grace. *The Colony. A History of Early Sydney*. Sydney: Allen & Unwin, 2009.
Kędzia, Paweł, Maciej Piasecki, and Marlena J. Orlińska. 'Word Sense Disambiguation Based on a Large Scale Polish CLARIN Heterogeneous Lexical Resources'. *Cognitive Studies* 15 (2015): 269–92.
Kessler, Lauren. *The Dissident Press, Alternative Journalism in American History*. Newbury Park: Sage, 1990.
Khachaturian, Lisa. *Cultivating Nationhood in Imperial Russia: The Periodical Press and the Formation of a Modern Armenian Identity*. New Brunswick, NJ: Transaction Publishers, 2009.
King, Andrew, Alexis Easley and John Morton, eds. *The Routledge Handbook of Nineteenth-Century British Periodicals and Newspapers*. Abingdon: Routledge, 2016.
Kitroeff, Alexander. 'The Transformation of the Greek American Press: the *National Herald* 1915–1939', *Etudes Helléniques* 25/2 (Autumn 2015): 125–38.
Knowlton, Edgar C. 'The Portuguese Language Press in Hawaii'. *Social Process in Hawaii* 24 (1960): 89–99.
Kouts, Gideon. *La Presse hébraïque en Europe: ses origines et son évolution de 1856 à 1897*, PhD dissertation, Université Paris 8, 1997.
Kouts, Gideon. *News and History: Studies in the History of Hebrew and Jewish Press and Communication* (in Hebrew). Jerusalem: The Zionist Library and Tel Aviv University, 2013.
Kouts, Gideon. *The Hebrew and Jewish Press in Europe*. Paris: Suger Press, 2006.
Kraemer, Gilles. *Trois siècles de presse francophone dans le monde. Hors de France, de Belgique, de Suisse et du Québec*. Paris: L'Harmattan, 1996.
Kreitz, Kelley. 'American Alternatives: Participatory Futures of Print from New York City's Nineteenth-Century Spanish-Language Press'. *American Literary History* 30, no. 4 (2018): 677–702.
Kreitz, Kelley. 'Telephonic Modernismo Latinidad and Hemispheric Print Culture in the Age of Electricity'. *English Language Notes* 56, no. 2 (2018): 90–103.
Kronenbitter, R. T. 'The Sherlock Holmes of the Revolution', in *Okhrana: The Paris Operations of the Russian Imperial Police*, edited by Ben B. Fischer, 47–64. Washington: History Staff of the Center for the Study of Intelligence, CIA, DIANE Publishing, 1999.

Krzyżanowski, Michał. *The Discursive Construction of European Identities. A Multilevel Approach to Discourse and Identity in the Transforming European Union*. Frankfurt am Main: Peter Lang, 2010.

Laqua, Daniel. 'Political Contestation and Internal Strife: Socialist and Anarchist Newspapers in London, 1878–1910', in *The Foreign Political Press in Nineteenth-Century London: Politics from a Distance*, edited by Constance Bantman and Ana Cláudia Suriani da Silva, 135–54. London: Bloomsbury Academic, 2019.

Lattek, Christine. *Revolutionary Refugees: German Socialism in Britain, 1840–1860*. London: Routledge, 2006.

Lazo, Rodrigo. 'Introduction: Historical Latinidades and Archival Encounters', in *The Latino Nineteenth Century*, edited by Rodrigo Lazo and Jesse Alemán, Kindle, 1–19. New York: New York University Press, 2016.

Lazo, Rodrigo. *Writing to Cuba : Filibustering and Cuban Exiles in the United States*. Chapel Hill: University of North Carolina Press, 2005.

Lee Hun-Yul. 'At the Crossroads of Migrant Workers, Class, and Media: A Case Study of a Migrant Workers' Television Project. *Media, Culture & Society* 34, no. 3 (2012): 312–27.

Library of Congress. 'Chronicling America Ethnic Press Coverage'. February 2022, https://public.tableau.com/app/profile/chronicling.america/viz/ChroniclingAmericaEthnicPressCoverageGraph/ethnicity_bar.

Liptack, Dolores Ann. *Immigrants and Their Church. Makers of the Catholic Community*. New York-London: McMillan, 1989.

Llorens, Vicente. *Liberales y románticos. Una emigración española en Inglaterra, 1823–1834*; Madrid: Castalia, 1979.

Lomas, Laura. *Translating Empire: José Martí, Migrant Latino Subjects, and American Modernities*. Durham: Duke University Press, 2008.

'Londyński "Dziennik Polski" staje się tygodnikiem', 17 July 2015, *Dzieje.pl*. https://dzieje.pl/aktualnosci/londynski-dziennik-polski-staje-sie-tygodnikiem.

Luca de Tena, Gustavo. *Noticias de América*. Vigo: Nigra, 1993.

Luconi, Stefano and Tintori, Guido, eds. *L'ombra lunga del fascio. Canali di propaganda fascista degli italoamericani*. Milan: M&B Publishing, 2004.

Luconi, Stefano. 'The Ethnic Press and the Translation of the U.S. Political System for Italian Immigrants in the United States, 1924–1941', in *Translating America: The Circulation of Narratives, Commodities, and Ideas Between Italy, Europe and the United States*, edited by Marina Camboni, Andrea Carosso, Sonia Di Loreto and Marco Mariano, 317–31. New York: Peter Lang, 2011.

Luconi, Stefano. *La diplomazia parallela. Il regime fascista e la mobilitazione politica degli italo-americani*. Milan: Franco Angeli, 2000.

Lüsebrink, Hans-Jürgen. 'Der Almanach des Muses und die französische Almanachkultur des 18. Jahrhunderts', in *Literarische Leitmedien. Almanach und Taschenbuch im kulturwissenschaftlichen Kontext*, edited by Paul Gerhard Klussmann and York-Gothart Mix, 3–15. Wiesbaden, Harrassowitz-Verlag, 1998.

Lüsebrink, Hans-Jürgen. '*Le livre aimé du peuple*'. *Les almanachs québécois de 1777 à nos jours*. Québec: Les Presses de l'Université Laval, 2014.

Lüsebrink, Hans-Jürgen. 'Les almanachs franco-américains des XIXe siècles et XX siècles: un média de communication et d'information populaire entre le Québéc et les communautés francophones aux États-Unis', in 'La recherche sur la presse: nouveaux bilans nationaux et internationaux' special issue, edited by Micheline Cambron and Stéphanie Danaux, 2013. http://www.medias19.org/index.php?id=15554.

Lüsebrink, Hans-Jürgen, and York-Gothart Mix. 'Kulturtransfer und Autonomisierung. Populäre deutsch-amerikanische und frankokanadische Kalender des 18. und 19. Jahrhundertzs. Prämissen und Perspektiven der Forschung'. *Gutenberg Jahrbuch*, 2002, 188–200.

Machado, Joe et al. *Power of the Spirit. A Portuguese journey of building faith and churches in California*. San Jose CA: Portuguese Heritage Publications of California, 2012.

Madianou, Mirca. 'Beyond the Presumption of Identity? Ethnicities, Cultures and Transnational Audiences', in *The Handbook of Media Audiences*, edited by Virginia Nightingale, 444–58. Malden, MA: Wiley, 2012.

Magnarelli, Paola, ed. *Il ricordo di viaggio. Un carteggio familiare di Luigi Albertini, 1921–1922*. Macerata: Eum, 2007.

Magrì, Enzo. *Luigi Barzini: una vita da inviato*. Florence: Pagliai, 2008.

Matsaganis, Matthew D., Sandra Ball-Rokeach and Vikki S. Katz. *Understanding Ethnic Media: Producers, Consumers, and Societies*. Thousand Oaks: Sage Publications, 2011.

Mckernan, Luke. 'Newspaper data and news identity', *The British Library Newsroom blog*, 18 October 2017. https://blogs.bl.uk/thenewsroom/2017/10/newspaper-data-and-news-identity.html.

Meadows, Bryan. 'Neo-Nationalism and Language Policy in the United States: A Critical Discourse Analysis of Public Discourse Advocating Monolingual English Use', in *Applied Linguistics and Language Teaching in the Neo-Nationalist Era*, edited by Kyle McIntosh, 17–49. Palgrave Macmillan Cham, 2020.

Menéndez Pelayo, Marcelino. *Historia de los heterodoxos españoles*. Madrid: Homo Legens, 2007.

Metykova, Monika. 'Only a Mouse Click away from Home: Transnational Practices of Eastern European Migrants in the United Kingdom'. *Social Identities* 16, no. 3 (2010): 325–38.

Miehe, Dorothea and Christopher Skelton-Foord. 'A Press for Natives and Immigrants. German Newspapers in the British Library', *British Library Newspaper Library News* 27 (1999): 8–10.

Miller, Martin A. 'The Transformation of the Russian Revolutionary Emigre Press at the End of the Nineteenth Century', *Russian History* 16, no. 2/4 (1989): 197–207.

Miller, Sally M. 'Distinctive Media: The European Ethnic Press in the United States', in *A History of the Book in America, Volume 4: Print in Motion: The Expansion of Publishing and Reading in the United States, 1880–1940*, edited by Carl F. Kaestle and Janice A. Radway, 299–311. Chapel Hill: University of North Carolina Press, 2009.

Miller, Sally M., ed. *The Ethnic Press in the United States. A Historical Analysis and Handbook*. New York-West Port-Connecticut-London: Greenwood Press, 1987.

Mirabel, Nancy. *Suspect Freedoms*. New York: New York University Press, 2017.

Mix, York-Gothart, Bianca Weyers and Gabriele Krieg, eds. *Deutsch-amerikanische Kalender des 18. und 19. Jahrhunderts/German-American Almanacs of the 18th and 19th Centuries. Bibliographie und Kommentar/Bibliography and Commentary*. Berlin/Boston: De Gruyter, 2012, 2 vols.

Molek-Kozakowska, Katarzyna. 'Media polonijne w Londynie a kształtowanie tożsamości polskich emigrantów po 2004 roku'. *Rocznik Biblioteki Głównej Uniwersytetu Opolskiego*, 91–100. Opole: Wydawnictwo Uniwersytetu Opolskiego, 2014.

Molek-Kozakowska, Katarzyna. 'Negotiating an Identity: The Mediated Discursive Self-Representation of the Polish Immigrant Community in the UK', in *Representing the Other in European Media Discourses*, edited by Jan Chovanec and Katarzyna Molek-Kozakowska, 158–81. Amsterdam: John Benjamins, 2017.

Molek-Kozakowska, Katarzyna. 'Fuzzy Identities in (Dis)Integrating Europe: Discursive Identifications of Poles in Britain Following Brexit', in *Fuzzy Boundaries in Discourse Studies: Theoretical, Methodological, and Lexico-Grammatical Fuzziness*, edited by Péter B. Furkó, Ildikó Vaskó, Csilla Ilona Dér, and Dorte Madsen, 55–76. Basingstoke: Palgrave Macmillan, 2019.

Molinari, Augusta, 'I giornali delle comunità anarchiche italo-americane', *Movimento operaio e socialista* II/1–2 (January–June 1981): 117–30.

Monteiro, George. *Caldo Verde is not Stone Soup: Persons, Names, Words and Proverbs In Portuguese America*. New York-Oxford-Berne: Peter Lang, 2017.

Moreno Alonso, Manuel. *La forja del liberalismo en España. Los amigos españoles de Lord Holland, 1793–1840*. Madrid: Congreso de los Diputados, 1997.

Moreno, Alonso, Manuel. *La generación española de 1808*. Madrid: Alianza Editorial, 1989.

Morrison, James. 'Re-framing Free Movement in the Countdown to Brexit? Shifting UK Press Portrayals of EU Migrants in the Wake of the Referendum'. *The British Journal of Politics and International Relations* 21, no. 3 (2019): 594–611.

Mouradian, Claire. 'La Caricature dans la presse arménienne du Caucase, d'un Empire l'autre', in *Russie, URSS, 1914–1991, Changements de Regards*, edited by M. Quarez, 40–7. Nanterre: BDIC, 1991.

Muhs, Rudolf. 'Max Schlesinger und Jakob Kaufmann: Gegenspieler und Freunde Fontanes', in Peter Alter and Rudolf Muhs (eds.), *Exilanten und andere Deutsche in Fontanes London*. Stuttgarter Arbeiten zur Germanistik 331, 292–326. Stuttgart: Hans-Dieter Heinz, 1996.

Muhs, Rudolf. 'Theodor Fontane und die Londoner deutsche Presse', *Jahrbuch der Deutschen Schillergesellschaft* 45 (2000): 36–61.

Muñoz-Sempere, Daniel. 'Culture identity and Political Dissidence in the Spanish Periodical in London', in Constance Bantman and Ana Clàudia Suriani da Silva (eds.), *The Foreign Political Press in Nineteenth-Century London*. London: Bloomsbury, 2017, 33–50.

Nakata, Martin. *Disciplining the Savages Savaging the Disciplines*. Canberra: Aboriginal Studies Press, 2007.

National Ethnic Press and Media Council of Canada. *Canada's Other Voices*. Website. http://nationalethnicpress.com/ethnic-press.

Nettelbeck, Colin, ed. *The Alliance Française in Australia 1890–1990 – an Historical Perspective*. Melbourne: Fédération des Alliances Françaises en Australie Inc. in association with the Institute or the Study of French-Australian relations, 1990.

Nieuws van de Groote Oorlog (2018), Gent: Viaaa. https://nieuwsvandegrooteoorlog.hetarchief.be.

Ogunyemi, Ola. 'Introduction: Conceptualizing the Media of Diaspora', in *Journalism, Audiences and Diaspora*, edited by Ola Ogunyemi, 1–14. Basingstoke: Palgrave Macmillan, 2015.

Pacyga, Dominic. *Polish Immigrants and Industrial Chicago*. Columbus: Ohio State University Press, 1991.

Pacyga. 'To Live Among Others: Poles and Their Neighbors in Industrial Chicago, 1865–1930'. *Journal of American Ethnic History* 16, no. 1 (1996): 55–73.

Panayi, Panikos. *German Immigrants in Britain during the Nineteenth Century, 1815–1914*. Oxford: Berg, 1995.

Pap, Leo. *The Portuguese-Americans*, Boston: Twayne Publishers, 1981.

Pap, Leo. 'The Portuguese Press', in *The Ethnic Press in the United States. A Historical Analysis and Handbook*, edited by Sally Miller, 291–302. New York-West Port-Connecticut-London: Greenwood Press, 1987.

Papacosma, Viktor. 'The Greek Press in America', *Journal of the Hellenic Diaspora* 5/4 (Winter 1979), 45–61.
Papadopoulos, Yannis. 'The Role of Nationalism, Ethnicity, and Class, in Shaping Greek American Identity, 1890–1927: an Historical Analysis', in *Identity and Participation in Culturally Diverse Societies: A Multi-Disciplinary Perspective,* edited by Assaad E. Azzi, Xenia Chryssochoou, Bert Klandermans, Bernd Simon. New Jersey: Wiley-Blackwell, 2010.
Park, Robert E. *The Immigrant Press and its Control*, New York: Harper & Brothers, 1922.
Pasikowska-Schnass, Magdalena. *Regional and Minority Languages in the European Union*, European Parliamentary Research Service, Briefing, September 2016. https://www.europarl.europa.eu/EPRS/EPRS-Briefing-589794-Regional-minority-languages-EU-FINAL.pdf.
Pedley, Malika and Alain Viaut. 'What Do Minority Languages Mean? European Perspectives', *Multilingua* 38, no 2 (2019), 133–9.
Pena-Rodríguez, Alberto. 'El periodismo portugués en California. Notas históricas sobre el *Jornal Português* de Oakland (1932–1997)'. *Estudios sobre el Mensaje Periodístico* 25, no. 1 (2019): 443–457.
Pena-Rodríguez, Alberto. 'Los inicios de la prensa portuguesa en los Estados Unidos de América'. *Revista Famecos. Mídia, Cultura e Tecnologia* 24 no. 2 (2017) (ID25558).
Pena-Rodríguez, Alberto. *News on the American Dream: A History of the Portuguese Press in the United States*. Tagus Press, 2020.
Pernicone, Nunzio. *Carlo Tresca. Portrait of a Rebel*. Oakland, Edinburgh, Baltimore: AK Press, 2010.
Pimott, William. 'The Yiddish Press 1890–1920: A Global History'. Research Project, Birkbeck Institute for the Study of Antisemitism. https://bisa.bbk.ac.uk/research/item/the-yiddish-press-1890-1920-a-global-history.
Pinson, Guillaume. *La Culture médiatique francophone en Europe et en Amérique du Nord, de 1760 à la veille de la Seconde Guerre mondiale*. Québec: Presses de l'Université Laval, 2016.
Portas, Alicja. 'Representations of Polish Migrants in British Media from the Perspective of "Moral Panic" Theory'. *Polish Journal of English Studies* 4, no. 1 (2018): 113–42.
Porter, Tim. 'Dismantling the Language Barrier: in an Effort to Crack the Burgeoning Hispanic Market, Major Newspaper Companies are Investing in New and Expanded Spanish-Language Editions', *American Journalism Review* 25 (2003), https://ajrarchive.org/Article.asp?id=%203415.
Poyo, Gerald Eugene. *With All, and for the Good of All: The Emergence of Popular Nationalism in the Cuban Communities of the United States, 1848–1898*. Durham: Duke University Press, 1989.
Prager, Leonard. 'A Bibliography of Yiddish Periodicals in Great Britain (1867–1967)', *Studies in Bibliography and Booklore* 9, no. 1 (1969): 3–32.
Proquest. 'Ethnic Newswatch'. http://www.proquest.com/products-services/ethnic_newswatch.html.
Qaisrani, Sajid Mansoor. *Urdu Press in Britain*. Islamabad: Mashal Publications, 1990.
Rabikowska, Marta. 'Negotiation of Normality and Identity among Migrants from Eastern Europe to the United Kingdom after 2004'. *Social Identities* 16, no. 3 (2010): 285–96.
Rapoport, Michel. 'Du journal papier à l'e-journal: La presse francophone de Londres aujourd'hui', in *Los medios en lengua extranjera. Diversidad cultural e integración*, edited by Juan Antonio García Galindo and Laura López Romero, 88–93. Granada: Editorial Comares, 2018.

Rasinger, Sebastian M. '"Lithuanian migrants send crime rocketing": representation of "new" migrants in regional print media'. *Media, Culture & Society* 32, no. 6 (2010): 1021–30.

Readex. 'American Ethnic Newspapers'. http://www.readex.com/content/american-ethnic-newspapers.

Reynolds, Henry. *An Indelible Stain?: The Question of Genocide in Australia's History*. Melbourne: Penguin Books Australia, 2001.

Rhodes, Leara D. *The Ethnic Press: Shaping the American Dream*. New York: Peter Lang, 2010.

Richet, Isabelle. 'The English-Language Press in Italy as Community Builder and Bridge Toward the Host Society', in *Los medios en lengua extranjera. Diversidad cultural e integración*, edited by Juan Antonio García Galindo and Laura López Romero, 105–12. Granada: Editorial Comares, 2018.

Rigoni, Isabelle and Eugénie Saitta. *Mediating Cultural Diversity in a Globalised Public Space*. New York: Palgrave Macmillan, 2012.

Robertson, Roland. *European Glocalization in Global Context*. Basingstoke: Palgrave Macmillan, 2014.

Rocha, Gilberta. *Dinâmica Populacional dos Açores no Século XX: Unidade. Permanência. Diversidade*. Ponta Delgada: Universidade dos Açores, 1991.

Rosemberg, Jean. *Studies in the French Presence in Australia*. Accessed 15 December 2019, https://www.isfar.org.au/resources/jean-rosemberg.

Rubio, Dolores, Antonio Rojas Friend, and Juan Francisco Fuentes. 'Aproximación sociológica al exilio liberal español en la Década Ominosa (1823–1833)', *Spagna contemporánea* 13 (1998): 7–20.

Ruiz Acosta, María José (ed.), *La prensa hispánica en el exilio de Londres, 1810–1850*. Salamanca: Comunicación Social Ediciones y Publicaciones, 2016.

Russo, Pietro. 'La stampa periodica italo-americana', in *Gli italiani negli Stati Uniti. L'emigrazione e l'opera degli italiani negli Stati Uniti d'America*, edited by Rudolph J. Vecoli et al., 494–8. Florence: Istituto di Studi Americani, 1972.

Russo, Pietro. *Catalogo collettivo della stampa periodica italo-americana, 1836–1980*. Rome: Centro Studi Emigrazione, 1983.

Rzepnikowska, Alina. 'Racism and Xenophobia Experienced by Polish Migrants in the UK before and after Brexit Vote'. *Journal of Ethnic and Migration Studies* 45, no. 1 (2019): 61–77.

Şahin, Sanem. 'Journalism of Turkish-Language Newspapers in the UK', in *Journalism, Audiences and Diaspora*, edited by Ola Ogunyemi, 68–83. Basingstoke: Palgrave Macmillan, 2015.

Saloutos, Theodore. *The Greeks in the United States*. Cambridge: Cambridge University Press, 1964.

Samuels, Timothy. 'The Poles are Coming!' Tonic Productions for BBC TV. 17 October 2013. https://vimeo.com/77151640.

Sánchez Mantero, Rafael. 'El exilio político en tiempos de Blanco White', *Archivo hispalense: Revista histórica, literaria y artística* 76, no. 231 (1993): 75–88.

Sánchez Mantero, Rafael. *Liberales en el exilio: la emigración política en Francia en la crisis del Antiguo Régimen*. Madrid: Rialp, 1975.

Sanjian, Ara. *Celebrating the Legacy of Five Centuries of Armenian-Language Book Printing, 1512–2012*. Exhibit Booklet. University of Michigan: Dearborn, 2012.

Sankey, Margaret. 'The Franco–Australasian Connection: Historical Studies in French Departments in Australia and New Zealand', *Journal of the Australasian Universities Language and Literature Association* 100, no. 1 (2003), 73–87.

Schoeps, Julius H. 'Der Kosmos: ein Wochenblatt der bürgerlich-demokratischen Emigration in London im Frühjahr 1851', *Jahrbuch des Instituts für Deutsche Geschichte [Tel Aviv]* 5 (1976): 212–26.

Shattock, Joanne (ed.). *Journalism and the Periodical Press in Nineteenth Century Britain.* Cambridge: Cambridge University Press, 2017.

Shaw, Ibrahim S. '"Human Rights Journalism": A Critical Conceptual Framework', in *Expanding Peace Journalism: Comparative and Critical Approaches*, edited by Ibrahim S. Shaw, Jake Lynch, Robert A. Hackett, 96–121. Sydney: Sydney University Press, 2011.

Siapera, Eugenia. 'Digital News Media and Ethnic Minorities', in *The SAGE Handbook of Digital Journalism*, edited by Tamara Witschge, C. W. Anderson, David Domingo and Alfred Hermida, 35–50. London: SAGE, 2012.

Slatter, John. 'Among British Liberals. Jaakoff Prelooker and the Anglo-Russian', *Immigrants and Minorities* 2, no. 3 (November 1983), 49–66.

Slatter, John. 'The Russian Émigré Press in Britain, 1853–1917', *Slavonic and East European Review* 73, no. 4 (1995), 716–47.

Spigelman, Ariel. 'The Depiction of Polish Migrants in the United Kingdom by the British Press after Poland's accession to the European Union'. *International Journal of Sociology and Social Policy* 3, no. 1–2 (2013): 98–113.

Stead, Evanghelia. 'Periodicals In-Between', *The Journal of European Periodical Studies* 4, no 2 (2019). DOI: https://doi.org/10.21825/jeps.v4i2.15755.

Stowell, Marion Barber. *Early American Almanacs: The Colonial Weekday Bible.* New York: Burt Franklin, 1977.

Stuer, Anny P. L. *The French in Australia.* Canberra: Department of Demography, Institute of Advanced Studies, Australian National University, 1982.

Sundermann, Sabine. *Deutscher Nationalismus im englischen Exil: zum sozialen und politischen Innenleben der deutschen Kolonie in London 1848–1871.* Paderborn: Ferdinand Schöningh, 1997. Veröffentlichungen der Deutschen Historischen Institut London 42.

Sverre Lovoll, Odd. *Norwegian Newspapers in America: Connecting Norway and the New Land.* Saint Paul: Minnesota Historical Society, 2010.

Sword, Keith, Norman Davies and Jan Ciechanowski. *The Formation of the Polish Community in Britain: 1939–1950.* London: University of London Press, 1989.

Taylor, Barry. *Foreign-Language Printing in London, 1500–1900.* London: The British Library Publishing Division, 2003.

The Belgian Press from The Great War (no date). https://belgianpressfromthegreatwar.be/en.

Thérenty, Marie-Ève and Alain Vaillant. Eds. *Presse, nations et mondialisation au XIXe siècle*, Paris: Nouveau Monde, 2010.

Tinker, Edward L. *Les Écrits de langue française en Louisiane au XIXe siècle. Essais biographiques et bibliographiques.* Geneva: Slatkine Reprints, 1975.

Tsow, Ming. 'Ethnic Minority Community Languages: A Statement', *Journal of Multilingual and Multicultural Development* 4, no 5 (1983): 361–84.

Turcato, Davide 'The Other Nation. The Places of the Italian Anarchist Press in the USA', in *Historical Geographies of Anarchism. Early Critical Geographers and Present-Day Scientific Challenges*, edited by Federico Ferretti, Gerónimo Barrera de la Torre, Anthony Ince and Francisco Toro, 40–64. London: Routledge, 2017.

Turcato, Davide, 'Transnational Italian Anarchism, 1885–1915', *International Review of Social History* 52/3 (2007): 407–44.

Tymozcko, Maria. 'Trajectories of Research in Translation Studies'. *Meta* 50, no. 4 (2005): 1082–1097.

Van Dam, Frederik. 'An Outpost of Modernism: The Diplomatic Design of Cosmopolis', *Victoriographies* 8, no. 2 (2018), 170–86. DOI: 10.3366/vic.2018.0304.

Vantomme, François. Ed. *Le Courrier Australien 1892–1945. Creating the French-Australian Connection since 1892*. Sydney: Le Courrier Australien Pty Ltd, 2019.

Vaz, August Mark. *The Portuguese in California*. San Francisco: IDES Supreme Council, 1965.

Vecoli, Rudolph. 'The Italian Immigrant Press and the Construction of Social Reality, 1850–1920', in *Print Culture in a Diverse America*, edited by James Philip Danky and Wayne A. Wiegand, 17–33. Urbana: University of Illinois Press, 1998.

Vellon, Peter. *A Great Conspiracy against Our Race. Italian Immigrant Newspapers and the Construction of Whiteness in the Early 20th Century*. New York: New York University Press, 2014.

Vicente, António Luís. *Os Portugueses nos Estados Unidos de América. Política de Comunidades e Comunidade Política*. Lisbon: Fundação Luso-Americana, 1998.

Vismanath, Katam and Pamela Arora. 'Ethnic Media in the United States: An Essay on Their Role in Integration, Assimilation, and Social Control'. *Mass Communication & Society* 3/1 (2000): 39–56.

Waddington, Keir. 'We Don't Want Any German Sausages Here!' Food, Fear, and the German Nation in Victorian and Edwardian Britain'. *Journal of British Studies* 52 (2013): 1017–1042.

Warrin, Donald and Geoffrey L. Gomes. *Land as Far as the Eye Can See. Portuguese in the Old West*. Washington: The Arthur H. Clark Company, 2001.

Weaver Matthew. 'Hate Crime Surge Linked to Brexit and 2017 Terrorist Attacks'. *The Guardian*, 16 October 2018. https://www.theguardian.com/society/2018/oct/16/hate-crime-brexit-terrorist-attacks-england-wales.

Weinhauer, Klaus, 'Terrorism between Social Movements, the State and Media Societies', in *The History of Social Movements in Global Perspective. A Survey*, edited by Stefan Berger and Holger Nehring. London: Palgrave Macmillan, 2017.

Wenzlhuemer, Roland. 'The Ship, the Media, and the World: Conceptualizing Connections in Global History', *Journal of Global History* 11 (2016): 163–86.

Werner, Michael and Bénédicte Zimmermann. 'Beyond Comparison: Histoire Croisée and the Challenge of Reflexivity', *History and Theory* 45 (February 2006): 30–50.

West-Sooby, John and Jean Fornasiero. 'Matthew Flinders through French Eyes: Nicolas Baudin's Lessons from Encounter Bay'. *The Journal of Pacific History* 52, no. 1 (2017), 1–14.

West-Sooby, John, Jean Fornasiero, and Lindl Lawton. Eds. *The Art of Science: Nicolas Baudin's Voyagers 1800–1804*. Mile End: Wakefield Press, 2016.

West-Sooby, John. Ed. *Discovery and Empire: the French in the South Seas*. Adelaide, Australia: University of Adelaide Press, 2013.

White, Anne. *Polish Families and Migration since EU Accession*. Bristol: Policy Press, 2011.

Wierietelny, Matylda. *Being Part of the City: Multilingual Manchester*, Film, 2019. https://youtu.be/awUoeKJzxj4.

Wilk, Przemyslaw. 'Construing the Other: On Some Ideology-laden Construals of Europeans in *The Guardian*', in *Representing the Other in European Media Discourses*, edited by Jan Chovanec and Katarzyna Molek-Kozakowska, 121–34. Amsterdam: Benjamins, 2017.

Williams, Jerry. *In Pursuit of Their Dreams. A History of Azorean Immigration to the United States*. North Dartmouth: Tagus Press, Center for Portuguese Studies and Culture-University of Massachusetts Dartmouth, 2007.

Wittke, Carl, *The German-Language Press in America*. Lexington: University of Kentucky Press, 1957.
Wodak, Ruth, Rudolf de Cillia, Martin Reisigl and Karin Liebhart. *The Discursive Construction of National Identity*. Edinburgh: Edinburgh University Press, 2009.
Works Progress Administration. *The History of Journalism in San Francisco. Volume 1: Foreign Journalism in San Francisco*. WPA: San Francisco, 1939.
Wynar, Lubomyr. 'The Study of the Ethnic Press', *Unesco Journal of Information Science* I, n°1 (1979), 56–62.
Yablon, Alex. 'The Rise of New York's Foreign-Language Newspapers', *New York Intelligencer*, 9 October 2014. https://nymag.com/intelligencer/2014/10/rise-of-new-yorks-foreign-language-newspapers.html.
Yardeni, Galia. *The Hebrew Press in Palestine (1860–1904)*. Hakibutz Hameuhad Publishers: Tel Aviv University, 1969.
Yeoman, James. *Print Culture and the Formation of the Anarchist Movement in Spain, 1890–1915*. London, NY: Routledge, 2019.
Yu, Sherry S. and Matthew D. Matsaganis, *Ethnic Media in the Digital Age*. New York: Routledge, 2019.
Zecker, Robert. '*A Road to Peace and Freedom*' *The International Workers Order and the Struggle for Economic Justice and Civil Rights, 1930-1954*. Philadelphia: Temple University Press, 2018.
Zecker, Robert. *Race and America's Immigrant Press: How the Slovaks Were taught to Think like White People*. New York: Continuum, 2011.
Zimmer, Kenyon. 'A Golden Gate of Anarchy: Local and Transnational Dimensions of Anarchism in San Francisco, 1880s–1930s', in *Reassessing the Transnational Turn: Scales of Analysis in Anarchist and Syndicalist Studies*, edited by Constance Bantman and Bert Altena, 100–17. London: Routledge, 2015.
Zimmer, Kenyon. *Immigrants against the State. Yiddish and Italian Anarchism in America*. Champaign, Ill.: University of Illinois Press, 2015.
Zubrzycki, Jerzy. 'The Role of the Foreign-Language Press in Migrant Integration'. *Population Studies* 12, no. 1 (1958): 73–82.

Index*

Note: References in *italic* and **bold** refer to figures and tables. References followed by "n" refer to endnotes.

Νέος Κόσμος 178
Англия (Angliya) 1
Пульс UK 1
130 Days in the Siege of Paris (Bril) 38

A Alvorada (The Dawn) 115, 116
Abyssinian Campaign by Britain 34
Acevedo, Manuel M. 169
Ackermann, Rudolf 167, 170–1
A Colónia Portuguesa (The Portuguese Colony) 112
actor-network theory 12
Albania 190n28
Albertini, Luigi 194
Alemán, Jesse 224
Alexander II (emperor of Russia) 97
Alexander III (emperor of Russia) 241–2
'Al hamedinot po ye-amer' 32
Aliens Bill 251–2, 253
Aliens Restriction Order 98
allophone journalism 24n68
allophone press 11, 19, 147
almanac(s) 81 *see also* French-language almanacs in United States
  Almanach Américain 83, 84, 86, 88
  Almanach, annonces de la librairie 84
  Almanach Chantant, dédié aux Dames 83
  Almanach de Hostetter pour les États-Unis 88
  Almanach de la Langue Française 81
  Almanach de la Louisiane 83, 85
  Almanach de la Renaissance 84
  Almanach des Adresses des Membres de l'Union Saint-Baptiste d'Amérique 90
  Almanach des Dames 83–4, 88, 90
  Almanach des Familles 81
  Almanach des Français en Californie 83
  Almanach des Graces 83–4
  Almanach des Muses 84
  Almanach du Commerce et de l'Industrie des États-Unis 88
  Almanach du Peuple 81, 85, 88–9
  Almanach et Directoire des États-Unis 89–90
  Almanach et Directorium Français des États-Unis 87
  Almanach Français de New York, composé principalement pour les populations françaises des États-Unis, pour 1848 88
  Almanach franco-américain et catholique 90
  Almanach Franco-Américain/French American Directory 87
  Almanach Franco-Californien. Petit Journal 'Directory' des Français de la Côte du Pacifique 83
  Almanach Hachette 89, 90
  Almanach illustré de Hostetter pour les États-Unis 83
  Almanach Louisiane 84
  Almanach Rolland 81, 88–9
  Almanack for 1639 81
  Almanacs of the United States 82
  evolution of 81–2
  German-language 82, 90
  identity model of 90
  printing of French immigrants in US 16
Alonso, Manuel Moreno 164
A Luta (The Struggle) 112
American ethnic press in foreign-language 109
American Legion magazine 118

---

* The Index was sponsored by the Institut universitaire de France

Ameryka-Echo (American Echo) 128
Ames, Nathanael 82
Amigo dos Cathólicos (The Friend of the Catholics) 114
anarchist movement 45, 58
    L'Adunata dei Refrattari's role in 73
    organizing and sustaining 52–5
    Paris-based Trial of the Thirty 48
anarchist periodicals 45–6, 49, 58–9
anarchist press 45, 59
    building shared culture 55–6
    intertextual networks 50–2
    personal and periodical mobility 49–50
    transnational 46–9
    variations in translations 56–8
Angiolillo, Michele 51
Anglo-Armenian Association (AAA) 261, 264, 267
Anglo-Belgian Exports 285, 287
Anglo-Belgian Trade Review 285
Anglo-German Friendship Gazette 98
Anglo-German press 93
    mapping circulation and readership 93–8
    and migrant integration 101–2
    readership of 98–100
    struggling to retain readers 103–5
    transcultural and translocal perspectives 98–100
The Anglo-Russian 237, 240–4, *241*, 248, 251, 252
    convergence of 248–9
    portrayal of Bourtzeff 252–3
anti-German sentiments in Britain 280–1, 294n11
anti-Turkish discourse 181
anti-Venizelos demonstration in Athens 184
Antillón, Isidoro 167
Aptak (The Slap) 273
Argentina:
    multilingual press in 3
    transnational anarchist press in 46
Argüelles, Canga 169
Arkun, Aram 260
Armenia (*Hayastan*) 261
Armenia: Iragir azgayin qałaqakan arevtrakan ew ayln (Armenia: Journal in Armenian Language) 260

Armenia/L'Arménie 259, 261, 272, 274
    Armenianness in cosmopolitan periodicals 261, 264–7
Armenian 274
    challenges of composing in 267–9
    language 259
    massacres (1894–6) 267
    national identity 261
    nationalist periodicals 260–1
Armenian/Armenian-language press in Britain 13, 259 *see also* *Armenia/L'Arménie*; *Hnch'ak* (The Bell); *Le Haïasdan*
Aptak 273
Armenian nationalism and 261
Azdarar 259
    cosmopolitan political 270–3
    diasporic periodicals 259–60
Armenianness (*hayapahpanum*) 259, 262–3
    challenges of composing in Armenian 267–9
    in cosmopolitan periodicals 261, 264–7
    through diasporic periodicals 260–1
Armenophile campaign in Britain 271
Ashkharhabar (New Armenian) 261
Asian and African Studies Department 8
The Astronomical Diary and Almanack for the Year... 82
Athenian Quixotism 186
Atlantis (Ἀτλαντίς) 178–9, 187
    digitalization 187n1
    about Eastern Question 180–2
    and 'National Schism' 183–6
    origins, actors, financing 179
The Atlas 104
A Tribuna Portuguesa 119
A União Lusitana-Hawaiana (The Lusitanian Hawaiian Union) 109
A União Portuguesa (The Portuguese Union) 109, 112, 114, 117
Aurora Hawaiana (Hawaiian Aurora) 109
Aus England essays (Fontane) 103
Ausonio Acrate (pseudonym) *see* Damiani, Gigi
Australia:
    'Australian Royalty' 207–8
    'Australians' 207

colonial history 207–8
multilingual press in 3
automated sentiment analysis 150–1
Aux Enfants (To the Children) 212
Aux Petits (To the Little Ones) 212
Aventine secession 69
Ávila, Artur Vieira 112
Ayer and Son periodical directory 2
Ayer's American Almanach 88
Azdarar (The Monitor) 259
Azef, Evno 250

Balch Institute in Philadelphia 7
Balfour, Edith 281
banda del matese 75n20
Ban, Oscar 7
Bantman, Constance 10, 13, 15
Barcelona Universal Declaration on Linguistic Rights (1996) 4–5
Barko, Ivan 208, 209–10, 211, 221n48
Barsotti, Carlo 194
Barzini, Luigi 194, 201n8
  editor's career in United States 194–6
  indulging to Italian fascism 197–200
  late days at *Il Corriere d'America* 200
  striving to keep *Il Corriere d'America* floating 196–7
Barzini, Luigi, Jr. 197
Barzini, Mantica 197
Becker, Bernhard 96
Bek, Israel 29
Belgian/Belgium:
  anthem in British journals 282–3
  national identity in exile 291
  transnational anarchist press in 46
Belgian exile press in Britain 279–80
  adaptive replication network 287–90
  language choice for refugees 283–7
  list of newspaper and journal titles 291–3
  online newspaper database 293–4n5
  periods for publication **286**
  readership of 287
  transnational networks **290**
  way for foreign-language press 282–3
Belgian refugees in Britain 279
  anti-German sentiments in Britain 280–1
  British sympathy 281–2

features of Wartime Belgian exile 291
German atrocities 280, 281
language choice 283–7
translation as transitional tool for 282–3
Belle Époque 189n20
Bello, Andrés 172
Benadusi, Lorenzo 15, 17
Beniamino De Ritis 195
Bergantz, Alexis 208, 211, 212, 221n48
Berneri, Camillo 66, 73, 75n20
Bertgues, Louis 50
Besa-Besën association 182
Bianchi, João António de 113
Bibliotheca Danica. Systematisk Fortegnelse over den danske Literatur fra 1482 til 1830, 24n68
Bilbo, Theodore 134
Bismarck, Otto von 33, 36
Black-White solidarity, *Rovnosť ľudu*'s campaigning for 126–8
Black, Asian, Minority Ethnic (BAME) 8
Blanco Crespo, José Maria *see* Blanco White, José María
Blanco White, José María 165, 166–8, 171, 174n3, 176n17
Blanco y Crespo, José María *see* Blanco White, José María
Bolivar, Simón 172
Bollettino della Sera 200
Bonaparte, Napoleon 164
Bourtzeff, M. Vladimir 246–8, 252–3
Brabançonne (Belgian national anthem) 282, 295n20
Bradley, Stephen Row 82
Brady, Tom 136
Brake, Laurel 10
Branco, Anibal 118
Brazil:
  multilingual press in 3
  transnational anarchist press in 46
Brickhouse, Anna 224
Bril, Yehiel 27, 44n27
  effort to publish *Ha-Levanon* in Paris 29–36
  first journalistic occupation 27
  London edition of *The Lebanon* 39–42
  Qol mevasser. Perah Levanon prospectus in Paris 29

role in publishing *Ha-Levanon* in Mainz 36–9
Britain:
Abyssinian Campaign 34
anti-German sentiments in 280–1
Armenian/Armenian-language press in 13
Belgian exile communities in 287–8
British-Armenian serials 274
British Brothers' League 251
British Coffee House 169
British Criminal Law 270
British *Directory Almanac* 90
British Library 8, 215
British Premier Salisbury 272
British sympathy on Belgian refugees 281–2
foreign political exiles and immigrants 12
French-language anarchist press in 13, **46**
non-English-language press 8–10, 13
political wisdom 168
research on Yiddish press in 9–10
tradition of welcoming political exiles 270
British Poles 145, 146
collective identities of 144
community needs 150
community spirit of 151
ethnic identities 155
identity split with Poles in Poland 153
interactional and discursive strategies 148
Polish-language media for 143
Brogan, Michael 221n48
Brum, João P. 113
Bryce, James 261, 271
Burke, Edmund 175n10
Burrows, Simon 10, 214
Burtsev Defence Fund 247
Burtsev, Vladimir 237, *238*
appraising 252–3
censorship for *Narodovolets* 244–6
exile to London 249–51
journalistic career 238–9
and *Narodovolets* 237, 240–4, *243*
public outcry at censoring 246–8
views on SR policies 248–9

The Business Courier 1
Butler, Nicholas Murray 189n25
Bykowski, Edward 134

Cabrilho, João Rodrigues 116, 117
Cabrillo Commentator, Discoverer of California 117
Cacara Jícara 226, 234n15
Cacella, Monsignor Joseph 112
Cahn, David 99, 101, 107n34
Cailliau, F. O. 210, 215
Calderón, Juan 170
Caleffi, Giovanna 75n20
Calfa 24n72
Callewaert, Juul 289
Cameron, David 144
Cammaerts, Emile 281
Camoesas, João 114
Campbell, Thomas 169, 176n17
Canada:
almanac periodicals 81
French-language almanacs 16
multilingual press in 3
Canadian News 215
Cánovas, Antonio 51
Cantelmo, Ercole 195
Cantelmo, Frank 195
Capt, Charles 50
Cardozo, Manuel S. 116
Cartas desde España (Campbell) 176n17
Carvalho, Eduardo de 115
Casimir-Périer, Jean 57
Castro, Josefina do Canto e 116
Catecismos (Catechisms) 175n8
Catholicism 170
Catolicismo Neto (Pure Catholicism) 170
Cellis, Mario De 195
Center for Migration Studies on Staten Island 7
Chadova, Elena 7–8
Charle, Christophe 53
Chernyi peredel (Black Partition) 254n11
Chicago Daily News 135
Christakis-Zografos, Georgios 182
'Chronicling America' project 106n2
'Civil Rights Congress' campaign 126, 133–4
Clark, Tom 113, 133
Clowes, Norris A. 13

code switching 279
Colleye, Hubert 287
Collier's Weekly 19n26
Colonial Sand & Stone Company 203n41
The Common People of Colonial America (Wechsel) 82
community language 5
The Confederate 95
Confédération Générale du Travail (CGT) 53
Connolly-Smith, Peter 7
Constantine (King) 182–6, 189n26, 191n49
Cooltura 156n6
Cooper-Richet, Diana 211
Coronado, Raúl 224
Correo político y literario de Londres (London Political and Literary Mail) 175n8
Corriere d'America:
  Barzini's role in 196–7
  first issue of 195
  as pro-fascist newspaper 198
  role in fascist propaganda 199–200
Corriere della Sera company 194, 195, 197, 202n17
Corte Real, João Vaz 117
Cortés, Hernán 117
Cosmopolis 211–13
  to bilateral relations 213–16
  Cosmopolis: An International Review 214
cosmopolitan/cosmopolitanism 212
  diasporic Armenian identity 274
  of *Le Haïasdan/L'Arménie/Armenia* 264–5
  political Armenian-language press 270–3
  readership 215
Cotta, Johann Friedrich 84
'Coups de tranchet' (skiving-knife strikes) 48
Crespi, Pio 195, 200
Cristo e Bonnot (Christ and Bonnot) 70
Crocco, Anthony 195
Cronaca sovversiva (Subversive Chronicle) 63–5, 64, 73, 74n4
Cuba Libre 232
Cuisinier, Henry 48

Cultivating Nationhood in Imperial Russia (Khachaturian) 260

da Câmara, Mário Bettencourt 114
Daels, Frans 289
da Gloria, Father Guilherme Silveira 114
Daily Express 251, 274
Daily Telegraph 215
Daily Worker 127
Damiani, Gigi 16, 63, 74 *see also* anarchist press
  art as political propaganda 70–2
  contribution to Italian-American anarchist press 68–70
  and *Cronaca sovversiva* 64, 64–5
  global networks of news and contacts 13
  and *Guerra Sociale* 65
  letters to Maraviglia 76n38
  professional and personal life trajectories 73
  and rise of fascism in Italy 65–8
  writing in exile in US 63–4
D'Andrea, Virgilia 71, 77n39
da Silva, Ana Cláudia Suriani 10
da Silva Leite, Joaquim Rodrigues 117
da Silveira, Pedro L. C. 112
Das Vaterland (Fatherland) 96, 104
Das Volk (The People) 96, 100–1, 105
Davis, Benjamin 133
Davis, Richard Harding 231
Day, Stephen 81
de-territorialization 279
Debagory-Mokrievich, V. K. 239
De Belgische Standaard (The Belgian Standard) 288, 289, **290**
Decadent movement 282
Decornoy, Jacques 189n20
Defence of the Realm Act (1914) 8
Deffendi, Giovanni 50
Delabarre, Edmund B. 117, 122n55
Delalande, Nicolas 53
de la Torriente, Maria Teresa 230
De Leijegalm voor Bisseghem en Omliggende (The Lys Echo for Bisseghem and Surrounding) 285
Delgado, José de Espronceda y 175–6n12
Demoor, Marysa 10
Denník Rovnosť ľudu see Rovnosť ľudu (Slovak) (Equality for the People)

De Paaschklok (The Easter Bells) 285
Depoilly, Louis 48
Der Bote aus London (The Messenger from London) 96
Derby, William Evans 240
Der Gartenlaube (The Bower) 95
Der Hoch-Deutsche Amerikanische Calender 82
Der Israelit (The Israelite) (Lehman) 38
Der Kosmos (The Cosmos) 13, 95, 101
Der Landstreicher (The Vagabond) 97
Der Rebell (The Rebel) 97
Der Sozialdemokrat (The Social Democrat) 97
Der Telegraph (The Telegraph) 95
Der Treue Verkündiger (The Faithful Messenger) 94, 99, 102, 104
Der Verkündiger 94
Deschamps, Bénédicte 193
De Stem Uit België (The Voice From Belgium) 284–5, 289, **290**
Deutsch-Australische Post 219n24
Deutsch-Englische Korrespondenz (German-English Correspondence) 100
Deutsche Londoner Zeitung (German London News) 94–5, 99, 100, 102, 104
Deutsche Zeitung (German News) 96
De Vlaamsche Stem (The Flemish Voice) 289, **290**
Dewhirst, Catherine 5
Diario de Noticias (Daily News) 112–16
diasporic mediascapes 9
Díaz-Leal, Laura Rubio 279
Dickens, Charles 165
Dictionary of Nineteenth-Century Journalism 10
Die Autonomie (Autonomy) 97
Die deutsche Presse (The German Press) 94, 104
Die Gartenlaube 106n14
Die Glocke (The Bell) 97
Dielli (The Sun) 182, 189n28
Die Neue Zeit (The New Age) 96, 100–2, 104
Die Philadelphische Zeitung 2
Diggins, John 199
dignity in Polish immigrants, articulations of 151

Dilke, Charles 248
Directory of US Newspapers of American Libraries, languages in *18*
diretta da Virgilia D'Andrea 77n39
'Divrey Hayamim' (History) 31
Doblado, Leocadio *see* Campbell, Thomas
Doctrina de Martí (Martí's Doctrine) 224, 226
Domani (Tomorrow) 71
Don't Forget Me 175n8
Dorgeel, Heinrich 96
Dragomanov, M. P. 239
Drake, Milton 81, 82
Droogstoppels (Boring But Funny) 289
Drucker, Louis 95
Dufoix, Stéphane 16
Duggan, Stephen 181, 189n25
Durán, Fernando 171
Dutch De Stem Uit België (The Voice From Belgium) 280
Dziennik Chicagoski (Daily Chicagoan) 135
Dziennik Polski (Polish Daily) 21n31, 129, 156n6
Dziennik Polski i Dziennik Żołnierza (The Polish Daily and Soldier's Daily) 21n31

Eastern Question 178, 180–2, 187, 188n8
Eastland, James 136
'Echo d'Europe' (Echoes from Europe) 49
ecumenical reconciliation 240–4
Edinger, Michel 30, 32
Education Reform Act (1988) 8
Edwards, Viv 5
El Alba (The Dawn) 170
Elatri, Bernard 209
El Diario 4
El Eco de Martí (Martí's Echo) 226
El Español (The Spaniard) 166–8
El Español Constitucional (The Constitutional Spaniard) 169
El Examen Libre (The Free Examination) 170
El Ibérico Gratuito (The Free Iberian) 1
El Instructor (The Instructor) 172
El Instructor o Repertorio de historia, bellas artes y letras (The Instructor or Repertoire of History, Fine Arts and Letters) 171

El Misisipí 232n1
El Mundo Nuevo (The New World) 224, 225
El Oriente (The East) 226
El País 4
El Reconcentrado (Brought Together) 230
El Repertorio Americano (The American Repertoire) 173–4
Engels, Friedrich 95
English-language (Paris-based) periodical 211
Escosura, Patricio de la 167
Espronceda y Delgado, José de 167
ethnic group in United States 3
Ethnic Media in the Digital Age (Yu and Matsaganis) 18
ethnic media in UK 9
'ethnic minority media' in North America 5
The Ethnic Press in the United States: a Historical Analysis and Handbook (Miller) 7
Ethnikos Kyrix (Εθνικός Κήρυξ) 178–9, 187
  digitalization 187n1
  about Eastern Question 180–2
  and 'National Schism' 183–6
  origins, actors, financing 179–80
Étrennes historiques et intéressantes contenant l'Abrégé géographique du royaume de France, avec un mélange curieux d'anecdotes, d'événements remarquables, &c. &c. pour l'année de grâce 1786 83
Etudiants Socialistes Révolutionnaires Internationationalistes (ESRI) 57
European Association of Daily Newspapers in Minority and Regional Languages (MIDAS) 4
European Charter for Regional and Minority Languages (1992) 4–5
European Council Directive (1977) 8
The European Review 166
Evans-Gordon, W. E. 251
Evening Despatch 283
Evening Star 184
Evolution et Révolution (Elisée) 57
Exhibition of the Jewish Press in Great Britain (Fraenkel) 10

'Éxilpresse' (Exile Press) 107n30
exopolities 16–17
Express News 4
Extra, Guus 4

Fabbri, Luigi 66, 68, 69, 73, 75n20
fact-checking of Anglo-German press 100–1
Fair Employment Practices Committee (FEPC) 132, 133
fascism:
  Barzini's involvement in 197–200
  Damiani's contribution against 68–70
  in Italy 65–8
Fedeli, Ugo 72
Federzoni, Luigi 202n17
Felice, Renzo De 69
Felici, Isabelle 13, 16, 199
Ferdinand VII (king of Spain) 163, 164, 165, 172, 175n10
Fernandez Sardino, Pedro Pascasio 169
Ferrer, Alicia Ferrández 5
Ferrero, Felice 195
Figueroa, Sotero 226, 228, 232
Figuras de la emigración 169
Flemish/Dutch language of Belgian refugees 283–7
Fontane, Theodor 100, 103
Foreign Agency (*Zagranichaia agentura*) 242
foreign-language journalism/press 3–4, 11, 15–19
  in Britain and the US 11–12
  history of 6–11
  titles 12–13
The Foreign-Language Press in Australia, 1848–1964 208
The Foreign Political Press in Nineteenth-Century London: Politics from a Distance (Bantman and da Silva) 10
Fraenkel, Josef 10
France:
  Belgian exile communities in 287–8, 291
  Belgian exile press in **288**
  Damiani's anarchist periodicals in Paris 69
  from *Ha-Levanon* to *Le Libanon* 29–36
  Libanon 30

multilingual press in 3
treating refugees as prisoners of war
    166
Francisco, Pedro *see* Francisco, Peter
Francisco, Peter 116, 118
Franco-Americains 86
Francophone Walloon refugees 284
Franklin, Benjamin 2, 6, 82
Fraternal Outlook 132, 134
free-mindedness of Anglo-German press
    100–1
Freedom 51, 245
freedom of Anglo-German press 100–1
Free Russia 239, 248
Freiheit (Freedom) 13, *14*, 96–7
French Armenophile movement 267
French-language (Australia-based)
    periodicals 207
French-language almanacs in United
    States 16, 83–4
  for bourgeoisie 84–5
  cultural transfer 90–1
  in New England States 85–90
  from *Cosmopolis* to bilateral relations
    213–16
  Le Courrier Australien 208–11, 215
  pedagogical uses of 211–13
French-language (London-based)
    periodicals 212
French-language press:
  anarchist communist papers in Britain
    and US **46**, 47–9
  anarchist press in Britain 13, 15–16
  exile press 10
  in Greater British context 12
  in London 209
*French Exile Journalism and European
    Politics 1792–1814* 10, 214
French Revolution 10, 165
Freycinet, Charles de 57

Gaelic language 5
Galiano, Alcalá 167, 168
Galignani, Giovanni Antonio 211
Galignani's Messenger 211
Galleani, Luigi 65, 66
Gamsenfels, Johann Lachmann von 102
Gartner, Lloyd 9
Gascoyne-Cecil, Robert 244, 255n16

Gazetje van Thielt (The Thielt Courier)
    289
Gazzetta del Massachusetts 193
Geehl, Heinrich *see* Dorgeel, Heinrich
Gennadios, Ioannis 181
Georgiou, Myria 9
German/Germany:
  atrocities on Belgian refugees 280,
    281
  economic migrants 100–1
  German-American newspapers 94
  German-language almanacs 82, 90
  German-language immigrant press
    10
  Ha-Levanon's French politics in
    Mainz 36–9
  multilingual press in 3
Germania 95
German-language press in Britain *see*
    Anglo-German press
Germinal 47, 51, 55, 63, 67, *67*
  Damiani's contribution to *68*, 69–70, 73
  publishing Daudé-Bancel's letters 56
  support of *Cronaca sovversiva* 65
  in United States 49, 58
  Zisly's role 57
Gibbons, Herbert Adams 180
Gilbert and Rivington printers 268–9
Gilson, Miriam 208, 211, 212, 215
Ginsburg, Baron Yudil 35
Giovanola, Luigi 195
Gladstone, Herbert John 281
Gladstone, William Ewart 266, 271, 281
Głos Ludowy (Polish) (The People's Voice)
    125–6
  advocacy of racial justice 137
  fighting Nazism and segregation
    128–30
  fighting to make lynching as federal
    crime 130–2
  for racial equality in unions 132–5
  surviving as dissident foreign-language
    newspapers 135–7
Goaziou, Louis 47–9, 51–3
Goethe, Johann Wolfgang von 94
Goffman, Erving 147–8
  basic needs of Polish immigrants
    150–1
  essay on face-work 152

Goldman, Emma 66
Golmiche, Xavier 56
Goniec Polski 156n6
Gordon, Judah Leib 36
Gori, Pietro 54
Gorter, Durk 4
Gossetti, Valentina 12
Gounaris, Dimitrios 185, 186
Grabar (Classical Armenian) 261
Grave, Jean 47, 55
Greek-Language press in United States 177 *see also* Megali Idea (the Great Idea)
   Atlantis 178–80
   ethnic identity creation and construction 191n41
   Ethnikos Kyrix 178–80
   newspaper publications from migrants **177**, 177–8
   readership terms 190n41
   Νέος Κόσμος 178
Greek-Ottoman War (1919–22) 188n7
The Greeks in the United States (Saloutos) 177
Grella, Egidio 195
Grève Générale/Lo Sciopero Generale 57–8
Gruesz, Kirsten Silva 224, 225
Guadalupe Hidalgo, Treaty of 223
Gubernatis, Angelo de 275n17
Guerra Sociale (Social War) 65
Guide Canadien-français ou Almanach des adresses de Fall River, et notes historiques sur les Canadiens de Falls River par H. A. Dubuque 88
Guinsburg, Baron Yudil 40

Ha-Levanon/Halbanon (The Lebanon) 15, 27
   first issue 27, *28*
   French politics in Mainz, Germany 36–9
   Hebrew edition *37*
   juggling with French press regime 29–36
   in London as *The Lebanon* 39, 39–42
   'Palestinian' orientation of 27
   political agenda 29
Ha-Maggid (The Storyteller) 27, 32, 43n16

Ha-Melitz (The Mediator) in St Petersburg 39
Ha-Tzvi (The Deer) in Jerusalem 40
Ha-Yom (Today) in St Petersburg 39
Ha-Zefira (The Dawn) in Warsaw 39
Hagopian, Garabed 261
Haïasdan 272
Haïka-schirtchan (cycle of Haïk) 268
Hale, Grace 125
Halukah 28, 35
Hamid II, Abdul 260, 261, 272
Hamon, Augustin 50, 51, 55
Hampton, Mark 15
Hans Ibeles in London (Johanna) 102
Harriman, Arthur R. 118
Hart, Charley 195
Harzig, Christiane 7
Haskalah (Jewish Enlightenment) movement 31, 36
Havatzelet (The Crocus) 29
Haymrket Massacre 51
The Hebrew Press in Palestine (Yardeni) 43n2
Hellenism, cradle of 181
Henry, Agnes 50
Hermann 95–6, 98, 100, 102, 105
Herter, Christian A. 118
Herzen, Alexander 270
Het Nachtlichtje (The Light at Night) 289
Hibben, Paxton 19n26, 181
Hirsch, Arnold 135
'historical guides' (*Guides dans l'histoire*) 86–7
Hnch'ak (The Bell) 260, 261, 270, 272–3, 274
Hoerder, Dirk 7, 126
Hoffnung-Garskof, Jesse 226, 228
Holt, Sally 5
Honey, Michael 130
honour in Polish immigrants, articulation of 151–2
House Un-American Activities Committee (HUAC) 126
How Do You Do (London-based newspaper) 95
Hughes, George 131
Hugo's French Journal 212
Hull Daily Mail 283
Hunter, Edward 6
Hürriyet (Freedom) 270

'idée nationale' 210
'identity model' of almanac 90
ideological internationalism 45
Il Carroccio, e Il Grido della stirpe 193
Il Corriere d'America 17
Illustrated London News 95
Illustrirte Familien-Zeitung (Illustrated Family Newspaper) 98
Il Martello (The Hammer) 63, 66, 66–8, 199
    Damiani's contribution to 68, 68–9
    Fabbri's appreciation for 69
Il Nuovo Mondo 199
Il Popolo Italiano 193
Il Progresso Italo-Americano 193, 194, 196, 200
Il Proletario 199
Il re fascista (The fascist King) 70
Imagining Armenia 266
immigrant language 5
immigrant minority languages 4–5
The Immigrant Press and Its Control (Park) 3
Immigration History Research Center in Minneapolis 7
In Many Voices: Our Fabulous Foreign-Language Press (Hunter) 6
Intelligencer 2
International free newspaper stands 2
International Labor Defense (ILD) 127, 131
international Transfopress network 11
International Workers Order (IWO) 126, 133
intertextual networks of anarchist press 50–2
Irish language 5
Israel:
    community divisions of *Ha-Levanon* in 27–9
    Ha-Tzvi in 40
Italian-language newspapers in United States 2, 193
    Corriere d'America 195, 196–7, 200
    Il Progresso Italo-Americano 193, 194, 196, 200
    problems with fascist regime 193–4
Italian radical anarchist periodicals in US:
    Cronaca sovversiva 64, 64–5

Germinal 67, 67
Il Martello 66, 66, 67–8
L'Adunata dei Refrattari 66, 67, 68
Italy:
    fascism in 65–8
    Italian colonies 199
    multilingual press in 3
    transnational anarchist press in 46

Jacobson, Mathew Frye 125
Jacques Bonhomme 215
Janvion, Emile 57
Jardim, Vasco de Sousa 118
J. C. Ayer (pharmaceutical company) 88
Jerome, Jerome K. 240
The Jewish Chronicle 41, 42
The Jewish Immigrant in England (Gartner) 9
Jewish World 41
Jim Crow law 132
Jornal Português (Portuguese Newspaper) 112, 114, 117
journalism without borders 15, 16
journalistic discourse of Portuguese-language press 116
Jóżwik, Arkadiusz 158n25

Kalendarium Pennsilvaniense, or America's Messenger 86
Kalisher, Zvi Hirsch 36
Kanellos, Nicolàs 7
Karl, Duke 94–5, 106n11
Kelley, Robin 130
Kelly, Harry 48, 51
Kemal, Mustafa 178
Kennedy, John F. 118
Kennedy, Robert 137
Khachaturian, Lisa 260
Khalturin, S. N. 255n14
King, Martin Luther 136
Kinkel, Gottfried 95–6, 100–2
Kirsop, Wallace 211
Kolettis, Ioannis 188n6
Kolokol (The Bell) 270
Kombi (The Nation) 189n28
Komitet Narodowy Amerykanów Polskiego Pochodzenia (KNAPP) 129
Kommunistische Zeitschrift (Communist Journal) 95

Konica, Faik Bey 190n28
Konofsky, Ervin 135
Kouts, Gideon 15
Kravchinsky, S. M. 254n12
Kreitz, Kelly 18
Krieg, Gabriele 82
Kropotkin, Peter 55, 57, 245
Ku Klux Klan (KKK) 129, 134
   KKK Lynchings 133
Kurier Wileński 4

La América (America) 224
La América Ilustrada 225
La Battaglia (The Battle) 64, 65
La Biblioteca Americana (The American Library) 173–4
'labour migrants' journalism in Europe and North America 7
La Capitale 193
La Colmena, periódico trimestre de Ciencias, Artes, Historia y Literatura (The Beehive, Quarterly Newspaper of Sciences, Arts, History and Literature) 172
La Diana 69
La Discusión (The Discussion) 230
L'Adunata dei Refrattari 63, 66, 67, 68
   Damiani's contribution to 68, 69, 70, 73
   interruption of Damiani's collaboration with 71–2
   Maraviglia's contribution to 76n38
   role in anarchist movement 73
   tribute to Damiani 73
La Folle d'Ostende 55
La Grève des Electeurs 55
La Grève Générale 48
La Grève Générale/Lo Sciopero Generale 53
La Grève Générale/Lo Sciopero Generale/The General Strike 58
La Habana Elegante (Elegant Havana) 226, 234n15
La Huelga General 57
LAJT Magazine see *Panorama Magazine*
La Métropole d'Anvers (The Metropolis of Antwerp) 280, 284, 285
La mia bella Anarchia (My Beautiful Anarchy) 72
L'Ami des Ouvriers 54

language choice:
   in Armenian diasporic identity 261, 264–5
   for Belgian refugees 283–7
language group 5, 7
l'Annuaire Louisianais 84
La Notizia 193
La Nueva República (The New Republic) 226
La Questione Sociale 54
L'Araldo 193
La Revista de Cuba Libre 224, 225–7
   fashioning female editorial voice 230–1
   futures of media and democracy 232
   printing revolution 227–30
La Revista Ilustrada de Nueva York (New York Illustrated Magazine) 224–6, 228, 234n25, 234n27
La Révolte 47, 55
La Société Mourante et l'Anarchie (Moribund Society and Anarchy) 55
La Staffetta Italiana: or, The Italian Post 11
latinidad 224, 232
La Tribuna d'America 193
La Tribune Libre (The Open Forum) 47, 49–51, 54
Lattek, Christine 101
Laursen, Ole Birk 59n1
Lausanne, Treaty of 188n9
L'Avant Garde (The Avant-Garde) 285
Lavater, Johann Kaspar 84
La Voce del Popolo 4
La Voce del Popolo Italiano 193
Laycock, Joan 266
Lazo, Rodrigo 224
LEAVE campaign against Polish migrants in Britain 144, 154
'Lebanon Honor' (*Kevod Ha-Levanon*) 35
Le Bouriscot, Bernard 209
Le Courrier Australien (The Australian Courier) (CA) 208–11, 214, 215
Le Courrier Belge (The Belgian Courier) 285
Le Cri de Londres (The Cry from London) 287
Le Franco-Belge (The Franco-Belge) 285

Le Haïasdan 259–61, *262–3*, 271, 272, 274
  Armenianness in cosmopolitan periodicals 261–7
  challenges of composing in Armenian 267–9
Lehman, Meir 38
Le Journal de Melbourne (The Melbourne Journal) 208
Le Libertaire 52
Le Mercure anglois 8
Le Moniteur Universel (The Universal Monitor) 32
Le Neptune (d'Anvers) (The Neptune of Antwerp) 285, 287, 296n38
Le Père Peinard 48, 52, 53–4
Le Petit étranger (The Little Foreigner) 212
Le Plébéien (The Plebeian) 50
Le Réveil des Mineurs 49
Le Rothschild 50, 52, 56, 57
Leroy, Achille 51
Les deux rivaux; ou un mariage au Bayou 83
Le Semeur contre tous les tyrans (The Sower against all Tyrants) 77n42
Les Paroles d'un révolté (Kropotkin) 57
Les Tablettes (The Columns) 288
Les Temps Nouveaux 51
Le Tocsin 47, 48, 50, 51, 53–6, 57
Le XXe Siècle **290**
L'Humanité Nouvelle (A New Humanity) 50, 52
Libanon 30, *30*, 32–3, 36
Liberal Triennium or Constitutional Triennium 174n6
Liberty 53
'librairie internationale' 51
Lilienblum, Moses Leib 36
L'Indépendance Belge (The Independent Belgium) 280, 284, 287, 296n38
lingua franca 267
Língua Portuguesa nos Estados Unidos (The Portuguese Language in the United States) 115
L'Italia 183, 193
'Little Greece' policy 184–5
Llorens, Vicente 165, 168, 169
L'Observateur français (The French Observer) 213, 215
L'Océanien (The Oceanian) 208, 220n34

London, England *see also* Spanish exiled liberals in London, England; Spanish-language media strategies in England
  Burtsev's exile to 249–51
  El Ibérico Gratuito 1
  French-language press in 209
  The Lebanon in 39, 39–42
Londoner Arbeiter-Zeitung (London Workers' News) 97
Londoner Correspondenz (London Correspondence) 99, 103
Londoner Courier (London Courier) 97, 102
Londoner deutsche Post (London German Post) 96, 104
Londoner deutsches Journal (London German Journal) 95, 100, 101, 104
Londoner deutsches Tageblatt (London German Daily) 97, 101, 104
Londoner deutsches Wochenblatt (London German Weekly) 94, 102
Londoner deutsche Zeitung 102
Londoner deutsche Zeitung und allgemeiner Anzeiger (London German News and General Advertiser) 95
Londoner Figaro-Chronik (London Figaro Chronicle) 97
Londoner Freie Presse (London Free Press) 97, 102
Londoner General-Anzeiger (London General Advertiser) 97, 98
Londoner Journal (London Journal) 97, 102
Londoner Zeitung: Hermann (London News: Hermann) *see Hermann*
The London Hotel & Restaurant Gazette 98
López, Fernando Durán 163
López, Marissa 224
L'Opinione and La Libera Parola 193
L'Opinion Wallonne (The Walloon Opinion) 287
Losada, Elías de 224, 228
Los Numantinos 167
Loxias 184
Lucetti, Gino 66
Ľudový denník see Rovnosť ľudu (Slovak) (Equality for the People)

Lugard, Frederick 281
Lugard, Lady 281
Luigi Roversi 195
Luotto, Andrea 195
Lüsebrink, Hans-Jürgen 16
Luso-Americano (Luso-American) 118, 119, 121n28
Luso-American press 115
Luzzatti, Luigi 195
lynching on Black community 130–2
Lyttelton, Alfred 281

Maandelijksche Katholieke Brieven (Monthly Catholic Letters) 285
Maine 225
Malatesta, Errico 65–8, 71, 73, 75n20, 77n42
Malato, Charles 48, 50, 53, 57
The Maltese Falcon 134
The Manchester Guardian 282
Manchester Nachrichten (Manchester News) 98
Maraviglia, Osvaldo 70, 76n38
Maria Stuart (play by Schiller) 102
Marsy, Claude Sixte Sautreau de 84
Mart (March) 273
Martí, José 224–6, 228, 232, 234n25
Martín, José de San 172
Marx, Karl 95, 96
Matras, Yaron 5
Matsaganis, Matthew 18
Matteotti, Giacomo 76n35, 198
Mazower, Mark 189n20
McCarthyism 6–7
Megali Idea (the Great Idea) 178, 187, 188n6
   Atlantis 178–80
   Ethnikos Kyrix 178–80
   and National Schism 182–6
   New York Greek-language press 180–2
Melville, William 242, 250–1
Mendibil Grao, Pablo León José 175n11
Mendíbil, Pablo de 167
Menéndez Pelayo, Marcelino 168
Michel, Louise 51, 54
Michigan Chronicle 128
Mikrasiates 186
Millerand, Alexandre 178

Miller, Sally 7
minority community printed press 5
minority languages 4–5
Miranda, Francisco de 172
Mirbeau, Octave 55
Mix, York-Gothard 82, 90
Miyares, Enrique Hernández 226, 234n15
modernismo 233n2
Moja Wyspa (My Island) 145, 154, 155
   automated sentiment analysis 150–1
   as ethnic press and role in identity manufacturing 146–8
   Goffman's need analysis 151–2
   impact of institutional voices in 148, 149
   role in Polish collective identities 145–6
   sources of **148**
   thematic categories 149, **149**
Molek-Kozakowska, Katarzyna 9, 19
Molière and Shakespeare, an international review of stage 215
Montefiore, Moses 42
Moore, Harry 134
Mora, José Joaquín de 166–7
Morgagni, Manilo 201n4
Morley, John 248
Morrogh, Patricio de la Escosura 176n13
Most, Johann 96
Mowbray, Charles 48, 49, 53
Mukhbir (The Informer) 270
Müller, Friedrich Max 275n17
multilingualism, UK debate on 8
Multilingual Manchester project 5
Musenalmanach 84
Museo Universal de Ciencias y Artes (Universal Science and Arts Museum) 171, 175n8
Musil, Charles 132

Napier, Robert 34
Napoleon III (president of France) 33, 36, 38, 271
Narodovolets 237, 240–4, *243*
   censorship for 244–6
   convergence of 248–9
   public outcry at censoring 246–8
Naród Polski (Polish Nation) 127

National Committee of Americans of Polish Extraction *see Komitet Narodowy Amerykanów Polskiego Pochodzenia* (KNAPP)
National Herald *see Ethnikos Kyrix* (Εθνικός Κήρυξ)
'National Schism' (*Ethnikos Dichasmos*) 182–6, 187
Nazarbek *see* Nazarbekian, Avetis
Nazarbekian, Avetis 261, 270, 272–4
Nazzaro, Pellegrino 195
Nedelia (The Week) 240
the Netherlands:
    Belgian exile communities in 287–8, 291
    Belgian exile press in **288**
    and nationalist affiliation **290**
Nettelbeck, Colin 211
Neue Rheinische Zeitung (New Rhenish News) 95
'New England' colonies 82
'new journalism' 13, 15
new minority languages 5
New Monthly Magazine 166, 169, 176n17
The New York Journal 231
New Yorský denník (New York Daily) 127
The New York Star 13
Nicholas II (emperor of Russia) 244
Nikitine, Nicolas 48, 50
Noli, Fan 182
non-English-language periodicals 1
non-English-language press 6
    Britain *vs.* United States 8
    émigré press 10
    historians of immigration/exile 9
    in North America 12
    publishing 13
    serial in Britain 9, 10
non-Latin-script periodical prints 18
Non molliamo 69
The Northern Whig 103
Nowak, Stanley 126, 128, 135
Nowy Świat (New World) 135–7
Nuestra America (Our America) 225, 234n25
N. W. Ayer & Son's American newspaper annual and directory 110

O Arauto (The Herald) 112
Observatory of Portuguese Emigration 110
Ocios de españoles emigrados (Pastimes of Spanish Émigrés) 169
O Colonial or Diario de Noticias 114
Odesskii listok (The Odessa Leaflet) 240
O Facho (The Mogul) 109
Ojetti, Ugo 202n17
O Jornal (The Newspaper) 114
O Jornal de Noticias (News Journal) 109
'Old Establishment' (*HaYishouv Ha-Yashan*) 28
Oliphant, Lawrence 41
Oliveira, Joaquim de 116
Olmedo, José Joaquín de 172
O Luso-Hawaiano (The Luso-Hawaiian) 109
'Ominous Decade' 166, 168
'omoethnis' 190n41
'omogenis' 190n41
Online Etymology Dictionary 213
Ons Blad (Our Journal) 285
Ons Vaderland (Our Native Land) 289, **290**, 296n49
O Progresso Californiense (The Californian Progress) 109
Orsini Affair 270
Orsini, Felice 271
The Other Languages of Europe 4
O Trabalho (The Work) 116
Ottoman Armenia 260, 265, 273
Ottoman nationalism 260
'Ottoman peril' 181
Ottoman surveillance 272–3
'Our muse' poem by Damiani 72

Packer, John 5
The Pakistani News 4
Paléologue, Maurice 250
Palestine:
    Eretz Israel 27, 37, 41
    fighting against *Haskalah* movement 31
    Ha-Levanon in 27–8
    Halukah 35
    Oliphant's Palestine settlement plans 41
Panciatichi, Francesco 195, 201n9

Panhellinios 179
Panorama Magazine 156n6
Paola, Pietro di 58
Paris, Treaty of 231
Park, Robert 3, 6, 7
Partiia narodnoi voli 254n11
Party of Socialists-Revolutionaries (SRs) 248–9, 250
Pasha, Musurus 270–1
Passos, John dos 118
Patkanian, Raphael 268
Patria (Fatherland) 224, 226
Pedley, Malika 4
Peirce, William 81
Peninsula War (1808–14) 164, 174n1
Pennsylvania Chronicle 82
Père Peinard 47, 48, 49, 51, 54, 55
Perovskaia, S. L. 255n14
Peru, multilingual press in 3
Peter Francisco Award 118
Peter Francisco Day 118
Peter Francisco Park 118
Peukert, Josef 97
Piñeyro, Enrique 224
Pitsos, Nicolas 17
'plural Britain' 8
'Polak na wyspie' (The Pole on the Isle) 145
Poles in Poland 144, 147, 153, 155
Polish-language online media 144, 155
  collective identities of Polish immigrants 144–5, 155
  MojaWyspa 145–52
Polish Cultural Organization (PSOK) 156n6
Polish diaspora/migrants in Britain 143, 156n6 *see also MojaWyspa* (My Island)
  collective identities 144–6
  LEAVE campaign against 144, 154
  mitigation strategies 152–4
Polish Express Media Group 156n6
The Polish Express 1
Polish festival 150
The Polish Observer 1
political exile 163
Polyzoidis, Adamantios T. 179, 181
Poor Little Belgium 281
Poor Richard's Almanack 82
Pope, Generoso 203n41

Porter, Tim 2
Portugalian, Mkrtitch 260–1
Portuguese journalism 110
Portuguese-language ethnic press in United States 109
  identity, cultural and ethnic perspective 119
  immigrant press as cultural instrument 112–16
  related to evolution of migratory flows 110–11
  role in promoting language and culture 111
  symbolic imaginary of Portuguese journalism 116–19
Pouget, Emile 48, 49
powroty 160n49
practical politics 168
Prager, Leonard 9–10
Prelooker, Jaakoff 239, 240, 247–51, 253
press censorship 12
  for *Narodovolets* 244–6
  for Russian émigré press in Britain 244–6
'presse allophone' 219n17
pride in Polish immigrants, articulations of 150–1
Protocol of Peace between Spain and United States 231
Punch 280

quota system for European immigrants in US 121n21

Rabe, Victor 55
Rachkovsky, P. I. 242, 244
racism in United States 135
  of European immigrants 125
  Głos Ludowy and *Rovnosť ludu* for racial equality 132–5
Rakenius, Karl 94, 106n8
Ranken, Ellis & Co. 269
Rankin, John 133
Rapoport, Michel 209
Rataev, Leonid 249, 250
The Rebel 48–50, 53, 55, 56
Reclus, Elisée 55, 57
Recuerdos (Memories) 168
Red Scare in US 66, 126, 135–6

Reed, Susan 13
regional and minority languages (RML) 4
Renan, Ernest 35
replication of Belgian exile press 279, 287–90
Retis, Jessica 5
Reuters Finanz-Chronik 98
Révolution chrétienne et révolution sociale (Malato) 57
Revue Australienne (Australian Review) 208
Rhodes, Leara D. 7
Richet, Diana Cooper 219n17
Ridley, Matthew White 248
Riego, Rafael del 174n6
Rocafuerte, Vicente 172
Rocha, João R. 118
Roediger, David 125
Ronge, Johannes 95, 106n15
Rossetti, Arthur 53
Rossetti, Helen 53
Rossetti, Olivia 53
Rothschild, Baron de 48
Rothschild, Baron Nathan Mayer 44n27
Rothschild, Nathan de 44n27
Rovnosť ľudu (Slovak) (Equality for the People) 125, 126
    campaigning for early Black-White solidarity 126–8
    about early civilizations in Egypt and China 129–30
    fighting to make lynching as federal crime 130–2
    for racial equality in unions 132–5
    surviving as dissident foreign-language newspapers 135–7
Rowell periodical directory 2
Russian-language revolutionary press 10
Russian émigré press in Britain 237
    convergence of *The Anglo-Russian* and *Narodovolets* 248–9
    ecumenical reconciliation *vs.* destruction of autocracy 240–4
    Public outcry at censoring Burtsev and *Narodovolets* 246–8
    Russian-language serials and censorship 244–6
    Russian language standing for liberty 249–52
    setting Russian scenes and exilic trajectories 237–40
The Russian Reformation Society (*Obshchestvo sodeistviia rossiiskim reformam*) 240
Russian State Archive of Social and Political History (RGASPI) 249
Russo, Pietro 2
Rzegocki, Arkady 153

Sacco-Vanzetti Case 66
Sachs, Schneur 40
Salazar, António de Oliveira 114
Saloutos, Theodore 177
Salvemini, Gaetano 198
Sánchez, José Joaquín de Mora y 175n8
Sapir, Yaakov 28
Sarolea, Charles 281
Sarrail, Maurice 186
Sasun massacre 266
Sauer, Christoph 82
Schiller, Friedrich 84, 102, 105
Schlesinger, Max 99, 103
Schulze, Gottfried 94
Scott, C. P. 248
Scully, Richard 5
Semanario Patriótico (Patriotic Weekly) 167, 174n3
Sempere, Daniel Muñoz 163
'Senegalese Tirailleurs' 186
serialized media 49
Serra, Rafael 224, 226, 232
Sevasly, Mihran 261
Shaw, Flora 281
The Sheffield Daily Telegraph 273
Shmavonian, Harutyun 259
Sigarroa, Rosario 229, 230
Simplicio (pseudonym) *see* Damiani, Gigi
Slatter, John 237
Slovak Workers Society (SWS) 125–6, 132
Society of Friends of Russian Freedom (SFRF) 247, 251–2
Sojourner Truth riots 128, 129
Sotiropoulos, Georgios 186
Sotiropoulou, Magdalini 186
Sotiropoulou, Vasilia 186
Souvenir d'Exil (Souvenirs of Exile) 285
Spada, Silvestro 67

Spanish-language media strategies in England:
  monthly periodicals 168–70
  periodicals in Latin American colonies 172–4
Spanish-language press in United States 4, 223–4
  El Misisipí 232n1
  La Revista de Cuba Libre 224, 225–32
  women-led publication 224–5, 228
Spanish exiled liberals in London, England 163
  collaboration with London publishing scene 170–2
  connection with British anti-absolutist circles 164–6
  during Peninsula War 164
  periodicals in Latin American colonies 172–4
  role in media and journalism 163
  Spanish cultural politics of 166–8
Spanish/Spain:
  colonies trade in America 170
  cultural politics in England 166–8
  transnational anarchist press in 46
Stefani Agency 193, 201n4
Stepniak-Kravchinsky 245
Stobsiade 8
Surrey Mirror 283
Svobodnaia Rossiia (Free Russia) 239
Switzerland, transnational anarchist press in 46
symbolic imaginary of Portuguese journalism 116–19
Szaniawski, Wojciech 150

Tageblatt 97
Talmadge, Herman 136
Tatanis, Petros 179–80, 183, 184
Taylor, Barry 163
Tchéraz, Minas 264, 265–7, 274, 275n17
The Telegraph 216
Temps Nouveaux 52
Teutsche Pilgrim, Mitbringende einen Sitten-Calender 82
't Gazetje van Tongerloo (The Tongerloo Gazette) 285
Theodoros 34, 35
Thusnelda 96

Tiber Publishing Company 195
Tiesa 1
Till, Emmett 136
The Times 104, 245, 282
Tocchati, James 53
The Torch 52–3
Tormento (poems by D'Andrea) 77n39
Townsend, Frederick Henry 280
trans-language phenomenon 10
transatlantic journalism 13, 15, 17
translations of Belgian exile press 282–3, 294n6, 295n20
transnational anarchist press 46–9
transnational and translational culture 279
Tresca, Carlo 66, 199
Treuttel, Jean-George 84
Tribune Independent 128
Tribune Libre 51–2, 57
Trigueiro, Manuel F. Martins 112
Truman, Harry 113, 134
Tsow, Ming 5
Tujague, François 85
Turner, John 51
Tydzień Polski (The Polish Week) 8, 21n31, 156n6

UK Chinese Times 1
UK Race Relations Act (1976) 8
Umanità Nova (New Humanity) 65–6, 68
Umanità Nova 77n53
United Kingdom (UK):
  debate on multilingualism 8
  ethnic media in 9
  Multilingual Manchester project 5
  multilingual press in 3
  non-English-language print heritage 8
United States (US):
  almanac printing of French immigrants 16
  English language in 6
  ethnic group in 3
  foreign political exiles and immigrants 12
  French-language almanacs in 83–5
  French-language anarchist communist papers **46**
  multilingual newsstands in New York City 3

multilingual press in 3
non-English-language press 8, 13
Portuguese immigrants in 110
quota system for European immigrants in 121n21
radical anarchist periodicals in 66–8
tradition of free community press distribution 2
'yellow danger/peril' 189n20
US Hispanic Literary Heritage Project 224

van de Perre, Alfons 289
Vantomme, François 209
Variedades o El Mensajero de Londres (Varieties or The London Messenger) 171
Vaz, August Mark 113
Veglia (Vigil) 69
Veglia anarchica mensile 77n39
Venizelos, Eleftherios 182–6
Viaut, Alain 4
Vicente, João Maria 109
Villalobos, Ángel de 172
Villavicencio, Antonio Alcalá Galiano y Fernández de 175n10
Villeval, Albin 221n47
Vita 70
Vlasto, Demetrius J. 179
Vlasto, Solon J. 179, 183, 184
Vogel, Johann Benjamin 94
VoilaSydney 209
Volkhovsky, Felix 245
Volontà (willingness) 71
von Aehrenthal, A. L. 252
Vrij België (Free Belgium) 289, **290**

Wanderungen durch London 103
War Refugees Committee (WRC) 281

Washington, George 118
The Washington Herald 183
The Waterloo Directory of English Newspapers and Periodicals: 1800–1900 9
Watson, Robert Spence 248
Wechsel, Louis 82
Weinhauer, Klaus 56
Welsh language 5
Werner, Michael 11
Weyers, Bianca 82
White-supremacist violence against Black civil-rights activists 133–4
Wiener, Joel H. 13, 15
Wilson, Daniel 48
Wittke, Carl 98, 103
Wroblewski, Charles 209–10, 215

Yardeni, Galia 43n2
Yearbook of Immigration Statistics 109, 110
'yellow danger/peril' 189n20
Yiddish press in Britain 9–10
Yorkshire Evening Post 283
Yu, Sherry 18

Zasulich, Vera 247, 255n34
Zecker, Robert M. 8, 16
Zeitung 240
Zemlia i volia (Land and Freedom) society 254n11
Zheliabov, A. I. 255n14
Ziarul romanesc 1
Zimmer, Kenyon 45, 58
Zimmermann, Bénédicte 11
Zimmern, Helen 103
Zisly, Henri 57
Zitron, Samuel Leib 31
Zubrzycki, Jerzy 7, 208, 211, 212, 215

www.ingramcontent.com/pod-product-compliance
Lightning Source LLC
Chambersburg PA
CBHW071758300426
44116CB00009B/1128